MUSIC THEN AND NOW

MUSIC THEN AND NOW

Thomas Forrest Kelly

HARVARD UNIVERSITY

W. W. NORTON & COMPANY

NEW YORK   LONDON

W. W. Norton & Company has been independent since its founding in 1923, when William Warder Norton and Mary D. Herter Norton first published lectures delivered at the People's Institute, the adult education division of New York City's Cooper Union. The firm soon expanded its program beyond the Institute, publishing books by celebrated academics from America and abroad. By midcentury, the two major pillars of Norton's publishing program—trade books and college texts—were firmly established. In the 1950s, the Norton family transferred control of the company to its employees, and today—with a staff of four hundred and a comparable number of trade, college, and professional titles published each year—W. W. Norton & Company stands as the largest and oldest publishing house owned wholly by its employees.

Editor: Maribeth Payne
Development Editor and Project Editor: Kathy Talalay
Development Editor: Harry Haskell
Manuscript Editor: Jodi Beder
Electronic Media Editor: Steve Hoge
Electronic Media Assistants: Nicole Sawa and Stefani Wallace
Assistant Editor: Ariella Foss
Associate Editor: Justin Hoffman
Marketing Manager: Amy Parkin
Director of Production, College: Jane Searle
Photo Editor: Stephanie Romeo
Photo Researcher: Julie Tesser
Permissions Manager: Megan Jackson
Page Layout: Carole Desnoes
Art Director: Rubina Yeh
Book Designer: Lissi Sigillo
Cover Design: Leah Clark
Music Typesetter: David Botwinik
Recordings Consultant: Allison Courtney Fitch Hirschey
Indexer: Marilyn Bliss
Proofreader: Barbara Necol
Composition: Jouve
Manufacturing: Courier, Kendallville

Library of Congress Cataloging-in-Publication Data

Kelly, Thomas Forrest.
  Music then and now / Thomas Forrest Kelly.—1st ed.
   p. cm.
  Includes bibliographical references and index.

ISBN 978-0-393-92988-1 (pbk.)

1. Music appreciation—Textbooks. I. Title.
MT6.K353 2013
780—dc23   2012013066

W. W. Norton & Company, Inc., 500 Fifth Avenue, New York, NY 10110-0017
wwnorton.com

W. W. Norton & Company Ltd., Castle House, 75/76 Wells Street, London W1T 3QT

1 2 3 4 5 6 7 8 9 0

Listening Guides xi

Listening Excerpts (alphabetical list) xiii

Metropolitan Opera Videos xvi

Author Videos (by chapter) xvii

Maps xvii

Preface xviii

CHAPTER 1 Fundamental Musical Concepts and Forms 2

Introduction • Some Basic Terms and Concepts about Sound • Musical Instruments • The Orchestra • Musical Forms • Chapter Review

Part 1 Music and Prayer: Medieval and Renaissance Music 19

Timeline: The Middle Ages • The Middle Ages • Arts and Ideas: The Middle Ages • Timeline: The Renaissance • The Renaissance • Arts and Ideas: The Renaissance • Style Comparisons at a Glance

CHAPTER 2 Friday, December 25, 1198, Paris: Christmas Mass at Notre Dame Cathedral 30

Introduction • The Setting • Christmas Day at Notre Dame • The Music • LG 1 Introit: "Puer natus est" • LG 2 Kyrie • LG 3 Alleluia: *Dies sanctificatus* • LG 4 Leoninus: Alleluia, *Dies sanctificatus* • LG 5 Perotinus: *Viderunt omnes* • Notre Dame Then and Now • Chapter Review

CHAPTER 3 Thursday, July 23, 1586, Harleyford Manor, England: William Byrd's Mass for Four Voices and Other Domestic Music 56

Introduction • The Setting • The Performance • The Music • Listening to the Music • LG 6 Byrd: Agnus Dei, from Mass for Four Voices • LG 7 Byrd: "This sweet and merry month of May" • LG 8 John Dowland: "Can she excuse my wrongs," for Voice and Lute • LG 9 Dowland: "Can she excuse my wrongs," arrangements • Renaissance Music Then and Now • Chapter Review

Part II Music and Speech: Baroque Music 83

Timeline: The Baroque Era• Baroque Musical Style • Style Comparisons at a Glance • Arts and Ideas: The Baroque Era

CHAPTER 4 Saturday, February 24, 1607, Mantua: Claudio Monteverdi's *Orfeo* 90

Introduction • The Setting • The Performance • Listening to the Music • LG 10 Toccata • LG 11 Opening Ritornello and Prologue • LG 12 "Vi ricorda, o boschi ombrosi" • LG 13 "Tu se' morta" • LG 14 "Possente spirto" • Listening Map of *Orfeo*'s Act 2 • *Orfeo* Then and Now • Chapter Review

CHAPTER 5 Tuesday, April 13, 1742, Dublin: George Frideric Handel's *Messiah* 118

Introduction • The Setting • The Performance • Listening to the Music • LG 15 "There were shepherds" • LG 16 "Comfort ye, my people" • LG 17 "Ev'ry valley" • LG 18 "And the glory of the Lord • LG 19 "Hallelujah" chorus • LG 20 "He trusted in God" • How Did It Go? • *Messiah* Then and Now • Chapter Review

CHAPTER 6 Friday, September 18, 1739, Leipzig: Johann Sebastian Bach at Zimmermann's Coffeehouse 146

Introduction • The Setting • The Performance • Listening to the Music • LG 21 Prelude and Fugue in C Minor, BWV 847 • LG 22 Suite in D Major, BWV 1068, Overture • LG 23 Concerto in F Major for Harpsichord, Two Recorders, and Strings (arr. from *Brandenburg* 4), BWV 1057, I • Bach Then and Now • Chapter Review

ParT III Music and Reason: Classical Music

ParT III Music and Reason: Classical Music 169

Timeline: The Classic Period • Political Events • Arts and Ideas: The Age of Enlightenment • Classic Musical Style • Style Comparisons at a Glance

CHAPTER 7 Monday, October 29, 1787, Prague: W. A. Mozart's *Don Giovanni* 176

Introduction • The Setting • The Performance • The Music • Listening to the Music • **LG 24 Act 1, Scene 1: "Notte e giorno faticar"** • **LG 25 Act 1, Scene 1: Ensemble** • **LG 26 Act 1, Scene 5: Catalogue Aria** • **LG 27 Act 1, Scene 9: "Là ci darem la mano"** • **LG 28 Act 1: Finale** • *Don Giovanni* Then and Now • Chapter Review

CHAPTER 8 Thursday, December 22, 1808, Vienna: Ludwig van Beethoven's Symphony No. 5 in C Minor 208

Introduction • The Setting • The Performance • The Music • Listening to the Music • **LG 29 First Movement** • **LG 30 Second Movement** • **LG 31 Third Movement** • **LG 32 Fourth Movement** • The Fifth Symphony Then and Now • Chapter Review

CHAPTER 9 November 1826, Vienna: A Schubertiade at Joseph von Spaun's 234

Introduction • The Setting • The Performance • Listening to the Music • **LG 33** *Die Forelle* (*The Trout*) • **LG 34** *Gretchen am Spinnrade* (*Gretchen at the Spinning Wheel*) • **LG 35** *Der Erlkönig* (*The Erlking*) • **LG 36 The "Trout" Quintet, IV** • Schubert Then and Now • Chapter Review

Part IV Music and Feeling: Romantic Music 257

Timeline: The Romantic Period • Politics, Economics, and Technology • Romantic Musical Style • Arts and Ideas: The Romantic Period • Style Comparisons at a Glance

CHAPTER 10 Sunday, December 5, 1830, Paris:
Hector Berlioz's *Fantastic Symphony (Symphonie fantastique)* 264

Introduction • The Setting • The Performance • The Music • Listening to the Music • LG 37 "Rêveries—Passions," I • LG 38 "Un bal," II • LG 39 "Scène aux champs," III • LG 40 "Marche du supplice," IV • LG 41 "Songe d'une nuit de sabbat," V • How Did It Go? • The *Fantastic Symphony* Then and Now • Chapter Review

CHAPTER 11 Thursday, March 13, 1845, Leipzig:
Felix Mendelssohn's Violin Concerto in E Minor 294

Introduction • The Setting • The Performance • The Music • Listening to the Music • LG 42 First Movement • LG 43 Second Movement • LG 44 Third Movement • How Did It Go? • The Violin Concerto Then and Now • Chapter Review

CHAPTER 12 Saturday, March 29, 1862, Paris:
Clara Schumann Performs Robert Schumann's *Carnaval* 316

Introduction • The Setting • The Performance • The Music • Listening to the Music • LG 45 "Préambule" • LG 46 "Arlequin" • LG 47 "Eusebius" • LG 48 "Florestan" • LG 49 "Chopin" • LG 50 "Pause" and "Marche des Davidsbündler contre les Philistins" • How Did It Go? • *Carnaval* Then and Now • Chapter Review

CHAPTER 13 Monday, August 14, 1876, Bayreuth:
Richard Wagner's *The Valkyrie (Die Walküre)* 344

Introduction • The Setting • The Performance • The Music • Listening to the Music • LG 51 Act 1, Prelude (Storm) • LG 52 Act 1, Scene 1: Siegmund and Sieglinde Meet and Fall in Love ("Wess' Herd dies auch sei") • LG 53 Act 1, Scene 2: Sieglinde and Siegmund in Love, and Siegmund's Sense of Foreboding • LG 54 Act 1, Scene 3: "Winterstürme wichen dem Wonnemond" • LG 55 Act 1, Scene 3: "Siegmund heiss' ich" • How Did It Go? • *The Valkyrie* Then and Now • Chapter Review

CHAPTER 14 Friday, December 15, 1893, New York: Antonín Dvořák's Symphony No. 9 in E Minor (*From the New World*) 372

Introduction • The Setting • The Performance • The Music • Listening to the Music • LG 56 First Movement • LG 57 Second Movement • LG 58 Third Movement • LG 59 Fourth Movement • How Did It Go? • The *New World* Symphony Then and Now • Chapter Review

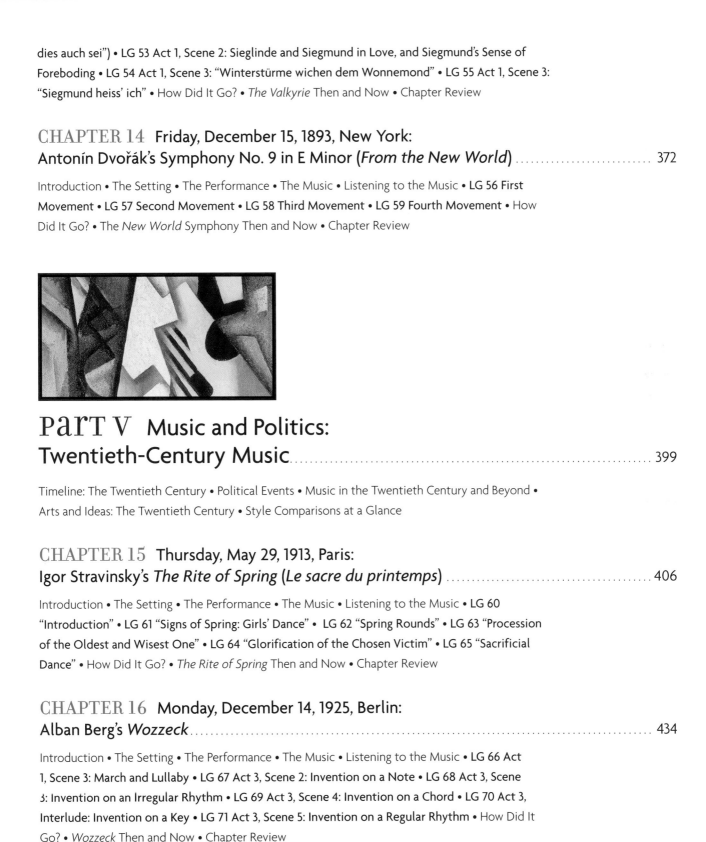

Part V Music and Politics: Twentieth-Century Music 399

Timeline: The Twentieth Century • Political Events • Music in the Twentieth Century and Beyond • Arts and Ideas: The Twentieth Century • Style Comparisons at a Glance

CHAPTER 15 Thursday, May 29, 1913, Paris: Igor Stravinsky's *The Rite of Spring* (*Le sacre du printemps*) 406

Introduction • The Setting • The Performance • The Music • Listening to the Music • LG 60 "Introduction" • LG 61 "Signs of Spring: Girls' Dance" • LG 62 "Spring Rounds" • LG 63 "Procession of the Oldest and Wisest One" • LG 64 "Glorification of the Chosen Victim" • LG 65 "Sacrificial Dance" • How Did It Go? • *The Rite of Spring* Then and Now • Chapter Review

CHAPTER 16 Monday, December 14, 1925, Berlin: Alban Berg's *Wozzeck* 434

Introduction • The Setting • The Performance • The Music • Listening to the Music • LG 66 Act 1, Scene 3: March and Lullaby • LG 67 Act 3, Scene 2: Invention on a Note • LG 68 Act 3, Scene 3: Invention on an Irregular Rhythm • LG 69 Act 3, Scene 4: Invention on a Chord • LG 70 Act 3, Interlude: Invention on a Key • LG 71 Act 3, Scene 5: Invention on a Regular Rhythm • How Did It Go? • *Wozzeck* Then and Now • Chapter Review

CHAPTER 17   Wednesday, January 15, 1941, Stalag VIIIA, Zgorzelek, Poland: Olivier Messiaen's *Quartet for the End of Time* 466

Introduction • The Setting • The Performance • The Music • Listening to the Music • LG 72 "Liturgie de cristal" (Liturgy of Crystal) • LG 73 "Vocalise, pour l'Ange qui annonce la fin du Temps" (Vocalise, for the Angel Who Announces the End of Time) • LG 74 "Abîme des oiseaux" (Abyss of the Birds) • LG 75 "Intermède" (Interlude) • LG 76 "Louange à l'Éternité de Jésus" (Praise to the Eternity of Jesus) • LG 77 "Danse de la fureur, pour les sept trompettes" (Dance of Fury, for the Seven Trumpets) • LG 78 "Fouillis d'arcs-en-ciel, pour l'Ange qui annonce la fin du Temps" (Tumult of Rainbows, for the Angel Who Announces the End of Time) • LG 79 "Louange à l'Immortalité de Jésus" (Praise to the Immortality of Jesus) • How Did It Go? • The *Quartet* Then and Now • Chapter Review

CHAPTER 18   Thursday, September 26, 1957, New York: Leonard Bernstein's *West Side Story* 498

Introduction • The Setting • The Performance • Listening to the Music • LG 80 Prologue • LG 81 "Jet Song" • LG 82 "Dance at the Gym" • LG 83 "Tonight" • LG 84 "America" • How Did It Go? • *West Side Story* Then and Now • Chapter Review

CHAPTER 19   Coda: Into the Twenty-First Century 526

Introduction • Listening to Modern Music • John Adams's *Doctor Atomic* • Chapter Review

APPENDIX   More Technical Matters A-1

Glossary A-9

Endnotes A-17

Credits A-27

Index A-31

ⓢ Listening Guides

1 Introit, "Puer natus est" (chant) 42

2 Kyrie (chant) 45

3 Alleluia, *Dies sanctificatus* (chant) 47

4 Leoninus: Alleluia, *Dies sanctificatus* (2-voice organum) 50

5 Perotinus: *Viderunt omnes* (4-voice organum) 52

6 Byrd: Agnus Dei, from Mass for Four Voices 67

7 Byrd: "This sweet and merry month of May" 69

8 Dowland: "Can she excuse my wrongs," for Voice and Lute 76

9 Dowland: "Can she excuse my wrongs," arrangements

    a) Four voices with lute 77

    b) Lute solo 78

    c) Harpsichord solo 78

    d) Consort of five viols and lute 79

    e) Mixed consort 79

10 Monteverdi: *Orfeo*, Toccata 104

11 Monteverdi: *Orfeo*, Opening Ritornello and Prologue 105

12 Monteverdi: *Orfeo*, "Vi ricorda, o boschi ombrosi" (Orfeo's Song), Act 2 108

13 Monteverdi: *Orfeo*, "Tu se' morta" (Orfeo's Lament), Act 2 109

14 Monteverdi: *Orfeo*, "Possente spirto" (Orfeo's Song), Act 3 111

15 Handel: *Messiah*, Recitative, "There were shepherds" 129

16 Handel: *Messiah*, Recitative, "Comfort ye, my people" 131

17 Handel: *Messiah*, Aria, "Ev'ry valley" 134

18 Handel: *Messiah*, Chorus, "And the glory of the Lord" 137

19 Handel: *Messiah*, "Hallelujah" chorus 139

20 Handel: *Messiah*, Fugue chorus, "He trusted in God" 141

21 Bach: Prelude and Fugue in C Minor, BWV 847 158

22 Bach: Suite in D Major, BWV 1068, Overture 161

23 Bach: Concerto in F Major for Harpsichord, Two Recorders, and Strings, BWV 1057,
Arranged from the Fourth *Brandenburg* Concerto, I 164

24 Mozart: *Don Giovanni*, Act 1, Scene 1, "Notte e giorno faticar" 193

25 Mozart: *Don Giovanni*, Act 1, Scene 1, Ensemble 194

26 Mozart: *Don Giovanni*, Act 1, Scene 5, Catalogue Aria 197

27 Mozart: *Don Giovanni*, Act 1, Scene 9, "Là ci darem la mano" 198

28 Mozart: *Don Giovanni*, Act 1, Finale 200

29 Beethoven: Symphony No. 5 in C Minor, Op. 67, I (Allegro con brio) 224

30 Beethoven: Symphony No. 5 in C Minor, Op. 67, II (Andante con moto) 227

31 Beethoven: Symphony No. 5 in C Minor, Op. 67, III (Allegro) 229

32 Beethoven: Symphony No. 5 in C Minor, Op. 67, IV (Allegro) 230

33 Schubert: *Die Forelle* (*The Trout*) 246

34 Schubert: *Gretchen am Spinnrade* (*Gretchen at the Spinning Wheel*) 247

35 Schubert: *Der Erlkönig* (*The Erlking*) 250

36 Schubert: The "Trout" Quintet, Piano Quintet in A Major, IV 253

37 Berlioz: *Fantastic Symphony*, I, "Rêveries—Passions" (Reveries—Passions) 283

38 Berlioz: *Fantastic Symphony*, II, "Un bal" (A Ball) 284

39 Berlioz: *Fantastic Symphony*, III, "Scène aux champs" (Scene in the Country) 285

40 Berlioz: *Fantastic Symphony*, IV, "Marche du supplice" (March to the Scaffold) 287

41 Berlioz: *Fantastic Symphony*, V, "Songe d'une nuit de sabbat" (Dream of a Witches' Sabbath) 288

42 Mendelssohn: Violin Concerto in E Minor, Op. 64, I (Allegro molto appassionato) 307

43 Mendelssohn: Violin Concerto in E Minor, Op. 64, II (Andante) 309

44 Mendelssohn: Violin Concerto in E Minor, Op. 64, III (Allegro molto vivace) 312

45 Schumann: *Carnaval*, "Préambule" (Preamble) 333

46 Schumann: *Carnaval*, "Arlequin" (Harlequin) 335

47 Schumann: *Carnaval*, "Eusebius" 336

48 Schumann: *Carnaval*, "Florestan" 337

49 Schumann: *Carnaval*, "Chopin" 338

50 Schumann: *Carnaval*, "Pause" and "Marche des Davidsbündler contre les Philistins"
(March of the League of David against the Philistines) 339

51 Wagner: *The Valkyrie*, Act 1, Prelude (Storm) 359

52 Wagner: *The Valkyrie*, Act 1, Scene 1, Siegmund and Sieglinde Meet and Fall in Love ("Wess' Herd dies auch sei") 360

53 Wagner: *The Valkyrie*, Act 1, Scene 2, Sieglinde and Siegmund in Love, and Siegmund's Sense of Foreboding 362

54 Wagner: *The Valkyrie*, Act 1, Scene 3, "Winterstürme wichen dem Wonnemond" 364

55 Wagner: *The Valkyrie*, Act 1, Scene 3, "Siegmund heiss' ich" 366

56 Dvořák: Symphony No. 9 in E Minor (*From the New World*), I (Adagio—Allegro molto) 386

57 Dvořák: Symphony No. 9 in E Minor (*From the New World*), II (Largo) 388

58 Dvořák: Symphony No. 9 in E Minor (*From the New World*), III (Scherzo: Molto vivace—Poco sostenuto) 390

59 Dvořák: Symphony No. 9 in E Minor (*From the New World*), IV (Allegro con fuoco) 392

60 Stravinsky: *The Rite of Spring*, "Introduction" 422

61 Stravinsky: *The Rite of Spring*, "Signs of Spring: Girls' Dance" 423

62 Stravinsky: *The Rite of Spring*, "Spring Rounds" 425

63 Stravinsky: *The Rite of Spring*, "Procession of the Oldest and Wisest One" 426

64 Stravinsky: *The Rite of Spring*, "Glorification of the Chosen Victim" 428

65 Stravinsky: *The Rite of Spring*, "Sacrificial Dance" 429

66 Berg: *Wozzeck*, Act 1, Scene 3, March and Lullaby 447

67 Berg: *Wozzeck*, Act 3, Scene 2, Invention on a Note 449

68 Berg: *Wozzeck*, Act 3, Scene 3, Invention on an Irregular Rhythm 452

69 Berg: *Wozzeck*, Act 3, Scene 4, Invention on a Chord 454

70 Berg: *Wozzeck*, Act 3, Interlude, Invention on a Key 457

71 Berg: *Wozzeck*, Act 3, Scene 5, Invention on a Regular Rhythm 459

72 Messiaen: *Quartet for the End of Time*, I. "Liturgie de cristal" (Liturgy of Crystal) 480

73 Messiaen: *Quartet for the End of Time*, II. "Vocalise, pour l'Ange qui annonce la fin du Temps"
(Vocalise, for the Angel Who Announces the End of Time) 481

74 Messiaen: *Quartet for the End of Time*, III. "Abîme des oiseaux" (Abyss of the Birds) 483

75 Messiaen: *Quartet for the End of Time*, IV. "Intermède" (Interlude) 485

76 Messiaen: *Quartet for the End of Time*, V. "Louange à l'Éternité de Jésus" (Praise to the Eternity of Jesus) 486

77 Messiaen: *Quartet for the End of Time,* VI. "Danse de la fureur, pour les sept trompettes" (Dance of Fury, for the Seven Trumpets) 488

78 Messiaen: *Quartet for the End of Time,* VII. "Fouillis d'arcs-en-ciel, pour l'Ange qui annonce la fin du Temps" (Tumult of Rainbows, for the Angel Who Announces the End of Time) 490

79 Messiaen: *Quartet for the End of Time,* VIII. "Louange à l'Immortalité de Jésus" (Praise to the Immortality of Jesus) 492

80 Bernstein: *West Side Story,* Prologue 515

81 Bernstein: *West Side Story,* "Jet Song" 516

82 Bernstein: *West Side Story,* "Dance at the Gym" 518

83 Bernstein: *West Side Story,* "Tonight" 519

84 Bernstein: *West Side Story,* "America" 521

⑤ Listening Excerpts (alphabetical list)

Bach: *Brandenburg* Concerto No. 4, I (harpsichord)

Bach: Brandenburg Concerto No. 4, I (original, followed by transcription)

Bach: Brandenburg Concerto No. 4, I (recorder)

Bach: Cello Suite No. 1, I

Bach: Prelude and Fugue in C Minor, BWV 847, opening of fugue

Bach: Sanctus, B Minor Mass

Bach: Suite in D Major, Air

Bach: Suite in D Major, Bourrée

Bach: Suite in D Major, Gavotte

Bach: Suite in D Major, Gigue

Bach: Suite in D Major, Overture (trumpet and drums)

Beethoven: Piano Sonata in C Minor, Op. 13 (*Pathétique*), III

Beethoven: Piano Sonata in C# Minor, Op. 27, No. 2 (*Moonlight*), III

Beethoven: String Quartet No. 9 in C Major, Op. 59 (*Rasumovsky*), No. 3, III, Minuet

Beethoven: Symphony No. 5, I, opening 4-note motive

Beethoven: Symphony No. 5, I, transition 1st to 2nd theme

Beethoven: Symphony No. 5, II, modulation

Beethoven: Symphony No. 5, II, opening

Beethoven: Symphony No. 5, III (double bass)

Beethoven: Symphony No. 9, IV, "Ode to Joy"

Berg: *Lyric Suite,* Allegro misterioso

Berg: Violin Concerto, I

Berg: *Wozzeck,* Act 1, opening

Berg: *Wozzeck,* Act 1, Scene 2, Andres's hunting song

Berg: *Wozzeck,* Act 1, Scene 3, March

Berg: *Wozzeck,* Act 3, Scene 3, Wozzeck's descent into madness

Berlioz, arr. Liszt: *Fantastic Symphony,* II

Berlioz: *Fantastic Symphony,* I, "Estelle" melody

Berlioz: *Fantastic Symphony,* I, first theme, following introduction

Berlioz: *Fantastic Symphony,* I, opening

Berlioz: *Fantastic Symphony,* I, recapitulation

Berlioz: *Fantastic Symphony,* I, theme returns in the middle

Berlioz: *Fantastic Symphony,* II, *idée fixe* theme

Berlioz: *Fantastic Symphony,* III, appearance of *idée fixe* with recitative-like passage

Berlioz: *Fantastic Symphony,* III (oboe and English horn)

Berlioz: *Fantastic Symphony,* IV, Coda

Berlioz: *Fantastic Symphony,* IV, "March to the Scaffold" (conjunct)

Berlioz: *Fantastic Symphony,* IV, "March to the Scaffold," dominant chord

Berlioz: *Fantastic Symphony,* IV, "March to the Scaffold," harmonic alteration

Berlioz: *Fantastic Symphony,* IV, "March to the Scaffold," march theme

Berlioz: *Fantastic Symphony,* V, *Dies irae,* originally performed by serpent and ophicleide

Berlioz: *Fantastic Symphony,* V, first theme, following introduction

Berlioz: *Fantastic Symphony*, V, Witches' Dance
Berlioz: *Harold in Italy*, I (viola solo)
Berlioz: *Romeo and Juliet*, IV, Scherzo

Bernart de Ventadorn: *Can vei la lauzeta mover*

Bernstein: *Candide* Overture
Bernstein: *Chichester Psalms*
Bernstein: *Mass*, Alleluia
Bernstein: *West Side Story*, "America"
Bernstein: *West Side Story*, "Cool," fugue
Bernstein: *West Side Story*, "Maria"
Bernstein: *West Side Story*, Prologue (drums)
Bernstein: *West Side Story*, "Something's Coming"
Bernstein: *West Side Story*, "Tonight"

Brahms: Violin Concerto in D Major, I

Byrd: Agnus Dei, from Mass for Four Voices, final major
    chord
Byrd: Agnus Dei, from Mass for Four Voices, middle section
Byrd: "Civitas sancti tui," from *Cantiones sacrae, Book 1*
Byrd: "The Galliarde for the Victorie," from *My Lady
    Neville's Virginal Book*
Byrd: Kyrie, from Mass for Four Voices
Byrd: "This sweet and merry month of May"
Byrd: "Ye sacred muses"

Chopin: Prelude, Op. 28, No. 11

Debussy: "Jeux de vagues," from *La mer (The Sea)*
Debussy: *Prelude to "The Afternoon of a Faun"*

Dowland: "Can she excuse my wrongs" (ensemble of viols)
Dowland: "Can she excuse my wrongs" (voice and lute)
Dowland: "Flow, my tears"
Dowland: "Semper Dowland, semper dolens"

Dvořák: *Humoresques*, Op. 101, No. 7
Dvořák: *Slavonic Dances*, Op. 46, No. 1
Dvořák: *Stabat Mater*
Dvořák: Symphony No. 9, I, 1st theme
Dvořák: Symphony No. 9, I (flute solo)
Dvořák: Symphony No. 9, I, melody with lowered 7ths
Dvořák: Symphony No. 9, II, opening
Dvořák: Symphony No. 9, II, 1st and 2nd phrases

Dvořák: Symphony No. 9, II, 3rd and 4th phrases
Dvořák: Symphony No. 9, II, 5th and 6th phrases

Earl of Essex Galliard (lute)
Earl of Essex Galliard (viols)
Earl of Essex Galliard (virginal)

"Goin' Home"

Gradual: "Viderunt omnes," chant

Gregorian chant: example of melismatic setting
Gregorian chant: example of neumatic setting
Gregorian chant: example of syllabic setting

Handel: *Acis and Galatea*, Sinfonia (baroque oboe)
Handel: *Messiah*, "And he shall reign for ever and ever"
Handel: *Messiah*, "And he shall reign for ever and ever"
    (disjunct)
Handel: *Messiah*, "And the glory of the Lord," opening
Handel: *Messiah*, "Behold, a virgin shall conceive"
Handel: *Messiah*, "For the Lord God omnipotent reigneth"
Handel: *Messiah*, "Hallelujah" chorus
Handel: *Messiah*, "He shall feed his flock"
Handel: *Messiah*, "He trusted in God," final minor chord
Handel: *Messiah*, "He trusted in God," opening
Handel: *Messiah*, "Rejoice," basso continuo
Handel: *Messiah*, "The trumpet shall sound"
Handel: *Messiah*, "Thus saith the Lord"
Handel: *Music for the Royal Fireworks*, "Réjouissance"

Haydn: Symphony No. 82, I, opening

Hildegard of Bingen: "O euchari in leta via"

Liszt: *Transcendental Etudes*, No. 4, "Mazeppa"

Machaut: "Puis qu'en oubli"

Mahler: Symphony No. 2, I (crescendo and explosion)

Melismatic organum

Mendelssohn: *Elijah* (oratorio)
Mendelssohn: *A Midsummer Night's Dream*, Overture
Mendelssohn: *A Midsummer Night's Dream*, Scherzo
Mendelssohn: *Songs without Words*, No. 6, "Spring Song"
Mendelssohn: Violin Concerto in E Minor, I, first theme

Messiaen: *L'Ascension,* "Transports de joie d'une âme devant la gloire du Christ qui est la sienne"

Messiaen: *Quartet for the End of Time,* "Abyss of the Birds" (clarinet)

Messiaen: *Quartet for the End of Time,* "Dance of Fury"

Messiaen: *Quartet for the End of Time,* "Interlude"

Messiaen: *Quartet for the End of Time,* "Praise to the Eternity of Jesus"

Messiaen: *Quartet for the End of Time,* "Tumult of Rainbows"

Messiaen: *Quartet for the End of Time,* "Vocalise"

Messiaen: *Turangalîla-symphonie*

Monteverdi: 1610 *Vespers*

Monteverdi: *Orfeo,* "Ahi! Caso acerbo"

Monteverdi: *Orfeo* (cornetts and sackbuts)

Monteverdi: *Orfeo* (2 cornetts with organ and lute)

Monteverdi: *Orfeo,* "E intenerito"

Monteverdi: *Orfeo,* opening ritornello (ensemble of violins, viola, and cello)

Monteverdi: *Orfeo* (recorders)

Monteverdi: *Orfeo,* Toccata

Monteverdi: *Orfeo,* "Vi ricorda, o boschi ombrosi"

Monteverdi: *Scherzi musicali*

Morley: Galliard, "Can she excuse my wrongs"

Mozart: Clarinet Quintet, II

Mozart: *Clemenza di Tito,* Overture

Mozart: *Dies irae,* from Requiem

Mozart: *Don Giovanni,* Act 1, Scene 9, "Là ci darem la mano"

Mozart: *Don Giovanni,* Act 1, Scene 12, "Non ti fidar"

Mozart: *Don Giovanni,* Act 1, Trio, "Protegga" (bel canto)

Mozart: *Don Giovanni,* Ottavio, "Il mio tesoro"

Mozart: *Don Giovanni,* Overture

Mozart: *Don Giovanni,* Overture, opening

Mozart: "Prague" Symphony, No. 38, IV

Mozart: Symphony No. 30, I, opening

Mozart: Symphony No. 40, I, opening

Mozart: Symphony No. 40, I, transition 1st to 2nd theme

Mozart: "Tuba mirum," from Requiem

Mussorgsky: "The Field Marshal"

"Old Folks at Home"

Palestrina: Kyrie, from *Missa Aeterna Christi munera*

Pentatonic scale

Perotinus: *Viderunt omnes,* 4-voice organum

"Puer natus est," opening notes

Reich: *New York Counterpoint*

Rodgers and Hammerstein: *Carousel,* Overture

Saltarello

Schoenberg: Five Piano Pieces, Op. 23, V

Schoenberg: Five Pieces for Orchestra, Op. 16, No. 4, *Farben*

Schoenberg: *Pierrot lunaire,* No. 1, *Mondestrunken* (Moondrunk), Sprechstimme

Schubert: "Death and the Maiden" Quartet, II

Schubert: *Der Erlkonig*

Schubert: *Die Forelle,* first verse

Schubert: *Die Forelle,* instrumental version

Schubert: *Gretchen am Spinnrade*

Schubert: String Quartet No. 10, IV

Schubert: "Unfinished" Symphony, I

Schubert: "Wanderer" Fantasy

Schubert: "Das Wandern," from *Die schöne Müllerin*

Schumann: *Carnaval,* "Chopin"

Schumann: *Carnaval,* "Paganini"

Schumann: *Carnaval,* "Pantalon et Columbine"

Schumann: *Carnaval,* "Pause"

Schumann: *Carnaval,* "Préambule," crashing chords

Schumann: *Carnaval,* "Préambule," octaves

Schumann: *Carnaval,* "Reconnaissance"

Schumann: "Im leuchtendem Sommermorgen," from *Dichterliebe*

Schumann: Piano Quintet, I

Schumann: Piano Sonata in F# Minor, I (theme from Clara's *Dance of the Phantoms*)

Schumann: Symphony No. 1, IV

C. Schumann: Piano Trio, IV (Allegretto)

Shostakovich: String Quartet No. 8 in C Minor, II

Sousa: "Stars and Stripes Forever" (piccolo)

Stravinsky: *The Firebird*

Stravinsky: *L'histoire du soldat*

Stravinsky: *Petrushka*

Stravinsky: *Requiem Canticles*

Stravinsky: *The Rite of Spring*, "Games of Rival Cities"

Stravinsky: *The Rite of Spring*, "Glorification of the Chosen Victim"

Stravinsky: *The Rite of Spring*, "Glorification of the Chosen Victim" (timpani)

Stravinsky: *The Rite of Spring*, "Introduction

Stravinsky: *The Rite of Spring*, "Procession of the Oldest and Wisest One"

Stravinsky: *The Rite of Spring*, "Procession of the Oldest and Wisest One" (tuba ostinato)

Stravinsky: *The Rite of Spring*, "Signs of Spring: Girls' Dance"

Stravinsky: *Symphony of Psalms*

"Swing Low" theme

Tchaikovsky: Violin Concerto in D Major, III

Varèse: *Deserts*, excerpt 7

Wagner: *Die Meistersinger von Nürnberg*, Prelude

Wagner: *The Rhinegold*, Prelude

Wagner: *The Rhinegold*, the Valhalla leitmotif

Wagner: *Tannhäuser*, Pilgrim's chorus

Wagner: *Tristan and Isolde*, Prelude

Wagner: *The Valkyrie*, "Du bist der Lenz"

Wagner: *The Valkyrie*, Hunding's leitmotif

Wagner: *The Valkyrie*, Hunding's tuba

Wagner: *The Valkyrie*, love leitmotif

Wagner: *The Valkyrie*, Sieglinde's pity leitmotif

Wagner: *The Valkyrie*, Siegmund's leitmotif, at end mixed with Sieglinde's

Webern: Five Pieces for Orchestra, Op. 10, No. 4

"Will you go walk in the woods so wild?"

▶ Metropolitan Opera Videos

Chapter 7: W. A. Mozart's *Don Giovanni*

Act 1, Scene I, "Notte e giorno faticar" —"Leporello, ove sei?"

Act 1, Scene 5, "Ah! Chi me dice mai"—"Chi è là?"— "Madamina, il catalogo è questo"

Act 1, Scene 9, "Là ci darem la mano"

Part IV: Music and Feeling: Romantic Music

Giacomo Puccini: *La Bohème*, Act II, "Quando me'n vo"

Giuseppe Verdi: *Rigoletto*, Act III, "La donna è mobile"—"Un di, se ben rammentomi"—"Bella figlia dell'amore"

Giuseppe Verdi: Act III, *La Traviata*, "Signora"—"Parigi, o cara"

Chapter 13: Richard Wagner's *The Valkyrie* (*Die Walküre*)

Act 1, Scene 3, "Winterstürme wichen dem Wonnemond"

Act 1, Scene 3, "Siegmund heiss' ich"

Act 3, Prelude, Ride of the Valkyries—"Hojotoho!"

Act 3, Scene 3, Magic Fire Music

Chapter 16: Alban Berg's *Wozzeck*

Act 3, Scene 2, "Dort links geht's in die Stadt"

Act 3, Scene 3, "Tanzt Alle; tanzt nur zu"

Act 3, Scene 4, "Das Messer? Wo ist das Messer?"

Interlude and Act 3, Scene 5, "Ringel, Ringel, Rosenkranz, Ringelreih'n!"

Chapter 19: Coda: Into the Twenty-First Century

John Adams: *Doctor Atomic*, Act I, Scene 3: "Batter my heart"

Author Videos (by chapter)

Chapter 1
Melody
Rhythm and meter
Phrase
Harmony
Expression

Chapter 2
Notation for chant and polyphony

Chapter 3
Imitation in Renaissance music
Rhythm in Dowland's "Can she excuse my wrongs"

Chapter 4
The use of basso continuo in *Orfeo*
Rhythm in Orfeo's song, "Vi ricorda," from Act 2

Chapter 5
Recitative in oratorio
Structure of the "Hallelujah" chorus in Handel's *Messiah*

Chapter 6
Bach's C Minor Fugue: subject and countersubject
Bach's C Minor Fugue: episode and sequence

Chapter 7
The aria "Notte e giorno faticar," from Mozart's *Don Giovanni*
The duet "Là ci darem la mano," from Mozart's *Don Giovanni*

Chapter 8
How to make a theme out of a motive in Beethoven's Fifth Symphony
Rhythmic unity of themes throughout Beethoven's Fifth Symphony

Chapter 9
Accompaniment in *Gretchen am Spinnrade*

Chapter 10
Berlioz's *idée fixe*

Chapter 11
Basic techniques in violin playing
A demonstration of violin virtuosity in Mendelssohn's Violin Concerto

Chapter 12
The Sphinxes and the A-S-C-H motive in Schumann's *Carnaval*

Chapter 13
The sword leitmotif in Wagner's *Valkyrie*

Chapter 14
Syncopation and the spiritual in the first movement of the *New World* Symphony

Chapter 15
Folklike melodies from *The Rite of Spring*
New sounds in "Signs of Spring: Girls' Dance," from *The Rite of Spring*
The building blocks of "Glorification of the Chosen Victim," from *The Rite of Spring*

Chapter 16
The use of note and rhythm in Act 3 of Berg's *Wozzeck*

Chapter 17
The nightingale and the blackbird in "Liturgie de cristal," from Messiaen's *Quartet for the End of Time*

Chapter 18
Meter and rhythms in "America," from Bernstein's *West Side Story*

Appendix
Scales
Harmony

Maps

Europc in 1050	21
Western Europe, ca. 1500	25
Europe, ca. 1610	84
Northern Italy around the time of *Orfeo* (1607)	92
Europe, 1815–48	170
Europe, ca. 1871	259
Europe during the Cold War (1945–91)	400

A "You Are There" Guide to Masterpieces of Western Music

This is a book for people who like to listen to music. It may be that some students who use *Music Then and Now* are not accustomed to hearing the music described in these pages, but all music has common elements. Even if we have varying tastes and like to listen to different music, we're all looking for that same something: what you might call aesthetic pleasure—that warm feeling in the pit of our stomachs. We know how we feel when we hear music we love.

Music happens in time; you can't listen faster or know what's going to happen next (unless, of course, you already know the music). Sometimes we get to know music passively, by noticing that we're hearing a piece we like, or by recognizing that we've heard it before. Many people do their listening this way—by letting it happen while doing something else. That's fine, and we're blessed with a lot of music that is available to us in many different ways.

But in this book we plan to listen a little more *actively*; to pay attention to what's happening, and to try to articulate why we like it—or don't. In a way it's the kind of listening we do at a concert, when a favorite artist or group plays music that we specifically want to hear. For some of us, it's rock music that we like, for others it's jazz, and for still others it may be the latest indie group.

That concert experience, of hearing music in real time, projects a particular kind of excitement: on a recorded track or video, we know that the music will be fine—no one distributes a *bad* performance except as a joke; but in a live situation, anything can happen—and it sometimes does. The excitement of watching and hearing performers walk tightropes of difficulty, of hoping it will go well, of feeling the tension and the effort that a musician puts into giving the very best possible performance, all this is part of the thrill of live performance—along with the fun of being physically present, with other people, when the music is happening.

This book is about such specific musical moments; it's about music, yes, but really about the process and the pleasure of hearing music. Each chapter discusses a precise moment in time, in which a new piece of music was given its first performance. The people who were there were the *only people in the world who had ever heard this music*: the sounds begin, the listeners don't know how it will continue, it spins itself out, and it ends. And if you weren't there you didn't hear it.

The chapters are arranged in chronological order and grouped by musical style periods, with general introductions for each group. If you choose, you can create a history of Western classical music using these examples. But taken another way, each chapter stands on its own as an exploration of a particular place and time, and more importantly, of the beauties of a specific musical moment.

The excitement of performance, and of the new, is what we seek to capture here. The music discussed in this book is now classic, in that it has stood the test of time and continues to be loved by listeners. But there was a moment when each piece was cutting-edge, contemporary, when no one had ever heard it before and no one was sure if it would ever be heard again; it is this moment that we want to capture, to regain the tension and anticipation of the new, and of the *now*, which is sometimes missing in modern concert and recorded performances.

We have chosen interesting moments, and beautiful pieces, in the hope that they will appeal both by their cultural context and by their intrinsic musical worth. The cultural context can be important when it tells us who the people were who first heard this music. What sort of music did they usually listen to? What did they expect? What might have surprised them? What else could they have done on that same day? When we place music in the THEN of its original time and place, we learn a lot about music, about people, and, most important, about ourselves and our own expectations and preferences.

When we return to NOW, we can consider the music just as music, and compare it with other music, either from our own time or from other times and places. This is a luxury that was not available to any of the people who listened to the music described in this book: until the twentieth century no one could hear any music unless they performed it themselves or were physically present when the music was played. And they would probably not have wanted to hear music from the past, or from the future. They wanted music for *now*. And so do we. But our now includes all times and all peoples.

In this book we will focus on one kind of music, and pay close attention to it. Western Classical music, or art music, often has a privileged place compared to other kinds of music. We are not claiming that this type of music is better, or more important, or more significant than other music—it's just the music that I like, that I hope you will too, and that many other people have also liked.

And to like it you need to pay close attention, to listen carefully, and to figure out how to describe what you hear. This book is designed to facilitate that process.

Using the Book

Music Then and Now is accompanied by many useful and instructive features that will help in the study of music. The chapters have a clear **three-part structure**— the setting, the music, and the performance—that unpacks both the musical and cultural meanings of each work. All chapters end with a **Then and Now** section that links the past to the present day.

The book begins with a brief unit on **Fundamental Musical Concepts and Forms**, teaching you how to listen and what to listen for; further details on elements are introduced as they are needed. Throughout this opening chapter, each music element is illustrated with brief excerpts from the core repertoire. When you read the historical chapters that follow, you will not only understand essential concepts, but the works will be familiar companions. **Instruments of the Orchestra** videos show each instrument family in action—strings, winds, brass, percussion—and five **Author Videos** walk you through the elements of music— Melody, Rhythm and meter, Phrase, Harmony, and Expression—illustrating each with pithy music examples. In addition, a short but important **Appendix** at the back of the book discusses the more intricate issues of music notation, including an Author Video on Scales.

There are five historical **Part Introductions**, and they give concise overviews of the major political, artistic, and intellectual trends in each period, including—

- **Arts and Ideas** boxes that present capsule accounts of some of the leading figures in literature, the arts, science, and history.

- **Style Comparisons at a Glance** boxes that list quick comparisons between successive eras, highlighting their similarities and differences.

- **Timelines** that set the musical events and venues in historical context.

THE MIDDLE AGES

	HISTORICAL EVENTS	MUSICAL EVENTS
476	**476** Fall of the Roman Empire **ca. 480–547** Benedict writes his *Rule*	**4th–7th centuries** Christianity spreads across Europe
600	**7th century** Rise of Islam **768–814** Reign of Charles the Great (Charlemagne)	**8th century** Repertory of Gregorian chant stabilized
800	**800** Charlemagne crowned emperor by pope **9th century** Raids of Europe by Vikings in the north, Arabs in the south **843** Treaty of Verdun divides Charlemagne's realm	**10th century** First notated books of chant **10th–11th centuries** Flourishing of tropes and sequences **1098–1179** Hildegard of Bingen
1000	**1099** First Crusade captures Jerusalem from Muslim rule	**11th century** Troubadours (Provençal poet-composers) flourish
1100	**1182** Main altar of Notre Dame Cathedral dedicated **1181/82–1226** St. Francis of Assisi	**12th–13th centuries** Trouvères (French poet-composers) and Minnesänger (German poet-composers) flourish **1150s–1201** Leoninus
1200	**1225–1274** St. Thomas Aquinas, Christian theologian	**ca. 1200** Perotinus
1300	**1308–1321** Dante Alighieri writes *Divine Comedy* **1305–1308** Giotto di Bondone paints fresco cycle in Arena Chapel, Padua **1305–1378** Popes reside in Avignon **1337–1453** Hundred Years' War (between France and England) **1346–1351** Black Death **1370–1371** Giovanni Boccaccio finishes revised *Decameron*, begun 1349 **1383** Geoffrey Chaucer begins *Canterbury Tales*	**1300–1377** Guillaume de Machaut, French poet and composer **ca. 1335–1397** Francesco (Landini) of Florence, composer of secular music
1400		

● Italy ● France ● England ● Germany ● Various

18

Features that are common to all chapters include **sidebars** that bring the cultural context alive—

WOLFGANG AMADÈ MOZART (1756–1791)

Mozart has a reputation as an inspired genius, a composer whose compositions have a perfection and a clarity that has rarely been equaled. Music is thought to have poured out of him in an inspired torrent.

The truth is a little more pedestrian. The talented son of a Salzburg violinist, Mozart and his sister, whom he called Nannerl, were toured around Europe, perhaps exploited, as child prodigies (see Figure 7.3). The young Wolfgang was employed, as his father was, by the prince archbishop of Salzburg. Tours with his father (throughout Italy, England, Germany, and Austria) made the son's talent well known. and Mozart decided to seek his fortune independently in Vienna, where he hoped to establish himself in a court-sponsored position and gain fame as an opera composer. He did not succeed, but his fame is now secure.

In Vienna, Mozart struggled to find his way as a composer. He organized concerts, created piano concertos for his own virtuoso performances, and composed symphonies, chamber music, and other works. Mostly, however, he sought commissions for operas, since that was where he felt his talent lay, and that was how composers achieved success. His *Abduction from the Seraglio* (*Die Entführung aus dem Serail*, 1782) was an enormous success, and on the strength of it he broke with the archbishop, defied his father, and married the singer Constanze Weber (see Figure 7.4). Unfortunately, the hoped-for continued success and financial security evaded him. He scored a hit with Da Ponte's libretto of *The Marriage of Figaro* (1785), which, along with *The Abduction*, made him famous in Prague before he traveled there in January 1787.

Don Giovanni was not, however, a success in Vienna. Despite his appointment as a Chamber Musician to the emperor, and despite further operatic ventures, including *Così fan tutte* (1790, libretto by Da Ponte) and *The Magic Flute* (*Die Zauberflöte*, 1791), a poor economy and Mozart's inability to manage his affairs left him and his family in increasingly difficult circumstances, and they repeatedly moved to smaller and cheaper apartments. He died from an unknown disease in December 1791, leaving behind his unfinished Requiem Mass.

Mozart was witty, amusing, full of fun and jokes, and loved puns and off color humor. He had a talent for complexity, as his skill at billiards and counterpoint attest; he even devised a set of dice that anyone could use to compose a minuet. His brilliant and impromptu lifestyle led to his reputation for tossing off his music, but there was actually a good deal of hard work involved in Mozart's efforts, and the clarity and perfection of his music is an achievement of a genius as well as a superb craftsman.

In addition to his operas, he is remembered for his symphonies and chamber music.

Ⓢ Mozart: Symphony No. 40, I, opening
Ⓢ Mozart: Clarinet Quintet, II
Ⓢ Mozart: *Dies irae*, from Requiem

MAJOR WORKS: Operas, including *Marriage of Figaro, Don Giovanni, Abduction from the Seraglio, Così fan tutte*, and *The Magic Flute*; 41 symphonies; chamber music, including *Eine kleine Nachtmusik*; about 23 piano concertos and other concertos; Masses and 1 Requiem (unfinished); and numerous keyboard works and songs.

■ Concise **Composer Biographies** summarize the personal details and professional activities of the composer's life, works, and style. A short list of principal works— with brief audio excerpts streaming from StudySpace (the student website)—helps you identify the composer's major contributions.

■ The **Closer Look** boxes provide additional information on important historical, musical, or social issues.

The Cult of the Virtuoso

The Italian word *virtuoso* (from a Latin root meaning skill) originally denoted a person who was proficient at something; it might be fencing, music, cooking, or practically any other activity. By the nineteenth century, it had come to mean a performer with almost superhuman skill as a singer or instrumentalist. There had been concertos, and expert players, long before Mendelssohn, but it was not until the early nineteenth century that the virtuoso performer came to inspire the kind of hero worship we now associate with an elite group of rock musicians and other pop idols.

In the 1830s, Niccolò Paganini dazzled all of Europe with his violin acrobatics; he performed what seemed to be miracles—indeed, some thought he was in league with the Devil, or was the Devil himself. At the same time Franz

Pierre Monteux Hears Stravinsky Play the *Rite*

With only Diaghilev and myself as an audience, Stravinsky sat down to play a piano reduction of the entire score. . . . The very walls resounded as Stravinsky pounded away, occasionally stamping his feet and jumping up and down to accentuate the force of the music. Before he got very far I was convinced he was raving mad.

■ **In Their Own Words** boxes allow composers, audiences, and critics to speak for themselves.

■ **You Are There** sidebars establish the setting for each musical event—who heard the music and where, and what they thought about it.

Mozart on Zerlina's Scream

Joseph Svoboda, the concertmaster, recollecting the rehearsal:

At the final rehearsal of the opera Mozart was not at all satisfied with the efforts of a young and very pretty girl, the possessor of a voice of greater purity than power, to whom the part of Zerlina had been allotted. The reader will remember that Zerlina, frightened at Don Giovanni's too pronounced love-making, cries for assistance behind the scenes. In spite of continued repetitions, Mozart was unable to infuse sufficient force into the poor girl's screams, until at last, losing all patience, he clambered from the conductor's desk on to the boards. At that period neither gas nor electric light lent facility to stage mechanism. A few tallow candles dimly glimmered

There are other features common to all chapters as well:

- **Key Terms** are boldfaced throughout and highlighted in red in the margins. Most of these terms are defined, for easy reference, in the **Glossary** at the back of the book, which offers clear and concise definitions.

- Many chapters feature a segment called **"How Did It Go?"** After reading about the contextual background and listening to the music—making up your *own* mind on how the music sounded—you'll have a chance to read about what *actually happened.*

- Each chapter ends with a **Chapter Review** that provides a **Summary of Musical Styles**, important terms to know (**Flashcards**), and a list of the **Interactive Listening Guides** (**iLGs**) and **Author Videos**. End-of-chapter material also includes resource and review materials—online **Chapter Quizzes, Listening Quizzes,** and **Music Activities**—all available on SudySpace, and will test your understanding of the music and facts in each chapter.

Marginal icons direct your attention to important media resources on StudySpace—

- Eighty-four **Interactive Listening Guides** highlight essential musical features of each work in real time and, along with the online Listening Quizzes, teach you how to listen critically to all musical styles and genres.

- Over two hundred short **Listening Excepts** —drawn from the core repertoire or from related works from all periods—highlight essential musical concepts and enable you to instantly make comparisons to other works across periods and genres.

- Thirty-two **Author Videos** linked to our online Listening Guides demonstrate *how* to listen and *what to listen for*. There is an Author Video for most of the pieces featured in the text.

- Metropolitan Opera Videos make you feel as if you're right there, placing you in front-row seats to enjoy stunning performances of *Don Giovanni, Die Walküre, Wozzeck, Doctor Atomic,* and others.

Full-color photographs and illustrations highlight and bring to life important ideas, architecture, people, and events from the text.

In addition, we've inserted some quick reference guides:

- A **Table of Listening Guides** (inside the front and back covers) gives quick and easy access to each Listening Guide in the book.

- All short **Listening Excerpts, Metropolitan Opera Videos,** and **Author Videos** are listed in the front of the book for easy reference.

- Important historical **Maps** give clear overviews of changing political boundaries throughout the history of the Western world.

About the Listening Guides

The **Listening Guides**—both in-text and online—highlight the essential musical features of each work in real time. These easy-to-follow guides will teach you how to listen critically to all musical styles and genres and will augment your listening and understanding. Icons in the green strip at the top of all in-text Listening Guides indicate, when applicable, the following:

- ⓢ: the work is available on StudySpace for streaming.
- **DVD**: the work is available on an mp3 disc.
- ▶: a Metropolitan Opera Video is available on StudySpace for streaming.
- 🎙: an Author Video to enhance your understanding of the work is available on StudySpace for streaming.

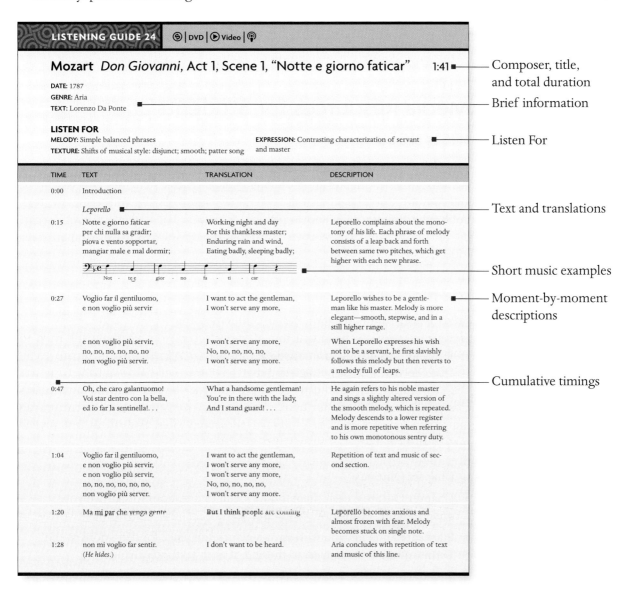

Labels pointing to the Listening Guide:
- Composer, title, and total duration
- Brief information
- Listen For
- Text and translations
- Short music examples
- Moment-by-moment descriptions
- Cumulative timings

LISTENING GUIDE 24   ⓢ | DVD | ▶ Video | 🎙

Mozart *Don Giovanni*, Act 1, Scene 1, "Notte e giorno faticar"   1:41

DATE: 1787
GENRE: Aria
TEXT: Lorenzo Da Ponte

LISTEN FOR
MELODY: Simple balanced phrases
TEXTURE: Shifts of musical style: disjunct; smooth; patter song
EXPRESSION: Contrasting characterization of servant and master

TIME	TEXT	TRANSLATION	DESCRIPTION
0:00	Introduction		
	Leporello		
0:15	Notte e giorno faticar per chi nulla sa gradir; piova e vento sopportar, mangiar male e mal dormir;	Working night and day For this thankless master; Enduring rain and wind, Eating badly, sleeping badly;	Leporello complains about the monotony of his life. Each phrase of melody consists of a leap back and forth between same two pitches, which get higher with each new phrase.
0:27	Voglio far il gentiluomo, e non voglio più servir	I want to act the gentleman, I won't serve any more,	Leporello wishes to be a gentleman like his master. Melody is more elegant—smooth, stepwise, and in a still higher range.
	e non voglio più servir, no, no, no, no, no, no non voglio più servir.	I won't serve any more, No, no, no, no, no, I won't serve any more.	When Leporello expresses his wish not to be a servant, he first slavishly follows this melody but then reverts to a melody full of leaps.
0:47	Oh, che caro galantuomo! Voi star dentro con la bella, ed io far la sentinella!. . .	What a handsome gentleman! You're in there with the lady, And I stand guard! . . .	He again refers to his noble master and sings a slightly altered version of the smooth melody, which is repeated. Melody descends to a lower register and is more repetitive when referring to his own monotonous sentry duty.
1:04	Voglio far il gentiluomo, e non voglio più servir, e non voglio più servir, no, no, no, no, no, no, non voglio più server.	I want to act the gentleman, I won't serve any more, I won't serve any more, No, no, no, no, no, I won't serve any more.	Repetition of text and music of second section.
1:20	Ma mi par che venga gente	But I think people are coming	Leporello becomes anxious and almost frozen with fear. Melody becomes stuck on single note.
1:28	non mi voglio far sentir. (He hides.)	I don't want to be heard.	Aria concludes with repetition of text and music of this line.

Every Listening Guide includes a recording of the music in both streaming and mp3 formats.

The LGs offer other important information as well (see sample LG, p. xxiii, for boldfaced terms):

- Each piece lists the **composer** and **title** as well as **brief information** about the work.
- The **total duration** of the piece is found to the right of the title. **Cumulative timings**, beginning with zero, run down the left side of each Listening Guide.
- A **Listen For** section spotlights the big ideas—the "can't miss" features of each work.
- **Text and translation**s, when appropriate, are given for all vocal works.
- **Short musical examples** are provided that identify themes and other important musical events.
- Detailed **moment-by-moment descriptions** allow you to follow the work throughout, carefully guiding your listening.

Media Resources for Students and Instructors

The Total Access Package includes full access to all online media, including streaming music, Chapter and Listening Quizzes, Music Activities, Videos, ebook, and more. A unique registration code comes automatically with each new textbook copy. Access couldn't be simpler for instructors. For students, this total access couldn't be richer. If you've got a new book, you have access to everything. That's total access.

FOR THE STUDENT

StudySpace: Your Place for a Better Understanding
StudySpace tells you what you should know, shows you what you still need to review, and then gives you an organized study plan to master the material.

Our effective and well-designed online resources will help you succeed in this course—StudySpace is unmatched in providing a one-stop study solution that's closely aligned with the textbook. This easy-to-navigate website offers you an impressive range of exercises, interactive learning tools, assessment, and review materials, including:

- **Chapter Outlines**.
- **Chapter Quizzes**: each chapter quiz includes questions to sharpen your understanding of historical contexts.
- **Flashcards** provide you with an at-a-glance reference for definitions to the Terms to Know that appear at the end of each textbook chapter.

- **Music Activities**: twelve activities are designed to get you thinking about musical connections and mastering concepts. Activities include brief exercises on Melody and Harmony, Rhythm and Meter, Keys (major/minor), Texture, Tempo and Dynamics, and the Instruments of the Orchestra. Style comparisons include musical examples that span chapters so you can assess your understanding of musical contrasts in specific eras—Middle Ages, Renaissance, Baroque, Classical, Romantic, and Modern.

- **Listening Quizzes**: each StudySpace listening quiz includes questions (with music excerpts) to help you grasp the important moments of the works covered in each chapter.

- **Playlists** combine all the selections for a chapter into an easily scanned and accessed listening menu. This section of StudySpace includes:

  - **Streamed audio selections** of all eighty-four listening guides covered in the book.

  - **Interactive Listening Guides** (**iLGs**) for every selection.

  - **Author Videos,** which tell you what to listen for.

  - **Metropolitan Opera Videos,** including scenes from Mozart's *Don Giovanni,* Wagner's *Valkyrie,* Berg's *Wozzeck,* and Adams's *Doctor Atomic.*

  - **Listening Excerpts:** over two hundred brief, illustrative excerpts that expand the reach of the works for each composer.

- **Ebook Links**: the ebook and StudySpace link seamlessly to one another. Each StudySpace chapter assembles a list connecting to the relevant sections of the ebook. Once in the ebook, links are available to music, iLGs, Listening Excerpts, and Videos.

Music Then and Now **mp3 + iLG Recordings Disc**

Providing an option for offline listening, the recordings disc assembles all twenty-eight works and their eighty-four corresponding iLGs into a rapidly accessible and stable platform. Also included on the disc are the **Author Video** lessons and, as a bonus, all additional **Listening Excerpts** are indexed to maintain a direct correlation between StudySpace and the disc to all the listening materials.

FOR THE INSTRUCTOR

Coursepacks

Available at no cost to professors or students, Norton coursepacks for online or hybrid courses are available in a variety of formats, including all versions of Blackboard and WebCT. With just a simple download from our Instructor Website, you can bring high-quality Norton digital media into a new or existing online course. Content includes chapter-based assignments, Test Banks and quizzes, interactive learning tools, and all content from the StudySpace website. This customizable resource includes:

- Links to all **StudySpace** content.
- Additional **Chapter and Listening Quiz Questions**.
- All **Assessment Activities** report to an individual course management gradebook.
- **Total Access Package** (*Music Then and Now* textbook registration code required) includes the following:
  - **Listening Quizzes**.
  - **All Playlist materials, including interactive Listening Guides.**
  - **Music Activities**.
  - **Ebooks links**.

Instructor's Resource Disc (IRD)

The ultimate tool for transition, this disc contains everything an instructor needs to start from scratch or to augment his or her music appreciation lectures. Contents include:

- Chapter PowerPoints, integrated with all the art from the book.
- Listening Guides, as they appear in the textbook (iLGs are not included on the IRD).
- Art JPGS and PowerPoints.
- Listening Excerpts—over two hundred short examples to illustrate a composers range beyond the primary repertoire covered in the LGs.
- Author Videos.

Instructor Website (wwnorton.com/instructors)

This instructor-only password-protected site features instructional content for use in lecture and distance education, including a Coursepack, Test-item files, PowerPoint lecture slides, images, figures, and more. The Instructor Website for *Music Then and Now* includes:

- Chapter PowerPoints, integrated with all the art from the book.
- Listening Guides, as they appear in the textbook.
- Art JPGS and PowerPoints.
- Test Bank.
- Instructor's Manual.
- Coursepack.

Test Bank, by Nathan C. Bakkum, Columbia College Chicago

The Test Bank includes over 1,300 multiple choice, true/false, short answer, and essay questions. Each question is identified with a topic, question type (factual, conceptual, or applied), and difficulty level, enabling instructors to customize exams for their students. The test bank is available in a variety of formats online and on a CD-ROM.

Instructor's Manual, by Blake Stevens, College of Charleston, and Annie Yen-Ling Liu, College of Charleston

The Instructor's Manual includes detailed teaching advice for new and experienced instructors alike. Each chapter offers:

- An overview and outline.
- A list of learning objectives.
- Lecture suggestions and class activities.
- Suggested writing assignments.
- Advice for responding to the challenges of teaching music appreciation.
- Supplemental repertoire and a detailed annotated bibliography of books and audiovisual resources.

In addition, the manual includes sample syllabi and advice for crafting writing assignments for music appreciation classes. It is available online as a PDF file.

Acknowledgments

This book began as a conversation with Maribeth Payne, Music Editor at W. W. Norton & Company, with whom I had collaborated on several projects in the past; and with Pete Lesser, currently Associate Director for Digital Media, who was the acquiring editor. They assured me that a new textbook is a lot of work, and that it requires many hands to bring it to completion. I had no idea how right they were. I had written books before, but never a textbook, and I have learned a great deal about collaboration, incremental improvement, repeated consultation, and the wonderful synergy that sometimes happens when many talented people bring their skills to bear on a single project.

No one individual—certainly not this author—can have all the skills, insights, and creative ideas that have made this book so much more interesting, comprehensive, and clear that I could ever have made it by myself.

The number of people who need to be credited for their substantial contributions is large, and if the list below seems almost numbing, please remember that these are not just names but individuals with talent and skill, each of whom has contributed something indispensable to the result that you hold in your hands.

From W. W. Norton, in addition to Maribeth Payne and Pete Lesser, Kathy Talalay, Developmental Editor and Project Editor, has worked tirelessly, patiently, and creatively with me (and with many others) as a sort of control center for the whole project, and it's hard to imagine ever doing any sort of project without her wit, her ceaseless help, and her gentle reminders. Ariella Foss, Assistant Editor, coordinated all the reviews, from generous generalists and outstanding experts, and prepared enormously useful summaries. Justin Hoffman, Associate Editor, coordinated and worked on the many ancillaries that make this project so comprehensive. Jane Searle, Director of Production, College, did all the production on this book, which requires a staggering amount of coordination.

Steve Hoge, Electronic Media Editor, ably and expertly created, coordinated, and tracked the outstanding media package for this book, assisted at Norton by Nicole Sawa and Stefani Wallace, Emedia Editorial Assistants, who coordinated the various aspects of electronic enhancements, including the listening guides and the many author videos. Online quizzes are by Rebecca G. Marchand (Longy School of Music, Boston Conservatory); Interactive Listening Guide programming is by John Husser; the Author Videos were produced by Erica Rothman of Nightlight Productions.

Stephanie Romeo, Photo Editor, managed the photo side of the book and selected the cover art. Indispensable in their areas of expertise are Megan Jackson, Permissions Manager; Leah Clark, Senior Designer, who designed the cover; and Rubina Yeh, Art Director.

A number of other experts have collaborated in this book, called into service by the publisher to contribute to the communal effort. Harry Haskell, and old and admired friend, improved much of the writing here in a crucial stage of creation. Jodi Beder, Manuscript Editor, improved the book at a later stage, and taught me much; she also helped develop Chapter 1, Fundamentals. Julie Tesser, Photo Researcher; Allison Courtney Fitch Hirschey, Recordings Consultant; David Botwinik, Music Typesetter; Randy Foster and Monica Combs at Naxos, have all contributed expertise in their particular areas that no one person could hope to match.

The book itself has been brought to its state of perfection with the expert help of Lissi Sigillo, Book Designer; Carole Desnoes, Page Layout; Scott Gleason, who vetted endnotes and in-text quotations, checked musical examples and some timings; Barbara Necol, proofreader; and Marilyn Bliss, Indexer.

I am particularly grateful to those colleagues who were kind enough to read and evaluate early versions of this material. Some of them are experienced teachers who have a good sense of what is likely to be effective and attractive to students; others, no less expert in those matters, also read specific chapters with a view to accuracy and clearness of interpretation. Nobody could be an expert about all the things in this book, and do not be fooled for a moment into thinking that the information herein is all my own; it is owed to a community of scholars and teachers to whom I hope to give back here just a bit of the gratitude I feel. Those teachers and scholars who read and commented are:

Nicole Baker (California State University, Fullerton)
Nathan C. Bakkum (Columbia College Chicago)
Anthony Barone (University of Nevada, Las Vegas)
Michael Beckerman (New York University)
Geoffrey Block (University of Puget Sound)
Cathryn Clayton (University of Utah)
Julie E. Cumming (McGill University)
Andrew Dell'Antonio (The University of Texas at Austin)
Robert Fallon (Carnegie Mellon University)
Lisa Feurzeig (Grand Valley State University).
David Gramit (University of Alberta)
Thomas Grey (Stanford University)

James Grier (University of Western Ontario)
James A. Grymes (University of North Carolina at Charlotte)
Patricia Hall (University of Michigan, Ann Arbor)
D. Kern Holoman (University of California, Davis)
Jennifer L. Hund (Purdue University)
Orly L. Krasner (City College, CUNY)
Jeffrey Kurtzman (Washington University in St. Louis)
Michael Marissen (Swarthmore College)
William McGinney (University of North Texas)
Gerald Moshell (Trinity College)
Nancy Newman (University at Albany)
Alison Nikitopoulos (Louisiana State University)
James Parsons (Missouri State University)
John Platoff (Trinity College)
Peter Schimpf (Metropolitan State University of Denver)
Glenn Stanley (University of Connecticut, Storrs)
Blake Stevens (College of Charleston)
Joseph N. Straus (Graduate Center, City University of New York)
Marie Sumner Lott (Georgia State University)
Andrew Talle (Peabody Conservatory of Johns Hopkins University)
R. Larry Todd (Duke University)
Mary Wolinski (Western Kentucky University)
Scott Warfield (University of Central Florida)
Susan Youens (University of Notre Dame)

Particular thanks go to those students, at Princeton and Harvard, who test-drove earlier versions of this material, and to their teachers, Wendy Heller and Ellen Exner.

Wendy Strothman helped bring this book into W. W. Norton's competent hands, and has followed its development with generosity and hospitality. Peggy Badenhausen, some of whose beautiful art appears here, has put up with the whole thing with characteristic patience and understanding.

—Tom Kelly
May 2012

MUSIC THEN AND NOW

CHAPTER 1

Fundamental Musical Concepts and Forms

▶ **VIDEOS**

- Instruments of the Orchestra (available on StudySpace)

🎙 **AUTHOR VIDEOS**

- Melody
- Rhythm and meter
- Phrase
- Harmony
- Expression

Introduction

"Music expresses that which cannot be said, and on which it is impossible to be silent."

—Victor Hugo

Music, even familiar music, can be very difficult to describe. We may only be able to say that we know what we like when we hear it. This chapter is an introduction to the conventional terms and concepts that are used to describe the music covered in this book, and it provides a good introduction to thinking about music. An Appendix at the back of the book (see pp. A-1–A-8) deals with more technical matters, including musical notation, and a Glossary provides definitions of all the main terms used (see pp. A-9–A-16). These, along with other online study materials, form the reference portion of this book.

Some Basic Terms and Concepts about Sound

We value music for its effect on us, and when we talk about it, this is often what we have to say: "I like this piece, I don't like that one; do you like the other one as much as I do?" Sometimes, however, we want to be more specific, to *describe* something about music, to let someone else know about the sound of something, to say what it was that we liked, to compare two or more songs. Ordinary language can be wonderful for poetic, suggestive descriptions ("It sounds like fleecy clouds on a summer afternoon"), but these mean different things to different people, and sometimes we may want to be more concrete.

This book covers a particular musical world: that of the European and American "classical" tradition, composers such as Bach and Beethoven, symphonies and operas and chamber music, Gregorian chant and *West Side Story*. As this music has evolved, a special vocabulary has evolved along with it, much as football, basketball, and soccer have their own vocabulary. Some of the terminology might be thought of as instructions, used by composers to tell performers how to understand what is on the page: for example, how fast to play, or in what mood. Other terms are descriptive, used by listeners who want to articulate what they hear, by music historians to place musical developments in a historical context, and by students of music to delve into the intricacies of what sets one musical style apart from another or makes a particular symphony great. The vocabulary we will look at is standard for talking about this music, and you will see it in concert programs and music reviews of similar music. (Other kinds of music, such as the classical music of India or China, and even jazz and blues, may use different musical instruments, scales, rhythms, and techniques; each tradition has its own musical vocabulary, and may require its own names for its special musical instruments, techniques, and features.) It may take some time and effort to learn the terms, because music itself is a wordless and ephemeral art, but for that very reason, the special vocabulary is useful, and can even help us hear music more clearly.

Music has many aspects, but all of them have to do with *sound* and *time*. Every sound, every event in music, has numerous ways in which it might be described. In addition, a single moment has numerous characteristics—it can be, say, loud, fast, high, polyphonic, played on a clarinet, and speeding up, all at the same time. The terms that follow are ways of separating out some of these variables that coexist. In this opening chapter we will use many examples from the pieces discussed in this book. Chapter 1, then, is not only a reference but also an introduction to the music to come.

NOTES AND MUSIC: PITCHED AND UNPITCHED

Sound has a definition in physics, but what we're interested in here is sound as we perceive it: a sensation that we perceive through our ears, created by the vibration of airwaves. We hear in the range of 20 to 20,000 vibrations ("cycles") per second (or hertz, abbreviated Hz). There are a lot of sounds in this world, and any of them could be music if we listen to them for pleasure ("That's music to my ears"). We define music more by *how* we behave toward the sound than *what* the sound actually is. By "noise" we usually mean sound that is not communicating anything and is annoying. But some music incorporates sounds that are usually thought of as noise: there's a string quartet with a helicopter, by Karlheinz Stockhausen, for example; a ballet with airplane propellers, by George Antheil; and a piece with a typewriter and a Wheel of Fortune, by Erik Satie.

Noise has a more specific technical meaning: sound without specific pitch. In music we distinguish between pitched and unpitched sound. By "pitch" we mean, technically, the frequency of the vibrations: if something vibrates 440 times per second, it is sounding the note that we call "A." It's also the note that the oboe plays when an orchestra tunes up, and the note that most tuning forks play (see Figure 1.1).

But there are sounds that contain many pitches and, as a result, we can't distinguish a single pitch: a waterfall, for example, has so many kinds of vibration that it has an unpitched sound. Many instruments, too, are unpitched, including cymbals, triangles, and most drums; and foot stamping, hand clapping, and finger snapping, all examples of unpitched sounds, are often used in music.

FIG. 1.1 A tuning fork, which produces a very pure tone.

 Melody

UP AND DOWN: PITCH AND MELODY

We speak of pitches as being higher and lower: women's and children's voices are higher in pitch than men's, and a trumpet plays higher than a tuba. (Interestingly, this use of spatial terms to describe pitch differences holds in various languages.) Higher notes vibrate faster: the A used for orchestra tuning, at 440 Hz (vibrations per second), is higher than what we call middle C, which is approximately in the middle of the piano keyboard, at about 262 Hz. We don't actually perceive the frequency of the vibrations, but they can be measured in a laboratory, and the vibrations are what's causing the difference we hear. The lowest note on most pianos (all the way to the left) is a low A at 27.5 Hz; the highest (all the way to the right) is a high C, at 4,186 Hz, although, as we shall see, because of overtones, we do make use of our hearing above this level. The word "note" is often used to mean pitch, as in "the note A," "the note B," and so on, but each note has other aspects too, which we'll discuss later.

We use the first seven letters of the alphabet to indicate the ascending series of notes: A, B, C, D, E, F, G (these correspond to white keys on a piano; see Figure

1.2). After G, the series repeats: the next note is again A, an **octave** (eight notes) above the previous A, and vibrating exactly twice as fast. (Some countries use syllables instead of letters: do, re, mi, fa, sol, la, ti. You can read more about note names in the discussion of musical notation in the Appendix as well as hear a Video about **scales**—collections of pitches arranged in ascending or descending order.) The other pitches we use, which we call sharps and flats, correspond to the black keys of the piano. Note that some cultures around the world, not to mention traditional American blues, use pitches that are not even in our system. But the systems of naming notes, whether A, B, C or do, re, mi, all reflect an interesting aspect of how humans around the world perceive pitch: we actually hear notes that are an octave apart as being the same in some fundamental way.

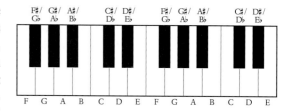

FIG. 1.2 Piano keyboard

When we put several notes together in sequence, we are creating what is called a **melody**: a series of musical notes designed to be sung or played in succession. We usually use the word *melody* for a series of notes that is somehow memorable, often because it is singable, or catchy in some way. We can't always say why it's memorable, but we can try to describe it. Later we'll talk about rhythm and meter, the other main elements of melody. But just in terms of pitch, we can talk about whether notes rise or fall, and whether the movement from one note to the next, the melodic motion, is **conjunct** (by step, to an adjacent pitch) or **disjunct** (skipping pitches). Some melodies are primarily conjunct ("My Country, 'Tis of Thee"); other melodies are primarily disjunct: "The Star-Spangled Banner" is a good example. You can often tell that a melody is disjunct if you try singing it: disjunct melodies tend to be harder to sing than conjunct melodies.

Many melodies are a mixture of conjunct and disjunct motion. Listen to the first segments or **phrases** of a melody from Berlioz's *Fantastic Symphony*. Each phrase begins with disjunct motion and ends with conjunct motion.

Ⓢ Berlioz: *Fantastic Symphony*, "March to the Scaffold" (conjunct)

Ⓢ Handel: *Messiah*, "And he shall reign for ever and ever" (disjunct)

Ⓢ Berlioz: *Fantastic Symphony*, I, first theme, following introduction

But there's more to say about disjunct melodies: how far apart are the pitches—how large are the melodic skips? We tend to hear larger skips as being more energetic, more dramatic (they are also harder to sing). We call the distance between two pitches an **interval**. The interval between two notes a letter name apart (e.g., A–B, F–G, G–A) is called a *second*; a *third* is the interval between two notes that skip a letter between (A–C, D–F, etc.), a *fourth* is one note wider (A–D, etc.), and so on.

Interval

TIME: RHYTHM, BEAT, AND METER

🎙 Rhythm and meter

Music happens in time, and the temporal aspect of music is often described in terms of rhythm and meter. Rhythm is the hardest word to spell in all of music, and it is the central fact of music: **rhythm** is the sequence of events in musical time. We perceive time, and rhythm, when we perceive change. A single unchanging and unending tone would be impossible to perceive as music, but once there are two notes, one after another, we have rhythm—and music becomes possible.

Most music that you are familiar with, as well as most of the music we will be discussing in this text, has an underlying pulse or **beat**, a regular unit of musical time, like the ticking of a clock, or a heartbeat. The speed of the beat is referred to as **tempo** (the Italian word for time), which is often given in terms of number of beats per minute (see metronome, below).

Meter is a grouping of beats. Regular meter in which beats are grouped in twos (*1-2, 1-2,* etc.), threes, or fours is common to most of the music in this book, and indeed, most of the music in our lives. Meter occurs naturally in the way we move, even breathe, and is central to music for dancing. Walking produces a meter of two beats, waltzing produces a meter of three beats. While most of us are familiar with meters of 1, 2, 3, 4, and 6, other meters are common in the traditional music of some cultures (for example, meters of 5 or 7 are common in Greek music). Occasionally a classical composer will try something unusual (one movement of a symphony by Tchaikovsky is in quintuple meter, *1-2-3-4-5*; so is the Dave Brubeck Quartet's *Take Five*), but duple and triple meter are the norm for most classical music, as well as the popular music you probably know. The earliest music we discuss, Gregorian chant (see Chapter 2), may have been sung with a feeling of beat, but it did not have a meter. Parts of Stravinsky's *Rite of Spring* (see Chapter 15) have frequently changing meter. But most music has a more or less regular meter. Meter is the yardstick by which we measure the passage of musical time.

Ⓢ Stravinsky: *The Rite of Spring,* "Signs of Spring: Girls' Dance"

Countless melodies have the same meter; it is the rhythm that gives them their distinctive temporal character. While meter is (normally) regular, rhythm is highly variable; it creates a sense of motion that is interesting mostly with respect to the underlying meter. In the following example, you'll note that the beats come regularly, *1-2-3, 1-2-3*: that's the meter, a triple meter where the first beat of each group (the **downbeat**) gets an accent but has the same length as the other beats. The rhythm—that is, the placement of the syllables, the timing of the events of the song—occurs sometimes at the same time as one of the beats (we say it comes "on the beat"), and sometimes between beats; and some of the syllables last longer than others, as in the familiar "Happy Birthday":

Downbeat

Meter:	3	**1**	2	3	**1**	2	3	**1**	2	3	**1**	2	
Rhythm:	Happy	birth-	day	to	you,		Happy	birth-	day	to	you,		

Meter:	3	**1**	2	3	**1**	2	3	**1**	2	3	**1**	2	3
Rhythm:	Happy	birth-	day,	dear	Wolf-	gang,	Happy	birth-	day	to	you!		

When we sing "Happy Birthday," we only sing the melody and its rhythm, we don't sing the meter—but we *feel* the meter, and that's what makes the rhythm interesting. (Incidentally, this song provides some good examples of a common, very characteristic uneven long-short rhythm often referred as *dotted rhythm*, discussed in the Appendix: each time the word "Happy" occurs in the song, it is sung as a long note followed by a much shorter one, all in the space of one beat. Also, you might have noticed the little symbol over "-gang." It's called a *fermata*; and if you think about how you sing the song, you might guess what it signifies.)

COMBINING PITCH AND RHYTHM

🎙 Phrase

Melodies

Melodies are a combination of pitch and rhythm—notes in time. There are further ways too, of thinking about melodies.

Melodies may have *regular* or *irregular rhythm*. "Twinkle, Twinkle, Little Star" is essentially regular: most of its notes are the same length. Some melodies have regular rhythmic patterns such as short-long or long-short-short, but others such as "The Star-Spangled Banner" are more irregular.

A melody may have *phrases of regular* or *irregular lengths*. The vast majority of songs you know—"Twinkle, Twinkle," "Old Folks at Home," "Take Me Out to the Ball Game," folk songs, show tunes, jazz standards, national anthems, hymns, and many more—are built of phrases of regular lengths. Regular phrases are rather like lines of poetry, one phrase suggesting an answering phrase, so that phrases tend to come in pairs, as in the opening of a duet from Mozart's *Don Giovanni*.

Ⓢ Mozart: *Don Giovanni,* Act 1, Scene 9, "Là ci darem la mano"

Many melodies in classical music don't have such regular phrases. Phrases of irregular lengths are particularly common in classical music written before 1750 and after 1900, as in Stravinsky's Introduction to *The Rite of Spring*.

Several other terms you will commonly see are closely related to melody. In some contexts, a melody is referred to as a **theme** (for example, "theme and variations" or "rondo theme") or a **subject** (the main melody of a fugue). Themes and subjects are essentially melodies that are used in some structural way, by being altered, for example, or by returning later in the music. Thus they become part of larger-scale musical form. Another important term is **motive**, indicating a small melodic unit, perhaps only two or three notes, that is, again, used in some structural way. A good example of a motive is the famous opening of Beethoven's Symphony No. 5, a four-note motive.

Stravinsky: The Rite of Spring, "Introduction"

Theme and subject

Motive

Beethoven: Symphony No. 5, I, opening 4-note notive

HARMONY

Harmony

One of the most characteristic—and pleasurable—aspects of Western music is the use of **harmony**. Harmony makes use of **chords**—collections of three or more pitches sounded together to produce a pleasing sound. Chords are commonly used to accompany melodies; and series of chords provide much of the sense of direction in music, of tension or of finality. Harmony is the art of arranging and ordering these sounds.

Chords

The interval names we mentioned earlier in relation to melody (seconds, thirds, etc.) are also useful in talking about **consonance** (notes that sound well together) and **dissonance** (notes that sound harsh together). Much of the dramatic and emotional impact of harmony has to do with the tension and relaxation created by the succession of dissonant and consonant intervals and chords.

Consonance and dissonance

Intervals and harmony are discussed at greater length in the Appendix.

FAST AND SLOW: TEMPO

Expression

Music seems to be going fast when there are many short notes close together. Generally we use the Italian word **tempo** (which means "time") to indicate the concept of speed in music.

Composers may indicate tempo by using an Italian word (see the list below). You'll notice that some of these words are about speed, but others are about mood. The list is far from complete—and not everyone agrees on how slow is "slow" or whether Largo is slower than Adagio—but generally, these terms are the most commonly used tempo indications, proceeding from slow to fast:

Grave	*grave, serious (very slow)*	Moderato	*moderate*
Largo	*broad*	Allegretto	*fairly happy (fairly fast)*
Adagio	*slow*	Allegro	*happy (fast)*
Lento	*slow*	Vivace	*lively*
Larghetto	*fairly broad*	Presto	*very fast*
Andante	*going, walking (somewhat slow)*	Prestissimo	*as fast as possible*

All of these terms can be modified in various ways: as diminutives, superlatives, and the like (adagietto, adagissimo), or by qualifying them (un poco adagio—somewhat adagio; allegro assai—very allegro). Or composers can give a description that combines mood, emotion, and speed in order to create a kind of feeling for the piece—for example, "Allegro ma non troppo con molta passione" (Fast but not too fast, with much passion).

Composers may choose to give tempo indications in their own language, or to give no indication at all. Much music before Mozart's time had little or no indication of tempo—you had to figure it out from the musical context.

Metronome

An alternative way to indicate tempo is by using a metronome. The original metronome was a mechanical device, an inverted pendulum, patented in 1815 by Johann Nepomuk Maelzel, a friend of Beethoven's. Nowadays most metronomes are electronic, but they work the same way: giving signals, usually clicks, at a speed selected by the user. A composer might give a metronome mark such as "♩ = 60," meaning that sixty notes of this length should fit into a minute. The metronome is then set at 60, so that it clicks sixty times in a minute (once per second, or the speed of a relaxed heartbeat), and the musicians adjust the performance accordingly.

Often a composer wants the performer to change tempo: speed up, slow down. There are conventional Italian indications for that too (the abbreviations are in italics), such as

accelerando, *accel.*	speeding up
ritardando, *rit.*, *ritard.*	slowing down
rallentando, *rall.*	slowing down
a tempo	back to the original speed
più mosso	faster (usually refers to the tempo of a new section)
meno mosso	slower (usually refers to the tempo of a new section)

While tempo indications are a communication from the composer to the performer, they also allow listeners to identify and distinguish sections of a piece of music, and to talk about how the music communicates to us. When we listen, we have our own sense of tempo. Once you are familiar with the tempo terminology, you might try assigning tempo designations as you are listening to a musical work.

 Expression

LOUD AND SOFT: VOLUME AND DYNAMICS

Sounds can be loud, soft, and everything between; they can stay at one level, or change slowly or quickly to a different loudness. In music, we use the word **dynamics** to refer to the level of loudness or softness of music. Traditionally (for historical reasons), many indications in written music are given in Italian, and this is generally true for dynamics: **piano** means soft, and **forte** means loud. (The instrument we know as the piano was originally named the **pianoforte** or the **fortepiano**: when it was invented in the eighteenth century, it was notable for being able to play gradations of soft and loud.) Here are some of the common terms for dynamics, and their abbreviations:

pianissimo	*pp*	very soft	fortissimo	*ff*		very loud
piano	*p*	soft	più forte			louder
mezzo piano	*mp*	somewhat soft	più piano			softer
mezzo forte	*mf*	somewhat loud	crescendo	*cresc.*		becoming louder
forte	*f*	loud	descrescendo	*decresc.*		becoming softer

SMOOTH AND ROUGH: TEXTURE

Most of the music we listen to consists of more than a single melodic line. Perhaps several different instruments play together, each with its bit of melody; or a chorus sings rich chords, all in the same rhythm; or a song has a chordal accompaniment on piano. We refer to these overall effects as **texture**.

Sometimes it is easiest simply to describe the individual elements, but there are some basic textures that are worth pointing out, because they can serve as categories that allow us to describe a much larger range of textures.

Monophonic texture refers to music with a single melodic line sounding the same thing at the same time—whether played or sung, performed on a single instrument or by a voice or voices and instruments playing in unison. Examples include the clarinet solo that forms the third movement of Messiaen's *Quartet for the End of Time*; the choir singing the Gregorian chant "Puer natus est"; the moment in Handel's "Hallelujah" chorus where the choir all sing "For the Lord God omnipotent reigneth"; and the opening of the middle movement, for clarinet, violin, and cello, in Messiaen's *Quartet for the End of Time*. (The last two of these are perhaps not *strictly* monophonic; the choir in the Handel, and the instruments in the Messiaen Interlude, are in octave—but octaves, as we've seen, sound almost like unisons.)

Homophonic texture refers to music where there are many notes at once, but all moving in the same rhythm. Examples are a choir or a congregation singing a hymn in harmony; the moment in the "Hallelujah" chorus where the chorus sings a series of "Hallelujahs" in the same rhythm; and the ensemble of trombones in Monteverdi's *Orfeo*.

The word "homophonic" is also used to apply to another texture: that of a *melody and accompaniment*, when this accompaniment may have something of a texture of its own. Examples include the opening melody of Mendelssohn's Violin Concerto, and the waltz theme from Berlioz's *Fantastic Symphony*.

Polyphonic texture refers to a web of autonomous melodies, each of which contributes to the texture and to the harmony but is a separate and independent strand in the fabric. Examples are the Agnus Dei from Byrd's Mass for Four Voices; the Fugue in C Minor, from Book 1 of Bach's *Well-Tempered Clavier*; and the section in the "Hallelujah" chorus where the choir sings "And he shall reign for ever and ever." In all three cases, the texture is also **imitative**, that is, each voice imitates the previous voice, singing or playing the same melody, often at a different pitch level. Polyphonic texture need not be imitative; Stravinsky provides one of the most complicated polyphonic textures in the introduction to *The Rite of Spring*, but it is not imitative.

Most textures are not all one texture or another. A singer and a guitar, for example, are not exactly homophonic, but close. A section of a polyphonic piece might be homophonic, or almost so. There are cases where two voices, often a melody and a bass line, are more important than other parts—for example, in the music of Handel and Bach, often the harmony is filled in by the harpsichord or other instruments, but it is still the melody and bass line that are dominant. A melody sung by a voice, with a rippling accompaniment on the piano, might be hard to classify as to texture. It's often best to give as clear a description of the texture as possible without relying on these categories. The terms of texture can be regarded as a shorthand, convenient ways that we—not the composer—sort music into categories for our own purposes of description.

Monophonic

ⓢ Messiaen: *Quartet for the End of Time*, "Abyss of the Birds" (clarinet)

ⓢ "Puer natus est," opening notes

ⓢ Handel: *Messiah*, "For the Lord God omnipotent reigneth"

ⓢ Messiaen: *Quartet for the End of Time*, "Interlude"

Homophonic

ⓢ Handel: *Messiah*, "Hallelujah" chorus

ⓢ Monteverdi: *Orfeo*, Toccata

ⓢ Mendelssohn: Violin Concerto in E Minor, I, first theme

Polyphonic

ⓢ Byrd: Agnus Dei, from Mass for Four Voices, middle section

ⓢ Bach: Prelude and Fugue in C Minor, BWV 847, opening of fugue

ⓢ Handel: *Messiah*, "And he shall reign for ever and ever"

▶ Video: Instruments of the Orchestra

Timbre

Musical Instruments

Musical tones, even if they have the same loudness, pitch, and duration, sound different if they come from different instruments. We call this quality **tone color** or **timbre**. We use various terms to describe tone color: reedy, nasal, piercing, mellow, dark—all are useful, but there are not really any technical terms for timbre.

The difference in quality between one sound source and another is related to the physical nature of sound and to the fact that almost any natural sound is not really one sound but many, consisting of what we hear as the fundamental pitch, and a great number of much softer overtones. (That middle C on the piano that we talked about in our discussion of pitch may vibrate at 262 Hz, but it also produces overtones that vibrate twice, three times, four times, five times as fast. See Overtones and the Harmonic Series, left.)

The tone colors of different human voices and of the various instruments vary in large part because the relative strengths of their overtones vary. A clarinet, for example, has relatively strong odd-numbered partials (the third, fifth, seventh, and so on, overtones); this is partly owing to the cylindrical shape of the inside of the instrument; a saxophone, conical on the inside, has a very different timbre.

In addition to the overtone signature that differentiates instruments from each other, there are differences resulting from how the air is set in motion (by striking, blowing, scraping, and so on), and how the vibration resonates within a soundbox (as with a violin or a piano) or within a tube (as with a flute). The combination of variables means that there is an enormous range of tone colors available, and we are able to enjoy and distinguish a great range of sounds. There is also music that is generated electronically, either by computers or synthesizers, and in these cases there is no other intermediary between the creation of the sound and us. (Electronically generated sounds, as in synthesizers, or electronically reproduced sounds, as in recordings, provide as wide a range of possibilities as the traditional acoustic instruments.)

Most of the music we will listen to in this book is made by traditional musical instruments. These—or at least the instruments we discuss in this chapter—are categorized by a combination of how they are made and how they are played. Acoustic instruments are sorted into **strings, winds,** and **percussion**. Winds are further categorized as **woodwinds** and **brass**. Keyboard instruments are really mechanical devices and can be wind (organ), string (harpsichord, in which strings are plucked), percussion (celesta, a mechanized xylophone), or electronic (synthesizer, Hammond organ). Although the piano has strings, it is often called a percussion instrument because its strings are struck with hammers.

Overtones and the Harmonic Series

Sound is created by vibrations, and the pitch of a sound is determined by the speed of those vibrations. **Overtones** are generated by secondary vibrations of whatever is vibrating, e.g., the string, the column of air, and so on. For example, a plucked harp string vibrates at its full length, which is known as its **fundamental pitch**. But at the same time, it is also vibrating in halves, producing a sound an octave higher: this is the first overtone, or **partial**; in thirds, giving a sound of an octave plus a fifth (the second partial); in quarters of its length (the third partial, two octaves higher), and so on. Each of these subsidiary vibrations is much less pronounced than the fundamental, and generally cannot be discerned individually. (Those of you who have played guitar or a bowed string instrument are probably already familiar with the phenomenon when you play harmonics.) We call the series of overtones, always the same in relation to any given fundamental pitch, the **harmonic series**. All these notes are present whenever a note is sounded.

▶ Video: Instruments of the Orchestra

Ⓢ Bach: *Brandenburg* Concerto No. 4, I (harpsichord)

STRINGS

String instruments are divided into plucked and bowed strings according to how the string is set in motion.

Plucked string instruments include the **guitar, mandolin, lute, harp,** and **harpsichord** (a sort of mechanized harp).

Bowed string instruments include the **violin** and its larger relatives: the **viola, cello,** and **string bass** or **double bass.** These instruments are the backbone of the symphony orchestra.

The **viola da gamba,** or **viol,** a six-stringed bowed instrument favored in the Renaissance and Baroque periods, familiar to Monteverdi, Handel, and Bach, fell out of use in the eighteenth century; today it is enjoying something of a revival because of a renewed interest in Renaissance and Baroque music. The most common viol is the bass, an instrument about the size and range of a cello, but it was often played in ensembles of treble, tenor, and bass instruments.

WOODWIND INSTRUMENTS

Woodwind instruments include flutes, oboes, clarinets, and bassoons; they are not all made of wood now, but they used to be. What they have in common is a length of tube with holes drilled through the side; these holes can be closed by keys or fingers, altering the vibrating length of the tube, thereby producing a range of notes. The means of setting the tube's air in motion varies: sometimes air is blown over a sharp edge (flute, recorder); sometimes a single piece of reed vibrates against a fixed mouthpiece (clarinet, saxophone); sometimes two narrow pieces of reed vibrate against each other (oboe, bassoon).

Many of these instruments come in a number of sizes. In addition to the familiar **flute** (which is played holding the tube crossways to the body and blowing across an open hole), there is the **piccolo,** a wonderful little flute that plays an octave higher than the flute. The most common other sizes are **alto flute** and **bass flute** (both quite rare, but Stravinsky uses them in *The Rite of Spring*).

The **recorder,** the favorite "flute" of the Renaissance and Baroque periods, is played by blowing directly into one end; it has a mouthpiece that directs air over a sharp edge.

The **clarinet** is a single-reed instrument, widely used in jazz, concert bands, and orchestras. It comes in various sizes; most common are the B-flat and A clarinets; there is a high-pitched clarinet in E-flat and a **bass clarinet.** A relative of the clarinet is the **saxophone,** rare in orchestras but widely used in jazz and popular music. Its most common sizes are soprano, alto, tenor, and baritone.

The **oboe** is a double-reed instrument; its alto version is the **English horn** (even though it is not English and is not a horn). Perhaps the most famous English horn solo in the classical repertory is the main theme of the slow movement of Dvořák's *New World* Symphony (see Chapter 14).

The **bassoon** is the bass instrument of the double-reed group; it has a long tube doubled up on itself so as to be manageable. The **contrabassoon** is an even lower instrument. A very famous bassoon solo is the opening melody of Stravinsky's *Rite of Spring* (see Chapter 15). Stravinsky has the instrument play so high that it can barely be recognized as a bassoon.

BRASS INSTRUMENTS

Brass instruments are usually made of brass, but what really sets them apart is the way sound is produced: the air column in their tubing is set in vibration with a cup-shaped mouthpiece into which the player buzzes her lips so that she becomes a sort of double reed. These instruments are generally the heavy artillery of the band or orchestra, the blaring, fanfare instruments, but they can also be used to play a beautiful lyrical melody.

Ⓢ Mendelssohn: Violin Concerto in E Minor, I, first theme

Ⓢ Monteverdi: *Orfeo,* opening ritornello (ensemble of violins, viola, and cello)

Ⓢ Beethoven: Symphony No. 5, III (double bass)

Ⓢ Dowland: "Can she excuse my wrongs" (ensemble of viols)

▶ Video: Instruments of the Orchestra

Ⓢ Dvořák: Symphony No. 9, I (flute solo)

Ⓢ Sousa: "Stars and Stripes Forever" (piccolo)

Ⓢ Bach: *Brandenburg* Concerto No. 4, I (recorder)

Ⓢ Messiaen: *Quartet for the End of Time,* "Abyss of the Birds" (clarinet)

Ⓢ Berlioz: *Fantastic Symphony,* III (oboe and English horn)

Ⓢ Dvořák: Symphony No. 9, II, 1st and 2nd phrases

Ⓢ Stravinsky: *The Rite of Spring,* "Introduction"

▶ Video: Instruments of the Orchestra

ⓢ Handel: *Messiah,*
"The trumpet shall sound"

The **trumpet**, in its simplest form, has been around for a long time. Through the age of Beethoven, it was a tube with a mouthpiece, about eight feet long, bent back on itself for ease of holding. With no valves or finger holes, it played only the notes of the harmonic series—only overtones.

In the nineteenth century, valves or pistons were added to the trumpet, which increased its flexibility enormously; each valve (or piston) added a lengh of tube to the instrument, and thus added another set of notes it could play; three valves make for eight different combinations, and it became possible to make shorter trumpets that could still play any note of the chromatic scale. The modern trumpet is such a valved instrument. Occasionally, as in Stravinsky's *Rite of Spring*, a composer calls for **piccolo trumpet** or a **bass trumpet.**

ⓢ Beethoven: Symphony No. 5, I
transition 1st to 2nd theme

The **horn** (or **French horn**), originally a hunting instrument, is a long coiled tube played with a cupped mouthpiece. Because of the coil, the *bell* or flaring end of the tube is close to the player, and it is possible not only to play notes of the harmonic series, but also to inflect those notes by pushing a hand into the bell of the instrument so that more notes are available. Not until Berlioz's time were horns fitted with valves, as were trumpets.

ⓢ Mozart: "Tuba mirum,"
from Requiem

Because of its slide, the **trombone** has the greatest flexibility of the brass instruments. It has existed in this form for a long time. Orchestral music only occasionally uses the trombone (commonly, the alto, tenor, and bass sizes), often to accompany vocal music, and often in relation to death, as in Mozart's Requiem.

ⓢ Wagner: *The Valkyrie,*
Hunding's tuba

The bass instrument of the brass family is the **tuba.** It was not invented until the nineteenth century, when Wagner, among others, particularly favored it.

▶ Video: Instruments of the
Orchestra

PERCUSSION INSTRUMENTS

Percussion instruments include those that use vibrating membranes, like drums and tambourines, and those that themselves vibrate, like blocks, gongs, and triangles. In the orchestra, the most-used percussion instruments are the **timpani** or **kettledrums.** For centuries these have been paired with trumpets in the orchestra; they are used that way by Handel, Bach, and Beethoven, so that when the trumpets play, the timpani are like the bass. Timpani are tuned to specific pitches (unlike most drums, and indeed triangles, blocks, gongs, and many other percussion instruments, which make unpitched sounds) and there are usually two (although Berlioz calls for four, and Stravinsky uses six in *The Rite of Spring*). Unpitched drums include bass drum and **snare drum.** Bernstein uses a group of four drums to make a jazzy, exciting effect in the Prologue of *West Side Story* (see Chapter 18).

ⓢ Bach: Suite in D Major,
Overture (trumpet and drums)

There is another category of pitched percussion instrument in which pieces of metal or wood, sized to produce specific notes (and often arranged like a piano keyboard), are struck with a mallet. These **mallet instruments** include xylophones, marimbas, vibraphones ("vibes"), and chimes. Mallet instruments can be used to play melody and harmony.

ⓢ Stravinsky: *The Rite of Spring,*
"Glorification of the Chosen
Victim" (timpani)

ⓢ Bernstein, *West Side Story,*
Prologue (drums)

The Orchestra

Many of the works in this book are for orchestra. The modern orchestra is a more or less standard ensemble characterized by an ensemble of string instruments, normally divided into five groups: first violins, second violins (there is no difference between the instruments: they just play different parts); violas; cellos; and double basses. To this central group are added woodwind, brass, and percussion

TABLE 1.1

Instrumentation in Orchestras through the Centuries

	Handel, *Messiah*	Beethoven , Fifth Symphony	Berlioz, *Fantastic Symphony*	Stravinsky, *The Rite of Spring*
Flute		2 (+piccolo)	2	5
Oboe	2	2	2	5
Clarinet		2	2	5
Bassoon	1	2 (+contrabassoon)	4	5
Horn		4	4	8
Trumpet	2	2	4	5
Trombone		3	3	3
Tuba			2	2
Percussion	1	2	4	5
Strings				
Violin 1	6	8	15	14
Violin 2	4	6	14	13
Viola	2	4	7	8
Cello	2	4	12	8
Double bass	1	2	8	7

instruments (see above, pp. 11–12). These are normally solo instruments, each playing its own part, while the strings play as groups—all the first violins on a single melody, and so on.

Modern symphony orchestras have a more or less standard size—rather like that of the Berlioz symphony in Table 1.1 above; they add or subtract players as the music warrants.

The original orchestras of the seventeenth century were made up of string instruments. Over the next two centuries, woodwinds and brass were added, usually as pairs of flutes, oboes, trumpets, and so on. In the nineteenth century the numbers of winds were often increased.

Table 1.1 lists the instrumentation of a few characteristic orchestras for pieces studied in this book, including the approximate numbers of strings used in the premieres of those works. Figures 1.3 and 1.4 show an image of a typical orchestra and the typical seating arrangement.

Musical Forms

 Phrase

Much of what makes music interesting has to do with contrast and familiarity, memory and surprise. "Have I heard this (melody, rhythm, harmony, and so on) before, or is this new?" Same or different, new or old; this is the essence of musical structure. When we hear something, we do not know whether we will hear it again. If we *do* hear it again, we hear it differently, because we already know it.

FIG. 1.3　Cincinnati Symphony Orchestra, Paavo Järvi, Music Director, 2005.

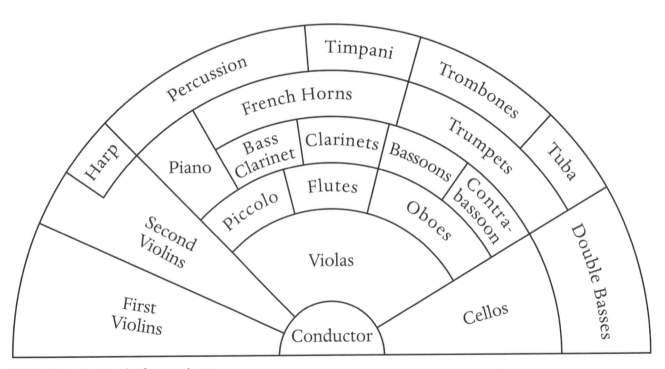

FIG. 1.4　Typical seating plan for an orchestra.

And if we do *not* hear it again, we hear the new thing in comparison to what we have already heard.

That's how music is made; and some very long musical structures are based on this very simple and basic principle.

Think of the song "Old Folks at Home." There is a first line ("Way down upon the Swanee River, far, far away"). What will happen next? This line does not sound like the end of a song, because it does not end on a final-sounding note. Will the next line be the same or different? When it comes ("That's where my heart is turning ever. . ."), we hear that it is the same music, but with different words; the ending, though, is a little different, and sounds more like a possible ending.

Now that we've heard two lines, there is a pattern; sing a line, sing it again; is this what will happen next? No: composers like to set up patterns so that we will expect something, and then surprise us with something new. The third line is very different indeed. It makes a big leap up to begin very high ("All the world is sad and dreary. . ."), and is totally different from the previous lines. What can happen next? After having given us a contrasting line, Stephen Foster (the song's composer) returns to the music of the opening for the fourth line; it sounds so familiar to us now—although we can't tell whether it's the melody of the first line or the second line, because they are the same at their beginnings; only at the end do we hear that it's the same music as the second line—the one that sounds like an ending—and this time it *is* an ending, the end of the first verse.

Patterns

All that musical experience, all that psychology, we might summarize by saying that "Old Folks at Home" has the musical form **AA'BA'** (**A'** is read as "A prime"; the "prime" sign, which you may know from math or science, here means that the second **A** is not quite the same as the first). This formula says a lot, but of course it omits a lot, because there are many songs that have this same shape; it's an effective musical shape, and perhaps that's why it gets used so often. (The famous tune in the last movement of Beethoven's Ninth Symphony uses this same form, though the musical content is quite different.) The formal diagram that we've invented is only a very small part of the story, but it is useful because it helps us see why the music has the effect on us that it does.

Forms

Suppose then that we wanted to create a larger form. We might put some different music next, another melody with the same general shape but different notes: **CC'DC'**. And then if we returned to our original melody afterwards, we'd have made a larger shape like this: **AA'BA' CC'DC' AA'BA'**. That's the shape that Beethoven and Dvořák use in the scherzos of the symphonies in this book: a first section, a second section, the first section again. Stepping back a little, we could call that form **ABA**, where now the letters stand for much longer sections of music (in this case, sections of four phrases each).

Larger forms

You can see that musical forms can get bigger and bigger, even when they are built on the basic psychological idea: same or different. And we have to remember that musical forms are not like architecture, in which you can see the whole building at once; in music there is only one instant—now. Everything else is either memory or expectation based on memory. This is the special pleasure of listening to music.

We will explore many musical forms and genres (categories) in this book; here's a partial list, including some important components of form:

Renaissance motet, imitative polyphony: pp. 23 and 62

Ritornello form: pp. 104–06

Baroque melodic phrases: pp. 130–32

Baroque fugue: p. 140 (Handel), pp. 157–60 (Bach)

Baroque concerto: pp. 163–65

Sonata form, or first-movement form: pp. 220–23 (Beethoven); p. 384 (Dvořák)

Symphony: p. 219

Classical genres: p. 223

Concerto first-movement form: pp. 305–07

There are really as many forms as there are pieces of music, and we will discuss many pieces in this book. Each deserves to be heard, listened to, and understood on its own terms.

It is this act of listening that makes the music work for us. The more attention we pay, the more we can hear and remember, and the more we can marvel at how effectively made the music is. Sometimes we listen to a piece we already know, and when we do we temporarily acquire the skills of really expert listeners: we know when to be surprised, we know when it's the end. But in a piece that is not so familiar, we have to be particularly sharp; in order to tell whether what we're hearing is new or old, we have to be able to hear the present, predict the future, and remember the past, all at the same time. Such listening requires careful concentration, but you will find that it is superbly rewarding.

Chapter Review

⑤ Multimedia Resources and Review Materials on StudySpace

Visit wwnorton.com/studyspace for review of Chapter 1.

What Do You Know?

Check the facts for this chapter. Take the online **Quiz**.

What Do You Hear?

Listening Quizzes and **Music Activities** will help you understand the musical concepts in this chapter.

🎙 Author Videos

- Melody
- Rhythm and meter
- Phrase
- Harmony
- Expression

Flashcards (Terms to Know)

Terms

beat	homophonic	polyphonic
brass instruments	imitative	rhythm
chords	interval	string instruments
conjunct	melody	tempo
consonance	meter	texture
disjunct	monophonic	theme
dissonance	motive	timbre
downbeat	octave	tone color
dynamics	overtone	winds
fundamental pitch	partial	woodwind instruments
harmonic series	percussion instruments	
harmony	phrase	

Instruments

string instruments
> bowed strings: violin, viola, cello, double bass; viola da gamba
> plucked strings: harp, guitar, lute, mandolin, harpsichord
> piano

woodwind instruments
> flutes: flute, piccolo, alto flute, bass flute; recorder
> double-reed instruments: oboe, English horn, bassoon; contrabassoon
> single-reed instruments: clarinet, E-flat clarinet, bass clarinet, saxophone

brass instruments
> trumpet; piccolo trumpet, bass trumpet
> (French) horn
> trombone (alto, tenor, bass)
> tuba

percussion instruments
> timpani (kettledrums)
> snare drum
> bass drum
> triangle
> mallet instruments (marimba, vibraphone, xylophone)

THE MIDDLE AGES

HISTORICAL EVENTS	MUSICAL EVENTS

476 Fall of the Roman Empire

ca. 480–547 Benedict writes his *Rule*

● **4th–7th centuries** Christianity spreads across Europe

7th century Rise of Islam

● **8th century** Repertory of Gregorian chant stabilized

768–814 Reign of Charles the Great (Charlemagne)

800 Charlemagne crowned emperor by pope

● **10th century** First notated books of chant

9th century Raids of Europe by Vikings in the north, Arabs in the south

● **10th–11th centuries** Flourishing of tropes and sequences

843 Treaty of Verdun divides Charlemagne's realm

● **1098–1179** Hildegard of Bingen

1099 First Crusade captures Jerusalem from Muslim rule

● **11th century** Troubadours (Provençal poet-composers) flourish

1182 Main altar of Notre Dame Cathedral dedicated

● **12th–13th centuries** Trouvères (French poet-composers) and Minnesänger (German poet-composers) flourish

1181/82–1226 St. Francis of Assisi

● **1150s–1201** Leoninus

1225–1274 St. Thomas Aquinas, Christian theologian

● **ca. 1200** Perotinus

1308–1321 Dante Alighieri writes *Divine Comedy*

● **1300–1377** Guillaume de Machaut, French poet and composer

1305–1308 Giotto di Bondone paints fresco cycle in Arena Chapel, Padua

● **ca. 1335–1397** Francesco (Landini) of Florence, composer of secular music

1305–1378 Popes reside in Avignon

1337–1453 Hundred Years' War (between France and England)

1346–1351 Black Death

1370–1371 Giovanni Boccaccio finishes revised *Decameron*, begun 1349

1383 Geoffrey Chaucer begins *Canterbury Tales*

● Italy   ● France   ● England   ● Germany   ● Various

PART I

Music and Prayer: Medieval and Renaissance Music

The Middle Ages

Historians often use the term **Middle Ages** or **medieval period** to describe the period from around 450 to 1450, of roughly one thousand years ("in medio" means "in the middle," in Latin, and the adjective "medieval" comes from the same word). But what "middle" are they talking about? Prior to the Middle Ages is a period called the Ancient or Classic era, which spans the Ancient Greek and Roman world to the fall of the Roman Empire in the fifth century C.E. After the Middle Ages is a period known as the **Renaissance**, with its revival of Classical learning and art beginning in the fifteenth century. The Middle Ages, then, is defined not by what it *is*, but by what it is *between*. It is also a defined by what it is not—neither Classic nor Renaissance—and by people who mostly valued the classical arts of the Greeks and Romans.

Renaissance

During this time that was neither Classic nor Renaissance, many important events took place—the emergence of modern European languages and their literatures; the formation of the countries of Europe; and the foundation of vital institutions such as universities and hospitals.

Perhaps most important, the medieval period saw the rise and spread of Christianity across the European theater. The Christian Church had extraordinary influence and importance in politics, in literature, and in the arts. It affected everyone, from monarchs to peasants. Throughout the Middle Ages, until the time of the Reformation in the sixteenth century (see below), there was just one church in the West, whose head was the pope.

Rise of Christianity

The church

The church had a centralizing presence. Its organization, international scope, continuing use of the Latin language, and uniform rituals and ceremonies unified the Western world. It was also the church that became the main outpost for education during most of the Middle Ages; as a result almost all the literature, art, and music that survives today was created in the name of religion. Only clerics (members of religious orders) were literate, and most of the significant literature was written and copied in church settings.

The church was heavily hierarchical (as, indeed, it is today), with the pope as the representative of Christ on earth, and a vast international network of bishops who represented the pope. Bishops were in charge of the clergy in their individual regions, called dioceses; each bishop had his official seat in a great church called a cathedral ("cathedra" is Latin for seat), and ruled over the many clergy in his area. Most cathedrals were in cities, and it is the schools associated with cathedrals (originally established for teaching the boys who sang cathedral services) that often gradually developed into groups of schools called universities.

Monasteries were familiar sights in medieval cities and in the countryside. Women and men who set themselves apart from the world to pray, read, and work lived a communal life, guided by *The Rule* written by Benedict of Nursia in the sixth century (see left). Benedictine monasteries were everywhere, and their monks copied books, founded schools, and sang music every day. It was not until the later Middle Ages, in the thirteenth and fourteenth centuries, that other kinds of monastic orders came into being and learning became separate from religious life.

In a time when people were encouraged to think seriously about their preparation for the afterlife, monasteries fulfilled the indispensable role of praying for the souls of the dead. Many people therefore provided endowments to monasteries—lands with incomes—to guarantee perpetual prayer on their behalf. As a result, some monasteries grew very wealthy.

Political power in the earlier Middle Ages was based on oaths of loyalty, the so-called feudal system, in which a hierarchy of kings, lords, and knights were knit together by vows of mutual support and defense. The castles and knights that for many of us comprise the standard image of the Middle Ages are aspects of this system—the lord's fortress on the one hand and the mounted warrior at the service of his lord on the other. Women's roles were indispensable, but women did not figure in the legal and political system except as dependents on fathers or husbands.

Beginning as early as the fifth century, the great kingdom of the Franks (stretching from northeastern Spain to central Europe) reached its apogee with its king Charlemagne (r. 768–814) but failed to achieve a lasting political unity. The Treaty

Treaty of Verdun

of Verdun (843) divided the realm into East, West, and Middle (Burgundy and the Low Countries) kingdoms. Although the three kingdoms as such did not last, this division was the basis of much of the rest of European history. The kings of England, Spain, and France (the West) and the Holy Roman Empire (the East) gradually centralized their powers (see Figure I.1, map of medieval Europe, p. 21). The pope, too, claiming higher authority, asserted his right to rule—a matter that led to frequent and long conflicts with secular rulers of the day.

Starting in the late eleventh century, rulers of the West launched a series of

The Crusades

Crusades, expeditions designed to recapture territories taken from the Christians

From *The Rule of St. Benedict*

St. Benedict of Nursia was born in the late fifth century in Italy and became the founder of one of the main traditions of Western Christian monastic communities. He wrote a kind of handbook on monastic living called The Rule of St. Benedict. The following excerpt gives an idea of the monks' daily (and nightly) routine:

In wintertime, that is, from the first of November until Easter, it seems reasonable to arise at the eighth hour of the night [about three a.m.], so that the brethren do so with a moderately full sleep after midnight and with their digestion completed. And whatever time remains after Vigils should be devoted to the study of the psalms and lessons by those brothers who lack sufficient knowledge of them. And from Easter, in turn, to the first of November, let the hour of rising be postponed so that Lauds, which are celebrated as the light of day sets in, are separated from Vigils by a brief interval in which the brothers may attend to the necessities of nature.

by Islamic invaders in the waning days of the Carolingian empire. Although the Crusades had a religious basis, the resulting political chaos had far-reaching social, cultural, and economic impact. While the Crusades failed in their goal of capturing and holding Jerusalem, they did succeed in recapturing Islamic-held parts of Spain, Portugal, and Italy.

The Franciscan and Dominican monastic orders arose during the thirteenth century, teaching, preaching, and ministering to the people. In addition, new technologies and goods from other cultures contributed to the welfare of humankind (clocks, silk) and to their destruction (cannons, gunpowder).

Fourteenth century

The fourteenth century was in some ways disastrous. A great famine ravaged the land at the beginning of the century. In the aftermath, the Holy Roman Empire disintegrated completely, and war and confusion dominated the political landscape. The papacy was contested, with two, even three, popes vying for authority, resulting in what became known as the papal schism. Under the influence of the French king, various popes resided for much of the fourteenth century in Avignon in southern France, far from Rome. Compounding the crisis was the Hundred Years' War (1337–1453)—actually a sporadic series of wars—the result of a long-standing territorial dispute between France and England.

Black Death

Adding to the misery, the Black Death (bubonic plague) recurred several times throughout the century, reducing the population of Europe sometimes by as much as half, and causing immense changes in society, especially in cities, while greatly increasing the cost of labor. But cities continued to grow in size and importance in the later Middle Ages, as a rising commercial and professional class contributed to the gradual decline of feudalism.

FIG. I.1 Map of Europe in 1050.

Religion, Literature, and the Arts

Schools and universities developed around monasteries and cathedrals, and learning flourished. The liberal arts were taught by masters, who transmitted and created knowledge in a system known as **Scholasticism,** a method of learning and teaching that emphasized reasoning. The main purpose of Scholasticism was to find answers to questions and to resolve contradictions. As these arguments were resolved, huge bodies of knowledge accumulated and were passed on in the schools and universities. One of the greatest works of medieval Scholasticism is **Thomas Aquinas**'s unfinished treatise, the *Summa Theologica*, proposing to explain all of theology.

Many writers and artists of the Middle Ages took pride in creating without seeking recognition, and by following authority. As a result, much of the art of the period is anonymous.

Religious art flourished, on walls as frescoes (see Figure I.2), on panels as altarpieces, and on other devotional objects decorated with gold, enamel, and precious stones. As interest in books grew, artists created handsome manuscripts—handwritten books on parchment—whose sometimes exuberant **illuminations** (decorative figures or illustrations) made them the finest and most precious surviving work of the period (see illustration, p. 19).

Romanesque architecture—named for the ancient Roman buildings it resembled—had given form to great churches of the earlier Middle Ages like

FIG. I.2 An eleventh-century mural in the Italian church of Sant'Angelo in Formis depicting one of the archangels.

MEDIEVAL MUSICAL STYLE

Ⓢ "Puer natus est," opening notes

Music of the Middle Ages survives in written documents, most of it religious. Music for church, called **Gregorian chant** (see p. 32), consisted mostly of Latin texts sung in unison by men's or women's voices without accompaniment (chant is monophonic in texture, meaning it has one melodic line). The rhythm of chant was flexible, so far as we can tell, although there are no specific rhythmic indications in the notation.

Some vernacular music survives from later in the Middle Ages, the work of poets in various parts of Europe, writing in their own languages (troubadours in Old Provençal, trouvères in Old French, Minnesänger in German). Their surviving

Strophic verse

music is mostly **strophic**, each verse of the poem being sung to the same music; the music itself sounds not so different from Gregorian chant.

Polyphony

Beginning in the eleventh century, techniques of **polyphony** were created in some of the great churches, to embellish the music of the liturgy. At first, polyphony consisted of singing a second melody along with the prescribed chant. By the twelfth century, such second melodies were more ambitious in style, and the chant

the abbeys of Cluny and Vézelay (see Figure I.3]. In the twelfth century this style gave way to the great Gothic cathedrals, like Notre Dame in Paris, with their pointed arches, soaring vaults, and walls filled with sumptuous stained-glass windows (see Figure 2.5, in Chapter 2).

In the pictorial arts, Giotto di Bondone, commonly known as **Giotto** (ca. 1267–1337), is most famous today for his magnificent frescoes of Jesus and Mary and the Last Judgment in the Arena Chapel in Padua (see Figure 2.2, p. 31), the cycle on the life of St Francis in the great basilica in Assisi, and the bell tower of the Cathedral of Santa Maria del Fiore in Florence. Giotto is credited with moving toward a more lifelike and natural depiction of the human form and is considered one of the first artists to bridge the artistic divide between the Middle Ages and the Renaissance.

Much of the Latin literature of the Middle Ages is about religion: sermons, commentaries on the Bible, and theological and other religious works based on the interpretation of authority. But the Middle Ages was also a time for growth of vernacular languages—English, French, Italian, Spanish, Portuguese, and German—and the beginnings of their literatures.

Dante Alighieri, commonly known as **Dante** (ca. 1265–1321), is considered the father of the Italian language. His expansive allegorical poem, the *Divine Comedy,* about a man's personal and spiritual journey toward salvation, is unlike earlier epic poems, such as the *Iliad* or *Odyssey,* which rely on myths and legends.

The Italian poet and writer **Giovanni Boccaccio** (1313–1375) wrote a collection of prose stories known as the *Decameron.* Set in Florence during the Black Plague, it portrays a changing medieval society, but it does so with a lighthearted attitude. Boccaccio's style was more down to earth than other writers of the time—his men and women more natural and unaffected.

London-born **Geoffrey Chaucer** (ca. 1343–1400) is best remembered for his *Canterbury Tales,* a collection of stories told by traveling pilgrims. The tales are

FIG. I.3 Sculpted figures adorn the central portal of the Romanesque basilica St. Madeleine in Vézelay, France, showing the Last Judgement.

by turns satirical, pious, ironic, bawdy, and damning, especially of the Catholic Church. His style is said to have been influenced by Boccaccio's tales.

itself, although still present, took a secondary role. Later still, two or three simultaneous voices were sometimes added to the original chant.

In some polyphonic chant settings, the melodies accompanying the chant were given additional texts, creating **motets.** A great repertory of these pieces arose, in which several texts might be sung, in more than one language, at the same time: perhaps a religious poem in Latin and a love song in French, together with a series of notes taken from a chant. The motet was a favorite sort of poetical-musical combination.

By the fourteenth century, composers had started creating a repertory of secular songs, mostly from France and Italy, in which the structure was not based on a preexistent chant or a "fixed melody" (**cantus firmus**) but on a new melody accompanied by one or more other melodies, perhaps played on instruments.

Many of the fundamentals of Western art music can be traced back to the Middle Ages. Our concepts for notating pitch and rhythm, as well as the development of polyphony, harmony, form, and structure, came from this enormous span of one thousand years.

Ⓢ Perotinus: *Viderunt omnes,* 4-voice organum

Motets

Ⓢ Machaut: "Puis qu'en oubli"

THE RENAISSANCE

HISTORICAL EVENTS	MUSICAL EVENTS

1350

1304–1374 Francesco Petrarca, known as the "Father of Humanism"

1400

1377–1446 Filippo Brunelleschi

● **1397–1474** Guillaume Dufay

1404–1472 Leon Battista Alberti

● **ca. 1410–1497** Johannes Ockeghem

ca. 1415–1492 Piero della Francesca

1431 Joan of Arc burned for heresy and witchcraft

1444–1514 Donato Bramante

● **ca. 1450–1521** Josquin des Pres

1453 End of Hundred Years' War

1473–1543 Nikolaus Copernicus

1492 First voyage of Columbus to America

1495–98 Leonardo da Vinci, *Last Supper*

1500

1501–04 Michelangelo Buonarroti, *David*

1509–1564 John Calvin, French Protestant reformer

1514 Niccolò Machiavelli, *The Prince*

1516 Thomas More, *Utopia*

1517 Martin Luther posts his 95 Theses, leading to Protestant Reformation

1519–1522 Ferdinand Magellan's voyage around the world

● **1525/26–1594** Giovanni Pierluigi da Palestrina

1528 Baldassare Castiglione, *The Book of the Courtier*

● **1530/32–1594** Orlande de Lassus

● **ca. 1540–1623** William Byrd

1545–1563 Council of Trent

● **1557/58–1602** Thomas Morley

1558–1603 Reign of Queen Elizabeth I

● **1563–1626** John Dowland

1564–1616 William Shakespeare

1564–1642 Galileo Galilei

1600

● Italy ● France ● England ● Germany ● Franco-Flemish

The Renaissance

The word **Renaissance** literally means "rebirth," but historians of literature, art, and architecture most often use it to refer to the rediscovery of the literature of ancient Greece and Rome that began in Italy at the start of the fifteenth century. Music has borrowed much of its terminology from the history of art, and the term "Renaissance" is no exception: we use it to describe music of the fifteenth and sixteenth centuries, when Renaissance art and culture were flourishing.

During these centuries, the kingdoms of Spain, France, and England and the Holy Roman Empire were frequently at odds with each other and with the pope, who was not only head of the church but also the ruler of a large portion of Italy. Burgundy, Mantua, and many other smaller areas were independently ruled by dukes and princes. Rulers great and small defined their nobility through prowess in warfare. But equally, they showed their standing through generous patronage of the arts; under their influence, painting, sculpture, poetry and music flourished. The greatest buildings from this time were paid for by these rulers, and even by the church itself.

Two influential books, both by Italians, reflect the Renaissance ideals of behavior stemming from secular courtly circles. Nicolò Machiavelli, a Florentine nobleman, wrote *The Prince* (*Il principe*) to describe how a ruler ought to behave; his recommendations of practicality, and his conclusion that a prince is better off being feared than loved, gave rise to the adjective "Machiavellian," used for sly and devious actions.

Nicolò Machiavelli

Baldassare Castiglione wrote *The Book of the Courtier* (*Il libro del cortegiano*) as a reflection of his experience at the Italian court of the duke of Urbino. In his text, he defines the ideal of a Renaissance courtier (a member of the court's circle)—how a

Baldassare Castiglione

FIG. I.4 Map of Western Europe, ca. 1500.

Ⓢ Dowland: "Can she excuse my wrongs" (voice and lute)

gentleman and a lady ought to behave, what skills they should have, and how they should treat each other. Courtiers should, he wrote, be educated; men should be athletic, that is, able to ride and fence; all should be musicians—for example, able to sing and play the lute—able to compose poetry (see p. 59). A gentleman or a lady should not display too much enthusiasm, should never show off, and should be modest and courteous. Throughout the Middle Ages, a gentleman showed his prowess through feats on the battlefield. Castiglione changed all that: now a gentleman had to be educated as well.

POLITICS

Courts

Renaissance monarchs surrounded themselves with nobles, artists, and with others who could lend splendor to their surroundings or their courts. Part of this princely environment included a court painter, a philosopher, an astrologer, and a court composer with his musicians, who were expected to perform both in church and in private, secular entertainments. The greater his artists and musicians, the greater the prince. Rulers such as the Medici family in Florence, the Este in Ferrara, and the Sforza in Milan vied with each other and with the popes for the services of the greatest artists and musicians.

Cities

After the disasters of the fourteenth century, economic stability and growth during the Renaissance allowed a rising merchant and professional class to accumulate wealth, and spurred a desire for education, leisure, and the arts. Cities formed republics based on commerce and trade; Florence and Venice in Italy are only two of many such republics that managed to retain a degree of democracy, and a degree of independence, from monarchs and popes. The freedom of the republic suggested the freedom to learn and to create. In addition, the creation of the printing press allowed the wide dissemination of literature, pictures, and music.

HUMANISM, REFORMATION, AND COUNTER-REFORMATION

Humanism, the study and learning related to knowledge about the world and about humankind, gradually replaced the medieval ideals of Scholasticism. In contrast with the focus on God and the church in the Middle Ages, the human spirit and the natural world now became subjects for intense scrutiny. Humans were considered a link between the mortal world and the spiritual one. This shift from a predominantly religious society to a more secular one created conflicts between traditional religion and the more "human" study of men and women and of their place in nature and

Martin Luther

history. Martin Luther was one of several reformers who, in seeking to privilege personal faith over ecclesiastical doctrine, ended by breaking away from the church in protest. These Protestants, as they were called, created the movement we now call the **Reformation.** The Catholic Church reacted (the **Counter-Reformation**) by making every attempt to regain lost territory, building ever grander buildings (culminating in Saint Peter's Basilica in Rome), and making efforts at excellence in preaching, in art, in architecture, and in music. Some countries remained predominantly Catholic (Italy, Spain, most of France), while others witnessed conflict between Protestants and Catholics that sometimes led to violence and bloodshed.

RENAISSANCE MUSICAL STYLE

While the revival of Classical learning was important to the literature of the Renaissance, the music of the Renaissance is *not* a rebirth of anything, but the continuation of the traditions and changes that came out of the Middle Ages. In fact, in music the Renaissance can be best understood as a time of continual and overlapping changes rather than as a unified style or movement.

As mentioned above, every Renaissance gentleman and lady, especially those who spent time at courts, was expected to be able to sing or play an instrument. Like dancing, riding, fencing, and creating poetry, music was practiced by anyone who had pretensions of belonging to polite society.

One result of this courtly world of the arts was that the music of the Renaissance, at least a good deal of it, did not distinguish between music for amateurs and music for professionals. Music was for everyone, and everyone was expected to appreciate and perform it. Music based on dances, and on popular song, gives us a view, almost for the first time, of music at all levels of society.

Despite the rise of secular courts, the church in the Renaissance, as in the Middle Ages, remained a powerful institution and patron of the arts; the foremost composers of the sixteenth century were still composers of church music, perhaps owing to the education and the stability that the church continued to provide. This is essentially the last time in history that the church would be in the musical avant-garde. By the seventeenth century it was the creators of instrumental and secular music—operas, concertos, and sonatas—who would herald the new. But in the Renaissance, as in the Middle Ages, it was church music that led the way.

Music and the church

This might seem odd to us today, when the music in churches and in other religious settings tends to be traditional and conservative, perhaps even old-fashioned. But during the Renaissance, musical innovations came in the form of Masses and motets. It was the singing, the praise of God, that was important, so important in fact that people often left endowments in their wills for the support of religious music. All over Europe, in court chapels and churches, expert professional choirs were customary. Indeed, most of the famous composers of the Renaissance started their careers as choirboys. Many of them (Guillaume Dufay, Josquin des Pres, Orlande de Lassus) came from the Low Countries (modern-day Belgium, Holland, and northern France), traveled to Italy, and performed in the choirs of princes or popes, sometimes staying on as composers in their newly adopted homes. Giovanni Pierluigi da Palestrina worked primarily in Rome; Johannes Ockeghem, in the court of the king of France; and Lassus, though he too was from the Low Countries and worked in Italy, finished his long career at the court of Munich. Two well-known composers from England—William Byrd and Thomas Morley—also sang in choirs as young boys.

Vocal polyphony is the norm in Renaissance music, and although the styles of the great composers are different from each other, they each created their most famous works for choirs of several voices, usually for the chapels of great princes or the churches or Rome. Although composers of the early Renaissance—Dufay, Ockeghem, Josquin—often based their Masses, and sometimes motets, on a **cantus firmus**—that is, a preexisting melody—by the sixteenth century the sound ideal was one of several, usually four or five, voices singing together, all in different ranges from soprano to bass, but all alike in having shapely melodies, and generally woven together with the technique of **imitation**.

Vocal styles

In imitation, a technique that has since become very familiar, one voice begins with a theme, or motive; the motive is taken up by the next voice while the first continues with new material; then the third voice begins to sing, using the same motive, and so on. This process of imitation, in the expert hands of a Byrd or a Palestrina, creates a seamless fabric of equal strands. The music achieves a classic, timeless quality that puts it on the same level as the great visual art of the Renaissance, and has made it a model for many kinds of music composed in later ages, as we will see.

Imitation

ⓢ Palestrina: Kyrie, from *Missa Aeterna Christi munera*

Science and Religion

In the spirit of humanistic learning, Greek literature was introduced to Renaissance scholars who learned the language and translated Plato and the Greek tragedies into Latin and made them widely available for the first time. The study of the ancient classics was intended to improve the mind, the spirit, and the society.

Along with this rediscovery and study there arose a new curiosity about the world beyond Europe—the worlds of Africa, Asia, and the New World—all of which were explored by adventurers such as Christopher Columbus and Ferdinand Magellan. It was an age of scientific inquiry as well, with both **Nikolaus Copernicus** (1473-1543) and **Galileo Galilei** (1564–1642) proving that the earth was not the center of the universe after all.

The Catholic Church, despite its best efforts, lost its unique position in the Christian world as a result of the Reformation; various religious reformers, like **Martin Luther** (1483–1546) in Germany and **John Calvin** (1509–1564) in Switzerland, challenged the authority of the church, and the theological bases of papal authority.

FIG. I.5 *The Legend of the True Cross: The Battle between Heraclius and Chosroes* (detail, ca. 1455-60), by Piero della Francesca, created with the new art of "perspective."

Literature and the Arts

From the lyric poetry of **Francesco Petrarca**, one of the earliest humanists (1304–1374), to the poems and plays of **William Shakespeare** (1564–1616), the works of great writers and poets showed what could be done to express humankind's highest and noblest thoughts

Mass The most usual kinds of sacred music were the **Mass** (settings of the invariable chants of the mass—**Kyrie, Gloria, Credo, Sanctus, Agnus Dei**) and the motet. Unlike the medieval, polytextual secular motet, these were imitative settings of sacred texts, almost always in the Latin that was the language of the church.

Sometimes Renaissance composers focus attention on a single voice—as in a solo song with accompaniment. And sometimes they add a lot of embellishment to the melodic lines, as when lutes or harpsichords—which cannot sustain long notes—need to find ways to keep the sound alive. But even in these other media, the melodic genius and classical balance of the Renaissance stand out. The main text of the piece is clearly understood, and, as in Renaissance painting, the subject shines through.

Within the church, organ music flourished. Outside the church, the great variety of instrumental music—for keyboards, for instrumental ensemble, and for combinations of voices and instruments—provided for recreation and entertainment: banquets, weddings, dances, and private music-making all benefited from the efforts of superb composers, and we benefit from it still today.

But let us first turn back to the roots of Western music—the Middle Ages—to a Christmas day in the twelfth century, in the city of Paris, and watch and listen to one of the most important aspects of the community: a Mass.

in elevated verse and in vernacular languages.

Among the great achievements of Western civilization are the art and architecture of the Renaissance.

The trend toward greater realism in art was enhanced by the study of anatomy; the pleasure taken by artists and viewers in the ideal human body, in sculpture and painting, stands in strong contrast to the medieval idea of shame at nudity.

The art of Piero della Francesca, Michelangelo Buonarroti, and Leonardo da Vinci depicted what marvelous creatures humans can be at their best; the rediscovery of perspective, and a new concern for realism in painting and sculpture, have made the work of Renaissance artists a model for the ages. **Piero della Francesca** (ca. 1415–1492) was a painter—and mathematician—from the early Renaissance, skilled in the relatively new art of "perspective" (see Figure I.5). His works are marked by a certain poise and serenity. **Leonardo da Vinci** (1452–1519), known primarily as a painter, was also a musician, an architect, an engineer, a scientist, and an inventor. His *Last Supper* reflects his intense interest in human expression, and his famous *Virgin of the Rocks*, his passion for natural settings (see Figure I.6). Michelangelo Buonarroti, known simply as **Michelangelo** (1475–1564), was a painter, a sculptor, and an architect. He is perhaps best known for the ceiling frescoes in the Sistine Chapel in Rome as well as his remarkably powerful sculptures, such as his *David*.

The architects of the Renaissance have left us great buildings, and great ideas: **Filippo Brunelleschi** (1377–1446), who built the great dome of the Cathedral of Santa Maria del Fiore in Florence, **Leon Battista Alberti** (1404–1472), the theorist of Renaissance architecture, and **Donato Bramante** (1444–1514), who finished the great church of St. Peter's in Rome (begun by Michelangelo). They reinterpreted the elements of Classical Greek and Roman architecture, producing magnificent buildings arranged to produce a sense of harmony, order, and human scale.

FIG. I.6 *The Virgin of the Rocks*, by Leonardo da Vinci. Mary's beauty is idealized, but she is surrounded by precisely rendered plants, flowers, and rock formations.

Style Comparisons at a Glance

MEDIEVAL MUSICAL STYLE	RENAISSANCE MUSICAL STYLE
Moves by step within narrow range	Emphasis on melody
Much monophonic music; polyphony is developed	Polyphonic texture
Simultaneous melodies create the concept of harmony	Polyphonic texture controls harmony
Polyphonic lines create strong dissonances	Polyphony favors smooth, consonant harmony
Vocal genres: Gregorian chant, vernacular song (both have polyphonic versions in the later Middle Ages)	Vocal genres: mainly Mass, motet, madrigal, and song
Very little instrumental music survives	Instrumental genres mainly keyboard or lute solos, often based on vocal styles, and music for instrumental ensemble

CHAPTER 2

FRIDAY, DECEMBER 25, 1198, PARIS:

Christmas Mass at Notre Dame Cathedral

🔧 CORE REPERTOIRE		🎙 AUTHOR VIDEOS
■ **LG 1** Introit, "Puer natus est" (chant)	■ **LG 5** Perotinus: *Viderunt omnes* (4-voice organum)	■ Notation for chant and polyphony
■ **LG 2** Kyrie (chant)		
■ **LG 3** Alleluia, *Dies sanctificatus* (chant)		
■ **LG 4** Leoninus: Alleluia, *Dies sanctificatus* (2-voice organum)		

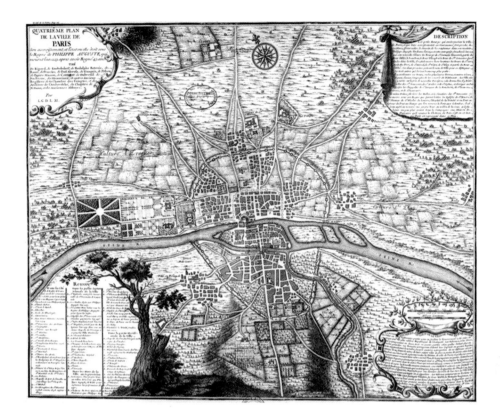

FIG. 2.6 A map of Paris in 1223. The large island in the middle of the Seine River is the site of the Cathedral of Notre Dame.

of the Catholic Church, which is another reason why most medieval books—Bibles, sermons, the lives of saints—have to do with belief and faith.

And then there is the music: thousands of medieval manuscripts filled with sacred music, almost all of them containing Gregorian chant created for the continuing praise of God. Chant is still sung today in countless churches and religious communities around the world. Like the church itself, it is part of an ongoing tradition that stretches back more than a thousand years. Today, chant is not confined to religious settings; it is frequently sung in concert halls by choirs of mixed voices, or by all-male or all-female ensembles. One of the most remarkable composers of the twelfth century was a German nun named Hildegard of Bingen (see biography, p. 36), whose compositions were designed for the nuns under her charge.

FIG. 2.7 Facade of Notre Dame Cathedral, Paris.

MEDIEVAL PARIS

Paris in the Middle Ages, as now, spread out on both sides of the Seine River. An island in the middle of the stream, the Île de la Cité, was the site of the original Roman settlement, and it was still the center of government and religious life in the 1100s. Paris's 200,000 inhabitants made it one of the largest cities in Western Europe. On the southern, "left" bank (as you face downstream) of the Seine, where the population was concentrated, stood the schools, monasteries, and student residences that would grow into the great University of Paris. Because Latin was the language of instruction and learning,

HILDEGARD OF BINGEN (1098–1179)

The first female composer whose name has come down to us, Hildegard was famous in her lifetime for her visions, prophecies, and richly imaginative religious poetry. Having taken her vows at age fourteen, she rose to become prioress of her convent in Germany and later founded her own monastic community at Rupertsberg, near Bingen. A very influential figure in her time, she was the author of mystical, dramatic, and theological texts. The highly idiosyncratic music that Hildegard wrote to accompany her Latin verses sounds like liturgical chant and follows many of its stylistic conventions. Like Gregorian chant, her songs were intended for use in religious services, as was her morality play *Ordo virtutum* (*The Order of Virtues*), which may have been performed at the dedication of the church at Rupertsberg in 1152. Today she is the most recorded known composer of sacred monophony.

MAJOR WORKS: *Scivias* (*Know the Ways*), poetry and visions; *Ordo virtutum* (*The Order of Virtues*); a music drama, not attached to liturgy; and numerous chants, hymns and other religious music.

Ⓢ Hildegard of Bingen: "O euchari in leta via"

Ⓢ Gradual: "Viderunt omnes," chant

FIG. 2.8 A typical street scene in Paris today, showing many surviving medieval buildings.

this area was called the Latin Quarter, as it still is today. Not until the marshes (in French, *marais*) north of the river were drained in the twelfth century did extensive commercial and residential districts spring up on the right bank.

Modern Paris, with its grand boulevards, stately architectural facades, and magnificent public spaces, is largely the result of nineteenth-century urban redevelopment. Medieval Paris, like all cities of the time, was a tangled web of narrow, winding streets, where most people lived in crowded, unhealthy conditions. (You can still get a sense of the medieval city in the densely populated *marais* district, just across the river from Notre Dame; see Figure 2.8.) A circuit of defensive walls, long since dismantled, surrounded the city, and King Philippe Auguste (reigned 1180–1223) had begun building a new royal palace called the Louvre. He also paved some of the streets and established a new central market called Les Halles.

The typical Parisian house in the 1100s was timber-framed, faced with plaster or a similar material, and roofed with thatch or reeds. The upper stories (many houses had as many as five floors) leaned out above the lower ones, shrouding the streets in a kind of perpetual dusk. A number of wooden bridges spanned the Seine, two of which crossed over the Île de la Cité. These bridges were lined on both sides with little shops, since that was where customers were most frequent. Elsewhere boatmen ferried passengers from one side of the river to the other. Clogged with docks, barges, fishing boats, and other craft, the Seine must have experienced frequent traffic jams.

The sound of chant Ⓢ was almost as familiar to medieval Parisians as the cries of street vendors or the noise of horses and carts. The city was home to many monasteries and other religious establishments, including one of the oldest and largest abbeys in France, St. Germain des Prés. The grounds of the Cathedral of Paris (of which Notre Dame was the centerpiece) was a little city in itself. Within the close—the land closed off from the rest of the city for the use of the cathedral—were the bishop's palace, houses for the clergy, several smaller churches, a school for the boys who sang in the cathedral choir (at the time, only males sang aloud in public worship, although women sang in their convents), and the schools of philosophy and theology that formed the nucleus of the future University of Paris.

NOTRE DAME CATHEDRAL

In 1198 the vast Cathedral of Notre Dame was about half complete; even so, it dwarfed every other building in the city. Construction began shortly after Maurice of Sully became bishop of Paris in 1160, and tradition says that Pope Alexander III himself laid the cornerstone. The eastern end of the church was complete—except for the roof—by 1177. Services seem to have started shortly after that, maybe as early as 1178. The main public part and the side-arms, with their dramatic flying buttresses (a special kind of arched support), were built between 1180 and 1220, and by 1225 the great west rose window was in place. The facade and towers were not finished until about 1250.

The Cathedral of Notre Dame could hold several thousand people (most large churches today hold many fewer; Saint Patrick's Cathedral in New York seats 2,200). For the major religious feasts, such as Christmas and Easter, the church could well be full of worshippers. Even before entering the cathedral, church-goers were meant to know that something important lay in store: the sculptures that adorned the facade were designed to tell them about this world and the world to come. The kings of Israel are sculpted in a row across the front. Below them, over the three doorways, are depictions of the Last Judgment (on the left), Saint Anne (mother of Mary, on the right), and Mary (to whom the cathedral is dedicated), holding the infant Jesus, in the center. All the portals are surrounded by statues of saints in niches (see Figure 2.9). This was the planned effect, at least; actually, the entrance wall with its sculpture was still under construction in 1198.

Inside, the public part of the cathedral, called the *nave* (from the Latin for ship, perhaps signifying a voyage to the afterlife), soars on lofty columns to a vaulted stone ceiling of stupendous height. The side-arms of the cross-shaped building, called the *transepts*, have walls filled with huge circular windows of stained glass, casting many-hued beams of light from above. The numerous windows—not just the big circles—are filled with colorful religious imagery (see Figure 2.10). However, all of the sunlight that passed through them was not enough to penetrate the cathedral's murky interior, which was illuminated by candles at all hours of the day and night.

The part of the cathedral in front of the main altar, called the *choir*, where the singers were positioned and the services were performed, was set off by a partition of carved and painted wood (it was replaced with a stone screen in the fourteenth century). It

FIG. 2.9 The central portal of Notre Dame Cathedral, showing Christ seated in judgment as the central sculptural detail.

FIG. 2.10 The famous south rose window from Notre Dame Cathedral depicting scenes from the New Testament.

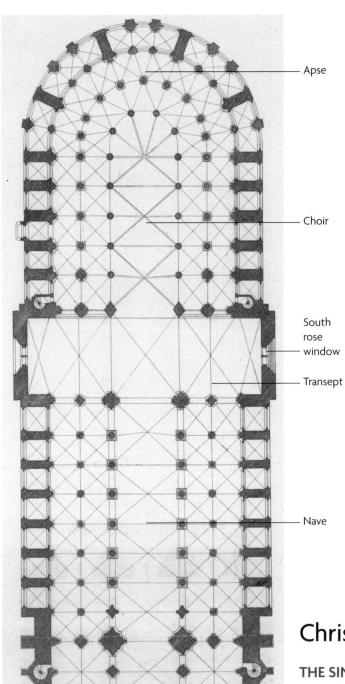

Apse

Choir

South
rose
window

Transept

Nave

FIG. 2.11 Diagram of Notre Dame
Cathedral.

was usual to furnish choirs with tapestries, hangings, rugs, banners, and paintings. Banks of choir stalls faced each other across the central aisle, each row a little lower than the one behind it, with long benches for the choirboys in front. Facing the altar, and closing the choir into a U-shape, were special seats for the highest dignitaries of the cathedral—the dean, the archdeacons, and the cantor and his assistant (see Figure 2.11).

In a city that had few public spaces, Notre Dame Cathedral was open to people from all parts of society. Nobles, clerics, and scholars mingled with tradesmen, merchants, and laborers. Everyone's attention was focused on what took place beyond the ornate screen that separated the nave from the choir, where the main altar and the seats for the clergy provided ceremonial space for the worship services. In the context of the cavernous space, the impressive sculpture, and the dazzling stained glass, it is only fitting that music should also play an important role in the overall experience.

The effect of chant in a gigantic and resonant cathedral is marvelously impressive. In fact, the acoustics of Notre Dame are almost perfect for this kind of music, which is designed to be a vehicle for prayer. The unaccompanied melody reverberates throughout the building, producing a sense of unity, of a group of singers melded into a single voice with a single purpose. This unity is an important aspect of chant, as it is of all public worship. For both performers and hearers, then, a Christmas Day service at Notre Dame must have been a richly rewarding experience.

Christmas Day at Notre Dame

THE SINGERS

As we have seen, the Cathedral of Paris was a large and busy place, with many buildings and many workers. The clergy were workers too. Foremost among their duties was the performance of the regular religious services at Notre Dame, the official seat of the bishop of Paris. The cathedral building and its operations were supervised by a small army of officials, organized in a complex hierarchy.

Cantor   The highest-ranking musical officer was the **cantor**. He "ruled" the choir (that is, kept good musical order in the services and started off the most important musical pieces), assigned solo parts to individual singers, and maintained and corrected the music books. By the late twelfth century, however, a subcantor had taken over most of these duties, because the cantor had so many official financial and legal matters to attend to. The subcantor was assisted by a *chancellor*, who had responsibility for assigning scriptural readings, appointing and rehearsing the readers, and looking after the nonmusical books containing prayers and readings for use in services.

The *canons*, clerics nominally in charge of the cathedral and expected to be present at all services, could (and usually did) hire replacements for themselves, since many of them had other things to do—teaching in the university, for example. These substitute canons were called *vicars* (hence our word "vicarious"). In order to have even the lowly job of vicar, a candidate had to know by heart all the psalms (the 150 poems of the Old Testament's Book of Psalms, usually attributed to King David) and all the pieces of chant required for every feast day in the church calendar.

Most of the regular singing at the cathedral was done by the *clerks of Matins*. (Matins was one of the eight services that clergy performed at designated hours of the day and night.) Solo parts were awarded to the most accomplished clerks. Finally, there were the choirboys in residence at the cathedral, who were instructed in music, Latin, and theology, and played an important role in the various services; they assisted in carrying incense and holy water, occasionally took turns as readers, and sang specific solo parts.

The singers

In all, the choir for Mass at Notre Dame numbered about forty men and eight boys—larger than a modern cathedral choir.

On major feast days like Christmas, the cantor himself stood in the choir of the cathedral holding the baton that symbolized the importance of his office. On such days he was one of four *rulers of the choir*, whose job was to go with their books to the person designated to begin the next chant and, when the time came, to sing the first few notes to him quietly so that he remembered the melody and started it at a convenient pitch.

The members of the singing clergy faced each other across the choir, in two ascending rows of stalls. Each place had a hinged wooden seat that flipped up like a modern stadium seat, with a small platform attached to the underside against which a singer, officially standing, could lean during longer services. The best singers stepped forward to perform the solos from the book placed on the elaborate reading desk, or *lectern*, that stood in the middle of the choir.

The Structure of the Mass Mass on Christmas Day began with the Introit, sung by the choir from the stalls, with a short solo section in the middle. The **Introit** (from the Latin word for "entrance") accompanied the procession of the bishop from the sacristy (a room, usually near the altar, in which sacred vessels, vestments, and books are kept) to his place in front of the altar. The next two chants, the **Kyrie** and the **Gloria**, were performed **antiphonally**, half of the choir alternating with the other half in a kind of question and answer. The bishop himself intoned the Gloria (that is, he sang the opening few words). After the Gloria, he greeted the community from the altar with the words "Dominus vobiscum" (The Lord be with you), to which they responded, "Et cum spiritu tuo" (And with your spirit). Then the bishop sang the first of the Mass's three prayers specific to Christmas. Everybody sat down and a cleric assigned for the day went to the reading desk in the middle of the choir and sang the Epistle (a reading from one of the letters of the New Testament).

Introit

Kyrie and Gloria

After the Epistle came the **Gradual** and the **Alleluia**, performed by solo singers in silk copes (long, capelike vestments) standing in the middle of the choir. These two pieces were ordinarily sung, like the rest of the Mass, in chant. But on this particular Christmas Day, in 1198, a marvelous thing happened: the Gradual and the Alleluia were heard in glorious *polyphonic* (multivoice) settings by two composers closely associated with Notre Dame, Master Leoninus and Master Perotinus.

Gradual and Alleluia

ⓢ Perotinus: *Viderunt omnes,*
4-voice organum

One of Perotinus's most magnificent four-voice pieces, *Viderunt omnes,* is a setting of the Gradual of the Christmas Mass, and we know that the bishop in that very year provided for the possibility of singing it in four parts. So, although we have no way of knowing for certain, we may well imagine that the congregation was hearing Perotinus's music for the first time in 1198.

The effect on the listeners crowded inside Notre Dame Cathedral was surely electrifying. Following immediately after the chanted and intoned sections of the Mass, the amazing outburst of polyphony must have been a little like the scene in the movie *The Wizard of Oz* in which Dorothy opens the door of her house in black-and-white Kansas and steps out into the full-color wonderland of Oz. No one who heard Perotinus's dazzling virtuoso showpiece could ever have listened to chant in the same way again. This celebration of the birth of Jesus also marked the birth of a new musical era.

MUSICAL SHAPE OF THE MASS

Proper

Ordinary

Before we listen more closely to the Mass, we need to understand something about its musical shape. The texts for certain chants of the Mass that vary from day to day, according to the church calendar, are collectively called the **Proper**; their names come from their function in the ceremony. The texts for other parts of the Mass, the **Ordinary,** do not change, although their melodies may vary. The five chants in the Ordinary are so called because they are always present in the *ordo*, the order of service. We refer to them by their opening words: Kyrie, Gloria, Credo, Sanctus, and Agnus Dei. (There is also a final dismissal, *Ite missa est*, usually sung to the melody of the Kyrie. See the Outline of the Mass, p. 41.) All of these chants are acclamations, that is, texts of praise or supplication.

And now, let's turn to the glorious music of the day.

The Music

🎵 LG 1   **THE MASS BEGINS: THE INTROIT**

The Mass begins with the Introit, sung by the choir from the choir stalls. The text from the Proper makes a fitting opening for the Christmas service: "Puer natus est nobis, et filius datus est nobis" (A boy is born to us, and a son is given to us). The piece is intoned by the cantor—that is, he sings the notes of the first word, "Puer," alone, both to give the pitch to the choir and to make sure everybody knows which chant is to be sung. The chant is moderately ornate, having sometimes two or three notes to a syllable (see LG 1, p. 42).

After the choir finishes the main part of the Introit, a soloist sings a verse from Psalm 97: "Cantate Domino canticum novum, quia mirabilia fecit" (Sing to the Lord a new song, for he has done marvels). The verse is sung to a melody that is always used for chanting the psalms, even though in this case only one verse of the psalm is actually sung. (It is possible that in the earlier Middle Ages whole psalms were sung at entrance processions; this single verse may be what is left of that tradition.)

The cantor then sings the **Doxology**, the verse of praise to the Father, the Son, and the Holy Spirit that is always added to the ends of psalms and sung to the same melody as the verse. Afterwards, the choir repeats the Introit, this time without the cantor's intonation (after all, they now know the starting pitch and the melody).

Outline of the Mass

Blue: Sung by Choir
Orange: Intoned by Celebrant or Reader

Proper	Ordinary
Introit	
	Kyrie
	Gloria
Collect	
Epistle	
Gradual	
Alleluia	
Sequence (on major feasts)	
Gospel	
	Credo
Offertory	
Secret (prayer said quietly)	
Preface	
	Sanctus
	Canon
	Pater Noster (Lord's Prayer)
	Agnus Dei
Communion	
Postcommunion prayer	
	Ite missa est

Many modern listeners might expect the opening song for Christmas to be particularly joyful, but Introits are always poised, melodious, and not particularly exuberant; they sound like Introits, regardless of the meaning of their words.

BACKGROUNDS: MUSIC AND RITUAL

Gregorian Chant In a church like Notre Dame, everything in the service was sung. Even the readings and the prayers were sung by the readers and the presiding bishop or priest. The many psalms recited by the religious community throughout the day were also sung. But there were particular places in the service where the music was more elaborate and where the main focus was the singing (instead of reading or praying). These pieces—the Gregorian chants—were the places where music came to the fore.

The singers of the medieval church thought that chant arose from the efforts of Pope Gregory the Great (reigned 590–604), hence the name Gregorian chant. But scholars now believe that the chant repertory may have been organized systematically in the eighth century, at least one hundred years *after* Pope Gregory. Whatever its origin, by the time of our Christmas Mass in 1198, chant (also called **plainchant** or **plainsong**) had been sung for a very long time.

Plainchant

LISTENING GUIDE 1 | DVD

Introit *Puer natus est*   2:00

DATE: 12th century (origin, 8th century)
GENRE: Gregorian chant, Proper of the Mass (Introit)

LISTEN FOR

MELODY: Little internal repetition: each phrase is different
FORM: Larger shape: Introit-Verse-Introit
TEXTURE: Neumatic style: approximately one to three notes per syllable

SCORING: Alternation of choir with solo singer
EXPRESSION: A sense of hovering: each phrase has repetitions of the same note

TIME	MUSIC, TEXT, AND TRANSLATION	DESCRIPTION
	INTROIT	
0:00	U-er * ná-tus est nó- bis, A boy is born to us,	The cantor sings up to the asterisk, the choir continuing. The piece begins with a big upward leap, then remains in a 3-note range, pausing on note D that was at the top of the leap.
0:07	et fí- li- us dá-tus est nó- bis : and a son is given to us;	Parallelism in words ("a boy"... "and a son") suggests the same big leap again, but this time the phrase sinks to the opening note of the initial leap.
0:16	cú-jus impé- ri- um whose power	Every note used so far is swept through, up to a note higher than any before; this is the musical high point at the center of the piece.
0:21	super hú- me-rum é- jus : is upon his shoulder:	The melody hovers, sinking slightly at the end.
0:31	et vocá- bi-tur nómen é- jus, and his name shall be called	Similar to the previous phrase, hovering then sinking.
0:40	mágni consí-li- i Ange- lus. the Messenger of great counsel.	The Introit concludes with leaps at the beginning of a phrase (note that leap between words "magni" and "consilii" is the reverse of the leap at the beginning); it concludes on the same note (G) that began the piece.
	VERSE	
0:51	*Ps.* Can-tá-te Dómino cánti-cum nó-vum : Sing to the Lord a new song,	The soloist sings a psalm verse to a standard formula; like all psalm-tones, it has two halves. The first half has an *intonation* (sung to first two syllables), a *recitation* on a single note (sung to middle syllables); and a *termination* (sung to last five syllables, "canticum novum").

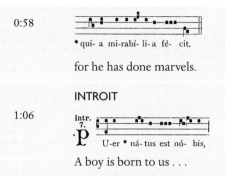

0:58

*qui- a mi-rabí- li-a fé- cit.

for he has done marvels.

The second half, sung here by choir, also has an intonation (two syllables), recitation (here only two syllables), and termination (five syllables).

INTROIT

1:06

Intr.
7.
·P
U-er * ná- tus est nó- bis,

A boy is born to us . . .

Entire Introit repeats.

Gregorian chant is sung in unison, blending many voices into a single sound. Chant has a practical purpose, since the singing voice is more readily audible than the spoken one, especially in large cathedrals, and singing a text helps keep a group together. Moreover, words and music reinforce each other, so that the effect of the text is in a way more than doubled. "For he that singeth praise, not only praiseth but only praiseth with gladness," wrote St. Augustine. Chant singing provides a symbolic sense of unity, not only within the community but also with those singing elsewhere, and with the faithful long departed and those yet to come.

The music of Gregorian chant reflects the accents, grammar, and syntax of the text. The shape of the melody lets you know about beginnings and endings, pausing places, and where the accented syllables fall. What the music does not reflect is the meaning of the words: it does not get quicker and livelier when the text speaks of joy, or slower and sadder when the text speaks of grief.

However, the style of the music is closely related to the role the piece plays in the service. A single text (for instance, "All the ends of the earth have seen the salvation of our God," from Psalm 97) may be sung in a number of different settings, ranging from the simple **syllabic** setting (each syllable of text has one note) used when the psalm is sung in the regular round of psalm-singing in the daily service to the musically complex version we will see in the Christmas Gradual.

The difference does not depend on the day—Easter or Christmas, for example— but rather on the function of the piece. Where the clear delivery of words is foremost—as with readings, prayers, and psalms—the musical setting is very simple and syllabic. Where the music is the primary focus, as in the Gradual and Alleluia**,** the setting is sometimes so elaborate that it is hard to keep track of the words. Florid melodies (known as **melismas**) of twenty or thirty notes sung to a single syllable are not uncommon; such pieces are said to be in **melismatic** style. In between are settings like the Introit, Offertory**,** and Communion that accompany specific actions; their so-called **neumatic** style may have two or three notes per syllable.

Ritual and Liturgy   By the twelfth century, chant had been sung in the Christian church for hundreds of years. Church services were essentially fixed; musical books prescribed exactly what ought to be sung on each occasion and where in the service it should happen. Worshippers felt part of an unbroken and unbreakable tradition; those who performed the ritual actions and sang the chants understood that these procedures had always been executed in this manner, and that identical celebrations were being held more or less simultaneously in every church throughout the Western world; that tradition continues to this day.

The complete round of ceremonies and rituals—everything that made up a sacred service—was called the **liturgy**, from a Greek word meaning "public work."

Syllabic, neumatic, and melismatic settings

ⓈGregorian chant: example of syllabic setting

ⓈGregorian chant: example of melismatic setting
ⓈGregorian chant: example of neumatic setting

Liturgy

FIG. 2.12 A diagram showing the eight daily services of the monastic Office and their distribution over the course of a day.

There are a few basic ideas concerning the liturgy that are worth knowing because they will help us understand why the people of the time attached such importance to the celebration of the Mass, spent so much time performing the rites, and tried so hard to make them as beautiful as possible.

Medieval men and women believed that praising God was not something to be done once or twice a week, but at all times. To them, worshipping God meant being not only in God's presence but also in the presence of the angels who sing around the throne of God, as described by the prophet Isaiah in the Bible. It was important to maintain a tradition ordained by the church, and to perform the sacred rites in a way that was pleasing to God. The best that humankind could produce, including architecture, sculpture, painting, and music, was in reference and submission to God.

The church calendar includes a Mass for every day of the year. As we have seen, the Mass, a reenactment of the Last Supper and the sacrifice of Jesus, is the central moment of Christian ritual; as such it contains the most elaborate ceremonies and music. The actions of the participants culminate in the transformation of bread and wine into the body and blood of Jesus, and all present are actors in this mysterious drama.

The Office   Besides the Mass, eight other services are performed at specified hours throughout the day; collectively, we call them the **Divine Office,** or **Office** (see Figure 2.12).

The liturgical cycle is deeply repetitive, marking out the hours, the days, and the seasons in the same way from year to year. Yet in another sense the liturgy is anything but repetitive, because its contents are constantly changing. There is a complete set of prayers, readings, and chants for every Sunday, every feast day, and every saint's day. This means that there is always an entrance chant at the Mass, but it is not always the same chant. The combination of regular, repetitive elements with the ever-changing repertory of contents makes the liturgy a many-faceted and highly intricate piece of machinery.

The main Mass of Christmas Day (Christmas, unusually, has three Masses) in 1198 was thus like every other Mass in its *structure* but different in its *contents* from all the other Masses that had been celebrated since the previous Christmas.

🔊 LG 2   THE MASS CONTINUES: THE KYRIE

The Kyrie is part of the Ordinary—that is, its words are always the same and are sung in every Mass. It is performed by the full choir. Unlike the other sections of the Mass, the Kyrie is sung in Greek.

The Kyrie is a ninefold invocation: each of the three phrases—"Kyrie eleison" (Lord, have mercy), "Christe eleison" (Christ, have mercy), and "Kyrie eleison" —is sung three times. The chant is sung antiphonally, with the two sides of the choir passing the florid phrases of music back and forth (see LG 2, p. 45). There is something mesmerizing about the repetitions, especially when the melody is particularly elaborate. Some of the shapeliest and most memorable melodies of the chant are to be found in Kyries.

The next chant is the *Gloria in excelsis*, a hymn of praise that, on Christmas, is begun by the archbishop himself and continued by the choir.

LISTENING GUIDE 2 | DVD

Kyrie   1:58

DATE: 12th century (origin, 10th century)
GENRE: Gregorian chant, Ordinary of the Mass (Kyrie eleison)

LISTEN FOR

MELODY: Florid, melismatic style, with many notes per syllable of text

FORM: Nine-fold pattern, 3+3+3

SCORING: Antiphonal performance, with two halves of choir singing in alternation

---

TIME	MUSIC, TEXT, AND TRANSLATION	DESCRIPTION
0:00	1. Kýri- e * e- lé- i-son. Lord, have mercy	The cantor begins the first few notes; one side of the choir continues with the melisma. This phrase begins fairly high and descends to its close.
0:13	*Kyrie eléison* Lord, have mercy	Opening *Kyrie* is repeated by the other side of choir. This alternation side-to-side continues to the end.
0:26	*Kyrie eléison* Lord, have mercy	Opening *Kyrie* is sung for a third time.
0:39	Chrí-ste e- lé- i-son. Christ, have mercy	The phrase begins on the same note as *Kyrie*, and its ending is the same; otherwise it is different and does not rise so high.
0:52	*Christe eléison* Christ, have mercy	*Christe* is repeated.
1:03	*Christe eléison* Christ, have mercy	*Christe* is sung for the third time.
1:16	Ký-ri- e e- lé- i-son. Lord, have mercy	Beginning with a large leap upward, this *Kyrie* begins with the same low note that ended the previous phrase, and ends with the same note (A) that began it.
1:26	*Kyrie eléison* Lord, have mercy	Previous *Kyrie* is repeated.
1:37	Ký-ri- e * **e- lé- i-son. Lord, have mercy	The previous *Kyrie* is lengthened by repeating the opening section, sung first by one side of choir, then by the other side. Final *eleison* is sung by both sides together.

⏻ LG 3   THE MASS CONTINUES: THE GRADUAL AND THE ALLELUIA

After the Kyrie and Gloria, the presiding priest sings the first prayer, and a reader intones the first reading, called the Epistle. Then follow the two most elaborate chants of a Mass, those that are reponses to the readings; they are purely musical moments, not intended to accompany any action or procession: they are musical meditations.

Both of them, the Gradual (so called because it is sung from the altar step or *gradus*) and the Alleluia, follow the performance pattern of the Introit, as we will see. Let us first listen to the Alleluia chant, *Dies sanctificatus* (see LG 3, p. 47).

Both the Gradual and the Alleluia require the skills of expert singers. But on this particular day in 1198, they were sung in polyphony, in a kind of composition that combines the music of the standard Gregorian chant with newly composed music sung at the same time. It is one of the triumphs of medieval music, and a specialty of Notre Dame Cathedral. A bit of background will help us to appreciate what we're about to hear next.

Embellishing the Liturgy   A sense of tradition, regularity, and unchangeability is essential to the medieval conception of worship. And yet there are artistic spirits in every generation who desire creative change. Even though new feasts in the calendar of the later Middle Ages sometimes required new chants, the creative era of Gregorian chant had essentially come to a close centuries earlier, when the complete repertory had been established. It might seem, then, that poets and musicians had very little chance to contribute creatively to the liturgy. We have evidence to the contrary, however—evidence of marvelous innovations that embellished and updated the medieval liturgy without changing or affecting the underlying tradition. Seeing how this was accomplished requires a medieval understanding of tradition and change.

If you sing all the words and the notes of the liturgy in the prescribed order, you are performing the rite as required by the church. But you are not necessarily required to perform the rite continuously and without interruption, or to do that and *only* that. These two loopholes in the liturgical regulations allowed for two large bodies of medieval musical creativity: tropes (and a special kind of trope, called sequences) and polyphony. While **tropes** (interpolated musical meditations or glosses on liturgical texts) and **sequences** (extensive poems appended to the Alleluia) continued to provide an outlet for creativity until the sixteenth century, worshippers at our Christmas Mass in 1198 witnessed another kind of innovation during the Gradual and Alleluia that in the long run would prove vastly more important.

Tropes and sequences

Another way of embellishing Gregorian chant was to sing something else *at the same time* as the liturgical melody. This practice is known as **polyphony**, music in which more than one note is sounded simultaneously, and it lies at the heart of Western musical culture. Polyphony—as distinct from monophony, music that consists of only one melodic line, such as chant—was one of the glories of the Cathedral of Notre Dame. It is here that we can identify the first great repertory of polyphonic church music attributed to specific composers.

Polyphony

The concept of performing two melodies at once is easy to understand. When two people sing a round such as "Row, row, row your boat," the two sections of the melody overlap is a kind of simple, two-part polyphony. It is a more complicated matter to write melodies that sound good together and create what we call harmony—the pleasing sound of several sounds together. It is perhaps a further challenge if one of the melodies already exists—say, in the form of a Gregorian chant.

LISTENING GUIDE 3 DVD

Alleluia *Dies sanctificatus* 1:45

DATE: 12th century (origin, 8th century)
GENRE: Gregorian chant, Proper of the Mass (Alleluia)

LISTEN FOR

MELODY: Mixture of syllabic and melismatic styles

FORM: Internal repetition: Alleluia is repeated at the end; phrases 1 and 3 of the verses use similar melody altered to fit different texts

SCORING: Alternation of choir and soloist

TIME	MUSIC, TEXT, AND TRANSLATION	DESCRIPTION
0:00	Lle-lú-ia. * Praise the Lord!	The cantor begins alone.
0:04	Lle-lú-ia. * Praise the Lord!	The choir repeats the opening "Alleluia," adding a melisma.
0:21	℣. Dí- es sancti-ficátus illúxit nó- bis : The holy day has enlightened us.	Verse, part 1: the soloist begins the verse: notice the melisma on "*no*-bis."
0:42	ve- ní-te géntes, et adorá-te Dómi-num : Come, ye peoples, and adore the Lord	Verse, part 2: notice the low melisma on "*ve*-nite" and the almost syllabic recitation in the middle.
0:58	qui-a hó-di- e descéndit lux má- gna For today has descended a great light	Verse, part 3: the music is very similar to part 1, with another melisma on "*mag*-na."
1:15	* su-per tér- ram. Upon the earth.	The final words are sung by the choir. The music is not related to the previous music.
1:25	Lle-lú-ia. * Praise the Lord!	The opening Alleluia, with melisma, is repeated by the choir.

In fact, the earliest surviving examples of polyphonic music are Gregorian chants to which a second melody has been added. In the simplest versions, the second voice is the same chant sung at a different pitch (as when two people sing the same song starting on different notes). In other early examples, the added melody

LEONINUS AND PEROTINUS

Trained at the University of Paris, Master Leoninus (active from the 1150s until about 1201) was not only a high-ranking canon of Notre Dame Cathedral but also a poet whose works were widely copied and highly praised. He seems to have started work on his *Great Book of Organum (Magnus liber organi)* in the 1180s. Leoninus may have been present at our Christmas Mass in 1198, but was probably far too senior to be called on to sing his own composition.

The Great Book of Organum contained music for major feast days throughout the year. **Organum** was the Latin word used to designate any piece of polyphonic music; it was also the name for a particular style, in which one voice sings a note of the chant while another voice sings a great many notes. Although this style is associated with the name of Leoninus, it is likely that it developed over time and that a whole body of singer-composers were involved with its creation.

This style of organum has a mesmerizing, improvisatory effect, but it also makes the performance of the chant very long. Partly to remedy this, Leoninus developed his so-called **discant style**, in which both the chant and the upper (added) voice move along at a good speed and in regular rhythms.

Leoninus was not the only composer of organum at Notre Dame. By 1198 a newer and more elaborate style had come into fashion. It is associated with the other composer of organum whose name is known to us, Master Perotinus (active in the late twelfth and early thirteenth centuries). According to an anonymous student at the University of Paris, *The Great Book of Organum* "was in use up to the time of Perotin the Great, who edited it and made very many better [substitute sections or clauses], since he was the best composer of discant, and better than Leonin. . . . Master Perotin [composed excellent four-voice works], like *Viderunt* and *Sederunt*, with an abundance of [harmonic color]; and also several very noble [three-voice works]."

The surviving copies of *The Great Book of Organum* include some gigantic four-voice pieces whose texts begin with the words *Viderunt* and *Sederunt*; these copies of the book must represent the revised version by Perotinus. One of these four-voice pieces, *Viderunt omnes*, is a setting of the Gradual of the Christmas Mass, which was heard perhaps for the first time in 1198.

has some degree of independence; it may move in the opposite direction from the chant, for example, or the distance between the two voices may vary so that the second voice has its own, separate melodic character.

All such early examples of polyphony have one thing in common: each note in the added voice corresponds to one note in the chant. This basic kind of polyphony was described in Latin as *punctus contra punctum* (point against point), from which we get our word **counterpoint**, the musical term for composing simultaneous independent melodies.

Counterpoint

The big breakthrough in polyphony came shortly before the time of our Christmas Mass, when composers decided that they could add *more than one note* to the new melodic line for *every note* of the original chant. This gave them much greater flexibility and fluidity in composing a new melody than the older note-against-note style, and their music began featuring flights of melody above longer notes of chant. At the same time, this newer style created new problems for singers by making coordination between the melodic lines more difficult, because the musical notation used for Gregorian chant did not provide for this kind of polyphony. It presented notes and matched them with the words, but gave no information about how long the notes lasted. (Scholars believe that singers of that time gave each note of chant approximately the same length.) In other words, the music was written down, but not in such a way that the relative lengths of the notes in the different parts were clear (see Early Musical Notation, p. 33).

Ⓢ Melismatic organum

These limitations persisted until composers at the Cathedral of Notre Dame devised a way of notating rhythms. Only then did it become possible to write down, and perform in a consistent and predictable way, complex polyphonic music. Credit for this innovation, as far as we know, goes to a composer, poet, and official of Notre Dame named Master Leoninus. His successor, Master Perotinus, wrote music that survives in an even more evolved system of rhythmic notation, characterized by amazing musical complexities. It was music by these two great composers that listeners at Notre Dame may have heard on Christmas Day in 1198 (see Leoninus and Perotinus, p. 48).

THE ALLELUIA IN POLYPHONY

 LG 4

Until Leoninus's time, the Alleluia at Notre Dame, as elsewhere, was performed in traditional Gregorian chant. This Christmas Mass, however, is different. The mode of performance alternates not only between soloists and choir, but between monophony (chant) and polyphony, as follows:

Alleluia (first few notes)	SOLOISTS (with polyphony)
Repeat Alleluia, with long melisma	CHOIR
Verse	SOLOISTS (with polyphony)
Last two words of verse	CHOIR
Repeat the long Alleluia	CHOIR (or solo and choir)

Only the solo singers needed to know how to sing in parts; the choir did what it always did, but the soloists enriched the air with "modern" polyphony. One of the surviving works in Leoninus's *Great Book of Organum* is a polyphonic version of the Alleluia of the Mass of Christmas—a two-voice setting of the solo portions listed above. The choral sections are not in Leoninus's book, because it is a book for the expert soloists. The choir knew what and when to sing; they could have relied on their standard chant books. The combination of soloists (singing from Leoninus's book) and choir made a single performance of the Alleluia.

Leoninus's polyphony switches between two styles. Most of the Alleluia is in **sustained-note organum**, or **pure organum**, in which one voice sings the notes of the original chant slowly, while a second voice performs a melody above it, using as many as twenty notes, in a free, improvised-sounding rhythm, for each note of the chant (see Figure 2.13).

Leoninus's second, or **discant**, **style** usually occurs when the original chant has a melisma—many notes on a single syllable. (In the Christmas Alleluia, melismas happen on the words "*no*-bis," "*ve*-nite," and "*mag*-na.") In these cases Leoninus arranges the chant in regular, repeating rhythmic patterns; here he chooses groups of four notes of equal length (or, for "*mag*-na," groups of three). In the upper part the rhythms consist of alternating long and short notes, producing a rhythmic pattern in a rapid triple meter. Listen to the chant version of the Alleluia again (see LG 3); now listen to Leoninus's version (see LG 4, p. 50).

FIG. 2.13 A version of Leoninus's setting of the Alleluia, *Dies sanctificatus* for Christmas. The manuscript is written in score, the chant voice (having many fewer notes) written below the added organum voice. The bottom four staves on this page, marked with large initial letters for each pair of staves, show the opening notes of the Alleluia, and the beginning of the verse *Dies sanctificatus.*

THE GRADUAL OF THE MASS: PEROTINUS, *VIDERUNT OMNES*

 LG 5

🎧 Notation for chant and polyphony

Viderunt omnes ("All shall see") is Perotinus's version of the Gradual of the Mass. In the order of service, the Gradual comes before the Alleluia, but we have saved it for last because its elaborate polyphonic style represents the culmination of the process that Leoninus initiated. *Viderunt omnes* is a magnificent piece, on a scale never before attempted; indeed, it might be considered a kind of Gothic cathedral of composition in itself.

LISTENING GUIDE 4 | DVD

Leoninus Alleluia, *Dies sanctificatus*   6:41

DATE: 12th century
GENRE: Organum (2 voices)

LISTEN FOR

RHYTHM: Difference between sustained-note organum (free rhythms) and discant style (repeating rhythmic patterns)

FORM : **ABA**, Alleluia, Verse, Alleluia repeated

SCORING: Alternation of two-voice polyphony and chant

TIME	TEXT	TRANSLATION	DESCRIPTION
0:00	Alleluia	Praise the Lord!	Sustained-note organum for the opening of the Alleluia; a slower voice sings the notes sung by the cantor in chant version (see LG 3).
0:46	Alleluia (repeated with melisma)	Praise the Lord!	The choir sings the opening Alleluia in chant style, with melisma.
1:07	Dies	The day	The verse begins in sustained-note organum; each slow note of the chant is accompanied by the additional voice moving in free, rhapsodic rhythm; it switches to discant style, both voices moving in regular patterns.
1:47	sanctificatus illuxit	sanctified has enlightened	Sustained-note organum continues.
2:07	nobis;	us;	Discant style. Return to sustained-note organum at the end.
2:38	Venite,	Come,	Discant style: both voices move in regular patterns, with four equal notes in chant, and again returning to sustained-note organum.
3:00	gentes, et adorate dominum;	ye peoples, and adore the Lord;	Sustained-note organum continues.
3:44	quia hodie descendit	for today has descended	Sustained-note organum continues.
4:31	lux magna	a great light	Discant style: both voices move in regular patterns, this time with three notes of equal length in the chant. Return to sustained-note organum at the end.
5:18	super terram.	upon the earth.	The choir sings the last two words of the verse in chant style.
5:32	Alleluia	Praise the Lord!	The opening intonation in sustained-note style.
6:12	Alleluia	Praise the Lord!	The choir continues with the melisma of the opening Alleluia.

Viderunt works in the same way as Leoninus's Alleluia in that it is a polyphonic setting of the solo portions of the chant, with the choir singing the rest. In these solo portions, however, the chant is accompanied not by one but by *three* added voices, each of which is independent of the others. The pattern is as follows:

Intonation (first two words)	SOLOISTS (with polyphony)
The rest of the Gradual	CHOIR
Verse	SOLOISTS (with polyphony)
Last two words of the verse	CHOIR

Some aspects of Perotinus's piece are familiar—the same alternation of polyphony and chant and the same alternation of sustained-note organum and discant sections (where the chant has a melisma). But what a difference there is between his music and Leoninus's! Those differences, mostly ones of scale, would have had magical effects on listeners in the twelfth century.

Since there are four voices, instead of Leoninus's two, Perotinus had to work especially hard to coordinate the different parts (see Figure 2.14). The clear rhythmic patterns of the sort that Leoninus used only in discant sections are now used everywhere, even in the sustained-note organum section. (This means that the rhapsodic-sounding upper voice of the Leoninus organum is a thing of the past.) There are compelling repetitions and exchanges among the upper voices, little patterns that ascend or descend, with slight changes; overall the effect is of a giant fabric woven from many small threads.

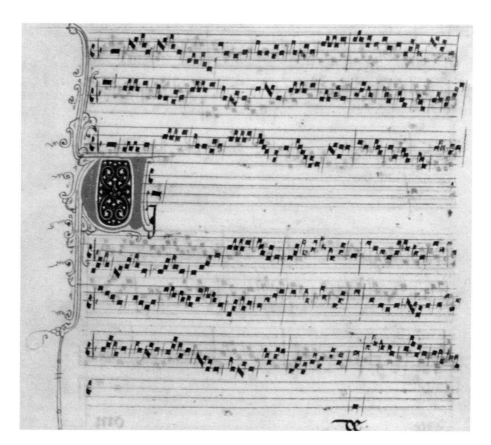

FIG. 2.14 Perotinus's four-voice organum setting of the gradual *Viderunt omnes* for Christmas. The manuscript is written in score, all four voices parallel, with the text written only under the lowest stave. Note the three active upper voices, and the very slow chant voice (which here has only one note per line).

LISTENING GUIDE 5 Ⓢ | DVD | 🎧

Perotinus *Viderunt omnes*   11:38

DATE: 12th century
GENRE: Organum (4 voices)

LISTEN FOR

RHYTHM: Swirling patterns of rhythms using long and short notes

HARMONY: Extreme lengthening of the original chant; each note of chant underlies many notes of polyphony

TEXTURE: Alternation of chant and polyphony, and within the polyphony, of sustained-note and discant styles

SCORING: Alternation of chant and polyphony

TEXT:
Viderunt omnes fines terrae salutare dei nostri.
Jubilate deo omnis terra.
All the ends of the earth have seen the salvation of our God.
Rejoice in God, all the earth.

VERSE:
Notum fecit dominus salutare suum:
ante conspectum gentium revelavit iusticiam suam.
The Lord has made known his salvation:
in the sight of the nations he has revealed his justice.

TIME	TEXT	DESCRIPTION
0:00	Vi(-derunt)	The opening chord is followed by many repetitions in a similar rhythmic pattern, while one voice holds the single note of a chant.
1:01	(Vi-)de(-runt)	Second note of the chant!
1:29	(Vide-)runt	Third syllable of the chant; this syllable has two notes from the original chant.
2:33	om(nes)	On this first syllable of the second word, Perotinus includes a section in discant style; the music then returns to sustained-note organum.
3:51	fines terrae salutare dei nostri. Jubilate deo omnis terra.	The choir sings the rest of the Gradual in chant.
4:49	No(-tum)	The soloists sing the verse: sustained-note organum continues.
5:55	(No-)tum	New syllable; the change of vowel affects the sound of the music.
6:19	fe(-cit)	Sustained-note organum continues.
7:10	(fe-)cit	Sustained-note organum continues.
7:44	do(-minus)	Sustained-note organum continues . . .
8:14	(do-)minus	leading to a pause.
8:21	sa(-lutare)	Discant section—the chant has a melisma on this syllable.
8:50	(sa-)lutare	Return to sustained-note style.
9:13	suum	Sustained-note organum continues.
9:35	ante	Sustained-note organum continues.
10:03	conspectum	Sustained-note organum continues.
10:25	gentium	Sustained-note organum continues.
10:44	revelavit	Sustained-note organum continues; final cadence for polyphony.
11:11	iusticiam suam.	The choir sings the end of the verse in chant.

The sustained-note organum sections are extended far beyond Leoninus's in length. Consider that over the opening note of the chant there are more than a hundred notes in each of the upper parts. (It makes you wonder how the chant was performed—did several singers sing the chant voice, taking turns breathing so as to sustain each note?) The piece is a long one, and it would be longer still if Perotinus, like Leoninus before him, did not insert a number of sections in discant, where the chant voice is given a brisk rhythm nearly as fast as the upper parts. There is one such section in the opening (on "*om*-nes") and one in the verse (on "*do*-minus").

No one could follow the original melody of the Gradual—or for that matter its words—in this sort of performance. And yet every note of the original chant gets performed, and every syllable is pronounced, even when the listener does not recognize or understand them. Apparently, it was sufficient to produce the words and notes in order, and the strict liturgical requirements would be fulfilled. Like the anonymous medieval artists who adorned the facade of Notre Dame Cathedral, often concealing their creations from viewers on the ground, Master Perotinus fixed his gaze on a higher authority. In *Viderunt omnes*, it must be God, not we, who is the intended listener to the chant; we have the good fortune to overhear it (see LG 5, p. 52).

Notre Dame Then and Now

The age of the great cathedrals could almost be called the Age of Leoninus and Perotinus, or the age of St. Thomas Aquinas (see p. 22). They all have in common the making of an enormous construction out of the ceaseless accumulation of many small elements. The cathedral, made as it is of a series of bays, each one with columns, windows, roof, vaults, and buttresses, becomes an impressive and majestic presence partly because of the similarity of many smaller parts: looking down the nave of a Gothic cathedral is looking at many repetitions. Likewise the logical series of propositions that adds up to the systematic philosophy of Aquinas is typical of the scholasticism of the time, in which one authority is confronted with another, with the intention of reconciling apparent differences.

The spellbinding music of Perotinus, with its enormous length made of many small repetitions, rather like a rose window of many brilliant small pieces of colored glass, never fails to inspire. The effect of *Viderunt omnes* and other polyphonic pieces must have been stunning in the context of an otherwise monophonic liturgy of chant. Sung in the stone choir of Notre Dame Cathedral by expert solo singers wearing exquisitely embroidered silk copes, the music would have been memorable and powerful—grand in both scale and effect.

Gregorian chant and polyphony existed side by side on this Christmas Day in 1198. The chant was considered timeless, a gift from the past to be transmitted to the future, while the polyphony was entirely up-to-the-minute, evolving as composers came and went and as tastes changed. Whatever church music is, it is not always the same thing—except, perhaps, for Gregorian chant, which, despite many changes in the world, is still being sung in the Catholic Church (and elsewhere too). Today Gregorian chant is heard in concerts as well as in churches, and it has continued to inspire composers of both secular and religious music. There is also a revival of interest in other kinds of medieval music that would not have been heard in church. The ancient and the new, the traditional and the innovative, are as much in evidence in our own world as they were at Notre Dame in 1198.

Chapter Review

Summary of Musical Styles

Two main musical styles are considered in this chapter: **monophonic** and **polyphonic** music. Both styles arise from the music of the medieval church, in which Gregorian chant is the main vehicle for music in worship.

Monophonic music
Gregorian chant is monophonic music, sung by a soloist or a choir, using the Latin text of the medieval church. Most of the texts are drawn from the Bible, especially the book of Psalms. The relation of text to music varies according to their relative importance; we can distinguish three styles:

- **Syllabic style:** each syllable of text has a single note, resulting in a sort of musical recitation. This style is used for places where the text needs to be clearly heard, for example, in readings and prayers.
- **Neumatic style:** each syllable may have several notes; this is the style for most musical pieces in the Gregorian repertory, such as the Introit of the Mass.
- **Melismatic style:** one or more syllables may have a very long **melisma**, a series of notes sung to a single syllable. The effect is one of great musical expansion, and the possibility that the text may be hard to understand.

Polyphonic music
In polyphonic music more than one note is sounded at the same time. This chapter draws examples from the musical elaborations practiced at the cathedral of Notre Dame in Paris. There, some of the Gregorian chants of the liturgy were embellished by the addition of one or more voices. This style of embellishment of chant was given the generic name of **organum**. Within the practice of organum, there are two chief styles:

- **Sustained-note organum** (or **pure organum**): one voice sings the notes of the original chant slowly, while one or more voices performs a melody or several melodies around it, using many notes for each note of the chant.
- **Discant style:** all voices sing in patterned rhythms; composers often use this style in places where the original chant has a melisma.

The two main composers of organum at Notre Dame are Leoninus and Perotinus. Leoninus, the earlier of the two, composed organum in two voices; the sustained organum sections feature a single upper voice with a free, improvised-sounding rhythm. Perotinus composed organum in three or even four voices; in his works, the sustained-note organum sections have upper voices with mesmerizing patterned rhythms.

ⓢ Multimedia Resources and Review Materials on StudySpace

Visit wwnorton.com/studyspace for review of Chapter 2.

What Do You Know?

Check the facts for this chapter. Take the online **Quiz**.

What Do You Hear?

Listening Quizzes and **Music Activities** will help you understand the musical works in this chapter.

ⓟ Author Videos

- Notation for chant and polyphony

Interactive Listening Guides

LG 1 Introit, "Puer natus est" (chant)
LG 2 Kyrie (chant)
LG 3 Alleluia, *Dies sanctificatus* (chant)
LG 4 Leoninus: *Dies sanctificatus* (2-voice organum)
LG 5 Perotinus: *Viderunt omnes* (4-voice organum)

Flashcards (Terms to Know)

Alleluia	neumatic
antiphonal	Notre Dame repertory
cantor	Ordinary
counterpoint	organum
discant	plainchant
discant style	plainsong
Divine Office	polyphony
Gloria	Proper
Gradual	pure organum
Gregorian chant	sequences
Introit	strophic
Kyrie	sustained-note organum
liturgy	syllabic
Mass	troubadours
melismas	trouvères
monophonic	

CHAPTER 3

THURSDAY, JULY 23, 1586, HARLEYFORD MANOR, ENGLAND:

William Byrd's Mass for Four Voices and Other Domestic Music

🎵 CORE REPERTOIRE		🎙️ AUTHOR VIDEOS

• **LG 6** Byrd: Agnus Dei, from Mass for Four Voices
 	
• **LG 7** Byrd: "This sweet and merry month of May"
 	
• **LG 8** Dowland: "Can she excuse my wrongs," for Voice and Lute
	• **LG 9** Dowland: "Can she excuse my wrongs," arrangements
	  a) Four voices with lute
	  b) Lute solo
	  c) Harpsichord solo
	  d) Consort of five viols and lute
	  e) Mixed consort
		• Imitation in Renaissance music
		• Rhythm in Dowland's "Can she excuse my wrongs"

Introduction

"I am not satisfied with our Courtier unless he be also a musician, and unless, besides understanding and being able to read music, he can play various instruments."

—Baldassare Castiglione, *The Book of the Courtier*, 1528

This chapter leaps four centuries and the English Channel to present an evening of music-making in a great English country house at the end of the Renaissance when the reign of Queen Elizabeth I (1558–1603) witnessed a golden age of the arts, a prolonged period of peace and general prosperity that allowed music, drama, and literature to flourish as never before. The playwrights William Shakespeare and Christopher Marlowe; the poets Edmund Spenser and Thomas Campion; and the composers William Byrd, John Dowland, and Thomas Morley are some of the bright stars in the Elizabethan galaxy of creative artists.

The musical fare on occasions such as the one we propose here typically featured a varied menu of secular and sacred music—dances, solo songs, **consort music** (the English name for ensemble music) for singers and instruments, and music for keyboard and lute. Some of the music was formal and compositionally complex, some more relaxed and designed purely for entertainment. Although the church continued to play a central role in Renaissance musical life, as it had in the Middle Ages, secular music (which had always existed) now became a major component of the written tradition: people were writing down music, and amateur musicians were learning to read music and to perform, in their homes, from written music. This burgeoning trend was linked to a new market for printed music. Amateurs rubbed shoulders with professional musicians, family members made music together. Almost everyone participated.

One such musical evening took place at Harleyford Manor in the summer of 1586. We know that William Byrd, one of the greatest composers of his day, was present and that his aristocratic host was a music lover. There is no record of the music that was performed, so I have taken the liberty of choosing a group of favorite works of the time. Although some of the pieces we will hear in this chapter were not published until several years after the house party in question, it was common in the sixteenth century for music to circulate in manuscript form long before it was printed. Byrd's Mass for Four Voices was written somewhat later, in the early 1590s, for private performance at a country house much like Harleyford Manor. In any case, these pieces are among the treasures of the musical Renaissance, and we would not want to miss them.

Ⓢ Byrd: "This sweet and merry month of May"

Ⓢ Dowland: "Can she excuse my wrongs" (voice and lute)

Ⓢ Morley: Galliard, "Can she excuse my wrongs"

Consort music

The Setting

HARLEYFORD MANOR

In July 1586, William Byrd attended a week-long gathering at a secluded estate in the county of Buckinghamshire, northwest of London, belonging to a wealthy

Music in an Elizabethan Country House

Meals at a country house like Harleyford Manor were often accompanied by music. As this job description from the 1580s suggests, musicians were generally considered servants and treated accordingly. Byrd was an exception; he would have sat with his host at the high table. (For a description of the instruments mentioned, see Elizabethan Musical Instruments, p. 72.)

At great feasts, when the Earl's service is going to the table, they are to play upon Shagbutte, Cornets, Shalms and such other instruments giving with wind. In meal times to play upon Viols, Violins, or other broken music. They are to teach the Earl's children to sing and play upon the Base Viol, the Virginals, Lute, Bandera or Cittern. In some houses they are allowed a mess of meat in their chambers, in other houses they eat with the waiters.

gentleman named Richard Bold. The composer's fellow guests were men and women of varying backgrounds, but they had one thing in common: they all refused to attend the services of the Protestant Church of England and to swear allegiance to Queen Elizabeth as head of the church. Known as recusants, these beleaguered members of England's Catholic underground had traveled to Harleyford Manor (see Figure 3.1) in utmost secrecy to meet two itinerant Jesuit missionaries: Father Henry Garnet, a musician and singer newly arrived from the Continent, and Father Robert Southwell, a noted poet. It was dangerous business being a Catholic.

An Elizabethan manorial estate—even a middling-sized one like Harleyford—was a self-contained community. English noblemen typically maintained one or more country residences in addition to a town house in London. Each was staffed by a "household" of a hundred or more servants and retainers. On special occasions, the lords of the manors welcomed visitors with much pomp and ceremony. Guests partook of elaborate feasts in the so-called great chamber, adorned with ornate tapestries and carved plasterwork, while more intimate gatherings were held in an adjacent withdrawing room or parlor. The periods between meals were filled with banquets (lavish buffets of sweets and drinks), dancing, music-making, and other festivities (see Music in an Elizabethan Country House, left). Once or twice a day, the lord's family, his household, and guests interrupted their revelries for quiet prayers in the private chapel or a corner of the great chamber.

Father Garnet's description of his stay at Harleyford gives some sense of the possibilities of a great house:

On reaching this gentleman's house, we were received, as I said before, with every attention that kindness and courtesy could suggest. We met also some gentlewomen who had come there to hide; and altogether we were eight days at the house. We were very happy, and our friends made it apparent how pleased they were to have us. Indeed, the place was most suited to our work and ministrations, not merely for the reason that it was remote and had a congenial household and company, but also because it possessed a chapel, set aside for the celebration of the Church's offices. The gentleman was also a skilled musician, and had an organ and other musical instruments, and choristers, male and female, members of his household. During those days it was just as if we were celebrating an uninterrupted octave [a liturgical term meaning a week of celebration] of some great feast.

Bold was a staunch Catholic who lived under constant threat of persecution, or even death, as England's sectarian conflict intensified in the late 1500s (see The English Reformation, p. 59). Bold prudently distanced himself from Elizabeth's court in London and maintained a low profile at Harleyford on the outskirts of

FIG. 3.1 A typical Elizabethan manor house (Harvington Hall). The original Harleyford manor, the site of this chapter's musical events, no longer exists.

Great Marlow, a sleepy market town beside the River Thames. (His responsibilities included custody of the royal swans, under a special grant from the queen.) There his family and servants—including a sizable complement of musicians—continued to practice their faith discreetly. Byrd, a fellow Catholic, had brought his own family to live in nearby Harlington, at least in part to keep them out of harm's way. According to another of Bold's guests,

> Mr Byrd, the very famous musician and organist, was among the company. Earlier he had been attached to the Queen's chapel, where he gained a great reputation: he had sacrificed everything for the faith—his position, the court, and all those aspirations common to men who seek preferment in royal circles as a means of improving their fortunes.

Byrd did indeed pay a price for his recusancy: fines were repeatedly levied against him (though they never seemed to amount to much), and his house was ransacked by the authorities in August 1586, shortly after the meeting at Harleyford. Thanks to his carefully cultivated relationship with the queen, however, his career barely skipped a beat. In 1575, Elizabeth had granted Byrd and his teacher, Thomas Tallis, a monopoly on the printing of music. They shrewdly dedicated their first publication, an anthology of Latin **motets** (choral pieces on sacred Latin texts), to their royal benefactor. Byrd went on to write another sacred piece ("Rejoice unto the Lord") to mark the twentieth anniversary of Elizabeth's ascendancy to the throne. As further pledges of his allegiance, he composed music to an English text that the queen had written in gratitude for the defeat of the Spanish Armada in 1588, as well as a **madrigal** (see p. 68) in her honor, "This sweet and merry month of May."

MUSIC IN ELIZABETHAN ENGLAND

Byrd and his fellow composers had ample reasons to ingratiate themselves with "Good Queen Bess." In addition to being a munificent patron of the arts, she was a gifted singer, lutenist (see Figure 3.2), and keyboard player. In their anthology of motets (1575), Byrd and Tallis praised her as an "outstandingly skilled" musician, "whether by the elegance of [her] voice or the nimbleness of [her] fingers." Elizabeth maintained an instrumental ensemble at St. James's Palace to entertain her at mealtimes, and an organist and a choir of men and boys to celebrate services in her private Chapel Royal. It is said that the queen's love of music was no less keen on her deathbed, when she summoned her court musicians to give a command performance so that "she might die as gaily as she had lived, and that the horrors of death might be lessened; she heard the music tranquilly until her last breath."

For the queen and most of her noble subjects, music was far more than a genteel pastime; it was an essential accoutrement of every cultivated person (see Figure 3.3). They took their cue from Baldassare Castiglione, whose classic book on courtly etiquette was published in Italy in 1528 and quickly became required reading throughout Europe. Castiglione has one of his model courtiers declare:

The English Reformation

The Church of England, also known as the Anglican Church, is one of the great Protestant churches that split off from the Roman Catholic Church in the early sixteenth century. In 1517 Martin Luther nailed his famous 95 theses (arguments) to a church door in Wittenberg; his protest of what he considered abuses in the Catholic Church led to the establishment of today's Lutheran Church. In 1534, England's King Henry VIII—the father of Elizabeth I—also broke with the Roman church: in defiance of the pope and many of his advisors, he declared himself supreme head of the Church in England.

In his desire for a male heir, Henry asked the pope to annul his marriage to Catherine of Aragon (the first of six wives) and allow him to wed Anne Boleyn (who would become Elizabeth's mother). When the pope refused, Henry denied the authority of Rome and set about systematically dismantling the wealth and power of the English clergy.

After Henry's death in 1547, the crown passed first to Edward, a sickly child who reigned only six years, and then to Elizabeth's half-sister Mary Tudor (daughter of Catherine); she lost no time in reversing her father's Reformation with a vengeance (she is known to history as "Bloody Mary.") By the time Elizabeth assumed the throne in 1558, at age twenty-five, sectarian conflict threatened to engulf the country. She pursued a middle course, steering England back into the Protestant fold while taking pains to appease her Catholic subjects.

My lords, you must know that I am not content with the Courtier unless he be also a musician and unless, besides understanding and being able to read notes, he can play upon divers instruments. For if we consider rightly, there is to be found no rest from toil or medicine for the troubled spirit more becoming and praiseworthy in time of leisure, than this; and especially in courts, where besides the relief from tedium that music affords us all, many things are done to please the ladies, whose tender and gentle spirit is easily penetrated by harmony and filled with sweetness.

Music was an integral part of official ceremonies, banquets, tournaments, and courtly entertainments, such as the one held in Queen Elizabeth's honor at Sudeley Castle in 1592, at which John Dowland—one of England's greatest Renaissance composers and performers—dazzled the monarch with his virtuosity on the lute.

If aristocratic patrons were the paymasters of this lively musical culture, its foot soldiers were the legions of amateur musicians from all walks of life. In the preface to his *Psalmes, Sonets, and Songs of Sadnes and Pietie* (1588), Byrd listed the advantages of learning to sing, regardless of one's wealth or social station (see Why Learn to Sing?, p. 61). This not only reflected the Renaissance ideal, expressed by Castiglione, that music is an indispensable social skill, but also may have helped to sell Byrd's own book.

FIG. 3.2 A miniature, by Nicholas Hilliard, of Queen Elizabeth playing the lute.

WILLIAM BYRD

Byrd was arguably the greatest of the many celebrated composers in Elizabethan England; certainly he was the most influential. Not only did he compose in virtually all the major forms and genres of the day—sacred music, secular song, instrumental music for consort and for keyboard—he also left a deep impression on a generation of younger composers, notably his pupils Thomas Morley and Thomas Weelkes. Byrd's work, like that of his contemporary William Shakespeare, is imbued with the confident, innovative, all-embracing spirit of the Elizabethan age (see biography, p. 62).

Byrd was a tough-minded man of business who successfully parlayed his extensive social connections into political and financial security. The dedicatees whose

FIG. 3.3 A ball at court. The couples in the foreground are dancing a pavan, to the accompaniment of musicians (lute, viol, and other instruments). Louis de Caullery (?1580–1621).

names grace his works are among the greatest of England's Catholic nobility. Prominent among them were the Earl of Worcester, who placed a special room in his London house at the composer's disposal, and Sir John Petre, whose largesse eased Byrd's later years.

Byrd's most powerful protector, of course, was Queen Elizabeth herself. Despite his stubborn refusal to acknowledge her spiritual authority, she permitted the composer to keep his titles (and salary) in the Chapel Royal, without having to perform the duties of the office. When Byrd's publishing monopoly generated a lower-than-expected profit, the queen compensated him with a lucrative lease on a manor in Gloucestershire. (Byrd owned many properties at various times in his life and was continually embroiled in real-estate litigation.) Elizabeth turned a blind eye to his association with Jesuits and saw to it that his fines for recusancy were knocked down. Byrd was evidently a jewel in the monarch's crown, even though people were arrested for owning his books and it was dangerous to be involved in singing one of his Masses. We know that two of the itinerant Jesuit missionaries at the weeklong gathering, Father Southwell and Father Garnet, were ultimately hanged (Father Garnet was also drawn and quartered).

The Performance

Richard Bold's guests might well have entertained themselves with all sorts of music, but what they cared about most passionately was their faith. Our proposed program begins, therefore, with a piece of sacred music for four voices that was perfectly suitable for music-making in a Catholic house. (Byrd's Mass seems to be intended for use as part of the liturgy, but nothing prevents its use elsewhere.) Next comes a sampler of Elizabethan secular music: a madrigal (a secular song for several voices) by Byrd followed by one of Dowland's most memorable songs, a piece so famous that it soon appeared in many different settings and arrangements. Although the song begins "Can she excuse my wrongs," many of the instrumental versions of it are called the "Earl of Essex Galliard," perhaps because the Earl of Essex was the author of the anonymous text of the song. The program might have gone like this:

1. Agnus Dei, from Byrd's Mass for Four Voices

2. Byrd's "This sweet and merry month of May"

3. Dowland's "Can she excuse my wrongs," for voice and lute

4. Five further versions of "Can she excuse my wrongs":
   a. Version for four voices and lute
   b. *The Earl of Essex Galliard*, lute version
   c. *The Earl of Essex Galliard*, keyboard version
   d. *The Earl of Essex Galliard*, viol consort version, from Dowland's *Lachrimae or Seaven Teares*
   e. *The Earl of Essex Galliard*, from Thomas Morley's *First Booke of Consort Lessons*

The program

Why Learn to Sing?

Reasons briefly set down by th'author, to perswade every one to learne to sing.

First, it is a knowledge easely taught and quickly learned, where there is a good Master, and an apt Scholler.

2 The exercise of singing is delightfull to Nature, & good to preserue the health of Man.

3 It doth strengthen all parts of the brest, & doth open the pipes.

4 It is a singuler good remedie for a stutting and stamering in the speech.

5 It is the best means to procure a perfect pronounciation, & to make a good Orator.

6 It is the onely way to know where Nature hath bestowed the benefit of a good voyce : which guift is so rare, as there is not one among a thousand, that hath it : and in many, that excellent guift is lost because they want Art to expresse Nature.

7 There is not any Musicke of Instruments whatsoeuer, comparable to that which is made of the voyces of Men, where the voyces are good, and the same well sorted and ordered.

8 The better the voyce is, the meeter it is to honour and serue God there with: and the voyce of man is chiefly to be imployed to that ende.

Omnis Spiritus Laudet Dominum
[Let every spirit praise the Lord]
    Since singing is so good a thing
    I wish all men would learne to sing.

WILLIAM BYRD (ca. 1540–1623)

William Byrd's early life is obscure, but he seems to have been musically active from an early age; as a teenager he sang in the Chapel Royal (the monarch's official church choir) under the Catholic Mary Tudor. In 1558, Mary died and her half-sister Elizabeth assumed the throne. Thus Byrd experienced both Catholic church music (sung in Latin) and Protestant music (in Latin and English) as it was revived under Queen Elizabeth. Despite his service to the Protestant court, he staunchly remained faithful to his Catholic roots.

In 1563 Byrd was appointed organist and master of the choristers at Lincoln Cathedral. By 1572, now married and the father of two children (he eventually had five), he was back in London as a Gentleman of the Chapel Royal, a very high-ranking and well-paying position. He sang in the choir and shared the organ-playing with the aging Thomas Tallis. Byrd was well connected, especially with influential fellow Catholics, and for more than twenty years he maintained his headquarters as composer and publisher in the capital city. A number of his works were covert protests against the persecution of Catholics, a fate that Byrd himself managed to avoid, probably by grace of the queen's protection.

Eventually, however, the rising anti-Catholic sentiment prompted him to seek refuge in Stondon Massey, Essex, where he passed his last three decades in seclusion and continued to practice his faith in secret. Along with keyboard music and songs, he published some overtly Catholic, and very beautiful, sacred music: three Masses—one each for three, four, and five voices—and two books of *Gradualia*, collections of settings of the liturgical texts of the Proper of the Latin Mass. Upon his death on July 4, 1623, he was memorialized in the records of the Chapel Royal as "a Father of Musick."

Byrd wrote vocal music of all kinds: secular madrigals and consort songs (accompanied by a group, or consort, of stringed instruments); sacred anthems in English, and sacred motets in Latin. Perhaps Byrd's greatest, and most movingly personal, religious works are the two collections of *Cantiones sacrae* (Sacred Songs), published in 1589 and 1591. Even with their rich polyphonic textures, these songs treat the themes of lamentation, oppression, and entreaty with a powerful directness.

A prolific keyboard composer, Byrd is associated with music for the virginal (a small harpsichord), which he elevated to a new level of sophistication. In 1591 he made a compilation of his best keyboard music for the Nevell family. *My Ladye Nevells Booke* was an enormously important and influential collection of popular dances, elaborate variations, free-form fantasies, and sundry other pieces. As this wide-ranging anthology demonstrates, Byrd was just as at home in the older contrapuntal style as he was in more up-to-date idioms.

Ⓢ Byrd: "Ye sacred muses"
Ⓢ Byrd: "The Galliarde for the Victorie," from *My Lady Neville's Virginal Book*
Ⓢ Byrd: "Civitas sancti tui," from *Cantiones sacrae, Book 1*

MAJOR WORKS: Over 180 motets; dozens of psalms and anthems; 4 Services; 3 Masses; secular songs; and works for keyboard and for viol consort.

The Music

RENAISSANCE POLYPHONY

There were many kinds of music in the Renaissance—vocal and instrumental, sacred and secular, public and domestic. Then as now, a piece of music was categorized according to its function and its stylistic attributes. One of the main contributions to music of this period, and one that has affected and informed music ever since, is the style of imitative polyphony (see below). And one of its most beautiful examples is the Agnus Dei from Byrd's Mass for Four Voices.

Polyphony   **Polyphony,** as we learned in Chapter 2, is music in which more than one note is sounded simultaneously. The term usually refers to two or more continuous melodies moving more or less independently, rather than to, say, a texture characterized by a single prominent melody with accompaniment.

Imitative polyphony   In **imitative polyphony** each of the melodies in the polyphonic texture is of more or less equal importance; that is, no one voice is "the melody," while the others are "the accompaniment." (We use the term **voices** for the individual melodies even when the polyphony is for choirs or instruments.) Note that equal importance does not mean that all the voices have the same range—four sopranos, for example. Rather, it means that all the voices, from high to low, are equally prominent in the overall polyphonic texture and move independently of one another. Not all multivoiced music written in the Renaissance is polyphonic in the sense of having voices of equal importance; many sixteenth-century madrigals, for example, clearly differentiate between the melodic line and the accompaniment, although the melody typically skips from one voice to another.

Voices

In imitative polyphony, one voice copies what another voice has just done, as in the familiar round "Row, row, row your boat." The basic idea could be pictured as follows:

```
M———-------------------
    M———-------------
        M———--------
            M———---
```

One voice sings something, a tuneful phrase of a few notes, represented here by M———. As it continues, a second voice begins to sing the same phrase, but usually in a different register (a **soprano**—the higher range of female voices—followed by an **alto**—the lower female range, for example), while the first voice continues singing other, harmonious music, here represented by dotted lines. A third voice (a **tenor**, say—a high male voice) enters after the alto, while alto and soprano continue to sing, using other material; and perhaps a fourth voice (a **bass**, perhaps) enters singing the same characteristic phrase—let's call it a **motive**. That whole process, in which each voice enters using the same motive (that is, each voice imitates the first) creates a **point of imitation.**

Soprano. alto, tenor, and bass

Motive

Ⓢ Byrd: Kyrie, from Mass for Four Voices

What happens next? Well, the voices could stop, by making a **cadence** (an effective musical close), and that would be the end of the piece (see Chapter 1). Or they could begin the same process again with another point of imitation, using the same motive or a different one. Indeed, this is how a lot of Renaissance music is made—using a series of points of imitation. Vocal pieces in particular are often guided by their texts, each successive phrase of text associated with a different motive.

Here is a diagram of a longer construction, made of three points of imitation. This is the middle section of the Agnus Dei of Byrd's Mass for Four Voices, in which three of the voices sing; each segment of text has its own motive, as follows:

Agnus Dei, (motive **A**)
    qui tollis peccata mundi, (motive **B**)
      miserere nobis (motive **C**)

Points of imitation

Ⓢ Byrd: Agnus Dei, from Mass for Four Voices, middle section

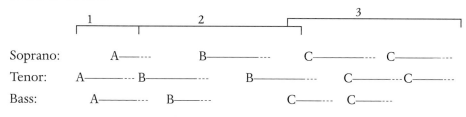

Agnus Dei, qui tollis peccata mundi,   miserere nobis

Imitation in Renaissance music

This section begins with three voices entering one after another using motive **A**; but note that they do not come to a cadence. Just as the soprano voice is finishing motive **A**, the tenor, after a brief **rest** (the musical term for a silence), begins another motive (it is common to give each voice an occasional pause, especially just before it is about to sing an important motive—the rest calls attention to the voice when it reenters). The other voices, in a different order this time, each enter with the new motive **B**; then the bass begins a new motive (**C**), which is imitated in the other voices, in another order still, until all voices have entered, and the three make a cadence.

There are problems with this scheme, however: isn't it likely to get boring, one point of imitation after another? How does a composer provide variety? There are, as you might suppose, a number of ways to keep things interesting. They include:

- *Varying the number of voices.* For example, one section of the piece might be composed for two or three voices, instead of the full complement.

- *Varying the texture.* Occasionally, a composer will insert a section in **homophony,** where all the voices sing the same words at the same time and in more or less the same rhythm.

- *Varying the imitation.* There are several ways of managing this, depending on whether the motive is fast or slow, angular or smooth, long or short. It is sometimes possible to overlap the motive with itself, so that the second voice enters before the first voice has finished the motive, and so on with other voices (a good example of this is the beginning of the Agnus Dei). Among the special types of imitation is **paired imitation**, in which two motives are combined:

```
A——————- - - - - - - - - - -
B——————- - - - - - - - - -
              A——————- - -
              B——————- - -
```

Cantus firmus technique

There are other ways, too, of creating textures and styles of composition. One is called **cantus firmus technique**, in which one voice sings a preexistent melody (a piece of Gregorian chant for the church, or some other previously composed melody) while the other voices weave a web of polyphony around it. This is no easy thing to do, but it is a means of ensuring a kind of unity in a multisection composition like a Mass (which normally has five different sections), if each section uses the same cantus firmus.

It is also possible, of course, to make polyphony that is not imitative at all. Voices can be independently beautiful, but without singing one another's music. Dowland's song is a bit like that, in its four-voice version: the voices are independent, but do not imitate each other.

Counterpoint

What Renaissance polyphony is really about is texture: the miraculous fact that several voices can be singing (or playing) at the same time, each voice a satisfyingly lovely melody in itself, and together produce marvelous harmonies. Another name for this kind of music is **counterpoint**; we have already encountered an early, and somewhat more austere, form of it in the music of Leoninus and Perotinus. The contrapuntal techniques that Byrd and his contemporaries developed to such a high degree have inspired admiration for centuries. In fact, composers still consider counterpoint an essential skill and study it in conservatories as part of their basic training.

The polyphonic tradition was second nature to the company assembled under Richard Bold's roof. Polyphony was the mother tongue of their musical culture and as such needed no explanation. They knew what to listen for in a piece of vocal polyphony, and when they heard Byrd's Mass, we can be sure they recognized it as a masterpiece of its kind.

Listening to the Music

BYRD: AGNUS DEI, FROM THE MASS FOR FOUR VOICES

LG 6

The Mass for Four Voices is one of three Masses that Byrd published late in his life (the others call for three and five voices, respectively). Although it was intended to be sung at private worship services attended by a small number of Catholic recusants, both the musical structure and the liturgical texts were the same as those used in the grand public Christmas Mass celebrated at Notre Dame in 1198. The five sections—Kyrie, Gloria, Credo, Sanctus, and Agnus Dei—are present in every Mass, and are the same texts found in thousands of polyphonic Masses by Byrd, Palestrina, Lassus, and other Renaissance composers. They are also used in Masses written by composers we will encounter later in this book, such as Bach, Mozart, Beethoven, Dvořák, and Bernstein.

The Latin words of the Agnus Dei (Lamb of God) are always the same as well. Three times the choir invokes Christ by that name; on the third repetition, the final phrase, "have mercy on us," is changed to "give us peace."

The words

> *Agnus Dei, qui tollis peccata mundi, miserere nobis.*
> *Agnus Dei, qui tollis peccata mundi, miserere nobis.*
> *Agnus Dei, qui tollis peccata mundi, dona nobis pacem.*

> Lamb of God, who take away the sins of the world, have mercy on us.
> Lamb of God, who take away the sins of the world, have mercy on us.
> Lamb of God, who take away the sins of the world, give us peace.

Byrd sets the words to music in a way that builds on the structure of the text: each phrase of the text is sung to a new motive, producing a series of points of imitation that becomes steadily denser in texture. Each motive is designed to be melodious and readily identifiable (so that we can easily hear the imitation), and also to fit well with the shape and accentuation of the words. As is generally true of such motives in imitative polyphony, the motives are most characteristic at their beginnings, and trail off into other material as our attention is drawn away from one voice to the entrance of the motive in another voice.

The motives

Each new motive is marked in the text below:

A———— B———————— C————
Agnus Dei, qui tollis peccata mundi, miserere nobis.

D———— E———————— F————
Agnus Dei, qui tollis peccata mundi, miserere nobis.

G———— H———————— I————
Agnus Dei, qui tollis peccata mundi, dona nobis pacem.

Canon

The opening "Agnus Dei" is sung by the altos and sopranos, the altos always leading, so that it sounds almost like a relaxed **canon** (a continuous imitation, one voice always following along after the other).

The three lines of text are set for an increasing number of voices; the first is given to soprano and alto; the second to soprano, tenor, and bass; and the final one to soprano, alto, tenor, and bass. The entry of the additional voices at the ends of the first two sections provides a couple of magical moments for this piece.

The structure

The general layout of the motives in the various voices is summarized in the diagram below. Capital letters stand for musical motives (all the As sound alike, etc.), with the words shown below. You can see that there are nine points of imitation (A through I), and that even though the words repeat ("Agnus Dei," for example, comes three times), the music does not—the "Agnus Dei" in each line of text has its own motive.

The diagram, of course, gives no idea of the beauty of Byrd's music, but it does show the structure and the increasing density of the piece.

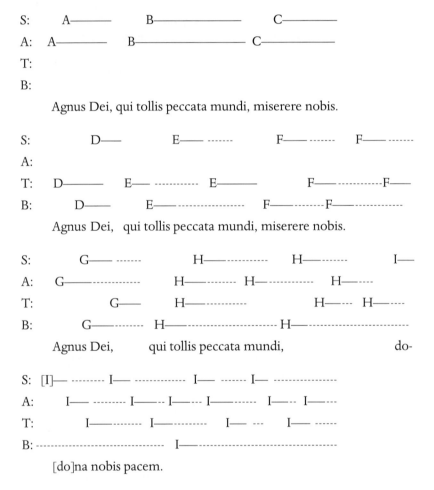

In the final "dona nobis pacem," the entrances come closer and closer together. As you listen, note how Byrd uses wrenching **suspensions**—sharply dissonant notes that clash with the prevailing harmonies—on strong beats to give the prayer an extra measure of passion and poignancy.

Suspensions

Perhaps this long, tension-filled, and beautiful plea was intended as a secret message to Byrd's fellow Catholics, who, like him, were awaiting an end to strife. Only at the end of the Agnus Dei does a brief ray of sunlight illuminate the final cadence (see LG 6, p. 67).

LISTENING GUIDE 6

Byrd Agnus Dei, from Mass for Four Voices

3:45

DATE: About 1592–93

GENRE: "Agnus Dei" section from a Mass

LISTEN FOR

FORM: Increasing lengths of section

TEXTURE: Points of imitation

SCORING: Increasing number of voices

EXPRESSION: Passionate suspensions at final "dona nobis pacem"

TIME	TEXT	MOTIVE	DESCRIPTION
0:00	Agnus Dei	Motive (**A**): Ag — nus De - i, Ag - nus De - i.	Alto begins; soprano enters while the alto is still singing the first note; imitation is closely over-lapped. The motive, with its highest and longest note at the beginning, has effect of a cry.
0:10	qui tollis peccata mundi	New motive (**B**): qui tol - lis pec - ca-	Alto followed by soprano. Note soprano leap to "tollis." Imitation is not exact.
0:21	miserere nobis	New motive (**C**): mi - se - re - re	Alto followed by soprano. Note repetition of words "miserere," alto singing three times, each higher and more intense, coming to a cadence.
0:41	Agnus Dei	New motive (**D**): Ag - nus De - i,	Tenor voice is added! The new motive (not the same as first "Agnus Dei") emphasizes "Dei." The tenor is followed by bass (also new!), then soprano. Alto rests throughout middle section.
0:50	qui tollis peccata mundi	New motive (**E**): qui tol - lis pec - ca - ta	While soprano is still singing (**D**) motive, tenor begins new motive (**E**), which is quicker and strives upward urgently. There are four entrances because tenor sings the motive twice.
1:08	miserere nobis	New motive (**F**): mi - se - re - re no - - - - - - - bis.	Bass begins—this motive is slower, and begins with stepwise downward motion. Each voice sings the motive twice: bass-soprano-tenor, bass-soprano-tenor, the last two accompanied by unusual repetition of the same figure in bass. Byrd is pointing us toward a strong cadence. To the three voices, a final voice is added (alto) to fill out the chord and to start the next motive.

(continued)

TIME	TEXT	MOTIVE	DESCRIPTION
1:37	Agnus Dei	New motive (**G**): Ag - nus De - i,	Motive's upward leap and downward scale give an impression of urgent yearning. Alto begins; soprano and bass enter simultaneously; the following tenor, alto, bass entrances closely overlap. Clear cadence with three voices.
1:55	qui tollis peccata mundi	New motive (**H**): qui tol - lis pec - ca - ta	Bass begins (**H**), followed by alto and tenor simultaneously; then soprano; alto. What appears to be a cadence, leads to further set of entrances: bass, soprano, tenor, alto, tenor. The sections are getting longer.
2:25	dona nobis pacem	New motive (**I**): do - na no - bis pa -	The new motive is full of suspensions (notes that begin harmonious and turn dissonant when other voices move). This is almost always the case with the notes for **do**-na **no**-bis. The effect, of piling dissonance on dissonance to an almost excruciating degree, is at odds with the peace that the text asks for. Bass provides a strong harmonic underpinning in long notes.
2:47	(dona nobis pacem *continues*)		Bass now joins in singing the motive, while the soprano sings long notes. Bass returns to long-note role, soprano holding high notes while inner voices continue the motive. There is a surprising—and finally peaceful—turn to a bright major-chord harmony for the final cadence.

♪ LG 7   BYRD: "THIS SWEET AND MERRY MONTH OF MAY"

Madrigal

The jovial, outgoing mood of Byrd's madrigal "This sweet and merry month of May" contrasts sharply with the intensity of the Agnus Dei. A **madrigal** is a polyphonic setting of a secular poem in a modern language—in this case, English. (Both the name and the musical genre were imported to England from Italy.) Many madrigal composers made a point of putting as many amusing details into their compositions as possible. They often chose poems describing birdsongs, rushing waves, chirping crickets, and so on, which gave them an opportunity to display

Word painting

their talent for **word painting**—that is, imitating the sounds described by the text.

The poem is a lighthearted salute to Queen Elizabeth (or Eliza, as she is somewhat familiarly called here). On this first day of May, the poet (Thomas Watson) and composer greet the beauteous "Queen of second Troy"—the implication is that Elizabeth is as beautiful as Helen of Troy. It was also believed that the English crown descended from the Trojans, and since the Trojans founded Rome, England was a New Rome (it was a lot to pack into a single compliment). Composer and poet beg the queen not to place too much value on their rhyme, or on a "simple toy"—a light literary and musical amusement:

This sweet and merry month of May,
While Nature wantons in her prime,
And birds do sing and beasts do play,
For pleasure of the joyful time:
I choose the first for holiday
And greet Eliza with a rhyme:
O beauteous Queen of second Troy
Take well in worth a simple toy.

Byrd's lively madrigal for six voices is essentially a secular counterpart of his serious sacred music. Here, as in the Agnus Dei, each new element of text calls for a new musical motive, which allows the words to be sung in a fairly natural rhythm (and therefore to be readily understood). In addition, the points of imitation are interspersed with sections of homophony, with varied rhythms and groupings of voices (see LG 7, below).

The poet's voice

This kind of multisectional, imitative music was used for a great deal of poetry in the Renaissance period. Interestingly, the poems often represent one person speaking, even though the musical settings may require several singers. In a sense, a group is playing the role of a single actor or poet: no one voice is the speaker, and no one voice has "the tune." The use of a group also allows for imitation and other effects that are impossible for a single singer to produce. The musical variety characteristic of the madrigal made it a favorite genre of listeners and performers in the sixteenth century.

LISTENING GUIDE 7   Ⓢ | DVD

Byrd "This sweet and merry month of May"   2:01

DATE: Published 1590
GENRE: Madrigal

LISTEN FOR
FORM: Each new element of text calls for a new musical motive
TEXTURE: Varied texture: homophony relieves the imitative texture
SCORING: Variety of groupings of the six voices
TEXT: Word painting: music reflects text meaning

TIME	TEXT	DESCRIPTION
0:00	This sweet and merry month of May	Paired imitation in the top pairs of voices (two sopranos, later joined by alto and tenor); note lighthearted scale on "merry merry month."
0:07	While Nature wantons in her prime,	New point of imitation, overlapped with previous cadence. Beginning in lowest two voices (bass and tenor); motive has a long note on accented syllable of "Nature," and then a dotted descending figure gives flippant tone on "wantons":

(continued)

TIME	TEXT	DESCRIPTION
0:17	And birds do sing and beasts do play	Divided into two motives, two points of imitation: "and birds do sing" (note twitter on "sing") is followed without cadence by "and beasts do play." A strong cadence ends section.

TIME	TEXT	DESCRIPTION
0:36	For pleasure of the joyful time:	Change of pace; triple rhythms connote pleasure and joy. "For pleasure" has one triple rhythm, "of the joyful time" has another, faster rhythm. Homophonic groups of 3, 4, or 5 voices.
0:43	I choose the first for holiday	Back to duple time. A point of imitation begins after cadence; voices gradually accumulate for a 6-voice cadence.
0:53	And greet Eliza with a rhyme:	The name "Eliza" repeats many times, like trumpet calls; the cadence is preceded by long series of same note (C) in soprano, calling everyone to attention. Cadence in all voices.
1:13	O beauteous Queen of second Troy	Solemn almost-homophony begins section after a rest (text now addresses the Queen directly); gradually gets more polyphonic, without being imitative.
1:29	Take well in worth a simple toy.	Section overlaps with previous section. Two 4-note motives "take well in worth":

and "a simple toy"

are combined in a number of inventive ways: above, below, overlapped. The two motives are combined in the bass.

All voices join in a cadence on "a simple toy."

JOHN DOWLAND

John Dowland was not present in person at Harleyford Manor, but most of Bold's houseguests would have known him by reputation as a leading light of English music and a virtuoso lutenist (see biography, p. 71). At twenty-three, Dowland was Byrd's junior by almost a generation. The two composers moved in different spheres and probably never met; but they were both Catholics, and they were surely familiar with each other's music.

Dowland's musical style and career path could scarcely have been more different

JOHN DOWLAND (1563–1626)

Born in England in 1563 (his precise birthplace is unknown), Dowland spent much of his life abroad in the service of various noble patrons. After a period in France in the 1580s, he worked and traveled in Germany and Italy, and ultimately accepted a lucrative post at the court of the king of Denmark in 1598. Dowland had converted to Catholicism in France and claimed that this prevented him from obtaining a post at the court of Queen Elizabeth (who had, of course, been willing enough to overlook Byrd's religion). Only late in life, after the queen's death, did he get a position as lute player for her successor, King James I, whom he served from 1612 until his own death in 1626.

Dowland is England's greatest composer of lute music and lute songs (that is, songs for solo voice with lute accompaniment). His solos for the instrument range from simple jigs to brilliant contrapuntal fantasias. Dowland's temperament was famously melancholy. One of his most beautiful lute pieces is titled "Semper Dowland, semper dolens" (Latin for "Always Dowland, always doleful"), a play on words that seems to

characterize both the man and his music. A case in point is his lute song "Flow, my tears," whose opening phrase—four notes descending stepwise—became a kind of musical shorthand for intense grief.

Dowland's arrangement of "Flow, my tears" for a consort of five viols is the first of seven **pavans** (a pavan is a slow, stately dance) that explore the possibilities of this four-note theme; they are the seven pieces that begin his *Lachrimae or Seaven Teares Figured in Seaven Passionate Pavans*. The book also includes some other, less doleful, music. Dowland, in his preface, described the collection as "this long and troublesome worke, wherein I have mixed new songs with olde, grave with light."

ⓢ Dowland: "Flow, my tears"
ⓢ Dowland: "Semper Dowland, semper dolens"

MAJOR WORKS: Numerous vocal works, including "Flow, my tears"; lute music, including fantasias, galliards, and pavans; consort works, including *Lachrimae, or Seaven Teares*.

from Byrd's. Despite his international fame, he found it difficult to get a good position at the English court; in part this may have been because of his religious convictions. Several published books of lute songs and a collection of ensemble music for viols have assured his immortality. In addition, a great deal of wonderful solo music for lute survives. The lute was a popular domestic instrument in Elizabethan times (see Elizabethan Musical Instruments, p. 72), and Dowland was its acknowledged master.

Renaissance composers tended to write for groups of instruments of the same family, but of different sizes. A "whole" consort of instruments is a group of the same type: a consort of lutes, a consort of viols, and so on. A mixed ("broken") consort groups instruments of different kinds, like those that play the pieces in Morley's *First Booke of Consort Lessons* (see LG 9 and figures on pp. 71 and 79).

It is characteristic of Renaissance music that it could be adapted for whatever vocal and instrumental forces were at hand. If at Bold's house there were not four singers, or four viol players, then some of the parts could be assigned to other voices or instruments. This flexibility is possible when the individual parts are not so specialized that they can be played on only one instrument (as is true of much instrumental music of the seventeenth century and later). And it is characteristic of Dowland's music that everybody wanted to sing and play it.

It's easy to imagine the company in Bold's great chamber joining together with instruments and voices to play and sing some of the finest and most popular music of the day. They lived in a time when a lot of music was made, not by professional musicians, but by people who simply liked music and poetry, and were able to savor them by writing poetry and singing and playing music themselves. They were lucky to live in a time when inspiration could be provided by the likes of Byrd and Dowland.

FIG. 3.4 A mixed instrumental consort; front to back: bass viol, harp, lute, and flute.

Elizabethan Musical Instruments

Instrumental music flourished during the Renaissance, as the center of musical life shifted from the great medieval cathedrals to royal courts and private estates like Harleyford Manor. Among the favorite instruments in Elizabethan households, both great and small, were the lute, the viol, and the virginal.

The **lute** (see Figure 3.2, p. 60) is a pear-shaped, flat-topped instrument held like a guitar and played by plucking the six (or more) *courses* (a course is one or two strings tuned to the same pitch). A series of frets, or ridges crossing the fingerboard, tells the player where to press down the fingers of the left hand to produce different notes. (The modern guitar has frets too, but they are bars set into the fingerboard rather than strings tied around it.) The sound of the lute resembles that of an acoustic guitar, but is softer.

Ⓢ *Earl of Essex Galliard* (lute)

Like the lute, the **viol**, or **viola da gamba**, has six strings and frets, but instead of being plucked by the fingers, they are played with a bow. Viols come in three basic sizes: the small treble viol, the middle-sized tenor viol, and the large bass viol. All are played vertically (like a cello rather than a violin), with the instrument resting on or between the player's legs. (Viola da gamba means "leg viol" in Italian, to distinguish it from the viola da braccio, or "arm viol," held like a violin.) Compared to the modern violin, viola, and cello, viols have a more subdued and less penetrating sound, in part because their strings are made of animal gut instead of metal. An ensemble of viols sounds something like a softer version of a modern string quartet.

Ⓢ *Earl of Essex Galliard* (viols)

The **virginal** is a small, oblong portable keyboard instrument whose strings are plucked (rather than being struck by hammers, as on a modern piano) by depressing a key. The origin of the word is not clear; some think the virginal, an instrument overwhelmingly English, is named for Elizabeth, the "Virgin Queen." Related to the virginal is the wing-shaped **harpsichord**, which plucks the strings in the same way and often has more than one keyboard. The organ, a keyboard instrument that sounds by means of air passing through long pipes, was (and is) most often found in churches.

Ⓢ *Earl of Essex Galliard* (virginal)

All these instruments—lute, viol, and keyboards—were popular among musicians at various levels of proficiency. Renaissance wind instruments, on the other hand, were mostly the province of professionals. They include the **recorder** (an end-blown flute), the **flute** (played by blowing across a hole in the side of the tube), the **shawm** (a loud, buzzy, double-reed instrument, ancestor of the modern oboe); and the traditional brass instruments: trombone (in England called the **sackbut**), trumpet, and horn. The **cornett**, a curved wooden horn with fingerholes like a recorder but played with a trumpetlike mouthpiece, was a favorite, especially among the Italians. (See Figures 3.4, 3.5, and 3.6 for images of some Renaissance instruments.)

Ⓢ Monteverdi: *Orfeo* (recorders)
Ⓢ Monteverdi: *Orfeo* (cornetts and sackbuts)
Ⓢ Monteverdi: *Orfeo* (2 cornetts with organ and lute)

 LG 8   **DOWLAND: "CAN SHE EXCUSE MY WRONGS"**

Dowland's song "Can she excuse my wrongs" is written for solo voice and lute, with an optional version for four voices (with additional alto, tenor, and bass vocal parts). It comes from his *First Booke of Songs or Ayres* of 1597, an enormously successful collection that was reprinted several times in the composer's lifetime. One reason for its popularity was its novel and convenient layout: instead of printing the four parts in separate partbooks, as was the norm, Dowland combined them in a single, large-format volume. Each song is spread across two facing pages, with the parts oriented in different directions (see Figure 3.5). Hence a group of singers and a lutenist can gather around a table and perform the piece using only one copy of the music.

The poem   Dowland's text is a poem by Robert Devereaux, the second Earl of Essex. Essex was a suitor to Queen Elizabeth (he is said to have proposed to her more than once). Ultimately, owing to Essex's rash disobedience, he was imprisoned and executed for treason. His poem may well be addressed to the queen; it is a lover's complaint about his mistress's failure to return his affection. (Note that when the poet refers to "*my* wrongs," he does not mean his own misdeeds, but the wrongs done *to him* by the lady.) Both verses of poetry are set to the same music; this is called

Strophic musical setting   a **strophic** musical setting. The six couplets of each verse are set to three musical sections, each of which is repeated. The first two sections have new words when

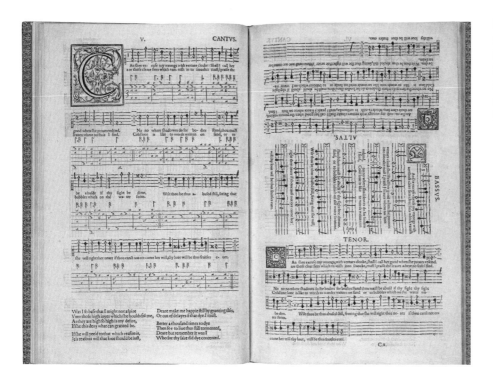

they are repeated; the third section repeats its words. The musical shape, then, of each of the two verses is **AABBCC**, as follows:

A *Can she excuse my wrongs with virtue's cloak?*
Shall I call her good when she proves unkind?

A *Are those clear fires which vanish into smoke?*
Must I praise the leaves where no fruit I find?

B *No, no: where shadows do for bodies stand,*
Thou may'st be abused if thy sight be dim.

B *Cold love is like to words written on sand,*
Or to bubbles which on the water swim.

C *Wilt thou be thus abused still,*
Seeing that she will right thee never?
If thou canst not overcome her will,
Thy love will be thus fruitless ever. (C repeats)

A *Was I so base, that I might not aspire*
Unto those high joys which she holds from me?

A *As they are high, so high is my desire:*
If she this deny what can granted be?

B *If she will yield to that which reason is,*
It is reason's will that love should be just.

B *Dear make me happy still by granting this,*
Or cut off delays if that I die must.

C *Better a thousand times to die,*
Than for to live thus still tormented:
Dear but remember it was I
Who for thy sake did die contented. (C repeats)

On one level, Dowland's song is an extraordinary study of triple rhythms, but his handling of the melody is no less brilliantly imaginative. The fifth couplet of each verse alludes to a popular tune of the day, surely known to everyone at Harleyford Manor, called "Will you go walk in the woods so wild?" In the first verse, the lute plays the popular tune once while the singer asks, "Wilt thou be thus abused still," and again, one step higher, at the words "seeing that she will right thee never." The quotation is a sly wink at the woman addressed in the poem, a wordless invitation to a lovers' tryst. The singer's repeated notes divert the listener's attention to the melody in the lute (it's the only thing moving, and it's moving in the same rhythm as the voice). In the four-voice version of the song, Dowland complicates the situation further by arranging for that same tune to be sung in canon between the alto and the tenor (see LG 8, p. 76).

Rhythm in Dowland's "Can she excuse my wrongs"

"Will you go walk in the woods so wild?"

FIG. 3.6 A plate from Michael Praetorius's treatise on musical instruments; depicted here are (starting on the left) bass viol, harpsichord, trombone, and two views of a bassoon.

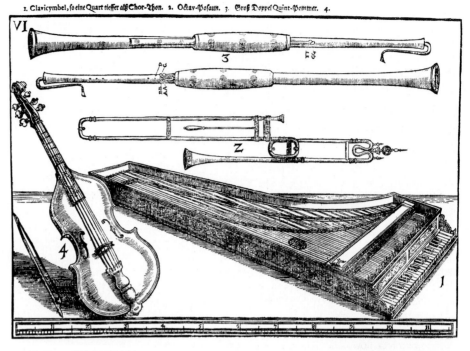

FIG. 3.7 A group of instruments played in procession: (back to front) a bassoon, a straight shawm, a curved cornett, two more straight shawms, and a trombone (or possibly a slide trumpet).

 LG 9

DOWLAND: "CAN SHE EXCUSE MY WRONGS" (*THE EARL OF ESSEX GALLIARD*)

Popularity of the song

"Can she excuse my wrongs" is one of many songs by Dowland that became hits throughout England and the Continent. Like a modern pop tune, it was disseminated in a variety of arrangements, so that it could be performed by virtually any combination of players and singers that happened to be available. In addition to the "original" version for voice and lute (and the alternative version with four voice parts, which could be either sung or played on viols), there are arrangements

Renaissance Dances

Much music written in the 1500s (and later periods) was originally intended for dancing. Like music-making, dancing was a social skill that members of the Elizabethan aristocracy took great pains to acquire. Most households of any pretension employed professional dancing-masters to teach the steps. Published manuals offered not only dance instruction but also tips on social etiquette (for example, "Spit and blow your nose sparingly"). Dance parties were held regularly at court and at houses like Harleyford Manor. In addition to showing off the dancers' grace and deportment, they afforded an opportunity for socially acceptable flirtation and matchmaking. Indeed, one leading dance writer of the day said that the main reason for learning to dance was to find a suitably accomplished wife or husband.

Renaissance dances go by many names—pavan, galliard, corrente, saltarello, branle, balletto, and so on—each characterized by distinctive rhythmic patterns, geometrical floor figures, and steps. To dance Dowland's *Earl of Essex Galliard*, for instance (or any galliard), you take three little hops on alternating feet ("Can she ex-"), then a big leap on the next foot ("-cuse"), hang in the air, and then put the two feet down quickly one after the other ("my wrongs"). The pavan, as represented by Dowland's famous *Lachrimae*, was comparatively sedate; one manual describes it as follows:

The pavane is easy to dance, consisting merely of two single steps and one double step forward, [followed by] two single steps and one double step backward. It is played in duple time; note that the forward steps begin on the left foot and the backward steps begin on the right foot.

FIG. 3.8 An Elizabethan couple dancing the Lavolta. This picture was long thought to be of Queen Elizabeth and the Earl of Essex.

---

for different instrumental ensembles and for solo lute, solo harpsichord, and solo bandora (a wire-strung cousin of the lute). The differences between these versions are subtle but telling, and the listeners at our imaginary concert would have taken pleasure in being able to pick them out (see LG 9, p. 77).

Arrangements

Dowland himself made an arrangement of his song for five viols and included it in his *Lachrimae or Seaven Teares Figured in Seaven Passionate Pavans*. There it is called *The Earl of Essex Galliard*, in honor of the queen's disgraced favorite, and the author of the text. Dowland may have had this kind of dance in mind all along, because the opening of the song—the six notes that accompany the words "Can she excuse my wrongs"—is a perfect example of **galliard** rhythm (see Renaissance Dances, above). The galliard was perhaps the Elizabethans' favorite social dance, and Dowland's arrangement for five instruments, even though it preserves the tune and the intricate rhythms of the song, also has enough regular rhythm to be an effective piece of dance music.

Galliard

We also have a version of *The Earl of Essex Galliard* for lute, arranged by Dowland; for keyboard (probably arranged from Dowland's song by somebody else); and a wonderful version from Thomas Morley's *First Booke of Consort Lessons* (see LG 9, p. 77). Morley, composer, author, and publisher, compiled pieces by various composers and arranged them for the marvelous mixed consort of flute (or recorder), violin or treble viol, bass viol, lute, cittern (a little wire-strung plucked instrument), and bandora. In this version, the lute plays a kind of solo role: it performs a decorated version of the melody when the various sections get repeated. Adding ornaments (they were called "divisions") was standard practice in the Renaissance, as it would be in the Baroque era, but in this case only a virtuoso like John Dowland would be able to do them justice.

LISTENING GUIDE 8 | DVD | 🎙

Dowland "Can she excuse my wrongs," for Voice and Lute   1:26

DATE: Published 1597
GENRE: Lute song

LISTEN FOR
RHYTHM: Three levels of triple rhythms
TEXTURE: Music repeated with new words

SCORING: Lute comes to foreground with a popular tune
TEXT: Lyrical setting of poem

TIME	FORM	TEXT	DESCRIPTION
		First musical section, repeated with new text	
0:00	A	1. Can she excuse my wrongs with virtue's cloak?	Two big upward leaps ("Can she ex-") followed by stepwise motion downwards that fills the gaps; opening triple rhythm becomes a slower triple:
0:07		2. Shall I call her good when she proves unkind?	Melody made of descending thirds. Fast triple turns to same slow version as above:
0:14	A	3. Are those clear fires which vanish into smoke?	Repeat music of line 1.
0:20		4. Must I praise the leaves where no fruit I find?	Repeat music of line 2.
		Second musical section, repeated with new text	
0:27	B	5. No, no: where shadows do for bodies stand,	Rhythm begins like that of line 1, but no leaps: melody has very narrow range:
0:34		6. Thou may'st be abused if thy sight be dim.	Rhythm and melody are similar to line 2, but with new ending, leaving a feeling of suspense:
0:41	B	7. Cold love is like to words written on sand,	Repeat music of line 5.
0:47		8. Or to bubbles which on the water swim.	Repeat music of line 6.

Third musical section, repeated with new text

| 0:54 | C | 9. Wilt thou be thus abused still, | Lilting triple rhythm, all on one note. Lute plays tune called "Will you go walk in the woods so wild?" a not-so-subtle, but unspoken, invitation to his mistress: |

Wilt thou be thus ab - us - ed still,

0:58		10. Seeing that she will right thee never?	Same lilting rhythm, one note higher (lute plays same tune, also one note higher).
1:02		11. If thou canst not overcome her will,	Still on a single note, melody is perhaps a picture of insistence.
1:05		12. Thy love will be thus fruitless ever.	
1:09	C	9. Wilt thou be thus abused still,	Repeat music for lines 9–12.
1:12		10. Seeing that she will right thee never?	
1:16		11. If thou canst not overcome her will,	
1:19		12. Thy love will be thus fruitless ever.	

LISTENING GUIDE 9 | Ⓢ | DVD

Dowland "Can she excuse my wrongs," arrangements 7:26

a) Four voices with lute
b) Lute solo
c) Harpsichord solo
d) Consort of five viols and lute
e) Mixed consort

DATE: Various arrangements of the late 16th century
GENRE: Various arrangements of a song

LISTEN FOR

FORM: Shape of the original song is retained
TEXTURE: Ornamentation of repeated sections
SCORING: Elaborate figuration for solo instruments (lute, harpsichord)

TEXT: All versions emphasize the quotation of "Will you go walk in the woods so wild?"

TIME	FORM	TEXT	DESCRIPTION
a) FOUR VOICES WITH LUTE			**1:24**
	First musical section, repeated with new text		
0:00	A	1. Can she excuse my wrongs with virtue's cloak? 2. Shall I call her good when she proves unkind?	Tune in soprano voice; the other voices provide harmony and rhythmic variety.
0:13	A	3. Are those clear fires which vanish into smoke? 4. Must I praise the leaves where no fruit I find?	Repeat music of lines 1–2.

(continued)

TIME	FORM	TEXT	DESCRIPTION
		Second musical section, repeated with new text	
0:27	B	5. No, no, where shadow do for bodies stand, 6. Thou may'st be abused if thy sight be dim.	The lower voices (alto, tenor, bass) are somewhat independent rhythmically in the interior of the phrase.
0:40	B	7. Cold love is like to words written on sand, 8. Or to bubbles which on the water swim.	Repeat music of lines 5–6.
		Third musical section, repeated with same text	
0:54	C	9. Wilt thou be thus abused still, 10. Seeing that she will right thee never? 11. If thou canst not overcome her will, 12. Thy love will be thus fruitless ever.	Alto and tenor sing melody of "Will you go walk in the woods so wild?" in canon; difficult to hear.
1:08	C	9. Wilt thou be thus abused still, 10. Seeing that she will right thee never? 11. If thou canst not overcome her will, 12. Thy love will be thus fruitless ever.	Repeat music of lines 9–12.

b) LUTE SOLO   1:39

TIME	FORM	TEXT	DESCRIPTION
		First musical section, repeated	
0:00	A	*The song's words are given here for reference* 1. Can she excuse my wrongs with virtue's cloak? 2. Shall I call her good when she proves unkind?	The lute provides melody, rhythm, and harmony.
0:15	A	3. Are those clear fires which vanish into smoke? 4. Must I praise the leaves where no fruit I find?	Repeat music of lines 1–2; note ornamentation in the lute.
		Second musical section, repeated	
0:30	B	5. No, no, where shadow do for bodies stand, 6. Thou may'st be abused if thy sight be dim.	The melody begins with many repeated notes.
0:45	B	7. Cold love is like to words written on sand, 8. Or to bubbles which on the water swim.	Repeat music of lines 5–6; ornamented.
		Third musical section, repeated	
1:01	C	9. Wilt thou be thus abused still, 10. Seeing that she will right thee never? 11. If thou canst not overcome her will, 12. Thy love will be thus fruitless ever.	Note emphasis in quotation of "Will you go walk in the woods so wild?" Insistent repeated notes in melody.
1:16	C	9. Wilt thou be thus abused still, 10. Seeing that she will right thee never? 11. If thou canst not overcome her will, 12. Thy love will be thus fruitless ever.	Repeat music of lines 9–12, ornamented.

c) HARPSICHORD SOLO   1:27

TIME	FORM	TEXT	DESCRIPTION
		First musical section, repeated	
0:00	A		(By now the tune should be familiar!)
0:14	A		Repeat music of lines 1–2; note the characteristic quick ornamentations of individual notes.

		Second musical section, repeated	
0:28	B		
0:42	B		Repeat music of lines 5–6.
		Third musical section, repeated	
0:57	C		
1:11	C		Repeat music of lines 9–12.

d) CONSORT OF FIVE VIOLS AND LUTE: *Earl of Essex Galliard*, from *Lachrimae or Seaven Teares*   1:29

		First musical section, repeated	
0:00	A		
0:14	A		Repeat music of lines 1–2; note the characteristic ornamentations of repeated sections.
		Second musical section, repeated	
0:28	B		
0:42	B		Repeat music of lines 5–6.
		Third musical section, repeated	
0:56	C		"Will you go walk" in lute and viol.
1:10	C		Repeat music of lines 9–12.

e) MIXED CONSORT: Galliard: *Can shee excuse*, from Morley's *First Booke of Consort Lessons*   1:27

		First musical section, repeated	
0:00	A		
0:14	A		Repeat music of lines 1–2; note the elaborate ornamentation by the lute.
		Second musical section, repeated	
0:27	B		
0:39	B		Repeat music of lines 5–6; lute ornamentation.
		Third musical section, repeated	
0:52	C		Note flute melody of "Will you go walk."
1:05	C		Repeat music of lines 9–12.

Renaissance Music Then and Now

William Byrd was recognized as a great composer in his lifetime, and his reputation continued to grow in the centuries after his death. If his music is not heard today as much as it might be, it must be because the style of Renaissance vocal polyphony to which he devoted the greater part of his genius is no longer in vogue. Like most of the music we'll encounter in this book, Byrd's is written in a language that came naturally to his contemporaries but feels less familiar to us. Now that we have seen how Byrd's music works and how skillfully it is put together, perhaps we can appreciate some of its nuances and hear how the individual motives weave themselves into a magical musical tapestry.

At first hearing, John Dowland's lute song may seem simpler and easier to follow than Byrd's multilayered polyphony. Yet despite its brevity, "Can she excuse my wrongs" is as sophisticated as any of Byrd's Masses, motets, or madrigals. Dowland's treatment of rhythm, melody, and word-setting is astonishingly intricate and subtle. Moreover, he could write polyphony with the best of them (even if his most grandly polyphonic pieces are not for voices but for solo lute). All of this explains why Dowland is regarded as one of the consummate masters of English song, a field in which he reigns supreme just as Byrd does in his.

Today, many of us pride ourselves on being good athletes, or skilled at video games, or attentive as students. We spend a lot of time practicing these skills because they are useful in modern society. In the same way, people in the Renaissance period worked hard to acquire skills that would make them useful members of their world. Music was as important for them as sports are for many of us today. Both activities teach the same basic lessons: if you have skill, you will be admired; people need to work together as a team; regular practice produces improvement. In sixteenth-century England, the growing number of people who could read music meant more people could enjoy complex polyphony, and it was because of these increased skills that the special talents of musicians like a Byrd or a Dowland could be appreciated and admired.

Chapter Review

Summary of Musical Styles

- **Imitative polyphony** is one of the main textures of the Renaissance: *imitative* because the voices engage in imitating each other; *polyphony* because there are several voices of equal importance. This texture can be used for voices or for instruments.

- A **point of imitation** is the use of a **motive** by all voices, one after another.

- **Accompanied song** makes a contrast with imitative polyphony. Here a single voice carries the main melodic interest, and the accompaniment is provided by an instrument, several instruments, or several voices.

- **Arrangements** are versions of a piece of music for some other medium. We have in this chapter a number of arrangements of what was originally an accompanied song ("Can she excuse my wrongs").

⊚ Multimedia Resources and Review Materials on Studyspace

Visit wwnorton.com/studyspace for review of Chapter 3.

What Do You Know?

Check the facts for this chapter. Take the online **Quiz**.

What Do You Hear?

Listening Quizzes and **Music Activities** will help you understand the musical works in this chapter.

Author Videos

- Imitation in Renaissance music
- Rhythm in Dowland's "Can she excuse my wrongs"

Interactive Listening Guides

LG 6 Byrd: Agnus Dei, from Mass for Four Voices
LG 7 Byrd: "This sweet and merry month of May"
LG 8 Dowland: "Can she excuse my wrongs," for Voice and Lute
LG 9 Dowland: "Can she excuse my wrongs," arrangements
    a) Four voices with lute
    b) Lute solo
    c) Harpsichord solo
    d) Consort of five viols and lute
    e) Mixed consort

Flashcards (Terms to Know)

accompanied song	motive
alto	paired imitation
arrangements	pavan
bass	point of imitation
cadence	polyphony
canon	recorder
cantus firmus technique	rest
consort music	sackbut
cornett	shawm
counterpoint	soprano
galliard	strophic
harpsichord	suspension
homophony	tenor
imitative polyphony	viola da gamba (viol)
lute	virginal
madrigal	voices
motet	word painting

THE BAROQUE ERA

HISTORICAL EVENTS	MUSICAL EVENTS

HISTORICAL EVENTS

1564–1642 Galileo Galilei
1571–1630 Johannes Kepler
1596–1650 René Descartes
1598–1680 Gian Lorenzo Bernini
1599–1660 Diego Velasquez

1600

1603 Death of Queen Elizabeth I
1606–1669 Rembrandt van Rijn
1607 Jamestown Colony founded
1608–1674 John Milton

1616 Deaths of Shakespeare and Cervantes
1620 Pilgrims land at Plymouth
1622–1673 Molière

1631–1700 John Dryden

1638 Louis XIV of France (to 1715)
1639–1699 Jean Racine

1642 (to 1649) English Civil War
1643–1727 Isaac Newton
1646–1716 Gottfried Leibniz
1648 Peace of Westphalia ends 30 Years War

1650

1666 Great fire of London

1692 Salem witch trials

1700

1711–1776 David Hume
1714 George I of England (to 1727)

1740 Frederick the Great of Prussia (to 1786)

1750

MUSICAL EVENTS

● 1567–1643 Claudio Monteverdi

● 1623 Death of William Byrd
● 1626 Death of John Dowland

● 1632–1687 Jean-Baptiste Lully

● 1653-1713 Arcangelo Corelli

● 1659-1695 Henry Purcell

● 1678-1741 Antonio Vivaldi
● 1683-1764 Jean-Philippe Rameau
● 1685-1750 Johann Sebastian Bach
● 1685-1759 George Frideric Handel

● Italy   ● France   ● England   ● Germany

PART II

Music and Speech: Baroque Music

W e chose a late Renaissance composer, William Byrd, and his contemporary John Dowland, as examples of Renaissance music at its best. And we portrayed a musical evening in 1596 as a point of departure to illustrate this music. In Part II we will start on the next period in music history—the Baroque—through an event that occurred in 1607—just eleven years later.

There were many stylistic changes between the Renaissance and the Baroque eras. But none of them happened overnight, and a good deal of overlapping occurred while these transformations were evolving. We will see, however, that Byrd and Dowland belong mostly on the Renaissance side of the balance, while Claudio Monteverdi—the man we are about to meet—belongs mostly in the Baroque era, at least for his opera *L'Orfeo* in 1607.

We will also see that things are never quite as simple as our hindsight might tempt us to think. Byrd and Dowland were already using elements from the later style, and in 1607 a musical play composed by Monteverdi, a master musician of the late Renaissance, combined elements from the older tradition with something uniquely new. That new element is what we now call Baroque music, which is about passion, communication, and language.

In the next three chapters we will discuss three significant composers from the **Baroque period**: Claudio Monteverdi, George Frideric Handel, and Johann Sebastian Bach. The word "baroque" originally referred to an irregularly shaped pearl, and in a way it is a perfect image for the music we are about to consider. Although

Renaissance vs. Baroque

Definition of baroque

the term was initially derogatory, the notion of a precious item—like a pearl—with a unique and characteristic shape, turns out to be an accurate description of Baroque music, but without the negative connotation.

The Baroque period extends roughly from 1600 to 1750. It was an age of absolute monarchs, of the rise of Louis XIV in France, of the emperors of Austria, and, after a difficult time of revolution and reformation, of the restoration of the monarchy under George I in England (see Figure II.1 map of Europe, below). Italy was a little different—it was a collection of smaller princely states, sometimes under the power of northern monarchs but always with the pope as the spiritual ruler of the Catholic Church and absolute temporal ruler of the area around Rome. This age of sovereignty extended overseas as well: Europeans continued to establish lucrative colonies throughout the world, creating a new, and cruel, world of colonialism.

Europe was also in the midst of a scientific revolution. Sir Isaac Newton discovered the laws of gravity, and the scientific world has never looked the same. Johannes Kepler showed that planets moved around the sun. Galileo Galilei improved the telescope and used it to prove that moons orbited the planet Jupiter. In the field of medicine, physician William Harvey studied the circulation of blood and the function of the heart. Other men and women studied diabetes

FIG. II.1 Map of Europe, ca. 1610.

and scarlet fever, and developed a cure for scurvy, a vitamin deficiency that often killed large numbers of passengers and crew on long-distance voyages. Italian physician Santorio Santorii measured human body temperature with his invention, the thermometer.

In art, in architecture, in literature and music, the Baroque was an age of grandeur, of spectacle, of drama, and of passion. An attempt to dazzle the eye with enormous scale and tiny detail at one and the same time was characteristic of the great architectural marvels of the day: the palace of the king of France at Versailles (imitated by many other monarchs); the colonnade leading the eye up to the entrance to St. Peter's Basilica in Rome (see Figure II.2). These grand structures were also enriched with countless detailed ornaments, of a kind that made the whole sparkle. A comparison with a sober and balanced monument of Renaissance architecture like Brunelleschi's Pazzi Chapel in Florence (see Figure II.3) makes clear that this Baroque style is meant to impress, to centralize, and to theatricalize.

The Baroque buildings look like stage settings, and this is indeed the period of drama, of gesture, of theater. The literature of the age is dramatic—it includes poets John Milton and John Donne in England; the classical playwrights Pierre Corneille, Jean Racine, and Molière in France; the adventure writer Miguel de Cervantes from Spain; and in Italy, the impressive theatrical display called opera (see Arts and Ideas, pp. 88–89). Because it involves grandeur, rhetoric, drama, passion, and elaborate presentations, but also, and most of all, music, opera is the perfect expression of Baroque art.

The idea of passion, of the expression of emotions by means of words, gestures, and actions, is central to Baroque art. Comparing Michelangelo's *David* (1501) with the ca. 1620 sculpture of *David* by the Baroque sculptor Gian Lorenzo Bernini makes clear that Bernini has in mind the expression—maybe even the exaggeration—of a particular moment: David's extreme focus is on the instant he hurls the stone at Goliath, and we are in no doubt about what he feels or the level of his effort (see Figures II.4 and II.5).

The painters and sculptors of the Baroque era emphasize an almost theatrical setting, in which characters are posed like actors, and demonstrate, through

LEFT, FIG. II.2 An aerial view of St. Peter's Basilica, Rome. The Renaissance church, the work of many famous architects, stands at the end of Bernini's immense, keyhole-shaped Baroque colonnade.

RIGHT, FIG. II.3 The Pazzi Chapel, in the cloister of the church of Santa Croce, Florence, is a masterpiece of Renaissance simplicity. Based on designs by Filippo Brunelleschi, it shows simple relationships of circles and squares.

Sculpture and painting

gestures, not only their actions but also their passionate feelings. The great works of Nicolas Poussin, of Rembrandt van Rijn, of Peter Paul Rubens, and of many others are all infused with this Baroque gestural quality.

It was generally understood during this period that human emotions were controlled by the "four humors"—blood, yellow bile, phlegm, and black bile. When the humors shifted and moved about the human body, they dictated the disposition of one's passions—or put more simply, how one felt. The passions were therefore external expressions of an inner state, and they could be codified, listed, explained, and described. And so it became possible, and desirable, to express each passion (or **affect**, as it was sometimes called, e.g., rage, anger, jealousy, love, or remorse; see Figure II.6) with specific language, specific gestures, or specific musical expression. This led to the stylized gestures of music and dance, to the careful delineations of the passions in opera, and to the efforts of Baroque composers to express each passion in music.

Baroque Musical Style

Ⓢ Monteverdi: *Orfeo:* "E intenerito"

Drama, passion, and language coalesced in one of the most important innovations of the Baroque musical style—the reciting style, called **stile recitativo** in Italian, or **recitative** (RESS-it-a-TEEVE) style in English, and defined as a type of singing that resembles speaking by following the natural rhythms of the text.

In the next chapter we will learn how the composer Claudio Monteverdi used this new style in his drama on the myth of Orpheus, a play in which *all the characters sing their parts* (we now call this kind of work an **opera**). Some characters sing their parts in the rhythm, and at the speed, that an actor would normally use in speaking.

The words are sung to a melody designed to emphasize the sound and sometimes the meaning of the words—accented syllables are set to longer and higher notes; the words accelerate if the character feels excited, or slow down if the character is sad; the accompanying harmonies are smooth or harsh, depending on the meaning. The result is not a tuneful melody but a melding of melody and language that emphasizes the language—as Monteverdi put it, in this style "the music should be the servant of the words and not the mistress."

What does he mean by that? Consider the differences between the Renaissance and the Baroque styles: a Renaissance composer often used a polyphonic web of continuous sound (as in Byrd's vocal music). A Baroque recitative presented a one-time delivery focused on a single text and melody. Consider also how differently the words and music are related: in the Renaissance, melodies are generated from groups of words, and each group repeats several times to create the texture ("dona nobis pacem, dona nobis pacem, dona nobis pacem"). In Baroque recitative, a once-through delivery by a single voice, in a rhythm that a person might use when speaking the words, creates the texture. Byrd seems to use the words to emphasize the music; in his operas, Monteverdi uses the music to focus our attention on the words.

By the time we get to later Baroque music, the idea of recitative remains, but it appears separate from other musical devices where music takes precedence over language (as in the "Hallelujah" chorus). Bach and Handel might seem very far removed from Monteverdi, but at the end of this section we will see what they all have in common, including their connection to William Byrd!

All music from the Baroque period shares some basic musical techniques. With

TOP, FIG. II.4 Michelangelo's famous statue of *David*, carved 1501–04. Calm and poised, the adolescent hero is depicted before his battle with the giant Goliath.

BOTTOM, FIG. II.5 *David*, by Gian Lorenzo Bernini, carved 1623–24. David, his face full of determination and strain, is in the act of launching the stone that will kill Goliath. His posture involves many curves.

this in mind, let us examine some of these, so that we can be on the lookout for them throughout the next few chapters.

A tendency toward musical polarization, with a *focus on a single melody,* is an important aspect of Baroque music. Whereas a Byrd motet consists of a web of equally important voices, Baroque music tends to focus attention on a single voice (or instrument), which becomes the main melody.

If the first pole, as it were, is the melody line, then the other pole is the **bass line** (Ⓢ "Rejoice," from Handel's *Messiah*)**,** the lowest sounding series of notes. Between the melody and the bass, instead of many other voices, we hear a series of chords played by a harpsichord, organ, lute, or some combination of them. This three-part structure—melody, bass, and chordal accompaniment—is more or less the standard Baroque sound. In fact, the continuous bass line, with its continuous chordal accompaniment, was called the **basso continuo** or the "continuous bass," by the Italians; in England it was known as **thoroughbass**. The sound of the harpsichord, so often used on modern recordings, is almost a guarantee that the music is from the Baroque era.

FIG. II.6 Drawings of facial expressions by Charles Le Brun (1619–1690). These images depict the various *passions,* the dramatic emotional states that are at the core of Baroque artistic expression.

Ⓢ Handel: *Messiah,* "Rejoice," basso continuo

The idea of bass lines and chords leads to another essential aspect of Baroque music, the use of **harmony** as a structuring device. By harmony we mean the choice of chords and their relationship to each other. This can be a deeply complicated matter, but some of the most basic and essential relationships are instantly recognizable. Take, for example, the common sequence of chords known as **dominant-tonic** (sometimes notated with the Roman numerals V-I). This progression simply means that the chord built on the fifth note of the scale is followed by the chord built on the first note of the scale (see Chapter 1 and Appendix for more information). Think, for example, of the last two words of "Happy Birthday—"to" is dominant, and "you" is tonic.

Another important aspect of harmony is how often the accompanying chords change. This is known as **harmonic rhythm**. Again, think of the difference between

Harmonic rhythm

Style Comparisons at a Glance	
RENAISSANCE MUSICAL STYLE	**BAROQUE MUSICAL STYLE**
Emphasis on melody	Emphasis on meaning of words
Polyphonic texture	Focus on a single melody
Polyphonic texture determines harmony	Harmony as structuring device
Modal harmony	Major and minor tonality
Sequences are avoided	Many melodies are extended using sequences
Vocal genres mainly Mass, motet, madrigal, and song	Vocal genres mainly opera and oratorio
Instrumental genres mainly keyboard or lute solos, often based on vocal styles	Instrumental genres mainly sonata and concerto

Science and Philosophy

The seventeenth and eighteenth centuries witnessed periods of enormous advances in science, partly because of the increased importance given to observation and measurement (rather than the rational logical philosophizing that had also been the basis of most of science). Knowledge of the universe, the natural world, and human medicine and physiology all made enormous strides.

Galileo Galilei (1564–1642), son of a famous Florentine musician involved in the birth of opera, improved the telescope, discovered the moons of Jupiter, and argued for the sun-centered solar system that had been posited by Nikolaus Copernicus. Galilei was tried as a heretic and ultimately confined to house arrest.

Johannes Kepler (1571–1630), the German astronomer, improved the telescope and is remembered for the laws of planetary motion.

In mathematics and physics, **Isaac Newton** (1643–1727) developed the basic laws of motion and gravitation,

FIG. II.7 The church of San Carlo alle Quattro Fontane by the Roman Baroque architect Francesco Borromini. The building seems to burst out of its little footprint.

fundamental to all successive science. Both he and the German mathematician and philosopher **Gottfried Leibniz** (1646–1716), independently of each other, invented the calculus.

Rationalism, based on the idea that logical structures can lead to truth, was characteristic of the period. One of its major figures was **René Descartes** (1596–1650), father of the "Cogito ergo sum" (I think, therefore I am) thesis. Descartes opposed the so-called empiricist philosophers who believed that knowledge comes from experience. These philosophers included **Thomas Hobbes** (1588–1679; his *Leviathan* was an important document in social thought), **John Locke** (1632–1704, famous for the idea that our mind begins as a *tabula rasa,* a blank slate), and **David Hume** (1711–1776).

Literature and the Arts

Descartes's treatise *The Passions of the Soul* is a good example of the traditional view of emotions as being distinct, clearly delineated, and describable. Emotions were thought to come from the changing balances in the body of the four humors, or bodily fluids (see p. 86). These emotions, or passions, were the

a melody whose accompanying chords stay the same—such as "Row, row, row your boat"—and one whose accompanying chords change often, like most Protestant hymns, such as "A Mighty Fortress Is Our God." Baroque music tends to prefer a very regular harmonic rhythm—that is, chord changes at a regular rate. This constancy provides an architectural sense of structure, giving the listener the impression that a piece is being created from regular-sized blocks of sound.

Melodic rhythm

Paralleling harmonic rhythm is the Baroque tendency to use regular **melodic rhythm**, that is, repeating the same pattern many times in a kind of mesmerizing regularity. This combination of regular melodic rhythm with slower but equally regular changes of harmony contributes to the Baroque impression of grand architecture decorated by a wealth of surface detail.

A Baroque melody tends to be like a sentence from an orator or a preacher: a rhetorical period intended to convince. A speaker begins with a statement or a gesture; continues with amplification in the form of examples, repetitions, or

subjects of painting, sculpture, literature, drama, and music. The clear distinction and expression of these passions is a key to all the arts of the Baroque.

The deaths of Miguel de Cervantes (*Don Quixote*) and William Shakespeare, both in 1616, left a large gap, filled by **John Dryden** (1631–1700), **John Milton** (1608–1674), and others in England, and by the dramatists **Lope de Vega** (d. 1635), **Tirso de Molina** (d. 1648), and **Calderón** (d. 1681) in Spain. The seventeenth century was the golden age of French drama, when under the reign of the "Sun King," Louis XIV, the playwrights **Jean Racine** (1639–1699), **Pierre Corneille** (1606–1684), and **Molière** (1622–1673) produced the great classic dramas of French literature. The depiction of the passions, and their display on the stage, reached a highly stylized climax.

Painters reveled in the depiction of passions, of figures in dramatic poses and highly charged moments. Many of the enduring masters come from this period: **Peter Paul Rubens** (1577–1640), **Rembrandt van Rijn** (1606–1669), **Diego Velasquez** (1599–1660), **Johannes Vermeer** (1632–1675), and **Nicolas Poussin** (1594–1665).

Baroque art is perhaps best seen in its architecture and sculpture. The Roman architects **Gian Lorenzo Bernini** (1598–1680) and **Francesco Borromini** (1599–1667) are the models for many who came later. They sought drama, expression, and grandeur. If their buildings sometimes look like a stage setting, it is probably no accident. Borromini's tiny San Carlo alle Quattro Fontane, with its undulating curves and niches, seems to burst out of its tiny space (see Figure II.7).

Bernini—architect of the keyhole colonnade in front of Saint Peter's Basilica in Rome—was a sculptor of astounding ability. His chapel arrangement depicting Saint Teresa of Avila in ecstasy shows the saint while an angel withdraws the arrow of divine love from her. The frenzy of her clothing, her open-mouthed awe, her curved, even twisted posture, create a powerful effect through the exaggeration of a variety of aspects (see Figure II.8).

In music, as in the other arts, the combination of passion, rhetoric, and drama worked to produce some grand expressive music and led to the combination of all of these in the medium we now call opera.

FIG. II.8 *Saint Teresa in Ecstasy* by the Roman sculptor and architect Gian Lorenzo Bernini. Note the saint's twisted posture, and the nervous folds of her garments.

intensification; and arrives at the concluding point: gesture, amplification, conclusion. Many Baroque melodies operate in this fashion. A perfect example is the opening melody of the chorus "And the glory of the Lord," from Handel's *Messiah*, which we'll hear in Chapter 5. The opening melodic gesture will fit the words "And the glory of the Lord," but we don't know this yet. A series of repetitions follows the opening gesture, a favorite Baroque technique called the **sequence**—a group of notes (or sometimes notes plus their harmony), repeated several times, at increasingly higher or lower pitch. In this case a four-note figure is repeated, each time lower; and then followed by the conclusion in the form of a **cadence** (the musical word for a close, like a semicolon or a period in writing).

This list of musical techniques may seem overwhelming at first, but your ears will get used to them, and they are concepts that will recur over and over again throughout our three case studies of Baroque music.

For now, let's have some music.

Ⓢ Handel: *Messiah*, "And the glory of the Lord," opening

Sequence

Cadence

CHAPTER 4

SATURDAY, FEBRUARY 24, 1607, MANTUA:

Claudio Monteverdi's *Orfeo*

CORE REPERTOIRE

- **LG 10** Toccata
- **LG 11** Opening Ritornello and Prologue
- **LG 12** "Vi ricorda, o boschi ombrosi" (Orfeo's Song), Act 2

- **LG 13** "Tu se' morta" (Orfeo's Lament), Act 2
- **LG 14** "Possente spirto" (Orfeo's Song), Act 3

AUTHOR VIDEOS

- The use of basso continuo in *Orfeo*
- Rhythm in Orfeo's song, "Vi ricorda," from Act 2

Introduction

"Tomorrow evening the Most Serene Lord the Prince is to sponsor [a play] in the main room in the apartments which the Most Serene Lady of Ferrara had the use of. It should be most unusual, as all the actors are to sing their parts; it is said on all sides that it will be a great success. No doubt I shall be driven to attend out of sheer curiosity, unless I am prevented from getting in by the lack of space. . . ."

— Carlo Magno, Mantua, February 23, 1607, to his brother Giovanni in Rome

Monteverdi in Mantua

By 1607 the forty-year-old composer Claudio Monteverdi was living in the city of Mantua, in northern Italy, with his wife, Claudia, a court singer, and his two surviving children. He had served the duke of Mantua as his chief musician for almost two decades, beginning as a string player and singer at court (see biography).

Although Monteverdi might have seemed to be enjoying the benefits of a successful life, in fact he had financial difficulties, and he felt underappreciated by his patron; his wife would die that year, leaving him with their small children to look after. But February 1607 also saw the first performance of his *Orfeo,* a play in which all the characters sang their parts. We call such a performance an **opera;** the term

CLAUDIO MONTEVERDI (1567–1643)

Claudio Monteverdi was born in Cremona, in northern Italy, the son of a physician. He was a musical prodigy; at about the age of twenty-three, having already published several musical collections, he moved to Mantua, where he served at the court of Vincenzo Gonzaga, duke of Mantua, until 1612. There, he married the singer Claudia Cattaneo. Monteverdi's duties as music director included composition, performance, and supervision of entertainments. While in Mantua he composed madrigals, instrumental music, ballets, and operas, and continued to publish his works and achieve substantial fame.

In 1613, after a miserable last few years in Mantua (the duke was succeeded by one who cared little for music, and the city was captured), Monteverdi was appointed *maestro di cappella* (master of the chapel) at St. Mark's Basilica in Venice, the most prestigious musical post in Italy. He remained there for thirty years, until his death in 1643. During the last years of his life, when he was often ill, he composed his two last surviving masterpieces, both operas: *Il ritorno d'Ulisse in patria* (*The Return of Ulysses,* 1641) and *L'incoronazione di Poppea* (*The Coronation of Poppea,* 1642) on the life of Roman emperor Nero. Remarkably, Monteverdi wrote these operas while in his seventies, when the average lifespan was probably in the forties.

Monteverdi's music spans the Renaissance and the Baroque eras, beginning with expressive madrigals, and concluding with operas in the innovative **recitative style** (see p. 86). His careful attention to the meaning and expression of words, and his harmonic daring, give his music a characteristic lively quality.

To hear the full range of Monteverdi's expression, listen to selections from his *Scherzi musicali* (Musical Jokes) of 1607 and his magnificent *Vespers of the Blessed Virgin* (1610), composed for the full vocal and instrumental grandeur of the Mantuan court.

Ⓢ Monteverdi: *Scherzi musicali*
Ⓢ Monteverdi: 1610 *Vespers*

MAJOR WORKS: Masses, motets, and operas, including *Orfeo* and *L'incoronazione di Poppea* (*The Coronation of Poppea*), 9 books of madrigals, *Vespers,* and other sacred work.

Ⓢ Monteverdi: *Orfeo,* "Vi ricorda, o boschi ombrosi"

did not exist in 1607, but this piece is one of the great foundations of that long tradition.

Presented in a small, narrow room at the duke's palace to an exclusive club of noblemen (a club called the *Accademia degl'Invaghiti,* or Academy of the Lovestruck), *Orfeo* was performed only twice, for small audiences. Monteverdi could not know that his musical play—which lasted all of ninety minutes—would become a key event in music history, and a beloved musical monument. We now think of it as the first great opera, the beginning of what would become a remarkable tradition combining drama and music.

The Setting

MANTUA IN 1607

In the beginning of the seventeenth century, Italy was made up of numerous and distinct geographical and political units (principalities, republics, and papal states), having their own currencies, capital cities, ambassadors, and governments. The balance of power was constantly shifting, with a seemingly endless series of wars and arranged marriages between princely families; those in power needed plenty of spies and armies to maintain (or extend) their position in the balance.

In Monteverdi's day, Mantua was one of the more important artistic and civic centers in Italy (see Figure 4.1, map of northern Italy, left) as well as the residence of the great Gonzaga family, which had ruled this northern city-state and its territories since the fourteenth century (see Figure 4.2). The city was rich; commerce and trade flourished; and the substantial Jewish population added significantly to the city's cultural life. Today much of the city still retains its medieval and Renaissance flavor, and if you walk the streets of the city's center, you will see many of its old buildings, grand palaces, and private houses, alongside huge piazzas designed for markets, public gatherings, and evening strolls (see Figure 4.3).

In 1607 the duke of Mantua, Vincenzo Gonzaga, who was only three years older than Monteverdi, was the absolute ruler of Mantua. He led an indulgent life—hunting, gambling, traveling, and pursuing his other pleasures of theater, music, and women. Like many Renaissance princes of his day, Vincenzo showed off his grandeur and nobility by joining the Holy Roman Emperor on military campaigns, spending lavishly, and being a generous patron of the arts. He also succeeded in dissipating a substantial amount of the family fortune.

Painters, architects, poets, dramatists, and musicians had all been employed by the Gonzaga family for generations to decorate their palaces and to entertain the many people—family, nobles, administrators—who formed

FIG. 4.1 Map of northern Italy around the time of *Orfeo,* showing Mantua as well as other important artistic and civic centers.

FIG. 4.2 A *The Expulsion of the Bonacolsi* (1494), by Domenico Morone, which shows the main piazza of the Ducal Palace in Mantua. The Bonacolsi were a noble family who were overthrown in a revolt backed by the rich and powerful Gonzagas.

the "court," as it was called, of a great prince. The palace at Mantua (see Figure 4.4), thought by some to be the biggest building in the world at the time, had grown over the centuries, and it now incorporated a medieval fortress, a large and looming church, a separate floor on a reduced scale for the court dwarves (who performed a variety of duties, including entertaining and serving), a grand riding ring, many courtyards and gardens, and over five hundred rooms and apartments. The court was an enormous operation that hired a huge number of people, including footmen, physicians, pharmacists, barbers, tutors, stewards, waiters, cooks, wood gatherers, alchemists, clock-winders, falconers, and carvers of meat, to mention only a fraction of the in-house staff.

Palace at Mantua

Duke Vincenzo had always been fond of music and the theater. He kept on staff a group of court musicians, led by Claudio Monteverdi, who was involved whenever music became a part of the many court entertainments. Monteverdi was constantly busy, said his brother Giulio Cesare Monteverdi,

> because of his responsibility for both church and chamber music, but also because of other extraordinary services, for, serving a great prince, he finds the greater part of his time taken up, now with tournaments, now with ballets, now with comedies and various concerts, and lastly with the playing of the two *viole bastarde* [rare solo stringed instruments].

FIG. 4.3 Modern-day Mantua during an evening stroll.

FIG. 4.4 The medieval Palazzo del Capitano, one of the many conjoined parts of the palace of the dukes of Mantua.

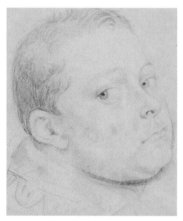

FIG. 4.5 Francesco Gonzaga, son of the reigning duke and the chief organizer of the first performance of *Orfeo*.

By 1607 Claudio Monteverdi was already a composer of some renown. He had published several books of music, and his reputation far exceeded the boundaries of Mantua. But he was still a servant. In 1608 he complained that "the fortune I have known in Mantua for nineteen consecutive years has given me more occasion to call it misfortune, and inimical to me, and not friendly." The duke expected all of his musicians to perform not only at the highest level but also in a variety of jobs. A letter from Monteverdi to Prince Francesco Gonzaga, the duke's eldest son (see Figure 4.5), gives us an idea of what was expected from these overworked court musicians: "His Highness the Prince . . . very much likes not only to hear a variety of wind instruments, he also likes to have the said musicians play in private, in church, in procession, and atop city walls; now madrigals, now French songs, now airs, and now dance-songs."

THE BIRTH OF OPERA

As we have read in the previous chapter, music played an important role in the sacred, civic, religious, and courtly life of the Renaissance. It was also important in drama; plays often included music, be it song, dance, or instrumental interludes performed between acts. In addition, the courts created lavish spectacles that included song, dance, magnificent costumes and stage effects, and large instrumental ensembles, all for the benefit of a small noble audience. But music's role in drama was about to become much more central.

Greek tragedy and opera

In the late-Renaissance Florence of the 1580s and 1590s, a small select group of Italian poets, composers, and intellectuals met regularly to discuss trends in art. Led by the nobleman and composer Giovanni de' Bardi, they sought to study and purify the arts of their day. Modern music had become corrupt, they decided, and their solution was to return to the style of ancient Greek tragedy, which some believed had been sung throughout. They believed that direct delivery of a text, through a single singing voice, would not distort the words or confuse the listener as to the emotional message of the text. As this group of experimenters expressed it, the singer became an orator, and the nuances of the music enhanced the rhetorical inflections of the text.

Monteverdi was well aware of the current intellectual trends, and his *Orfeo* was based on these Florentine ideals. It was called a "fable in music," that is, a play in which "all the actors are to sing their parts" (as one of the people present at the premier wrote).

Imagine, for a second, what it must have been like in 1607, for the first time witnessing this scene of people standing on stage, looking at each other and singing. Somehow you needed to accept the idea of a world in which singing was the sound of speaking.

Why would anyone have sat through this new form of entertainment? We do now, of course, because we like the idea that music and drama can happen at the same time and that each can enrich the other. But in 1607, people were not accustomed to this concept, and they attended this fable in music as much out of curiosity as anything else.

This particular opera stands at the beginning of a long tradition; other representatives of this tradition will also appear in this book. Those works come from later times, when opera was the absolute height of the arts, when every city had its own opera house, and when high technology and fabulously expensive stars came together in major events at high prices. But it was this early fable in music (*favola in musica;* see Figure 4.6), this small, experimental piece, that would remain such a formidable and enduring monument.

THE STORY OF ORPHEUS (ORFEO)

Presenting an opera about Orpheus—the greatest musician who ever lived, according to the myths—was a good idea, for two reasons. First, the story was familiar. In 1607 every cultured member of society would have known about the legend of Orpheus, the demigod son of Apollo who falls in love with the beautiful mortal Eurydice. When Eurydice dies, the desperate Orpheus resolves to do what no human has ever done—descend to the world of the dead and bring her back to life. He crosses the River Styx, where the boatman Charon (Caronte) ferries the souls of the dead to the underworld, and succeeds, with the help of Pluto's wife Proserpine, in convincing Pluto to release his beloved Eurydice—but on one condition: Orpheus may lead Eurydice out, but he must not look back to see whether she is following him.

This is the critical issue at the center of the myth. Orpheus's head and heart are at war: his reason tells him that he must not look back, but his heart urges him otherwise. His passion ultimately gets the better of him, he looks back, and Eurydice disappears into eternal darkness while Orpheus is thrust back into the daylight in which he will have to wander alone, forever. We understand this story when we hear it, because we enact it every day—our heart tells us one thing and our head tells us another. (See Figures 4.7–4.9 for illustrated examples of the Orpheus myth through time.)

The other reason that makes the Orpheus myth such a good choice is that an opera about Orpheus is an opera about *music.* What better subject for a play in music than a story about the greatest musician who ever lived? Orpheus is the son of Apollo, who is the god of the sun but also the god of balance in all

FIG. 4.6 Title page of Monteverdi's 1615 publication of the score of *Orfeo*. It reads "The *Orfeo*, fable in music, by Claudio Monteverdi . . . presented in Mantua in the year 1607, and newly reprinted."

FIG. 4.7 A sixth-century mosaic from a church in Libya depicting Orpheus playing a four-stringed instrument.

things (note the connection: Apollo knows how to keep emotions in check) and the god of music (note the other connection: the greatest musicians of heaven *and* earth, Apollo and Orpheus). In addition, Orpheus is such a fine singer that birds fall silent and stones weep when he sings. What a challenge to a composer—to put music into the mouth of Orpheus!

The music throughout Monteverdi's *Orfeo* is glorious, and the message, addressed to the learned members of the Academy, is emotional but also philosophical: balance in all things. Orpheus loses when he lets his heart overpower his reason. He lives, as we all do, in a world between reason and passion. Overhead, in the heavens, where Apollo drives the chariot of the sun through the skies every day, is the realm of purity and light, of reason and balance. And below our feet is the underworld, ruled by passionate Pluto, who long ago snatched Proserpine from the world of the living because of his lust for her. In Monteverdi's opera, she pleads for the lover Orpheus, understanding his plight only too well.

Orpheus is like us in living in the world between. He looks back when he shouldn't, and the result is the loss of everything he cares about. He is out of balance at the end, and his father Apollo rescues him, bringing his inconsolable son up to heaven.

Orfeo is about classical figures, but it is also about human beings, and that was part of its appeal to the noblemen of Mantua, and why it still appeals to us today. The author of Monteverdi's text, Alessandro Striggio, was a poet, and also a lawyer, a musician, and a diplomat who had served the duke as ambassador. He was well educated in the classics, and he was particularly aware of the work of Ottavio Rinuccini, the Florentine nobleman who had been one of the early experimenters in writing poetry for singing. Rinuccini had written a drama about Orpheus and Eurydice, which Striggio knew and tried to emulate.

Striggio took great care to make sure his play resembled a familiar (to that elevated audience) classical Greek or Roman tragedy, complete with prologue,

FIG. 4.8 Orpheus rides over the Styx, by Eduard Engerth (1818–1897), from the Vienna Opera House.

long poetic speeches, and a chorus that comments on what is happening. Sometimes the chorus members are the nymphs and shepherds who inhabit the pastoral scene, and sometimes they are the spirits of the underworld. But in either case, they all participate in the action and comment on it: at the news of Eurydice's death, the chorus cries out "Ahi! Caso acerbo!" (Oh, bitter fate!); but they follow this outburst with a little lesson: "Mortal man should not trust frail joy; it suddenly flees away, and often at the greatest height the precipice is nearby." Monteverdi displays his musical wit in portraying the sudden fleeing away, the great height, and the deep plunge; it's a little madrigal, of the sort he was already famous for.

As in a Greek tragedy, each act of the play ends with a great choral ode—a series of pieces for chorus and soloists that brings each of the five dramatic units of the play to a close. There is action followed by reflection, which would become a time-honored device in later opera.

Ironically, this effort at historical re-creation, the attempt to present drama as it had been presented to the ancient Greeks, had the contrary effect: it created a new cutting-edge art form.

FIG. 4.9 *The Song of Orpheus*, by twentieth-century American artist Barnett Newman (1905–1970).

The Performance

PREPARATIONS

You might imagine that Francesco Gonzaga, as eldest son of the duke of Mantua, and the one organizing the production of *Orfeo*, would not have had any trouble gathering the singers and the musicians or creating the sets and the costumes that were needed to present this play for the Academy, but it was not so easy. A temporary theater had to be built in the palace, sets constructed and painted, costumes made, and rehearsals held. And most problematic of all was getting the right singers.

We actually know more about the first performance of *Orfeo* than we do about almost any other performance of its time because Monteverdi's published score survives; it is really a memory book, a souvenir program for those who were not fortunate enough to be there. It describes what actually *happened* on that particular occasion, rather than how one should perform the piece in the future. There are many little references scattered throughout the music. "This sinfonia [an instrumental piece] was played very quietly," reads one typical remark, "with *viole da braccio*, and organ, and a *contrabasso de viola da gamba*."

We also have information about some of the musical personnel who were employed by the duke and who must have taken part in the performance. In addition we have a series of letters from Francesco Gonzaga—as he tries to organize the performance—to his brother Ferdinando. We know where the performance was given and who must have created the sets. And yet there is still a lot we will never know.

What might seem to us the strangest of all the circumstances that we do know about is that *Orfeo* was sung by an all-male cast. The beautiful Eurydice, on whom the plot turns; Proserpine, queen of the underworld; the feminine Music (La Musica), who sings the prologue; and the female personification of Hope

All-male cast

Plot of Orfeo

Orfeo is based on the ancient Greek myth of Orpheus, who tries to rescue his deceased lover, Eurydice, from the underworld.

- Opening Toccata. 🔊 **LG 10**

PROLOGUE

- Prologue (La Musica) invites the audience to hear the story of Orpheus (Orfeo) and his powers to tame the world with his singing and playing of the lyre. 🔊 **LG 11**

ACT 1

- Orpheus and Eurydice celebrate their wedding, each singing a song.
- The act ends with the chorus singing "Ecco Orfeo" (Here is Orpheus).

ACT 2

- The Chorus continues in celebration, and Orpheus sings his song "Vi ricorda, o boschi ombrosi" (Do you remember, o shady woods). 🔊 **LG 12**
- A Messenger tells Orpheus that Eurydice has died.
- Orpheus sings his poignant "Tu se' morta" (You are dead) about the impermanence of happiness. 🔊 **LG 13**
- Orpheus vows to go to the underworld to rescue Eurydice by using his power of love through song to convince Pluto (god of the underworld) to free her.
- Act 2 ends with the Chorus singing "Ahi! Caso acerbo!" (Oh, bitter fate!).

ACT 3

- Hope guides Orpheus to the entrance of the underworld, where at the River Styx he meets Charon (Caronte), the ferryman, who carries souls down to the underworld.
- Orpheus attempts to charm Charon by singing "Possente spirto" (Mighty spirit), but to no avail. 🔊 **LG 14** Charon falls asleep to soft music and Orpheus steals Charon's boat.

ACT 4

- Pluto's wife Proserpine is moved by Orpheus's plight, and convinces her husband to release Eurydice.
- Pluto agrees, but on one condition: that Orpheus not look back.
- Orpheus and Eurydice begin their ascent from Hades.
- Impelled by doubt, Orpheus looks back; Eurydice vanishes before his eyes.
- Orpheus is ejected, against his will, into the upper world.

ACT 5

- Orpheus, consumed by grief, cries out and is answered by the lone voice of Echo.
- Orpheus becomes angry, vowing to reject all women.
- His father, Apollo, descends from the heavens to console his son. He promises to take Orpheus to the heavens, where his disconsolate son can look forever upon the image of Eurydice in the stars.
- Father and son ascend to heaven. A final chorus and dance.

Women singers at court

(La Speranza), who leads Orpheus to the edge of the underworld, were all sung by men. (See Plot of *Orfeo*, above.)

It is not that there weren't spectacularly good women singers in Mantua. The duke had gathered together a famous group of women singers like the similar *concerto delle donne* in Ferrara (a group of professional female singers renowned for their technical and artistic virtuosity, whose signature style of florid, highly ornamented singing brought prestige to Ferrara and inspired composers of the time). Not only was Francesco's father, Vincenzo, a competitive man, wanting to keep up with rival courts, but he was known to have a weakness for the ladies, so it might seem strange that he would not employ some of his outstanding women singers. But on this occasion, and apparently on all previous occasions, the duke refused to allow his women singers to appear before a public audience. Only a year later, in 1608, did he allow a woman to appear in an opera.

With the shortage of singers for women's roles in *Orfeo*, Francesco Gonzaga sought to "borrow" a **castrato** from the Grand Duke of Tuscany by way of his brother Ferdinando. (A castrato was a male singer who was castrated before his voice changed—such singers were in great demand and were famous for their powerful voices. Today castrato roles are usually sung by women or by countertenors.) On January 5, 1607, Francesco Gonzaga wrote a letter to his brother requesting to borrow a castrato from the Grand Duke's stable of singers:

Castrato

> I have decided to have a play in music performed at Carnival [the festivities before the beginning of Lent] this year, but as we have very few sopranos here, and those few not good, I should be grateful if Your Excellency would be kind enough to tell me if those castrati I heard when I was in Tuscany are still there.

Ferdinando succeeded in locating a good singer; but he was slow in arriving, wrote Francesco:

Arranging for the singers

> February 9: . . . I had expected that the castrato would have arrived by now, and indeed it is essential that he should be here as soon as possible. He will now have not only to play the part that was sent to him, but also to learn that of Proserpine, as the singer who was to take the role can no longer do so. So I am awaiting him from day to day with great eagerness, as without him the play would be a complete failure.

Francesco was frantic; but finally the singer—Giovanni Gualberto Magli—arrived to sing the roles of Proserpina and the Prologue (La Musica), and at least one other female role in the play.

> February 16: . . . the castrato arrived yesterday. . . he knows only the prologue, and seems to think that he will not have time to learn the other part before the Carnival; in which case I shall have no choice but to postpone the performance of the play until Easter. This morning, however, he began to study not only the music, but the words as well; and if he were able to learn the part (although it does contain too many notes ["troppo voci"], as Your Excellency says), he would at least know the melody, the music could be altered to suit his needs, and we would not waste so much time ensuring that he knows it all by heart. . . .

We also know the names of some of the other singers. The role of Eurydice was most likely played by Girolamo Bacchini, a *soprano castrato* who was a composer and also a priest. He may have been hired because he had a beautiful voice—Eurydice's role, though brief, has two exquisite speeches—or perhaps because he was short and therefore fit the part. We do know that he was later referred to as that "little priest [*pretino*] who played Eurydice in the *Orfeo* of the Most Serene Lord Prince."

The singers

The star of the show, however, was Francesco Rasi, a singer in the employ of the duke of Mantua. Rasi was not only a famous singer but a published poet and composer as well. He was described in his role of Orpheus as "that signor Francesco Rasio, so famous for his excellence in his profession that everyone agrees that there are few in the world who can excel him." He was a handsome, jovial man, with a strong voice; his singing was sometimes described as angelic. Rasi sang, according to one critic, "with a range consisting of many notes, and with exquisite style and passage-work [rapid ornaments], and with extraordinary feeling and a particular talent to make the words clearly heard." Monteverdi surely had Rasi in mind when composing the role of Orpheus.

THE INSTRUMENTS

Although Monteverdi was creating a play for a small, elite audience, he did so for one of the richest court establishments in the world. No expense, apparently, was spared, and in the arena of instrumental colors, *Orfeo* is much richer than almost anything else we know of from the period, except for the entertainments written for the grandest princely events.

The instruments in *Orfeo* represent a panorama of the sounds of the time. Monteverdi followed two basic principles: (1) that instruments be used in groups of similar sound (a group of strings, or flutes, or trombones, for example—rather than a mixture of different types) and (2) that melody instruments not play while characters are singing. The instruments that played in groups were usually either in pairs or in groups of five, as outlined below:

Paired instruments

Recorders ("flautini"), used in Acts 1 and 2, suggestive of shepherds' pipes in the charming ritornello.

Violins, as well as a pair of "violini piccioli alla francese," probably little dancing-masters' pocket violins, used just once, in the sequence of songs in Act 2.

Cornetts, used in the underworld acts, sometimes to enrich the ensemble of trombones, and on one occasion heard by themselves in "Possento spirto," Orfeo's virtuoso appeal to Caronte. Cornetts—not to be confused with the modern trumpetlike instrument—are a family of wooden instruments with finger holes like a clarinet or other woodwind but with a small cupped mouthpiece like a trumpet's. A cornett has a beautiful silvery sound that some likened to the human voice.

Groups of 5

Trumpets, used in the opening Toccata.

Stringed instruments, two groups of five, one in the front and one backstage, each group ranging from high (violin) to low (cello).

Trombones played in the underworld scenes, Acts 3 and 4.

Three viole da gamba are sometimes added to one of the string groups. In Orfeo's song "Possente spirto" there is a splendid solo for harp, which is the earliest surviving solo music for that instrument. Perhaps this represents Orpheus's lyre. Monteverdi calls for an "arpa doppia," a double harp that has some extra strings so that it can play sharps and flats.

And then there were the instruments that played the accompaniment, the basso continuo (see p. 101), comprising at various times harpsichords, wood and reed organs, chitarroni, harp, viole da gamba, and contrabasses (see pp. 72 and 156).

Later in his life, when Monteverdi lived in Venice and wrote opera for commercial opera houses, his orchestras were very small: four or five string players and a harpsichord would often be enough. But here in Mantua, where Monteverdi was at the head of a large musical establishment, and where splendor was expected, the array of instruments was as grand as anyone could imagine.

It was a group of instruments specific to the musical personnel of Mantua. We know the names of some of the expert performers who worked for Monteverdi, and, as if happens, they correspond almost exactly with the virtuoso parts in *Orfeo*. The two Rubini brothers were accomplished violinists; Monteverdi's pupil Giulio Cesare Bianchi was an expert on the cornett; and there was a consummate harpist named Lucrezia Urbana who was probably present (she appears in payment records from 1603 to 1605, although the ones from 1607 are missing). These are precisely the solo instruments that Monteverdi used in his virtuoso songs for Orpheus.

THE VOICE AND ITS ACCOMPANIMENT

When any of the characters on stage sang, they were accompanied by one or more instruments that could play chords—the lute, organ, harpsichord, or, as in Act 3, a buzzy reed organ called a **regal**. But the actual *notes* for these instruments were not written out by Monteverdi. Instead, he provided a kind of shorthand in the score: a series of bass notes, which gave the player a sense of the required harmony. The player was expected to improvise an appropriate chord for each bass note. When Monteverdi thought there might be some confusion on what exactly he wanted, he gave extra signs to indicate, for instance, a major chord or a minor chord (see Appendix, pp. A-6–A-7 or how the notes should be arranged in the chord. This shorthand notation was called **figured bass**, and the continuous bass melody to represent chordal accompaniment was called **basso continuo**, as we mentioned in the Part Opener. These were techniques used not only by Monteverdi but by many other composers and performers of the day (see Figure 4.10).

Figured bass and basso continuo

🎙 The use of basso continuo in *Orfeo*

While sometimes Monteverdi specified what the accompanying instruments should be, most of the time he did not. But we do learn a couple of things from his indications in the score: one is that characters were not specifically associated with one instrument or another (except for Caronte, who is accompanied by the regal). Another is that sometimes a melody instrument—usually a cello—played the bass notes along with the chordal "continuo" instruments. (We will see later that the music of Handel and Bach always used a melody instrument—again, usually the cello—to accompany the chord-playing instrument.)

Speaking and Singing   The singing itself presented another kind of problem: if all the characters are singing their parts, what happens when one of the characters wants to "sing" a song—how is that to be distinguished from speaking? How can a character sing, as it were, more? It is a problem that all opera composers face in one way or another, and how they work this out is one of the more interesting things to listen for.

In the case of the story of Orpheus, it is particularly important because Orpheus himself is a singer. So how does Monteverdi make a contrast between speaking and singing? *Song*s tend to be rhythmic, fall into regular phrases, and

FIG. 4.10 Orfeo's song at the beginning of Act 2, from Monteverdi's original printed score. Orfeo's music, with its words, is the top line of music; below it is a series of notes that provide the basso continuo for accompanying instruments.

often repeat the words. They *sound* like songs. In *speaking*—even in opera—the words are recited, without repeating them, in a rhythm designed to make them understood. In a song like Orfeo's "Vi ricorda, o boschi ombrosi," from Act 2 (we will hear more of it, in detail, in LG 12), Monteverdi has given us a lively tune, many repeated lines, and a characteristic rhythmic pattern that repeats. The musical contrast between "Vi ricorda" and the Messenger's announcement of Eurydice's death ("Ahi! Caso acerbo!") could not be stronger. The Messenger has an angular, nonrepeated melody that reflects her anguished emotion. The words are delivered as if she were crying out in anguish, and aside from the rhetorical repetition of the exclamation "Ahi!," there is no repetition of either words or of musical phrases.

Ⓢ Monteverdi: *Orfeo,* "Vi ricorda, o boschi ombrosi"

Ⓢ Monteverdi: *Orfeo,* "Ahi! Caso acerbo"

SATURDAY, FEBRUARY 24, 1607

Arriving for the performance, if we were members of the Academy, we would have entered the palace from the public square, going into the ground-floor rooms that served as a sort of transitional space between the public and private parts of the palace. We would then have entered the room where the musical play was about to take place.

The "theater"

There is some good historical evidence on where the performance was given—in a room measuring about twenty-eight by thirty-nine feet—with its vaulted ceiling still intact. It was fitted up as a temporary theater and was barely large enough for the small membership of the Academy (see Figure 4.11). The room is still part of the palace, although it is now used as commercial and office space.

For the production, three windows on the right were curtained to enhance the theatrical lighting created by candles and reflectors; these provided the proper atmosphere for *Orfeo*. At the far end of the room was a proscenium stage covered with a curtain, in front of which a large number of instrumentalists were seated and behind which, presumably, the costumed players and backstage instrumentalists were preparing.

Antonio Maria Viani, the painter, architect, and Prefect of the Ducal Fabric (he was in charge of all the buildings), was famous for his skill in constructing theaters

FIG. 4.11 A reconstruction of the room in which *Orfeo* was performed, created by P. Guillou for the Museé de la Musique, Paris. Recent research suggests that the stage was at the short end of a room on the ground floor of the palace.

and machines (such as flying clouds) for the court; he was surely the designer of the platforms, the scenery, and the decorations.

The performance began when the lights were lowered, the candles behind the stage were lit, and the audience was in place.

We do not have any pictures of how the stage was arranged or of the costumes or the performers. The sets do not survive, but they are described for us by the singers.

"Be silent," says the Prologue, "let this river, these hills, these trees, all attend to the story of Orfeo." And later, when Orpheus is ejected from the underworld after he loses Eurydice forever, he too describes the fields and rocks and mountains that he once loved and now hates.

In the middle of the play, the set changes to depict the underworld (the instrumentation changes as well, from the light timbre of violins to the deeper, darker trombones and cornetts). The new scene is described to Orpheus (and to us) by La Speranza (Hope), who leads Orpheus to the boundaries of the lower world. Here are the dark marshes, she says, there is the boatman who rows the dead across the river; and over there is the realm of Pluto.

It was all there on the stage (or more likely, painted on the set). Two relatively simple sets, two set changes (probably done with a quick change of painted side panels and backdrop), and perhaps one machine: Apollo's "flying cloud."

There are ongoing debates as to whether or not the small room would have allowed for a *deus ex machina* (literally, a god from a machine), in this case a crane-like machine allowing Apollo to descend from the heavens to rescue Orpheus from his madness, at the end of his increasingly unbalanced soliloquy. Orpheus, towards the end of his dialogue with the mountain echo, rejects all womankind forever because the one woman he loves is lost. Apollo comes down in a cloud to save his son from the irrationality of imbalance. He takes Orpheus with him into the heavens, where he can contemplate Eurydice's beauty in the sun and the stars. They sing a dazzling duet as they rise in Apollo's cloud; the shepherds sing a chorus and perform a final dance. If indeed there was a *deus ex machina*, it would only have added to the breathtaking spectacle of this first production.

According to what we know, the performance went well, despite the slightly rushed rehearsals. There was a small cast, on a small stage, in a small room. Even though there are many characters in *Orfeo*, there were surely not many singers. We know that Magli sang three roles, and other singers probably performed more than one role, given how many characters appear only once and never return: La Musica, La Speranza, Caronte, Plutone (Pluto), Proserpina, and Apollo. The chorus, too, is not really a chorus (which we would normally define as a vocal ensemble with several singers on each part) but an ensemble made of those people who are on stage—never more than six or seven at a time. The whole play could be acted and sung by a group of nine singers, and might have lasted about ninety minutes. In such a small room most of the audience would probably have stood, but it would have been considered a privilege just to be there.

Deus ex machina

Listening to the Music

TOCCATA

 LG 10

Orfeo begins with a blast from the trumpets, a fanfare. Monteverdi calls it a **toccata,** a word meaning "touched," a term (more often used for a keyboard work)

LISTENING GUIDE 10   Ⓢ | DVD |

Monteverdi *Orfeo*, Toccata   1:36

DATE: 1607

GENRE: Fanfare, played three times

LISTEN FOR

HARMONY: A single harmony throughout the entire piece

FORM: Opening, martial-sounding toccata played by trumpets; repeated by strings and recorders, then by all the instruments

SCORING: The same music played three times but with varied instrumentation for each playing

TIME	FORM	DESCRIPTION
0:00	Toccata, 1st time	Five trumpets.
0:30	Toccata, 2nd time	Strings, recorders, lutes, and keyboards.
0:59	Toccata, 3rd time	All instruments together.

suggesting that the performers need to "touch" their instrument with great dexterity, in other words, to create a kind of showpiece.

Monteverdi tells us in the score that the toccata should be performed three times: the first is surely to call the audience to attention, the second to announce the arrival of the duke, and the third to signal the start of the play (see LG 10, above). The curtain rises, and the Prologue begins.

🔊 LG 11   **PROLOGUE**

In a play, especially one modeled on classical antiquity, a prologue is a device that introduces the audience to the action that will follow. In this case the Prologue is a *person* (La Musica), the personification of Music. She addresses the audience ("You noble descendants of kings"); calls for their attention; tells what the story will be, specifically about the power of Orpheus, whose music is so commanding that it can move the gods; and describes the set. She sings five varied verses of a song, *Ritornello* alternating with an instrumental piece (a **ritornello**) played by stringed instruments (violins, violas, violoncellos) with lute and harpsichord. Monteverdi calls these short pieces ritornellos because they continue to "return" throughout the opera. We hear this particular ritornello five times in the Prologue, so we become quite familiar with it. This ritornello comes in two versions, long and short. Before and after La Musica sings, we hear the long version (four phrases), like bookends; and between stanzas, we hear the short version (three phrases), as interludes.

The Prologue introduces us to the basic premise of Monteverdi's musical plan: a character has a line of poetry to deliver; she will sing it in more or less a spoken rhythm, with an accompaniment that provides a harmonic foundation but does not intrude by playing anything that might distract from the speaker/singer. The speaking/singing alternates with music played by groups of instruments, often in the form of recurring, easily recognizable ritornellos. (See LG 11, p. 105.)

LISTENING GUIDE 11 | DVD

Monteverdi *Orfeo*, Opening Ritornello and Prologue   5:53

DATE: 1607

FORM: Strophic variation

LISTEN FOR

MELODY: Melody is similar, but not identical for each strophe

HARMONY: Harmony is the same for each strophe

TEXT: Lines of 11-syllable Italian poetry. Text delivered in a spoken rhythm

La Musica sings five verses; each verse uses **strophic variation**: the same basic melodic shape and the same series of harmonies, with variations.

TIME	FORM	TEXT	TRANSLATION	DESCRIPTION
0:00	**Ritornello A**			Ritornello made of 4 similar phrases.
0:15	**Ritornello A**	Repeated		Ritornello repeated.
0:33	**Verse 1**	Dal mio permesso amato a voi ne vegno,	I come to you from my beloved River Permessus,	Prologue accompanied by harpsichord.
		Incliti eroi, sangue gentil de Regi	Renowned heroes, noble blood of kings	Note that she sings with the same rhythm an actor might use if speaking these lines.
		Di cui narra la fama eccelsi pregi,	Whose high praises are told by Fame,	
		Né giunge al ver perch'è troppo alto il segno.	Nor do they reach the truth, since the standard is too high.	
1:20	**Ritornello B**			This ritornello consists of phrases 2–4 of Ritornello A.
1:33	**Verse 2**	Io la Musica son, ch'ai dolci accenti	I am Music, who in sweet accents	In this verse, singer accompanied by harpsichord.
		So far tranquillo ogni turbato core,	Know how to calm any troubled heart,	Melody is a varied version of the other verses.
		Ed or di nobil ira, ed or d'amore,	And now with noble anger, now with love,	
		Posso infiammar le più gelate menti.	I can inflame the coldest minds.	
2:15	**Ritornello B**			
2:28	**Verse 3**	Io su cetera d'or cantando soglio	I am used to singing with golden lyre	In this verse, singer accompanied by harpsichord.

(continued)

TIME	FORM	TEXT	TRANSLATION	DESCRIPTION
		Mortal orecchio lusingar talora,	And charming every mortal ear,	Melody is a varied version of the other verses.
		E in guisa tal de l'armonia sonora	And in this way to inspire souls to long	
		De le rote del ciel più l'alme involglio.	For the sonorous harmonies of heaven's lyres.	
3:10	**Ritornello B**			
3:23	**Verse 4**	Quinci a dirvi d'Orfeo desio mi sprona,	Thus desire urges me to tell you of Orfeo,	In this verse, singer accompanied by harpsichord.
		D'Orfeo che trasse al suo cantar le fere,	Of Orfeo who attracted wild beasts with his singing,	Melody is a varied version of the other verses.
		E servo fe' l'inferno a sue preghiere,	And made Hades his servant with his prayers,	
		Gloria immortal di Pindo e d'Elicona.	The immortal glory of Pindus and Helicon.	
4:03	**Ritornello B**			
4:17	**Verse 5**	Or mentre i canti alterno, or lieti, or mesti,	Now, while I alternate happy and sad songs,	In this verse, singer accompanied by harpsichord.
		Non si mova augellin fra queste piante,	Let no bird move among these trees,	Melody is a varied version of the other verses.
		Né s'oda in queste rive onda sonante,	Nor let any wave make a sound on these banks,	
		Ed ogni auretta in suo camin s'arresti.	And let every breeze halt in its course.	Note that verse ends with a suspended effect.
5:14	**Ritornello A**			
5:30	**Ritornello A**	Repeated		

LG 12

The use of basso continuo in *Orfeo*

Rhythm in Orfeo's song "Vi ricorda," from Act 2

SONG: "VI RICORDA"

The action proper takes place in the fields of Thrace (in Greece) where nymphs and shepherds have few cares and many delights. The pleasures of this ideal world are depicted by Monteverdi in songs, and those songs allow him later to make a stark contrast between singing and speaking, and between happiness and its opposite.

In order to understand and appreciate the contrast, let us begin with a song. In Act 2, Orfeo sings a song with four verses, in which he describes how happy he is now (he is in love with Eurydice), and how it contrasts with his former unhappiness. The poet gives Monteverdi a four-line stanza for the first verse:

Vi ricorda, o boschi ombrosi,   *Do you remember, shady woods,*
De' miei lungh'aspri tormenti,   *My long and bitter torments,*

> *Quando i sassi, ai miei lamenti,*   *When the stones, at my lamenting,*
> *Rispondean fatti pietosi?*   *Replied with their own sadness?*

If the vowels are elided as marked below (which is how they would be sung, and how Italian poetry is scanned), it's clear that each line has eight syllables, alternately stressed and unstressed:

VI ri**COR**d<u>a o</u> **BOS**chi <u>om</u>**BRO**si,
DE' m<u>iei</u> **LUNGH**'aspr<u>I</u> tor**MEN**ti,
QUANd<u>o i</u> **SAS**s<u>i ai</u> **MIEI** la**MEN**ti
RIspon**DEAN** fat**TI** p<u>ie</u>**TO**si?

But Monteverdi makes a longer song out of it, by repeating some of the lines. Here is the text as Orfeo sings it:

> *Vi ricorda, o boschi ombrosi,*
> *Vi ricorda, o boschi ombrosi,*
> *De' miei lungh'aspri tormenti,*
> *Quando i sassi, ai miei lamenti,*
> *Rispondean fatti pietosi?*
> *Vi ricorda, o boschi ombrosi,*
> *Vi ricorda, o boschi ombrosi.*

You'll hear that the first line of text is sung to two different melodies, and that Monteverdi makes a refrain out of those two phrases by repeating them at the end of the verse. You could make a musical diagram of the song as **AB cde AB** (where capital letters are used for music that is repeated).

Interestingly, Monteverdi makes this song out of only two note lengths: a short note, and a note twice as long. So, using the symbols S and L for the notes, we could sketch the rhythm of the first line as SSLSLSLL

Each verse is preceded by a ritornello in the same characteristic rhythm as the verses. It's the same sort of alternation we know from the Prologue (except that here there are not two forms of the ritornello; see LG 12, p. 108).

LAMENT: "TU SE' MORTA"

 LG 13

The use of basso continuo in *Orfeo*

We focus here on Act 2, where Monteverdi makes the stark contrast between song and speech. Shepherds sing and dance, but the celebration is interrupted when Silvia, a friend of Eurydice's, rushes on stage with terrible news, describing how Eurydice has been bitten by a serpent and is dead. Orfeo, overcome with grief, finally speaks: in the heart-wrenching lament "Tu se' morta" (You are dead) he addresses himself to Eurydice, even though she is not there. He seems to be in a state of disbelief. He then vows to go to the underworld to rescue his beloved. In this speech, one of Monteverdi's finest examples of recitative style, Orfeo is using poetic rhetoric, and Monteverdi uses striking harmonies, a variety of jagged and smooth melodies, and changing rhythms to give as much added emotion as he can to what is a speech, not a song. Orfeo speaks more or less in the rhythm that an actor would use in speaking this text, but the value added by the music is incalculable (see LG 13, p. 109).

As Orfeo's world literally breaks apart, the chorus joins in a final ode of lament that combines madrigal and recitative styles. Pages 113–15 provide a map to the whole of Act 2, which should allow you to follow the sudden shifts in musical styles.

LISTENING GUIDE 12 | DVD |

Monteverdi *Orfeo*, "Vi ricorda, o boschi ombrosi" (Orfeo's Song), Act 2

2:38

DATE: 1607

GENRE: Strophic song with ritornello

LISTEN FOR

RHYTHM: Lively rhythm made of long and short notes

FORM: Repetition of opening lines and music at the end of each verse, as a refrain

TEXTURE: Alternation of music for strings with music for voice and basso continuo

TEXT: Song text in 8-syllable poetic lines

TIME	FORM AND TEXT	TRANSLATION	DESCRIPTION
	Orfeo returns to the stage, and with this song Act 2 begins.		
0:00	**Ritornello**		Ritornello made of 4 phrases with different melodies but very similar rhythms. Meter alternates 2 and 3.
	Verse 1		
0:12	Vi ricorda, o boschi ombrosi,	Do you remember, shady woods,	
	Vi ricorda, o boschi ombrosi,	Do you remember, shady woods,	Opening words are repeated to a new melody.
	De' miei lungh'aspri tormenti,	My long and bitter torments,	
	Quando i sassi, ai miei lamenti	When the stones, at my lamenting	
	Rispondean, fatti pietosi?	Replied with their own sadness?	
	Vi ricorda, o boschi ombrosi,	Do you remember, shady woods,	Opening words are repeated to the original melody.
	Vi ricorda, o boschi ombrosi?	Do you remember, shady woods?	Second phrase of melody, slightly varied.
0:37	**Ritornello**		Same ritornello as before.
0:50	**Verse 2**		Same melody as verse 1.
	Dite, allor non vi sembrai	Say, did I not seem to you	
	Dite, allor non vi sembrai	Say, did I not seem to you	
	Più d'ogni altro sconsolato?	More desolate than anybody else?	
	Or fortuna ha stil cangiato	Now fortune has changed her style	
	E ha volti in festa i guai.	And had turned troubles into a festival.	
	Dite, allor non vi sembrai	Say, did I not seem to you	
	Più d'ogni altro sconsolato?	More desolate than anybody else?	
1:15	**Ritornello**		Same ritornello as before.
1:28	**Verse 3**		Same melody as verse 1.
	Vissi già mesto e dolente,	Then I lived sad and sorrowful,	
	Vissi già mesto e dolente,	Then I lived sad and sorrowful,	
	Or gioisco e quegli affanni	Now I rejoice, and those worries	

Che sofferti ho per tant'anni	That I suffered for so many years
Fan più caro il ben presente.	Make my present joy more precious.
Vissi già mesto e dolente,	Then I lived sad and sorrowful,
Vissi già mesto e dolente.	Then I lived sad and sorrowful.

1:53	**Ritornello**	Same ritornello as before.
2:06	**Verse 4**	
	Sol per te, bella Euridice,	Only through you, beautiful Eurydice,	Same melody as verse 1.
	Sol per te, bella Euridice,	Only through you, beautiful Eurydice,
	Benedico il mio tormento:	I bless my torment:
	Dopo 'l duol viè più contento,	After sorrow there's more contentment,
	Dopo il mal viè più felice.	After evil, more happiness.
	Sol per te, bella Euridice,	Only through you, beautiful Eurydice,
	Sol per te, bella Euridice.	Only through you, beautiful Eurydice.	The piece is brought to a close.

LISTENING GUIDE 13   Ⓢ | DVD | 🎙️

Monteverdi *Orfeo*, "Tu se' morta" (Orfeo's Lament), Act 2   2:43

DATE: 1607

LISTEN FOR

HARMONY AND MELODY: Recitative style uses harmony and melody to emphasize emotional moments

THEMES: Text painting: low notes for "abysses," high notes for "stars"

EXPRESSION: Change of mood: lament at first, resolution later

TEXTURE: Solo voice with basso continuo

TIME	TEXT	TRANSLATION	DESCRIPTION
	Orfeo, having learned the news of Eurydice's death, laments in a speech addressed to his departed beloved.		
0:00	Tu se' morta	You are dead,	Accompaniment is sustained chords played by organ and chitarrone. Orfeo begins with a highly dissonant interval (1), a diminished 4th. His second note (2) creates dissonance with the accompaniment as well. Both show his bitterness and anguish.
0:14	se' morta, mia vita	dead, my life,	Repetition of "se' morta" (3) has similar dissonance but with new chord; "vita" (life) (4), however, is a bright, shining major chord.

(continued)

TIME	TEXT	TRANSLATION	DESCRIPTION
0:25	ed io respiro?	and I breathe?	Sudden shift of harmony (5) from bright major (life), recollecting the beautiful Eurydice, contrasts with Orfeo's own situation (minor chord).
0:31	Tu se' da me partita,	You, gone away from me,	Orfeo rephrases the same question, but with greater emphasis. He speaks faster and starts on higher note (6) than before, but drops to same dissonant note as in first phrase.
0:39	se' da me partita, per mai più,	gone away, and never,	Repetition of "sei da me partita" has similar dissonance as before, but with new chord.
0:51	mai più non tornare ed io rimango?	never more to return, and I remain?	On last word (7), bass lags behind—a picture of "remaining" behind.
0:56	No! No, che se I versi alcuna cosa ponno	No! No, if verses can do anything	Orfeo changes from grief to resolve—in middle of his second "No," he decides what to do.
1:06	n'andrò sicuro a più profondi abissi,	I will surely go down to the deepest abysses,	Descending melodic line and low notes on "abissi."
1:13	e intenerito il cor del re del ombre	and having softened the heart of the king of darkness	Chromatic melody (descending half steps) on "intenerito" represents his softening.
1:27	meco trarrotti a riveder le stelle;	I'll draw you up with me to see the stars again.	Ascending melody, high notes on "stelle" (stars).
1:39	o se ciò negherammi empio destino	Or if cruel fate denies this to me,	Dissonant note on "empio" (cruel).
1:48	rimarrò teco, in compagnia di morte.	I'll remain with you, in the company of death.	Low melody for Hades; unusual ("blue note") effect just before "morte" (death).
2:03	Addio terra, addio cielo, e sole, addio.	Farewell heaven, farewell earth, and sun, farewell.	His farewell salute, each time higher as he addresses earth, sky, sun.

LG 14   SONG: "POSSENTE SPIRTO"

Act 3 opens on the banks of the river that leads to the kingdom of Pluto, the underworld where the spirits of the dead reside. Orpheus, abandoned by his guide Hope (La Speranza), tries to convince Charon, the ferryman, to take him across to Eurydice, even though mortals are not allowed to cross the river.

Monteverdi saves his most dazzling music for this moment; Francesco Rasi, the singer of the role of Orfeo, has the task of creating his most persuasive musical argument. In his song "Possente spirto," he summons up all of emotion, and all of music, in his plea. Striggio provides a classic poetic form, a *capitolo*, of five three-line stanzas and a final four lines; Monteverdi gives Rasi stupendously difficult and virtuosic music, and the superb instrumentalists of the court of Mantua are engaged in embellishing his music; violins, cornetts, harp, and a trio of strings, insert commentaries, interludes, and ritornellos between the lines of his song and at the ends of the verses. As Orfeo reaches his intense conclusion, he is accompanied by a quartet of strings—the only place in the opera where singing is accompanied by anything other than the instruments of the basso continuo. The song is virtuosity at its height, Monteverdi's and Rasi's expression of what the greatest singer of myth can do (see LG 14, below).

LISTENING GUIDE 14 | DVD

Monteverdi *Orfeo*, "Possente spirto" (Orfeo's Song), Act 3   8:49

DATE: 1607

LISTEN FOR

SCORING: Rich variety of solo instruments. In the last verse, strings accompany Orfeo

EXPRESSION: Highly virtuosic singing: this is one way to impress Charon

FORM: Melody instruments punctuate the lines, and perform a series of ritornellos

---

TIME	TEXT	TRANSLATION	DESCRIPTION
	Verse 1		
0:00	Possente spirto . . .	Powerful spirit . . .	First line interrupted by pair of solo violins, one following the other.
0:16	. . . e formidabil nume,	. . . and formidable deity,	Virtuosic fast notes in violin.
0:33	Senza cui far passaggio a l'altra riva	Without whom a soul loosed from its body	Virtuosic violins again.
0:50	Alma da corpo sciolta in van presume,	Presumes in vain to cross to the other shore,	Vocal line is even more virtuosic, with more fast notes.
1:16	**Ritornello**		Violins, now playing together, close the verse with what Monteverdi calls a ritornello (even though it does not return).
	Verse 2		
1:45	Non viv'io no . . .	I am not alive, no, . . .	First line interrupted by a pair of cornetts, one following the other.
1:57	. . . che poi di vita è priva	. . . since my beloved wife	
			Cornetts.
2:09	Mia cara sposa, il cor non è più meco,	Is deprived of life, my heart is no longer with me,	

(continued)

TIME	TEXT	TRANSLATION	DESCRIPTION
			Cornetts.
2:25	E senza cor com'esser può ch'io viva?	and without a heart, how can it be that I live?	
2:43	**Ritornello**		Cornetts, now playing together, close verse with ritornello (that does not return).
	Verse 3		
2:59	A lei volt'ho il cammin . . .	I have turned my steps toward her . . .	First line is interrupted by solo harp ("arpa dopia")
3:20	. . . per l'aër cieco,	. . . through the blind air,	
			Harp.
3:34	A l'inferno non già, ch'ovunque stassi	Not yet to Hades, for wherever is found	
			Harp.
3:55	Tanta bellezza il paradiso ha seco.	Such beauty, Paradise is there.	
4:25	**Ritornello**		Harp closes verse with ritornello (that does not return).
	Verse 4		
5:19	Orfeo son io . . .	I am Orfeo, . . .	First line interrupted by trio of two violins and cello.
5:47	. . . che d'Euridice i passi	. . . who follow Eurydice's steps	
			Trio.
6:02	Seguo per queste tenebrose arene,	Through these shadowy sands,	Instruments do not provide an interlude between these two lines.
6:17	Ove già mai per uom mortal non vassi.	Where no mortal man has yet trod.	Instead, trio accompanies close of Orfeo's last line. No ritornello at end of this verse.
	Verse 5		
6:39	O de le luci mie luci serene;	O serene light of my eyes;	Verse sung straight through, without the vocal fireworks of preceding verses.
6:52	S'un vostro sguardo può tornarmi in vita,	If a glance from you can return me to life,	
7:04	Ahi, chi nega il conforto a le mie pene?	Ah, who denies comfort to my pains?	Orfeo repeats this passionate last line. Again, no ritornello at end of verse.
	Verse 6		
7:48	Sol tu, nobile dio, puoi darmi aita,	Only you, noble god, can give me help,	Singing even more simply, Orfeo is accompanied by "halo" of four strings.
8:04	Né temer déi che sopra un'aurea cetra	Nor should you fear, since I arm my fingers	
8:12	Sol di corde soavi armo le dita	Only with sweet strings on a golden lyre	
8:28	Contra cui rigida alma invan s'impetra.	Against which a rigid soul arms itself in vain.	Note that this verse has four lines, while the others had three.

LISTENING MAP OF *ORFEO*'S ACT 2

FORM	TEXT/TRANSLATION	PERFORMING FORCES	DESCRIPTION
PART I: SINGING			
A. Orfeo returns			
Song 1: Ritornello 1		Five-part strings, with basso continuo (= b. c.)	Slow triple meter, but with many syncopations and other devices to make it irregular.
Song 1: Verse (Orfeo)	Ecco pur ch'a voi ritorno . . . I'm now returning to you. . .	Orfeo, with b. c	Begins like the sinfonia. Six musical phrases (4 text phrases, some repeated); each with almost the same rhythm.
B. Invitation to music			
Song 2: Ritornello 2		Two "little French violins" with b. c.	Duple meter; 4 violin phrases, each introduced by a series of quick rising notes in the bass.
Song 2: Verse 1	Mira ch'a se n'alletta . . . Here is a shady place . . .	A shepherd, with b. c.	Note the quick surprise of the last line.
Song 2: Ritornello 2		Two "little French violins" with b. c.	Repetition of ritornello 2.
Song 2: Verse 2	Su quest'erbosa sponda . . . Here is a grassy bank . . .	A shepherd, with b. c.	Same melody as verse 1.
Song 3: Ritornello 3		Two "ordinary violins" with b. c.	Quick triple time.
Song 3: Verse 1	In questo prato adorno . . . Here's an enchanting meadow . . .	Two shepherds	They sing in harmony, in the same rhythm; meter derives from the ritornello.
Song 3: Ritornello 3		Two "ordinary violins" with b. c.	Repetition of ritornello 3.
Song 3: Verse 2	Qui Pan dio de' Pastori . . . Here Pan the God of Shepherds	Two shepherds with b. c.	They sing in harmony, in the same rhythm; meter derives from the ritornello.
Song 4: Ritornello 4		Two recorders with b. c.	Quick duple time.
Song 4: Verse 1	Qui le Napee vezzose . . . Here the nymphs gather . . .	Two shepherds with b. c.	They sing in harmony, in the same rhythm; meter derives from the ritornello.
Song 4: Ritornello 4		Two recorders with b. c.	Repetition of ritornello 4.
Song 4: Verse 2	Dunque fa degno Orfeo! . . . So Orfeo, sing! . . .	Chorus of shepherds with b. c.	They sing in harmony, based on the music of verse 1.
C. Orpheo's song			
Song 5: Ritornello 5		Five-part strings and b. c.	Meter alternates 2 and 3.
Song 5: Verse 1	Vi ricorda, o boschi ombrosi . . . Remember, shady woods . . .		Meter alternates like ritornello. Seven musical phrases, using 4 lines of poetry.

(continued)

FORM	TEXT/TRANSLATION	PERFORMING FORCES	DESCRIPTION
Song 5: Ritornello 5		Five-part strings with b. c.	Meter alternates 2 and 3.
Song 5: Verse 2	Dite all'hor non vi sembrai . . . Before, I was sad . . .	Orfeo with b. c.	Same music as verse 1.
Song 5: Ritornello 5		Five-part strings with b. c.	Repetition of ritornello 5.
Song 5: Verse 3	Vissi già mesto e dolente . . . I lived in sadness . . .	Orfeo with b. c.	Same music as verse 1.
Song 5: Ritornello 5		Five-part strings with b. c.	Repetition of ritornello 5.
Song 5: Verse 4	Sol per te, bella Euridice . . . But now I've met Eurydice . . .	Orfeo with b. c.	Same music as verse 1.

PART II: RECITATIVE

A. News and reactions

	Mira, deh mira, Orfeo. . . Orfeo, sing again . . .	A shepherd with b. c.	In lyrical style, inviting Orfeo to sing again.
Recitative	Ahi! Caso acerbo! Terrible news!	Sylvia, the messenger, with b. c.	Very angular melody, delivered in speech rhythm; a shepherd interrupts her twice.
Recitative	D'onde vieni? . . . Whence do you come? . . .	Orfeo, Sylvia with b. c.	A dialogue, in which Sylvia tells Orfeo that Eurydice is dead; quick, passionate lines.
Recitative	In un fiorito prato . . . In a flowery meadow . . .	Sylvia with b. c.	Messenger tells how Eurydice died. Her speech rises and falls, quickens and slows, to show her feelings and the nature of what she is describing.
Recitative	Ahi! Caso acerbo! Terrible news!	A shepherd with b. c.	Takes up Sylvia's cry.
Recitative	A l'amara novella . . . Orfeo is almost dumbstruck . . .	A shepherd with b. c.	
Recitative	Tu se' morta! . . . You are dead! . . .	Orfeo with b. c.	His bitter lament, and his resolve to rescue her.

B. Code ode of lament

Refrain: Chorus	Ahi! Caso acerbo! Terrible news!	Chorus of shepherds with b. c.	They take up Sylvia's cry, in recitative rhythm.
Chorus	Non si fidi uom mortale . . . Mortal man should trust fortune . . .	Chorus of shepherds with b. c.	The chorus continues with reflections on fate, in madrigal style.
Recitative	Ma io . . . I will hide myself forever . . .	Sylvia with b. c.	
Sinfonia: introduction to shepherds' lament		Five-part strings with b. c.	Slow duple meter; the whole thing repeats.

Lament, part 1	Chi ne consola . . . Who can console us . . .	Two shepherds with b. c.	A combination of recitative and madrigal style.
Refrain: Chorus	Ahi! Caso acerbo! Terrible news!	Chorus of shepherds with b. c.	Repetition of refrain.
Lament, part 2	Ma dove . . . But where is comfort?	Two shepherds with b. c.	A combination of recitative and madrigal style.
Refrain: Chorus	Ahi! Caso acerbo! Terrible news!	Chorus of shepherds with b. c.	Repetition of refrain.

C. Closing ritornello

| Ritornello | | Five-part strings and b. c. | The same ritornello that began the Prologue now concludes the first part of the drama. |

Orfeo Then and Now

The audience, in that ground-floor room in the palace at Mantua, knew their classical literature well. They knew how Italian poetry should sound, and their ears were accustomed to Monteverdi's music. They were acquainted with his *Scherzi musicali* ("musical jokes"—a collection of them had been published that same year, 1607); each of these little pieces alternates a lively ritornello with a tuneful song (like the songs in Act 2). They knew his famous madrigals, which were elaborately polyphonic settings of Italian poetry (like many of the choruses in *Orfeo*). They knew his sacred music, and much other music now lost to us. What they did *not* know—unless they happened to have been at a few experiments in Florence—was this new **recitative style**, the ***stile recitativo,*** in which actors sing their speaking parts. That focus on the voice, on the natural delivery of words in speech rhythm, would have far-reaching implications. The use of instrumental ritornellos as musical bookends would also have a long career in music. These elements, along with the basso continuo, the improvised chordal accompaniment to solo melodies, were part of the new experiment, and they were to become hallmarks of Baroque musical style.

The audience

Recitative style

But in Mantua, on that February day in 1607, it was all new. Nobody had heard this piece before, and they probably expected never to hear it again. A second performance was given ("for the ladies of the court"), and then the piece was retired. It was, after all, only a one-time composition for a specific occasion and a private audience.

We do not know much about how the spectators reacted to the two performances; but if two contemporary witnesses are typical, then it seems that people were fascinated by this new thing, not yet called opera, and that they thought Monteverdi's solution was beautiful and moving. Giovanni Striggio, the brother of the play's author, was captivated by the idea of *Orfeo* because it was something new. He wrote to his brother:

Contemporary accounts

> Having recounted as well as I know how the fable of Orpheus, your excellency's own work, to my wife, I have such a powerful desire to see it performed that I could not deny her such a just request to hear it, both because it is your honor's creation, and because it is a new thing.

In the summer of the same year Monteverdi's friend Cherubino Ferrari wrote to the duke of Mantua:

> Monteverdi is here in Milan, staying with me; and every day we talk about Your Highness and vie with one another in paying tribute to your virtues, your goodness and your royal manners. He has shown me the words and let me hear the music of the play which Your Highness had performed, and certainly both poet and musician have depicted the inclinations of the heart so skillfully that it could not have been done better. The poetry is lovely in conception, lovelier still in form, and loveliest of all in diction; and indeed no less was to be expected of a man as richly talented as Signor Striggio. The music, moreover, observing due propriety, serves the poetry so well that nothing more beautiful is to be heard anywhere.

It is only in the twentieth century that interest was revived in *Orfeo*, and gradually it has assumed a place of honor in the realm of opera—not as a museum piece, but as a passionate expression of a myth that continues to speak to us all.

Monteverdi, now thought of as the composer of the first great opera, might be surprised to know that we still love his piece four hundred years later. In music, change is not the same as progress. Many great operas have been written since, but musicians still agree with Ferrari: no music serves poetry better, or is more beautiful, than that of Monteverdi's *Orfeo*.

Chapter Review

Summary of Musical Styles

The main musical impact of *Orfeo* is the contrast between singing and speaking style.

- Singing style is accomplished by strophic songs, in which each verse uses the same music but with different words. Lively rhythms, regular phrases, and repetitions of words mark this style

- Speaking style (*stile recitativo*, or **recitative style**) is characterized by a delivery of the words in approximately the rhythm that an actor would use on stage; simple chordal accompaniment provides a setting, but not a distraction from the delivery of the text.

- A ritornello is often used to articulate larger forms. Ritornellos are short, usually lively instrumental pieces that introduce each verse of a song.

ⓢ Multimedia Resources and Review Materials on StudySpace

Visit wwnorton.com/studyspace for review of Chapter 4.

What Do You Know?

Check the facts for this chapter. Take the online **Quiz**.

What Do You Hear?

Listening Quizzes and **Music Activities** will help you understand the musical works in this chapter.

Author Videos

- The use of basso continuo in *Orfeo*
- Rhythm in Orfeo's song, "Vi ricorda," from Act 2

Interactive Listening Guides

LG 10 Monteverdi: *Orfeo*, Toccata
LG 11 Monteverdi: *Orfeo*, Opening Ritornello and Prologue
LG 12 Monteverdi: *Orfeo*, "Vi ricorda, o boschi ombrosi" (Orfeo's Song), Act 2
LG 13 Monteverdi: *Orfeo*, "Tu se' morta" (Orfeo's Lament), Act 2
LG 14 Monteverdi: *Orfeo*, "Possente spirto" (Orfeo's Song), Act 3

Flashcards (Terms to Know)

basso continuo	opera
cadence	recitative
castrato	*stile recitativo* or recitative style
figured bass	strophic variation
harmony	toccata

CHAPTER 5

TUESDAY, APRIL 13, 1742, DUBLIN:

George Frideric Handel's *Messiah*

CORE REPERTOIRE

- **LG 15** Recitative, "There were shepherds"
- **LG 16** Recitative, "Comfort ye, my people"
- **LG 17** Aria, "Ev'ry valley"
- **LG 18** Chorus, "And the glory of the Lord"
- **LG 19** "Hallelujah" chorus
- **LG 20** Fugue chorus, "He trusted in God"

AUTHOR VIDEOS

- Recitative in oratorio
- Structure of the "Hallelujah" chorus in Handel's *Messiah*

Introduction

"Handel wore an enormous white wig, and, when things went well at the Oratorio, it had a certain nod, or vibration, which manifested his pleasure and satisfaction. Without it, nice observers were certain that he was out of humour. At the close of an air, the voice with which he used to cry out, CHORUS! *was extremely formidable indeed."*

—Charles Burney, *An Account of the Musical Performances in Westminster-Abbey* (London, 1785)

George Frideric Handel composed *Messiah* to entertain a public that had heard a lot of opera. For some time he had been shifting his attention to a new kind of entertainment called an **oratorio**, a grand religious drama written in the style of an opera but without opera's expensive trappings. Handel was an astute business-man, and his experience as a manager of opera companies in London had taught him that the combination of good music, fancy sets, and high-priced singers was as much a recipe for financial ruin as it was for great art.

Oratorio

Like all of Handel's oratorios, *Messiah* was designed to fill theaters during the six-week Lenten season—a penitential season of the Christian year leading up to Easter—when only sacred works were allowed on stage in England. Although its subject matter—the birth, suffering, and resurrection of Jesus—is religious, *Messiah* sounds like an opera and it appealed to audiences in much the same way. Handel was a devout believer, but it was not only piety that motivated him to compose *Messiah*. He wrote it for the same reason he wrote his operas: to sell tickets and make money. And his plan worked. Not only was *Messiah* a huge success in Handel's lifetime, it continues to be one of the world's favorite pieces (see Figure 5.1).

Ⓢ Handel: *Messiah,* "Hallelujah" chorus

FIG. 5.1 This is the first page of Handel's autograph composing score of *Messiah*. The score was begun ("Angefangen") on Saturday, August 22, 1741, and finished on September 14.

Opera had been a popular form of entertainment in England and on the Continent since the time of Monteverdi more than a century earlier. Audiences came to Handel's operas expecting to hear portions of dialogue, set in recitative style, alternating with songs and interspersed with choruses and instrumental pieces. That is what they heard at the opera, and that is what they heard at the oratorio. Yet *Messiah* also differs significantly from Handel's operas, in ways that Handel himself invented. These differences served him and later composers so well that he is better remembered today for his oratorios than for his many operas. Indeed, the "Hallelujah" chorus from *Messiah* might be the best-known and most frequently performed piece of classical music ever written. Ⓢ

The Setting

GEORGE FRIDERIC HANDEL

George Frideric Handel was a German composer who studied in Italy and spent most of his life in England, although his English was never very good. Along the way he acquired a talent for swearing in three languages and a fondness for food and drink, as mature portraits of him attest. (See biography, below, and Figure 5.2.) In London, where he had lived since 1712, he was well known as a composer and producer of operas. But the 1740–41 season had been an economic disaster, and Handel was thinking of getting out of the opera business. Just then he received an invitation from the duke of Devonshire, the Lord Lieutenant of Ireland (the king of England's appointed administrator), to give some concerts in Dublin. He accepted and stayed for nine months, from late 1741 to August 1742.

George Frideric Handel (1685–1759)

Handel was one of the leading composers of the eighteenth century, a musician of cosmopolitan background and international renown. He helped introduce the Italian operatic style to England, where he combined it with his own brand of energetic German music making. His works were rich in melodic variety, contrasting textures, and dramatic expression. His invention of the English oratorio has made him a permanent fixture in the musical world.

Born to a respected family in Halle in 1685, Handel was raised to be a lawyer; his musical inclinations were so strong, however, that even though he entered the university, he soon left to join the orchestra of the famous opera house of Hamburg. Several operas of his were produced there, beginning when he was eighteen.

Handel traveled to Italy in 1707, where for three years, mostly in Rome, he absorbed the Italian style and composed sacred music, Italian oratorios, and other works.

Appointed music director to the elector of Hanover, Handel absented himself in London, where he began an illustrious career in opera. His employer at Hanover became King George I of England, and it was some time before the elusive employee was reconciled with the king. (The story that Handel's famous *Water Music* was designed as a peace offering is charming but apocryphal.)

In 1719 the Royal Academy of Music was organized to produce opera in the King's Theater, and Handel was engaged to find singers and compose music. Supported by the king and the great nobles, the opera company was Handel's chief occupation until 1727. He was in charge of recruiting and rehearsing the great opera singers of the day, as well as composing music for them to sing. Other operatic ventures after 1727 engaged Handel's attention in London, but he also began to interest himself in oratorio.

Having produced several oratorios in the 1730s (including *Saul* and *Israel in Egypt*), and having composed (but not performed) *Messiah*, Handel was well equipped to produce a series of concerts in Dublin in 1741 and 1742. His later career in London consisted mostly of performances of oratorios (*Solomon, Joshua, Judas Maccabaeus*, and others), along with many revivals of *Messiah*.

Handel was a composer of international significance; he wrote many pieces for state occasions, including the music for the coronation of King George II and the *Fireworks Music*, to celebrate the peace of Aix-la-Chapelle (1748). He was single all his life. He was handsome in youth, portly in age, and revered universally. At his death in 1759 he was buried in Westminster Abbey.

Ⓢ Handel: *Music for the Royal Fireworks*, "Réjouissance"

MAJOR WORKS: Over 4 dozen Italian operas, including *Rinaldo* and *Giulio Cesare*; English oratorios, including *Messiah, Israel in Egypt,* and *Saul*; orchestral suites, including *Music for the Royal Fireworks* and *Water Music*; and numerous keyboard and chamber works.

Handel composed *Messiah* shortly before he left London, in the summer of 1741, and it had its first performance in the Irish capital the following April. Its phenomenal success confirmed his decision to turn his back on the operatic stage once and for all.

OPERA

In the course of his long career, Handel composed concertos (pieces for orchestra and solo instruments; we'll meet them in the next chapter), chamber music, keyboard music, and much else. But since opera was at the top of the social and economic scale, opera is what he worked hardest at. It was also what he did best and what he was most famous for. If we want to hear Handel's *Messiah* as he meant it to be heard, it is important to understand the styles and conventions of early eighteenth-century opera.

Like many other composers in the 1720s and 1730s, Handel devoted most of his energy to the genre known as **opera seria** (serious opera). A "serious" opera is one that features historical or mythological personages of high standing—kings, queens, emperors, generals, princesses, and the like. These characters invariably express their noble thoughts in Italian, regardless of the language of the audience. Most opera seria plots are not terribly believable, but that is not the point. The point is to create a series of situations in which characters can come to understand and express certain feelings. The plots are designed to showcase the widest possible range of emotions, while giving the most important characters the greatest number of songs.

FIG. 5.2 A caricature of Handel, entitled "The Charming Brute," by Joseph Goupy, from around 1754. Handel's skill at the keyboard, and his skill at the table, are given equal prominence, and though he is depicted as a boar, he is wearing his famous white wig.

Structure of opera seria

The basic structure of an opera seria is entirely dictated by convention, even if the details are seldom predictable in the hands of a master like Handel. Each of the three acts consists of alternating recitatives and songs, much like those we heard in Monteverdi's *Orfeo*. The recitatives, accompanied by harpsichord (or occasionally by organ or lute) and cello, are dialogues or monologues delivered in speech rhythm. These are the parts of the show in which the plot advances. For example, a messenger may enter and report that the enemy army is in sight. This announcement might prompt the main character to step forward and sing an elaborate song (called an *aria* in Italian) about the clangor of arms and the trumpet's call to battle. After he leaves the stage, his wife may sing a recitative lamenting that he has put his life in danger. Then she too moves downstage to pour out her heart in a passionate aria before making her exit.

An opera seria, in other words, is like a film punctuated by a series of still photographs or freeze-frames. If the recitatives move the action forward in cinematic fashion, the arias are moments in which time stands still as we explore with the character how she or he feels.

Conventional elements

The conventions of opera seria may seem strange, or even silly, to us. But if we reflect on the conventional elements in our own pop culture (for example in sitcoms, detective stories, and music videos), we realize that conventions exist for our pleasure and convenience; they give us what we want in an efficient, if non-realistic, way. So it was with opera seria. In the eighteenth century almost every cultivated person in Europe understood and liked this kind of music, and this way of delivering it.

ORATORIO

Oratorios and operas are alike in that they are performed in a theater and have plots and characters. The recitatives and arias in oratorios are composed in an essentially operatic style. There are important differences, however. First, oratorios are not staged or acted; the singers wear concert dress and perform alongside the orchestra on stage. Second, Handel's oratorios are sung in English, not operatic Italian, which must have made a significant difference to audiences in London and Dublin.

Third, oratorios deal almost exclusively with religious subjects, mostly taken from the Old Testament. Finally, the chorus plays a more prominent and substantial role in oratorios than it does in most operas.

As mentioned above, during the penitential season of Lent it was forbidden to produce operas, which the religious authorities considered profane. Handel observed this prohibition by presenting oratorios instead (see Figure 5.3). They had the same musical effect as operas, but were deemed acceptable by virtue of their spiritually uplifting subjects (although their plots could be just as blood-curdling as those of operas). Oratorios had a practical advantage as well: they were comparatively inexpensive to produce, having neither sets nor costumes, and needing few if any superstar Italian opera singers (see A London Critic Goes to the Oratorio, left).

The stories of Handel's oratorios were generally drawn from biblical narratives featuring kings and heroes such as Solomon, Saul, Joshua, and Samson, and heroic women such as Esther and Athalia. The texts were arranged in rhyming verse by a poet, or librettist, who fleshed out the characters' motivations, actions, and dialogue. The stories often had a double meaning. For example, when an Israelite hero wins a battle in an oratorio, the chorus is apt to sing, "God save the King! Long live the King!" Handel's audience understood that it was not only the king of Israel who was being praised, but also King George of England, and that Israel represented England in its triumph.

A London Critic Goes to the Oratorio

Among other things, the writer is making fun of the use of Italian opera singers to sing in English. Note also the street clothes of the singers ("in their own Habits"). Handel's "pulpit" is surely the organ from which he presided.

"Haven't you been at the Oratorio?" says one. "Oh, if you don't see the Oratorio you see nothing," says t'other; so away goes I to the Oratorio, where I saw indeed the finest Assembly of People I ever beheld in my very Life, but, to my great Surprise, found this Sacred Drama a mere Consort [concert], no Scenery, Dress, or Action, so necessary to a Drama; but H–l was placed in Pulpit (I suppose they call that their Oratory). By him sat Senesino, Strada, Bertolli and Turner Robinson, in their own Habits. Before him stood sundry sweet Singers of this our *Israel*, and Strada gave us a Hallelujah of Half an Hour long; Senesino and Bertolli made rare work with the *English* Tongue, you would have sworn it had been *Welsh*. I would have wished it *Italian*, that they might have sung with more ease to themselves, since, but for the Name of *English*, it might as well have been *Hebrew*.

Messiah is like Handel's other oratorios in some ways and unlike them in others. It is typical in that it is sung in English, is not staged, and consists of recitatives, arias, and choruses. It is unusual in that its words are drawn directly from the Bible and the Book of Common Prayer, the standard book of worship in the Church of England, or Anglican Church; the text is not rearranged into rhyming couplets. Moreover, there are no characters in *Messiah*. The soprano, alto, tenor, and bass soloists do not represent persons who carry out actions and feel emotions that are expressed in their arias. These two features make *Messiah* almost unique in Handel's output.

DUBLIN

When Handel arrived in the late fall of 1741, Dublin was the second city of the British Empire, adorned with handsome public buildings, churches, and houses in the contemporary Georgian style (see Figure 5.4). Most of the newer construction was on the north side of the river Liffey. To the south lay old Dublin, with its medieval castle, its two Anglican cathedrals (both in a sad state of disrepair), the tranquil precincts of Trinity College, and the seat of the Irish Parliament. The latter body was almost powerless; Ireland was essentially ruled from London, with the Lord Lieutenant (an appointed English nobleman) enforcing Protestant English domination over the Catholic Irish majority.

The outstanding figure in Dublin's small but vibrant cultural community was the sharp-witted, Irish-born contrarian Jonathan Swift, the author of *Gulliver's Travels* and other political satires, who was dean of St. Patrick's Cathedral at the time of Handel's visit. Much of the city's music, opera, and theater, however, was imported from England and elsewhere. Dublin even had one theater, the Crow Street Music Hall, devoted to "the practice of Italian Musick." So when Handel brought his new works in the Italian style to the Irish capital, he was sure of finding a receptive public.

Many of Dublin's musical organizations were associated with hospitals, prisons, and other charitable institutions. Concerts were often presented in support of needy persons, offering patrons the double satisfaction of enjoying music while doing good works. Handel not only donated the proceeds from the first performance of *Messiah* to charity, but for many years thereafter gave an annual performance of the oratorio in London in aid of an orphanage called the Foundling Hospital.

The Charitable Music Society, which sponsored weekly concerts for the relief of persons in debtors' prison, was responsible for the construction of the New Music Hall in Fishamble Street, on the south bank of the Liffey. It opened in 1741, just in time for Handel's arrival. This theater, also called Mr. Neale's Music Hall (after the music publisher who was president of the Music Society), served as the venue for all of Handel's concerts, including his performances of *Messiah* (see Figures 5.5 and 5.6).

FIG. 5.3 The rehearsal of an oratorio. Here performers and audience are at close quarters, and the rehearsal seems almost as much a social event as a musical one. Handel may be the figure on the right of the harpsichordist.

The Performance

PREPARATIONS

Immediately after crossing the Irish Sea from Chester, the "celebrated Dr. Handel" (as the newspapers referred to him) announced a series of six concerts to begin toward the end of December. Another six concerts took place between

FIG. 5.4 A view from Capel Street, looking over Essex Bridge, Dublin, by the acclaimed Irish engraver and watercolorist James Malton. From *A Picturesque and Descriptive View of the City of Dublin* (1792–99).

FIG. 5.5 A nineteenth-century engraving of the entrance to Mr. Neale's New Music Hall, opened in 1741, as it then appeared.

mid-February and early April 1742. None of these dozen programs included *Messiah*; mostly they consisted of oratorios that Handel had already presented in London, mixed with organ concertos—allowing him to show off his virtuosity at the keyboard—and other instrumental music. The performances were given on a subscription basis, all six concerts in each series being sold as a set.

As a rule, Handel had specific performers in mind when he wrote a piece of music. *Messiah* was an exception: he composed it several weeks before he left for Ireland, without knowing what performers he would find there. None of the other pieces Handel brought to Dublin had been composed especially for the occasion, so he made do with the resources that were available, tailoring his existing music to the strengths and weaknesses of individual performers.

As it happened, the score of *Messiah* needed surprisingly little adjustment for its Dublin premiere. Handel had at his disposal an excellent orchestra called the State Music of Ireland, led by the violinist Matthew Dubourg. The all-male chorus was made up of boys and men from the choirs of the two cathedrals, Christ Church and St. Patrick's. The male soloists were drawn from the same pool of local singers, but the women soloists included a professional opera singer, Christina Maria Avolio, and a celebrated singing actress, Susannah Cibber, both of whom were well known on the London stage.

Handel employed a relatively spare orchestra in *Messiah*. The original score calls for a core ensemble of strings (first and second violins, violas, and cellos, presumably with double-basses playing along with the cellos), to which two trumpets and **kettledrums** (large bowl-shaped drums with a parchment head) are added for grand moments like the "Hallelujah" chorus. Although most of Handel's other oratorios feature solos for violin, oboe, flute, or other instruments, there are no solo instruments in *Messiah* except for a single trumpet, pretty obviously needed, in the aria "The trumpet shall sound."

Kettledrums

Handel almost always added oboes and bassoons when the string orchestra was larger than about ten players, and it seems likely that he did so on this occasion.

FIG. 5.6 The interior of the Music Hall in which *Messiah* was first performed. This view shows the hall after extensive renovations (1791), but it retains the general shape and dimension of the building.

It was possible, and indeed customary, to create parts on the spot by having the oboes play along with the violins (or with the sopranos and altos), and the bassoons with the cellos. We have no direct evidence of oboes and bassoons in the Dublin *Messiah*, but two different sets of parts survive from later performances, so we know that the practice was common in the eighteenth century. (Bach used oboes and bassoons to reinforce the strings in his D Major Orchestral Suite, as we will see in the next chapter.)

Rehearsals for *Messiah* must have been relatively straightforward. Handel changed two tenor arias to recitatives, possibly because the arias were too difficult for the tenor soloist. (It was not a purely artistic decision, apparently, since Handel reinstated the arias as soon as he began to produce *Messiah* in London.) He shortened and tightened up a few numbers, and transposed a couple of arias to new keys for voices that he hadn't heard when he composed the piece, but essentially he left the music as he had composed it.

On the whole, Handel was pleased with the quality of the musicians in Dublin. After the first of his twelve subscription concerts, he wrote to Charles Jennens (see Figure 5.7), the man who had selected and arranged the words for *Messiah*:

FIG. 5.7 Charles Jennens (1700–1773), Handel's acquaintance who assembled the words for *Messiah*.

> The Nobility did me the Honour to make amongst themselves a Subscription for 6 Nights, which did fill a Room of 600 Persons, so that I needed not sell one single Ticket at the Door, and without Vanity the Performance was received with a general Approbation. Sig^{ra} Avolio, which I brought with me from London pleases extraordinary, I have form'd an other Tenor Voice which gives great Satisfaction, the Basses and Counter Tenors are very good, and the rest of the Chorus Singers (by my Direction) do exceeding well, as for the Instruments they are really excellent, Mr Dubourgh being at the Head of them, and the Musick sounds delightfully in this charming Room, which puts me in such Spirits (and my Health being so good) that I exert my self on my Organ with more than usual Success.

TUESDAY, APRIL 13, 1742, 12 NOON

The first performance of *Messiah* was a special benefit for its three charitable sponsors. It was not part of either of Handel's subscription series, and for once he had nothing to do with the business arrangements (see *The Dublin Journal . . .* Announces the First Performance of *Messiah*, right). The premiere was preceded by a public dress rehearsal, rather like a "preview" of a Broadway show, open only to those who had bought tickets to the performance. Thus most of the audience heard the piece twice—once on April 8, and again five days later. (The performance was originally planned for April 12, but was postponed a day, to April 13.) Apparently, the rehearsal went very well. According to one newspaper account, "Mr. Handell's new Grand Sacred Oratorio, called, The MESSIAH, was rehearsed . . . to a most Grand, Polite and crouded Audience; and was performed so well, that it gave universal Satisfaction to all present; and was allowed by the greatest Judges to be the finest Composition of Musick that ever was heard, and the sacred Words as properly adapted for the Occasion."

What sort of people made up this "Grand, Polite and crouded Audience"? In Handel's own words, they included "the Flower of Ladyes of Distinction and other People of the greatest Quality," as well as "Bishops, Deans, Heads of the Colledge, the most eminent People in the Law as the Chancellor, Auditor General, &tc."

The *Dublin Journal* and *Dublin News-Letter* Announce the First Performance of *Messiah*

For Relief of the Prisoners in the several Gaols, and for the Support of Mercer's Hospital in Stephen's Street, and of the Charitable Infirmary on the Inns Quay, on Monday the 12th of April, will be performed at the Musick Hall in Fishamble Street, Mr. *Handel's new Grand Oratorio, call'd the* MESSIAH, in which the Gentlemen of the Choirs of both Cathedrals will assist, with some Concertoes on the Organ, by Mr. Handell. Tickets to be had at the Musick Hall, and at Mr. Neal's in Christ-Church-Yard, at half a Guinea each. N.B. No Person will be admitted to the Rehearsal without a Rehearsal Ticket, which will be given gratis with the Ticket for the Performance when pay'd for.

The audience

FIG. 5.8 Fashionable dress for ladies included substantial hoop skirts and trains. For Handel's concerts in Dublin the ladies were asked to come "without their hoops."

Susannah Cibber in the Eyes of Contemporaries

Charles Burney, an 18th-century music historian, said that her voice was "a mere thread, and knowledge of Music, inconsiderable; yet, by a natural pathos, and perfect conception of the words, she often penetrated the heart, when others, with infinitely greater voice and skill, could only reach the ear." When she sang the aria "He was despised," according to a story that might or might not be true, the Reverend Dr. Delaney was so moved, despite Mrs. Cibber's reputed immorality, that he shouted, "Woman, for this be all thy sins forgiven thee."

These distinguished members of the leisure class were free to go to a concert that started at noon and could afford the half-guinea (about three month's wages in today's economy). As few people who fell into that category would have been either native Irish or Catholics, we can assume that almost all of Handel's listeners were of English extraction and belonged to the Church of England.

People began arriving at the Music Hall as soon as the doors opened at 11 a.m. on April 13. They came by horse-drawn carriage, in sedan chairs carried by servants, and on foot (see Figure 5.8). Fishamble Street, narrow and winding, was prone to traffic jams on the days of Handel's concerts. The nearly seven hundred people filled the hall to overflowing for the midday performance. The complete *Messiah*, including two intermissions, would have lasted until shortly after 3 p.m. This schedule gave everyone sufficient time to get home for dinner, the main meal of the day, which was served about 4 p.m. The daytime performance also saved the management considerable expense in candles.

Even though almost everybody knew the words of *Messiah* from hearing them read in church, most ticketholders probably bought wordbooks that printed the full text. The wordbook does not tell us which solo singers sang which recitatives and arias; but, by a stroke of luck, one anonymous listener took the trouble to pencil in the names of the singers beside each section of text, giving us an accurate idea of how Handel divided up the solo responsibilities.

The caliber of the Dublin singers was not, by and large, equal to that of the operatic superstars whom Handel was used to hiring for his London seasons (and whose exorbitant salaries made producing operas so difficult). The soloists were professional singers mostly drawn from Dublin's cathedral choirs; the choir singers were basses, tenors, **countertenors** (men singing alto in falsetto voice), and boy sopranos; in *Messiah* the solo soprano parts were sung by women rather than by choirboys. Christina Maria Avolio, an Italian opera singer whom Handel had brought over from London, seems to have made a very good impression. Handel had known Signora Avolio for a long time and would employ her on several later occasions.

A lucky find was Susannah Cibber, a famous actress and singer who had also worked with Handel in London. Although Mrs. Cibber's alto voice was not particularly powerful, her skill at expressing the meaning of the words made her performances captivating. Handel used her dramatic abilities to full effect in *Messiah* (see Susannah Cibber in the Eyes of Contemporaries, at left).

According to the annotated wordbook, a certain Mrs. Maclaine also sang in the performance, though she was not mentioned in the reviews. Handel had met her in Chester, on his way to Ireland, and invited her, along with her organist husband, to travel to Dublin to help with his concerts.

As members of the cathedral choirs, the male soloists were well known to Dublin audiences, if not to Handel, and the remaining arias and recitatives were divided up among them. The soloists included altos William Lamb and Joseph Ward, tenor James Bailey, and basses John Mason and John Hill. Although Handel seems to have been pleased with Bailey ("I have form'd an other Tenor Voice which gives great Satisfaction," he told Jennens), he felt compelled to make adjustments for the other men to ensure that his music did not exceed their abilities.

Because the two cathedral choirs shared many singers (and even had the same choirmaster), it is not easy to know exactly how many people were in the chorus for *Messiah*. If all the choristers participated, they probably numbered about sixteen men (singing alto, tenor, and bass) and eight boy sopranos. The three women joined in the choruses, as did the five male soloists.

Handel presided over the performance at the keyboard (at the harpsichord during the oratorio), with Mr. Maclaine accompanying on the organ. One of the attractions of Handel's concerts was his dazzling organ playing, and during the pauses between the three parts of *Messiah* he played concertos with the orchestra on a small portable organ that he had brought from London. The manuscript scores of some of Handel's organ concertos contain only the orchestral music, with brief indications of where the organ solos begin and end. It must have been wonderful fun to watch him improvise the solo parts, nodding to the orchestra whenever it was their turn to come in (see Charles Burney Describes Handel Playing the Keyboard, right).

> ## Charles Burney Describes Handel Playing the Keyboard
>
> Indeed, his hand was then so fat, that the knuckles, which usually appear convex, were like those of a child, dinted or dimpled in, so as to be rendered concave; however, his touch was so smooth, and the tone of the instrument so much cherished, that his fingers seemed to grow to the keys. They were so curved and compact, when he played, that no motion, and scarcely the fingers themselves, could be discovered.

The singers and instrumentalists arranged themselves around Handel on stage. The soloists must have been close enough for him to follow the flexible speech rhythms of their recitatives on the keyboard, but not too far away from the chorus, since the soloists were expected to sing the choruses as well. The chorus probably stood behind and on both sides of the small orchestra. Typically for the time, there was no conductor as such; Handel started each movement from his perch at the harpsichord and organ, while Matthew Dubourg kept the orchestra together by gesticulating with his body and violin bow.

Listening to the Music

Many of us have heard *Messiah*; some of us even have sung it. Handel's familiar score tells a long story in a series of short pieces, each of which is a self-contained musical expression. As we have seen, the experience, for Handel's listeners, was a lot like going to the opera. For us it is a bit different: even if we are regular operagoers—and most of us probably are not—the operas we are most likely to listen to have little in common with the "serious" operas of Handel and his contemporaries.

The first thing we hear in *Messiah* is an instrumental overture; this was the standard way for Handel (and almost every other composer) to open both operas and oratorios. (In an opera house, the curtain usually rises at the end of the overture. There was no curtain in the Music Hall, but Handel observed the convention anyway.) Like almost all of Handel's overtures, this one begins with a slow, stately introduction, followed by a livelier section in which the instruments come in one after another in imitation, producing a **fugue** (see p. 140). The overture form with two continuing sections is called a French overture; we will consider it in more detail when we li sten to Bach's Suite in D Major in Chapter 6. After the overture comes a series of recitatives, arias, and choruses.

THE SHAPE OF THE ORATORIO

Three-part form

Messiah is divided into three parts, like the acts of an opera, each of which ends with a grand chorus. The first part is made up of triplet units consisting of a recitative, an aria, and a chorus. The second part is a sequence representing the Passion, Resurrection, and the spread of the Gospel of Christ. It features a long series of contrasting choruses, culminating in the famous "Hallelujah" chorus. The third part, drawn mostly from the funeral service, is a reflection on triumph over death. The final chorus, a grand "Amen" fugue, caps an oratorio that expresses, in both words and music, a Christian view of God's promise to humankind and of our hope for eternal life. (Parts 1 and 2 are often performed on their own during the Christmas season.)

Text

Charles Jennens, Handel's acquaintance who assembled the words for *Messiah,* selected scriptural texts that tell of the promise of the coming of the Messiah, of the birth and suffering of Christ, and of the promise of resurrection. All of these texts were well known to Handel's audiences. But most of the narrative is told in oblique ways. Often Jennens chooses an Old Testament text to narrate a Christian event ("For unto us a child is born"). He uses many texts from the Old Testament prophets, and few from the New Testament Christian texts that relate narrative events.

Musical connections

Although each aria, recitative, and chorus in *Messiah* is a discrete musical number, in several places Handel seems to be making an effort to connect one movement to another. The aria "O thou that tellest good tidings to Sion," for instance, is thematically linked to the ensuing chorus. Similarly, the narrative of the shepherds and the angels in the soprano recitative "There were shepherds" flows directly into the angels' chorus "Glory to God." Such connections make it clear that *Messiah* is not an anthology of miscellaneous pieces that might well have been assembled in some other order, but a carefully planned sequence of numbers designed to produce maximum musical and dramatic effect.

The texts of *Messiah* are not metered or rhymed, like poetry, but their inherent rhythmic quality and melodiousness make it seem almost as though they were written to be sung. Whether Jennens had recitatives, arias, or choruses in mind for specific texts is not known, but the groupings of three that Handel put together work very well with Jennens's selections.

Now let's take a closer look at these three musical genres.

🎙 Recitatives in oratorio

RECITATIVES

A recitative is just what it says: a recitation. The words are sung in essentially the same rhythm in which they would be spoken, with a simple chordal accompaniment played on a keyboard instrument and a cello. (In Handel's day, as in Monteverdi's, the so-called basso continuo instruments, those that played chords, improvised their parts, taking the unadorned bass line as a guide.) This is the standard,

Recitativo secco

default variety of recitative and is called **recitativo secco** ("dry" recitative), because it has no orchestral accompaniment.

In operas, *recitativo secco* is generally used for extended dialogues between characters, to advance the plot and prepare for the next aria. In *Messiah*, by contrast, most of the recitatives consist of only a few words—for example, "Behold, a virgin shall conceive and bear a son, and shall call his name Emmanuel: 'God with us.'"

In the other kind of recitative, **recitativo accompagnato** (accompanied recitative), the orchestra provides an accompaniment while the soloist sings the text in a generally spoken rhythm. The orchestra—usually the strings alone, augmented by the continuo instruments—might also play an introduction to set the mood of the text. Accompanied recitatives are typically saved for moments of high intensity or for passages where a series of contrasting emotions are presented one after another.

"There were shepherds" In opera, *recitativo accompagnato* is much rarer than *recitativo secco*. In *Messiah*, however, a large proportion of the recitatives are accompanied; some are very short, others of a more substantial nature. A good illustration of the difference between the two kinds of recitative is the passage in which the solo soprano describes the announcement of the birth of Jesus to the shepherds (see LG 15). The alternation of *secco* and accompanied recitative is clearly intended to paint a musical picture of the presence of angels—first one, and then many.

Handel: *Messiah*, "Behold, a virgin shall conceive"

Recitativo accompagnato

LG 15

Handel *Messiah*, Recitative, "There were shepherds"   1:24

DATE: 1742
GENRE: Oratorio (recitative)

LISTEN FOR
FORM: Alternation between *recitativo secco* ("dry" recitative, with continuo accompaniment) and *recitativo accompagnato* (recitative with orchestral accompaniment)

TEXTURE: Pictorial effects in orchestra
TEXT: Words delivered in a generally spoken rhythm

TIME	TEXT	DESCRIPTION
0:00	There were shepherds abiding in the field, keeping watch over their flock by night.	*Recitativo secco*: solo soprano sings words in a speaking rhythm, with chordal accompaniment by continuo instruments (harpsichord and cello).
0:15	And lo, the angel of the Lord came upon them, and the glory of the Lord shone round about them; and they were sore afraid.	*Recitativo accompagnato*: orchestra joins in, perhaps depicting flutter of angel wings.
0:33	And the angel said unto them: Fear not, for behold, I bring you good tidings of great joy, which shall be to all people. For unto you is born this day in the city of David a savior, which is Christ, the Lord.	Return to *recitativo secco*.
1:08	And suddenly, there was with the angel a multitude of the heavenly host, praising God, and saying . . .	*Recitativo accompagnato*: orchestral accompaniment even more active, depicting multitude of angels. Ending designed to lead directly into chorus that follows, "Glory to God."

LISTENING GUIDE 15   DVD

Ⓢ Handel: *Messiah*, "Thus saith the Lord"

A composer may have other reasons for choosing accompanied recitative—for instance, when a character is expressing particularly strong and active emotions, as in "Thus saith the Lord." The violent chords interjected by the orchestra take their cue from the lines: "yet once a little while, and I will shake the heavens and the earth, the sea and the dry land." The bass soloist doesn't just "speak" the text, he dramatizes and intensifies its meaning by embellishing the words "shake" and "desire" with long garlands of sixteenth notes, and singing some phrases more than once.

"Thus saith the Lord" is not pure recitative, but it is still far from being an aria. In fact, the category of recitative covers a broad expressive range, from the simplest and most straightforward recitations to more lyrical pieces that combine the characteristics of recitatives and arias. The distinction between recitative and aria will be clearer when you have a good idea of what an aria is like; we will listen to an example of Handel's arias in a moment.

LG 16

"Comfort ye, my people"   At the extreme aria-like end of the recitative spectrum is the tenor's *recitativo accompagnato* "Comfort ye, my people," the first music that is sung in *Messiah* (see LG 16, p. 131). This piece is in two parts, the first lovely and songlike, the second ("The voice of him that crieth in the wilderness: Prepare ye the way of the Lord") agitated and recitative-like. The recitative opens with a tender orchestral introduction, characterized by softly pulsing repeated notes in the strings. This beautiful passage will be a recurring musical motif that reinforces the central meaning of the text.

ARIAS

We use the Italian word *aria* to denote the more elaborate pieces for voice and orchestra that are found in operas and oratorios. For these pieces Handel composed, and his audience expected, something quite specific. An **aria** (or song, as it was called in England) is the place where the action pauses and the music takes over. It is generally intended to express one or two specific emotions and their corresponding musical moods. Several aspects of Handel's arias are of particular interest to us: musical phrases, musical motives, word painting, ritornellos, and larger shape.

Musical phrases

In an aria, the words provide the vehicle for musical phrases. It is the construction and juxtaposition of these phrases that we listen for, not the straight, once-through delivery of the text as in a recitative. For example, in *Messiah*'s first aria, which comes directly after "Comfort ye, my people," the aria has this text:

> *Ev'ry valley shall be exalted,*
> *And ev'ry mountain and hill made low;*
> *The crooked straight, and the rough places plain.*

But what we actually hear is something different:

> *Ev'ry valley,*
> *Ev'ry valley shall be exalted*
> *shall be exalted*
> *shall be exalted*
> *shall be exalted*
> *And ev'ry mountain and hill made low . . .*

and so on, with key words and phrases repeated for purely musical effect. (We'll have more to say about this wonderful aria when we consider Handel's skill at word painting.)

LISTENING GUIDE 16   Ⓢ | DVD | 🎙

Handel *Messiah*, Recitative, "Comfort ye, my people" 2:47

DATE: 1742
GENRE: Oratorio (*recitativo accompagnato*)

LISTEN FOR
TEXTURE: Interweaving of orchestral and vocal themes
EXPRESSION: Change of mood toward the end

TEXT: Varied settings of the words "comfort" and "comfortably"

TIME	TEXT	DESCRIPTION
0:00		Smooth, harmonious theme as introduction:
0:14	Comfort ye,	Simple statement of falling, 3-note theme by soloist (tenor), echoed by orchestra:
0:19	Comfort ye, my people;	Orchestra begins opening theme again; singer has elaborate version; orchestra repeats 3-note "Comfort ye" theme.
0:34	Comfort ye	Singer's part marked "ad libitum," meaning he is invited to ornament freely.
0:45	Comfort ye, my people.	Orchestra begins opening theme again, then repeats "Comfort ye" theme.
0:58	Saith your God, saith your God.	Orchestra punctuates tenor's words with "Comfort ye" theme.
1:08	Speak ye comfortably to Jerusalem, speak ye comfortably to Jerusalem	Orchestra begins opening theme again, accompanying singer's text and punctuating the end with "Comfort ye" theme.
1:35	And cry unto her that her warfare, her warfare is accomplished.	This time singer takes lead, while orchestra accompanies with opening theme. At the end, orchestra punctuates with "Comfort ye" theme.
1:54	That her iniquity is pardoned	On last word, orchestra plays beginning of opening theme.
2:03	That her iniquity is pardoned.	Beginning on singer's last note, orchestra plays opening theme (first time since the beginning that it appears in its entirety), but in different key.
2:26	The voice of him that crieth in the wilderness: Prepare ye the way of the Lord, make straight in the desert a highway for our God.	Mood and style change abruptly from "comfort" to "cry": orchestra punctuates vocal part with single chords.

Music and words convey meaning in different ways. In a recitative, the words are delivered more or less as they would be in spoken dialogue; they are meant to be clearly understood, since the point is to convey information about the characters and plot. In an aria, on the other hand, music takes precedence over speech.

The point is to express an emotion, to reflect on an event or an idea presented in the foregoing recitative, and the music takes all the time it needs.

Musical motives

A couple of basic ideas that Handel uses in composing arias are worth bearing in mind. First, each aria is made of a small number of short, recognizable musical motives, which almost always relate to some aspect of the words. For each phrase of the text, Handel selects one (and only one) musical idea to associate with it. In "Ev'ry valley," for example, the first two words are always sung to a particular tune (with slight variations). The same is true for other phrases, such as "the crooked straight" and "the rough places plain."

The idea of associating each phrase of the text with its own recognizable tune is characteristic of a great deal of Handel's vocal music. It wasn't an invariable rule—think of "Comfort ye, my people," where Handel uses the same musical motive repeatedly in the orchestra part, while varying the vocal line—but that, of course, is not an aria.

Musical phrases

Handel's second basic idea is to string these phrases of text together into what we might call musical sentences. Some of these sentences are long and elaborate in structure, the kind of thing that Handel's audiences were used to hearing from the mouths of actors, preachers, and lawyers. Typically, such lofty rhetorical utterances consisted of three elements: *gesture*, *amplification*, and *conclusion*. For example, take this well-known passage from the King James version of the Bible (1 Corinthians 13:11):

When I was a child,	(gesture)
I spake as a child,	(amplification)
I understood as a child,	
I thought as a child;	
But when I became a man	(conclusion)
I put away childish things.	

If Handel (or almost any other Baroque composer) were using this sentence as the text of an aria, he would most likely set the opening statement to a memorable musical gesture or motive. The middle section would elaborate on that idea, often

Sequence and cadence

by means of one or more **sequences** (short passages of music that are repeated several times, at progressively higher or lower pitches.) Then he would bring the phrase to a close with a **cadence** (the musical equivalent of a period or full stop). Many such phrases can be found in the first aria in *Messiah*, "Ev'ry valley" (see LG 17), and in many other arias. Handel also uses this gesture-sequence-cadence structure in instrumental pieces, such as the ritornellos of "Ev'ry valley" and of the chorus "And the glory of the Lord" (see LG 18), as we will see in a moment.

The point of an aria, as we have said, is to explore an emotion, to make the listener understand how the character, or the singer, feels at a given moment. Words such as "I weep with grief" can convey clear messages in an aria. But music can also send expressive signals without using words: tempo (fast or slow), key (minor or major), melody (angular or smooth), harmony (regular or unusual)—all these contribute to giving the listener a sense of the mood in an aria.

Word painting

One musical technique that Handel loves to exploit whenever opportunity knocks is **word painting** (we first encountered this technique in Chapter 3). This means just what you might expect—painting a colorful musical picture of whatever the words are saying. Sometimes Handel focuses on the big picture and sets the mood for an entire piece. For example, the aria "He shall feed his flock" begins with what any eighteenth-century listener would have recognized as music about the outdoors and the keeping of sheep. The flowing rhythm is that of a **siciliana**,

Ⓢ Handel: *Messiah*, "He shall feed his flock"

an Italian dance associated with pastoral scenes, and the allusion is reinforced by the bagpipe-like drone of the bass. We know that the aria is about sheep and shepherds before the singer opens her mouth. An even more obvious example of setting the mood is the opening of the aria "The trumpet shall sound," which features the only instrumental solo in *Messiah*.

Sometimes Handel "paints" on a more intimate scale, associating musical ideas with words and phrases, rather than with whole pieces. Particularly good examples are found in "Ev'ry valley," where Handel illustrates the word "exalted" either by writing a high note or by giving the singer an elaborate sequence, moving from a low pitch to an ever more exalted place. The phrase "and ev'ry mountain and hill made low" starts on a very high note and descends to the bottom of the tenor range. The next phrase of text, "the crooked straight," provides another contrast: Handel follows a jagged, crooked melody with smooth, sustained notes. He does something similar with "and the rough places plain," except that here he seems to be making a kind of musical pun, using a long-held note on the word "plain," as if it referred to a topographical feature.

Word painting is so intuitively obvious to most of us that it seldom needs to be pointed out. Indeed, one of the pleasures of listening to Handel's music is observing how he goes about doing what we know he is going to do all along. Music has an infinite number of ways of depicting both physical phenomena (birdsong, moving water) and intangible qualities and emotions (rage, softness, flatness). Handel used a great variety of them at one time or another.

A typical aria starts with an orchestral introduction, which is repeated at the end and is often used, in whole or in part, as interludes during the aria. The term for a passage of music that returns over and over is **ritornello**. It was a favorite device of composers in the Baroque era; we have met ritornellos in Monteverdi, and we'll encounter them again when we listen to Bach's Concerto in F for Harpsichord, Two Recorders, and Strings.

Ritornello

"Ev'ry valley" The opening ritornello of an aria (or a chorus) usually contains music that the singer will perform later. Listen to "Ev'ry valley," for instance. It begins with the motive that we will come to associate with the words "Ev'ry valley shall be exalted," and it continues with a sequence based on a figure that will accompany "the crooked straight." We don't yet know what the words will be, but the ritornello has given us the mood of the piece, the tempo, and some basic musical ideas, so that when the singer comes in we are already on familiar ground (see LG 17, p. 134).

🎧 LG 17

Not all ritornellos begin with the singer's music. Sometimes the composer has a good reason for making the orchestra paint a sound picture that doesn't lend itself to vocal performance. The aria "Thou shalt break them," for example, has a violent, jerky ritornello that suggests someone hurling things to the ground ("Thou shalt break them in pieces like a potter's vessel"). The ritornello is regularly used to accompany the singer, but it is not itself melodious or singable.

Likewise, the opening ritornello, and much of the accompaniment, of the aria "Why do the nations so furiously rage together?" feature a rapid, frenzied figure in the strings that has some characteristics in common with the vocal part but is unique to the orchestra.

Now that we know something about the ingredients that Handel uses in making his arias, we can begin to appreciate their overall structure and shape. In a typical Handel aria, the singer develops one or more of the basic ideas suggested by the text, pausing now and then for the orchestra to play a shortened version

Larger shape

LISTENING GUIDE 17 | DVD

Handel *Messiah*, Aria, "Ev'ry valley"   3:10

DATE: 1742

GENRE: Oratorio (aria)

TEXT: *Ev'ry valley shall be exalted,*
And ev'ry mountain and hill made low.
The crooked straight, and the rough places plain.

LISTEN FOR

FORM: Large-scale form:
| ritornello | **A** | shortened ritornello | **A'** + cadenza | ritornello |

SCORING: Opening and closing orchestral ritornello based on vocal themes

TEXT: Word painting: "exalted," "low," "crooked," "plain"

THEMES: Small number of themes, each tied to a phrase of text

Musical Theme Color and Letter Labels:

    V = valley, C = crooked, M= mountain, P = plain, K = cadence

TIME	TEXT/FORM	DESCRIPTION
	Ritornello (V C K)	
0:00	*Opening section* V1 V2 V2	Begins with upward figure (V1, which will accompany text, "Ev'ry valley") followed by downward figure (V2) played twice.
0:06	*Continuation section* C1 C2 C3 K	Wavering figure (C1, which will accompany text, "the crooked straight") played as a sequence 3 times ascending in pitch, followed by a **cadence** (K).
0:14	*Closing section* C3 K	Repetition of crooked theme, C, an octave lower, followed by a final cadence, K, to close the ritornello.
	A section	
0:19	Ev'ry valley (V1)	Singer announces valley theme V1, repeated by orchestra.
0:23	Ev'ry valley (V1) shall be exalted (V2) Shall be exalted (V2 extended) Shall be exalted (V2) Shall be exalted (V2 extended)	Main theme and continuation (V1, V2), extension. Singer engages in virtuosic (**melismatic**) word painting. Orchestra interjects, punctuates with V1.
0:50	And ev'ry mountain and hill made low. (M)	Vocal line introduces new theme (M). "Mountain" is highest pitch, "low" is lowest (word painting). Orchestra follows with statement of crooked theme, foreshadowing new text to come. (C)
0:55	The crooked straight (C1) And the rough places plain (P1) The crooked straight The crooked straight (imitative) And the rough places plain, And the rough places plain.	Crooked motive (from opening ritornello) now underlines text, and alternates with fourth motive (P) throughout next section. Orchestra imitates vocal line; themes are traded back and forth, mutations of C and P occur, connect, and interact with each other until cadence K after final statement of "rough places plain."

Abbreviated ritornello (V)

1:25	C K	Orchestra plays brief interlude with a fragment of crooked theme plus cadence.

A′ section (A elaborated) + cadenza

1:30	Ev'ry valley (V1)	Singer begins with the same "announcement" of valley theme (V), in different key from opening.
	Ev'ry valley (V1) shall be exalted (V2)	Opening theme continued and extended, just as in first **A section**, but extensions and melismas are new. Again, orchestra punctuates with V1 theme.
	Ev'ry valley (V1) Ev'ry valley shall be exalted (V1, V2)	
2:03	And ev'ry mountain and hill made low.	Text painting not as dramatic as before, but "mountain" still high point, "low" still lowest.
2:06		As in **A section**, orchestra follows with statement of crooked theme, heralding new text to come. (C)
	The crooked straight (C1) The crooked straight The crooked straight And the rough places plain (P) And the rough places plain And the rough places plain	Crooked theme, cadence motive, after second statement of the plain motive P. We expect final cadence K, which is the combination we have heard closing each section (both ritornellos plus the **A section**).
2:32	The crooked straight (**fermata**) And the rough places (cadenza) plain (Cadence- K)	Instead, orchestra's last chord is deceptively not final. Fermata (hold) over last statement of "straight" while singer embellishes word "places" and cadences (finally) on "plain."

Closing orchestral ritornello

2:48	V	C	K	Exact repetition of opening ritornello.
	V1 V2 V2	C1 C2 C3 K	C3 K	

of the ritornello. Usually toward the end Handel provides an opportunity for the soloist to show off her or his most elaborate decorated melodies. This is followed by a passage where the music pauses, the accompaniment thins out, and the singer is invited to supply a **cadenza** (an ornamented version of the final cadence). Then the orchestra closes with another statement of the ritornello.

Cadenza

The basic shape of most arias, then, can be described as ritornello-voice-ritornello, where the central vocal section is quite a bit longer than the framing ritornellos, and may include fragmentary portions of the ritornello. This is the outline of "Ev'ry valley" and of most of the other arias in *Messiah*. A couple of them, however, have a more complicated structure: the soloist sings a contrasting section following the second orchestral ritornello, after which the entire opening portion of the aria is repeated, with its concluding ritornello.

Da capo arias

This larger three-part form was standard for opera arias in the period. The contrasting middle section allows the singer afterwards to return to the opening music and sing it from the beginning (*da capo*, in Italian). The reprise is not a simple repetition, however. In light of the intervening music, the singer (and the audience) has a new understanding of the meaning of the words the second time around. Moreover, the reprise gives the soloist an opportunity to show off improvised ornamentation. Handel's singers would try to outdo each other with their dazzling fast-note passages, scales, and other embellishments, particularly in the cadenzas.

Although Handel wrote hundreds of **da capo arias** in his operas, *Messiah* includes only two: "He was despised" and "The trumpet shall sound." Why so few? In the first place, Handel wanted *Messiah* to be reasonably concise and to move along quickly. In the second, he did not intend the music for opera singers, and few oratorio singers were capable of the dazzling virtuosity that opera audiences expected in the *da capo* sections.

CHORUSES

The pieces sung by the full chorus are among the crowning beauties of *Messiah*, as they are of Handel's other oratorios. Indeed, most of the grandeur and glory of these works is generated by the choruses. The "Hallelujah" chorus in *Messiah* has thrilled listeners for more than two and a half centuries; for many of us, it is the first music that comes to mind when we think of oratorio (or of Christmas).

Handel had one basic method for making a chorus, although he inflected it in countless and endlessly imaginative ways. The idea is this: take the text, slice it into brief phrases, compose a musical motive for each phrase, and assemble the chorus using these motives as building blocks. Put that way, writing a chorus sounds easy. But the truly difficult part, and what sets Handel apart from more pedestrian composers, is inventing the right motives to go with the different phrases of the text and combining them in a musically satisfying composition.

LG 18

"And the glory of the Lord" Consider the first chorus in *Messiah*, "And the glory of the Lord," which completes the first triplet unit of recitative ("Comfort ye, my people"), aria ("Ev'ry valley"), and chorus. Handel divides the text into four lines or phrases:

> *And the glory of the Lord*
> *shall be revealed*
> *and all flesh shall see it together*
> *for the mouth of the Lord hath spoken it.*

Once you've heard the entire chorus, you can sing the tune of any of the four lines, because Handel invents a characteristic melody to which those words are always (or almost always) sung.

The opening ritornello is a classic of the type gesture-sequence-cadence, where the first two elements actually serve to introduce tunes we will come to associate with words; the opening gesture, or motive, is set to the music of "And the glory of the Lord," and the following sequence is set to the melody of "shall be revealed" (although of course we don't know this yet, unless we've already heard the chorus).

LISTENING GUIDE 18 | DVD

Handel *Messiah*, Chorus, "And the glory of the Lord"   2:38

DATE: 1742
GENRE: Oratorio (chorus)

TEXT: *And the glory of the Lord*
shall be revealed
and all flesh shall see it together
for the mouth of the Lord hath spoken it.

LISTEN FOR

TEXTURE: Contrast of textures: homophony and polyphony
SCORING: Use of orchestra (which plays the same motives) to provide breathing space and articulate the main sections

THEMES: Four motives, each based on one phrase of the text

TIME	FORM	DESCRIPTION
	*I: First two motives (**G** and **R**) introduced and combined*	
0:00	Ritornello **G+R**	First two motives make up classic statement-plus-sequences ritornello. Lively dancelike rhythm clearly established. Note upward-tending motive followed by downward-tending motive.
0:10	**G**	Opening phrase ("And the glory . . ." = **G**) stated once by altos and repeated, harmonized in homophony, with melody in the bass.
0:17	**R|R** **|G**	Second motive ("shall be revealed" = **R**) combined in various voices (tenor, bass, soprano), then combined with motive **G**.
0:34	**G**	Homophonic statement of **G**, melody in bass.
	*II: Second two motives (**F** and **M**) introduced and combined*	
0:40	Ritornello	Orchestra plays sequences based on **R**.
0:45	**F**	Third motive ("and all flesh . . ." = **F**) sung by altos and tenors; it consists of the same few notes 3 times.
0:53	**M** **F**	Fourth motive ("for the mouth . . ." = **M**) sung 3 times, each time combined with motive **F**, of strong, repeated notes, in other voices.
	III: All motives combined. This section is bookended by homophonic statements of first and last motives, and provides contrast with **counterpoint** *by brief section treating motive* **F**	
1:17	Ritornello (**G**)	Orchestra plays opening motive, but in new key (the dominant).
1:21	**G**	Homophonic statement of **G**, with melody in bass.
1:24	**F**	Second motive in various voices, combining in half cadence.
1:28	**M** **G**	Motive **M** in upper voices combines with motive **G** in tenor and bass.
1:39	**F**	Third motive in alto, tenor, bass, combining at end.
1:53	**G|G|R** **|R|F**	Solo statement culminating in soprano's high note of **A**, followed by combination of motives **G** and **R**, then **R** and **F**, closing on a homophonic "together" (!).
2:13	**M**	Final section is two grandiose statements of final motive.

The chorus is in a lilting triple meter, rather like a minuet (a favorite dance of the time), and its four motives, one for each phrase of text, are used in wonderful combinations (see LG 18, p. 137).

Many other choruses are constructed in this same way: a series of ideas, each based on one phrase of the text, which are introduced successively, and then combined in various ways.

LG 19

Structure of the "Hallelujah" chorus in Handel's *Messiah*

"Hallelujah" chorus In the "Hallelujah" chorus, the opening word is sung ten times before the second phrase is announced: Handel is clearly not in a hurry to get through the words. But what he does do is create a remarkable series of patterns and expectations.

That opening series of "Hallelujahs" is actually two groups of five, each group being made of what we might call two longs, two shorts, and an extra-long (HAA-le-lu-jah, HAA-le-lu-jah, hallelu-jah, hallelu-jah, hal-LE-E-lu-JAH). Five are sung in homophony, and then the same sequence is repeated, but in a different key. Handel is setting up patterns of pairs, smaller and larger, that keep us expecting something, which sometimes satisfies us when we get it, and often surprises us when we don't.

Monophony vs. homophony

Only after those ten "Hallelujahs" does the chorus announce, in unison (or we might call it **monophony**—everyone doing the same thing at the same time—to contrast with **homophony**), the second musical idea, "For the Lord God omnipotent reigneth." This is sung twice, each followed by four short "Hallelujahs."

Now that the first two ideas are present, Handel shows what he can do; in a blaze of polyphony (different melodies being performed at the same time), he creates a web of combinations of the two themes.

The central phrase of this chorus, "The kingdom of this world is become the kingdom of our Lord, and of his Christ"—unlike any other theme in this chorus, and unlike almost any theme in any chorus—is sung only once, the first half very soft, and the second half very loud. It is the central event of this chorus, and perhaps the central message of the oratorio, and it stands right in the middle of this chorus. There were two motives before it, and there are two phrases to come.

Imitation

Next comes the phrase "And he shall reign for ever and ever," and with it Handel produces a classic piece of polyphonic writing. The voices enter one at a time, each singing the phrase, and then continuing with other music as the next voice enters. This technique of **imitation**—a common technique in the Renaissance as well—is an effortless way to teach us the melody, and to teach us about counterpoint (the art of combining simultaneous melodies), because we hear the melody first all by itself, then with only one other voice, then with two other voices (more difficult to hear, but by then we know the melody that much better). When the final voice enters with the melody, we can proudly pick it out of the increasingly complex texture.

The chorus proceeds with the trumpetlike statement of "King of Kings, and Lord of Lords" (not much of a melody, just repeated notes, but very effective and easy to hear), punctuated with "Hallelujah." Handel concludes the chorus with a mighty combination of all themes (except the solemn central one), finishing with an increasingly excited series of "Hallelujahs."

This very symmetrical and carefully constructed chorus is somehow held together with the glue of "Hallelujah"—little exclamations that appear throughout, rather like sparkling stars (see LG 19, p. 139).

In addition to the basic general procedure, which Handel used to produce a profusion of choruses, there are two special types of chorus in *Messiah* that deserve our attention: fugue choruses and duet choruses.

LISTENING GUIDE 19 | DVD |

Handel *Messiah*, "Hallelujah" chorus

3:41

DATE: 1742
GENRE: Oratorio (chorus)

LISTEN FOR

FORM: Repetitions of blocks of material in new keys
TEXTURE: Clear contrasts of texture: monophonic, homophonic, polyphonic

THEMES: The short-version "Hallelujah" used as punctuation and countermelody throughout the piece

TIME	TEXT	DESCRIPTION	FORM
	*Part 1: Two motives (**A** and **B**), treated separately, then combined*		
0:06	Hallelujah, hallelujah, hallelujah, hallelujah, hallelujah	Homophonic: two "Hallelujahs" in same rhythm, two in a shorter rhythm, one in long rhythm.	**A** HHhh**H**
0:15	Hallelujah, hallelujah, hallelujah, hallelujah, hallelujah	Same music as before, but in different key.	HHhh**H**
0:24	For the Lord God omnipotent reigneth	All voices and instruments in unison: monophony.	**B**
0:31	Hallelujah, hallelujah, hallelujah, hallelujah,	"Hallelujah" 4 times in short rhythm.	hhhh
0:35	For the Lord God omnipotent reigneth	Monophony as before, but in different key.	**B**
0:41	Hallelujah, hallelujah, hallelujah, hallelujah,	"Hallelujah" 4 times in short rhythm, as before, but in new key.	hhhh
0:46	For the Lord God omnipotent reigneth (combined with "Hallelujah")	The two motives combined; "For the Lord…" appears in bass, soprano, and tenor, with other voices using "Hallelujah" as countermelody.	**A + B**
	*Part 2: Single motive (**C**), not repeated*		
1:11	The kingdom of this world is become	Homophonic; very quiet.	**C**$_1$
1:21	the kingdom of our Lord, and of his Christ	Homophonic; very loud.	**C**$_2$
	*Part 3: Two motives (**D** + **E**), treated separately, then combined*		
1:29	And he shall reign for ever and ever	Homophonic: voices enter in imitation: bass, tenor, alto, soprano.	**D**
1:50	King of Kings, Hallelujah, hallelujah, hallelujah, hallelujah,	Homophonic statement with 4 "Hallelujahs."	**E**$_1$ hhhh

(continued)

TIME	TEXT	DESCRIPTION	FORM
1:56	and Lord of Lords, Hallelujah, hallelujah, hallelujah, hallelujah,	Homophonic statement with 4 "Hallelujahs."	E_2 hhhh
2:03	King of Kings, Hallelujah, hallelujah, hallelujah, hallelujah,	Same as before, but in different key.	E_1 hhhh
2:09	and Lord of Lords, allelujah, hallelujah, hallelujah, hallelujah,	Same as before, but one note higher.	E_2 hhhh
2:16	King of Kings, Hallelujah, hallelujah, hallelujah, hallelujah,	Same as before, but one note higher.	E_1 hhhh
2:22	and Lord of Lords, (King of Kings and Lord of Lords)	One note higher for sopranos; chorus accompanies with full motive in homophony.	$E_1 (E_1 + E_2)$
2:29	And he shall reign for ever and ever King of Kings and Lord of Lords Hallelujah	Combined: "And he shall reign" in bass, then soprano, alternated and combined with shorter version of "King of Kings, Hallelujah."	D + E + hh
3:19	Hallelujah	Final cadence.	H

Fugue Choruses A **fugue** is a polyphonic composition based on a single theme, which is introduced in imitation in all voices at the beginning of the piece and recurs thereafter in various voices (see also the discussion of the fugue in Chapter 6, pp. 157–60). The fast portion of the overture to *Messiah,* after the stately opening section, is a fugue for strings.

Fugue structure Different fugues behave differently, but they all have three things in common:

- Each is based on a melody called the **subject.**
- There is an **exposition** section in which each voice enters in turn with a **statement** of the subject.
- There are entries of the subject in various voices, often alternating with **episodes** in which the subject is not present in its entirety.

There are several fugue choruses in *Messiah,* including the somber "And with his stripes we are healed" and the grand "Amen" chorus that concludes the oratorio.

LG 20 **"He trusted in God"** Handel probably selected "He trusted in God" for fugal treatment because it represents the shouts of many passers-by (the recitative that introduces it says "All they that see him laugh him to scorn"): all four vocal parts in the chorus have the same mocking words but sing them at different times. Starting with the lowest voices, basses, tenors, altos, and sopranos in turn sing "He trusted in God that he would deliver him: let him deliver him, if he delight in him." This angular and solid melody is the only theme the chorus will have. After all the

LISTENING GUIDE 20 | DVD

Handel *Messiah*, Fugue chorus, "He trusted in God" 2:15

DATE: 1742

GENRE: Oratorio (chorus)

TEXT: *He trusted in God
that he would deliver him:
let him deliver him,
if he delight in him.*

LISTEN FOR

THEME 1: Repetitions of a single theme (the subject). Beginning of subject:

He trust-ed in God that he would___ de-liv-er him; let him de-liv-er him,

TEXTURE: Contrapuntal texture

THEME 2: Almost continuous presence of the connecting theme "let him deliver him" (derived from the subject)

SCORING: S, A, T, B = Soprano, Alto, Tenor, and Bass

TIME	DESCRIPTION	TIME	DESCRIPTION
0:00	Subject in B.	1:05	Episode.
0:09	Subject in T, B continues.	1:10	Beginning of Subject in T.
0:18	Subject in A, TB continue.	1:15	Episode.
0:28	Subject in S, TBA continue.	1:22	Subject in B.
0:37	Episode.	1:31	Episode.
0:43	Beginning of Subject in B.	1:40	Subject in S.
0:45	Subject in A.	1:49	Episode.
0:54	Beginning of Subject in T.	1:54	Subject in B; cadence.
0:56	Subject in S.		

voices have entered, Handel alternates sections in which the melody is being sung in one of the voices with episodes where it is not being sung. In the episodes of this fugue, Handel repeatedly uses a little figure set to the words "let him deliver him" to give a unified sense to the fugue chorus (see LG 20, above).

Duet Choruses One of the special features of *Messiah*, not shared with his other oratorios, is a group of choruses that Handel adapted from a set of Italian duets that he had written earlier. There are four of these choruses, and they are among the chief delights of *Messiah*. You would never guess that they were adaptations unless you knew what to look for. The giveaway is the long stretches of music in which only one or two of the four voices are singing. This makes for a light, airy quality that the other choruses in *Messiah* lack.

The four duet choruses are "For unto us a child is born;" "His yoke is easy;" "All we, like sheep, have gone astray," and "And he shall purify the sons of Levi." What is remarkable about them, apart from their beauty, is the fact that the music fits the words so well, considering that it was composed for completely different texts.

The music of "For unto us," for example, originally accompanied a duet whose text begins as follows:

DUET TEXT	DUET TRANSLATION	*MESSIAH* TEXT
No, di voi non vo' fidarmi,	No, I will not trust you,	For unto us a child is born,
cieco amor,	blind love,	unto us
crudel beltà	cruel beauty	a son is given

We can only marvel at Handel's ability to transform a sassy duet about not being fooled in love a second time into this lovely and spirited chorus. (The conversion of the words is not perfect; there's a curious emphasis, in *Messiah,* on the word "For.") He takes the two solo voices of the duet and parcels them out among the four voices of the chorus, adding, by way of punctuation, music that was not in the duet: the homophonic outbursts of "Wonderful, counselor, the mighty God, the everlasting father, the prince of peace." These powerful choral interjections make a striking contrast with the dancing rhythms of the duet portions, which consist largely of **melismas** (long florid passages) with almost no accompaniment except continuo.

How Did It Go?

Handel's score was hardly revolutionary, and it seems to have made a good impression on the Dublin audience; one eyewitness wrote that *Messiah* was received "with the greatest applause." Unfortunately, we know little more than that about the first performance. Musical journalism was in its infancy in the 1740s, and the reports that appeared in the Dublin papers were more enthusiastic than informative. Here is what an anonymous writer had to say about the premiere:

> On Tuesday last Mr. Handel's Sacred Grand Oratorio, the Messiah, was performed at the New Musick-Hall in Fishamble-street; the best Judges allowed it to be the most finished piece of Musick. Words are wanting to express the exquisite Delight it afforded to the admiring crouded Audience. The Sublime, the Grand, and the Tender, adapted to the most elevated, majestick and moving Words, conspired to transport and charm the ravished Heart and Ear.

"The most finished piece of Musick," says the writer; by this he probably means that *Messiah* is finely crafted, a well-made example of something that is recognizable and well understood. We all know about recitatives, arias, and choruses, the writer seems to say, and we agree about how to judge them. *Messiah* is a good version of an oratorio, consisting of familiar elements, all fashioned the way we expect, and very satisfactory.

"The Sublime, the Grand, and the Tender": these adjectives seem to describe the emotional effect of Handel's music. In eighteenth-century parlance, *sublime* referred to that which is awe-inspiring and surpasses understanding. *Grand* and *tender* denote the contrast between the splendid and intimate, public and private. The writer seems to be suggesting that a full range of emotions is expressed in the music, which combines with the well-known sacred text ("the most elevated, majestick and moving Words") to "transport and charm the ravished Heart and Ear." We use our ears to hear and judge music, but ultimately it is the heart that tells us whether we like it—whether it produces the feeling that only great art can give.

Messiah Then and Now

Dubliners had one more chance to hear *Messiah*, on June 3, 1742, before Handel left Ireland. Back in London he was preoccupied for a time with preparations for his oratorio *Samson* and didn't get around to reviving *Messiah* until the following spring. From that time forward the work took on a life of its own, being performed with increasing regularity and to mounting acclaim, in different versions adapted to different performers and circumstances.

By the time Handel died in 1759, performances of *Messiah* had become annual events in cities and towns all over England. (No one knows for sure how the custom started of standing during the "Hallelujah" chorus; for one explanation, see Rising to the "Hallelujah" Chorus, right.) The eighteenth-century *Messiah* craze culminated in 1784, when some five hundred singers and instrumentalists joined forces during the great Handel commemoration at London's Westminster Abbey, where the composer was buried. As the tradition took root in other countries, the oratorio was presented in everything from intimate chamber versions, similar to the one the Dublin audience heard, to large-scale audience "sing-alongs."

We may not be as accustomed as Handel's audience was to hearing music that is made up of recitatives, arias, and choruses; nor is our culture one in which Anglican Christian values, and their associated texts, are taken for granted. And yet there is something about *Messiah* that still appeals powerfully to many listeners, not only in predominantly Christian countries, but all around the world. It must be what the newspaper writer said: the ravishing combination of "the Sublime, the Grand, and the Tender."

What might have been surprising to Handel's contemporaries, and is perhaps less so to us, is the fact that the words were taken from Scripture. This was not Handel's usual practice (he usually had a poet rework the story), and because the subject matter of *Messiah* is not an Old Testament drama but central doctrine of the Christian faith, he was evidently concerned about performing it in a concert hall or a theater, in front of a paying—rather than a praying—audience. Later, when he presented *Messiah* in London, he often advertised it simply as "a new sacred oratorio," with no mention of its highly evocative title.

In many Western cultures, the sacred and the secular occupy mostly separate spheres. Many people have the idea that sacred texts are only suitable for music intended to be heard in a church; or that music set to sacred words must have a character different than other kinds of music. But Handel drew no such clear distinction between oratorio and opera. The music he wrote for "Why do the nations so furiously rage together?" might just as well be sung by an operatic hero who is venting his bloodthirsty rage. In both cases, Handel is expressing the pictorial, narrative, or emotional content of the words.

Nevertheless, the musical similarity between opera and oratorio must have worried him. It certainly worried at least one critic, who signed himself Phila-lethes (Greek for "Lover of the True") in a London paper in 1743:

> An *Oratorio* either is an *Act of Religion*, or it is not; if it is, I ask if the Playhouse is a
> fit *Temple* to perform it in, or a Company of *Players* fit *Ministers* of *God's Word*, for in
> that Case such they are made.

Rising to the "Hallelujah" Chorus

This account, written years after the London premiere, may be apocryphal, but the custom is widely observed to this day.

When Handel's *Messiah* was first performed [in London], the audience was exceedingly struck and affected by the music in general; but when that chorus struck up, 'For the Lord God Omnipotent reigneth,' they were so transported that they all, together with the king (who happened to be present), started up, and remained standing till the chorus ended: and hence it became the fashion in England for the audience to stand while that part of the music is performing.

In the other Case, if it is not perform'd as an *Act of Religion*, but for *Diversion* and *Amusement* only (And indeed I believe few or none go to an *Oratorio* out of *Devotion*), what a *Prophanation* of *God*'s Name and Word is this, to make so light Use of them?

The role that religion plays in our lives is different for each of us. Somehow, though, Handel's music seems to have escaped his own time and place and become a universal statement of humanity. We feel that *Messiah* belongs to us at least as much as to the upper-crust, England-oriented Dubliners for whom it was first performed. Handel seems to have wanted it that way: not only did he perform *Messiah* regularly for charitable purposes in the remaining seventeen years of his life, he bequeathed a set of performance materials to the orphanage that still owns them. *Messiah* has continued to do good work for centuries.

If he were alive today, Handel might be surprised to find that *Messiah* is frequently presented in churches, with at least some sort of religious purpose in mind, in addition to the ubiquitous concert performances that are so much a part of our musical experience, particularly during the Christmas season. Then again, the evidence suggests that he saw his oratorio as both an "act of religion" and a commercial venture. In fact, *Messiah* had already become so famous and so popular in Handel's lifetime that he would probably just nod his wig in pleasure and satisfaction.

Chapter Review

Summary of Musical Styles

In *Messiah*, the main musical types are **recitative, aria**, and **chorus**.

- **Recitative:** solo voice that follows the inflection of the text
  General characteristics of recitative:
  Sung by a single voice, delivering the text in speech rhythm.
  Accompaniment consists of chords (usually harpsichord or organ) plus cello.
  Types of recitative:
  Recitativo secco: as above, simple chordal accompaniment.
  Recitativo accompagnato: accompaniment by orchestra.

- **Aria:** a song for a single voice with orchestra
  General characteristics of arias:
  Often opens and concludes with an orchestral ritornello.
  The vocal part has many text repetitions to accommodate elaborate musical structures.
  The singer's music may include difficult **melismas**, and may have a **cadenza** at the end.

- **Chorus:** movements for chorus (**sopranos, altos, tenors, basses**) plus orchestra
  General characteristics of choruses:
  Tend to attach a musical motive to each phrase of text.
  Variety of texture.
  Often begin, like arias, with an orchestral **ritornello**.
  Two special types of chorus in *Messiah*:
  Fugue chorus: a polyphonic chorus based on a single theme.

Duet chorus (these are unique to *Messiah*): chorus arranged from Handel's Italian duets for two voices and basso continuo. They feature many passages of light texture, in which only two of the choral voices sing at a time.

ⓢ Multimedia Resources and Review Materials on StudySpace

Visit wwnorton.com/studyspace for review of Chapter 5.

What Do You Know?

Check the facts for this chapter. Take the online **Quiz**.

What Do You Hear?

Listening Qizzes and **Music Activities** will help you understand the musical works in this chapter.

🎙 Author Videos

- Recitative in oratorio
- Structure of the "Hallelujah" chorus in Handel's *Messiah*

Interactive Listening Guides

LG 15 Handel: *Messiah*, Recitative, "There were shepherds"
LG 16 Handel: *Messiah*, Recitative, "Comfort ye, my people"
LG 17 Handel: *Messiah*, Aria, "Ev'ry valley"
LG 18 Handel: *Messiah*, Chorus, "And the glory of the Lord"
LG 19 Handel: *Messiah*, "Hallelujah" chorus
LG 20 Handel: *Messiah*, Fugue chorus, "He trusted in God"

Flashcards (Terms to Know)

aria	imitation	ritornello
cadence	kettledrums	sequences
cadenza	melismas	siciliana
countertenor	monophony	statement
da capo aria	opera seria	subject
episodes	oratorio	word painting
exposition	recitativo accompagnato	
fugue	recitativo secco	

CHAPTER 6

FRIDAY, SEPTEMBER 18, 1739, LEIPZIG:

Johann Sebastian Bach at Zimmermann's Coffeehouse

🔊 CORE REPERTOIRE

- **LG 21** Prelude and Fugue in C Minor, BWV 847
- **LG 22** Suite in D Major, BWV 1068, Overture
- **LG 23** Concerto in F Major for Harpsichord, Two Recorders, and Strings, BWV 1057, I

🎙 AUTHOR VIDEOS

- Bach's C Minor Fugue: subject and countersubject
- Bach's C Minor Fugue: episode and sequence

Introduction

> *"Musicum Collegium is a gathering of certain musical connoisseurs who, for the benefit of their own exercise in both vocal and instrumental music and under the guidance of a certain director, get together on particular days and in particular locations and perform musical pieces. Such collegia are to be found in various places. In Leipzig, the Bachian Collegium Musicum is more famous than all others."*
>
> —Johann Heinrich Zedler, 1739

Many people consider Johann Sebastian Bach the greatest musician who ever lived. It is probably a silly game to rate composers as if they were sports teams or refrigerators, but in the Western tradition there is hardly any doubt that Bach, Beethoven, and Mozart stand in the very top rank as composers whose music combines inspiration with skill, moves us by its beauty, and awes us with the intricacy of its construction.

What affects people about Bach's music is his unique way of balancing technical mastery with expressive sounds; a command of form that allows him to write long, involved pieces in which we always know where we are; and an ability to spin out contrapuntal melodies enmeshed in a texture of harmony and color that can be richer than any other musical fabric. In fact, some of his compositions seem almost beyond human conceiving.

But in Leipzig in 1739, Bach was not known as the world's greatest musician. He was not even the most famous composer in Germany. Georg Philipp Telemann (1681–1767), Handel, and a number of others enjoyed reputations larger than his. Bach was simply the local cantor, that is, the music director of Leipzig's four main churches, and he had been working hard at that demanding job for sixteen years.

Like many church musicians, then and now, Bach had another job on the side: he organized a concert series in Gottfried Zimmermann's coffeehouse (see Figures 6.1 and 6.3), a favorite gathering place for Leipzig's prosperous merchants and intellectuals. The weekly programs not only featured secular vocal and instrumental music by Bach and his contemporaries, but also allowed him to show off his virtuosity on the keyboard. We plan to attend one of those concerts, but first let's take a look at the fifty-four-year-old composer and the city with which he was most closely associated.

Bach's mastery

FIG. 6.1 Activities at the Leipzig Kuchengarten, in Gaststätte, south of Leipzig, drawn in 1746. This was the summer home of Zimmermann's coffeehouse, the site of Bach's Collegium concerts.

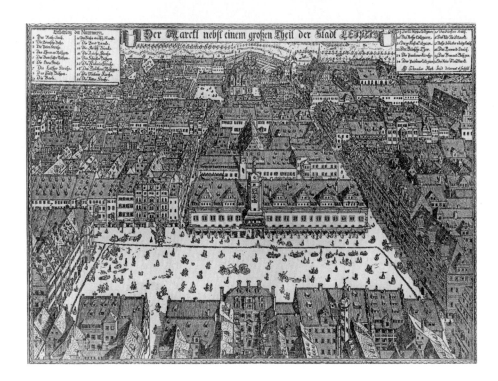

FIG. 6.2 The market square in Leipzig, 1712. Copperplate engraving by Johann Georg Schreiber.

The Setting

JOHANN SEBASTIAN BACH IN LEIPZIG

Johann Sebastian Bach was much admired by colleagues and students alike, but, to repeat, he was not the household name he is today. He was a musician of standing in a sizable middle-European city. With its 30,000 inhabitants, Leipzig was an important town (see Figure 6.2), but it was not a cultural center like Paris or Rome, nor was it the capital of a great prince capable of providing limitless resources and leisure to the musicians who worked for him. Bach was a municipal employee who served at the pleasure of city officials. His middling salary was adequate to support his large family but little more; only the extra income he earned from giving music lessons and other activities enabled him to publish some of his music at his own expense.

Bach came from a long line of court, town, and church musicians, more than seventy in all, stretching back to the late sixteenth century. (See biography, p. 149.) In fact, the Bach family was a musical dynasty, one of the greatest in history. Johann Sebastian's great-grandfather was a baker by trade who enjoyed playing the cittern (a plucked instrument resembling a lute: see p. 72); his musical seed bore much fruit in later generations.

Before coming to Leipzig, Bach had served as capellmeister (music director) to the prince of Anhalt-Cöthen, an enlightened patron who employed musicians of the highest caliber in his house band. "There I had a gracious Prince," he wrote to a friend, "who both loved and knew music, and in his service I intended to spend the rest of my life." In Cöthen Bach put the finishing touches on some of his most beloved works, including the first part of *The Well-Tempered Clavier* and the six *Brandenburg* Concertos. But when the Prince reduced the size of his musical establishment (his new wife did not share his enthusiasm for music), Bach seems to have started looking for another job—which is how he happened to move to Leipzig in 1723.

FIG. 6.3 The exterior of Zimmermann's coffeehouse, the building on the right, ca. 1750. Detail of a copperplate engraving by Johann Georg Schreiber.

Despite his impressive qualifications, Bach was not the Leipzig Town Council's first choice to replace the highly esteemed Johann Kuhnau as cantor of St. Thomas's Church (see Figure 6.4). The position had already been offered to the more famous Telemann, who declined, and to Johann Christoph Graupner, who failed to obtain a release from his employer. One thing that seems to have tipped the scales in Bach's favor was his willingness to put in long hours in the classroom: in addition to supplying music for Leipzig's four principal churches, the cantor served on the faculty of the city-run St. Thomas School (see Figure 6.4). The fifty-five resident St. Thomas boys were expected to sing at church services, and instructing them in music took up a lot of Bach's time. He taught no fewer than seven classes, as well as giving private lessons in instrumental and vocal music. He also offered a general music class, for the entire student body, which met four days a week.

Bach's apartment in the school building, next door to St. Thomas's Church, was a beehive of activity, said one of his sons (see C.P.E. Bach Describes His Father's Reputation, right). People were constantly coming and going—not only the composer's beloved second wife, Anna Magdalena (who was an accomplished singer herself), and his numerous offspring, but also pupils, school and ecclesiastical officials, visiting dignitaries, and, not least, copyists diligently writing out parts for performance in church or by the ensemble of university musicians that Bach directed.

> ## C.P.E. Bach Describes His Father's Reputation
>
> No master of music was apt to pass through this place without making my father's acquaintance and letting himself be heard by him. The greatness that was my father's in composition, in organ and in clavier playing, was far too well known for a musician of reputation to let the opportunity slip of making the closer acquaintance of this great man if it was at all possible.

JOHANN SEBASTIAN BACH (1685–1750)

Johann Sebastian Bach, revered as a composer, teacher, performer, and master of counterpoint, was the descendant, husband, and father of musicians. He assimilated and summarized the major musical styles of his time, even though his whole life was lived in a small area of Germany.

The youngest of eight children (and the father of many), Bach learned music as part of his family heritage. At age eighteen he was appointed church organist in Arnstadt, and his professional career developed in three stages: organist (two positions, Arnstadt and Mühlhausen), director of chamber music (two positions, Weimar and Cöthen, 1708–23), and director of church music (Leipzig, 1723–45). Bach was known in his time as a virtuoso performer on harpsichord and organ; as a composer of keyboard music; and, to those who lived in Leipzig or who had the privilege of hearing his music at court, as the creator of grand secular and sacred music. He was also a trusted teacher: of his own musical children, of the students in the Leipzig choir school, and of his private students; much of his keyboard music is designed to help students become better players and composers.

Bach seemed to think in counterpoint. Almost all of his music is conceived as a harmony of simultaneous voices, and from his solo music for violin and cello to the grandest of his **cantatas** and Passions, there is a highly controlled sense of structure and counterpoint. This is perhaps what gives him the reputation as a cerebral musician, but it takes only a little experience with the breadth of his music to hear the expressive depths of his creations.

Among his most enduring compositions are some that will be sampled in this chapter: *The Well-Tempered Clavier* for keyboard and the *Brandenburg* Concertos for orchestra. But there is a wealth of other materials—organ music (including the Toccata and Fugue in D minor), church cantatas (over two hundred), his last masterwork, *The Art of Fugue,* and much more. To hear the extremes of his range, listen to an excerpt from a suite for solo cello, and another from perhaps his grandest creation, the Mass in B Minor.

ⓢ Bach: Cello Suite No. 1, I
ⓢ Bach: Sanctus, B Minor Mass

MAJOR WORKS: Over 200 sacred vocal works, including *St Matthew Passion, St. John Passion*, and 30 secular cantatas; orchestral music, including 4 suites and 6 *Brandenburg* Concertos; and many organ and keyboard works, including *The Well-Tempered Clavier* and *The Art of Fugue.*

FIG. 6.4 St. Thomas's Church and choir school, where Bach lived and worked from 1723 until he died in 1750. Copperplate engraving (1723) by Johann Gottfried Kruegner.

The Collegium Musicum was only one of many extra activities—playing for weddings and funerals, giving lessons and concerts, maintaining organs and harpsichords, serving as an expert consultant on organ design, and so on—that kept Bach in a state of perpetual motion. Even with four student assistants to shoulder some of the burden, he must have found the organization of lessons and classes at St. Thomas's, not to mention preparations for weekly church services and Collegium concerts, extremely taxing.

On top of all this, Bach was responsible for providing a substantial piece of sacred music for use in church almost every Sunday of the year. Bach's church cantatas are among the marvels of Western music. Indeed, it seems almost impossible that schoolboys could have done justice to such richly inventive and formidably complex works. Bach might have been expected to write less demanding music, given that he sometimes had only a week to compose, copy, and rehearse each cantata. But he was clearly committed to providing the best music he was capable of, regardless of practicality. Bach had very high standards; his music lessons and rehearsals must have been as frightening as they were inspiring.

The convivial "cavaliers and ladies" who frequented Zimmermann's coffeehouse were hardly in the mood for religious instruction. They came to be fed and entertained, and, luckily for them, Bach was happy to accommodate their tastes. Not only did he write music for sundry vocal and instrumental combinations in most of the popular forms, genres, and styles of the day, he was also a better-than-average violinist and violist and had a pleasant singing voice. Above all, he was celebrated far and wide as a keyboard player, especially on the organ. By all accounts he was a brilliant improviser, capable of extemporizing variations on a single theme for two hours or more without a break. And his technique was the envy of all his contemporaries (see Bach's Keyboard Playing, p. 151).

Today Bach's compositions are the foundation of many keyboard player's repertoire. He wrote a prodigious amount of music for organ and harpsichord, including such well-known collections as *The Little Organ Book*, *The Well-Tempered Clavier*, the *Goldberg Variations*, the Partitas, the *French* and *English Suites*, and the two- and three-part Inventions and Sinfonias. These works were designed partly for pleasure, partly to display Bach's skills as a composer and performer, and partly for pedagogical purposes.

Teaching was a major part of Bach's job in Leipzig, an obligation that he could not have avoided even if he had wanted to. In fact, he had a strong desire to pass on his skills and knowledge to his children, several of whom became notable musicians in their own right (see Figures 6.5 and 6.6); Bach boasted that he could put together an entire concert of vocal and instrumental music without looking outside his own family. The basic lessons that Bach hoped to impart, at least to his keyboard students, are expressed on the handwritten title page to the Inventions and Sinfonias:

> wherein the lovers of the clavier, and especially those desirous of learning, are shown a clear way not alone (1) to learn to play clearly in two voices but also, after further progress, (2) to deal correctly and well with three *obbligato* [non-optional] parts; furthermore, at the same time not alone to have good *inventiones* [ideas] but to develop

the same well and, above all, to arrive at a singing style in playing and at the same time to acquire a strong foretaste of composition.

In a manner of speaking, Bach summed up his own accomplishment in the words "not alone to have good *inventiones* but to develop the same well." We will see that he excelled at doing just that—figuring out absolutely everything you can do with a musical idea.

Bach wrote an eclectic mix of music, ranging from the suites for unaccompanied violin and cello to works for larger ensembles, such as the four orchestral suites, the six *Brandenburg* Concertos, and concertos for various instruments with orchestra. But because of the nature of his job, much of Bach's music from his Leipzig years is church music. There are two-hundred-odd surviving cantatas and several other major sacred works for voices and orchestra, including the two great **Passions** (narrations of the suffering and death of Jesus) according to St. John and St. Matthew, to say nothing of the monumental Mass in B Minor. And the range and brilliance of his organ music has never been surpassed.

In the last chapter we saw how Handel combined recitatives, arias, and choruses to make a great work on a religious subject, the oratorio *Messiah*. This chapter might well have been devoted to Bach's similar combinations, to his work as a musical theologian (for he was a deeply religious man), and indeed, the grand sounds of Bach's sacred music repay any amount of listening.

Because we have already explored the genre of oratorio, however, it seems a good idea to take the opportunity to focus on another aspect of Bach's creative personality: his achievement as a performer and composer of popular instrumental music.

Baroque music was full of well-understood types, some of which we have already encountered, including the fugue, recitative, aria, and chorus. So complete was Bach's mastery of each of these forms and genres that he can be said to have summarized and defined them once and for all. He was, in a way, the last great Baroque composer, a multifaceted genius who embodied the spirit of an entire age.

One thing that Bach did not do, mostly because of the circumstances of his life and the opportunities that came his way, was work in an opera house. For many of his contemporaries, opera was the highest goal of music and musicians, a blend of music and drama cast in the form of recitatives and arias that thrilled audiences with their virtuosity and expressive effects. While Handel was making a splendid (and lucrative) career in London's opera houses, Bach was content to stay in Germany and work mainly in places where opera was not central to musical life.

LEIPZIG AND THE COLLEGIUM MUSICUM

Leipzig's ruler, the elector of Saxony, resided in splendor in the nearby city of Dresden, and Bach more than once applied for a position at his court. But Leipzig, too, had much to recommend it. A big, busy, prosperous town, it was enclosed by a massive wall, with fortified bastions and seven gates, and by moats. The four main gates, which gave their names to the city's four residential quarters, were equipped with drawbridges, guard towers, and tollbooths. A second line of gates ringed the suburbs, serving both for defense and for collecting excise taxes on merchandise coming into and out of the city.

Leipzig was known for its excellent system of pipes and aqueducts, which distributed water from the river Pleisse to houses throughout the city. According to a 1725 description, "The water systems of this city have the healthiest sources of the freshest

Bach's Keyboard Playing

B ach is said to have played with so easy and small a motion of the fingers that it was hardly perceptible. Only the first joints of the fingers were in motion; the hand retained even in the most difficult passages its rounded form; the fingers rose very little from the keys, hardly more than in a trill, and when one was employed, the other remained quietly in its position. Still less did the other parts of his body take any share in his play, as happens with many whose hand is not light enough.

FIG. 6.5 Johann Sebastian Bach's son Carl Philipp Emanuel Bach (1714–1788), eminent composer and author.

FIG. 6.6 Another of Bach's son's, Wilhelm Friedemann Bach (1710–1784), also a composer. Like his father, Wilhelm was known for his improvisatory skills.

FIG. 6.7 A view of the market square in Leipzig during one of the three annual trade fairs. Engraving, ca. 1850, after a drawing by Ludwig Rohbock.

FIG. 6.8 An impromptu outdoor concert; some have imagined that this might be Bach with his Collegium Musicum.

water, and there is hardly any little street to be found without several fountains, which have all been repaired in recent years." One of the newest fountains adorned the square in front of St. Thomas's Church, near where Bach and his family lived. It portrayed a lion (the symbol of Leipzig) holding the city's shield in its right forepaw, while jets of water spewed from the left.

The wealth of the city came from the thrice-yearly trade fairs for which Leipzig is still famous (see Figure 6.7). Thousands of people thronged the streets and squares at New Year's, Easter, and St. Michael's Day (September 29), when merchants from all over the world came to display their wares. The huge influx of visitors enriched the city's tradesmen, merchants, innkeepers, and coffeehouses, and created a brisk demand for concerts and other entertainments.

Leipzig's prosperity was most impressively visible in its grand public buildings and gardens, and in the splendor of its private homes. In the sixteenth-century Town Hall hung portraits of all the noble rulers of the House of Saxony and their ladies; from its balcony the town pipers and fiddlers held forth most mornings at 10 a.m. The municipal library, founded in 1677, housed not only books and manuscripts but a noteworthy collection of statuary and art. Leipzig's church steeples were rivaled in height by the palatial houses of four or five stories, with their slate roofs and multicolored, carved-stone facades.

The presence of Germany's most prestigious university, dating from 1409, greatly enhanced Leipzig's cultural and intellectual life. Bach himself was no stranger to academia: both his immediate superior, the rector of the St. Thomas School, and the vice rector held professorships at the University of Leipzig. Bach depended on university students to fill in for absent choirboys in church on Sundays. Moreover, the cantor of St. Thomas's automatically held a joint appointment as director of music for the university, which meant that Bach had the privilege—as well as the duty—of providing music for four religious services that marked the traditional academic calendar.

Bach's industry and energy were almost superhuman. So busy was he composing church music, and training musicians to perform it on Sundays and feast days year in and year out, that it would seem he had little time for anything else. And yet he was glad of the chance to present a regular series of public concerts during his precious free weekday hours. Perhaps Bach wanted an outlet for his nonreligious music; perhaps he wanted to display his instrumental virtuosity; perhaps he wanted to provide a showcase for other performers; maybe he even hoped to earn a little extra money. At any rate, six years after moving to Leipzig he became the director of an ensemble of university students who called themselves a **Collegium Musicum**, a musical college (see Figure 6.8).

Two such groups had been active in Leipzig for many years. One was run by a church organist named Johann Gottlieb Görner and performed regularly at Enoch Richter's coffeehouse. The other, and more distinguished, Collegium had been founded by Telemann in 1701. By the time Bach took over, in 1729, the ensemble had been closely associated for half a dozen years with Herr Zimmermann's well-appointed coffeehouse on the fashionable Catharinenstrasse, just off Leipzig's main marketplace. The "Bach Collegium" performed in a spacious music room that could accommodate an orchestra and upwards of 150 listeners. Concerts took place on Friday evenings in the winter, with additional performances on Tuesday evenings during the three weeks of each of the annual fairs. On Wednesday afternoons in the summer, the performers moved to Zimmermann's suburban coffee garden outside the city's eastern gate.

Public concert series of this sort were rare in the early eighteenth century (see Public Concert Series, right), and music-hungry Leipzigers flocked to hear Bach's and Görner's Collegia. An announcement published in 1736 described both groups as "flourishing," adding that

> The participants in these musical concerts are chiefly students here, and there are always good musicians among them, so that sometimes they become, as is known, famous virtuosos. Any musician is permitted to make himself publicly heard at these musical concerts, and most often, too, there are such listeners as know how to judge the qualities of an able musician.

The Bach Collegium was not, then, a bunch of amateurs sight-reading their way through easy music in the presence of casual listeners who were oblivious to their mistakes. These were serious concerts, directed by one of the most serious musicians in the world, presented to a serious and discerning audience. Solo music, orchestral music, music for voices and orchestra—all sorts of music, almost all of it contemporary, was in the repertoire of Bach's Collegium. Zimmermann's, one imagines, offered an agreeable change from the liturgical music at St. Thomas's.

That such highbrow musical fare was on the menu at an eatery was not as surprising as it sounds. Zimmermann's had little in common with the typical modern American coffee shop; a jazz club would be a closer approximation. The importance of coffeehouses for city dwellers in Bach's day is hard to exaggerate. Coffee was a fairly recent import from the East, and by the late 1600s a coffee craze was sweeping across Europe and America (see Figures 6.9 and 6.10). Various addictive and stimulating qualities were attributed to the inky brew, which made it all the more appealing. (Bach's "Coffee Cantata" is about a headstrong girl who wants nothing but coffee, while her father wants her to take a husband.)

According to one contemporary report, at Beyer's coffeehouse in Leipzig's Brühl Street (across from the slightly higher-priced Richter's, where the Görner Collegium played), customers could order "a serving of chocolate, cooked in water (6 groschen) or in milk (5 groschen), coffee, tea, a bottle of Merseburg or Mannheim beer, a glass of Orsade [barley water] and lemonade, a serving of Bavaroise or warm beer served in a cup." (A game of billiards cost 6 pfennigs during the day, 1 groschen at night, and the evening menu featured bread and butter with hot roast meat or sausage.)

Whether modest establishments like Beyer's or imposing townhouses like Zimmermann's, coffeehouses were places where all sorts of people could gather to

Public Concert Series

Until the late 1600s, concerts were almost exclusively private or semiprivate affairs, given under the auspices of the aristocracy or the church. But in 1673, the English violinist John Banister had the novel idea of opening his house in London to paying customers, announcing that "this present Monday, will be musick performed by excellent Masters, beginning at four o'clock in the afternoon and every afternoon for the future precisely at the same hour." Other musical entrepreneurs followed suit, and public subscription concerts, held in venues ranging from salons and concert halls to taverns and pleasure gardens, soon became a popular feature of British musical life.

With the rise of an affluent middle class in other European countries, the custom spread in the early eighteenth century to Italy, France, and Germany. By 1750, Leipzig, Frankfurt, and Hamburg all boasted self-sustaining concert series that were not dependent on princely patronage. Admission was open to anyone who could afford the price of a ticket, which in the case of Bach's Collegium was three groschen—the same as two tickets to the theater or the cost of knitting one shirt.

LEFT, FIG. 6.9 A coffee vendor, from a German engraving , ca. 1730.

RIGHT, FIG. 6.10 Advertisement for a London coffeehouse, ca. 1700. The craze for coffee was international.

gossip and read newspapers, and where business could be conducted in a relaxed and congenial atmosphere. The better to attract customers (and whet their appetites), proprietors generally offered some kind of entertainment, which at Zimmermann's meant Bach's Collegium Musicum.

The Performance

Bach Collegium The members of the Bach Collegium were mostly students at the University of Leipzig, but it seems that some of Bach's private pupils, as well as his sons, occasionally took part in the concerts at Zimmermann's. Professional town musicians and members of the academic community at large also seem to have joined in. All told, the pool of musicians available to Bach came to well above fifty, not counting the special guest artists who were invited to perform solos from time to time.

As with his church choir, Bach supervised every detail of the weekly Collegium programs, from planning to execution. Known for his quick temper and rough-and-ready sense of humor, he was adept at running rehearsals and enforcing discipline. As noted in his obituary, "In conducting he was very accurate, and of the tempo, which he generally took very lively, he was uncommonly sure." Rehearsal time was precious, just as it is in orchestras today, and Bach placed a premium on efficiency. Carl Philipp Emanuel Bach testified that his father knew how to get the best from his players:

> The placing of an orchestra he understood perfectly. He made good use of any space. He grasped at first glance any peculiarity of a room. . . . He heard the slightest wrong note even in the largest combinations. As the greatest expert and judge of harmony, he liked best to play the viola, with appropriate loudness and softness. In his youth, and until the approach of old age, he played the violin cleanly and penetratingly, and this kept the orchestra in better order than he could have done with the harpsichord.

Bach served as the Collegium's full-time director for a total of about ten years, during which time he directed more than five hundred concerts, each one lasting some two hours. Unfortunately, no printed programs—or, indeed, any other evidence—survive to give us a clear idea of what the concerts were like. What we do have is some of the music that Bach prepared for performance in Leipzig, an assortment of vocal and instrumental works designed to cater to current tastes: Italian cantatas and opera arias, German orchestral and chamber music, and various pieces that Bach either composed for the coffee concerts or arranged from music previously written for other purposes. Although church music was obviously unsuitable for a coffeehouse, Bach wrote a number of secular, or "moral," cantatas for the Collegium, including the aforementioned "Coffee Cantata" on the subject of addiction—an appropriate theme for Zimmermann's coffee-drinking and tobacco-smoking clientele.

The program proposed here is entirely imaginary. The date of September 18, 1739, is one on which an actual Collegium concert took place, but we have no way of knowing what the audience at Zimmermann's heard on that or any other night. All three pieces on our program are ones that Bach performed in Leipzig (even though some originated at an earlier date), and all three are perennial audience favorites: *The program*

1. Prelude and Fugue in C Minor for harpsichord, from *The Well-Tempered Clavier*, BWV 847*

2. Suite for Orchestra in D Major, BWV 1068

3. Concerto in F Major for Harpsichord, Two Recorders, and Strings, BWV 1057, arranged from the fourth *Brandenburg* Concerto

The C Minor Prelude and Fugue are part of Bach's famous collection of preludes and fugues in all the major and minor keys, titled *The Well-Tempered Clavier*. The pieces can be played on any keyboard instrument (*clavier* is the generic term for keyboard), but since Bach did not include a pedal part, as he usually did for his organ music, we can assume that the preludes and fugues were intended for harpsichord or **clavichord**, or possibly for the newfangled **fortepiano**, a precursor of today's piano (see Figures 6.11, 6.12 and 6.13). **The Well-Tempered Clavier**

The orchestral suite is entertainment music, pure and simple—grand and extroverted and full of lively dance rhythms. It was originally composed for the court musicians of Cöthen, an elite professional ensemble, and we can easily imagine it diverting the aristocratic guests at one of the prince's elegant musical soirées.

The harpsichord concerto is a version of a concerto for violin with two recorders that Bach had written some years earlier and presented with five others to the margrave of Brandenburg—hence their collective name, the *Brandenburg* Concertos. The six concertos feature extravagant virtuosity and richly varied orchestrations. When Bach revived this one for the Collegium, he transformed the solo violin part into a dazzling harpsichord solo, undoubtedly for himself to play.

Despite his limited geographical orbit—he spent his entire life within one small area of Germany—Bach was a cosmopolitan composer who moved with ease from a "German" prelude and fugue to a "French" suite to an "Italian" concerto. Each of these national types was well known in the eighteenth century, and Bach's listeners would have recognized them instantly. From the first measures of the fugue, with its single strand of melody, they would look forward to a brilliant outpouring of counterpoint; the opening of the suite, with its slow, stately, long-short rhythm, was a sure sign that a fast imitative section would follow; and from the very title of the concerto, the audience would know to expect a piece in three contrasting movements, fast-slow-fast, that pitted the solo harpsichord against a full orchestra.

---

* The BWV (Bach Werke Verzeichnis) numbers refer to the catalogue of Bach's works by Wolfgang Schmieder. Most writers about Bach, and most printed programs and reviews, use these numbers to avoid confusion.

LEFT, FIG. 6.11 A two-manual harpsichord. The strings are plucked by quills attached to the ends of the key-levers; no dynamic control is possible, except by using and combining the different sets of strings, which vary the tone quality.

TOP, FIG. 6.12 A clavichord. The strings are struck by tangents, light metal bars that touch the string, determine the pitch of the note, and remain in contact with the string while the note is sounding. This allows the player to vibrate the note and to vary the dynamics within the very quiet range of this instrument.

BOTTOM, FIG. 6.13 A fortepiano. This instrument, which was quite new in Bach's time, strikes the strings with a hammer, which allows the player to vary the dynamics from loud to soft (this is where the instrument gets its name). It is the early version of the modern piano. This particular image is a Stein fortepiano from 1790.

Listening to the Music

At a few minutes before 8 p.m., the smartly dressed audience, well plied with food and drink and abuzz with anticipation, take their seats in Zimmermann's concert room. A variety of music is on the program, ranging from harpsichord solos to music for full orchestra; some rearrangement of chairs and music stands will be required in the course of the evening, and perhaps a little retuning of the harpsichord. (Harpsichords tend to go out of tune if the temperature rises, as often happens in a crowded room. Fortunately, Bach is an expert tuner.) The concert room is well equipped; Zimmermann's even has its own set of musical instruments that some of the students in the orchestra have borrowed for the evening. Bach has previously had one of his own harpsichords delivered here.

PRELUDE AND FUGUE IN C MINOR, BWV 847 LG 21

The Well-Tempered Clavier has long been viewed as a Mount Everest, the highest pinnacle of the keyboard player's art. Indeed, it was Beethoven's dazzling execution of these four dozen **preludes and fugues** on the piano that first brought him fame in Vienna a generation after Bach's death. The composer's own performance on the harpsichord must have been even more impressive. According to his first biographer, Johann Nikolaus Forkel, Bach had "acquired such a high degree of facility and, we may almost say, unlimited power over his instrument in all the keys that difficulties almost ceased to exist for him."

The pairing of a prelude and fugue in the same key was something of a specialty for German composers, although there are many examples from other countries as well. As a rule, a prelude bears no thematic relationship to its corresponding fugue. In fact, the prelude can take almost any form, whereas the fugue is always a contrapuntal piece of the kind we are about to hear.

Prelude   In the C Minor Prelude, both hands are extremely busy executing a repeating pattern—two identical units of eight notes each—that sounds like a finger exercise. Every sixteen notes—that is, every measure—the pattern shifts slightly, a shift that corresponds with a change in harmony.

As soon as our ears get used to the mesmerizing regularity of the surface patterns, we start to hear the much slower regularity of the shifting harmony. The music gradually works its way down the keyboard until it seems to hit bottom (the bass note remains fixed for four sixteen-note patterns). Then, after twenty-four chords, the repeating pattern finally gives way to a series of broken chords in the same relentless sixteen-note rhythm, followed by a wonderfully rhapsodic, improvised-sounding ending that seems to evaporate into thin air (see LG 21).

Fugue   After a short, pregnant pause, the C Minor Fugue begins, as all fugues do, with a single voice introducing the main theme, or subject (see Chapter 5, p. 140, for the initial discussion of a fugue). The audience at Zimmermann's perks up: they know what to expect in a general way, but they also know that Bach is full of surprises. The fugue cannot be predicted from the prelude, except that it is sure to make a pleasing contrast and be in the same key. The composer's fingers tap out the catchy melody, based on a five-note motive (short-short-long-long-long), and the fugue is under way. (See LG 21, p. 158.)

Writing fugues was to Bach what singing is to birds—it was second nature. Fugues, and the techniques that produce them, pop up everywhere in his work—most notably the forty-eight fugues of *The Well-Tempered Clavier* and the amazing collection of fugues, all different but all on the same theme, in his *Art of Fugue*. Fugues appear as well in the suite and concerto featured later on in our program. All told, Bach wrote hundreds of fugues, each one unique. The C Minor Fugue is a particularly fine specimen, with a memorable tune and a structure as brilliant as it is sturdy.

The Latin word *fuga* means "fleeing" or "chase," and the fugue is aptly named in that one voice chases another. (The individual lines in a fugue are called voices, even if the piece is instrumental, because the composer sees to it that all the lines remain distinct.) In order to differentiate the voices, the composer gives them independent parts. (If all the lines moved up and down together, it would sound like one voice, not several.) The combination of individual, independent voices is called **counterpoint** (from putting one note against another, *punctus contra punctum* in Latin), and the resulting musical texture is called **polyphony**. We know polyphony well from the music of William Byrd, and from some music of Handel.

A fugue, then, can be defined as a polyphonic (many-voiced) composition based on a single theme or **subject**. Each voice enters in turn with a statement of the subject, after which appearances of the theme in one voice or another alternate with passages (called **episodes**) in which the complete subject is not present.

This is the standard textbook definition of a fugue, but it doesn't begin to do justice to the marvelous variety of formal schemes that are possible in this kind of music. Nor does it reflect the importance of harmony in contrapuntal writing. Polyphony is the easiest thing in the world to produce, unless you want it to be harmonious. That's where the challenge comes—in making several independent melodies add up to a sound that produces pleasing harmonies.

Bach's C Minor Fugue: subject and countersubject

Counterpoint and polyphony

Bach's C Minor Fugue: episode and sequence

LISTENING GUIDE 21

Bach Prelude and Fugue in C Minor, BWV 847   3:05

DATE: 1722–23
GENRE: Prelude and Fugue (3 voices)

LISTEN FOR

IN PRELUDE

MELODY: Highly disjunct sequence of notes
RHYTHM: Perfectly regular rhythm in opening section
TEXTURE: Simple pattern, changing every 16 notes

IN FUGUE

MELODY: Two countersubjects, made of 16th notes (1st countersubject) and 8th notes (2nd countersubject)
RHYTHM: Rhythmic motive used repeatedly to make fugue subject
TEXTURE: Sequences using motives from subject and countersubject

TIME	FORM	DESCRIPTION
	PRELUDE	
0:00	Theme with shifting harmonies	Repeated pattern in steady 16th-note rhythm, like a finger exercise:
0:44	Transition	Broken chords in same rhythm.
0:52	Ending section	Freely rhapsodic, like improvisation.
	FUGUE	
1:25	First entrance of subject	**Subject** melody:
		Catchy tune in repeated rhythmic pattern (short-short-long-long-long).
1:31	Second entrance of subject; first countersubject	**Countersubject** melody (green):
		Second voice performs subject in combination with new melody in first voice, beginning with downward scale.
1:37	Episode 1 (passage in which subject is incomplete)	Upper voice plays beginning of subject three times in sequence, each time a step higher. Lower voice accompanies with rising scale (inverted countersubject), also a step higher each time.
1:42	Third entrance of subject; second countersubject	Bass voice takes up subject, combined with first countersubject in top voice and new music (second **countersubject**, blue) in middle voice:

		(Second countersubject is difficult to hear when other two voices are playing subject and first countersubject.)
1:48	Episode 2	Beginning of subject imitated in two voices, combined with downward scale (inverted countersubject) in bass.
1:53	Subject	Subject in top voice, accompanied by two countersubjects.
1:58	Episode 3	Rising scale in top voice (inverted countersubject), accompanied by figures derived from second countersubject.
2:04	Subject	Subject appears in middle voice, accompanied by two countersubjects.
2:10	Episode 4	Closely related to Episode 1, but with voices reversed.
2:18	Subject	Subject in top voice; both countersubjects present.
2:24	Episode 5	Closely related to Episode 2, but longer. Beginning of subject imitated in two voices, combined with downward scale (inverted countersubject) in bass.
2:36	Subject	Subject in bass, both countersubjects present; surprise halt.
2:45	Final cadence; echo of subject	Subject played in soprano as a sort of fade-out of the last bass note.

We have considered fugues in the context of Handel's *Messiah*, where the overture and the chorus "He trusted in God" are both composed as fugues. Fugues were a favorite procedure of Baroque composers, but Bach was the consummate master of fugue (see C.P.E. Bach Describes How His Father Listened to Fugues, right).

A related aspect of fugues (which is also typical of Renaissance motets and much other music) is the technique called **imitation**—the process of having one voice sing or play the music that another voice has just finished. It is a good way of letting us hear individual voices, because the more familiar we are with the theme that is being imitated, the more easily we can pick it out of an increasingly complicated texture.

Imitation

In a fugue, each entrance of the subject is a kind of imitation. So once you have heard the subject, you already know what the second voice will do: it will enter by repeating the subject at a different tonal level (in this case, five steps higher). The job of a composer is to figure out what the *first* voice should do when the second voice enters. At this point in the C Minor Fugue, Bach has the first voice execute a fast downward scale, followed by a regular pattern of stepwise eighth notes, with one big leap in the middle.

As it turns out, this same music is played *every* time the subject appears. It is always used in another voice to accompany the subject, sometimes below it, sometimes above. We call it a **countersubject**. As you listen to the C Minor Fugue, watch for the telltale descending scale every time you hear the subject. A countersubject has to be composed very carefully, because it needs to sound good both above and below the subject.

Countersubject

After the appearances of the full subject in the two upper voices comes a short passage in which we hear only part of the subject. This little diversion, or episode, provides a bridge to the third appearance of the subject in the bottom voice. This

C.P.E. Bach Describes How His Father Listened to Fugues

When he listened to a rich and many-voiced fugue, he could soon say, after the first entries of the subjects, what contrapuntal devices it would be possible to apply, and which of them the composer by rights ought to apply, and on such occasions, when I was standing next to him, and he had voiced his surmises to me, he would joyfully nudge me when his expectations were fulfilled.

time it is combined with the countersubject in the top voice and music that we haven't heard before—a second countersubject—in the middle voice.

Exposition

By the end of the first eight measures, all the basic musical material of the fugue has been presented. We call this section the **exposition**. Thereafter the piece continues with appearances of the subject in different voices and different keys, alternating with episodes of various kinds.

One of the amazing things about Bach's C Minor Fugue is that essentially every note is derived from one of the three main ideas: subject, countersubject, and second countersubject. There is no flab in this fugue. In places where none of the voices is playing the subject, there are episodes. Those episodes are all cast in the form of sequences, which are made of bits of the themes. This kind of frugality is a hallmark of Bach and is extremely difficult to accomplish.

🔊 LG 22   SUITE IN D MAJOR, BWV 1068

Having begun our concert with a harpsichord solo, played by the composer himself, we continue with a piece that calls on the full resources of Bach's Collegium: a suite for large orchestra made up of strings (first and second violins, violas, cellos, and double basses), winds (two oboes and a bassoon), three trumpets, and kettledrums. The Suite in D Major is music in the grand manner, scored for an orchestra of the same size as that for Handel's *Messiah* (compare openings of Handel's *Messiah* to Bach's Suite in D Major). It is easy to picture Bach leading the performance from the concertmaster's music stand, violin in one hand, bow in the other, as we know he liked to do.

The suite is written in the French style, which explains why Bach uses French titles and tempo marks. It consists of six **movements** (a movement is a self-contained part of a longer work; the term comes from the French word for speed or tempo); the first is an Overture (*ouverture* is the French word for "opening") followed by a slow, lyrical Air and a series of quick dances. All except the Air feature wind instruments, trumpets, oboes, and bassoons, and it is worth pausing to consider how Bach uses them. In his day, as in ours, trumpets typically conveyed a sense of grandeur and royalty. In the Overture, Bach uses the three trumpets (in conjunction with the kettledrums) mostly for emphasis and rhythmic punctuation. Occasionally, though, the trumpeters get to play a real tune—in the first-movement fugue, for instance, where Bach twice gives the subject to the first trumpet, and also in the two Gavottes and the final Gigue (see The Baroque Trumpet, left).

Ⓢ Handel: *Acis and Galatea*, Sinfonia (baroque oboe)

The two oboes, on the other hand, almost never have music of their own. There are two places in the fast section of the Overture where they play an accompaniment in long notes, but everywhere else they "double"—that is, play along with—the first or second violins. (This is what oboes do most of the time in Baroque orchestral music.) Where Bach's texture is polyphonic, as in the fugue, the two oboes reinforce the first and second violins equally; elsewhere, as in the introduction of the Overture and most of the dances, they double only the first violins, emphasizing the principal melodic line. The Baroque oboe has a slightly more penetrating sound than its modern counterpart, as you can hear in this passage from Handel's *Acis and Galatea*. Ⓢ

The Baroque Trumpet

Baroque trumpets consisted of a simple length of brass tubing with a mouthpiece on one end and a flared opening, or bell, at the other. The tubing was coiled or bent, to make the instrument easier to hold, but there were no valves or other devices to help the player change pitches. As a result, trumpeters could only produce the notes that occur in the natural **overtone series**, which meant that they were rarely called upon to play melodies or switch from one key to another.

The Baroque trumpet is extremely hard to play: the trumpeter needs astounding control to produce the right notes. In his early years in Leipzig, Bach had at his disposal a superb player named Gottfried Reiche, whom he must have had in mind when preparing the D Major Suite for its first performance in 1731. By 1739, however, Reiche had been dead for five years. (He suffered a stroke the day after he played a particularly difficult part in one of Bach's cantatas.) We can only speculate how his successor, one Ulrich Ruhe, acquitted himself on this occasion. But the trumpet's majestic sound must have made a brilliant effect in Zimmermann's concert room.

Ⓢ Handel: *Messiah*, "The trumpet shall sound"

Bach Suite in D Major, BWV 1068, Overture   10:12

DATE: ca. 1729–31
GENRE: French Overture

LISTEN FOR

RHYTHM: Stately, dotted rhythm of opening section
FORM: Two-part form (slow introduction followed by lively fugue)

SCORING: Rich orchestration, highlighted by oboes and trumpets

TIME	FORM	DESCRIPTION
0:00	Slow introduction	**Dotted figures** and scales predominate. Texture focuses on soprano voice (violins and oboes) and bass line (cellos, double basses, bassoon, and keyboard).
1:23	Slow introduction, repeated	
	FUGUE	
	A—Opening section	
2:42	Exposition	Texture changes to 4-voice polyphony. Fugue subject introduced in each of the string parts in turn, with oboes doubling first and second violins:
2:59	Subject in violins, add trumpets	First violins play subject, then extend it and play it again, this time with trumpets.
3:10	Subject in bass, add trumpets	Subject in bass voice leads to cadence, bringing first section of fugue to an end.
	B—Episode plus subjects	
3:19	Episode 1	First violins have long solo in 16th notes, with string accompaniment.
3:35	Subject in strings, add winds	While violins continue rapid motion, subject appears in second violins; violas; second violins again; violas again; a brief extension of first-violin material.
3:51	**C**—Subject in bass, other instruments	Subject stated by basses (twice), first violins (twice), and basses again. Violins and oboes weave polyphonic lines above, with trumpets providing harmonic background.
	B—Episode plus subjects	
4:17	Episode 2	Similar to Episode 1: first violins have long solo in 16th notes, with string accompaniment. Oboes and trumpets gradually add their voices.
4:38		Subject reappears in second violin and viola (add oboes).
4:54	**A**—Opening of fugue returns	
5:30	Return of opening tempo and rhythm	Stately, dotted rhythms return in an abbreviated variant of the introduction. The Overture seems about to reach its end, but instead . . .
6:22	Repetition of fugue	Whole fugue repeats. The exposition, however, does not begin with a single voice. Instead, while first violins restate the subject, the accompanying voices continue playing rather than leaving subject unaccompanied as in the beginning.
9:10	Return of opening tempo and rhythm	After another hearing of "second introduction," this gigantic movement comes to rest on a sonorous D-major chord.

ⓈBach: Suite in D Major, Air

The second movement of the Suite, a hauntingly beautiful Air (the French word for a song or opera aria) scored for strings alone, has one of Bach's most famous tunes. (The tune is sometimes called "Air on the G String," from a much later arrangement in which the melody is played on the violin's lowest string, which is tuned to a G.) In one version of the piece, Bach assigned the tune to a single violin, but even when it is performed by several players, the melody has the limpid beauty of a solo aria gliding lyrically over a rhythmically steady bass. Unusual for Bach, the Air has almost no internal repetition. Apart from a brief sequential passage in each of the two sections, the melody is always new, inspired, and passionate. Note, too, how Bach invests the inner voices with contrapuntal interest, allowing the second violins and violas to speak up now and then from within the polyphonic texture.

The four dances that round out the Suite—a pair of Gavottes, a Bourrée, and a Gigue—are relatively uncomplicated. Like almost all Baroque dances, they are in two parts, each of which Bach marks to be repeated, producing an **AABB** form. (In Bach's orchestral suites the repeats are just that—literal repetitions—but it was customary for smaller ensembles to vary the repeats of dance movements with ornaments.) The two Gavottes are played in sequence, the first repeated after the second, producing an overall shape of **AABB CCDD AABB**.

ⓈBach: Suite in D Major, Gavotte

ⓈBach: Suite in D Major, Bourrée
ⓈBach: Suite in D Major, Gigue

Bach's listeners knew a **gavotte** when they heard one—it is a dance with four-beat rhythm, always beginning with two upbeats followed by a strong downbeat. The other two dances are also characterized by distinctive rhythms and clear phrases. A **bourrée** is always in a quick four-beat meter, with a single upbeat; and a **gigue** features quick triple rhythm. Audiences in the eighteenth century took this kind of stylistic shorthand for granted; it pleased them to be able to recognize what kind of dance they were listening to in the first few seconds.

The Air and dances make for wonderful listening, but the Overture is far and away the meatiest part of the Suite. Indeed, the first movement takes at least as long to perform as the other five put together. It, too, follows a well-known pattern, being a French overture of the type that had been familiar to opera-goers since the mid-seventeenth century. French overtures did indeed originate in France as opening movements of theater pieces, but they were not, by Bach's time, exclusive to opera, French or otherwise. As we saw in the last chapter, for instance, there is a French overture at the beginning of Handel's *Messiah*.

Overture

Bach's Overture begins with a slow opening section, marked by stately dotted rhythms and suspensions, that highlights the rich sonority of the orchestra. The second part is an energetic fugue—an orchestral one, this time. Bach has to decide how many voices to compose (there are four, most of the time) and which instruments to assign to which voice. Unlike the keyboard fugue, where every voice has the same basic timbre, the orchestral fugue allows the composer to differentiate the parts by means of instrumental tone color. In other words, Bach's scoring, or **orchestration**, is another way of helping us pick out the individual contrapuntal voices.

Orchestration

In structural terms, the Overture can be described as an introduction followed by a fugue and a brief return to the stately opening. The entire fugue and the closing slow music are repeated, so that the overall form is:

Opening slow music

Fugue

Closing slow music

Fugue

Closing slow music

The fugue itself has a similarly clear and symmetrical shape. The opening section (**A**) presents the exposition and additional appearances of the subject. It is followed by section **B**, consisting of the episode plus subjects, and section **C**, with the subject in the bass and other instruments. Then the first two sections are repeated in reverse order. The **ABCBA** pattern of the fugue, in turn, is repeated in the larger scheme of the Overture, as noted above. (See LG 22, p. 161.)

A piece on such a big scale surely made an unforgettable impression at Zimmermann's coffeehouse, where the audience sat close enough to the performers for the music to have its full effect. Listening to the Overture straight through, it is possible hear the melodic and rhythmic patterns that contribute to its sense of symmetry and proportion.

CONCERTO IN F MAJOR, BWV 1057, ARRANGED FROM THE FOURTH *BRANDENBURG* CONCERTO

 LG 23

Transcription

This concerto is a **transcription**, or arrangement, of one Bach had written years earlier in Weimar and included among his six *Brandenburg* Concertos. (Bach was an inveterate arranger of his own works, as well as of those of others.) In Leipzig, he revived it as a virtuoso showpiece for harpsichord, and the intended performer can hardly have been anyone but Bach himself. The original version featured a violin soloist, but it was really a triple concerto, with two "echo recorders" (*flauti d'echo*) sharing the limelight. Arranging it for keyboard involved more than simply transferring the notes and harmonies from one instrument to another; the violin and the harpsichord have very different qualities. Listen to an excerpt from the original and the rearranged versions, and see if you can hear the difference.

Ⓢ Bach: *Brandenburg* Concerto No. 4, I (original, followed by transcription)

Concerto

A **concerto** in Bach's time was a three-movement work featuring a contrast between an orchestra and one or more solo instruments. The first movement, moreover, almost invariably used the ritornello form. Bach had adopted the idea when studying the concertos of the Venetian composer Antonio Vivaldi (1678–1741). Such a movement begins and ends with an orchestral **ritornello** (a musical passage that returns). The middle section is devoted to solo material, with occasional reappearances of all or part of the ritornello in various keys. The ritornello idea was neither new nor unique to Bach—it is used in Monteverdi's *Orfeo*, Handel's *Messiah*, and countless other pieces—but it is nevertheless a basic principle of a lot of Bach's music. The last movement of this concerto also uses ritornello form.

Important to Bach was the idea that the opening ritornello should contain all the essential musical material for the movement. In fact, the ritornello is a carefully wrought composition, almost a concerto in itself. It consists of a series of sections, some of which sound like themes and others like developments. Bach took great pains in composing ritornellos, because in doing so he was working out all the possibilities implicit in the themes. He used the ritornello idea not just for concertos but for choral movements, arias, and many other kinds of music.

In the F Major Concerto, the ritornello of the first movement (the movement has no title or tempo marking) includes a six-bar theme that keeps popping up in different guises, usually with the voices switched. The result is a long stretch of music that falls into clearly defined sections. Between the ritornellos come stupendous solo passages, mostly featuring the harpsichord, but often with the recorders added, and with punctuation from the strings. But even in these solo developmental sections, the music is related to something in the ritornello—the harpsichord takes off on some idea already present, and develops it by elaborate figuration and changing keys. The ritornello sets not only the tempo, but also the emotional stance of the movement—in this case one of lively, quirky energy.

LISTENING GUIDE 23   Ⓢ | DVD

Bach Concerto in F Major for Harpsichord, Two Recorders, and Strings, BWV 1057, Arranged from the Fourth *Brandenburg* Concerto, I   6:36

DATE: Originally composed ca. 1720

GENRE: Concerto

LISTEN FOR

FORM: Opening ritornello recurs throughout movement in various keys and combinations of instruments

TEXTURE: Variety of solo techniques (scales, arpeggios, very rapid notes)

SCORING: Solo instruments: harpsichord and two recorders

TIME	FORM	DESCRIPTION
0:00	Ritornello, section 1 (**AAB**)	First section of ritornello begins with characteristic **arpeggio** figure (**A**):
0:05		Motive **A** repeats with the two recorders switching parts. Starts in F major, moves to dominant (C major), then returns to home key.
0:10		**B** section, beginning with rising **sequence** (each recorder performs scales up and down) and cadential passage with repeated notes in downward patterns.
	Ritornello, section 2 (**AACB**)	
0:20		Section 2 begins with figure **A** played twice, followed by a middle section (**C**) that features recorders in smooth parallel passages.
0:42		Version of the earlier cadence (**B**) follows.
	Ritornello, section 3 (**AAD**)	
0:50		Section 3 begins with two **A**s, followed by new section (**D**) that begins with syncopated rising figure (accompanied by the repeated-note figure from **B** above) and concludes with jerky and arresting final cadence.
1:14	Solo section 1	Mostly harpsichord, with interjections of opening chords and arpeggios of **A** in recorder and orchestra. Concludes with element **C** in orchestra.
2:03	Ritornello (**AACD**)	Abbreviated version of the ritornello (in D minor).
2:22	Solo section 2	Harpsichord and recorders, with punctuation from orchestra. Bits of **A**; harpsichord goes wild.
3:09	Ritornello (**AAC**)	Same sequence as section 3 of main ritornello. Here, in B-flat major.
3:33	Solo section 3	Short section based on rising and falling scales, with hints of **A**.

3:59	Ritornello (**CB**)	This is from middle section of main ritornello. Modulates through several keys.
4:19	Solo section 4	Recorders accompanied by harpsichord; concludes (like solo section 1) with **C** in orchestra.
4:52	Ritornello (**AD**)	Ritornello, section 3, in A minor.
5:15	Ritornello, sections 1–3	Full, opening ritornello, in original key (F major).

The ritornello is worth getting to know well before listening to the whole first movement of the concerto. There are three sections of the ritornello; listen to them until you can remember which is which.

The appearances of the ritornello are linked by chains of sequences (restatements of a pattern) whose repeating units vary in length from one to four measures. Each of these units is easily remembered, each concludes with shorter sequences, and Bach finishes the ritornello with a strong and rather quirky cadence. (See LG 23, p. 164.)

Middle movement

The middle movement of the concerto, in slow triple time, rearranges the instruments, pitting the harpsichord against everyone else. In the beginning, the recorders join with the strings in a chorus, leaving the harpsichord to reply alone. Short phrases become longer ones, and gradually the harpsichord takes off on some interesting solo tangents, some of which are highly chromatic (using semitones of the scale). There is a sense of passion, of yearning, of expectation, that makes a strong emotional contrast to the outer movements. The movement ends on a cadence that holds us in suspense, waiting to see what trick Bach has up his sleeve this time.

Finale

The finale combines two musical elements that Bach excelled at—fugue and ritornello. Orchestral sections that present the fugue subject in various voices alternate with solo episodes for harpsichord and recorders, and these episodes are based on ideas taken from the subject. Bach saves his big surprise for last: a **stretto**, which in a fugue means using the subject as a counterpoint to itself. Just before the end the violins and recorders play the subject a half-note apart. Then, as if astonished by their own ingenuity, everybody stops and plays a wild chord. The stop-and-go with wild chords happens twice more before we gallop to a final statement of the subject, overlapped between bass and soprano.

This scintillating display of virtuosity must have elicited a thunderous ovation, especially with the composer himself at the harpsichord. And who wouldn't be impressed, not only by this concerto, but by the range and variety of Bach's music? If Bach's contemporaries emphasized his prowess as a church composer and organist, his claim to immortality rests largely on pieces like these, learned and artfully constructed but at the same time accessible and delightfully engaging. It is worth remembering that Bach spent more time in Leipzig directing the Collegium than conducting cantatas in church. It was time well spent.

Bach Then and Now

As renowned as Bach was during his lifetime, few of his contemporaries would have predicted that he would come to be viewed by many as the greatest composer who ever lived. He was, after all, the Leipzig Town Council's *third* choice for the post of cantor. Even in 1723 he was thought of as a composer whose music was intellectual and cerebral, too complicated for a time when musical tastes were turning to simpler melodies.

After his death in 1750, Bach was honored as a master of fugue and counterpoint, but for many years his music was more respected than performed. His settings of Lutheran hymns continued to be studied as examples of harmony; his preludes and fugues remained the cornerstone of keyboard practice; and church musicians continued to play many of his organ works. For the most part, however, Bach was eclipsed, and the qualities that made his music great—his passionate expression of emotions, his dancing rhythms, his astounding inventiveness—were forgotten.

Mendelssohn and Bach   Felix Mendelssohn's revival of the titanic *St. Matthew Passion* in Berlin in 1829 started the process of bringing Bach back into the consciousness of listeners. The founding of the German Bach Society in 1850 was another important milestone in the nineteenth-century Bach revival. Just as the great museums of Europe and America sparked a new appreciation for the artistic artifacts of the past, so antiquarian interest contributed to the rediscovery of Bach, opening the door to a treasure-house of music that is now universally admired.

That Bach could make an economical piece of music and compose flawless, elegant counterpoint was never in doubt. But such technical skill matters only to professionals, unless the music that results is beautiful. Many believe that Bach's music demonstrates the amazing combination of workmanship and ingenuity that is found only in the rarest of artistic creations. Every one of his pieces is full of life and clearly expresses a feeling, a mood, or a passion.

Bach has a privileged place in modern musical life—not only in churches, where his organ music has always been revered, but on the concert stage as well. Performances of the great Passions and the B Minor Mass are regularly sold out, and several ensembles have undertaken complete cycles of his more than two hundred church cantatas. Keyboard students continue to delight in the inexhaustible variety of his preludes, fugues, and suites. The concertos are prized by harpsichordists, pianists, and violinists, and no cellist or violinist can ignore his dazzling solo music for their instrument.

In short, Bach's music is one of the central pillars of the Western tradition. The standards it demands of listeners are as high as those he imposed on himself.

Chapter Review

Summary of Musical Styles

Two common techniques in Baroque music are **ritornello** and **fugue.** They are not limited to Bach's music and are related to music from earlier and later styles.

- **Ritornello:** in its simplest form expressed as a refrain that returns after a succession of other materials. In Baroque music, ritornello form is used in a variety of kinds of piece, including:

    Concerto: many concertos, especially those by Vivaldi and Bach, have in their first movement (and often in other movements as well) an opening orchestral ritornello, usually with very characteristic music, which returns, in whole or in part, in the course of the movement. The solo instrument or instruments have music that may or may not be based on the music of the ritornello.

Aria: many arias are set in ritornello form. As in a concerto movement, an opening orchestral ritornello sets the mood, and often presents the main musical themes before the singer begins. The ritornello returns, in whole or in part; it is almost always repeated at the end.

- **Fugue:** a polyphonic imitative composition using a single theme. Fugues vary widely in formal shape and are written for all sorts of media, from keyboard to orchestra to chorus. Characteristic elements of a fugue are:

  Subject: the theme on which the fugue is based.

  Exposition: the opening section of the fugue, in which each of the voices enters in turn with the subject.

  Countersubject: a melody, which recurs regularly in another voice whenever the subject is played or sung.

  Episode: a passage of music in which the subject is not heard in its entirety; episodes are often based on motives from the subject or countersubject.

ⓢ Multimedia Resources and Review Materials on StudySpace

Visit wwnorton.com/studyspace for review of Chapter 6.

What Do You Know?

Check the facts for this chapter. Take the online **Quiz**.

What Do You Hear?

Listening Quizzes and **Music Activities** will help you understand the musical works in this chapter.

ⓟ Author Videos

- Bach's C Minor Fugue: subject and countersubject
- Bach's C Minor Fugue: episode and sequence

Interactive Listening Guides

LG 21 Bach: Prelude and Fugue in C Minor, BWV 847
LG 22 Bach: Suite in D Major, BWV 1068, Overture
LG 23 Bach: Concerto in F Major for Harpsichord, Two Recorders, and Strings, BWV 1057, Arranged from the Fourth *Brandenburg* Concerto, I

Flashcards (Terms to Know)

bourrée	exposition	Passions
clavichord	fortepiano	polyphony
Collegium Musicum	gavotte	preludes and fugues
concerto	gigue	ritornello
counterpoint	imitation	subject
countersubject	movements	transcription
episode	orchestration	

HISTORICAL EVENTS	MUSICAL EVENTS

1700

1694–1778 Voltaire

1709–1784 Samuel Johnson

1712–1778 Jean-Jacques Rousseau

1723–1792 Joshua Reynolds

1725

1732–1809 Franz Joseph Haydn

1741–1807 Angelica Kauffman

1741–1828 Jean-Antoine Houdon

1746–1828 Francisco Goya

1748–1825 Jacques-Louis David

1749–1832 Johann Wolfgang von Goethe

1750

1750 Death of Bach

1752 Benjamin Franklin's discoveries in electricity

1756–1791 Wolfgang Amadè Mozart

1757–1822 Antonio Canova

1759 Death of Handel

1759–1805 Friedrich Schiller

1770–1827 Ludwig van Beethoven

1775

1775–1817 Jane Austen

1776 Signing of the American Declaration of Independence

1789 George Washington inaugurated as first president of the United States

1789 Storming of the Bastille opens French Revolution

1795–1821 John Keats

1797–1828 Franz Schubert

1800

1802 Napoleon Bonaparte declared First Consul for Life

1815

1815 Battle of Waterloo ends Napoleon's career

1815 Congress of Vienna

● Italy   ● France   ● England   ● Germany/Austria

Music and Reason: Classical Music

The next group of chapters deals with composers and musical compositions that are the cornerstones of the Western repertory of classical music. Mozart, Beethoven, Schubert—these are names we regularly see on concert programs in symphonic concerts, chamber music events, and solo recitals. The modern orchestra is essentially designed to fit Mozart's and Beethoven's symphonies, and today's chamber-music repertory is based around the string quartets and other pieces by these three composers.

A curious thing about this group is how close together they are, in time and in place. Mozart knew Beethoven, Beethoven probably knew Schubert (we know that Schubert admired Beethoven's music); and they all lived in Vienna (although only Schubert was a native of the city). What it was about Vienna that attracted so many musicians is something of a mystery. True, it was the capital of a very large and powerful multinational empire, and a crossroads of culture; but there were other cities in Europe—Paris and London, for example—that were large and important, but they did not produce this blazing constellation of composers (see Figure III.1, map of Europe, p. 170).

Vienna

This period in music—roughly 1750 to 1825—is known as the **Classic period**, and the music is known as **Classical music** (the capital "C" distinguishes the name from classical music in general). Classical music includes the works of Mozart, Beethoven, and Schubert (along with those of their contemporaries like Joseph Haydn) and represents the era in which instrumental music became as important as vocal music. Ironically, despite its far-reaching influences, Classical music actually spans a short moment in time, encompassing what might be a single lifetime.

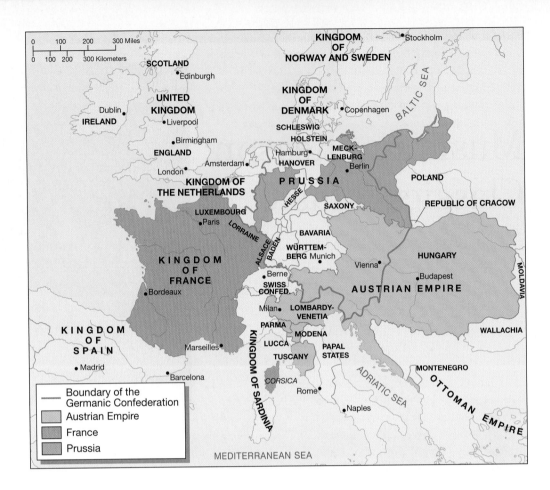

FIG. III.1 Map of Europe, 1815–48.

Mozart, Beethoven, and Schubert produced works against which all subsequent music was measured. It has balance, composure, and breadth, and was created alongside a growing awareness of the kinship of humanity, the worth of the individual, and the power of reason. These new ideas were reflected in the music, but differently for each composer.

Mozart's opera *Don Giovanni*, for example (with its masterful plot by Lorenzo Da Ponte), can be seen as a subversive work in a repressive and authoritarian society: the opera makes a certain amount of social commentary, observing fine distinctions among aristocrats, peasants, and those in between, as well as ways in which one group abuses or outsmarts another.

Beethoven's fiery and heroic music, representing triumph through struggle, also reflects the period; and we know that in much of his music, and especially in his third and ninth symphonies, Beethoven was conscious of the human struggle for individual liberty. The Third Symphony (now called the *Eroica*—"Heroic") was originally dedicated to Napoleon, whom Beethoven admired, but he canceled the dedication when Napoleon proclaimed himself Consul for Life. The Ninth Symphony, in its last movement, proclaims the brotherhood of humankind in the words of the German poet Friedrich Schiller's *Ode to Joy*.

Schubert is a composer who not only represents a wider urban access to music, but also looks ahead to the music of future composers: much of his music is personal, private, contemplative or inward-looking in a way that Mozart's or Beethoven's often are not. We will see that in the next generation, and the next

Ⓢ Mozart: *Don Giovanni*, Overture

Ⓢ Beethoven: Symphony No. 9, IV, "Ode to Joy"

Ⓢ Schubert: *Gretchen am Spinnrade*

section of this book, the interior life of the individual, the emotions of the soul, and the artistic experience become the central subjects of the Romantics.

All three of our musicians managed to make independent livings as composers. They might have preferred lucrative appointments as court composers or as imperial chamber musicians, but they did not receive them. Rather they operated in a world that was witnessing the beginnings of the *business* of music—public concert halls, music publishing, magazines and newspapers about music. It was really the birth of modern concert life, and in a way we have emulated it ever since.

The term "classic" in art usually refers to something that is timeless, whose qualities are enduring and have a balance and serenity that can't be disturbed. This is true of music from this period as well—it has certainly stood the test of time (but so has the music of Bach). We might instead call it **Enlightenment** music, or music of the **Age of Reason.**

The Age of Reason

Political Events

A growing emphasis on the power of reason and the rights of the individual was a challenge to the church and to the established authority of hereditary monarchs. It led to the American Declaration of Independence ("We hold these truths to be self-evident, that all men are created equal, that they are endowed by their Creator with certain unalienable Rights"), which resonated around the world, most notably in France, where rising dissatisfaction led to the French Revolution, beginning with the storming of the Bastille prison on July 14, 1789 (see Figure III.2), and continuing in various phases through the abolition of class distinction, the dissolution of the monarchy, and the execution of the royal family and many of the aristocracy.

French Revolution

FIG. III.2 *Storming of the Bastille*, by Jean Houel. This landmark event, July 14, 1789, marks the start of the French Revolution and is still celebrated as the main national holiday in France.

The late eighteenth and early nineteenth centuries encompassed the American Revolution, the French Revolution, the conquest of Europe by Napoleon, and his subsequent defeat. In societies ruled by absolute monarchs such as Austria, there was a growing sense of individual rights; the French "Declaration of the Rights of Man" and the American Declaration of Independence were both part of this rising tide of concern for civil liberties.

The publication of books and newspapers allowed for ready dissemination of ideas; the coffeehouses of Vienna, Paris, and London provided the space for people to read about and discuss the issues of the day; and the emerging lending libraries began to make a range of books available to customers. The loosening of class ties in society also produced a situation in which one might be able to attend a concert simply by paying for a ticket (rather than, say, because one was a member of a noble's court).

This was an age in which human reasoning (rather than divine inspiration or historical authority) became valued as a source of power and knowledge. Benjamin Franklin, Voltaire, Jean-Jacques Rousseau, and the creators of the French *Encyclopédie* all sought to increase human knowledge in the interest of increasing human goodness.

A desire for balance and reason led away from the theatrical and rhetorical postures of Baroque art toward a classicizing trend that is readily seen in art and architecture, and in the balanced phrases and forms of Classical music.

Science and Philosophy

Characteristic of Enlightenment ideals is the notion that knowledge can be accumulated and disseminated. New advances in science—"natural philosophy," as it was called—were made by Benjamin Franklin, Antoine Lavoisier, Carl Linnaeus, and others. The crowning glory of the Enlightenment and its most typical creation is the magnificent *Encyclopédie* (1751–85), an illustrated, thirty-five-volume publication of articles on every possible subject, seeking to contain all of human knowledge (see Figure III.3). An English-language effort in the same direction was the *Encyclopaedia Britannica*, first produced in Edinburgh, 1768–71.

Benjamin Franklin (1706–1790) was a publisher (*Poor Richard's Almanack*), an inventor, a scientist, and a musician, in addition to being a statesman. He signed the Declaration of Independence and the Constitution of the United States, and was ambassador to France from 1778 to 1785.

Voltaire (1694–1778), the witty essayist, outspoken philosopher, and satirical playwright, was a strong advocate of civil rights and of social reform. Voltaire's *Candide*, a mockery of the optimist philosophy of Leibniz (see p. 88) remains one of his most popular works. He wrote a philosophical dictionary and was a substantial contributor to the *Encyclopédie*.

Jean-Jacques Rousseau (1712–1778) was a professional music copyist in Switzerland before he became a famous novelist and philosopher. His novel *Emile, or On Education*, is about the preparation for responsible citizenship. Like Voltaire, he was an important contributor to the *Encyclopédie*. His *Social Contract* is among the most significant works of political philosophy, affecting many of the thinkers of the time. He wrote a dictionary of music, and a light opera called *Le devin du village* (*The Village Sage*, 1752) that was enormously popular.

The Arts

In the visual arts, the sculptors **Antonio Canova** (1757–1822) in Italy and **Jean-Antoine Houdon** in France (1741–1828, sculptor of Voltaire, Washington, Napoleon, and Franklin) managed to find considerable expression in often reserved and balanced forms.

In England, the painter **Joshua Reynolds** (1723–1792) specialized in portraits. At a time when most people of color were represented as servants, Reynolds's *Study of a Black Man* (see Figure III.4)—probably a portrait of Samuel Johnson's servant Francis Barber, a former Jamaican slave—afforded the sitter a measure of respect.

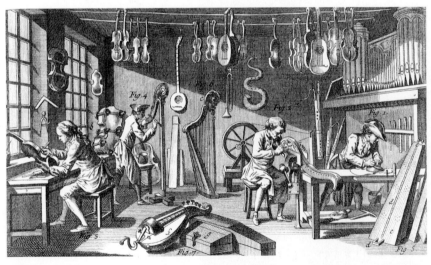

FIG. III.3 An illustration from the *Encyclopédie*, edited by Denis Diderot and Jean le Rond d'Alembert. The work sought to illustrate and explain all the arts and sciences. Here we see the interior of an instrument-maker's shop.

FIG. III.4 A portrait of Francis Barber, ca. 1770, by Sir Joshua Reynolds. The subject is thought to be a servant of Dr. Samuel Johnson.

FIG. III.5 The church of St. Mary Magdalene (La Madeleine) in Paris, a neoclassic church built on the model of the Pantheon in Rome.

The **Neoclassical** trend—a turning away from the ornamental Baroque toward order, symmetry, and simplicity—can be seen in the paintings of **Jacques-Louis David** (1748–1825). His big canvases create grandeur out of this turbulent period and catalogue his own personal turmoil.

Angelica Kauffman (1741–1807), the Swiss-born Austrian artist who worked in England and Rome, painted many historical scenes as well as imaginary portraits of Shakespeare and illustrations of scenes from his plays. She was the most successful female painter of the eighteenth century, and retains her fame today.

Francisco Goya (1746–1828), painter to the kings of Spain, produced handsome official portraits as well as darkly sinister works depicting the horrors of war. His *Caprichos*—a set of prints and etchings representing the weaknesses of human society—lead us out of the clarity of the Classical style toward the inwardness of Romanticism.

Neoclassicism is clearly represented in the architecture of the time. Thomas Jefferson's Monticello and George Washington's Mount Vernon in different ways reflect the traditions of classical architecture, and monumental buildings were often made in conscious reflection of classical models (see Figure III.5).

Literature

Samuel Johnson (1709–1784), the subject of a famous biography by James Boswell, single-handedly created the first important dictionary of the English language. Johnson was an essayist famous for his style and wit, and his *Lives of the Poets* and annotated edition of Shakespeare are lasting contributions to criticism.

This was the beginning of the age of the novel, and although Voltaire, Johnson, and others wrote them, the lasting works in English are by **Jane Austen** (1775–1817). Her novels *Sense and Sensibility* (1811), *Pride and Prejudice* (1813), *Mansfield Park* (1814), and *Emma* (1816) give us realistic social commentary and earned her a permanent place in literature, although her fame came only later in the nineteenth century.

One of Germany's most famous poet and playwright was **Johann Wolfgang Goethe** (1749–1832), the author of the two-part drama *Faust*, which was enormously influential in literature and the arts. His novels *The Apprenticeship of Wilhelm Meister* and *The Sorrows of Young Werther*, along with many plays, essays, and philosophical works, have made him a household name in world literature.

Poet and philosopher, **Johann Friedrich Schiller** (1759–1805) was another of Germany's leading dramatists. He was a close friend of Goethe's, and his plays have been the standard fare in Germany and served as the inspiration for numerous operas, including *Maria Stuarda*, *William Tell*, *Turandot*, and *Don Carlo*. Parts of his poem *Ode to Joy* were incorporated into the last movement of Beethoven's Ninth Symphony.

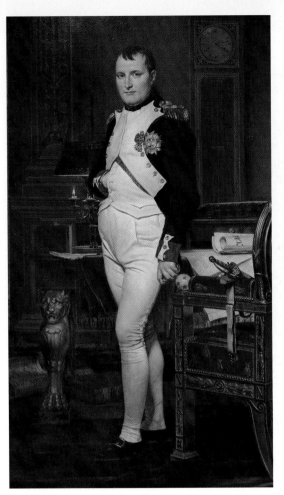

FIG. III.6 Napoleon Bonaparte as emperor of France, by the court painter Jacques-Louis David (1748-1825).

The monarchies of England, Austria, Spain, and other European countries kept a nervous eye on developments in America and in France, and reacted in different ways: things became increasingly democratic in England, increasingly repressive in Austria.

The figure of Napoleon Bonaparte looms over much of this period (see his portrait, Figure III.6, left). He was a brilliant young army officer, and his combination of military and political talent brought Napoleon to the height of authority in France; he seized power in 1799 and was proclaimed Consul for Life, and ultimately emperor (he was crowned in the presence of the pope in 1804). Napoleon conquered most of Europe in his short time in power; Italy, Spain, Germany, and Austria were under his control, but the invasion of Russia in 1812 was his downfall. Exiled to the island of Elba, his escape and return to military strength was finally overcome by the combined European forces at Waterloo (1815).

At the Congress of Vienna (1815), representatives of the great powers of Europe met to agree on the boundaries of post-Napoleonic Europe. Beethoven wrote a cantata for the Congress.

It is also said that the Congress of Vienna marks the beginning of a new style of dress for gentlemen: long trousers that came down to the tops of the shoes. Until now proper attire had consisted of knee breeches with stockings. To consider the differences in attire between the two gentlemen in the foreground of Bernardo Bellotto's painting of the Mehlmarkt in Vienna (about 1760; see p. 211) and the figures in Julius Schmid's painting of the Schubert circle (painted in the late 1800s but representing the 1820s; see p. 234) is to see the enormous changes that took place in European society in these few years: from the highly decorated, polite, refined world of eighteenth-century aristocratic Europe to the Enlightenment, post-revolutionary bourgeois urban society of 1820s Vienna.

Classic Musical Style

From a technical point of view, we might say that Classical music represents a music of poetry, in direct contrast to the Baroque, which we suggested was a music of rhetoric, that is, of prose. The shift from Baroque rhetoric to tuneful phrases makes possible a new kind of form-building, based on keys and on multiple moods and themes within an individual movement. The basso continuo was no longer present, and a simpler melody and accompaniment, with varied rhythms, was a typical texture.

Melody

The music of this period relies on melodies that come in paired phrases, like rhymed lines of poetry. You might think of "Twinkle, twinkle, little star" as such a representative melody (Mozart actually wrote a set of piano variations on the tune). You'll hear many other such melodies in the chapters to come: a question phrase followed by an answer phrase; another pair of phrases, and so on. A great example is the duet "Là ci darem la mano" from Mozart's *Don Giovanni*, in which an artful seduction scene is built up from just such balanced phrases.

Ⓢ Mozart: *Don Giovanni*, Act 1, Scene 9, "Là ci darem la mano"

This is the age of the **symphony**, that marvelous kind of composition that is made of a series (usually four) of separate compositions (called **movements,** from the French word for speed) designed to be played in order and to provide a comprehensive experience for the listener. Unlike Baroque movements (arias, concerto movements, and so forth), which are designed to develop a single mood and which have one single musical intention, Classical movements tend to have at least two themes, designed to contrast with each other, to create a tension, and then to resolve it. Using relatively simple melodies, but putting them in a context of other melodies and other keys, composers of Classical music created some of the grandest and most lasting of musical forms, and some of the music that lies at the heart of the high art of Western culture.

Symphony

Style Comparisons at a Glance

BAROQUE MUSICAL STYLE	CLASSIC MUSICAL STYLE
Motoric rhythm	Varied rhythms
Long melodies using sequences	Themes made from paired phrases
Polarity of melody and bass	Focus on melody with subsidiary accompaniment
Basso continuo always present except for solo instrumental works	No basso continuo
Movements based on a single idea	Movements based on several themes
Genres: opera, oratorio, sonata, concerto	Genres: symphony, string quartet, concerto, opera, song

CHAPTER 7

MONDAY, OCTOBER 29, 1787, PRAGUE:

W. A. Mozart's *Don Giovanni*

🔧 **CORE REPERTOIRE**	▶ **VIDEOS**	🎙 **AUTHOR VIDEOS**
▪ **LG 24** Act 1, Scene 1, "Notte e giorno faticar"	▪ Act 1, Scene 1: "Notte e giorno faticar" —"Leporello, ove sei?"	▪ The aria "Notte e giorno faticar," from Mozart's *Don Giovanni*
▪ **LG 25** Act 1, Scene 1, Ensemble	▪ Act 1, Scene 5: "Ah! Chi me dice mai"—"Chi è là?"—"Madamina, il catalogo è questo"	▪ The duet "Là ci darem la mano," from Mozart's *Don Giovanni*
▪ **LG 26** Act 1, Scene 5, Catalogue Aria	▪ Act 1, Scene 9: "Là ci darem la mano"	
▪ **LG 27** Act 1, Scene 9, "Là ci darem la mano"		
▪ **LG 28** Act 1, Finale		

Introduction

"As the company is so small, the impresario is in a perpetual state of anxiety and has to spare his people as much as possible, lest some unexpected indisposition should plunge him into the most awkward of all situations, that of not being able to produce any show whatsoever! So everything dawdles along here because the singers, who are lazy, refuse to rehearse on opera days and the manager, who is anxious and timid, will not force them."

Mozart, October 15, 1787, writing from Prague to a friend

There are many candidates for the title of *Greatest Opera Ever Written*. Tastes change, fashions come and go, and opera lovers and experts often disagree about what makes an opera great. The fact that *Don Giovanni* ranks at or near the top of everybody's list says a lot about Mozart's ability to fascinate, dazzle, and move us with his dramatic music more than two hundred years after his death.

The music

What does an opera written at the end of the eighteenth century for a second-string opera company in a provincial capital have to say to us? And why are we still listening to it? It goes without saying that the first answer has much to do with Mozart's music, but plenty of operas that have beautiful music don't succeed on stage. Other factors must help account for *Don Giovanni*'s permanence in the operatic canon.

The drama

A second element is drama—what happens on stage and how the action is amplified, explained, and projected by the music. In creating *Don Giovanni*, Mozart had the advantage of working with one of the most skillful librettists of his day—indeed, one of the greatest in history—an Italian poet and dramatist named Lorenzo Da Ponte. He and Mozart wrote three operas together—the two others are *The Marriage of Figaro* (*Le nozze di Figaro*) and *Così fan tutte* (often translated, freely, as *Women Are Like That*)—and all of them are masterpieces.

The performance

A third factor in an opera's success is the quality of the performance. It is possible, of course, to think of *Don Giovanni* apart from a specific performance. A musical work is in some sense an independent idea that gets realized in different ways on different occasions, and one could argue that the greatness of *Don Giovanni* shines through even in a poor performance. But because a performance is the only time when music, words, and action all happen at the same time, it follows that only a performance can make us fully appreciate the quality of the work. Mozart composed his opera with a particular performance in mind—he knew the theater and he knew the singers, and it is he who brought all the elements together in an opera that fit its company the way a glove fits a hand.

Don Giovanni is based on the famous story of Don Juan, the insatiable lover who chases women, seduces them to add to his collection, and treats them as objects. A highly unattractive character, without a doubt. And yet, as an archetype of a certain kind of raw sexual appetite and power, Don Juan has appealed to many playwrights, composers, poets, novelists, and even filmmakers. One reason may be that his unsavory story contains the ingredients for high drama as well as low farce.

The particular version of the story that Mozart and Da Ponte used is at once richly comic and deeply serious. For most of the opera Don Juan/Giovanni is a swashbuckling, no-holds-barred seducer, evil but funny. In the end, though, he meets his punishment, confronted by a judge in the form of a stone statue who drags him down to Hell. The statue is the image of the virtuous Commendatore, whom Don Giovanni kills in a duel at the beginning of the opera. By presenting the legend of Don Juan as a morality tale disguised as comedy, Mozart and Da Ponte made it palatable for genteel eighteenth-century audiences.

Music, mood, and action   Mozart's music fits the characters and situations amazingly well. Even more impressive is the way he uses the music to move the action along. In Monteverdi's *Orfeo* and Handel's *Messiah,* as we've seen, the music reflects a series of moods, one mood at a time; the action takes place mainly when the singers aren't busy telling us about their feelings. In *Don Giovanni,* however, Mozart is able to cause a single person, or a group of people, to act in real time—to change their minds, their partners, their positions, while the music is going on, almost as a result of the changes in the music.

The close fit between music and action is one of Mozart's special gifts. It explains why audiences in the twenty-first century continue to laugh at Don Giovanni's amorous exploits—and perhaps shudder at his exemplary fate.

The Setting

PRAGUE IN 1787

The city of Prague, now the capital of the Czech Republic, was second in importance to Vienna in the Austro-Hungarian Empire. It was the capital of Bohemia, which was one of many territories controlled by Emperor Joseph II of Austria. Bohemia had once revolted against Austria, and the new "Bohemian" nobility installed by its imperial rulers did all they could to make Prague an Austrian city.

FIG. 7.1 The Charles Bridge, begun in the fourteenth century and finished in the fifteenth. Lined with statues, it was Prague's only bridge across the Moldau River when Mozart visited.

FIG. 7.2 An exterior view of Count Nostitz's Theater (the light-colored building in the middle distance). Officially opened in 1783, it was the site of the first performance of Mozart's *Don Giovanni*.

Bisected by the Moldau River (Vltava in Czech), Prague was, and is, an exceptionally beautiful city. The splendid Charles Bridge (see Figure 7.1), lined by a double row of Baroque saints carved in stone, connected the ancient Kleinseite ("small side") on the west bank, with its medieval castle and monastery, to the Altstadt, or Old Town, the biggest and busiest part of the city. East and south of Old Town lay the Neustadt, or New Town, which despite its name traces its origins to the fourteenth century.

Most of Prague's 100,000 residents were bilingual. Although Czech was spoken in homes and shops, German was the language of business and culture. Even the city's architecture was largely imported: the magnificent Church of St. Nicholas on Old Town Square, erected in 1735, is typical of the fancifully ornate Baroque structures designed in the seventeenth and eighteenth centuries by German or Italian architects, most of whom came to Prague by way of Vienna. Many of the nobles who built grand palaces and supported the arts in Prague preferred to spend their time in the imperial capital. *Language*

Although Prague wasn't in the same cultural league as Vienna, it had a remarkably rich musical life. A German observer from around the time of *Don Giovanni*'s premiere was impressed with the locals' love of music: "Nowhere does one find so many children going about with instruments, especially the harp, and although very young, nevertheless earning their living." Music seemed to be everywhere—in taverns, on the streets, and in private homes. Yet despite the frequency of aristocratic house concerts and musical parties, it was not until 1783 that Prague had a theater for the general public. *Musical life*

Count Nostitz's Theater, built by the governor general of Bohemia, stood in a square by itself on the east bank of the river in Old Town (see Figure 7.2). The inscription above its imposing neoclassical portico, "Patriae et Musis" (Latin for "To the native land and the Muses") reflected the count's desire to bring the arts together here. It was in this theater that the premiere of *Don Giovanni* took place in October 1787. Four years later, Mozart's opera *La clemenza di Tito* (*The Clemency of Titus*), written to celebrate the coronation of Leopold II as king of Bohemia, made its debut on the same stage. *Count Nostitz's Theater*

ⓢ Mozart: *Clemenza di Tito*, Overture

Among the oldest and best-preserved opera houses in Europe, Count Nostitz's Theater was later renamed the Estates Theater and eventually became part of Prague's National Theater. Despite massive flooding in 2002, it is still standing and still giving productions of Mozart's operas.

THE BONDINI OPERA COMPANY

Credit for developing the Prague audience's appetite for opera belongs largely to an Italian singer and manager named Pasquale Bondini. After making his reputation as a bass in Prague and Dresden, he started an opera company of his own, which alternated between a winter season in Prague and a summer season in Leipzig, Germany. Bondini also hired theater companies to present German plays for part of the season, organized balls and casino evenings, and was generally in charge of major entertainments throughout the city of Prague (see A Description of Pasquale Bondini, left).

Not surprisingly, Italian opera was Bondini's specialty. As we saw in the Monteverdi chapter, Italy was the birthplace of opera, and by the late eighteenth century its progeny had spread all over the Western world, from St. Petersburg, Vienna, and Prague to London, Dublin, and Philadelphia. (Paris was an exception: the chauvinistic French professed to like nothing but their own opera.) Italian opera was generally considered the highest form of entertainment, where poetry, music, and drama came together in the presence of the most elegant and fashionable people. And the Italian style of singing, known today as **bel canto** (literally, beautiful song), was held up as the model of taste and technique.

(S) Mozart: *Don Giovanni*, Act 1, Trio, "Protegga" (bel canto)

Regardless of where the performances took place, Italian operas were almost invariably sung in the original Italian. Apparently, it didn't bother German, Russian, English, and American audiences that they couldn't understand the words. At least it was practical, since the singers were usually Italians. Every town of any size in Italy had an opera house that produced several new works each year. In addition, most major cities outside Italy had opera companies that were typically run by Italian *impresarios* (the Italian word for managers) like Bondini, who naturally favored singers and composers from the home country.

In Mozart's time, as in ours, many opera singers had international careers that took them from place to place, performing a year here, a year there, depending on who hired them and at what pay. This network of (mostly) Italian singers transcended the borders of geography, language, and politics. The system worked well, producing a fairly homogeneous product that was in constant and almost universal demand.

The Bondini Opera Company in Prague consisted of seven singers, all of them Italian, all trained in Italian opera houses, and all employed in each of the operas he presented. Many of the singers had performed with the company for several years.

In 1786, Bondini had produced another Italian opera by Mozart, his comic masterpiece *The Marriage of Figaro*, which the newspaper *Prager Oberpostamtszeitung* described as an unprecedented sensation. The overwhelming success of that production led Bondini to commission Mozart to write *Don Giovanni*, which turned out to be a singular stroke of good fortune, for Bondini as well as for posterity.

Bondini was neither a salaried court composer, like Monteverdi, nor the manager of a princely theater. He was an independent contractor who needed to

A Description of Pasquale Bondini

This impresario offers good salaries, and pays promptly, a reputation he has built up over many years. He is an Italian, he has an honest character, and one can trust his word. He was formerly a good comic actor. . . . He is likewise the impresario of the local Italian opera buffa. We have already said that Prague has an extraordinary taste for music and it is very happy with this opera, and this is a sign that it must be good. Herr Bondini furthermore spares no expense in acquiring the best and newest scores, in paying good men and women singers so that they are happy to work with him. . . . He has all the requisite knowledge of how to harmonize his own gifts with those of many others, and a certain dryness of character restrains the presumptuous ones with whom he must often surround himself.

earn a living for himself and his employees. Nor, despite the largesse of its noble founder, did Count Nostitz's Theater operate like a court opera house, subsidized by a royal patron and thereby obligated to respond to his wishes. Its purpose was to please the public, who voted with their feet and their purses. In 1787, they voted for more Mozart.

The Performance

Wolfgang Amadè Mozart lived in Vienna, some 150 miles southeast of Prague, where he was trying very hard to secure an official position at the court of Emperor Joseph II. (Mozart himself never used the version of his name that we are most familiar with today, except when he jokingly signed a letter "Wolfgangus Amadeus Mozartus.")

FIG. 7.3 Leopold Mozart, with his two talented children, Maria Anna (called "Nannerl" by her brother) and Wolfgang.

WOLFGANG AMADÈ MOZART (1756–1791)

Mozart has a reputation as an inspired genius, a composer whose compositions have a perfection and a clarity that has rarely been equaled. Music is thought to have poured out of him in an inspired torrent.

The truth is a little more pedestrian. The talented son of a Salzburg violinist, Mozart and his sister, whom he called Nannerl, were toured around Europe, perhaps exploited, as child prodigies (see Figure 7.3). The young Wolfgang was employed, as his father was, by the prince archbishop of Salzburg. Tours with his father (throughout Italy, England, Germany, and Austria) made the son's talent well known. and Mozart decided to seek his fortune independently in Vienna, where he hoped to establish himself in a court-sponsored position and gain fame as an opera composer. He did not succeed, but his fame is now secure.

In Vienna, Mozart struggled to find his way as a composer. He organized concerts, created piano concertos for his own virtuoso performances, and composed symphonies, chamber music, and other works. Mostly, however, he sought commissions for operas, since that was where he felt his talent lay, and that was how composers achieved success. His *Abduction from the Seraglio* (*Die Entführung aus dem Serail*, 1782) was an enormous success, and on the strength of it he broke with the archbishop, defied his father, and married the singer Constanze Weber (see Figure 7.4). Unfortunately, the hoped-for continued success and financial security evaded him. He scored a hit with Da Ponte's libretto of *The Marriage of Figaro* (1785), which, along with *The Abduction,* made him famous in Prague before he traveled there in January 1787.

Don Giovanni was not, however, a success in Vienna. Despite his appointment as a Chamber Musician to the emperor, and despite further operatic ventures, including *Così fan tutte* (1790, libretto by Da Ponte) and *The Magic Flute* (*Die Zauberflöte*, 1791), a poor economy and Mozart's inability to manage his affairs left him and his family in increasingly difficult circumstances, and they repeatedly moved to smaller and cheaper apartments. He died from an unknown disease in December 1791, leaving behind his unfinished Requiem Mass.

Mozart was witty, amusing, full of fun and jokes, and loved puns and off-color humor. He had a talent for complexity, as his skill at billiards and counterpoint attest; he even devised a set of dice that anyone could use to compose a minuet. His brilliant and impromptu lifestyle led to his reputation for tossing off his music, but there was actually a good deal of hard work involved in Mozart's efforts, and the clarity and perfection of his music is an achievement of a genius as well as a superb craftsman.

In addition to his operas, he is remembered for his symphonies and chamber music.

ⓢ Mozart: Symphony No. 40, I, opening
ⓢ Mozart: Clarinet Quintet, II
ⓢ Mozart: *Dies irae,* from Requiem

MAJOR WORKS: Operas, including *Marriage of Figaro, Don Giovanni, Abduction from the Seraglio, Così fan tutte,* and *The Magic Flute*; 41 symphonies; chamber music, including *Eine kleine Nachtmusik*; about 23 piano concertos and other concertos; Masses and 1 Requiem (unfinished); and numerous keyboard works and songs.

A child prodigy, he had been composing operas and other kinds of music from a very early age, as well as playing piano and violin under the tutelage of his affectionate but domineering father, Leopold Mozart, who died in the spring of 1787. Wolfgang, who was thirty-one years old at the time and at the peak of his powers, had only four more years to live. (See biography, p. 181.)

Mozart's travels in Germany, France, and Italy had made him an international superstar. He visited Prague for the first time in January 1787, partly to savor the recent triumph of *The Marriage of Figaro* (which had had its premiere in Vienna the previous spring). During his month-long stay in the Bohemian capital, he gave a number of public and private concerts, including the premiere of his delightful "Prague" Symphony. He also conducted a special performance of *Figaro,* at which, according to one account, "At once the news of his presence spread in the stalls, and as soon as the overture had ended everyone broke into welcoming applause."

ⓢ Mozart: "Prague" Symphony, No. 38, IV

Mozart loved it all, and Prague loved Mozart. After attending a high-society ball on his first night in the city, he wrote to a friend: "I looked on . . . with the greatest pleasure, while all these people flew about in sheer delight to the music of my 'Figaro,' arranged for contradances and German dances. For here they talk about nothing but 'Figaro.' Nothing is played, sung or whistled but 'Figaro.' . . . Nothing, nothing but 'Figaro.' Certainly a great honour for me!" Both the composer—who always seemed to be pressed for cash—and Bondini were eager to capitalize on his success. So when the impresario offered him the fee of 100 ducats for his next opera, Mozart didn't have to think twice. (The sum was about half of the admittedly small annual fee that Mozart would later be paid as Imperial Chamber Musician.)

PREPARATIONS IN VIENNA

Lorenzo Da Ponte

Upon returning to Vienna in February, Mozart enlisted the services of the court poet Lorenzo Da Ponte (see biography, p. 183), an ordained priest (despite his Jewish background), a libertine, a political liberal, and, above all, a brilliant crafter of opera librettos. (A **libretto**—"little book" in Italian—is the text of an opera.) A prodigious worker, Da Ponte was much sought after by composers, and Mozart was lucky to get him. The Italian claims in his wonderful memoirs that he was working on three librettos at the same time—morning, afternoon, and evening.

Libretto

Da Ponte called *Don Giovanni* a *dramma giocoso* (literally, a playful drama)—the usual term for a play or libretto that mixes serious and comic elements. In putting the story together, he took care to include both kinds of character: three purely serious nobles (the Commendatore, Donna Anna, and Don Ottavio), three purely comic peasants (Zerlina, Masetto, and Leporello), and two so-called *mezzo carattere*

FIG. 7.4 Constanze Weber (1762-1842), a singer from a well-known musical family, married Mozart in 1782.

Characters in *Don Giovanni*

The Commendatore, a Spanish grandee (bass)
Donna Anna, his daughter (soprano)
Don Ottavio, her fiancé (tenor)
Don Giovanni, a licentious young nobleman (baritone)
Leporello, his manservant (bass)
Donna Elvira, a lady of Burgos (soprano)
Zerlina, a peasant girl (soprano)
Masetto, her fiancé (bass)

Lorenzo Da Ponte (1749–1838)

Part scholar and part adventurer, Lorenzo Da Ponte began and ended his career in the classroom. As a young man he taught at seminaries in Italy (he entered the priesthood in 1773), but a series of run-ins with the authorities, who disapproved of his liberal political views and compulsive womanizing, prompted him to take refuge in Germany. It was there that he discovered his talents as a poet, translator, and librettist. A recommendation to the Austrian court composer Antonio Salieri brought him to Vienna in 1781, and two years later Emperor Joseph II appointed him poet to the court theater.

In the next decade, Da Ponte produced librettos for operas by Salieri and Martín y Soler, as well as his three immortal collaborations with Mozart: *The Marriage of Figaro, Don Giovanni,* and *Così fan tutte.* After the emperor's death in 1790, he fell out of favor at the court and decided to try his luck in Paris and London. In 1805, bankruptcy forced him to decamp once again, first to rural Pennsylvania and then to New York City, where he reinvented himself as a grocer and bookseller, became an American citizen, and tried with some success to build an audience for Italian opera. Despite his checkered past, his eminence was such that Columbia College appointed him professor of Italian in 1825, a post he held until his death.

Da Ponte's opera librettos reveal a mastery of dramatic characterization and pacing that is nearly equal to Mozart's. In his *Memoirs,* he wrote that "poetry is the door to music, which can be very handsome, and much admired for its exterior, but nobody else can see its internal beauties if the door is wanting." Da Ponte often adapted preexisting texts by Italian, French, and German playwrights; *Don Giovanni,* for example, is partly based on Carlo Goldoni's play *Don Giovanni Tenorio.* Coincidentally, another Don Juan opera, by the Italian composer Giuseppe Gazzaniga, had its premiere in Venice in February 1787, and Da Ponte borrowed freely from its libretto as well.

---

parts that are both comic and serious (Don Giovanni and Donna Elvira). (For the cast of characters, see p.182.) Mozart must have had some role in shaping the libretto, although we can't be sure what it was. It was he, after all, who knew the singers in Prague, which ones could act, and how their voices sounded.

When Mozart was asked to write a new opera for the Bondini Opera Company, he knew that it could have no more than seven singers and that the roles should be tailored to the members of this particular company. (*Don Giovanni* actually has eight parts, but two of them, Masetto and the Commendatore, were sung by the same person.) The fact that he was already familiar with most of the singers from their performance of *The Marriage of Figaro* several months earlier made it possible for him to compose with specific voices and talents in mind even before he left Vienna for Prague. Mozart said he liked to make an aria that fit a singer "as perfectly as a well-made suit of clothes"

The singers

We'll meet the members of the Bondini Company in a moment. First, though, you will want to familiarize yourself with the story of *Don Giovanni.* Plots of operas are seldom dramatic marvels; their purpose is to get people singing, in lots of different situations. And that's what happens here, thanks to Da Ponte's genius as a poet and librettist (see Plot of *Don Giovanni,* p. 184).

PREPARATIONS IN PRAGUE

Because some of the manuscript paper that Mozart used in his handwritten score of *Don Giovanni* was made in Prague, we know that he continued working on the opera almost until the day of the premiere. (Analysis of paper and manufacturers' distinctive watermarks has taken much of the guesswork out of dating

⏵ *Plot of* Don Giovanni

The opera takes place in Seville, Spain, in the 17th century.

ACT 1

- Leporello, waiting for his master outside the Commendatore's house, complains about the monotony of his life in the comic aria "Notte e giorno faticar" ("Working night and day"). 🔊 **LG 24** ⏵ **Video**
- Donna Anna emerges, pursued by Don Giovanni. The Commendatore, rushing out to save his daughter, is killed by Giovanni in a duel. 🔊 **LG 25**
- The grieving Anna is comforted by Don Ottavio.
- Donna Elvira, another of Don Giovanni's conquests, gives voice to her anger in the aria "Ah! Chi mi dice mai" ("Oh, who can tell me"). Leporello makes light of his master's lechery in the famous Catalogue Aria 🔊 **LG 26** ⏵ **Video,** but Elvira, implacable, vows to avenge herself.
- Near Don Giovanni's palace, peasants are celebrating the approaching marriage of Zerlina and Masetto. Giovanni orders his manservant to take the others inside and proceeds to win Zerlina's heart in the famous duet "Là ci darem la mano" ("There we will wed"). 🔊 **LG 27** ⏵ **Video** Elvira bursts in, denounces her seducer, and spirits Zerlina away.
- Anna, belatedly recognizing Giovanni as her father's assassin, bitterly accuses him to Ottavio in the aria "Or sai chi l'onore" ("Now you know who sought to steal my honor"). (For a later production of the opera in Vienna, Mozart at this point inserted a soothing aria for Ottavio, "Dalla sua pace" ["On her peace"].) The defiant Giovanni sings a drinking song, "Fin ch'han del vino" ("As long as there's wine").
- In the garden of Giovanni's palace, Zerlina coquettishly begs Masetto to forgive her infidelity.
- In the finale of Act 1 (🔊 **LG 28**) Masetto catches Giovanni ogling Zerlina again. The nobleman responds by inviting the couple inside to dance. In the ensuing confusion, he lures Zerlina into a side room, she screams for help, and Giovanni tries to pin the blame on Leporello. Elvira, Anna, and Ottavio, who have come to the ball disguised, strip off their masks and confront Giovanni, who flees.

ACT 2

- Giovanni and Leporello switch clothes so that servant and master can woo Donna Elvira and her maid, disguised as each other. Giovanni sings his famous serenade "Deh, vieni alla finestra" ("Oh, come to your window"), accompanied by a mandolin.
- Masetto arrives, leading a posse of peasants out for Giovanni's blood. Giovanni, still masquerading as Leporello, sends them on a wild goose chase and gives Masetto a thrashing.
- The deceptions continue in a complicated sextet that takes place in the courtyard of Donna Anna's palace. Anna, Ottavio, Elvira, Zerlina, and Masetto unmask Leporello (who is still sporting his master's finery); the frightened servant, pleading for mercy, slips away.
- After singing his aria "Il mio tesoro" ("My treasure"), Ottavio places Anna in the others' care and sets off to notify the police.
- Meeting by chance in a cemetery that night, Don Giovanni and Leporello are brought up short by the voice of the Commendatore issuing from the dead man's statue. At Giovanni's insistence, Leporello invites the statue to dinner.
- Ottavio expresses his impatience to wed Donna Anna, who rebukes him for dishonoring the memory of her murdered father.
- Giovanni is interrupted at dinner by Elvira, who begs him to mend his ways, but to no avail. Next to arrive is the Commendatore's statue. As Giovanni shakes his icy hand, flames rise up and engulf the unrepentant sinner.
- In the almost obligatory happy ending, all (except Giovanni) rejoice in a moralizing chorus.

musical manuscripts.) At the beginning of October, local newspapers trumpeted the arrival of "our celebrated Herr Mozart" and his wife Constanze, who was seven months pregnant. Lorenzo Da Ponte arrived close on their heels, ready to make whatever last-minute revisions were needed before he returned to Vienna to attend to his other commitments.

Although the Mozarts stayed at an inn close to the theater, the fun-loving composer stole away as often as he could to a friend's suburban villa, where he and Da Ponte reveled in the company of local gentry and celebrities, including the librettist's old comrade-in-lechery Giacomo Casanova. (The legendary Casanova, whose name would become a byword for womanizing, was finishing up his own kiss-and-tell memoirs and may have had a hand in revising the libretto for *Don Giovanni* after Da Ponte's departure.) A contemporary who saw Mozart in action described him as the life of the party. "He anticipated the day of the premiere as though it were a carnival. He paid extravagant court to the ladies, played all kinds of tricks, talked in rhyme, which gave him especial pleasure, and everyone let him do anything he wanted as if he were a child or a very young man."

The first performance of *Don Giovanni* was scheduled to coincide with a visit by Archduchess Maria Theresa, and time was of the essence. In principle ten days were available for rehearsals, but in practice Mozart found that there were only five, since the cast refused to rehearse on days when they had a performance. (Such insubordination would never have been tolerated at the court theater in Vienna.) Even though Mozart had sent much of the music in advance, the Bondini Company simply were not ready in time. The opening night was postponed and the archduchess had to be content with *The Marriage of Figaro*.

Mozart, who was used to working on tight schedules, fumed. "The stage personnel here are not as smart as those in Vienna, when it comes to mastering an opera of this kind in a very short time," he complained to a friend. "Secondly, I found on my arrival that so few preparations and arrangements had been made that it would have been absolutely impossible to produce it on the 14th, that is, yesterday."

To be sure, there was a great deal to be done. Even if all the singers had mastered their parts ahead of time, they still had to sing them to Mozart's satisfaction, commit them to memory, and practice their movements on stage. Like all comedies, *Don Giovanni* involves a lot of sight gags and other details that are funny only if they are perfectly timed and acted. Normally, it would have been Da Ponte's job to see to all this in rehearsal (there were no professional stage directors in the eighteenth century), but since he stayed in Prague only a week or so, the cast—with Mozart's help, no doubt—had to work out a lot of the stage business as they went along.

This wasn't such a tall order as it sounds. The singers in Bondini's troupe were all professionals, the style of acting was well known to them, and they were used to working together. Don Giovanni was played by the twenty-one-year-old Luigi Bassi (see Figure 7.5). He was renowned for his fine baritone voice, but even more for his acting. According to a contemporary report, "The worth of this artist is known; he is a splendid comic, and in his gestures an excellent actor, a complete connoisseur of mime, and—he doesn't exaggerate." Bassi's impersonation of Leporello in Act 2 must have been great fun to watch.

The **prima donna**, or leading lady, of the company was the soprano Caterina Bondini, the impresario's wife. Not surprisingly, perhaps, Mozart gave her more solo music than anybody else. As Zerlina, she had some wonderfully simple, folk-like melodies to sing. The fact that she was pregnant with her fifth child probably made her portrayal of the warm-hearted peasant girl all the more sympathetic. Zerlina's scream from backstage in the finale of Act 1, when Giovanni is presumably pawing her, is perhaps the greatest scream in all of opera; Mozart went to extraordinary lengths to get the effect he wanted (see Zerlina's Scream, p. 186).

FIG. 7.5 An engraving of Luigi Bassi as Don Giovanni. Presumably he is singing his second-act serenade to Elvira's maid. It is our only picture claiming to represent the original production, but it is not very accurate: Bassi should be wearing Leporello's clothes.

Prima donna

Mozart on Zerlina's Scream

Joseph Svoboda, the concertmaster, recollecting the rehearsal:

At the final rehearsal of the opera Mozart was not at all satisfied with the efforts of a young and very pretty girl, the possessor of a voice of greater purity than power, to whom the part of Zerlina had been allotted. The reader will remember that Zerlina, frightened at Don Giovanni's too pronounced love-making, cries for assistance behind the scenes. In spite of continued repetitions, Mozart was unable to infuse sufficient force into the poor girl's screams, until at last, losing all patience, he clambered from the conductor's desk on to the boards. At that period neither gas nor electric light lent facility to stage mechanism. A few tallow candles dimly glimmered among the desks of the musicians, but over the stage and the rest of the house almost utter darkness reigned. Mozart's sudden appearance on the stage was therefore not noticed, much less suspected, by poor Zerlina, who at the moment when she ought to have uttered the cry received from the composer a sharp pinch on the arm, emitting, in consequence, a shriek which caused him to exclaim: "Admirable! Mind you scream like that tonight!"

FIG. 7.6 An engraving of Teresa Saporiti, a member of the Bondini Opera Company in Prague, who played the role of Donna Anna.

Ⓢ Mozart: *Don Giovanni*, Ottavio, "Il mio tesoro"

Teresa Saporiti (see Figure 7.6), the Donna Anna, was Caterina Bondini's twenty-four-year-old sister. According to a not-very-flattering 1782 report, she was "a complete beginner as an actress, and halfway so as a singer; not so gifted, however, in her figure." Donna Elvira was played by Caterina Micelli, the third-ranking woman of the company. We don't know much about her, but Mozart was familiar with her voice and gave her the jagged, somewhat hysterical music that often characterizes Elvira—the one woman in the opera in whom Don Giovanni meets his match.

Both Anna and Don Ottavio (the tenor Antonio Baglioni) had difficult, florid music appropriate for personages of high rank. Indeed, Ottavio's second-act showpiece "Il mio tesoro" ("My treasure" Ⓢ) was so hard that Mozart had to compose an alternate aria when he revised the opera for a performance in Vienna with a different Ottavio. As the newest member of the company, Baglioni was unknown to Mozart, and there are conflicting reports of his performance. One critic said that he blended "acting and singing in the most masterful way," while another complained that he "industriously collected all the bad habits of Italian artists and nonartists."

Felice Ponziani, the bass who played Leporello, had sung the title role in *The Marriage of Figaro*. He was good at fast delivery of text (Mozart gave him plenty of this kind of **patter song**), and his talents as a comedian must have come in handy when he had to dress as his master, sing with his mouth full, imitate the Commendatore's statue, and perform other tricks.

The bass Giuseppe Lolli was double-cast as the Commendatore and Masetto. After the Commendatore's statue made his appearance at the end of the opera, Lolli had only moments to change costume and come back on stage as Masetto for the big finale. Lolli must have been equally versatile as a singer, because he had to perform noble music as the Commendatore, unearthly music as the statue, and peasant music as Masetto.

It's not hard to guess why Mozart held off composing some of the music for *Don Giovanni* until he got to Prague. The charming chorus of peasants in the first act, for example, probably wasn't written earlier because Mozart didn't know whether Bondini would pay extra for a chorus, and if so, whether it would be any good. Don Giovanni's beautiful serenade in Act 2 was composed in Prague too; maybe Mozart wanted to be absolutely sure that it would be a perfect fit for Bassi's voice. As for the overture, there are all sorts of stories about the ink being still wet on the orchestra's parts at the first performance.

MONDAY, OCTOBER 29, 1787, 7 P.M.

After one last infuriating delay (see Mozart Grows Impatient, p. 187), the premiere was finally set for October 29.

Count Nostitz's Theater was small by modern standards, seating about eight hundred people (see Figure 7.7). The ornate, horseshoe-shaped auditorium was decorated with white and gold, and the five tiers of boxes along the side and back walls glittered with candlelight and the jewels of the ladies. (In the days before gas

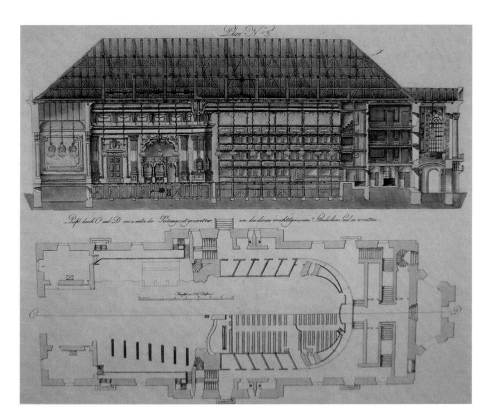

FIG. 7.7 A contemporaneous engraving of Count Nostitz's Theater. Like most eighteenth-century theaters, it has a series of boxes in tiers around the auditorium; an orchestra pit at ground level, and on the stage, a series of wings that can be used to change settings.

ⓢ Mozart: *Don Giovanni*, Overture, opening

and, later, electrical lighting, theaters were notorious firetraps.) The opening night had long been sold out, and the audience was abuzz with excitement. Everyone was eager to see whether Mozart's latest work would be as successful as Prague's favorite opera, *The Marriage of Figaro*.

Mozart himself conducted the performance. There were cheers when he entered the hall and took his place at the piano to lead the orchestra and accompany the recitatives. (The piano of Mozart's day, with its wooden frame and smaller dimensions, looked quite different from today's steel-framed versions; see Figure 7.8.) The orchestra was arranged at a long music desk so that the players faced each other in two lines; the piano was at one end so that Mozart, sitting sideways to the stage, could look down the lines of players, and also could glance toward the singers.

The slow introduction of the overture began with two massive chords ⓢ that send a subliminal signal that *Don Giovanni* was not a comic opera, pure and simple: there would be good tunes and plenty of laughs, but the murder that started the plot would ultimately be avenged. The audience would later recognize these same terrifying chords when they returned at the end of the opera, now featuring the dark sonorities of trombones, accompanying the entrance and speech of the Commendatore's statue.

The stage of Count Nostitz's Theater, like that of all theaters at the time and many theaters still, had painted panels on each side, and a painted backdrop. Scene changes were made by sliding the panels in or out and changing the backdrop, all in full view of the audience. (It was not until the nineteenth century

Mozart Grows Impatient

After the premiere was put off a second time, Mozart wrote to a friend in frustration:

It was fixed for the 24th, but a further postponement has been caused by the illness of one of the singers. As the company is so small, the impresario is in a perpetual state of anxiety and has to spare his people as much as possible, lest some unexpected indisposition should plunge him into the most awkward of all situations, that of not being able to produce any show whatsoever! So everything dawdles along here because the singers, who are lazy, refuse to rehearse on opera days and the manager, who is anxious and timid, will not force them.

FIG. 7.8 A piano of the sort preferred by Mozart. It is much smaller and lighter in sound than today's steel-framed models. Mozart accompanied the recitatives and conducted *Don Giovanni* from an instrument like this one.

that theaters began lowering the front curtain during an act to conceal scene changes.)

A scene could be played on a "short" set—that is, one where the backdrop was placed near the front of the stage, creating a shallow playing area. A "long" set could then be prepared behind it, which was revealed by removing the backdrop and changing the front panels. The alternation of long and short sets allowed for more or less instant scene changes and continuous action. This was especially useful in *Don Giovanni*, because, as we will see, it had many scenes (see Figure 7.9).

Although there are no surviving records of the scenery used in the Prague production, we can readily imagine the surprising spectacle that the audience witnessed in the next-to-last scene, when the fires of Hell rose up to swallow Don Giovanni as the orchestra reprised the fateful music heard at the beginning of the overture. As small as Count Nostitz's Theater was, its stage equipment was far more sophisticated than the simple machinery available to Monteverdi in Mantua. There was plenty of space overhead from which scenery and people could be lowered, and winches for raising and lowering and sliding. And there was a trapdoor, indispensable for the flames of Hell and the infernal chorus who welcome Don Giovanni to a "worse evil." A cloud of smoke, the simulation of the flames of Hell—perhaps with torches—and other special effects were meant to make the audience gasp as the miscreant tumbled to his infernal doom.

FIG. 7.9 An eighteenth-century set design for a graveyard. This might resemble the graveyard scene in *Don Giovanni* in which the statue of the murdered Commendatore speaks, and accepts Don Giovanni's invitation to dinner.

The Music

OPERA SERIA AND OPERA BUFFA

Eighteenth-century Italian opera comes in two basic types: **opera seria** (serious, or tragic, opera) and **opera buffa** (comic opera). Opera seria, as we saw in connection with Handel, generally deals with mythical or historical subjects. The human characters are all gods or members of the nobility—kings, queens, princes, princesses, knights, generals, and so forth—and behave in elevated fashion. Mozart and Handel both wrote splendid examples of serious opera.

Opera seria

Comic opera, on the other hand, is not peopled exclusively with nobles. An opera buffa (which is what Mozart himself called *Don Giovanni*) can have servants, drunks, buffoons, or any sort of character at all. There is no expectation that everybody must act in a high-minded fashion. Indeed, it is the mixture of people of various social ranks that often causes the complications in the plots of comic operas like Mozart's *Così fan tutte*, as well as in operas like *Don Giovanni* that straddle the line between comedy and tragedy.

Opera buffa

Nowadays we are not much used to plays and operas based on differences in social class. At the end of the eighteenth century, however, such distinctions were very important, and it could be risky to make fun of them. The French Revolution, which attempted to do away with hereditary social distinctions, would break out in 1789, and the tendencies toward individual liberties and self-expression that we call by the general name of the Enlightenment were firmly resisted by the old regime, even in such relatively enlightened courts as that of Emperor Joseph II of Austria.

To depict servants outwitting their masters on the stage, or a valet singing a serenade to a noble lady, might be dangerously subversive to the social order. Consequently, in Austria, France, and most other European countries, any opera or play produced in public had to be approved by official censors before it could be performed. Pierre Beaumarchais's *Marriage of Figaro*—the comedy on which Mozart and Da Ponte based their opera—was considered so incendiary that it was banned in Paris and Vienna for several years.

Opera and the censors

Composer and librettist were on safer ground with *Don Giovanni*; after all, no one could object to seeing a notorious libertine getting his just deserts. (In case anyone missed the point, the subtitle of the opera was *Il dissoluto punito,* or *The Libertine Punished.*) Ironically, Mozart himself was no respecter of social rank or privilege, as his often scatological and sometimes blasphemous letters show. In a way, he was the precursor of the self-employed composers and virtuosos of the nineteenth century, who considered themselves the equals of princes and prelates. As for Da Ponte, the parallels between his roguish, playboy behavior and Don Giovanni's venal sins would not have been lost on his contemporaries.

MUSICAL STRUCTURE

Recitatives Musically speaking, the first thing most people probably notice in a performance of *Don Giovanni* is the difference between recitative and other kinds of music. Recitatives, as we saw in our discussions of Monteverdi's *Orfeo* and Handel's *Messiah*, are the passages where the singers are accompanied by harpsichord or, later, piano. (In Prague, Mozart himself was the accompanist, although a second pianist was probably on hand to take over while he was

▶ Video, Mozart: *Don Giovanni,*
"Leporello, ove sei?"

conducting and to reinforce the large ensembles.) The pianist plays brisk, short chords while the characters advance the plot in dialogue, usually delivered at talking speed and with speech inflections. The music of Mozart's recitatives is pretty formulaic; this is not the part of the opera that makes us weep—although it may well make us laugh if we understand what's being said. The places where Mozart uses accompanied recitatives, by contrast, are among the most passionate places in the work.

Between stretches of recitative come the musical pieces—solo arias, duets, trios, quartets, and larger ensembles—that are accompanied by the orchestra and are the main reason most people go to the opera. These pieces are the building blocks of larger units called numbers, scenes, and acts. *Don Giovanni* has two acts, which are divided into twenty-four (musical) numbers and thirty-seven (dramatic) scenes. The latter are just like scenes in a stage play and usually, but not always, correspond with changes of scenery.

Mozart composed scenes as a series of individual musical numbers—that is, arias and ensembles, connected by recitatives. Sometimes a single scene can encompass quite a lot of action. The opening number of *Don Giovanni*, for instance, includes Leporello's opening aria, the entrance of Donna Anna, Don Giovanni, and the Commendatore, and the swordfight resulting in the Commendatore's death, all in one continuous sequence.

The longest scenes in *Don Giovanni* are the finales of the two acts, which consist of various kinds of music, uninterrupted by recitatives, and can easily last a full quarter of an hour. Da Ponte's view of a finale was this: "Everybody sings; and every form of singing must be available—the *adagio*, the *allegro*, the *andante*, the intimate, the harmonious, and then—noise, noise, noise; for the *finale* almost always closes in an uproar."

Arias The distinction between recitative and aria, in Mozart's operas as in the music of Handel and Bach, is dramatic as well as musical. When an aria is being sung, time generally slows down or stops: it's like a freeze-frame in a film, a moment in which a character reflects on or explains something (Leporello's "Notte e giorno faticar"), exclaims in joy or outrage (Elvira's "Ah! Chi mi dice mai"), or reacts to the unfolding of the plot (Anna's "Or sai chi l'onore"). One thing Mozart's arias do not do, as a rule, is advance the action very much. This is what allowed him, when revising the opera for Vienna, to omit Don Ottavio's first-act aria and substitute an easier one for the new tenor in Act 2.

▶ Video, Mozart: *Don Giovanni,*
"Notte e giorno faticar"

▶ Video, Mozart: *Don Giovanni,*
"Ah! Chi mi dice mai"

A good librettist, and a good composer, will arrange it so that everybody has an appropriate amount of music to sing. Almost every character in *Don Giovanni* gets two arias. Donna Anna's are serious, grand, and virtuosic, as befits a lady of noble rank. Donna Elvira's arias, both in Act 1, are not so grand, because she is less noble and is so flustered that she can't be properly reflective. Zerlina's arias sound like folk tunes, but they are longer and more complex than we might expect of a peasant girl (until we remember that the original Zerlina was the prima donna of the company).

Leporello sings his "Notte e giorno faticar" at the beginning of the opera and his Catalogue Aria a few scenes later. Poor Don Ottavio gets only one aria (although today tenors usually can't resist singing both "Dalla sua pace"—inserted later for the Vienna production—and "Il mio tesoro"). Don Giovanni has, among other things, a terrific serenade ("Deh, vieni alla finestra") and a rousing drinking song ("Fin ch'han del vino"). Nevertheless, the title character in the opera doesn't have a single full-scale aria; perhaps it's because Giovanni doesn't really reflect on his actions (or their consequences).

Ensembles   Mozart's great dramatic contribution is in the ensembles, where several characters not only sing beautiful music but advance the plot at the same time. There are ensembles in which everybody speaks at once, but expressing different ideas and feelings—this works especially well in the finales. There are ensembles in which characters change their minds: Zerlina, for example, feels very differently toward Don Giovanni at the end of their duet "Là ci darem la mano" than she did at the beginning.

There are also larger ensembles of considerable musical and emotional complexity. For example, the first-act quartet "Non ti fidar, o misera" ("Don't trust him, poor thing") involves Donna Anna and Don Ottavio, who are seeking Don Giovanni's help (not knowing that he's the murderer); Donna Elvira, who tries to warn them; and Giovanni, who brushes Elvira off ("The poor girl, she's crazy, my friends"), while pretending to be willing to find and punish the offender (that is, himself).

The finale of Act 1—involving a change of scene, a variety of tempos and moods, a minuet heard first through the window from outside Don Giovanni's house and then from inside as the first of three simultaneous dances and culminating in Zerlina's famous scream from offstage—rewards many listenings. The finale concludes with a last-minute burst of adrenaline, the so-called **stretta,** where things go faster, everybody sings, and all is confusion. That's what eighteenth-century audiences expected in this sort of comic opera. Nobody composed it better than Mozart, and nobody wrote it better than Da Ponte.

THE ORCHESTRA

The orchestra in Prague was full of extraordinarily good players. Bohemia in general, and especially Prague, was known for excellent musical training, and Bohemian musicians were employed throughout Europe. The players in the opera orchestra were residents of Prague, not Italians who traveled with the Bondini Company. Their jobs were not full-time, since they played for the opera only when the company was in town. Nevertheless, they were very well respected; the woodwind players, in particular, were famously competent, and Mozart's music plays to their strengths.

The orchestra for the Prague performance of *Don Giovanni* was small by today's standards. The string section consisted of six violins—three firsts and three seconds—and two each of violas, cellos, and double basses. (By comparison, a modern opera orchestra might have twelve first violins and ten seconds.) There were also pairs of flutes, oboes, clarinets, bassoons, and French horns. Pairs of trumpets and kettledrums completed the regular roster.

This was a typical orchestra of Mozart's time. Beethoven would recognize it, and indeed would write for just such an orchestra on many occasions. If a larger ensemble was needed, more string players would normally be added, without increasing the number of woodwinds.

The score of *Don Giovanni*, however, called for a number of extra players. Three small stage bands are needed in the finale of Act 1 (this is a common operatic device—we'll encounter it again in Alban Berg's opera *Wozzeck*); there is a small woodwind group, typical of the house-music of the nobility, that entertains Don

▶ Video, Mozart: *Don Giovanni*, "Là ci darem la mano"

ⓢ Mozart: *Don Giovanni*, Act 1, Scene 12, "Non ti fidar"

Stretta

Extra musicians

Giovanni at his solitary banquet in Act 2; and there are the three sinister trombones that accompany the Commendatore's statue when it speaks at the end of the opera.

Trombones often seem to be associated with the space beyond the grave. Mozart uses them in his Requiem (a setting of the Latin Mass for the dead), including a stunning trombone solo; and Monteverdi, as we have seen, uses a choir of trombones in *Orfeo* to represent the realm of Pluto and to accompany the chorus of infernal spirits.

Mozart: "Tuba mirum," from Requiem

Listening to the Music

When Mozart entered *Don Giovanni* in the handwritten catalogue of his works, he included the indication "Pieces of music. 24." By this he meant the number of orchestral sections, arias, ensembles, and so on. Each number is a separate piece of music, complete in itself, and often containing several sections in different tempos and moods. (In this sense, *Don Giovanni* is a traditional "number opera," as distinct from the "through-composed" music dramas of Richard Wagner, which we'll consider in Chapter 13.)

All two-dozen numbers in *Don Giovanni* repay repeated listening and close study. But since we don't have time to listen to the entire opera (it takes about two and a half hours to perform), we will focus on a few characteristic pieces that give a sense of the variety of music in the opera, and of the careful balance of music and drama that Mozart and Da Ponte achieved.

LG 24

The aria "Notte e giorno faticar," from Mozart's *Don Giovanni*

Video

ACT 1, SCENE 1: "NOTTE E GIORNO FATICAR"

Leporello sets the scene, musically and dramatically, with his opening song. Don Giovanni's manservant sings with three distinct voices: his normal complaining voice, which is angular and jumpy ("Working night and day for this thankless master"); another, smooth and melodious, when he imitates his master ("What a handsome gentleman! . . . I want to act the gentleman"); and a third when he is frightened by the approach of Giovanni and Donna Anna ("But I think people are coming . . . I don't want to be heard"). The aria is a brilliant illustration of Mozart's uncanny ability to characterize moods, social levels, and people (see LG 24, p. 193).

LG 25

ACT 1, SCENE 1: ENSEMBLE

The ensemble that follows Leporello's aria is a little opera in itself. Don Giovanni and the noble Donna Anna emerge from her father's house after what we later learn was an attempted rape. The Commendatore rushes out, sword in hand, to protect her. A challenge is issued, a duel is fought, the libertine murders the Commendatore, and the plot is set in motion. This is a superb example of how the action can advance in ensembles (see LG 25, p. 194).

LG 26

Video

ACT 1, SCENE 5: CATALOGUE ARIA

Leporello's Catalogue Aria, which occurs a little later in Act 1, after Donna Elvira has put in her appearance, is one of the classics of the opera repertory.

Mozart *Don Giovanni*, Act 1, Scene 1, "Notte e giorno faticar" — 1:41

DATE: 1787

GENRE: Aria

TEXT: Lorenzo Da Ponte

LISTEN FOR

MELODY: Simple balanced phrases

TEXTURE: Shifts of musical style: disjunct; smooth; patter song

EXPRESSION: Contrasting characterization of servant and master

TIME	TEXT	TRANSLATION	DESCRIPTION
0:00	Introduction		
	Leporello		
0:15	Notte e giorno faticar per chi nulla sa gradir; piova e vento sopportar, mangiar male e mal dormir;	Working night and day For this thankless master; Enduring rain and wind, Eating badly, sleeping badly;	Leporello complains about the monotony of his life. Each phrase of melody consists of a leap back and forth between same two pitches, which get higher with each new phrase.
	[musical notation: Not - te e gior - no fa - ti - car]		
0:27	Voglio far il gentiluomo, e non voglio più servir	I want to act the gentleman, I won't serve any more,	Leporello wishes to be a gentleman like his master. Melody is more elegant—smooth, stepwise, and in a still higher range.
	e non voglio più servir, no, no, no, no, no, no non voglio più servir.	I won't serve any more, No, no, no, no, no, I won't serve any more.	When Leporello expresses his wish not to be a servant, he first slavishly follows this melody but then reverts to a melody full of leaps.
0:47	Oh, che caro galantuomo! Voi star dentro con la bella, ed io far la sentinella!. . .	What a handsome gentleman! You're in there with the lady, And I stand guard! . . .	He again refers to his noble master and sings a slightly altered version of the smooth melody, which is repeated. Melody descends to a lower register and is more repetitive when referring to his own monotonous sentry duty.
1:04	Voglio far il gentiluomo, e non voglio più servir, e non voglio più servir, no, no, no, no, no, no, non voglio più server.	I want to act the gentleman, I won't serve any more, I won't serve any more, No, no, no, no, no, I won't serve any more.	Repetition of text and music of second section.
1:20	Ma mi par che venga gente	But I think people are coming	Leporello becomes anxious and almost frozen with fear. Melody becomes stuck on single note.
1:28	non mi voglio far sentir. (*He hides.*)	I don't want to be heard.	Aria concludes with repetition of text and music of this line.

Mozart *Don Giovanni*, Act 1, Scene 1, Ensemble   3:34

DATE: 1787   **TEXT:** Lorenzo Da Ponte

GENRE: Operatic ensemble

LISTEN FOR
FORM: Dramatic pacing; plot is advanced   **EXPRESSION:** Character exposition

TEXTURE: Shifts of musical style

TIME	TEXT	TRANSLATION	DESCRIPTION
0:00	*An interjection from orchestra introduces two new characters.*		
	Donna Anna		Dialogue between Donna Anna and Don Giovanni (with asides from Leporello) is set not as a speechlike **recitative** but as a **trio.** This emphasizes dramatic conflict among the three characters.
0:05	Non sperar, se non m' uccidi, ch' io ti lasci fuggir mai.	Do not imagine that you can get away unless you kill me.	
			Donna Anna's opening melody is forceful, and rises and falls with conviction.
	Don Giovanni		
0:12	Donna folle! Indarno gridi: chi son io tu non saprai.	Crazy woman! No point in screaming: you will not learn who I am.	Don Giovanni begins to imitate her melody but then shifts to his own version.
	Leporello		Three characters sing during this section. Anna and Giovanni either sing together or trade off phrases. They often insistently repeat their own version of melodies. Much of Leporello's music is similar to his opening aria, but he also occasionally imitates the melodies of others.
0:16	(Che tumulto!. . . Oh, ciel, che gridi! Il padron in nuovi guai!)	(What a noise! . . . Heavens, what shouts! My master's in trouble again!)	
	Donna Anna		
	Gente! Servi! Al traditore!	People! Servants! To the traitor!	
	Don Giovanni		
	Taci, e trema al mio furore.	Silence, and fear my fury.	
	Donna Anna		
	Scellerato!	Villain!	
	Don Giovanni		
	Sconsigliata!	Fool!	
	(Come furia disperata mi vuol far precipitar.)	(This desperate fury will undo me.)	
	Donna Anna		
	Come furia disperata ti saprò perseguitar.	I'll pursue you like an enraged fury.	

Leporello
(Sta' a veder che il malandrino
mi farà precipitar.)

(It looks as though this libertine
will undo me.)

Commendatore (rushing in)

1:24
Lasciala, indegno!
Battiti meco!

Leave her, wretch!
Fight with me!

Orchestra interrupts, changes to **minor key**, and introduces the Commendatore. This section is also a trio, but with the Commendatore, Giovanni, and Leporello. The Commendatore begins with forceful fanfare-like statement, characterized by repeated notes and downward leaps.

(Donna Anna, hearing the Commendatore, leaves Don Giovanni and goes back in the house.)

Don Giovanni

Va': non mi degno di pugnar teco.

Ha! I do not deign to fight you.

Giovanni imitates the end of the Commendatore's phrase but mocks it.

Commendatore

Così pretendi da me fuggir?

Is this how you think you can escape me?

Leporello

(Potessi almeno di qua partir!)

(If I could only get out of here!)

The two never sing together, but only trade off phrases. Leporello's ascending and descending lines are full of anxiety.

Don Giovanni

Misero! Attendi, se vuoi morir.

Wretch! Wait, if you want to die.

2:12
(They fight; Don Giovanni gives the Commendatore a mortal wound.)

Battle music: the high and low instruments duel in a series of fast upward runs.

Commendatore

4:08
Ah, soccorso! . . . Son tradito. . . .
L'assassino . . . m'ha ferito . . .
E dal seno palpitante . . .
sento . . . l'anima . . . partir . . .

Oh, help! . . . I'm betrayed. . . .
The assassin . . . has wounded me . . .
And in my beating breast . . .
feel . . . my spirit . . . departing. . . .

The Commendatore has the last word, but is mortally wounded.

Don Giovanni

(Ah! già cadde il sciagurato . . .
Affannosa e agonizzante,
già dal seno palpitante
veggo l'anima partir.)

(Ah! The villain is already fallen . . .
gasping and agonizing,
already from his beating breast
I see the spirit departing.)

Pace suddenly slows down to **andante** (a walking tempo). New, slower tempo reflects seriousness of what has just happened. Orchestral accompaniment becomes simpler. The three characters' singing overlaps more completely, and harmonic and melodic shifts reflect their awareness of the gravity of the Commendatore's murder.

Leporello

(Qual misfatto!
qual eccesso!
Entro il sen, dallo spavento,
palpitar il cor mi sento.
Io non so che far, che dir.)

(What a tragedy!
What excess!
In my breast, I feel
my heart palpitate with fear.
I don't know what to do or say.)

(Here the Commendatore dies.)

Like the opera itself, the aria is a blend of comedy and horror that describes Don Giovanni's callous exploitation of women in graphic detail. Leporello shows Elvira the list of his master's conquests, divided up by countries; Spain has the most, with a thousand and three—so far. In the second part of the aria the servant tells how to charm each type of woman: blond, dark, slim, large, and so on. (He tactfully refrains from specifying which category Elvira falls into.)

The Catalogue Aria is a very funny song with extremely dark overtones. Giovanni slips away from the outraged Elvira just before the aria begins, urging Leporello to "tell her everything." As we will see later in the opera, it's not the only time he leaves his manservant to pick up the pieces. The song gives the baritone a chance for acting, mockery, quick and witty language, and multiple changes of voice (see LG 26, p. 197).

LG 27

The duet "Là ci darem la mano," from Mozart's *Don Giovanni*

Video

ACT 1, SCENE 9: "LÀ CI DAREM LA MANO"

This duet of seduction, one of Mozart's most famous melodies, is actually a marvel of balance between formality and reality. Don Giovanni and Zerlina start singing verses to the same tune, in graceful ⁴⁄₄ time, although they want entirely different things. (He: "Let's go, my love, from here." She: "I'd like to, and I wouldn't like to; My heart is a little afraid.") As Giovanni becomes more and more insistent, the characters begin to alternate lines, with accompanying changes in the orchestra; and we can hear Zerlina wavering until Giovanni's final "Andiam!" (Let's go!) overpowers her, and they switch to a swinging homophonic triple rhythm, sinuous and sensuous (see LG 27, p.198).

LG 28

ACT 1: FINALE

The finale of Act 1 is a triumph of drama and music, Da Ponte and Mozart at their best. The drama is one that brings all the characters together, inexorably, towards the sort of confrontation that complex plots are designed around. Don Giovanni manages to convince Masetto that Zerlina didn't see him; he leads both of them off to his house. The nobles—Elvira, Anna, Ottavio—now knowing that Don Giovanni is the murderer, disguise themselves and vow revenge. A ballroom scene includes one of Mozart's most famous moments: three couples begin to dance, each to a different tune (three dance bands play on stage); Anna and Ottavio dance the noble minuet; Don Giovanni engages Zerlina in a contradanse; and Leporello distracts Masetto in a comic "Teisch" (German dance, or waltz); the sound of three dances at the same time is amazing. Zerlina screams from offstage, all hell breaks loose, Don Giovanni appears pretending that it was Leporello's fault; they all attack him and he escapes as the curtain falls (see LG 28, p. 200).

Act 2   All our examples are from Act 1. There is, of course, much more music, and more complexity, to discover on your own in Act 2. It includes a wonderful double seduction, in which Don Giovanni dresses as Leporello, and vice versa, so that he can seduce Elvira's maid. But Elvira comes to the balcony instead, and Don Giovanni hides behind Leporello and sings to Elvira so that she will think that the figure she sees is Don Giovanni, and that he is singing. Neither is true, but she's fooled. And then, when (again!) Leporello has to take Elvira off his master's hands, Don Giovanni takes his mandolin and sings a beautiful serenade to the maid; its melody is like the one he just sang to Elvira, but it's rather high in pitch, and may represent a disguised voice. Luigi Bassi has more chance to display his acting skill, since he has to pretend to be Leporello, send the others away in an aria, and disarm Masetto and beat him, all without being recognized.

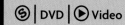

Mozart *Don Giovanni*, Act 1, Scene 5, Catalogue Aria   5:36

DATE: 1787

GENRE: Aria

TEXT: Lorenzo Da Ponte

LISTEN FOR

MELODY: Comic quality of the quick speech at the beginning   **TEXTURE:** Witty orchestral accompaniment at the beginning

FORM: Two-part form, quick section followed by lyrical one

TIME	TEXT	TRANSLATION	DESCRIPTION
0:00	**A section** (Allegro) *Leporello*		Orchestra sets lively rhythm, as Leporello shows his book to Elvira.
	Madamina, il catalogo è questo Delle belle che amò il padron mio; un catalogo egli è che ho fatt'io; Osservate, leggete con me.	Little lady, this is the catalogue Of the beauties my master loved, A catalogue I made myself; Look, read with me.	
0:22	In Italia seicento e quaranta; In Alemagna duecento e trentuna; Cento in Francia, in Turchia novantuna; Ma in Ispagna son già mille e tre.	In Italy 640; In Germany 231; 100 in France, 91 in Turkey; But in Spain, already 1003.	Quick orchestral phrase alternates with catalogue entries; pause to prepare "but in Spain, already 1003," with "1003" emphasized and repeated.
0:51	V'han fra queste contadine, Cameriere, cittadine, V'han contesse, baronesse, Marchesane, principesse. E v'han donne d'ogni grado, D'ogni forma, d'ogni età.	There are peasants, Maids, citizens, There are countesses, baronesses, Marchionesses, princesses; And women of all classes, All shapes, all ages.	Recitation of various kinds of women is presented in short phrases, speeding up and coming to an inconclusive cadence.
1:07	In Italia seicento e quaranta; In Alemagna duecento e trentuna; Cento in Francia, in Turchia novantuna; Ma in Ispagna son già mille e tre.	In Italy 640; In Germany 231; 100 in France, 91 in Turkey; But in Spain, already 1003.	Same words as before, but different music, leading to a similar pause before "Spain."
1:38	V'han fra queste contadine, Cameriere, cittadine, V'han contesse, baronesse, Marchesane, principesse. E v'han donne d'ogni grado, D'ogni forma, d'ogni età.	There are peasants, Maids, citizens, There are countesses, baronesses, Marchionesses, princesses; And women of all classes, All shapes, all ages.	Repeated words, similar music, except that cadence is a final one, concluding first part of aria.
2:00	**B section** (Andante con moto) Nella bionda egli ha l'usanza Di lodar la gentilezza, Nella bruna la costanza, Nella bianca la dolcezza.	With blondes he usually Praises their gentleness; With a brunette, faithfulness; With white hair, sweetness.	Second section begins in slow triple meter with regular phrases. Note military sound on "costanza," and sinuous sweetness of "dolcezza."

(continued)

TIME	TEXT	TRANSLATION	DESCRIPTION
	Vuol d'inverno la grassotta, Vuol d'estate la magrotta; È la grande maestosa, La piccina è ognor vezzosa.	In winter he wants chubby, In summer skinny; The big one is majestic, The small one charming.	New, **dotted rhythm**, leads to comical depictions of "maestosa," "piccina."
3:33	**B section** (music repeated, with variation) Delle vecchie fa conquista Pel piacer di porle in lista; Sua passion predominante È la giovin principiante. Non si picca — se sia ricca, Se sia brutta, se sia bella; Purché porti la gonnella, Voi sapete quel che fa.	He conquers the old ones For the pleasure of listing them; His predominant passion Is for the young beginner. Doesn't matter if she's rich Or ugly or beautiful; If she wears a skirt, You know what he does.	Same music as for "Nella bionda," with sinister harmonic turn on "lista." Back to the dotted rhythm. The "nella bionda" music leads to the final line, which is repeated.

LISTENING GUIDE 27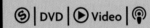

Mozart *Don Giovanni*, Act 1, Scene 9, "Là ci darem la mano"   3:08

DATE: 1787

GENRE: Duet

TEXT: Lorenzo Da Ponte

LISTEN FOR

MELODY: A folk song–like melody becomes increasingly fragmented

FORM: Two-part form, (**A**) a slow seduction followed by (**B**) a lively, dancelike second section

SCORING: Use of flute and bassoon to echo the voices of Don Giovanni and Zerlina

TIME	TEXT	TRANSLATION	DESCRIPTION
0:00	*Don Giovanni* Là ci darem la mano, La mi dirai di sì, Vieni, non è lontano, Partiam, ben mio, da qui.	There we will wed, There you'll say "yes," Come, it's not far, Let's go, my love, from here.	**A Section:** Seduction Don Giovanni sings what seems to be a verse from a folk song; it's relatively formal, and has nothing of urgency, only charm. There are two pairs of phrases, each a sort of question-and-answer. First and third lines have same music, second and fourth are slightly different.
0:20	*Zerlina* Vorrei, e non vorrei; Mi trema un poco il cor: Felice, è ver, sarei, Ma può burlarmi ancor.	I'd like to, and I wouldn't like to; My heart is a little afraid: I'd be happy, it's true, But you may still be tricking me.	Zerlina sings a second verse; she too is being formal, using the same music for completely different sentiments. She repeats her last line, to close this section.

Time	Italian	English	Commentary
0:44	DG: Vieni mio bel diletto! Z: Mi fa pietà Masetto; DG: Io cangierò tua sorte; Z: Presto non son più forte . . . DG: Vieni!	DG: Come, my delight! Z: Masetto won't like it; DG: I'll change your fortune; Z: Soon I won't be strong enough . . . DG: Come!	Now things get warmer: the music is in a new key; they take turns singing single lines, each having his or her own music, and repeating music for a second line. Zerlina's last line is wavering, but she manages to hold on. Don Giovanni's commanding "Come!" leads us back to the original key and original music.
1:12	DG: Là ci darem la mano, Z: Vorrei, e non vorrei, DG: La mi dirai di si, Z: Mi trema un poco il cor DG: Partiam, ben mio, da qui. Z: Ma può burlarmi ancor.	DG: There we will wed, Z: I'd like to, and I wouldn't, DG: There you'll say "yes," Z: My heart is a little afraid; DG: Let's go, my love, from here. Z: But you may still be tricking me.	The music and words are the same as before, but with important differences: 1) Characters now take turns singing lines of the same song, but no longer as formal verses. 2) When Don Giovanni sings, he is accompanied by an instrument in Zerlina's range (a flute); when she sings, she's accompanied by an instrument in his range (a bassoon).
1:38	DG: Vieni mio bel diletto! Z: Mi fa pietà Masetto! DG: Io cangierò tua sorte; Z: Presto non son più forte . . . DG: Andiam! Z: Andiam!	DG: Come, my delight! Z: Masetto won't like it! DG: I'll change your fortune; Z: Soon I won't be strong enough . . . DG: Let's go! Z: Let's go!	Second section as before, but they alternate single lines, in original key. At last Zerlina, in her wavering final line, loses her resolve, and music subsides downward, as she finally obeys Don Giovanni's final command.
2:07	*Both* Andiam, andiam, mio bene, A ristorar le pene D'un innocente amor.	Let's go, let's go, my love, To heal the pains Of an innocent love.	**B Section** begins Now the two voices are one, and the dance-like second section is sensuous, full of gaiety and frolicking.

More confusion, more splendid arias and ensembles follow; in a graveyard the statue of the Commendatore speaks, terrifying Leporello and inspiring Don Giovanni to invite the statue to dinner. The final scene is in Don Giovanni's house, where Leporello serves the meal (stealing bits as he goes), and a band plays selections from favorite operas. (This band echoes in a way the triple dance-music at the end of the first act.) The third tune is actually a favorite from *The Marriage of Figaro*, and Leporello says "I know this one all too well"—an inside joke, since Ponziani, now playing Leporello, had sung that very song when he played the role of Figaro, and everybody in the audience knew it.

Act 2, Final scene

The statue appears, accompanied by trombones and by the terrifying chords that began the overture; he gives Don Giovanni a last chance to repent. He refuses, the floor opens and Don Giovanni disappears among the flames and demons of Hell. Everybody else runs onstage (Masetto has to change from his Commendatore's costume), and there is a quick lively finale, where each character announces what he or she will do next—find a new master, join a convent, get married. That, they sing, is the end for those who do evil. And it's the end of an amazing opera.

LISTENING GUIDE 28 | DVD

Mozart *Don Giovanni*, Act 1, Finale   8:08

DATE: 1787
TEXT: Lorenzo Da Ponte

LISTEN FOR
HARMONY: Abrupt shifts of key   **SCORING:** On-stage orchestra plus main orchestra
EXPRESSION: Dramatic pacing   **TEXTURE:** Three simultaneous dances of different characters

TIME	TEXT	TRANSLATION	DESCRIPTION
	Scene 21: Don Giovanni, Leporello, Zerlina, Masetto, peasants, musicians, servants, Donna Anna, Donna Elvira, and Don Ottavio.		
0:00	*(Donna Anna, Donna Elvira, and Don Ottavio enter masked.)*		Full orchestra plays, with fanfare motives and rhythms. At first, characters exchange polite pleasantries.
	Leporello Venite pur avanti, Vezzose mascherette!	Come forward, handsome maskers!	
	Don Giovanni È aperto a tutti quanti, Viva la libertà!	It's open to all; long live Liberty!	
	Donna Anna, Donna Elvira, and Don Ottavio Siam grati a tanti segni Di generosità.	We are grateful for so many Signs of generosity.	
	All Viva la libertà!	Long live Liberty!	Eventually, Leoporello leads all in singing the refrain "Viva la libertà!"
1:25	*Don Giovanni* (*to the musicians*) Ricominciate il suono! (*to Leporello*) Tu accoppia i ballerini.	Start playing again! And you, pair up the dancers.	Don Giovanni invites stage orchestras to play. One orchestra of winds and strings plays a stately minuet for the nobility.

(Don Ottavio dances the minuet with Donna Anna.)

Leporello
Da bravi, via ballate!   Bravo! Dance away!
(*They dance.*)

Donna Elvira (to Donna Anna)
Quella è la contadina.   That is the peasant girl.

Donna Anna (to Don Ottavio)
Io moro!   I'm dying!

Don Ottavio (to Donna Anna)
Simulate!   Pretend!

Don Giovanni, Leporello (ironically)
Va bene in verità!   It's really going very well!

Masetto
Va bene in verità!   It's really going very well.

Don Giovanni (to Leporello)
A bada tien Masetto.   You keep Masetto away.   Second orchestra consisting of violins and
(to Zerlina)   bass begins to tune.
Il tuo compagno io sono,   I'll be your partner;
Zerlina vien pur qua!   Zerlina, come this way!

2:33   *(He begins to dance a contradance with Zerlina.)*

Leporello (to Masetto)
Non balli, poveretto!   You're not dancing, poor fellow!
Vien quà, Masetto caro,   Come on, dear Masetto,
Facciam quel ch'altri fa.   Let's do like the others.

(He forces Masetto to dance.)

Masetto
No, no, ballar non voglio.   No, I don't want to dance.

                                                This orchestra plays a lively **contradance**:
                                                Leporello and Masetto dance.

Leporello
Eh, balla, amico mio!   Oh, dance, my friend!

Masetto
No!   No!

Leporello
Sì, caro Masetto!   Yes, dear Masetto!

Donna Anna (to Ottavio)
Resister non poss'io.   I cannot resist.

Donna Elvira, Don Ottavio (to Donna Anna)
Fingete per pietà!   Do pretend, please!

(continued)

TIME	TEXT	TRANSLATION	DESCRIPTION

Don Giovanni

Vieni con me, vita mia!
(Dancing, he leads Zerlina away)

Come with me, my love!

Third group plays faster and wilder peasant dance called a **Deutscher**: Don Giovanni and Zerlina dance.

Each dance becomes associated with a different group of characters, and the confusion of the scene is reflected in simultaneous playing of the three dances in three different meters. This confusion covers Don Giovanni taking Zerlina away against her will. Her scream brings the dancing to a halt.

Masetto

Lasciami! Ah no! Zerlina!
(He tears himself away from Leporello.)

Leave me alone! Ah no! Zerlina!

Zerlina

Oh Numi! son tradita! . . .

Oh Heavens! I'm betrayed! . . .

Leporello

Qui nasce una ruina.

A disaster is hatching here.

Donna Anna, Donna Elvira, and Don Ottavio (from outside)

3:21 L'iniquo da se stesso,
Nel laccio se ne va!

The evil man is stepping
into the trap!

Zerlina (from within)

3:31 Gente, aiuto. . . !
(She screams)

People, help. . . !

Zerlina

Aiuto! . . . aiuto! . . . gente!

Help! Help!

Donna Anna, Donna Elvira, and Don Ottavio

Soccorriamo l'innocente!

Let's help the innocent girl!

(The instrumentalists exit.)

Masetto

Ah, Zerlina!

Ah, Zerlina!

Zerlina (from inside, on the other side)

Scellerato!

Criminal!

Donna Anna, Donna Elvira, and Don Ottavio

Ora grida de quel lato!
Ah gettiamo giù la porta!

Now she screams from that side!
Knock down the door!

Zerlina

Soccorretemi! o son morta!

Help me, or I'm dead!

Donna Anna, Donna Elvira, Don Ottavio, and Masetto

Siam qui noi per tua difesa!

We are here to defend you!

Don Giovanni

4:06   (*Entering with sword in hand, pulling Leporello by the arm, he pretends that he is to blame.*)

Ecco il birbo che t'ha offesa!	Here's the culprit who offended you!	Music slows and simplifies as Don
Ma da me la pena avrà!	But I shall punish him!	Giovanni tries to convince guests that
Mori, iniquo!	Die, evil one!	Leporello abducted Zerlina.

Leporello

Ah, cosa fate?   Ah, what are you doing?

Don Giovanni

Mori, dico!   Die, I say!

Don Ottavio

Nol sperate!	Don't try it!	Music intensifies, the three nobles reveal themselves and confront Don Giovanni.

Donna Anna, Donna Elvira, and Don Ottavio

L'empio crede con tal frode	The evil one thinks that he can
Di nasconder l'empietà.	hide it with this fraud.

(*They remove their masks.*)

Don Giovanni

Donna Elvira!	Donna Elvira!	His surprise is expressed in recitative-like interjections.

Donna Elvira

Sì, malvagio!   Yes, evil one!

Don Giovanni

Don Ottavio!   Don Ottavio!

Don Ottavio

Sì, signore!   Yes, signore!

Don Giovanni   (*to Donna Anna*)

Ah, credete. . . .   Ah, believe me. . . .

All except Don Giovanni and Leporello

Traditore! Tutto già si sa!   Traitor! We now know everything!

Donna Anna, Donna Elvira, Zerlina, Don Ottavio, Masetto

5:52	Trema, trema, o scellerato!	Tremble, you criminal!	Tempo becomes allegro and characters
	Saprà tosto il mondo intero	Soon the whole world will know	threaten Don Giovanni and Leporello.
	Il misfatto orrendo e nero	The black and horrendous misdeed,	They respond in different ways. First is
	La tua fiera crudeltà!	Your proud cruelty!	in a whisper accompanied by music that
	Odi il tuon della vendetta,	Listen to the sound of revenge,	accompanied their entrance in the finale.
	Che ti fischia intorno;	Whistling all around you;	
	Sul tuo capo in questo giorno	Today its lightning bolt	
	Il suo fulmine cadrà!	Will strike your head!	

Leporello

È confusa la sua testa,	He doesn't know what to do,	Second response includes lots of repetition
Non sà più quel ch'ei si faccia,	His head is confused,	of individual phrases.
E un orribile tempesta,	And a horrible storm, oh God!	
Minacciando, o Dio, lo va!	Is threatening him.	

(continued)

TIME	TEXT	TRANSLATION	DESCRIPTION
	Ma non manca in lui coraggio, Non si perde o si confonde, Se cadesse ancora il mondo, Nulla mai temer lo fa!	But he doesn't lack courage, He doesn't get lost or confused, Even if the whole world collapses, Nothing can make him afraid.	
	Don Giovanni È confusa la mia testa, Non so più quel ch'io mi faccia, E un orribile tempesta, Minacciando, o Dio, mi va! Ma non manca in me coraggio, Non mi perdo o mi confondo, Se cadesse ancora il mondo. Nulla mai temer mi fa!	I don't know what to do, My head is confused, And a horrible storm, oh God! Is threatening me But I don't lack courage, I don't get lost or confused, Even if the whole world collapses, Nothing can make me afraid.	Third response is a quick rising scale of repeated notes that shows great anxiety and contrasts with slower rhythm of other characters.
			The Finale ends solidly in C major, with quick ascending runs emphasizing the tonality.

Don Giovanni Then And Now

Mozart's audience in Prague knew the style of his music, they knew the singers in the Bondini Opera Company, and they knew the players in the orchestra. Most of them came to the theater predisposed to enjoy themselves, and it seems they did. The only newspaper review we have of the premiere is quite brief:

> [On] Monday, the 29th, the Italian Opera Company gave the ardently awaited opera by Maestro Mozard [*sic*], *Don Giovanni, or the Stone Banquet*. Connoisseurs and musicians say that Prague has never heard the like. Herr Mozard conducted in person; when he entered the orchestra he was received with threefold cheers, which again happened when he left it. The opera is, moreover, extremely difficult to perform, and everyone admired the good performance given in spite of this after such a short period of study. Everybody, on the stage and in the orchestra, strained every nerve to thank Mozard by rewarding him with a good performance. Much expenditure was required for the chorus and scenery, all provided splendidly by Herr Guardasoni [the manager of the Bondini Company].

Don Giovanni vs. The Marriage of Figaro

Behind the anonymous writer's measured praise lurks a hint that *Don Giovanni* was perhaps not quite as wildly popular as *The Marriage of Figaro*. The reference to "connoisseurs and musicians" suggests that Mozart's music was too sophisticated for the average operagoer. (It wasn't then, and it isn't now.) Although the sets clearly made a favorable impression, not much is said about the singing, an omission that would be unusual in an opera review today. The critic seems to acknowledge that the performance was far from perfect when he rather tepidly describes it as "good," while calling attention to the limited rehearsal time.

FIG. 7.10 A modern production of *Don Giovanni* by the English National Opera, London, presented in December 2010.

Still, Mozart and his librettist had every reason to be pleased. Guardasoni, the composer reported to Da Ponte, was beside himself after the premiere, exclaiming, "Long live Da Ponte! Long live Mozart! All impresarios, all virtuosi must bless their names. So long as they live we shall never know what theatrical poverty means." The Bondini Company continued to perform *Don Giovanni* in Prague, Warsaw, and other cities, and the opera became especially popular (in various translations and adaptations) with German and French audiences.

Mozart himself arranged to have the opera produced a few months later in Vienna, where he hoped to improve both his reputation and his employment prospects. As usual, Mozart adapted the music to fit the capabilities of the new cast and what he believed to be the taste of the local audience.

This time, unfortunately, *Don Giovanni* was a flop. After *The Marriage of Figaro*, the Viennese public was expecting something light and frivolous; instead Mozart gave them complexity tinged with tragedy. At a party after the premiere, according to one published account, the guests made no attempt to conceal their disappointment. Someone asked Mozart's mentor, Franz Joseph Haydn, then at the height of his fame, for his opinion. Haydn was apparently not willing to take a position about the opera: "I cannot settle the argument," the older composer said. "But one thing I know, and that is that Mozart is the greatest composer that the world now has."

Haydn's judgment was seconded by Emperor Joseph II, who told Da Ponte, "The opera is divine; possibly, just possibly even more beautiful than *Figaro*. But such music is not meat for the teeth of my Viennese!" To which Mozart replied. "Give them time to chew on it!"

Audiences have been chewing on *Don Giovanni* and its devilishly charismatic antihero ever since. In fact, the afterlife of Mozart's opera is as interesting as the story of its creation. Don Giovanni (alias Don Juan) became one of the most potent archetypal figures of the Romantic Era, celebrated and reviled in music, drama, and literature. Lord Byron wrote an epic poem about him, E.T.A. Hoffmann a novella, Richard Strauss a symphonic tone poem. Frédéric Chopin and

Don Giovanni, the archetype

Franz Liszt reworked themes from Mozart's opera for the piano. And playwrights like Alexander Pushkin and George Bernard Shaw found new meaning in the age-old tale.

Fascination with the ill-fated libertine continued to grow in the twentieth century and shows no signs of waning. There have been countless interpretations and reinterpretations of the Don Giovanni story in every artistic medium imaginable, including film. But the opera that Mozart and Da Ponte wrote in 1787 for a little-known Italian impresario in Prague towers above them all, thanks to its incomparable blend of music and drama, comedy and tragedy.

Chapter Review

Summary of Musical Styles

- Short, balanced phrases create tuneful melodies.

- Eighteenth-century Italian opera comes in two basic types: **opera seria** (serious, or tragic, opera) and **opera buffa** (comic opera). Opera seria generally deals with mythical or historical subjects. Opera buffa can have any sort of character, including servants, drunks, and buffoons.

- Although there are **arias** in Mozart's operas, much of the music, and the action, takes place in **ensembles** (duets, trios, etc.) where several characters sing at once.

- Many of the individual musical numbers have more than one section. Mozart usually has a very good reason for changing tempo and style: something has changed.

- Mozart's orchestra has more variety than Handel's: there are flutes, oboes, clarinets, bassoons, horns, trumpets, and trombones. He treats the instruments imaginatively, as in the use of flute and bassoon to echo the voices of Don Giovanni and Zerlina.

- The singing in *Don Giovanni* is mostly in tuneful phrases; occasionally very florid music is sung, mostly by members of the nobility.

ⓢ Multimedia Resources and Review Materials on StudySpace

Visit wwnorton.com/studyspace for review of Chapter 7.

What Do You Know?

Check the facts for this chapter. Take the online **Quiz**.

What Do You Hear?

Listening Quizzes and **Music Activities** will help you understand the musical works in this chapter.

⦿ Author Videos

- The aria "Notte e giorno faticar," from Mozart's *Don Giovanni*
- The duet "Là ci darem la mano," from Mozart's *Don Giovanni*

Interactive Listening Guides

LG 24   Mozart: *Don Giovanni*, Act 1, Scene 1, "Notte e giorno faticar"
LG 25   Mozart: *Don Giovanni*, Act 1, Scene 1, Ensemble
LG 26   Mozart: *Don Giovanni*, Act 1, Scene 5, Catalogue Aria
LG 27   Mozart: *Don Giovanni*, Act 1, Scene 9, "Là ci darem la mano"
LG 28   Mozart: *Don Giovanni*, Act 1, Finale

⏵ Videos

Act 1, Scene 1: "Notte e giorno faticar"—"Leporello, ove sei?"
Act 1, Scene 5: "Ah! Che me dice mai"—"Chi è la?"—"Madamina, il catalogo è questo"
Act 1, Scene 9: "Là ci darem la mano"

Flashcards (Terms to Know)

andante	opera seria
bel canto	prima donna
dotted rhythm	recitative
libretto	trio
opera buffa	stretta

CHAPTER 8

THURSDAY, DECEMBER 22, 1808, VIENNA:

Ludwig van Beethoven's Symphony No. 5 in C Minor

🔧 **CORE REPERTOIRE**	🎙 **AUTHOR VIDEOS**	
▪ **LG 29** First movement, Allegro con brio ▪ **LG 30** Second movement, Andante con moto ▪ **LG 31** Third movement, Allegro [Scherzo and Trio] ▪ **LG 32** Fourth movement, Allegro [Finale]	▪ How to make a theme out of a motive in Beethoven's Fifth Symphony ▪ Rhythmic unity of themes throughout Beethoven's Fifth Symphony	

Introduction

> *"Notwithstanding the fact that several mistakes were made, which I could not help, the public accepted everything enthusiastically. . . ."*
>
> —Beethoven, January 7, 1809, letter to his publisher

A symphony, to many traditional concertgoers, is the highest achievement not only of Classical music (music of the Classic period) but of classical music—that is, Western art music as a whole. And Beethoven's Fifth Symphony may be the ultimate realization of this genre. It is certainly one of the most often heard and readily recognized symphonies.

Actually, it was Beethoven who created the idea of the symphony as one of the noblest vehicles for great art. Not long before his time, a symphony was essentially an opening act—it was loud, and was usually placed at the beginning of a concert (or even an opera) to catch the audience's attention and to get them to quiet down. The genre itself emerged from other lighter instrumental types—such as multi-movement opera overtures and the kind of one-movement instrumental piece sometimes called *sinfonia*. In the hands of the brilliantly inventive Franz Joseph Haydn it had become an international concert standard, and with Mozart, especially in his later symphonies, it had already became a work of high art. The symphony is now the central form of our concert life.

Beethoven and the symphony

Ⓢ Haydn: Symphony No. 82, I, opening

Ⓢ Mozart: Symphony No. 30, I, opening

Beethoven himself conducted the first performance of his Fifth Symphony in Vienna in 1808, using it as a kind of curtain-raiser for the second part of a very long concert, a concert that he organized at his own expense, to earn some money. The concert, lasting three and a half hours, was very long, wrote an observer, and very loud, and the hall was very, very cold. No one at the time mentioned how Beethoven's Fifth was the grandest and most heroic symphony ever heard.

The Setting

VIENNA IN 1808

Vienna was at this time a cultural crossroads. It had become the capital of a large multinational empire whose subjects spoke German, Italian, Hungarian, Czech, Polish, and a host of other languages. It would remain a multilingual, multicultural society until the end of the First World War.

Vienna was a fortified city surrounded by strong defensive walls (see Figure 8.1, map of Vienna) beyond which lay an open space, the Glacis, where no permanent building was allowed. The Glacis had been established as a defensive zone during the period in the sixteenth and seventeenth centuries when Vienna was attacked and sometimes besieged by the armies of the Ottoman Empire. The open space made it easy to see if cannons were being moved into firing range of the city walls.

It was also a court city, with political power centered in the palace of the emperors of Austria. (The larger Holy Roman Empire had been dissolved in 1806 as a

FIG. 8.1 A view of Vienna in the eighteenth century. The medieval center of the city is surrounded by fortified walls; outside this is the Glacis, an open area, with the suburban portion of the city beyond. The Danube flows along the edge of the Glacis.

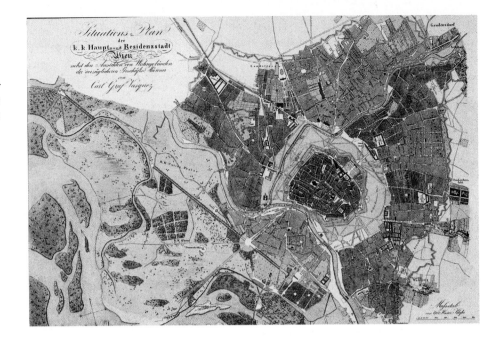

result of the conquests of Napoleon; see map, p. 170). The great urban Hofburg Palace housed various buildings and offices needed for the court bureaucracy. Other palaces included the beautiful Schönbrunn Palace just outside the city, and the Belvedere Palace, built in the early eighteenth century for the military hero Prince Eugene of Savoy (see Figure 8.2). Vast imperial lands had been opened to the public as parks: the Prater, a hunting preserve (now a park), and the Augarten, a pleasure garden (a place opened to the public for recreation) where concerts were held in the summer.

Vienna was also an aristocratic city, with grand palaces for the nobility. Many of these families were patrons of Beethoven and dedicatees of his published works. Some of the patrons connected with Beethoven at the time of the Fifth Symphony were Prince Lobkowitz, who had a special concert hall in his palace in which Beethoven's Third Symphony had been given its first performance; Count Oppersdorf, who maintained his own orchestra, and who commissioned the Fourth and Fifth Symphonies; and Countess Erdödy, a good pianist and a good friend, in whose house Beethoven lived for a short time in 1808.

And, finally, it was a Catholic city, centered on the medieval cathedral of Saint Stephen, the Stefansdom, whose spire can still be seen from almost anywhere in Vienna. Other churches, large and small, as well as the many monasteries, contributed to the religious aspect of the city. The clergy and the church hierarchy set and enforced moral standards and also supported a great deal of music in the churches, affording employment to many of Vienna's musicians.

The old city of Vienna looks today much as it did to Beethoven (see Figures 8.3 and 8.4). The dense web of medieval streets that make up the inner city opens occasionally to reveal a great square, a splendid church, or a coffeehouse where newspapers and magazines are provided for patrons who expect to

The English Physician Richard Bright Describes Vienna in 1814

After some time I walked into the streets,—a service of danger; for most of them are narrow, and the sides, which are paved with flat stones for the convenience of walking, and are, on that account, greatly praised throughout the whole empire, are so little elevated above the carriage tract, that the foot passenger has no safety but in the judgment of the charioteer, who frequently risks an encounter with your feet, rather than with the wheels of a passing carriage.... When, by courage or good luck, I could snatch an opportunity to cast a look upwards, I observed that many of the houses were large, and handsomely built, and all of them very high; but, owing to the narrowness of the streets, there is a prevailing gloom, and it is only in a few of the more open parts that the real beauty of the buildings can develop itself. The shops display a considerable variety of goods, though frequently a square glazed case of patterns hanging at the door is the only mark by which the nature of the shopkeeper's dealings is indicated. Besides this, a small board, projecting into the street from above each door, bears some painted sign, as the Golden Fleece, the Scepter, the Schwarzenburg Head, or the Holy Ghost.

FIG. 8.2 The Belvedere Palace in Vienna, about 1820.

pass an hour reading or talking. The Hofburg Palace and St Stephen's Cathedral, the town palaces of the noble families, great churches and monasteries, and the many apartment buildings still stand today (see The English Physician Richard Bright Describes Vienna in 1814, p. 210).

Outside the inner walls, beyond the open Glacis, were the suburban areas, which consisted of more Baroque palaces with their gardens, splendid churches, public buildings such as hospitals, schools, and barracks—and more apartment buildings. The Glacis and the inner walls gave the city its characteristic look. In the mid-nineteenth century, however, the walls were replaced by grand boulevards, the so-called Ring, and the Glacis is now occupied by museums, theaters, a new opera house and concert hall, and government buildings.

Most people lived in apartments, varying in cost—as apartments always do—according to their location and size. Rents were paid twice a year (usually around St. George's Day, April 24, and St. Michael's Day, September 29), and Beethoven often began to worry about finding a new apartment as rent-day approached. He lived in various Viennese dwellings throughout his life in the city, moving more than two dozen times during his thirty-five years there.

In apartment buildings, the ground floor was given over to shops. On the next two floors were the most expensive rentals—above the dust and noise of the street but without too many stairs to climb. On the upper floors lived tradesmen and servants with their families. Apartments were crowded (it has been estimated that in 1815 the average Viennese apartment housed thirty-three people), and it is perhaps partly because of a lack of privacy that people took at least one meal a day in a restaurant.

TOP, FIG. 8.3 The Graben, one of Vienna's busiest streets. The Pestsaüle (Plague column) was built by Emperor Leopold I (1658–1705) in thanksgiving for the city's recovery from the plague.

BOTTOM, FIG. 8.4 *The Mehlmarkt* (Flour Market) by Bernardo Bellotto (1721–1780).

Living conditions

Living conditions were close and not particularly healthful. The air was full of dust in summer and smoke in winter; disease was widespread in a time before antiseptics and antibiotics. Many people suffered from lung problems, digestive ailments, and sexually transmitted diseases. Life expectancy was relatively low, and infant mortality was high. The average lifespan for a man was between thirty-six and forty years, for a woman, between forty-one and forty-five. Beethoven, who lived to the age of fifty-six, was considered an old man when he died.

Musical life

Vienna enjoyed a rich artistic life of concerts, theaters, and opera. Music could be heard in many of the churches where orchestras and choruses regularly performed at mass. In the theaters, orchestras performed overtures and other kinds of music between acts of popular plays. Two official opera houses, and others besides, presented works mostly in Italian but sometimes in German. Many people were amateur musicians who enjoyed singing or playing instruments together in private gatherings. For people at all levels of society, music was everywhere.

But actual "public" concerts were few. Musical societies gave performances of chamber music or sacred music, and sometimes outdoor concerts; and the Musicians' Society occasionally put on grand events. But regular series of concerts by a symphony orchestra did not exist, nor was there any public hall specifically built for concerts. This is very different from our own time, where almost every large city has a concert hall, an orchestra that plays in it, and a standard series of symphony concerts. In Vienna, if you wanted to give a concert, you had to find and rent a hall, engage and pay an orchestra, and usually compose the music yourself, in addition to arranging for publicity, the box office, and all the logistics that a concert requires. In 1808 most concerts were one-time events arranged by an individual for profit. Nevertheless, there were plenty of occasions for the playing of a symphony.

BEETHOVEN IN VIENNA

Independent professional

Beethoven was a virtuoso pianist, conductor, and composer, and one of the first to earn an independent living in each of these various roles. Most musicians had few choices for economic survival. Their best solutions were either to gain government jobs, which meant performing in the orchestras of the court chapel or one of the official court theaters, or to be hired as a court composer or chamber musician. Failing this, they could piece together a living by giving lessons, by performing in public for paying audiences, or by selling their own compositions.

Various ways of earning an income as a composer were possible. The composer could dedicate a work to a patron, who would then be expected to give a monetary gift in return. Or the patron might pay a fee to commission a composition from a composer; the patron would then maintain the exclusive right to have the work performed for six months (after which the composer could sell it to a publisher). Or the composer could deal with a publisher directly.

Ⓢ Beethoven: Piano Sonata in C Minor, Op. 13 (*Pathétique*), III

Beethoven did all of these: he was known in Vienna as much for his virtuosity on the **pianoforte** (today we shorten this to **piano**) as for his composition, at least in his earlier years in the city. His dazzling, almost brutal, playing attracted attention, and his sonatas for piano and concertos for piano and orchestra were designed partly for him to play and partly for others to buy in order to try to emulate his playing. For much of his career, Beethoven more often played in private concerts and recitals sponsored by his aristocratic patrons than in public concerts (called *Akademien*), and he sometimes expressed resentment about playing "on command."

He gave lessons and attempted, with varying degrees of success, to give concerts and sell his compositions to patrons and publishers. Over time most of these endeavors were quite profitable, which we know because of the large estate left upon his death to his nephew Karl.

Beethoven is rightly considered one of the first composers to establish himself as an independent professional, doing business for himself and composing whatever he liked. He not only enjoyed his independence but also seems to have cultivated a somewhat prickly attitude, which completes the picture of composer as artist rather than composer as servant or employee.

Beethoven was a famously difficult tenant, and moved many times—twice in 1808 alone. For several years he had lived in an apartment, although an inadequate one, that shared a building with the Theater an der Wien (see Letter from Beethoven Complaining about His Apartment, right), which he was able to use to receive visitors. Sometime in 1808 he moved to a large, solid edifice built into the medieval city wall. His apartment, on the top floor with a good view, consisted of five rooms. In the fall of 1808 he moved once again, this time across the street, to an apartment in the house of Countess Erdödy, Beethoven's friend and patron and a great lover of music. (Beethoven dedicated to her two piano trios, Op. 70, that were composed in her house, as well as two cello sonatas, Op. 102.) But she made the mistake of intervening in a squabble between Beethoven and his servant, infuriating Beethoven, and ultimately he lasted only six months at her house.

Beethoven became a recognized character in Vienna, and his daily schedule, as described by a contemporary, went roughly as follows: up at daybreak, he had breakfast and went straight to his desk to work until midday (perhaps with time out for a short walk; see Figure 8.5). Dinner followed (the main meal, in the middle of the day), then a long walk (twice around the city, said one observer). Toward evening, he would often go to a tavern to read papers and talk. Evenings were spent at the theater, in company, or making music. He was usually in bed by 10 p.m., but sometimes stayed up late when particularly busy. He always carried a notebook with him in which he jotted down musical ideas, and the survival of many of these notebooks gives us a rare view into the creative life of one of the great composers (see biography, p. 214).

There are numerous descriptions of Beethoven's appearance, varying in their reliability. The common denominator, however, was that he was a short, stocky, and powerfully built man. "Short and thickset," goes one description, "broad across the shoulders, short neck, large head, rounded nose, dark-brown complexion; he always leaned forward a little in walking. In his boyhood they used to call him 'der Spagnol' [the Spaniard] in our house."

Beethoven was deeply concerned with the ideas of freedom and human liberty that characterized the thinking of the eighteenth century—a period in Western history we now call the Age of Enlightenment (see Part Opener III). Intellectually this movement ranged from the French Encyclopédistes, who sought to classify human knowledge, to the biting social satires of Voltaire, the romantic poetry of Johann Wolfgang von Goethe, the rational philosophical thoughts of Thomas Hobbes and David Hume in England, and the practical and humanistic philosophies of Benjamin Franklin and Thomas Jefferson in America.

Letter (1808) from Beethoven to Joseph Sonnleitner, Complaining about His Apartment in the Theater an der Wien

My brother has told you of my changing lodgings; I have occupied this one conditionally until a better one can be found. The chance came already some time ago and I wanted to assert my right then with *Zitterbarth* [previous owner of the theater], at which point Baron Braun became owner of the theatre. The rooms occupied by the *painter* above and which are clearly adequate only for a servant, need only to be vacated, then my apartment could be handed to the painter, and the affair would be settled. —Since in my apartment the servant must sleep in the kitchen, the servant I now have is already my third—and this one will not stay long with me either; without considering its other inconveniences.—I know beforehand that if it depends upon the decision of Herr *Baron* again, the answer will be *no*. In that case I shall look for something elsewhere immediately. Already I am used to the fact that he has nothing good to say about me—let it be—*I shall never grovel*—my world is elsewhere.

FIG. 8.5 Johann Peter Lyser's (1803–1870) depiction shows Beethoven on a walk in Vienna. The image was reproduced in the periodical *Cäcilia* in 1833.

LUDWIG VAN BEETHOVEN (1770–1827)

Ludwig van Beethoven merged clarity of form with power of expression. His music bridges, and combines, the periods of Classical balance and Romantic passion, and his symphonies, string quartets, and piano sonatas stand at the apex of their genres. He was also well known for his concertos, chamber music, his one opera (*Fidelio*), and two Masses.

Beethoven came from a musical family in Bonn, but at the age of twenty-two he moved to Vienna for good. There he studied for a time with the composer Franz Joseph Haydn. He rapidly made a reputation as a virtuoso pianist, sought after for salons and public concerts, and became known as an exceptional composer as well: by 1799 five different publishing houses had printed his music.

Beethoven had important patrons to whom he dedicated compositions, gave lessons, and in whose houses he performed and sometimes lived. He was fiercely independent, even abusive at times. He never achieved the security of a government or other official position, and partly as a result learned to make his own way.

He began to sense the possibility of real fame at about the same time as the onset of his devastating and progressive deafness. His so-called Heiligenstadt Testament, a letter of wrenching sadness written at his summer lodging in the suburban town of Heiligenstadt in 1802, acknowledged his deafness and his despair. Turning almost exclusively to composition, Beethoven produced some of his most lastingly popular works. After the concert of 1808, Beethoven gave another public concert in 1814, at the height of his popularity. It would be his last public performance.

Increasingly famous and increasingly isolated because of his deafness, Beethoven turned to introspective smaller genres—piano sonatas, string quartets, and other works for smaller ensembles. He gave his last concert in 1824; it included his Ninth Symphony and portions of his Solemn Mass (*Missa solemnis*). He died, a world-famous composer with a large estate, in March of 1827. His funeral procession down the streets of Vienna was witnessed by over 10,000 people.

Ⓢ Beethoven: Piano Sonata in C♯ Minor, Op. 27, No. 2 (*Moonlight*), III

Ⓢ Beethoven: Symphony No. 9, IV, "Ode to Joy"

Ⓢ Beethoven: String Quartet No. 9 in C Major, Op. 59 (*Rasumovsky*), No. 3, III, Minuet

MAJOR WORKS: Orchestral works, including nine symphonies; concertos, including five for piano, one for violin, and a triple concerto; chamber music, including string quartets, piano trios, sonatas for violin and for cello; 32 piano sonatas, including Op. 13 (*Pathétique*) and Op. 27 (*Moonlight*); one opera (*Fidelio*); Mass in C Major and *Missa solemnis*.

Social and political climate

The movement toward equality expressed by the Enlightenment was a difficult concept in an autocratic and monarchical society like Austria. The emperors of Austria ruled over a large empire of many nationalities, and they maintained a tight grip on their constituencies: there were censors, spies, and secret police everywhere. In order to get anything published, or to perform a play, an opera, or a song in public, official approval from the censors was needed. To receive permission to marry meant providing evidence of education, good conduct, loyalty to the government, and the means of supporting a family. This highly structured—and, to our modern minds, repressive—society was not unlike that of other monarchies. And it is partly as a result of this repression that people began investigating their own individual worth in relation to liberty and freedom.

It was also the Age of Revolution. The American Revolution, and then the French Revolution starting in 1789, had given many people, including Beethoven, hope for wider liberty. Thus he was devastated when Napoleon Bonaparte declared himself emperor of France in 1804. Disillusioned that his idol was well on his way to becoming a tyrant, Beethoven angrily removed the title "Bonaparte" from the original title page of his Third Symphony.

In this social and political climate, Beethoven premiered his Fifth Symphony. At the time, in 1808, Beethoven was in his prime, still active as a performer. Together with the lofty ideals embodied in this particular work, Beethoven designed the December 22 concert to show himself off as performer and composer, and to make a little money.

The Performance

PREPARATIONS

What we now call a "concert" was called an *Akademie* in Beethoven's Vienna (we'll call them "Academies"). It was normally a one-time event, organized most often by a virtuoso performer to display her or his talents, and was the main form of public concert in Vienna and elsewhere. The event might highlight an exotic instrument, in which case the concert was considered a kind of novelty. Or perhaps—and more often—it would focus on a particular touring virtuoso, showing off skills in singing or playing and presenting some flamboyant pieces. Only occasionally, as in the concert we are about to consider, was the main attraction a composer. But only rarely does such a composer come along.

An Academy, even when given by a virtuoso soloist on violin or piano, usually included a variety of musical genres: overtures, symphonies, vocal music, variations, and improvisations by the main performer. Symphonies were mostly used to begin the program (to get the audience's attention) and sometimes also at the end. It was up to the organizer to recruit and rehearse the orchestra and other performers, and to make certain that the event received official approval and was advertised properly. Because virtuosos often composed much of their own music, one could expect to hear at least some new music. In fact, the more modern it was, the better. For most people, newer music, all things being equal, was better than old.

Academies

For his 1808 Academy, Beethoven first had to find a place to give the performance. Obviously he needed a large enough space to accommodate an audience of several hundred in order to pay the expenses. Since no purpose-built concert halls existed, the choices were relatively limited. There was the grand ballroom of the Hofburg Palace, a fine space for some events, but it required too much setting up for a concert. There was also the indoor riding ring attached to the palace, a cavernous and beautiful space, sometimes used for concerts, but much bigger than what Beethoven needed.

Most suitable, and most often used for Academies, were theaters, of which there were several in Vienna. The two official court theaters, one used for plays and one for operas, were available for rent when there were no performances scheduled. (There were also small theaters in the suburbs, but these were not roomy enough for the composer's needs.) Beethoven settled on the Theater an der Wien, famous for its large size and spectacular scenery (see Figure 8.6). He knew it well; not only had he previously performed two versions of his opera *Fidelio* there, but as we saw, he also had rented

FIG. 8.6 The Theater an der Wien, where Beethoven's concert took place, is the building on the left.

An Advertisement for Beethoven's Concert

On Thursday, December 22, Ludwig van Beethoven will have the honor to give a musical Akademie in the Royal Imperial Private Theater-an-der-Wien. All the pieces are of his composition, entirely new, and not yet heard in public.

First part:
1. A Symphony entitled: "A Recollection of Country Life," no. 5
2. Aria
3. Hymn with Latin text, composed in the church style with chorus and solos
4. Pianoforte concerto played by himself

Second part
1. Grand symphony in C minor, no. 6
2. Sanctus, with Latin text, composed in the church style with chorus and solos
3. Fantasia for pianoforte alone
4. Fantasia for the pianoforte which ends with the gradual entrance of the entire orchestra and the introduction of choruses as a finale

Boxes and reserved seats are to be had in the Krugerstrasse No. 1074, first story. Beginning at half past six o'clock.

an apartment in the building. In recognition of his charitable contributions—that is, for his prior performances, which had been presented gratis in other Academies—Beethoven received official permission to give this concert for his own benefit.

Academy programs were long. If you were going to get dressed up and get yourself to the theater—which was not always easy—you would not have wanted it otherwise. Music, after all, only happened "live," and if you did not know how to perform music yourself, you could only hear it if you were present when it was performed.

This Academy of 1808, however, was exceptionally long: it included two of Beethoven's recent symphonies; two extracts from his recent Mass in C Major for chorus and orchestra (the censors did not allow performances of liturgical music for money, so these pieces were called "hymn with Latin text"); the very beautiful Fourth Piano Concerto, played by Beethoven himself; an improvisation at the piano, also performed by Beethoven; a vocal aria; and finally, a piece for all the performers—orchestra, piano, and chorus (the Choral Fantasy)—to close the program. (See An Advertisement for Beethoven's Concert, left.)

It was a spectacular event, full of brand-new music (except for one aria, *Ah! Perfido* that he had written twelve years earlier). Beethoven placed his symphonies at the beginning of each part of the concert. Both symphonies were new, and he numbered them in the order in which they were played, although he ultimately published and numbered them in reverse order.

Instead of closing with a symphony as would have been typical of the times, Beethoven composed a special piece for this concert, one that purposely included all the performers at this event—orchestral players, pianist, solo singers, and chorus. At his next public performance, in 1824, Beethoven used this same strategy, ending his concert with the exuberant Ninth Symphony, written for solo singers, chorus, and orchestra.

IN THE THEATER

The Theater an der Wien was seven years old; it had been opened in 1801 by Emanuel Schikaneder, whose company had commissioned Mozart's opera *The Magic Flute*. Standing somewhat apart from the official government-run court theaters, it was large and famous for elaborate stage machinery and for productions of "magic operas" like Mozart's. It had five tiers of boxes and a floor divided into two sections: at the front, benches, and at the back, reserved individual seats, with a sort of gangway between the two (see Figure 8.7). This was typical of theaters at the time, which were built to accommodate sightlines and stage settings rather than to optimize the acoustics for music. When an orchestra is placed on the stage of a theater, part of the sound inevitably disappears up into the flyspace above the stage. (This does not happen in opera, because the orchestra is on the floor of the hall, in the *orchestra pit*, and the singers generally come downstage, in front of the proscenium arch, to sing their arias.)

The theater's orchestra was accustomed to playing opera arias and overtures, not difficult symphonies like the Symphony in C Minor. There were only a few rehearsals, because of expense and scheduling difficulties. Many things went wrong

FIG. 8.7 The interior of the Theater an der Wien; it was famous for spectacular scenery, animals on stage, and magical effects.

in the concert. The soprano, already a replacement, had terrible stage fright and could barely sing. There had been numerous difficulties throughout the rehearsals themselves, with Beethoven knocking over one of the two choirboys who held lamps for him. The choirboys were there because Beethoven usually knocked the candles off his piano, and the boys were supposed to be able to dodge Beethoven's manic movements. (See two accounts of the first performance, pp. 217 and 218.)

Beethoven himself tried to put the best possible light on the first performance of his Fifth Symphony, described in a letter to a publisher a couple of weeks later:

> Notwithstanding the fact that several mistakes were made, which I could not help, the public accepted everything enthusiastically. . . . The musicians were particularly angry because, when a blunder was made through carelessness in the simplest, plainest place in the world, I stopped them suddenly and loudly called out *"Once again"*—Such a thing had never happened to them before. The public showed its enjoyment at this.

Beethoven played the piano solos himself and conducted the orchestra as well. His conducting style was energetic—as noted above—a little different from that of most of his contemporaries. Given that this concert, like most others of the time, had a pickup orchestra of musicians who, though good players, did not ordinarily play together, we could not expect the sort of finesse and polish that is characteristic of today's best orchestras. What's more, for today's orchestras these are familiar, favorite pieces, while in 1808 they were difficult contemporary music. And so the conducting may have been more involved with keeping things together than with delicate shades of expression.

An Account, Perhaps Exaggerated, of an Incident at the Concert

Beethoven was playing [his new concerto], but forgot at the first *tutti* [passage for full orchestra], that he was a Soloplayer, and springing up, began to direct in his usual way. At the first *sforzando* he threw out his arms so wide asunder, that he knocked both the lights off the piano. . . . The audience laughed, and *Beethoven* was so incensed . . . that he made the orchestra cease playing, and begin anew. *Seyfried*, [the conductor] fearing, that a repetition of the accident would occur at the same passage, bade two [choirboys] place themselves on either side of *Beethoven*, and hold the lights in their hands. One of the boys innocently approached nearer, and was reading also in the notes of the piano-part. When therefore the fatal *sforsando* came, he received from *Beethoven's* out thrown right hand so smart a blow on the mouth, that the poor boy let fall the light from terror. The other boy, more cautious, had followed with anxious eyes every motion of *Beethoven*, and by stooping suddenly at the eventful moment he avoided the slap on the mouth. If the public were unable to restrain their laughter before, they could now much less, and broke out into a regular bacchanalian roar. *Beethoven* got into such a rage, that at the first chords of the solo, half a dozen strings broke. Every endeavour . . . to restore calm and attention were for the moment fruitless. The first *allegro* of the Concerto was therefore lost to the public.

An Eyewitness to the First Performance of the Fifth Symphony: Johann Friedrich Reichardt, Composer and Writer

accepted the kind offer of Prince Lobkowitz to let me sit in his box with hearty thanks. There we continued, in the bitterest cold, too, from half past six to half past ten, and experienced the truth that one can easily have too much of a good thing—and still more of a loud. Nevertheless, I could no more leave the box before the end than could the exceedingly good-natured and delicate Prince, for the box was in the first balcony near the stage, so that the orchestra with Beethoven in the middle conducting it was below us and near at hand; thus many a failure in the performance vexed our patience in the highest degree. Poor Beethoven, who from this, his own concert, was having the first and only scant profit that he could find in a whole year, had found in the rehearsals and performance a lot of opposition and almost no support. Singers and orchestra were composed of heterogeneous elements, and it had been found impossible to get a single full rehearsal for all the pieces to be performed, all filled with the greatest difficulties.

Many, many millions of people have listened to this symphony since that day in 1808. Because the music is so familiar, it may be difficult to imagine hearing it for the first time, to be among the Viennese audience who paid such close attention to the contemporary music of their time, but let's give it a try.

The Music

WHAT IS A SYMPHONY?

Because symphonies were so often performed, most people in Beethoven's audience had probably listened to dozens of them. These early-nineteenth-century listeners expected a symphony to behave in a certain way—in fact, that is how they knew it *was* a symphony. Beethoven also expected a symphony to in certain conventions—to begin loudly, for example, or to consist of several movements, each in a different mood. But as a creative composer Beethoven also wanted to craft something other than the standard, traditional symphony. We cannot know why Beethoven composed music in the symphonic genre. Perhaps it was simply what people expected of him; that is, he was matching the conventions of the day. But by using a conventional form so well understood by his Viennese peers, he knew they would be much more capable of appreciating and following what was new, special, and exceptional.

A **symphony** is first and foremost a multimovement *composition for orchestra*, usually without voices or instrumental soloists. In this very broad sense we have already seen the word *symphony*, or *sinfonia*, used by Monteverdi, Handel, and Mozart.

Today an orchestra is defined as an ensemble of instrumentalists centered on players of stringed instruments (violins, violas, violoncellos, double basses), in which more than one player performs each part. This distinguishes a string orchestra from various chamber-music ensembles like string quartets, where there is only one player per part.

Typical eighteenth-century orchestra

Beethoven wrote his Fifth Symphony for a typical eighteenth-century orchestra. The fact that he was able to publish his Fifth Symphony so soon after its debut attests to its arrangement for a standard orchestra. The strings were typically divided into first violins, second violins (there weren't any physical differences in the instruments, only in their music), violas, cellos, and double basses. The double basses sometimes had independent parts, but just as often they played the same part as the cellos an octave lower.

To the strings were added woodwind, brass, and percussion instruments. Woodwinds included flute, oboe, clarinet, and bassoon. In this symphony, as in most symphonies, Beethoven called for two of each instrument.

The brass instruments included two French horns and two trumpets. A pair of kettledrums accompanied the trumpets and provided the only percussion sounds in Beethoven's Fifth.

This setup also describes today's standard orchestra. But composers tend to modify the orchestral makeup in order to suit their own creative needs. In the Fifth, for example, Beethoven actually adds more instruments at the end: a piccolo (very high flute), a contrabassoon (very low bassoon), and three trombones all join in the last movement. In other symphonies, Beethoven also deviates from the standard: he uses three horns in his Third Symphony; a piccolo and two trombones in the Sixth; and four horns, piccolo, contrabassoon, triangle, cymbals, and bass drum in the Ninth. Every composer, of course, has the right to call for a different size and composition of the orchestra; but most of Beethoven's Fifth Symphony is written for a "standard" orchestra of the sort that was customary at the time, and that has been the standard orchestra ever since.

SYMPHONIC FORM

Beethoven uses the classical symphony as his model—a model that consists of a series of four separate pieces, each designed to provide a satisfying musical experience; when the pieces are listened to in sequence, the result suggests a larger psychological and aesthetic journey. The symphony as a genre had essentially been defined by Haydn and Mozart.

The four parts of a symphony are called **movements**, from the French word *Movements* for tempo, because each part tends to "move" at different speeds. A typical four-movement symphony starts with a first movement, often the longest of the four, followed by a slow movement, a **minuet and trio**, and a lively finale. The box below describes each movement in more detail.

MUSICAL STYLE

Music written in the Classical style deviated considerably from the norms of Baroque music.

Themes You will remember that Baroque music tends to have melodies that resemble prose sentences, extended by **sequences** but not generally arranged in paired phrases. In contrast, the main melodies of Classical pieces—what we call

Standard Symphonic Model and the Fifth Symphony

I. *The first movement:* This is a strong, outgoing piece, with a lively or serious character, and is often the weightiest movement in the symphony. It may be preceded by an introduction in a slower tempo. Normally, as in this symphony, it is in **first-movement sonata form** (see p. 220). 🔊 **LG 29**

II. *The slow movement:* The second movement is almost always contemplative or lyrical and tends to progress at a more relaxed, even very slow, speed. This movement is usually in a different key from the other three. Slow movements may also contain dramatic passages that present strong contrasts to the lyrical quality of the opening. In the Fifth Symphony the movement is in a modified version of **variation form** (see p. 221). 🔊 **LG 30**

III. *The minuet:* It is reasonable to ask what is left after a fast movement and a slow movement. We can consider the third movement as a kind of seventh-inning stretch, a moment of relaxation. It is cast in a dance form, usually a **minuet** (see p. 221), but one that is intended not to be danced but rather

as pleasant listening. It has the regular rhythms and phrases expected from dance music. The minuet is followed by a contrasting section called a "trio," after which the whole minuet is played again. 🔊 **LG 31**

IV. *The last movement,* or *finale:* The final movement is fast, usually livelier and more lighthearted than the first, and is designed to send the audience away feeling happy, maybe even whistling a tune. While finales are often in **rondo form** (see p. 221), the Fifth Symphony uses sonata form for the last movement as well as the first. 🔊 **LG 32**

This description of a symphony can be applied accurately to hundreds of symphonies written by Haydn, Mozart, Beethoven, and many other composers. They followed the pattern because it was—and is—a good one; it gives listeners a varied and rounded experience, and makes it possible to compare one symphony with another, one finale with another.

themes—often consist of pairs of phrases with similar music. Two pairs of phrases can and often do make a very satisfactory theme, like the four musical phrases of many folk or folklike songs (think of the four lines of "Swanee River," or the four phrases that begin Mozart's "Là ci darem la mano").

Ⓢ Mozart: *Don Giovanni*, Act 1, Scene 9, "Là ci darem la mano"

Variety   While Baroque music generally seeks to express a single emotion or feeling in a piece (think of the arias in Handel's *Messiah*), a symphonic movement often presents two or more musical themes with differing sounds, thereby providing a contrast of moods. Listen to the contrasting themes in each of the four movements of Beethoven's Fifth to hear how it differs from the Baroque style.

Theme and Transition   In a Classical symphony, there is often a difference between music that is a theme, where a clear and memorable melody is presented, and music that is not thematic. The nonthematic music tends to be active, agitated, and deliberately unclear about key. (This is a little like the difference, in Baroque music, between a motive and a sequence that follows from it, or between the subject and the episodes in fugues.) If you feel a bit uncertain or hesitant at some point in your listening, or feel the tension level rise, it is likely that the composer means to create this effect, so that the arrival at a new theme can be a moment of release. Listen to the transition between the two themes in the first movement of Beethoven's Fifth and in the first movement of Mozart's Symphony No. 40.

Ⓢ Beethoven: Symphony No. 5, I, transition 1st to 2nd theme

Ⓢ Mozart: Symphony No. 40, I, transition 1st to 2nd theme

MUSICAL FORMS

There are various ways in which one might structure the overall form of a whole movement. Here are some of the most common forms.

First-movement form (or sonata form, or sonata-allegro form)   First-movement **sonata form** is a vessel so flexible that it can provide a basic framework for many hundreds, even thousands, of movements without seeming in any way rigid, conventional, or overused. It is the most complex, and the most frequently found, of the musical forms in the Classic period, and has continued in use ever since. It can almost be viewed as a psychological progression, and is often described in the following way:

Parts of sonata form

A. **Exposition.** A theme is presented. Then a transitional passage leads to a new mood and a new key. At this point, one or more contrasting themes are presented. A final passage leads to a conclusion, which stays in the new key. This whole section provides a rounded musical experience, but it seems incomplete because it does not end in the original key. The whole exposition is repeated from the beginning.

B. **Development.** A new section follows that is related to one or both of the previous themes but that raises the energy level, and the anxiety level, by various stratagems designed to confuse or mislead, so that the listener is relieved when the next section occurs. At the end, a **retransition** leads, sometimes urges, us back toward the home key.

C. **Recapitulation.** The opening theme returns, just as in the beginning. A transitional passage similar to the first one leads to a repetition of the second theme or group, but this time in the original key. The concluding passage from before (this time in the original key) brings the movement to a close. (Sometimes there is a repetition of sections B and C.) The conclusion makes us feel more at "home."

In addition, there is sometimes an introduction, usually in a different, slower tempo, before the movement itself gets started; and an ending section, called a **coda** ("tail," in Italian) added to the end of the recapitulation, to close the movement as a whole.

Coda

This very general outline accounts for the formal shape of many movements, not only of symphonies but also of sonatas for one or more instruments (which is why it is sometimes called "sonata form"), string quartets and other varieties of chamber music, and in modified form also for concertos for piano, violin, or other solo instrument with orchestra.

Beethoven's Fifth Symphony uses this formal design for the first and also the last movement.

Theme and variations This is one of the simplest forms to hear because it involves the same melody repeated a number of times. The melody, however, changes with each new presentation, usually by the addition of embellishments that involve increasingly faster notes while the basic tempo and the underlying harmonies remain the same. Often this pattern of increasing complexity is altered toward the end, usually in the next-to-last variation, by some striking contrast: changing from major to minor (or vice versa), changing the key, using a suddenly slower tempo, or some combination of these; this is often followed immediately by a rousing final variation. **Variation form** is sometimes used for slow movements of symphonies, but not often for other movements (although Beethoven does use a variation form in the last movement of his Third Symphony). The slow movement of the Fifth Symphony uses variation form, but in a relatively complex way.

Variation form

Minuet and trio This is the standard form for the symphony's third movement and is based on the triple rhythms and regular phrases of the eighteenth-century's favorite ballroom dance. Essentially it consists of a minuet, a trio (another minuet with contrasting orchestration), and a repeat of the minuet. The initial minuet is made up of two separate sections: the first part (we can call it **A**) usually consists of several pairs of phrases; the whole first part is repeated (**AA**). Then the second part (**B**) begins with a series of phrases related to, but different from, the first part. This section starts where the first part left off and brings us back to music reminiscent of the minuet's beginning. The whole second part is also repeated: we might diagram the minuet as **AABB**. The trio, which contrasts with the minuet in key, mood, and theme, is also made of two parts, each of which is repeated: **CCDD**. Finally, the minuet is played again, this time usually without repeats. The overall form of a typical minuet and trio movement could be given as **AABB CCDD AB**. Beethoven often preferred to use a sort of speeded-up minuet that he called a **scherzo** (Italian, for "joke"); it is faster than a minuet but retains the same form.

Minuet

Trio

Scherzo

Rondo form The basic idea in rondo form is that a melody (let's call it **A**), usually lighthearted and easy to remember, alternates with other material. We can diagram the basic idea like this: **AbAcAdA** . The chief delight for most listeners in a rondo is waiting for the familiar theme to return, and composers like to toy with listeners by delaying this return with playful anticipation. Sophisticated versions of the rondo are often used for the finales of symphonies, sometimes including recurrences of other material (for example, **AbAcAbA**) and the use of different keys for the various parts, all of which makes for a structure and effect that goes beyond the simple multiple returns of a theme. (Beethoven does not happen to use this form in the Fifth Symphony).

Individual movements, often using forms like those just described, are normally assembled into series to make a larger form. The box on page 223 gives a brief overview of some of the typical larger forms that were usual during the Classic period. Many of these are named more for their performing forces than for their forms.

Listening to the Music

How to make a theme out of a motive in Beethoven's Fifth Symphony

What might we hear when listening to the first movement of Beethoven's Fifth Symphony? Melodies, of course. But in Beethoven we will hear a different sort of melody from the shapely and expressive ones by Mozart; Beethoven's musical material is often formed from motives, which can be assembled into melodies.

We also hear qualities of the orchestral sound, perhaps the varying sounds of different instruments, the loudness or softness of certain passages. The overall form is also something we might notice, but we might be less conscious of the structure of the piece than of other, more immediate elements. Form is important, both for composer and listener, because it provides direction or an outline of how a movement can be expected to progress. As a listener, form is not necessarily what we hear first, or perhaps at all. Often we simply pay attention to a melody, or a lush sound, or a surprising new effect. But even these observations are made *in context*, and when we notice that a phrase is being repeated or that something sounds similar to (or different from) a passage that came earlier, we are paying attention to form, whether we realize it or not.

Form

Form can give us a sense of gratification. How does this work? When the first part of a minuet is repeated, for example, we are conscious of the repetition. We may hear this repetition slightly differently than we heard the same music at the beginning of the piece, in part because it is not new anymore and in part because now we are better equipped to notice more details that might have gone by too quickly the first time. When the first part of the minuet comes back for the third time, after the trio, we may well feel a sense of coming home, as if we have returned from a voyage.

Exposition in sonata form

In the more complex sonata form, the same ideas are present but in a more intricate manner. The opening part—the exposition—is a voyage in itself because it involves two themes (and two keys), with transitional and closing materials that separate the themes. It seems like a complete experience, although vaguely incomplete because it settles into a key different from the beginning key. When the whole exposition is repeated we get a second chance, as with the minuet form, to become familiar with the music before the composer begins the next section. Even within the exposition, the basic idea of same and different, familiar and new, is continuously present.

Development in sonata form

The development is also a combination of new and old. We recognize that this section generally deals with familiar material; but the composer also wants to take us as far afield as possible, or, in musical terms, to explore what interesting things can be done with the musical material of the exposition. The development is the place of highest tension, and it provides us with a sense of distance from the familiar. At the retransition to the recapitulation—and the moment of arrival at the now-familiar first theme—we feel a sense of relief.

Larger Classical Genres

Many compositions of the Classic period are given names that describe the performing forces (e.g., string trio) rather than the music itself. This is a practical matter, of course, but also reflects that whatever the performing forces, the contents are probably similar: several movements, in contrasting tempos, usually involving at least one movement in sonata form. Some large genres are likely to have four movements in the shape Fast (sonata form)—Slow—Minuet—Fast. These four-movement pieces include the string quartet and the symphony. Others, like the sonata and the concerto, are more likely to have three movements, omitting the minuet.

Compositions for two or more solo players (as opposed to orchestral compositions, which have more than one player on each string part) are generally called **chamber music** because of their suitability for performances in intimate spaces. Let us look at some of the typical genres from this period:

Sonata. This term can be applied to an instrumental piece for piano alone or for piano and another instrument (often violin, cello, or a solo woodwind instrument). Most Classical sonatas have three movements.

String Quartet. One of the favorite Classical ensembles, a string quartet consists of a first and a second violin, a viola, and a cello, which makes the string quartet like a solo version of an orchestra but without winds or brass. Some of the greatest works of Haydn, Mozart, Beethoven, and Schubert are written for string quartet, which are often in four movements, like those of a symphony.

Trio, Quartet, Quintet, etc. Compositions for various combinations of strings and winds are usually named according to the number of players. One of Beethoven's most popular pieces in his own time was the Septet for Strings and Winds, Op. 20. Such pieces often follow the form of the symphony.

Serenade. A serenade can be for a chamber group or for an orchestra. It is seldom highly serious, being a concert version of music played outdoors during the evening. It usually has more than four movements, including two or more minuets or other dance movements.

Concerto. Written for one (or sometimes more than one) virtuoso solo instrument with orchestra, a concerto usually has three movements. The first is a modified version of sonata form (with two expositions, one for the orchestra and one for the soloist); this is followed by a slow movement, and a finale often in rondo form.

Symphony. The chief genre of orchestral music in the Classic period, it generally is cast in four movements. In the hands of Haydn, Mozart, and Beethoven it progressed from an extended sort of overture into the grandest achievement of orchestral music.

Recapitulation in sonata form

The recapitulation is all familiar material—or is it? In the exposition, the transition from the first to the second theme moves from one key to another. In the recapitulation, the composer keeps us in the home key; the second theme and closing material here are also in this same key. So even in the recapitulation, whose psychological purpose is to make us feel solidly at home in the familiar, there is still an element of the new, which may be part of what keeps us interested.

Beethoven notably expanded the proportions of the standard first-movement form, largely through longer developments and codas. But he used his skill in developing themes from assemblages of motives to engage in a sort of continuous development throughout. This is particularly notable in the first movement of the Fifth Symphony (see LG 29, p. 224).

Beethoven's listeners were accustomed to hearing pieces that employed the standard first-movement shape, and maybe they were so familiar with it that they seldom described it in precisely these terms. In fact, the dramatic shape of the form seems to be one that arises naturally: situation (first theme), tension (new key, new theme), crisis (development), resolution (recapitulation). In that sense it would seem to recreate itself every time a composer sat down to write an extended movement; he would not have to think about the "rules" of a preordained sonata form.

Music writers and listeners do think of sonata form that way today, however, and listening for the form is one very interesting way of trying to find and keep one's bearings in the course of a long symphonic movement. There are plenty of other ways to listen, and the combination of enjoying the sounds of the moment with a sense of where we are, where we've been, and where we might (or might not) be going, is part of the fun of music.

LG 29 Beethoven: Symphony No. 5, I

LISTENING GUIDE 29 | DVD |

Beethoven Symphony No. 5 in C Minor, Op. 67, I   6:56
(Allegro con brio)

DATE: 1807–08

LISTEN FOR

MELODY: Themes developed from simple motive: short-short-short-long

FORM: Difference in sound between stable (thematic) portions and unstable (transitional or developmental) portions

SCORING: Moments of solo instruments: horn, oboe, bassoon

EXPRESSION/DYNAMICS: Dynamic contrasts (loud and soft); crescendos over long stretches of repeated motives

TIME	FORM	DESCRIPTION
	Exposition	
0:00	First theme, C minor	Four-note motive (SSSL), twice, with pauses. Note the down-up-down melodic direction when motive is played twice:
0:06		Motive statements combined into theme.
0:17		Motive as fanfare, higher than before.
0:20		Motive statements combined into theme, continued. Note the crescendo, and the extension of the motive from SSSL to SSSLLL.
0:41	Transition	Probably the shortest transition in symphonic music:
		Horn call derived from combining the motive with the melodic shape of the down-up-down of the opening.
0:43	Second theme, E♭ major	Lyrical second theme, in woodwinds, heard against rhythmic accompaniment of the 4-note motive:
		Begun by violins, crescendos to . . .
1:02	Closing theme, E♭ major	Gradually transitions from smooth, regular melody to original motive. Cadence in E♭ major.
1:20	**Exposition Repeated**	
	Development	
2:39		Opening fanfare, announced by horn call:

2:44		Begins like exposition, but in a different key (F minor).
3:14		Version of transition theme.
3:25		Focus on the two central notes.
3:34		Two notes reduced to one, interrupted once. Gradual decrescendo.
3:45		Second outburst of motive, repeated, leading to . . .

Recapitulation

3:57	First theme, C minor	Opening fanfare. Harmonized, not unison as before.
4:03		Motive statements combined into theme. The orchestration is different; note pizzicato in double basses.
4:14		Pause as before (but no motive as fanfare). Oboe cadenza:

4:26		Motive statements combined into theme, continued. Not quite the same as before, because it does not move to a new key.
4:46	Transition	Bassoons play the "horn call."
4:47	Second theme, C major	

| 5:11 | Closing theme, C major | Gradually transitions from smooth regular melody to original motive. Just when the symphony could end, cadencing in C major . . . |

Coda

| 5:30 | | Key is unclear. Basic motive, fortissimo, halting for statements of motive in woodwinds. |
| 5:42 | Polyphonic section, C minor | |

Opening motive reduced to two notes, as in development, but the two notes are faster here. Motive combined with smooth new theme.

| 5:58 | | Two notes become 4-note motive: |

6:24	Apparent closing cadence, C minor, leading to . . .	
6:28	Opening fanfare of original 4-note motives	Harmonized, like the recapitulation; the listener imagines that the recapitulation is being repeated.
6:36	Opening of first theme	The listener *really* thinks the recapitulation is being repeated.
6:41	Closing cadence, C minor	Loud, emphatic, interrupting the theme.

WHAT IS SPECIAL ABOUT THE FIFTH SYMPHONY?

The Fifth Symphony is one of the most frequently played pieces of classical music. Its four-note opening motive is associated with fate, with the struggle for victory in the Second World War (the rhythm of the motive—short, short, short, long—matches the letter V in Morse code—dot, dot, dot, dash—thus the theme's connection to the word and concept of "victory"). The work is strong, extroverted, and heroic. Its sense of unity derives from two ideas: first, Beethoven's careful tying together of the whole symphony by using related themes (see below); and second, the sense of goal-orientation throughout the symphony, beginning in the key of C minor and ending in a blaze, in the key of C major, as if the composer were going from darkness to light.

 Rhythmic unity of themes throughout Beethoven's Fifth Symphony

The relation of themes is easy to hear (see Unity of Themes, below). The first movement is tightly woven from versions of a single idea—the short-short-short-long motive that begins the movement and generates almost all the music in the movement. And the core rhythmic idea of that motive extends to the other movements of the symphony—a practice unique to Beethoven at this time. Although each movement has its own independent character, each also has at least one theme recalling the original rhythmic idea: the secondary theme in the slow movement (see LG 30, p. 227); the horn-call second idea in the scherzo (see LG 31, p. 229); and the second theme in the finale (see LG 32, p. 230).

LG 30 Beethoven: Symphony No. 5, II

According to his biographer Anton Schindler, not always a reliable witness, Beethoven, when asked about the opening four-note motive, said, "Thus Fate pounds on the gate." Some think that it is Beethoven's fate, surely his growing deafness, that Beethoven meant—if, of course, he said it at all. But whether he did or didn't, it remains true that he created and employed a unifying motive that recurs throughout the work.

Unity of Themes in Beethoven's Fifth Symphony

One of Beethoven's specialties was making long compositions out of short motives. The motive that he used to construct the whole first movement, **short-short-short-long**, keeps reappearing in all four of the movements.

MOVEMENT I: The opening four notes give the motive and its rhythm:

MOVEMENT II: The secondary theme, preceded by its two-note dotted upbeat, includes the four-note rhythm:

MOVEMENT III: The horn-call second theme in the scherzo uses the same rhythm:

MOVEMENT IV: The second theme of the finale uses a triplet version, much livelier, of the same rhythm:

Beethoven Symphony No. 5 in C Minor, Op. 67, II   9:18
(Andante con moto)

DATE: 1807–08

LISTEN FOR

MELODY: Different ways of making variations on a melody
FORM: Alternation of two themes (**A** and **B**)
TEXTURE: Varieties of accompaniment texture

SCORING: Orchestra treated in groups: strings, woodwinds, and brass

TIME	FORM	DESCRIPTION
0:00	**Theme A,** A♭ major	Violas and cellos play theme:
		The ending, prolonged, adds strings and winds. **Theme A** in clarinets and bassoons modulates to loud C major.
1:10	**Theme B,** C major	Brass and timpani, with triplet accompaniment in the strings:
1:25	Transition	Mysterious harmonies lead back to A♭ major.
1:50	**Theme A,** var. 1, A♭ major	Violas and cellos again, smooth 8th notes; same long ending as before; same transition to . . .
2:57	**Theme B,** var. 1, C major	Same theme in brass, faster accompaniment in the strings:
3:12	Transition	Same harmonies as before, with ominous accompaniment in cellos.
3:38	**Theme A,** var. 2, A♭ major	Violas and cellos play 32nd notes, pizzicato accompaniment:

(continued)

TIME	FORM	DESCRIPTION
3:55	**Theme A,** var. 3, A♭ major	Violins take up same version.
4:13	**Theme A,** var. 4, A♭ major	Loud: cellos and basses play same version but *forte*.
4:36	"Meditations" on **Theme A,** A♭ major	
5:26	**Theme B**, var. 2, C major	
5:49	Transition	Tentative, gradually accelerating but very soft.
6:08	**Theme A,** var. 5, A♭ minor	Quiet; theme in dotted notes in woodwinds:
6:30	Transition	Constructed of ascending and descending scale passages.
6:46	**Theme A,** var. 6, A♭ major	Very loud, soft for the repeated endings:
7:31	**Coda**	New, faster tempo; related to "meditations" earlier and to many closing gestures of main theme.

Beethoven also connects the last two movements, lending a further sense of unity to the symphony. The scherzo doesn't really end at all, but leads into a transitional passage to the surprisingly triumphant opening of the finale, and the last two movements become inseparable. (See LG 31, p. 229, and LG 32, p. 230.)

The arrival at heroic C major——the change to a major key and the bombastic entrance of brass and drums—at the beginning of the last movement is dazzling. We know exactly when that moment arrives by its theme, even though the scherzo never really ends; and the moment is emphasized by new instruments—the highest (piccolo) and lowest (contrabassoon) available, and some heavy artillery in the form of three trombones, all of which have waited until now to play.

The transition from C minor to C major, epitomized in the motion from the scherzo to the finale, is in fact at the heart of the whole symphony, a sort of musical depiction of struggle ending in triumph. This may be why Beethoven hammers out the final C major chord so many times at the close of the symphony. Somehow, we've earned it.

Perhaps Beethoven felt personal emotions that paralleled the musical ones when he was planning this symphony. The drama of struggle, motion, and ultimate triumph is one that many people sense in the music, and if it represented something personal for Beethoven, it also represents something personal for many of his listeners.

In purely musical terms, in 1808 it was an interesting and fairly novel concept to link the movements of a symphony together in this way, making a much longer piece of music. The symphony is a marvel of concision in its individual movements, and a marvel of continuity when it is considered as a whole piece lasting half an hour.

LG 31 Beethoven: Symphony No. 5, III

LG 32 Beethoven: Symphony No. 5, IV

Beethoven Symphony No. 5 in C Minor, Op. 67, III (Allegro)   4:56

DATE: 1807–08

LISTEN FOR

MELODY: Famous solo passages for the double basses

FORM: Transition to last movement, without any break

TEXTURE: Fugal texture in the trio

SCORING: Ominous solo timpani at the final transition to last movement; theme played by horns, related to opening motive of first movement

TIME	FORM	DESCRIPTION
	Scherzo	
0:00	Opening theme, C minor	Begins with cellos and double basses, answered by winds. Notice halts:
0:18	Second theme, C minor to E♭ minor	Begins with horns:
0:36	Opening theme, B♭ minor	
0:56	Second theme, C minor to F minor	
1:13	Opening theme, C minor	Combines with second theme, long crescendo to cadence.
	Trio	
1:43	First part, C major	Lively fugue, begins with cellos and double basses:
1:58	First part, repeated	
2:14	Second part, C major	Fugue restarts, but with halting steps in the basses:
2:42	Second part, repeated	Fades away, transition to . . .
	Scherzo	
3:13	C minor	
3:30	Second theme	Reorchestrated; spooky and quiet.
3:48	Opening theme, repeated, C minor	Pizzicato.
4:15	Second theme, C♯ minor	
4:31		Extended, shift from minor to major, transition without interruption to finale!

LISTENING GUIDE 32

Beethoven Symphony No. 5 in C Minor, Op. 67, IV (Allegro) 11:02

DATE: 1807–08

LISTEN FOR

MELODY: Theme 1 outlining C-major triad. Theme 2 uses triplets, reminiscent of motive from first movement

FORM: Sonata-allegro form. Transition to recapitulation is borrowed from the third movement.

Very long coda; ending has many repetitions of the tonic chord

SCORING: New instruments are added to the orchestra: piccolo, contrabassoon, three trombones

TIME	FORM	DESCRIPTION
	Exposition	
0:00	First theme	Fanfare-like heroic first theme in C major:
0:36	Transition, C major to G major	Lyrical transition begins with fanfare of horns and woodwinds:
		modulates to G major.
1:02	Second theme, G major	Forceful melody in triplet rhythm is reminiscent of motive from first movement:
1:31	Closing theme, G major	Descending figure featuring clarinet and violas:
		leads back to . . .
2:03	**Exposition Repeated**	
	Development	
4:07	Part 1: Modulating, climaxing in loud dominant chord	Based on the second theme.
5:43	Part 2: Transition to recapitulation	Meter and tempo change; return to second theme of Scherzo, in new guise. Ends in rapid crescendo, leading to . . .
	Recapitulation	
6:14	First theme, C major	As before.

6:50	Transition, C major	Remains in home key.
7:22	Second theme, C major	Remains in home key.
7:50	Closing theme, C major	Descending figure; remains in home key.
	Coda (C major)	
8:21	Section 1	Based on second theme.
8:55	Section 2	Based on transition theme, accelerates to . . .
9:52	Section 3	Presto: based on closing theme, culminates in a version of opening theme.
10:23	Conclusion	Almost endless repetitions of final harmony.

The Fifth Symphony Then and Now

Beethoven's listeners did not know, of course, that they were hearing a symphony that would become one of the best known and most played of all time. They thought they were going to a concert by one of the leading composers of their day and that they would be fortunate enough to hear a good deal of music for the money they paid. The audience was probably more interested in listening to Beethoven play his piano concerto and improvise a fantasia, and in hearing the large pieces for chorus and orchestra, than in listening to the symphonies.

Viennese audiences knew about symphonies, and they knew how to judge the Symphony in C Minor. They knew what to expect and when to smile or be surprised when something new and unexpected happened. But how they actually judged the Fifth is hard to say, since we have almost no written recollections of that first hearing.

They were experts at contemporary music, which Beethoven's Fifth was at the time. They had listened to a large repertoire of music from their own time and place, music composed in a fairly uniform style (we now call it Viennese Classical music). When they heard a new piece, they could readily categorize it and know what they liked about it, what was pedestrian, and what was exceptional. They didn't have to like a new piece, but from a technical listening standpoint they were experts at listening to it.

In some respects, the Fifth Symphony was fairly normal. It was about the same length as symphonies by Haydn and Mozart, and it conformed to the standard four movements and to the shapes and emotional content they were accustomed to hear. Perhaps they appreciated the extreme terseness of the first movement, the fact that it was built tightly from a single, very small idea. This was consummate Beethoven, and if they knew his music they would have smiled. Or perhaps they were gripped by the strong emotions that Beethoven's passionate

The Critic and Composer E.T.A. Hoffmann on Beethoven's Fifth Symphony, 1810

It is certainly not merely an improvement in the means of expression (perfection of instruments, greater virtuosity of players), but also a deeper awareness of the peculiar nature of music, that has enabled great composers to raise instrumental music to its present level.

Mozart and Haydn, the creators of modern instrumental music, first showed us the art in its full glory; but the one who regarded it with total devotion and penetrated to its innermost nature is Beethoven. The instrumental compositions of all three masters breathe the same romantic spirit for the very reason that they all intimately grasp the essential nature of the art; yet the character of their compositions is markedly different. . . .

Beethoven's music sets in motion the machinery of awe, of fear, of terror, of pain, and awakens that infinite yearning which is the essence of romanticism. He is therefore a purely romantic composer. Might this not explain why his vocal music is less successful, since it does not permit a mood of vague yearning but can only depict from the realm of the infinite those feelings capable of being described in words?

music arouses in many of his listeners, then and now (see E.T.A. Hoffman on Beethoven's Fifth Symphony, p. 231). It was a symphony of standard shape, but vessels of the same shape can hold water or champagne.

Today, most of us do not know much about any one style of music, and audiences for classical music typically do not prefer new music to old. Many people will go much more readily to hear Beethoven's Fifth Symphony than to hear the latest work by a leading composer of today. While this may be regrettable, it is also important to remember that we do not all listen to just one kind of music. We are blessed with a variety of musics to choose from, and we can choose any pieces, from any time and place, and any culture in the world, to listen to at any time. We are not limited to listening to music only when someone gives a concert. We probably would not want to swap the richness that we have in the twenty-first century for the expertise of Beethoven's listeners. But we may never have that acute experience of listening—fully listening—to a brand-new piece, with fully expert ears.

It might be interesting to find out, if we attended a concert featuring Beethoven's Fifth, how many in the audience had never heard the work before. The proportion would probably be small. But how lucky those few would be!

Chapter Review

Summary of Musical Styles

- The **symphony**—a composition for orchestra, without voices or instrumental soloists—is one of the major instrumental genres of the Classic period. Beethoven's Fifth Symphony may be the ultimate realization of this genre.

- In a Classical symphony, there is often a difference between music that is a theme, where a clear and memorable melody is presented, and music that is not thematic. The nonthematic areas tend to be active, agitated, and deliberately unclear about key.

- While Baroque music generally seeks to express a single emotion or feeling in a piece, a symphonic movement usually presents two or more musical themes, in contrasting style, within the same movement, thereby providing a rich contrast of moods within a single, longer movement.

- A typical four-movement symphony starts with a substantial first movement in **sonata form**, followed by a **slow movement**, a **minuet and trio**, and a **finale** that is usually upbeat and lively.

- The **first-movement sonata form** consists of **exposition**, **development**, and **recapitulation**. Sometimes a **coda** is added to the end of the recapitulation, to close the movement. Beethoven's Fifth Symphony uses this design for the first and last movements.

- One of Beethoven's specialties was unifying the symphony. The motive that he used to construct the whole first movement, short-short-short-long, reappears in the other three movements. His ability to compose long stretches of music by weaving together multiple versions of a small motive is displayed throughout the symphony, especially in the transitional and development sections.

⊛ Multimedia Resources and Review Materials on StudySpace

Visit wwnorton.com/studyspace for review of Chapter 8.

What Do You Know?

Check the facts for this chapter. Take the online **Quiz**.

What Do You Hear?

Listening Quizzes and **Music Activities** will help you understand the musical works in this chapter.

🎙 Author Videos

- How to make a theme out of a motive in Beethoven's Fifth Symphony
- Rhythmic unity of themes throughout Beethoven's Fifth Symphony

Interactive Listening Guides

LG 29 Beethoven: Symphony No. 5 in C Minor, Op. 67, I (Allegro con brio)
LG 30 Beethoven: Symphony No. 5 in C Minor, Op. 67, II (Andante con moto)
LG 31 Beethoven: Symphony No. 5 in C Minor, Op. 67, III (Allegro)
LG 32 Beethoven: Symphony No. 5 in C Minor, Op. 67, IV (Allegro)

Flashcards (Terms to Know)

chamber music	recapitulation
coda	retransition
development	rondo form
exposition	scherzo
first-movement sonata form	sonata form
minuet and trio	symphony
movements	variation form
pianoforte, piano	variations

CHAPTER 9

NOVEMBER 1826, VIENNA:

A Schubertiade at Joseph von Spaun's

🔊 **CORE REPERTOIRE**	🎙️ **AUTHOR VIDEOS**	
▪ **LG 33** *Die Forelle* (*The Trout*) ▪ **LG 34** *Gretchen am Spinnrade* (*Gretchen at the Spinning Wheel*) ▪ **LG 35** *Der Erlkönig* (*The Erlking*) ▪ **LG 36** The "Trout" Quintet, IV	▪ Accompaniment in *Gretchen am Spinnrade*	

Introduction

"I went to Spaun's where there was a big, big Schubertiade . . . a huge gathering. . . . I was moved almost to tears. . . . When the music was done, there was grand feeding and then dancing."

—Diary of Franz von Hartmann, 1826

The particular event we imagine here took place eighteen years after the premiere of Beethoven's Fifth Symphony, and four years before the premiere of Berlioz's *Fantastic Symphony (Symphonie fantastique)*. But why have another chapter situated within this narrow window of time? Because a Schubertiade allows us to turn our attention to smaller-scale, private music-making. Many of our chapters and our pieces deal with lavish ceremonial or public events, music composed on a grand scale for a large—or at least important—audience. Such music is appropriately imposing in its length and performing forces, and designed to be performed by expert professional musicians, usually in the hope of making money or of satisfying a patron.

But ours is a private event. Beginning in 1821, Vienna became host to numerous events known as **Schubertiades,** intimate social gatherings named for the composer Franz Schubert, who was the main attraction at these gatherings and who provided the music—almost always his own—to entertain a circle of close friends. Such events were not designed to make money, nor were they music on a grand scale. They were informal evenings given over to socializing, eating, drinking, dancing, and lots of music.

Schubertiades

We do not know exactly which pieces were performed on which evenings during Schubert's lifetime, or indeed the dates of all the gatherings. But we do know the names of many of the works performed and even what some of these evenings were like. This chapter, therefore, is not about a specific piece of music but rather about an evening—a Schubertiade—that *might* have taken place. We will listen to some of Schubert's most famous music and imagine what occurred and who performed, meet some of his close friends, and try to establish how some of his works might have been received.

Let us pause a moment to consider the term **chamber music**—music performed by a small number of people for a small audience—that is, in a chamber, not in a concert hall. (Much chamber music *does* get performed in concert halls these days, but that's another matter.) Songs, string quartets, music for solo instrument with piano, and various other combinations are typical. Each performer has his or her own part—we do not see or hear a group of eight first violins, for example, as we would in an orchestral setting—and most chamber music is intended as much for the pleasure of the players as for the audiences. The essential trait of this music is its intimate, close-up quality, which is often missing from orchestral music. In these smaller works, there can be an attention to detail, the composer can write for an audience of experienced listeners, and the performance is private and privileged.

Chamber music

Ⓢ Schubert: String Quartet No. 10, IV

In addition, chamber music is designed, at least in part, for the amateurs in music—in this case, "amateur" has a positive connotation as someone who loves music—and to give pleasure to friends.

The Setting

VIENNA IN 1826

We have already seen something of Beethoven's Vienna in the previous chapter. In the eighteen intervening years between the premiere of Beethoven's Fifth Symphony and our evening with Schubert, Vienna had seen many changes. From 1805 through 1815, the city was repeatedly occupied by Napoleon's troops. In 1814, a conference of ambassadors of European states convened in Vienna to redraw the continent's political map (see map of Europe, p. 170) and to settle other issues arising from the numerous wars, including the French Revolution and the Napoleonic Wars, as well as the dissolution of the Holy Roman Empire. It was a time of major upheaval, and the Congress of Vienna took almost a year to finalize the settlement, which occurred nine days before Napoleon's final defeat at Waterloo.

The period after the Congress of Vienna and before the revolution of 1848 is sometimes called "Biedermeier," after a fictional newspaper character—Gottfried Biedermeier, a self-confident middle-class schoolmaster. It is a time of growing middle-class institutions, a widening access to the arts, and an increased emphasis on domestic institutions—a period that moves from the heroic to the homey. In such a context, the music of Franz Schubert—himself a schoolmaster and the son of a schoolmaster—reflects its time: the music is personal, intimate, and domestic, and it was, in Schubert's era, most often heard in private gatherings.

Vienna was a crowded and dirty city. As in Beethoven's time, living conditions were close and not particularly healthful. Many women died in childbirth; orphaned children were raised by relatives. Schubert's father married twice and had nineteen children, only nine of whom survived into adulthood. Schubert's brother Ferdinand married twice and had twenty-eight children, of whom twelve survived. Countless children were illegitimate, at least officially, because their parents could not meet the stringent requirements of education and wealth that were necessary for marriage. In such crowded living conditions, coffeehouses and taverns were gathering places for refreshment and conversation—and sometimes music.

Entertainments were many. Opera, theater, and concerts were frequent, and public concerts had now become almost regular events (see J. F. Reichardt on the Viennese Theater, above left). The Society of Musical Artists presented occasional large-scale concerts, and the Society of Friends of Music, an organization of amateurs, gave evenings of orchestral and choral music as well as Thursday-evening concerts of chamber music. Schubert's compositions were occasionally presented on one or another series.

Music-making was not limited to the public sphere. A growing bourgeoisie increasingly cultivated music in the home, among family members and gatherings called **salons** at the houses of the well-to-do. Schubert's regular musical activities with his friends were paralleled all over Vienna (see Music-Making in the Home, left).

J. F. Reichardt on the Viennese Theater

In the city and in the suburbs five theaters of the most varied sort give performances all the year round. At the two court theaters in the city itself, one sees everything outstanding in the way of grand and comic opera, comedy, and tragedy that Germany produces—and, in some measure, Italy and France as well. . . . On days when no play is scheduled, all these theaters give great concerts and performances of the most important ancient and modern music for church and concert hall. Aside from this, all winter long there are frequent public concerts, by local and visiting musicians, and excellent quartet and amateur concerts by subscription. . . . All the great public diversions and amusements are enjoyed by all classes without any abrupt divisions or offending distinctions—in these respects, Vienna is again quite alone among the great cities of Europe.

Music-Making in the Home

A view of musical life in Biedermeier Vienna:

The number of amateurs is immense. In almost every family of several members there is an amateur. Pianos are certainly never missing in prosperous houses, and in narrowly built houses often the comic situation arises that the parties must make appointments regarding the hours in which they want to practice. Very often one hears in a house violin playing on the ground floor, piano on the first floor, flute on the second, singing and guitar on the third, while, into the bargain, in the courtyard, a blind man exerts himself on a clarinet.

SCHUBERT IN VIENNA

Schubert, son and brother of schoolteachers, was expected to become a schoolteacher himself (see biography, p. 238). For a while, he did serve as a teacher, but it was obvious early on that he was not cut out for the family profession.

In keeping with the emphasis on learning by his father and brothers, Schubert was educated in good schools (he had won an audition and sung for some years as a soprano in the Court Chapel). He learned a good deal of music by playing violin in a school orchestra, becoming a competent player and improviser on the piano. And he was fortunate enough to have studied composition with the famous court composer Antonio Salieri (who used to treat him and his other students to ice cream).

Living sometimes at home, sometimes alone, but most often with one or more of his circle of friends (see Figure 9.1), Schubert was active with groups, clubs, and societies that combined a concern for human betterment with a desire for art and "agreeable pastimes." Typically the friends in his circles were not fellow musicians, but poets, painters, theater people, government officials, and bureaucrats (see pp. 242–43 for a description of some of his friends).

Physically, Schubert was short and stocky. He was described by a fellow seminary student as

> strongly developed, firm bones and firm muscles, rounded rather than angular. Neck short and powerful; shoulders, chest and pelvis broad and finely arched; arms and thighs rounded; hands and feet small; his walk brisk and vigorous. His head, which was rather large, round and strongly built, was surrounded by a shock of brown curly hair . . . . His eyes, which were soft and, if I am not mistaken, light brown in colour and which burned brightly when he was excited, were heavily overshadowed by rather prominent orbital ridges and bushy eyebrows. . . . Nose medium size, blunt, rather turned-up. . . . On his chin the so called beauty dimple.

He was also known for his insouciant attitude toward his own physical appearance:

> Because of his short sight he always wore spectacles [see Figure 9.2], which he did not take off even during sleep. Dress was a thing in which he took no interest whatever: consequently he disliked going into smart society, for which he had to take more trouble with his clothes.

We know less about Schubert as a person than we might like. The picture most often painted of him is of a private, affable individual, devoted to his friends; a man who never succeeded in the realm of "public" music—of operas and symphonies and publishers—but whose intimate and heartfelt songs and piano pieces charmed the world around him and eventually the world at large.

Those who were privileged to witness Schubert at work were impressed by how the music seemed to pour out of him (although in truth, Schubert maintained that it was not as easy as it seemed). Years later, the lawyer Leopold von Sonnleithner would describe what he remembered of Schubert, the composer:

> Anyone who has seen him of a morning occupied with composition, aglow, with his eyes shining and his speech changed, like a somnambulist, will never forget the impression. . . . It was interesting to see him compose. He very seldom made use of

FIG. 9.1 Moritz von Schwind's drawing of Franz Schubert (center), the composer Franz Lachner (left), and playwright Eduard von Bauernfeld, all drinking wine.

franz schubert (1797–1828)

Schubert lived only to the age of thirty-one, but in his short life, passed almost exclusively in Vienna, he created music that captivated his friends—and an increasingly wider circle of admirers.

At the age of eleven he became a choirboy in St. Stephen's Cathedral. A student at the prestigious Imperial and Royal City College, he continued to play piano and violin, impressing everyone around him. After passing his exams in 1814, Schubert took a job at his father's school. All the while, however, he was working as a composer.

Realizing that he could not continue as a schoolmaster forever, Schubert tried other possibilities, never quite achieving the economic stability he sought. Gradually gaining recognition for his compositions, through private and occasional public performances, Schubert continued to compose symphonies, operas, piano music, and especially, songs.

By 1823 Schubert had contracted a disease—most likely syphilis—from which he would die. Scholars agree on Schubert's passionate sexual drive, though not on its objects—his sexual orientation has been the subject of much discussion.

Schubert served as a torchbearer at Beethoven's funeral in 1827. He died the following year, but not before performing at the last Schubertiade, on January 28, and giving a final public concert of his own music on March 26. When Schubert died, on November 19, he had been reading the quintessentially American author James Fenimore Cooper and listening to a Beethoven string quartet performed at his bedside.

Schubert's musical style is lyrical, often songlike, and famous for its expressive use of harmony. Even in his larger pieces, like the sonatas and fantasias for piano, or the symphonies, beautiful melody and harmonic richness are typical hallmarks.

Ⓢ Schubert: "Wanderer" Fantasy
Ⓢ Schubert: "Unfinished" Symphony, I
Ⓢ Schubert: "Das Wandern," from *Die schöne Müllerin*

MAJOR WORKS: Over 600 Lieder, including *Der Erlkönig* (*The Erlking*), the song cycles (groups of related songs) *Die schöne Müllerin* (*The Beautiful Miller's Daughter*) and *Winterreise* (*Winter's Journey*); 9 symphonies, including the "Unfinished"; chamber music, including the "Trout" Quintet (Piano Quintet in A Major) and the "Death and the Maiden" Quartet (String Quartet in D Minor); 22 piano sonatas and other short piano pieces; 6 Masses; and numerous operas and choral works.

---

the pianoforte while doing it. He often used to say it would make him lose his train of thought. . . . He would . . . bite his pen, drum with his fingers at the same time, trying things out, and continue to write easily and fluently, without many corrections, as if it had to be like that and not otherwise. And how right he was!

His facility with composing was just one of several half-truths about the young Schubert. That he was unsuccessful in the realm of public music was also not entirely true. Schubert did in fact have success in the theater—he *did* have several pieces performed in the major theaters; he *did* involve himself with the composition of symphonies and other large-scale works; and he *did* ultimately gain considerable success from his published works. Nor was he the paragon of good-natured humor so often depicted.

Schubert and Beethoven   Although Schubert and Beethoven inhabited the same city, they lived in very different worlds. Beethoven was not a native, but his virtuosity managed to attract a following of rich aristocrats who provided support and admired him. He was esteemed by a wide international public who knew his works, in part because of their extensive publication. Even though he could be difficult and stubborn, tending toward the solitary, he had a small circle of loyal supporters.

Schubert was, to an extent, Beethoven's opposite. He was a native of Vienna, born twenty-seven years after Beethoven, grew up among friends, and lived among them his whole life. He did not move in high social circles, and his prolific compositional output, unlike Beethoven's, did not attract public recognition. Although works of his were published during his lifetime, these were mainly smaller works such as songs and piano pieces (e.g., dances and marches). His audience was made up of close friends and associates interested in the music, literature, and the arts. The lottery official and dramatist Eduard von Bauernfeld (1802–1890), one of Schubert's inner-circle friends, recalled how he met the young composer, and how a group of friends formed:

> I was sitting thus in my den, one evening in February 1825, when my boyhood friend, [the painter Moritz von] Schwind, brought Schubert to see me, who meanwhile had already become famous or, at least, well known. We were soon on intimate terms with one another. At Schwind's request I had to recite some crazy youthful poems of mine; we then went to the piano, where Schubert sang and we also played duets, and later to an inn till far into the night. The bond was sealed, we three friends remained inseparable from that day on. But others too grouped themselves round us, mostly painters and musicians, a circle of people, with a zest for life and with similar aims and ideas, who shared together their joys and sorrows.

Schubert's life was essentially a private one. He was described as outgoing and friendly, but behind the scrim was a dark side. Bauernfeld characterized him as having "a double nature, the Viennese gaiety being interwoven and ennobled by a trait of deep melancholy. Inwardly a poet and outwardly a kind of hedonist." More than one obituary also reflected on his dual disposition: "Falsity and envy were utter strangers to him; his character was a mixture of tenderness and coarseness, sensuality and candour, sociability and melancholy." He was known for the heavy drinking noted by several of his friends; there were many late evenings at taverns, where Schubert was never one to hold back.

Music was for many of Schubert's contemporaries as much a pastime as it was an art. Many houses had pianos, and it was customary for people to learn to play and to sing, and to entertain each other at social gatherings. Relatively simple music for voice with piano accompaniment was much favored. Vocal ensembles, sometimes on humorous subjects, were meant to entertain. Music for two people to play at one piano ("four-hands") gave young people a chance to sit close. And there was lots of dance music; Schubert's dances for the piano number in the hundreds, and he was well know for improvising dance music for his friends, making up an endless stream of schottisches (a popular ballroom dance), waltzes, German dances—whatever was wanted.

The compositions that Schubert's contemporaries would have considered serious music were designed for other places. His concert arias, chamber music, overtures, and symphonies were intended for aristocratic salons or for the more public performances at musical societies, which were increasingly presenting concerts of chamber and orchestral music.

But the demand was for entertainment, not art. Publishers wanted dances and songs, and they begged Schubert and others to keep it simple. One aspect of Schubert's genius is that he was able to take the music of the salon and turn it into high art.

Indeed Schubert was himself, in a sense, an amateur, in that he sang his songs and played the piano, without thinking of himself as a professional performer. His voice, said Bauernfeld, was a composer's voice, "halfway between a gentle tenor and a baritone, his manner of performance simple and natural, sensitive, without any affectation." As a pianist and accompanist, Bauernfeld said that "without being a virtuoso he was wholly adequate as an accompanist and made up in intelligence and feeling what he lacked in technical perfection."

FIG. 9.2 A pair of Schubert's eyeglasses, resting on a manuscript of his music. Schubert never took his glasses off, even in bed.

Music as a pastime

FIG. 9.3 An 1827 pastel, by Joseph Teltscher, showing (left to right) Johann Baptist Jenger (an amateur pianist), Anselm Hüttenbrenner (a composer), and Franz Schubert.

Schubert was one of the more widely published—and purchased—composers in Vienna in the 1820s. His first publication was the song *Der Erlkönig* (*The Erlking*, a child-stealing forest spirit), which would become one of his most famous works. It had been no easy matter getting the piece published, but a public performance by the well-known opera singer Johann Michael Vogl, on March 7, 1821, helped turn the tide. The concert, given in the Kärntnertortheater (the site of the premiere of Beethoven's Ninth Symphony), was an annual event presented by the Society of Noblewomen for the Promotion of the Good and the Useful. These concerts were important social events, and Schubert's song was a hit, along with two of his pieces for vocal ensemble—*Das Dörfchen* (*The Little Village*), for two tenors and two basses, and *Gesang des Geistes uber den Wassern* (*Song of the Spirit over the Waters*), for four tenors and four basses. Anselm Hüttenbrenner (see Figure 9.3), who played the piano (and later published an *Erlkönig Waltz*), reported that

Vogl sang so splendidly and with such enthusiasm that *Erlkönig* had to be repeated. I played the accompaniment on a new grand piano by Konrad Graf. Schubert, who could have played his own compositions as well as I, was too shy to be induced to do so; he contented himself with standing near me and turning pages.

Critics paid attention: "excellently sung by Vogl; it made a great effect. A masterpiece of musical painting," wrote one; Vogl's "bold performance broke down the barriers for the simple and modest master, and presented the new prince of song," wrote another. It is no wonder, then, that Schubert chose *Erlkönig* to be his first published work.

But even before the concert, Schubert's works had begun to circulate outside his own circle. A Dresden newspaper reported enthusiastically that the young composer

has set to music several songs by the best poets (mostly Goethe), which testify to the profoundest studies combined with genius worthy of admiration, and attract the eyes of the cultivated musical world. He knows how to paint in sound, and the songs *Die Forelle, Gretchen am Spinnrade,* and *Der Kampf*, surpass in characteristic truth all that may be found in the domain of song. They are not yet published but go from hand to hand only in manuscript copies.

The publication of *Erlkönig* was organized by the court official and musical patron Leopold von Sonnleithner: he and a few others paid the cost of publication. Schubert called the song his Opus 1, and dedicated it to Sonnleithner. The first printing of about two hundred and fifty copies sold out immediately.

Thereafter, publishers were less reticent to print his works—at least his songs and smaller piano works. *Gretchen am Spinnrade,* originally composed in 1814, became Opus 2 (see An Article about "Gretchen," p. 241). From then on, Schubert's songs were published in groups, not individually, and the young composer began to make a decent income from them.

Schubert desperately wanted to compose operas and have them produced. In 1820, he had succeeded in getting two operas staged: *Die Zwillingsbrüder* (*The Twin Brothers*) at the Kärntnertortheater, and *Die Zauberharfe* (*The Magic Harp*) at another theater. But a change of management at the Kärntnertortheater (the Italian impresario Domenico Barbaja took over in 1821, and Vogl and others were dismissed) meant that Schubert's chances of having works presented there faded fast. Barbaja brought Gioacchino Rossini, the reigning king of opera, for a triumphant visit to Vienna, and no one else stood a chance in the shadow of his huge popularity. Despite the inaccessibility of the opera—or perhaps at least partly because of it—Schubert in the 1820s composed some of his finest works, though many of them remained unfinished (like the well-known "Unfinished" Symphony).

Schubert did not seek the company of other musicians (with some exceptions such as Vogl) but rather of painters, poets, dramatists, and other artists. He also avoided teaching music—either piano lessons or composition—although this was a regular source of income for almost any practicing musician at the time.

By 1826, at the time of the Schubertiade described by Franz von Hartmann in his diary and excerpted at the beginning of this chapter, Schubert was ill. His poor health caused considerable torment, both physical and mental. The duality that always existed in his personality—the creative, aspiring, positive composer Schubert, and the hard-drinking, depressive, reclusive and sometimes rude, private Schubert—was made even more prominent by illness. It limited his ability to travel and to work, and it focused his thoughts, partly on some important compositions and partly on his inevitable mortality, reflected in pieces such as the "Death and the Maiden" String Quartet, and the two timeless song cycles on Wilhelm Müller's poems: *Die schöne Müllerin* and *Winterreise*, each of which deals with unrequited love followed by death.

In a letter to his friend the painter Kupelwieser, he poured out his sadness and nostalgia, using the words from Goethe's character Gretchen (from *Faust* and from Schubert's now-famous song):

> "My peace is gone, my heart is sore, I shall find it never and nevermore," I may well sing every day now, for each night, on retiring to bed, I hope I may not wake again, and each morning but recalls yesterday's grief. Thus, joyless and friendless, I should pass my days, did not [my friend the painter Moritz von] Schwind visit me now and again and turn on me a ray of those sweet days of the past.

After Schubert's death, Schwind wrote to a mutual friend:

> I have wept for him as for a brother, but now I am glad for him that he has died in his greatness and has done with his sorrows. The more I realize now what he was like, the more I see what he has suffered.

An Article about "Gretchen"

This article from the Vienna Sammler, *May 1, 1821, appeared anonymously but was written by Josef Hüttenbrenner; Count Fries, to whom the song was dedicated, paid Schubert a handsome fee and was also a patron of Schubert's friend Anselm Hüttenbrenner, brother of the author of the article.*

At Cappi & Diabelli's on the Graben, has just been published: "Margaret [Gretchen] at the Spinning-Wheel," from Goethe's "Faust," by Herr Franz Schubert. . . . This composition has been distinguished by unanimous applause at several private concerts, and every lover of song has looked forward eagerly to the public appearance of a composition which does so much honor to a pupil of the great masters Salieri and Vogl.

Margaret's state of mind, in which the feelings and sensations of love, of pain and of rapture take turns, are so affectingly depicted by Schubert's music that a more heart-stirring impression than that left by his musical picture is scarcely imaginable. Apart from that, the composition is also remarkable for its pianoforte part, which so successfully sketches the motion of the spinning-wheel and develops its theme in such a masterly way. The little song, "Margaret at the Spinning-Wheel," must in fact be conceded to have as much originality and uniqueness as Beethoven's "Adelaide" and Mozart's "To Chloe" and "Evening Musings."

The Performance

Schubert's music had a close following among his friends and acquaintances, and these regular musical gatherings, centered on Schubert's music, occurred often, sometimes every week. The audience—probably not the right term for a group of friends—ranged from a small number of people to as many as a hundred, usually

FIG. 9.4 Joseph von Spaun, who was an imperial councilor and lottery director, close friend of Franz Schubert, and host to many Schubertiades.

in the home of one of Schubert's wealthier friends. Schubert's music was at the center of it all; piano music and songs, followed by drinking, eating, and dancing (the dance music often improvised by Schubert on the spot).

There were no printed or written programs, and it is difficult now to know exactly what music was performed at which Schubertiade, or even when most of them took place. But they were important events for those who attended, and also an outlet for Schubert's effusive musical and social disposition.

Many of Schubert's lifelong friends would have been at these evenings, chief among them Joseph von Spaun, Franz von Schober, Moritz von Schwind, Leopold Kupelwieser, Franz Grillparzer, Johann Baptist Mayrhofer, and Eduard von Bauernfeld.

Joseph von Spaun (1788–1865; see Figure 9.4), the host for the evening mentioned at the head of this chapter, had been Schubert's friend since the composer lived in a school dormitory. His support for Schubert included attempts to interest Goethe in Schubert's settings of the poet's texts.

Franz von Schober (see Figure 9.5), also a longtime friend of Schubert's, was not always the best influence on his companion. An aspiring poet and actor, talented but undisciplined, Schober never quite amounted to anything and was, in a way, the opposite of Schubert: he was lazy and unmotivated and had led a life of leisure. He came from a wealthy family and succeeded in squandering much of his own fortune. Schubert occasionally lived with Schober and his mother (the two men jokingly referred to themselves as "Schobert"). In fact, the first report of a Schubertiade was from an evening at Schober's:

> Franz [von Schober] invited Schubert in the evening and fourteen of his close acquaintances. So a lot of splendid songs by Schubert were sung and played by himself, which lasted until after 10 o'clock in the evening. After that punch was drunk, offered by one of the party, and as it was very good and plentiful the party, in a happy mood anyhow, became even merrier; so it was 3 o'clock in the morning before we parted.

Moritz von Schwind and Leopold Kupelwieser

The two painters, Moritz von Schwind and Leopold Kupelwieser, were also longtime friends of Schubert's, and from them we know something of how a Schubertiade looked and how Schubert passed some of his time (see Figure 9.6). They also made many sketches of Schubert as a young man, which portray the progression of the composer from a slim, almost cherubic-looking boy to a plump and more studious-looking adult.

Literary figures at these Schubertiades included Franz Grillparzer (he would give Beethoven's funeral oration), Johann Baptist Mayrhofer (Schubert lived with him for a time and set forty-seven of his poems), and Eduard von Bauernfeld (see above).

This group of friends—both literary and artistic—along with relatively highly placed officials, would have comprised the guests at a typical evening of music, dance, food, and drink. Musicians were few at these gatherings, except for the pianist Josef von Gahy and of course the one other person of great significance to Schubert: the singer Vogl (see Figure 9.7).

A star baritone at the court opera (until the arrival of Barbaja), Vogl became the most important and sympathetic interpreter of Schubert's songs. He was twenty-nine years older and probably provided a paternal influence not supplied by Schubert's own father. He was characterized as a difficult personality but was enamored of Schubert's music and did what he could to promote the younger man's career. Indeed, as we have seen, it was a performance by Vogl of *Erlkönig* that turned the tide in Schubert's career. In addition, it was Vogl who encouraged

FIG. 9.5 Franz von Schober, actor and poet, was also a close friend of Franz Schubert. This is in a painting by Leopold Kupelwieser, from 1822.

FIG. 9.6 Schubert and his friends playing charades at Atzenbrugg Castle, Lower Austria, as depicted in a watercolor by Leopold Kupelwieser, from 1821.

Schubert to write for the theater, and the early successes in opera and operetta had everything to do with Vogl (he played both of the twin brothers in the 1820 production of Schubert's *Die Zwillingsbrüder)*. At this Schubertiade, as at so many others, Vogl would have been the chief singer, and Schubert his accompanist.

Listening to the Music

We have selected four works for this particular Schubertiade, consisting of some of Schubert's best-loved music: the first two published songs—*Der Erlkönig* and *Gretchen am Spinnrade*—and the tuneful *Die Forelle* (*The Trout*). Schubert used the melody of *Die Forelle* to create his sumptuous and now famous "Trout" Quintet for piano and strings, included here as the last piece to give us an idea of how he reworked one of his own compositions to fit another genre.

Schubert has been called the master of the song, or **lied** (plural, **lieder;** German for "song") because he turned the genre of song into high art. The genre itself has a long history, going back to the Middle Ages, when French and German poets created settings of love poetry. Mozart, Beethoven, and others wrote songs, but it was not a significant part of their output. The songs of Schubert and others grow from the tradition of song in popular culture, rather than from the theatrical arias in operas. We sometimes call them **art songs** to distinguish them from folk songs, popular songs, and the like.

For Schubert the lied became an inspirational matrix. His songs are not reminiscent of the opera house but are inspired versions of beautiful melodies, more like folk songs than like arias. But his ability to find just the right unforgettable melody and an accompaniment that

FIG. 9.7 Moritz von Schwind's portrait of the singer Johann Michael Vogl, with Schubert at the piano.

TABLE 9.1		
Forms at a Glance: Song Types		
FORM	MUSIC	TEXT
Strophic	Music is repeated for each strophe of the poem.	The poem is made up of several strophes; each strophe has the same shape (lines, accents, etc.) but different words.
Modified Strophic	Music is repeated for each strophe of the poem, except for such variations as the composer chooses to make.	The poem is made of several strophes; each strophe has the same shape (lines, accents, etc.) but different words.
Through-Composed	Music does not repeat for each strophe; new text is set to new music for the length of the text.	The poem may take almost any shape—including strophic with multiple verses.

perfectly matches the mood of the song impressed and moved his listeners right from the beginning. And his songs are not simple to sing; they are full of surprises and challenges for the singer, the pianist, and the listener. Between 1810 and 1828 he wrote more than six hundred lieder, using texts from more than one hundred poets. Vogl told a story that when he sang Schubert a song that the composer had left with him a few weeks before, Schubert cried "That's not bad! Who is it by?"

Audience for songs   A number of factors encouraged the audience for songs: the growth of the middle classes with an appetite for domestic music-making, the rise of the piano as an instrument in the home, and a growing fashion for songs in a direct and simple style, which developed partly as a reaction to the complexity and artifice of the Italian opera aria, with its elements of display and its international star singers. As interest in poetry increased, so did Schubert's audience, and his acquaintance with many poets provided him with material and inspiration. His sources ranged from the great texts of Goethe to the latest works of his friends. The German lied would have a long and distinguished history, with Schubert as its founding father. Robert Schumann, Hugo Wolf, and many other composers would continue Schubert's traditions of song.

Song types   In Schubert's day, song forms usually fell into three categories: **strophic, modified strophic**, and **through-composed** (see Table 9.1, Forms at a Glance, above). Just as audiences today look forward to hearing their favorite tunes at a rock concert, right down to the lyrics and song structure, so too would Schubert's friends have anticipated spending an evening with some comfortably familiar styles and forms. His audience probably had heard hundreds of songs by Schubert and other composers. Some songs were simple and strophic (same music, same text in every strophe), some had a twist of new music and verses integrated with the familiar (modified strophic), and others conformed to the through-composed style—music that followed the text so closely that every musical phrase was different.

Finally, we get to our evening of song, dance, and refreshment. Vogl stands by Schubert, who is seated at the piano. The room is small and crowded, the women fanning themselves from the heat generated by too many bodies. Schwind is in the corner, sketching, and is that Schober over there, drinking a little too much for his own good?

Let us begin. . . .

DIE FORELLE (THE TROUT)

 LG 33

When Schubert began playing *Die Forelle* (1817) for his friends, it probably struck them as another one of his lovely, uncomplicated songs. They were in for a surprise. A short piano introduction sets the mood, then two verses sung to the same music followed.

But what begins as a simple strophic song turns into a not-so-clear-cut parable, with a bite at the end, literally and figuratively. The song is in modified strophic form. The poem, by Christian Friedrich Daniel Schubart, spins a fishing tale of a trout that finally gets caught. Or so it seems; but the poem is drenched in sexual symbolism: the trout is a maiden, the angler a seducer, the twitching fishing rod is surely suggestive, the onlooker is a rival suitor. The original poem has four verses, of which Schubert wisely omits the fourth, a kind of moralizing advice to other trout not to fall prey to seducers.

He makes a wonderful tricky song out of the first three verses, luring us into a sunny, happy, outdoor scene in the first two verses, only to snare us with the hook of his music, in the third verse, in the same sort of trap that parallels the meaning of the words.

The piano introduction is charming and guileless, bouncy and bright, with an unforgettable rhythmic pattern.

Piano introduction

The singer performs the first verse (we, like his listeners at the Schubertiade, don't know for sure that it is the first of several verses—we can only be sure when this music is repeated with new words—but it does seem like that kind of song). The poem paints an innocent outdoor scene of a trout in a brook, and the music matches it in sunny simplicity. When the second verse arrives we are not surprised; there is the same piano introduction, the same melody, but the words have just a hint of something ominous. We suspect the trout might be in for trouble. And there it is: the third verse is suddenly very different. What before seemed innocent enough, now is full of bitter humor. In the same way that the fisherman lures in the trout, Schubert's apparently simple setting lures in the listener. Perhaps the innocent melody of the last line, referring back to the opening music, is Schubert's way of smiling at all of us, his listeners, for being snagged—just like the gullible trout. (See LG 33, p. 246.)

First verse

Second verse

Third verse

GRETCHEN AM SPINNRADE
(GRETCHEN AT THE SPINNING WHEEL)

 LG 34

Accompaniment in *Gretchen am Spinnrade*

This song, Schubert's Opus 2, has remained one of his best-loved works. It was the first lied Schubert set to words by the famous poet and dramatist Johann Wolfgang von Goethe, who was still alive when Schubert composed the work.

In this scene from Goethe's *Faust,* Gretchen, a young woman, is sitting alone at her spinning wheel. She is thinking about Faust, the handsome young man she recently met, who seduced and abandoned her. We can imagine her staring sadly off into the distance; as she works at her spinning, Gretchen's mind turns to the past, and she becomes alternately despondent, nostalgic, and desperate.

Goethe built something of a refrain into the poem ("Meine Ruh' ist hin"— My peace is gone"), and Schubert makes even more of it: Gretchen reviews her memories and emotions, and three times is brought up short by a return to reality, to her spinning wheel, and to her cares. There are gripping harmonic shifts as her thoughts wander and then come back to the present, and she repeats the words "Meine ruh' ist hin. . . ." The return of these words, and of the key in which they are set, gives the song a rondo-like form. The spinning wheel itself, portrayed though a rapid rising and falling figuration in the accompaniment, twirls continuously while Gretchen spins, thinks back, and regrets.

When she finally comes to the memory of Faust's kiss (perhaps a euphemism), she forgets what she's doing. The wheel stops. But Gretchen realizes that it is all an illusion and sadly returns to the spinning wheel—we hear it starting up haltingly, and returning to its regular rhythm with her regular refrain, "My peace is gone. . . ." It is a bleak moment. Her sad refrain is left unfinished at the end of the song— the spinning wheel alone goes on. (See LG 34, p. 247.)

LISTENING GUIDE 33   ⑤ | DVD

Schubert *Die Forelle* (*The Trout*)   2:09

DATE: Final version published December 1820
TEXT: Christian Friedrich Daniel Schubart

TEMPO: Allegro

LISTEN FOR

MELODY: Regular four-phrase melody for each of the first two verses, the last phrase repeated (**AA'BCC**)

FORM: Modified strophic: third verse has different music

TEXTURE: Piano introduces "rippling" accompaniment

TIME	FORM	TEXT	TRANSLATION	DESCRIPTION
0:00				Introduction is charming and guileless, bouncy and sunny, with unforgettable rhythmic pattern that moves between upper and lower register (right and left hands).
0:10	A	In einem Bächlein helle, Da schoß in froher Eil'	In a bright little brook There shot in merry haste	Classic 4-phrase tune, with each phrase 4 measures long. The first two phrases (**A** and **A'**) have the same simple beginning and different, more active endings. The first verse describes an innocent outdoor scene.
	A'	Die launige Forelle Vorüber wie ein Pfeil.	A capricious trout: It shot past like an arrow.	
	B	Ich stand an dem Gestade Und sah in süßer Ruh'	I stood on the shore And watched in sweet peace	The third phrase (**B**) can be heard as a short phrase stated twice, in varied form.
	C	Des muntern Fischleins Bade Im klaren Bächlein zu.	The cheery fish's bath In the clear little brook.	The final phrase (**C**) begins with the same rhythm, but not notes, of the first two phrases. It is repeated, words and music, in slightly ornamented version, to close the verse.
	C	Des muntern Fischleins Bade Im klaren Bächlein zu.	The cheery fish's bath In the clear little brook.	
0:44	A	Ein Fischer mit der Rute Wohl an dem Ufer stand,	A fisher with his rod Stood at the water-side,	When the second verse arrives we are not surprised: same introduction, same melody, although the words have just a hint of something ominous. The music is exactly the same for verse 2.
	A'	Und sah's mit kaltem Blute, Wie sich das Fischlein wand.	And watched with cold blood As the fish swam about.	

B	So lang dem Wasser Helle,	So long as the clearness of the water	
	So dacht' ich, nicht gebricht,	Remained intact, I thought,	
C	So fängt er die Forelle	He would not capture the trout	
	Mit seiner Angel nicht.	With his fishing rod.	
C	So fängt er die Forelle	He would not capture the trout	
	Mit seiner Angel nicht.	With his fishing rod.	

TIME			
1:20	Doch endlich ward dem Diebe	But finally the thief grew weary	The third verse is suddenly different: minor replaces major; chords replace rippling figures; the key changes; melody is not melodious; phrases are irregular.
	Die Zeit zu lang. Er macht	Of waiting. He stirred up	
	Das Bächlein tückisch trübe,	The brook and made it muddy,	When text refers to muddy stream, Schubert muddies texture, abandoning the rippling accompaniment. Irregularity of voice and piano highlight the twitching rod as the fish is caught.
	Und eh' ich es gedacht,	And before I realized it,	
	So zuckte seine Rute,	His fishing rod was twitching:	
	Das Fischlein zappelt d'ran,	The fish was squirming there,	The last line surveys the betrayed fish, returning to the carefree music of the other verses and the original key. What at first seemed innocent now feels ironic.
	Und ich mit regem Blute	And with rushing blood	
	Sah die Betrog'ne an.	I gazed at the betrayed fish.	

LISTENING GUIDE 34   ⓢ | DVD | 🎙

Schubert *Gretchen am Spinnrade*
(*Gretchen at the Spinning Wheel*)   3:18

DATE: October 1814

TEXT: Johann Wolfgang von Goethe

TEMPO: Etwas schnell (somewhat fast)

LISTEN FOR

HARMONY: Moves to various keys, but returns to D minor for refrain ("Meine Ruh' ist hin")

FORM: Through-composed; note Gretchen's increasing excitement, punctuated by a refrain ("Meine Ruh' ist hin")

TEXTURE: Piano accompaniment representing a spinning wheel

TIME	TEXT	TRANSLATION	DESCRIPTION
0:00			The spinning wheel itself, portrayed marvelously in the accompaniment, twirls continuously as Gretchen thinks.
0:03	Meine Ruh' ist hin,	My peace is gone,	As she spins, she sings of her sadness.
	Mein Herz ist schwer,	My heart is heavy,	
	Ich finde sie nimmer	I will find it never	
	Und nimmermehr.	And never more.	

(continued)

TIME	TEXT	TRANSLATION	DESCRIPTION
0:19	Wo ich ihn nicht hab' Ist mir das Grab, Die ganze Welt Ist mir vergällt.	Where I do not have him, That is the grave, The whole world Is bitter to me.	Gretchen thinks, in her first episode, of Faust, the man she has lost.
	Mein armer Kopf Ist mir verrückt, Mein armer Sinn Ist mir zerstückt.	My poor head Is crazy to me, My poor mind Is torn apart.	
0:46	Meine Ruh' ist hin, Mein Herz ist schwer, Ich finde sie nimmer Und nimmermehr.	My peace is gone, My heart is heavy, I will find it never And never more.	She sinks into her previous sadness, repeating the same music.
1:03	Nach ihm nur schau' ich Zum Fenster hinaus, Nach ihm nur geh' ich Aus dem Haus.	For him only, I look Out the window, Only for him do I go Out of the house.	In the next episode her thoughts turn to Faust, whom she obviously still loves. As she thinks of his physical appearance, she becomes more agitated. The music turns to happier major keys, Faust's noble bearing is portrayed with a few bold notes, and when Gretchen comes to the memory of his kiss, she forgets what she's doing, and the wheel stops—the change of a single note in the piano turns the chord on "kiss" into a bitter one.
	Sein hoher Gang, Sein' ed'le Gestalt, Seines Mundes Lächeln, Seiner Augen Gewalt,	His tall walk, His noble figure, His mouth's smile, His eyes' power,	
	Und seiner Rede Zauberfluß, Sein Händedruck, Und ach, sein Kuß!	And his speech's Magic flow, The touch of his hand, And ah, his kiss!	
1:47	Meine Ruh' ist hin, Mein Herz ist schwer, Ich finde sie nimmer Und nimmermehr.	My peace is gone, My heart is heavy, I will find it never And never more.	Gretchen comes to herself, realizes that it's an illusion, and sadly returns to the spinning wheel—we hear it starting up haltingly, and returning to its regular rhythm with her regular refrain, "My peace is gone. . . ."
2:11	Mein Busen drängt sich Nach ihm hin. Ach, dürft' ich fassen Und halten ihn,	My bosom urges itself toward him. Ah, might I grasp And hold him,	In a third episode Gretchen expresses her passion and her desire, and at her mounting urgency the music rises higher and higher until her climactic highest note.
	Und küssen ihn, So wie ich wollt, An seinen Küssen Vergehen sollt!	And kiss him, As I would wish, At his kisses It should die!	
2:55	Meine Ruh' ist hin, Mein Herz ist schwer.	My peace is gone, My heart is heavy.	And then she falls back into her sad refrain, which is left unfinished at the end of the song, and her melody too is left unfinished—the spinning wheel alone goes on.

DER ERLKÖNIG (THE ERLKING)

LG 35

The form of this song is complex. It is essentially through-composed, since each stanza has different music. But at the same time, a musical motive suggesting fear is repeated in several of the stanzas, giving the song an element of the strophic.

The text is again by Goethe; the poem is made up of rhythmic, four-line strophes, but is really a disastrous three-way conversation framed by two short narratives. There are four characters—the narrator, the father, the son, and the evil Erlking. In the poem, the father, clutching his son, gallops furiously on his horse, seeking the safety of home. The Erlking, smooth and sinister, beckons to the child. The child cries to the father, who cannot see the Erlking (does the father perhaps think this vision is a symptom of his child's illness?). The closing narration, with its chilling last word, tells us the fateful outcome: "In his arms the child was dead."

Schubert produces a terrifying accompaniment in the piano, extremely difficult to play because of the almost incessant repeated notes in the right hand. The effect of the accompaniment is highly suggestive of a sinister wild ride in a storm. (It is similar to the storm at the beginning of Act 2 of Wagner's *Die Walküre*, which we'll hear in Chapter 13.)

The dialogue is delivered by a single singer, but Schubert manages to differentiate each character. The father sings in the lower part of the range, the son sings higher, and the Erlking sings in the middle. While the boy comes under more and more pressure, his speeches—each beginning with "Mein Vater, mein Vater" (My father, my father)—get progressively higher as the tension mounts. Schubert is able to differentiate the voices further by changing the accompaniment for the Erlking's persuasive lines. It is a song filled with dread, panic, and, finally, pure sorrow. (See LG 35, p. 250.)

This is the song that made Schubert's reputation. Vogl's singing, as we have seen, was stunning. *Der Erlkönig* was a perfect vehicle for him: it allowed his dramatic powers full range by playing four characters—man, child, Erlking, and narrator—all in a single song. It became a personal milestone for Schubert, and remains a favorite of music listeners today.

These three songs provide a range of possibilities for setting poems to music. They do not of course exhaust the possibilities, any more than Schubert exhausted them in his six-hundred-plus songs. But they range from the modified strophic in *Die Forelle* to the more or less completely through-composed *Gretchen am Spinnrade* and *Erlkönig*. The intricacies of phrasing, of accompanying figures, of harmonic shifts, even in songs that seem to be among the simplest, are worthy of careful study.

It is hard to say what exactly makes Schubert's songs so magical. Among their expressive elements, we might name the endlessly inventive melody, the piano as equal partner, the use of the keyboard not only to mirror the text but to interpret and comment upon it. The expressive use of harmony is especially noticeable in Schubert, and it is in these smaller pieces that he can use shifts from major to minor, the surprising moves to new keys, in ways that seem intimate and particularly personal. Schubert's music often seems to turn from the public toward the private and inward.

LISTENING GUIDE 35 | DVD

Schubert *Der Erlkönig (The Erlking)* 4:26

DATE: 1815
TEXT: Johann Wolfgang von Goethe

TEMPO: Etwas lebhaft (somewhat lively)

LISTEN FOR
MELODY: A narrative, with characters, though performed by one singer:

Narrator: middle register, minor mode

Father: low register, minor mode

Son: high register, minor mode

Erlking: medium register, major mode

FORM: Through-composed
TEXTURE: Thundering piano accompaniment; listen for changes in the piano

TIME	TEXT	TRANSLATION	DESCRIPTION
0:00			Piano introduction; rapid triplets suggest speed and agitation. Menacing minor motive in left hand.

0:24	*Narrator*
	Wer reitet so spät durch
	    Nacht und Wind?
	Es ist der Vater mit seinem Kind;
	Er hat den Knaben wohl in dem Arm,
	Er faßt ihn sicher, er hält ihn warm.
		Who rides, so late, through
		    night and wind?
		It is the father with his child.
		He has the boy in his arms
		He holds him safe, he keeps him warm.
			The opening line sets the sinister tone. In this through-composed verse each line is different, though most include some repetition. The verse modulates from minor to major and back again, and the pounding accompaniment captures the sense of terror.

0:59	*Father*
	"Mein Sohn, was birgst du
	    so bang dein Gesicht?"
	Son
	"Siehst, Vater, du den Erlkönig nicht?
	Den Erlenkönig mit Kron' und Schweif?"
	Father
	"Mein Sohn, es ist ein Nebelstreif."
		"My son, why do you hide
		    your face so anxiously?"
		
		"Father, do you not see the Erlking?
		The Erlking with crown and cloak?"
		
		"My son, it's a wisp of fog."
			Father's voice is in a lower register; son's is higher, with agitated leaps.
			
			The father speaks in low, consoling tones.

1:34	*Erlking*
	"Du liebes Kind, komm, geh mit mir!
	Gar schöne Spiele spiel' ich mit dir;
	Manch' bunte Blumen sind an dem
	    Strand,
	Meine Mutter hat manch gülden
	    Gewand."
		"You lovely child, come, go with me!
		Many beautiful games I'll play with you;
		Some colorful flowers are on the
		    shore,
		My mother has many golden robes."
			The Erlking sings softly, in a major key. Piano accompaniment is somewhat different for this verse.

Son

2:00   "Mein Vater, mein Vater, und hörest du nicht,
       Was Erlenkönig mir leise verspricht?"

"My father, my father, can't you hear,
What the Erlking quietly promised me?"

The son cries out, higher than before, and without waiting for an interlude between verses. There is a taut chromatic line in the voice.

Father

"Sei ruhig, bleib ruhig, mein Kind;
In dürren Blättern säuselt der Wind."

"Be calm, stay calm, my child;
It's the wind rustling in the dry leaves."

The father, singing smoothly, is perhaps only pretending to be calm.

Erlking

2:23   "Willst, feiner Knabe, du mit mir gehen?
       Meine Töchter sollen dich warten schön;
       Meine Töchter führen den nächtlichen Reihn,
       Und wiegen und tanzen und singen dich ein."

"Do you want to come with me, fine lad?
My daughters should be waiting for you;
My daughters lead the nightly dances,
And will rock and dance and sing you to sleep."

The Erlking tries a new strategy; he is singing faster now. The piano accompaniment is different again, both from his previous verse, and from the "hoofbeat" accompaniment.

Son

2:41   "Mein Vater, mein Vater, und siehst du nicht dort
       Erlkönigs Töchter am düstern Ort?"

"My father, my father, can't you see there,
The Erlking's daughters in that gloomy place?"

The son sings higher still, once again with a tight chromatic line.
.

Father

"Mein Sohn, mein Sohn, ich seh es genau:
Es scheinen die alten Weiden so grau."

"My son, my son, I see it well:
The old willows look so gray."

The father, also higher than before, and more agitated, pretends to see. The melody has more leaps.

Erlking

3:12   "Ich liebe dich, mich reizt deine schöne Gestalt;
       Und bist du nicht willig, so brauch ich Gewalt."

"I love you, your beautiful form entices me;
And if you're not willing, I shall use force."

The Erlking, singing softly of love, in a major key, ends with a threat, minor key, fortissimo.

Son

"Mein Vater, mein Vater, jetzt faßt er mich an!
Erlkönig hat mir ein Leids getan!"

"My father, my father, he's grabbing me now!
The Erlking has wounded me!"

The child cries out, singing the highest notes in the song.

Narrator

3:39   Dem Vater grauset's,
           er reitet geschwind,
       Er hält in Armen das ächzende Kind,
       Erreicht den Hof mit Müh' und Not;
       In seinen Armen das Kind war tot.

The father shudders;
    he rides swiftly,
He holds in his arms the moaning child.
He arrives at home in urgent need;
In his arms, the child was dead.

The narrator, rushing, describes the father's wild ride for home. The line rises and then falls.

The piece ends abruptly as the piano suddenly stops; the voice concludes with mournful recitative.

⚡ LG 36   **THE "TROUT" QUINTET**

Chamber music for strings was sometimes included in Schubertiades; the "Trout" Quintet for piano and strings is included in this program not because it is representative of what was performed during one of these evenings, but because it allows us to see how Schubert refashioned one of his own pieces for a different medium and a different genre—and because it is such wonderful music.

The "Trout" Quintet is not typical chamber music, in part because of its unusual instrumentation. The standard ensemble for string chamber music is the string quartet (two violins, one viola, and one cello). We have a large and fascinating repertory of pieces for this combination, with contributions from Haydn, Mozart, Beethoven, Schubert, and beyond. Adding a piano to a string quartet produces a *piano quintet* (even though the name sounds like a quintet of pianos). It makes sense in a way to compose for piano quintet, since it is simply a matter of adding one instrument to the familiar ensemble of the string quartet. There are other kinds of chamber music with piano, too, like the piano trio (piano, violin, cello).

Scoring   But the "Trout" Quintet has an unusual scoring: piano, violin, viola, cello, and double bass. This particular grouping, like the piece itself, comes from a specific event in Schubert's life.

When Schubert was twenty-two, he and Vogl took a summer trip to Steyr, Vogl's Austrian birthplace, and attended regular musical evenings at the home of Sylvester Paumgartner, a wealthy amateur cellist. Paumgartner mentioned how much he liked Schubert's song *Die Forelle*, and suggested a quintet to Schubert, to match the unusual scoring and structure of an existing quintet by Johann Nepomuk Hummel (the composer's own arrangement from his earlier septet).

Even though the quintet has a double bass part, which allows the cello to relax somewhat, Paumgartner struggled with the cello part. Schubert must have overestimated his friend's ability, and the work remained unpublished, and little played, in Schubert's lifetime.

The quintet follows the structure of a small symphony, except that there is an added movement: between the scherzo and the finale is a set of variations on Schubert's song *Die Forelle*. It would not be the only time Schubert returned to one of his earlier songs to create a larger instrumental piece (he does so in his "Death and the Maiden" String Quartet, using his song of the same name, and in his "Wanderer" Fantasy for the piano, using his song *The Wanderer*).

Ⓢ Schubert: "Death and the Maiden" Quartet, II

There are six variations in all, each one varied by instrument and accompaniment, with a few varied by key as well. The variations are arranged as follows:

Theme: strings

Variation 1: Piano plays decorated theme, with string accompaniment.

Variation 2: Viola has theme, echoed by piano.

Variation 3: Double bass has theme; elaborate piano countermelody.

Variation 4: Minor key: contrasts of loud and soft; theme is barely present except as a shape.

Variation 5: New slower tempo; cello plays theme, highly altered; a transition leads to . . .

Variation 6: Major key; violin and viola alternate phrases of the theme; piano and violin alternate playing the figuration from the original accompaniment of the song.

LISTENING GUIDE 36 | DVD

Schubert The "Trout" Quintet, Piano Quintet in A Major, IV   7:14

DATE: 1819
MEDIUM: Piano quintet: violin, viola, cello, double bass, and piano

TEMPO: Andantino (moving, or walking, somewhat; a little faster than Andante)

LISTEN FOR

MELODY: The theme is decorated in various ways
HARMONY: Major, except for Variation 4, in a minor key
FORM: The theme is the melody of the song *Die Forelle*; but where the song's verse had four phrases with the last

repeated, **AA′BCC**, the theme here repeats each half, **AA′ AA′ BCC BCC**.

TEXTURE: The theme is passed from one instrument to the other; note varied accompaniments

TIME	FORM	DESCRIPTION
0:00	Theme	Violin plays theme, with homophonic accompaniment in strings. Both phrases of melody repeated:
0:58	Variation 1	Piano plays theme in octaves, with trills; strings accompany; note *pizzicato* (plucked) double bass.
1:51	Variation 2	Viola plays theme, echoed by the piano. Violin plays decorative filigree in countermelody.
2:47	Variation 3	Cello and double bass play theme. Piano plays elaborate counterpoint in octaves.
3:37	Variation 4	Sudden shift to minor key, rhythm changes to triplets. Contrasting loud and soft. Harmony is altered. Theme essentially disappears; the shape is all that's left.
4:34	Variation 5	Tempo is slow; the music is in a new key. Cello plays altered version of the theme:
		Harmony is changed; there is a coda that provides transition to . . .
5:58	Variation 6	Bright, sunny, final version; violin and cello alternate phrases of theme; piano plays figuration from original song. Closes quietly.

The quintet provides a wonderfully lighthearted view on the different ways in which to treat a straightforward tune. (See LG 36, above.)

Surely in any performance where there was a piano and Schubert was present, he would have been the pianist. His friend Stadler said about his playing, "To see and hear him play his own pianoforte compositions was a real pleasure. A beautiful touch, a quiet hand, clear, neat playing . . . full of insight and feeling."

In our Schubertiade in 1826, there was surely dancing after the songs and the quintet. Perhaps Schubert improvised the dance music as he usually did. Lucky for us that he wrote so much of it down.

Schubert Then and Now

Schubert's life was tragically short—Grillparzer's inscription on his tombstone read, "The art of music here entombed a rich possession, but even far fairer hopes"—and we can only imagine what he might have composed had he lived as long as Beethoven.

The differences between the two composers are worth pointing out. Beethoven's music is often thought of in general terms as heroic, public, monumental, designed for large spaces and virtuoso performers, even though he composed songs and much chamber music. Schubert, on the other hand, although he too composed symphonies and operas, produced much of his music for private use, in homes and salons. Beethoven's music frequently is built from a small motive that gets worked out in all its possibilities; Schubert's music is often made of lyrical melodies, whether songs or not. Each, of course, produced music of the "other" kind, but the comparison allows us to think about the different functions that music can have in the world.

It's difficult to classify Schubert, if in fact composers need to be assigned style periods. Is he a Viennese Classicist, like Haydn, Mozart, and Beethoven? Well, yes, he is: his forms, his procedures, the kinds of pieces he wrote, are just the kinds of works that Vienna was used to. And yet there is something in Schubert's lyricism, in the personal aspect of his music, that leads us to think of him as a forerunner of the Romantic movement. Mozart the perfectly balanced, Beethoven the titanic hero, represent some aspects of what we call Classical music; and although Schubert's music includes these aspects as well, the lyrical, introspective quality of his music, the individual features of his songs, the sense of a single person expressing something personal, are all hallmarks of what, in the next section, we call Romantic music.

But it may be best not to classify beauty.

Chapter Review

Summary of Musical Styles

Schubert's music shares many characteristics with Beethoven and Mozart as well as with the Romantic composers who followed him.

He shares the **Classic** traits of
- themes with balanced phrases;
- the use of traditional symphonic and operatic forms;
- the use of keys to articulate form.

With the **Romantics** he shares
- a fondness for **miniatures** (his many songs and short piano pieces may be compared to those of Robert Schumann—see Chapter 12);
- the use of character pieces for a major portion of his output;
- the creation of music for performers of moderate ability.

Characteristic of Schubert above all are
- a gift for unforgettable, lyrical melodies;

- an ability to characterize a situation with a few simple strokes and a perfect accompaniment;
- a dramatic use of sudden shifts of key (*Die Forelle* and *Der Erlkönig*).

⑤ Multimedia Resources and Review Materials on StudySpace

Visit wwnorton.com/studyspace for review of Chapter 9.

What Do You Know?

Check the facts for this chapter. Take the online **Quiz**.

What Do You Hear?

Listening Quizzes and **Music Activities** will help you understand the musical works in this chapter.

🎙 Author Videos

- Accompaniment in *Gretchen am Spinnrade*

Interactive Listening Guides

LG 33 Schubert: *Die Forelle* (*The Trout*)
LG 34 Schubert: *Gretchen am Spinnrade* (*Gretchen at the Spinning Wheel*)
LG 35 Schubert: *Der Erlkönig* (*The Erlking*)
LG 36 Schubert: The "Trout" Quintet, Piano Quintet in A Major, IV

Flashcards (Terms to Know)

art song
chamber music
lied (pl. lieder)
modified strophic
salons

Schubertiades
song cycle
strophic
through-composed

THE ROMANTIC PERIOD

HISTORICAL EVENTS	MUSICAL EVENTS

1800

MUSICAL EVENTS

1797–1828 Franz Schubert

1803–1869 Hector Berlioz

1805–1847 Fanny Mendelssohn Hensel

1809 Death of Haydn

1809–1847 Felix Mendelssohn

1810–1856 Robert Schumann

1810–1849 Frédéric Chopin

1813–1883 Richard Wagner

1813–1901 Giuseppe Verdi

1815 Battle of Waterloo

1819–1901 Reign of Britain's Queen Victoria

1825

1825 Erie Canal opens

1827 Delacroix, *Death of Sardanapalus*

1819–1896 Clara Schumann

1827 Death of Beethoven

1830 July Revolution in France

1830 Victor Hugo's play *Hernani* premiers in Paris

1831 Cyrus McCormick invents the first successful mechanical reaper

1833–1897 Johannes Brahms

1837 Samuel F. B. Morse develops the telegraph

1839 Charles Dickens, *Oliver Twist*

1840–1893 Peter Ilyich Tchaikovsky

1841–1904 Antonín Dvořák

1848 Revolutions and uprisings in numerous European countries (Italy, France, Belgium, Austrian Empire, and others)

1848 Marx and Engels, *Communist Manifesto*

1850

1851 Herman Melville, *Moby-Dick*

1856–1939 Sigmund Freud

1859 Darwin, *On the Origin of Species*

1861–65 American Civil War

1869 Suez Canal opens

1870–71 Franco-Prussian War, collapse of the Second French Empire

1870–71 Unifications of Germany and Italy

1875

1877 Thomas Edison invents the phonograph

1895 Wilhelm Roentgen discovers X-rays

1900

Italy   France   Russia   Germany/Austria

PART IV

Music and Feeling: Romantic Music

During the so-called **Romantic era** the arts in general reflected an interest in the inner life of the mind and the heart. Artists emphasized the individual, the emotional, the visionary, the exotic, the sublime, and the spontaneous. We often use the term in a circumscribed way, to refer to love; but the nineteenth-century Romantic movement, which did concern itself with love and with many other things internal to human beings, was a much larger artistic movement.

Romantic era

The term "romantic" was originally associated with literature, and defined a movement that preferred the natural to the artificial. You will remember that balance and composure were essential to the eighteenth century; at that time the arts were often praised when they were "most artificial," that is, fashioned on purpose by human hands, not discovered or found to be naturally occurring. Clothing, architecture, and landscape, for example, were rigorously constrained according to generally agreed norms.

Romanticism was an effort to break free of these accepted forms, boundaries, and genres that artists began to consider stifling and oppressive. It was a time of experimentation and a yearning for the new. Anything that occurred in nature—even nature itself—was fascinating. Nineteenth-century gardens can be seen as a metaphor for the Romantic movement: instead of carefully tended and clipped *parterre* flower beds, people now preferred what they called English gardens (see Figure IV.1)—trees, grass, and flowers planted in curves to look natural or untamed (even if they weren't). Romantic artists were interested in that which was not managed by humankind.

Romanticism

FIG. IV.1 A painting of a typically "Romantic" English garden at Stourhead in England; natural vistas, lawns, and curving borders contrast sharply with the geometrical, ornamental gardens of the eighteenth century.

Politics, Economics, and Technology

The nineteenth century saw the beginning and end of the American Civil War, the reign of Queen Victoria, the collapse of nations and the building of new ones. It was an age of empire-building and colonization. The century also witnessed industrialization and the creation of the railroad, the invention of the telegraph, aspirin, and the light bulb, even the safety pin and blue jeans.

Nationalism

After Napoleon's defeat in 1815, the British navy enforced the growing power of Great Britain in the world. On the European continent, **nationalism**—the desire to create and maintain political states to represent cultural zones, languages, or commonly held cultures—led to the unification of Germany and of Italy. The Holy Roman Empire (which had included Austria, Hungary, Bohemia, and a number of other cultural areas) was dissolved, and the German (Prussian) Empire grew in strength. Otto von Bismarck, the great Prussian chancellor, managed, by gradually weakening Austria and winning a war with France (the Franco-Prussian War of 1870–71), to unify Prussia and a group of German-speaking principalities to form a unified German empire. The Italian Risorgimento ("Resurgence") resulted in a unified Italy created from former holdings of Austria, the papacy, and a number of smaller principalities (see Figure IV.2, map of Europe, p. 259.)

Industrial Revolution

The mechanization of industry—the Industrial Revolution—effected many changes in the economy and in society. Europe's population doubled in the course of the century, and the rising concentration of population in cities led to the increasing importance of the middle class.

Railways and telegraphs made travel and communication much easier and faster, gas lighting in cities made life more comfortable, increased printing of newspapers and books reflected a growing literate society, and by the end of the century electricity and the telephone were about to change the world.

Slavery and colonialism

Slavery was abolished—at least in name—everywhere. The American Civil War (1861–65), fought in part over this issue, devastated a nation growing in world importance. This was also an age of imperialism, in which European powers

FIG. IV.2 Map of Europe, ca. 1871.

sought to increase their prestige and their economies by acquiring colonies that were governed—some might say exploited—from Europe: a colony was a rich source of raw materials as well as a purchaser of the manufactured goods of the European colonizer. Large portions of the non-European world were divided up among the European powers.

Romantic Musical Style

Classical vs. Romantic music

The composers of the nineteenth century continued to do what Mozart, Beethoven, and Schubert had done: compose operas, orchestral music, chamber music, and songs. The continuity of musical forms, however, is contrasted by a strong musical difference in expression. Whereas the music we think of as Classical strives for a kind of universality, in which its beauty lies in objectivity—balance, form, order, and clarity—Romantic music, while constructed from the same materials, seeks to express subjectivity—emotions and passions, which are present not so much in society as in the individual, and not so much in human constructs as in nature. Although there is no absolute dividing line between Classical and Romantic music, we can sense a polarity, a balance between music as form, and music as expression of emotion or feeling. On each side of the Classic-Romantic divide, both ends of the polarity are found: Mendelssohn can be as Classical as Mozart, and Beethoven can be as Romantic as Berlioz. But the trend in music of the nineteenth century, as in the other arts, is toward Romanticism.

Science and Philosophy

Three great thinkers of the nineteenth century, each conversant in a very different area of knowledge, affected human thought and activity in ways almost unprecedented in the history of modern times. **Charles Darwin** (1809–1882), an eminent naturalist, developed the theory of natural selection and explained the process of evolution. His *On The Origin of Species* (1859) and *The Descent of Man* (1871) were enormously influential—as they still are—and produced a devastating challenge to religion and to many aspects of the biological sciences.

Karl Marx (1818–1883) was a theorist of capitalism and value; with Friedrich Engels he published *The Communist Manifesto* in 1848 (a year of over fifty revolutions throughout Europe). Marx argued that value is accrued through human labor and that capitalism tended to deprive workers of the value of this labor. The working class, he argued, would ultimately rise up in revolution and bring on a true communist society. The first part of his other major work, *Das Kapital* (*Capital*), was published in 1867, the rest after his death. Marx's theories became the basis of revolutions and new governments during the late nineteenth and early twentieth centuries.

Sigmund Freud (1856–1939), the creator of psychoanalysis, developed theories of how the unconscious mind functioned, and originated the idea of the sexual origin of neuroses. His theories of human psychology have profoundly affected how we think, although his influence was not widely felt until the twentieth century.

The Arts

This was the century that began to value the past: the great medieval cathedrals were restored and museums were established for the study of ancient art and culture. In the visual arts, the century began with the *neoclassicism* so favored by Napoleon. The refined work of Italian sculptor **Antonio Canova** (1757–1822) and the cerebral French painters **Jacques-Louis David** (1748–1825) and **J.A.D. Ingres** (1780–1867) represented a beauty of balance and decorum. But sculpture became more individual and expressive at the end of the century, culminating in the works of **Auguste Rodin** (1840–1917). The Romantic painters soon followed suit, with the later works of **Francisco de Goya** (1746–1828), **Théodore Géricault** (1791–1824), and **Eugène Delacroix** (1798–1863) depicting nature, emotions, and anything that reflected the inner self and the forces of the sublime. Color and atmosphere became the province of the English artist **J. M. W. Turner** (1775–1851; see Figure IV.3) and of the American artist **James McNeill Whistler** (1834–1903). Another

FIG. IV.3 J. M. W. Turner's (1775-1851) famous painting *The Morning after the Wreck*, 1835-45. Effects of light and atmosphere and the depiction of a hazy view of nature are typical of Turner's work.

FIG. IV.4 Vincent van Gogh, *Wheat Field with Cypresses*. 1889. The Dutch painter's strong colors and emphatic brushwork make his paintings unmistakable.

American painter, Thomas Cole (1801–1848), was known for his realistic portrayals of the American landscape and its wilderness. His detailed and elaborate works combine panoramic images with moralistic insights, often depicting nature as all-powerful.

Realist painters like **Jean-Baptiste-Camille Corot** (1796–1875) and **Gustave Courbet** (1819–1877) turned to the depiction of everyday life. In the latter part of the century, **impressionism** sought to portray the visual impression of a moment. Impressionist paintings often show clear brush strokes, each bearing a separate touch of color; the attempt to convey the impression of changing light is frequently attached to everyday subject matter. Painters like **Edouard Manet** (1832–1883), **Paul Cézanne** (1839–1906), **Claude Monet** (1840–1926), and **Vincent van Gogh** (1853–1890; see Figure IV.4) created a new way of looking at color, light, and movement.

Literature

In the nineteenth century the novel was a leading literary form, appealing to the wide middle-class readership. Novels explored the relationship of people to each other and to society, and also examined the inner emotional life of the characters. A long list of writers—**Charles Dickens** (1812–1870; *Oliver Twist, Bleak House*), **Anthony Trollope** (1815–1882; the Palliser novels), and **George Eliot** (Mary Ann Evans, 1819–1880; *Middlemarch*), in England; **Honoré de Balzac** (1799–1850; *The Human Comedy*), **Victor Hugo** (1802–1885; *Notre Dame de Paris*), and **Gustave Flaubert** (1821–1880; *Madame Bovary*), in France; **Edgar Allen Poe** (1809–1849; "The Fall of the House of Usher") and **Herman Melville** (1819–1891; *Moby-Dick*), in the United States; **Fyodor Dostoevsky** (1821–1881; *The Brothers Karamazov*), **Leo Tolstoy** (1828–1910; *War and Peace*), in Russia—all contributed to a genre that catered to an increasing, and increasingly literate, middle class.

Poetry flourished as well. The Romantic poets of the early years of the century include British writers **William Wordsworth** (1770–1850), **George Gordon Byron** (1788–1824), **Samuel Taylor Coleridge** (1772–1834), **John Keats** (1795–1821), and **Percy Bysshe Shelley** (1792–1822). Later English poets include **Alfred Tennyson** (1809–1892) and **Robert Browning** (1812–1889). Romanticism crossed the Atlantic through the works of poets like **Henry Wadsworth Longfellow** (1807–1882); **Walt Whitman** (1819–1892) and **Emily Dickinson** (1830–1886) were among the American poets whose Romantic style combined with more innovative and modern leanings. In Germany, **Heinrich Heine** (1797–1856) allowed a folkloristic element into the classical German tradition of Goethe. And in France, poets like **Charles Baudelaire** (1821–1867), **Paul Verlaine** (1844–96), and **Arthur Rimbaud** (1854–91) ushered in a new literary trend called symbolism.

The nineteenth century is the age of folklore and of the "rediscovery" of childhood as a state different from adulthood. A host of children's literature soon appeared—**Louisa May Alcott**'s (1832–1888) *Little Women* and **Rudyard Kipling**'s (1865–1936) *The Jungle Book*, for example—as well as music for children to listen to and learn, and special clothing and activities for them (before the nineteenth century children had been dressed and treated essentially as little adults).

The kind of idealism and self-reliance associated with the American view of the world and politics—and flavored by Romanticism—appears nowhere more strongly than in the works of American transcendentalists **Ralph Waldo Emerson** (1803–1882), **Henry David Thoreau** (1817–1862), **Bronson Alcott** (1799–1888), and his daughter Louisa May Alcott.

FIG. IV.5 The violinist Niccolò Paganini was such an astounding virtuoso that some said that he was in league with the Devil. In this caricature the Devil teaches him how to play the violin.

Ⓢ Mendelssohn: *Songs without Words*, No. 6, "Spring Song"

The towering figure of Beethoven cast a huge shadow. Composers were so full of admiration for his exceptional gifts and achievements that some felt a need to move away from the monumental toward the personal, working in the areas of chamber music, piano music, and song. These smaller, intimate works, sometimes called **miniatures**, were suitable for private performance in middle-class salons and are one of the hallmarks of nineteenth-century music. Ⓢ This repertory was useful to, and encouraged by, the growing number of amateur musicians, and by the fact that music was becoming part of the education of young people.

At the same time, the symphony, established by Beethoven as the highest form of instrumental music, did continue in a variety of ways. Berlioz used the symphony to express his inner emotional life (see Chapter 10) and to tell a story. Composers like Dvořák and Tchaikovsky sought to communicate something local or national in their symphonies (see Chapter 14). And the late Romantic composers Anton Bruckner and Gustav Mahler, full of inspiration from Richard Wagner, produced some of the grandest and longest symphonies ever written.

Harmony and melody were all expanded during the nineteenth century. Composers experimented with new chord forms, unusual key contrasts, and mixtures of major and minor modes, as well as highly charged and expressive harmonies, especially through the use of **chromaticism** (see p. A-6). Tone color, too, was the subject of much expansion. It is no surprise, then, that the orchestra grew in size—increasing its range of color expression—and that many of the instruments saw technical advances, allowing the use of the full chromatic scale, which in turn offered composers new levels of harmonic and melodic expression.

This was also the age of the **virtuoso**. The Romantic accent on the individual was important in the development of this musical role. Franz Liszt at the piano and Niccolò Paganini on the violin are the most famous of many Romantic virtuosos—soloists who played music so difficult and dazzling that they were believed by some to be possessed by the Devil himself (see Figure IV.5).

There had been virtuoso performers before, of course. Bach, Mozart, and Beethoven had all been valued in their time at least as much for their impressive performance as for their great compositions. On the opera stage, singers had always been stars, as they always would be. But the nineteenth century witnessed the rise of the career of the solo performer, as a person set apart from the rest of humanity. The cult of the artistic hero began perhaps with Beethoven but was furthered by the virtuosos and by the notion that an artist-composer feels, suffers, and creates in ways that are not available to ordinary people.

Opera   The nineteenth century was also the great period of opera. The lyric theater was everywhere, of central importance socially and musically. The Italians—with the early lyrical Gaetano Donizetti (1797–1848; *Lucia di Lammermoor*) and Vincenzo Bellini (1801–1835; *Norma*); then the incomparable Giuseppe Verdi (1813–1901; *Rigoletto, La Traviata, Aida*), followed by Giacomo Puccini (1858–1924; *La Bohème, Tosca*)—created a body of work that will never fade. Elsewhere Richard

Wagner (see Chapter 13) brought German opera to heights that would be hard to reach for anyone less talented than Richard Strauss (1864–1949; *Der Rosenkavalier*). In France, always somewhat independent, the tradition of grand opera, full of spectacle, began with Daniel François Esprit Auber (1782-1871; *Fra Diavolo*) and Giacomo Meyerbeer (1791–1864; *Robert le Diable, Les Huguenots*), and was carried on by Berlioz (1803–1869; *Les Troyens*), Charles Gounod (1818–1893; *Faust*), and others.

We might also call the nineteenth century the century of nationalism, not only in politics but also in music. Dvořák and many others sought to represent their own nation or culture with music that included local elements, folk melodies, and descriptive harmonies that would represent Moravia, or Bohemia, or Finland, or Denmark, or Russia, while remaining at the same time within the great tradition of art music.

The period covered here is not long: Berlioz's *Fantastic Symphony* is from 1830, Dvořák's *New World* Symphony from 1893—a period not much more than the forty-one years between Mozart's *Don Giovanni* and Schubert's 1828 evening. Yet works by the composers of the Romantic era represent the majority of pieces performed on modern concert programs; their works have become the core of the standard concert repertory. These composers don't all have chapters in this book, but you've surely heard of many of them: Chopin, Schumann, Liszt, Brahms, Tchaikovsky, Verdi, Grieg, Sibelius, Musorgsky, Rimsky-Korsakov, to name a few.

The musical selections we're about to hear—and many we won't hear because of limited space in this book—have become the most popular works of today's concert stages and opera houses. Perhaps what attracts us is the combination of music that is meant to be personal—that speaks to the soul—with the lyrical melodies, the lush harmonies, and the original and imaginative forms characteristic of the Romantic century.

▶ Video, Verdi: *Rigoletto*, "La donna è mobile"—"Un di"—"Bella figlia dell'amore"

▶ Video, Verdi: *La Traviata*, "Signora"—"Parigi, o cara"

▶ Video, Puccini: *La Bohème*, "Quando me'n va"

Ⓢ Mussorgsky: "The Field Marshal"

Style Comparisons at a Glance	
CLASSIC MUSICAL STYLE	**ROMANTIC MUSICAL STYLE**
Themes made from paired phrases	Themes often folklike
Straightforward harmonies	Harmonies based on chromatic scale, mixtures of major and minor modes, unusual key contrasts
Genres: symphony, string quartet, concerto, opera, song	Genres: many miniatures—piano solos, songs, character pieces—as well as symphony, concerto, and opera
Sonata form prevails in many movements	Various extensions and variations of sonata form are tried
Music is expressive of itself	Music seeks to express personal, interior emotional experiences; it is sometimes used for narrative purposes
Music is international	Music seeks to express local, cultural, and national traditions

CHAPTER 10

SUNDAY, DECEMBER 5, 1830, PARIS:

Hector Berlioz's *Fantastic Symphony* (*Symphonie fantastique*)

◉ CORE REPERTOIRE

- **LG 37** "Rêveries—Passions" (Reveries—Passions), I
- **LG 38** "Un bal" (A Ball), II
- **LG 39** "Scène aux champs" (Scene in the Country), III
- **LG 40** "Marche du supplice" (March to the Scaffold), IV
- **LG 41** "Songe d'une nuit de sabbat" (Dream of a Witches' Sabbath), V

◉ AUTHOR VIDEOS

- Berlioz's *idée fixe*

Introduction

"How we shivered in horror before the scaffold, rendered by such beautiful images of such startling veracity that they aroused, right in the middle of the execution, a thunder of applause that nothing could stop."

—From the review in *Le Temps*, December 26, 1830

Paris in 1830 was the center of the civilized world, at least in the eyes of its three-quarters of a million inhabitants, and it was there that the young Hector Berlioz set out to make a name for himself. Using money from an important prize he had won, he paid to put on a concert that would feature his new Romantic symphony, called the *Fantastic Symphony* (in French, *Symphonie fantastique*). The work attracted a modest amount of attention from the press—though not as much as Berlioz would have liked. Since that day it has become one of the most frequently played works in the standard repertory. Besides being a fine, and quite avant-garde, piece of music on its own, it has the unusual feature of narrating a plot set in the natural world.

We have already seen how music and words work together to tell a story in an opera like Mozart's *Don Giovanni* or a song like Schubert's *Gretchen am Spinnrade* (*Gretchen at the Spinning Wheel*). But what happens when there are no words? There is plenty of precedent for narrative music in the past, and the question of how, or whether, music can narrate things outside itself is one that fascinates many people. It became especially urgent in the Romantic era, when music was called upon to describe not only natural phenomena but also interior states of the soul. The term **program music**, meaning music that describes something or tells a story, relates to the first performance of this symphony, at which Berlioz distributed a printed program to the audience explaining the story behind—or perhaps inside—the music.

And a whopping good story it is. The *Fantastic Symphony* is typical of the Romantic movement in literature and the other arts in that it focuses on the creative artist, on the interior life of the emotions, on the supernatural, and on romantic love. The highlights of this unspoken drama include the imagined execution by guillotine of the lovesick hero and his opium-induced visions of a witches' dance of the dead.

The *Fantastic Symphony* seemed avant-garde to its listeners in 1830, partly because the story itself was adventurous, and partly because the idea that music could describe such matters without the help of words was relatively novel and controversial. Many listeners found the symphony "difficult" or distasteful. Quite a few, however, recognized Berlioz's work for what it was: a terrific symphony in the tradition of Beethoven. In fact, the *Fantastic Symphony* still seems so shockingly modern today that it's surprising to learn that it comes so early in the history of nineteenth-century Romantic music, and so early in the career of its young composer. Berlioz remains *the* pioneer of program music.

It is a first symphony by an almost unknown composer. The sheer force of its sound, which was thoroughly new and imaginatively wrought, helps to explain why the music is still so vivid today. The crazy flying woodwinds at the end of the

Program music

ⓢ Berlioz: *Fantastic Symphony*, IV, "March to the Scaffold," march theme

ⓢ Berlioz: *Fantastic Symphony*, V, Witches' Dance

last movement, the stunning noise of the harps at the beginning of the second movement, and the spooky beginning of the finale all create a new world of sound.

The Setting

PARIS IN 1830

Paris was then, as it is now, a grand metropolis, even though many of the improvements that modern visitors associate with the city had not yet been realized. The vast network of broad, tree-lined boulevards, the enormous train stations, the palatial opera house, the Eiffel Tower, the underground metro—all this and more lay in the future. The Arc de Triomphe under construction at the top of the Champs-Élysées was in 1830 four stone stumps. Even the magnificent Palace of the Louvre, which was both a royal residence and a public art museum, was woefully dilapidated and awaiting restoration. At that time the Tuileries Palace (which later burned) stood in front of the Louvre, closing its courtyards; it was the scene of the July Revolution (see below) in 1830, during which Berlioz, across the river, was competing for the composition prize that helped bring him to public attention.

The French Revolution had turned the social and economic world upside down at the end of the eighteenth century, and Emperor Napoleon Bonaparte had temporarily turned it right-side up again, with France at the top. After Napoleon's defeat at Waterloo in 1815, the map of Europe was redrawn and the French monarchy restored. Fifteen years later, a few months before the premiere of the *Fantastic Symphony,* history repeated itself (see map of Europe, p. 259). During three days of fighting in the streets (known in France as "Les Trois Glorieuses," the "Three Glorious Days," or the July Revolution), the people of Paris made barricades of paving stones and succeeded in forcing King Charles X from his throne. The new constitutional monarch, Louis-Philippe, who styled himself the "citizen king," was careful to have no crown in his official portraits (see Figure 10.1).

Despite the king's bow to popular democracy, the July Revolution ushered in a period of political instability, with factions jockeying for power in what the Marquis de Lafayette (the hero of both the French and the American Revolutions) optimistically called "the best of all republics." Economically, however, day-to-day life in the French capital didn't change as quickly or dramatically as the political landscape. The streets on which the newly empowered members of the middle and working classes strode so confidently remained cramped, badly lit, and mostly unpaved, especially in the congested labyrinth that surrounded the royal enclave on the Right Bank of the Seine River. (Berlioz's modest apartment on the Rue de Richelieu was a few blocks northeast of the Louvre.) Residents still emptied their chamberpots onto public thoroughfares, where carriages competed for space with the new multicolored public omnibuses (see Figure 10.2).

For all that, Paris offered a wide range of civilized amenities, including a cultural life as lively and varied as was to be found anywhere in Europe. The Parisians' pride in French classical drama—enshrined at the venerable Comédie Française—was if anything surpassed by their passion for opera. The main institution for the performance of opera was known then, as now, as the Opéra (its formal name was the Royal

FIG. 10.1 Louis-Philippe, duke of Orléans, who was installed as king of the French after the July Revolution of 1830.

FIG. 10.2 The Rue Saint-Denis, Paris, in the 1830s. Apart from the major squares and monuments, streets were often crowded and messy.

FIG. 10.3 The Opera House on the Rue Le Peletier, the main opera house of Paris.

Academy of Music; see Figure 10.3). It was housed on the Rue Le Peletier, just off the Boulevard des Italiens, in a theater that was grand but built in a hurry (the former one burned down) and was meant to be temporary. The Opéra catered to the public's growing appetite for grand opera—works with complicated historical plots and spectacular settings, such as Daniel Auber's *La muette de Portici* (*The Mute Girl of Portici*; see Figure 10.4) and Gioachino Rossini's *Guillaume Tell* (*William Tell*). New gas lighting allowed for spectacular novel effects. Those whose tastes ran to lighter fare or supernatural plots frequented the Opéra-Comique and the Italian Opera.

The Opéra

Berlioz and most of his fellow French musicians were trained at the Paris Conservatory (see Figure 10.9, p. 274), one of the first public music schools in the world. (It was founded during the French Revolution to provide players for military marching bands.) The director in 1830 was Luigi Cherubini, an eminent Italian composer known for his high standards and strict sense of discipline and decorum. Berlioz incurred Cherubini's displeasure even before he officially enrolled at

Paris Conservatory

FIG. 10.4 A performance of *La muette de Portici* at the Opera, with the famous eruption of Mount Vesuvius in the background. A benefit performance of this opera was given on the same day as Berlioz's concert.

the school, when he innocently entered the building through the door reserved for female students. As much as he chafed at Cherubini's seemingly arbitrary rules, though, he valued the solid musical education he received from the Conservatory's excellent faculty. Eventually, Berlioz would have the satisfaction of seeing his own treatise on orchestration used by students at his alma mater. (**Orchestration** is the art of using instruments well and combining them in effective ways.)

Conservatory concerts

François-Antoine Habeneck, the enormously influential conductor of the Opéra and professor at the Conservatory, had founded a series of Sunday afternoon concerts in the auditorium of the Conservatory, which were well attended and highly respected. The Société des Concerts du Conservatoire, a cooperative society of eighty-six of the top instrumentalists in Paris, was in fact one of the earliest concert orchestras in the world. Habeneck was a devotee of Beethoven; among other works by the German master, he introduced Parisians to the Fifth Symphony in April 1828, in a concert that Berlioz attended.

ROMANTICISM

You could not be in Paris, and involved in the arts, without being swept up in the literary and artistic movement known as Romanticism (see p. 257). Romantic revolutionaries like Berlioz sought to break out of the rule-bound traditions of art.

Victor Hugo

Victor Hugo's play *Hernani*, premiered in Paris in 1830, is a defining moment in the Romantic movement. A historical potboiler seething with intrigue and passion, it flaunted the time-honored conventions of classical drama. Hugo's depiction of unbridled emotions and his use of everyday, unpoetic language provoked an outbreak of hooting and hissing at the first performance. Berlioz and the playwright's other supporters countered with an equally vociferous defense, and the experience convinced the young composer that he and Hugo were kindred spirits.

Romantic writers, musicians, and painters were interested in nature, in the

FIG. 10.5 *The Death of Sardana-palus* (1827), by Eugène Delacroix. Sardanapalus, the decadent Assyrian ruler, refusing to be captured by his enemies, gathered all his riches and his women in his palace, and burned it to the ground with everyone and everything inside. Berlioz won the Rome Prize for his cantata based on the story of Sardanapalus.

outdoors, in everything that was not created and managed by humankind. They were interested, too, in exotic lands and distant eras; this is the time when the French began to value and restore the great Gothic cathedrals. (Notre Dame was in such a disgraceful state of disrepair by the mid-nineteenth century that Hugo and others led a campaign to save it as a national treasure.) The supernatural—ghosts, demons, large black birds and bats, fiery stagecoaches, lightning and thunder, apparitions—features largely in Romantic art, music, and literature; in fact, a ballet of the ghosts of nuns was one of the attractions of Giacomo Meyerbeer's opera *Robert le diable*.

Above all, Romantic art concerned itself with the heart, with feelings, the struggles and passions of individual human beings, and with the soul (see Figure 10.5). That is why there is such interest in religion (there are religious subjects in the operas of the time—Halévy's *La Juive*, Meyerbeer's *Les Huguenots*, not to mention the dancing ghosts of nuns in *Robert le diable*), in drugs (Berlioz read De Quincey's *Confessions of an English Opium Eater*), and perhaps most of all, in love. The emphasis on nature, the supernatural, religion, and drugs already mark the *Fantastic Symphony* as a quintessentially Romantic work. But the real subject of the symphony is Berlioz's tempestuous love life, which in turn revolved around the lives of three women who had captured his highly impressionable heart.

HECTOR BERLIOZ

Short and red-headed, with a beaky nose, Hector Berlioz (pronounced *Bear*-lee-oze) thought he looked like an owl. As a medical student in Paris in the early 1820s, Hector Berlioz concealed his musical aspirations from his father. Dr. Louis-Joseph Berlioz, a well-to-do physician in the southeastern French town of La Côte Saint-André, had groomed his eldest child for a medical career; when he discovered that Hector had no intention of following in his footsteps, he cut off his son's allowance, hoping to bring him back to his senses. Hector, however, was appalled by the thought of becoming a doctor, and determined to give himself "body and soul to music," and for many years father and son were estranged. It took the winning of the prestigious Rome Prize to convince his parents that a musical career was possible and permissible.

Forced to fall back on his own resources, Berlioz took several part-time jobs to make ends meet while he pursued his studies at the Conservatory. He worked as a singer in the chorus of a theater, taught guitar at a school for young women, read proofs for a music publisher, and wrote occasional pieces of music journalism. All the while he longed to be a great composer. He managed to get part of a Mass and one or two other pieces performed; he also worked hard on a couple of operas, though with little hope of seeing them produced. Berlioz had been thinking about Shakespeare's *Romeo and Juliet*, and was captivated by Goethe's drama *Faust*. Finally, at the beginning of 1830, he conceived the idea of writing a symphony that would tell a story—the story of the sufferings of a Romantic artist very like himself. (See biography, p. 270.)

ESTELLE, HARRIET, AND CAMILLE

The first of the composer's muses, Estelle Duboeuf, was his first love (see Figure 10.6). Six years older than Berlioz, she lived in a village near where he visited his grandfather. When he was twelve, he fell madly and secretly in love with her. When they parted at the end of his stay, he poured out his sadness in a song, and the melody of that song is woven into the first movement of the *Fantastic Symphony*.

FIG. 10.6 A photograph of the aged Estelle Duboeuf whom the young Hector Berlioz fell in love with at the age of twelve, when she was eighteen.

Ⓢ Berlioz: Fantastic Symphony, I, "Estelle" melody

Hector Berlioz (1803–1869)

A highly imaginative composer of an experimental, even avant-garde bent, Hector Berlioz was also a distinguished conductor, especially of his own music, and a prolific and talented writer on music (his memoirs make engrossing reading). He is admired especially for his orchestral compositions, and his classic treatise on orchestration is still in print. Among his early works, mostly lost or unfinished, are a *Solemn Mass*, recently rediscovered, and an opera *Les francs-juges* (sometimes translated as *The Judges of the Secret Court*), never finished. His first big success came in 1830, when he gave a concert of his own works that included the new *Fantastic Symphony*.

Strongly influenced by literature, by Shakespeare's plays, by nature, and by passion, Berlioz was a naturally dramatic composer. His programmatic symphonies, including *Harold in Italy* (purportedly based on Byron's narrative poem *Childe Harold's Pilgrimage*), which has a prominent viola solo, and *Romeo and Juliet*, helped make his reputation abroad.

Berlioz made strenuous but essentially unsuccessful efforts to establish himself as a leading composer. He gave concerts of his own music; after 1835, he conducted most of these himself. Above all, he strove to succeed in opera, where he could earn the most fame. But here success also eluded him, even though his operas (including *The Trojans, Beatrice and Benedict*, and *Benvenuto Cellini*) are among the most wonderful creations of the genre. For several years he earned most of his income, and considerable respect, from his writings about music.

Berlioz's late years were mostly bitter ones, marked by the deaths of his first wife, the actress Harriet Smithson; his son Louis, a naval officer; and his second wife, the singer Marie Recio. Consoled by his correspondence with Estelle Duboeuf, the love of his childhood, he died on March 8, 1869.

Ⓢ Berlioz: *Harold in Italy*, I (viola solo)
Ⓢ Berlioz: *Romeo and Juliet*, IV, Scherzo

MAJOR WORKS: 3 operas (*The Trojans, Beatrice and Benedict*, and *Benvenuto Cellini*); 4 symphonies, (*Fantastic Symphony, Lélio, Harold in Italy*, and *Romeo and Juliet*); choral music, including a Requiem Mass and *La damnation de Faust* (*The Damnation of Faust*); songs and song cycles.

FIG. 10.7 Harriet Smithson, about 1822. The Shakespearian actress captivated Parisians in the 1820s, including Hector Berlioz; his love for her is the subject of his *Fantastic Symphony*.

Harriet Smithson was a famous English actress who took Paris by storm in the late 1820s (see Figure 10.7). She infatuated Berlioz as Ophelia in Shakespeare's *Hamlet*: "The impression made on my heart and mind by her extraordinary talent, nay her dramatic genius, was equaled only by the havoc wrought in me by the poet she so nobly interpreted." Then he saw her portray the heroine in *Romeo and Juliet*, and "by the third act, scarcely able to breathe—as though an iron hand gripped me by the heart—I knew that I was lost." Berlioz tried to bring himself to Smithson's attention, but she was so famous, and he so insignificant by comparison, that little came of it at first—except the *Fantastic Symphony* itself, which tells the story of his unrequited love for Harriet.

Eighteen-year-old Camille Moke was a piano instructor at the school where Berlioz taught guitar (see Figure 10.8); she later went on to become a celebrated performer. They had a brief affair—apparently more serious on his part than on hers—and it was probably she who repeated to Berlioz (or perhaps invented) rumors that damaged Smithson's reputation. In any event, she succeeded in turning Berlioz, at least temporarily, against the actress, and it is the torment of that rejection that drives the plot of the symphony.

The story the symphony tells doesn't end in 1830, however. After the first performance, Berlioz was engaged to Camille, only to be jilted a few months later for another man with brighter prospects. Harriet was finally attracted to Berlioz and became his wife in 1833; they had a long and mostly unhappy marriage. As for Estelle (whom Berlioz called his "stella montis," the "star of the mountain" that beckoned him from afar): as an elderly widow, she received Berlioz in her house in Lyons, nearly half a century after their last meeting. The tenderness she may once have felt for him was, if anything, stronger, and he wrote to her faithfully for the rest of his life.

PROGRAM MUSIC

Berlioz's symphony tells the tale of an artist and his loves; its first title is *Episode from the Life of an Artist* (the subtitle is *Fantastic Symphony*). The box below shows Berlioz's titles for the five movements with their conventional Italian tempo indications that stand at the head of countless symphonic and other pieces (see Chapter 1, p. 7). Both the first and the last movements have slow introductions (Largo and Larghetto, respectively) before the main part of the movement, in a fast tempo (Allegro agitato, Allegro), begins. The middle movement is the slow movement; it is preceded by a Waltz (*Valse*) and followed by a march marked "Allegretto non troppo" (not too fast).

FIG. 10.8 A portrait of Camille Moke, around 1830. Berlioz was engaged to Moke, but while he was in Rome, she married another man.

Movement Titles

Épisode de la vie d'un artiste: Symphonie fantastique en 5 parties
(Episode from the Life of an Artist: *Fantastic Symphony* in Five Movements)

I. Largo—Allegro agitato e appassionato assai: "Rêveries—Passions" (Reveries—Passions)
II. Valse, Allegro non troppo: "Un bal" (A Ball)
III. Adagio: "Scène aux champs" (Scene in the Country)
IV. Allegretto non troppo: "Marche du supplice" (March to the Scaffold)
V. Larghetto—Allegro: "Songe d'une nuit de sabbat" (Dream of a Witches' Sabbath)

Each of the five movements can stand on its own; for many listeners they add up to a musical experience as satisfying as any of Beethoven's four-movement symphonies. In addition to the music there is a narrative, in which Berlioz tells us his story (see the Listening Guides for each narrative). The printed program handed out at the concert (and published several times in newspapers beforehand) offered the following explanation:

> The composer's purpose has been to develop the musical aspects of different situations in the life of an artist. The plan of the instrumental drama, lacking the assistance of words, needs to be explained in advance. The following program should thus be considered as though it were the spoken text of an opera, serving to introduce the movements, whose character and expression it motivates.

The *Fantastic Symphony* is about the inner life of a young artist, and the artist in question is the composer himself. Buffeted by a wave of passions (represented by the sad "Estelle" melody in the slow introduction of the first movement), he falls in love with a young woman; her theme—representing Harriet—begins the main part of the first movement. The artist sees her at a ball (the waltz) and thinks about her in the countryside (the slow movement). He realizes she does not love him, and he poisons himself with opium. But the dose is not enough to kill him, and instead he has visions—of killing his beloved and being marched to his execution (the fourth movement), and of a witches' gathering—surely inspired by Goethe's *Faust*—in which she joins in a diabolical dance (the last movement).

Romantic elements   Berlioz's "program" has all the requisite Romantic ingredients. The love interest, of course, is front and center throughout. The sounds of nature, including shepherds and distant thunder, are heard in the slow movement. The religious consolations that close the first movement are echoed at the end by the church bells and by the *Dies irae* chant, sung at funerals, which Berlioz transforms into a grotesque dance tune. The mind-expanding drugs the artist takes give rise to the exotic visions of the last two movements. The supernatural element comes in the last movement, where the hero witnesses his own funeral and the strange witches' sabbath.

Program music vs.   The concept of program music had much resonance for Romantic composers;
absolute music   music can be an expression not only of visible things but also of feelings (we will see in later chapters how the music of Schumann, Wagner, and Dvořák reflects the ideas we find in Berlioz's symphony). As part of the reaction against Romanticism in the early twentieth century, the notion of program music was rejected by modernist composers like Igor Stravinsky and Arnold Schoenberg, the teacher of Alban Berg (see Chapters 15 and 16). In fact, the division between program music and what some call "absolute" music (can we really say that Beethoven's Fifth Symphony has no extra-musical meaning?) is far from being clear. It is perhaps more a spectrum than an opposition; and the nature of musical meaning—of how music means anything, and what that meaning is—is a discussion that will always be with us.

But at the beginning of the nineteenth century, program music was still fresh and exciting. It helps explain why Berlioz's *Fantastic Symphony* sparked a great deal of comment and controversy. Many people were simply curious to find out what sort of "symphony" the *Fantastic Symphony* was and whether music on its own could indeed, as Berlioz claimed, tell a story.

The Performance

First attempts   Berlioz attempted to get his symphony performed even before it was finished. Early in 1830, he made arrangements for a spring concert at the Théâtre des Nouveautés, where he sang in the chorus. He convinced the management to let him try out a couple of movements in the theater, but the rehearsal was a complete disaster, mostly because there were not enough chairs and music stands. The fiasco that Berlioz describes so amusingly in the memoirs he wrote later in life was probably not so amusing to him as a young man. The following passage gives a taste of the vivid and entertaining prose style that makes both his narrative and his critical writing so delightful:

> When the day came for the rehearsal, and my orchestra of a hundred and thirty tried to arrange themselves on the stage, there was nowhere to put them. The tiny pit, when pressed into service, barely accommodated the violins. From all over the theater an uproar arose that would have driven a much more sanguine composer demented. People were calling for desks [music stands], while the carpenters strove to knock together something that would do instead. The scene-shifter went about swearing and searching for his flats and his struts. There were cries for chairs, for instruments, for candles; the double basses were short of strings; there was no place anywhere for the drums. The orchestral attendant did not know where to begin. Bloc [the theater conductor] and I were in thirty-seven different places at once; but it was all to no avail. The situation had got beyond control. It was a rout.

Plans for the concert had to be abandoned, but Berlioz's fortunes soon took a turn for the better: that summer, on his fourth attempt, he finally succeeded in winning the Rome Prize (Prix de Rome), an honor awarded by the Academy of Fine Arts of the venerable Institute of France that provided the winner with a gold medal, a performance of the prize-winning work, a paid fellowship for five years, and a two-year residency at the French Academy (the Villa Medici) in Rome. The academic aspects of the contest were not to Berlioz's liking—contestants were all given the same text and required to set it to music within a limited time—but he swallowed his pride and wrote his cantata *La mort de Sardanapale* (*The Death of Sardanapalus*), keeping back from the judges the great orchestral finale that depicts the destruction of King Sardanapalus's palace; he thought they would think it too daring. Locked into a room where he, like the other contestants, was sequestered during the competition, he heard the clamor of the July Revolution outside his window without knowing what it was.

Rome Prize

Suddenly, everything changed for Berlioz. There was a ceremony at the Institute of France, where the medal was awarded. The cantata was duly performed, although the climactic orchestral conflagration fizzled ("Ten million curses on all musicians who do not count their rests," Berlioz grumbled in disgust). Now that he had the fame—and the cash—needed to put on his own concert, he began preparations to use the hall of the Paris Conservatory and the services of their orchestra and celebrated conductor.

PREPARING THE PERFORMANCE

As the sole producer of the concert, Berlioz was responsible for virtually everything. He rented the hall, engaged the players, and papered the house with tickets for his friends. (Since it was not one of the Conservatory's regular subscription concerts, he had to work especially hard to attract an audience.) Thanks to the receipts that Berlioz meticulously filed in a folder that survives today, we know that he paid a music copyist to make parts for the orchestra, as well as additional parts for this larger orchestra for existing pieces that were to be performed earlier on the program (his opera overture and cantata). On top of all that, he had to pay the firemen and police who protected the building, the wood and coal merchant who provided fuel for heat, the ushers who handed out the programs, and on and on. All in all, it was an expensive proposition.

The concert hall of the Paris Conservatory, inaugurated in 1811, was—and is—a splendid space (see Figure 10.9; it was restored in the 1980s and can still be seen today). Decorated in mint green and cream, the horseshoe-shaped auditorium has a painted cyclorama of several wooden panels at the back of the stage to reflect the sound outward. In Berlioz's time, the floor was divided into orchestra (in the front, with seats) and parterre (in the rear, with benches). There were three levels of boxes, with an amphitheater above them up against the roof (these were the "cheap" seats). Including standing room, the hall could hold about a thousand listeners, but crowding made the hall uncomfortably hot. (One concertgoer complained that a Turkish bath was pleasant by comparison.) The acoustics, however, were splendid; in such a space—small by modern standards—the Conservatory orchestra must have sounded like a gigantic chamber ensemble in the sense that each individual instrument can be heard clearly.

Concert hall

The arrangement of the orchestra (and chorus, when one was present) was designed to maximize these advantages. The chorus was arranged at the front, with the conductor standing in the middle. At the back of the chorus sat first and

Arrangement of the orchestra

FIG. 10.9 The concert hall of the Paris Conservatory. The hall is relatively small, and audience members said that the heat resembled a Turkish bath.

FIG. 10.10 An ophicleide, the bass instrument of the brass family, used by Berlioz in the first performance of the *Fantastic Symphony*.

second violins and violas; and above them, on four tiers of risers, were the cellos and double basses on the right, and the woodwinds on the left, with the brass and percussion above and behind them at the very back. (The four harps that Berlioz calls for in the second movement of the *Fantastic Symphony* were placed at the front of the orchestra in pairs, two on the left and two on the right of the stage.) This seating, with the loudest instruments farthest from the audience, produced a remarkably transparent, well-balanced sound. The effect must have been stunning.

The Conservatory orchestra was not a student group: it was an all-star ensemble that included players from the Opéra and other orchestras. Berlioz later considered it the best orchestra in the world, in the best arrangement possible. In his famous book, published years later, on how to write for the orchestra, he used the Conservatory orchestra as his model. Although his music is complex, he knew that the orchestra could handle it.

THE INSTRUMENTS

The Conservatory orchestra was essentially a somewhat expanded version of the orchestra for which Beethoven wrote his Fifth Symphony. But Berlioz calls for some slightly unusual instruments—unusual for us, that is, but not for a Parisian audience in 1830. There were four bassoons in his orchestra because the Conservatory orchestra, like the Opéra orchestra, had four bassoons. Berlioz also used a beautiful tenor oboe, the **English horn**—a rarity outside of Paris in those days; it plays a shepherd's call in alternation with the oboe in the slow movement of the *Fantastic Symphony*.

The brass section was large: there were two newfangled piston trumpets; four French horns; three trombones; and, as the foundation for the section, an **ophicleide** (see Figure 10.10). Invented in France in 1817, the ophicleide was a rather ungainly instrument with a peculiar fingering system; it was soon replaced by the tuba.

The last movement of the symphony features two bells (imitating church bells) and a **serpent** (see Figure 10.11), a snake-shaped bass instrument with fingerholes and a brass mouthpiece, which was used in churches to accompany the singing of chant. (It is a bass relative of the cornetts in Monteverdi's *Orfeo*.) Berlioz, despite that fact that he thought the serpent a remarkably ugly-sounding instrument, called for it to play the *Dies irae* chant, so that everybody would identify it as religious music. He used another instrument he disliked, the squeaky little **E-flat clarinet** (then mostly found in military bands), to play the diabolically transformed theme of the beloved after she has joined the witches. ⑤

This was an orchestra on the forward edge of technology, using instruments of the latest sort, the best players, and a composer committed to making the most of all available possibilities.

On the day of the concert, Berlioz went to a music shop and acquired fourteen mutes for violins. (Mutes are small wooden clamps that attach to the bridge of the violin and give it a softer, darker, more mysterious sound.) The symphony as ultimately published called for muted violins to play the beautiful "Estelle" melody at the beginning of the first movement. Perhaps Berlioz thought of the wonderful effect of the mutes only on the morning of the concert.

FIG. 10.11 A serpent, used in military bands and in churches as a bass instrument; it was used at the premiere of the *Fantastic Symphony* to accompany the chant melody in the finale.

⑤ Berlioz: *Fantastic Symphony*, V, *Dies irae*, originally performed by serpent and ophicleide

THE CONDUCTOR

François-Antoine Habeneck (1781–1849; see Figure 10.12), who taught violin at the Conservatory as well as conducting the orchestra, was one of the more illustrious musicians in Europe, so Berlioz was glad to secure his services. Habeneck built the Conservatory orchestra from scratch into a marvelously disciplined, responsive ensemble that many observers (not just Berlioz) considered the finest orchestra of it is time. It was Habeneck and this orchestra who introduced the symphonies of Beethoven to Parisian audiences. The precision of the orchestra's playing was legendary; one critic likened it to a machine in perfect working order.

Habeneck's impact on the art of conducting was considerable. Endowed with a phenomenal memory, he typically conducted from the first violin part alone, although for a piece as novel and complex as Berlioz's *Fantastic Symphony*, he may have used the full score.

In some ways, Habeneck was a tempting target for ridicule. Despite his self-effacing manner, he seemed to take perverse pleasure in shaming hapless musicians for their lapses. "At every wrong note," recalled one member of the audience, "he turned around and pointed out the culprit to the vindictive public with his violin-bow." Such behavior helped give rise to the popular stereotype of the conductor as an autocratic *maestro*.

FIG. 10.12 François-Antoine Habeneck, professor at the Paris Conservatory and conductor of the Opéra orchestra. As conductor of the Conservatory Concerts, he was engaged by Berlioz to conduct the first performance of the *Fantastic Symphony*.

THE PRESS AND THE AUDIENCE

In an attempt to gain additional publicity for his concert, Berlioz announced that proceeds would benefit those who had been wounded in the July Revolution. He sent an obsequious letter to King Louis-Philippe explaining his plan, mentioning his recent Rome Prize, and inviting the monarch to attend. He did not expect the king to be there, and he wasn't; but Berlioz did receive the customary three hundred francs from the royal accounts.

As a music journalist and an employee of a music publisher, Berlioz knew better than most how to use the press to his advantage. He had been sending notices to the newspapers since earlier in the year, when he made his first plans for the concert at the Théâtre des Nouveautés; and versions of his printed program had appeared in several papers. His publicity campaign succeeded in attracting attention, both positive and negative. A writer for the newspaper *Le Figaro* was intrigued by the novel programmatic aspects of the upcoming symphony:

> This is the first time that anyone has tried to give an exact meaning to instrumental music. Until now, a symphony has been a development, more or less successful, of a melodic idea without a specific signification, and where the composer's only perceptible purpose has been to make a pleasing piece of music. M. Berlioz's symphony is a novel. It tells you a story with instruments.

The influential critic François-Joseph Fétis, by contrast, regarded Berlioz's attempt to depict narrative events in music as fundamentally misguided: "It is perhaps a misunderstanding of the aims of art to want to apply oneself to painting material facts or to express abstractions, and to need to resort to explanations is enough proof of its inability to do these things." Berlioz was upset by the criticism, and with good reason: Fétis would become an enemy of his music for a long time. When he read Fétis's notice on November 27, he went back to the printer and ordered an additional run of the already printed program, in which he made a few revisions (see Figure 10.13), notably a long footnote answering Fétis' criticisms, which began:

> It is not at all a matter of copying exactly what the composer has tried to present in orchestral terms, as certain persons seem to think; on the contrary, it is precisely in order to fill in the gaps which musical language unavoidably leaves in the development of dramatic thought, that the composer has had to resort to written prose to explain and justify the plan of the symphony . . . . Those who make the curious accusation against which the musician must defend himself fail to realize that if he really entertained the exaggerated and ridiculous opinions about the expressive power of his art that are laid at his door, then by the same token he would have thought this program to be merely a kind of duplication, and hence perfectly useless.

FIG. 10.13 The first page of Berlioz's program, showing the beginning of the very long footnote Berlioz inserted to respond to his critics.

Episode

DE

LA VIE D'UN ARTISTE,

SYMPHONIE FANTASTIQUE, EN CINQ PARTIES,

Par Hector Berlioz,

EXÉCUTÉE POUR LA PREMIÈRE FOIS LE 5 DÉCEMBRE 1830,

Au Conservatoire de Musique de Paris.

Programme.

Le compositeur a eu pour but de développer, DANS CE QU'ELLES ONT DE MUSICAL, différentes situations de la vie d'un artiste. Le plan du drame instrumental, privé du secours de la parole, a besoin d'être exposé d'avance. Le programme suivant doit être considéré comme le *texte parlé d'un opéra,* servant à *amener* des morceaux de musique dont il *motive le caractère et l'expression* (1).

RÊVERIES. — PASSIONS.

(Première partie.)

L'auteur suppose qu'un jeune musicien, affecté de cette maladie qu'un écrivain célèbre appelle le *vague des passions,* voit pour la première fois une femme qui réunit tous les charmes de

(1) Il ne s'agit point en effet, ainsi que certaines personnes ont paru le croire, de donner ici la reproduction exacte de ce que le compositeur se serait efforcé de rendre au moyen de l'orchestre; c'est justement, au contraire, afin de combler les lacunes laissées nécessairement dans le développement de la pensée dramatique par la langue musicale, qu'il a dû recourir à la prose écrite pour faire comprendre et justifier le plan de la symphonie. L'auteur sait fort

SUNDAY, DECEMBER 5, 1830, 2 P.M.

"At precisely two o'clock," wrote one observer, "Habeneck, the chief of this marvelous troupe, in which there is not a soldier who has not commanded somewhere or who is not worthy of command, struck his stand with the point of his bow, and the profoundest silence immediately reigned in the hall, where a swarm of brilliant young women of taste had been listening loudly only a short time before."

The complete program for the concert—almost exclusively music by Berlioz—was as follows:

Two *Mélodies irlandaises* (Irish Melodies) for chorus and piano

The cantata *La mort de Sardanapale* (*The Death of Sardanapalus*)

A violin solo by Joseph Mayseder (a Viennese violinist-composer), played by Chrétien Urhan

Fantastic Symphony

The audience

It was a well-balanced program of the sort the Conservatory audience was used to. It included orchestral music, solo instrumental music, choral music with piano, and a cantata for voice and orchestra. What set it apart from a typical Conservatory program is that all the music was modern; Habeneck's orchestra did not normally play the music of living composers. (Cherubini's music was the exception, but he was the Director.)

Although Berlioz had done everything he could to publicize the event, the hall was far from full. He bought most of the tickets himself, evidently to give away. Among the prominent musicians in the audience were Gaspare Spontini and Giacomo Meyerbeer, whose operas were hugely popular in Paris, and nineteen-year-old Franz Liszt, the virtuoso pianist and avant-garde composer. Liszt and Berlioz had met just the day before, discovered a mutual love of Goethe's *Faust*, and became fast friends. Camille Moke (Berlioz's current love interest) was there with her mother. Madame Moke did not want her daughter to marry a provincial musician, but she relented after the Rome Prize and the success of this concert. Since Berlioz was to be safely out of the way in Rome for an extended period, she allowed them to become engaged.

Berlioz's composition teacher, Jean-François Le Sueur, was ill and could not come to the concert; Cherubini, who had never been fond of Berlioz or his music, refused to attend. Also absent was Harriet Smithson: she was across town at the Opéra, preparing to play the title role in Auber's *Muette de Portici*. (The plot of the opera turns on a character who never speaks a word, and since Miss Smithson could neither sing nor speak French, the part was a perfect fit.) The performance was a benefit for the English Shakespeare Company, which Smithson directed. Probably because many members of Berlioz's orchestra were also involved in that performance and could not be late, Habeneck refused to encore the "March to the Scaffold," even though the audience liked it so much that they shouted for it to be played again.

Berlioz on stage

A reviewer for the newspaper *Le Temps* spotted Berlioz on stage at the performance, most likely in his favorite place at the back of the orchestra, playing in the percussion section:

Here is a young man, lanky, skinny, with long blond hair [did his red hair look blond in the light?] whose disorder has something that reeks of genius; all the traits of his bony form are drawn forcefully, and his large deep-set eyes, under a large forehead, dart jets of light. The knot of his cravat is tightened as though with rage; his suit is elegant because the tailor made it elegant, and his boots are muddy because his impetuous character refuses to sit still and be pulled along in a carriage, because the activity of his body must match the activity going on in his head. He runs about among the hundred musicians who fill up the stage of the Conservatoire, and although all these regulars in the Conservatoire orchestra make up perhaps the most admirable orchestra ever heard, he begs, he growls, he entreats, he excites each one of them.

The Music

The *Fantastic Symphony* is one of the most often played, mentioned, and studied pieces in the symphonic repertory. It is the creation of a young genius whose experience at age twenty-eight was limited. Moreover, Berlioz put the symphony together in a big hurry, much of it from material that he had already composed for other purposes. It's no surprise, then, that he didn't publish the symphony for almost fifteen years, and that when he did publish it, it differed in a number of ways from the version that was performed in 1830. It's his published version that is normally performed now; and indeed some aspects of the 1830 version will never be recovered, since the earliest surviving source for the symphony is a somewhat revised version that Berlioz brought back with him from Italy in 1832.

Berlioz and Beethoven

Berlioz was a great admirer of Beethoven. He had heard some of the master's symphonies at the Conservatory concerts and had come to know others through his musical proofreading. "Beethoven," he declared, "opened before me a new world of music, as Shakespeare had revealed a new universe of poetry."

The structure of the *Fantastic Symphony* is symmetrical, with first and last movements in fast tempos, a slow movement in the middle, and two lighter, action-based movements, a waltz and a march, in the second and fourth positions. Whereas Beethoven uses a minuet (or a speeded-up minuet called a scherzo) to provide a kind of light relief either before or after the slow movement, Berlioz includes a pair of dancelike movements, before and after the slow movement, so that the symphony has five movements and a balanced musical shape.

In narrative terms, one might divide the symphony into two parts rather than five: the first three movements, which describe events more or less in real time—sadness and love in the first movement, a ball in the second, a contemplative scene in the country in the third; and the last two movements, which represent the crazy, drug-induced visions in the composer's mind. But the story line isn't the only thing that ties the various parts of the *Fantastic Symphony* together into an artistic unit. The symphony also features a musical device to which Berlioz gives narrative meaning: the use of the same theme, but in varied form, in each of the five movements.

🎙 Berlioz's *idée fixe*

THE *IDÉE FIXE*

In the printed program, Berlioz described this device as follows:

> Through an odd whim, whenever the beloved image appears before the mind's eye of the artist, it is linked with a *musical thought* whose character, passionate but at the same time noble and shy, he finds similar to the one he attributes to his beloved. This melodic image and its model pursue him incessantly like a double *idée fixe*. That is the reason for the constant appearance, in every movement of the symphony, of the melody that begins the first *allegro*.

We use Berlioz's term ***idée fixe*** to describe this recurrent melody. The term means "fixed idea," a sort of obsession, or monomania, which focuses the artist (or the listener) on one thing and one thing only. This is what he means by a "double" *idée fixe*: that the artist-hero is fixed on one thing—the beloved—and that we the listeners, like him, are fixed on one thing—the melody.

This wonderful tune consists of four long phrases (see Table 10.1, The Four Phases of the *Idée fixe*, below; the timings refer to LG 37). The first two phrases are related in a sort of question-answer relationship (what we call **antecedent** and **consequent** phrases); each phrase is nervous and **disjunct** (with jagged leaps between the notes) at its beginning, and smooth and **conjunct** (with the notes moving stepwise) at its end. The third phrase is rather like a sequence, rising higher and higher in a yearning pattern, and the closing phrase is a little like the first two, in that its motion is initially disjunct, then conjunct.

TABLE 10.1

The Four Phrases of the *Idée fixe*

5:33   First phrase: an initial phrase with a disjunct, rising line and jagged rhythm that concludes with very smooth, downward long notes; the phrase ends on a half cadence.

5:40   Second phrase: an answering phrase with the same rhythmic and melodic profile, but different notes, concluding with a full cadence.

5:46   Third phrase: a contrasting phrase, really consisting of four short phrases (the fourth extended). Each phrase begins with same rhythmic profile, and each reaches upwards (like the first two phrases), each time to a higher note.

6:01   Fourth phrase: a final phrase, different from all the others, but similar in the jagged profile of its beginning and the relatively smooth shape of its end (except for one spectacular leap down and back up).

TABLE 10.2

Appearances of the *Idée fixe*

Movement	Position	Idée fixe	Accompaniment
I	First theme, following introduction	Flutes and first violins in unison.	Unaccompanied, then accompanied by lower strings in pulsing, heartbeat rhythm.
	Development, introduced by solo horn and strings	Flute, clarinet, and bassoon.	A composite, throbbing arpeggio in the accompanying strings.
	Recapitulation	Brass, woodwinds, violas; the melody is squared off like a march.	Very loud, full orchestra, fast notes in violins.
	Coda	The beginning of the melody in contrapuntal imitation in the woodwinds.	Minimal accompaniment by double basses with long notes in horns.
II	Second theme	Waltz rhythm, flute and oboe, later flute and clarinet.	Tremolos in strings; occasional fragments of the movement's main waltz theme.
	Coda	Clarinet solo, first two phrases.	Horns and harps.
III	Transition between variations 2 and 3	Flute and oboe.	The phrases of the *idée fixe* are separated by vigorous tremolos in the upper strings, and a sort of raging recitative-like passages in the lower strings and bassoons.
	Coda	The opening notes of the first phrase only, by woodwinds in imitation.	The opening notes of the main theme of this movement, played by strings in imitation; long notes in horns.
IV	Coda	The opening of the *idée fixe* comes at the very end of this movement; it is unaccompanied but interrupted by a crash imitating the stroke of a guillotine.	
V	First theme, following introduction	Solo clarinet played from afar, following a loud tutti; then the *idée fixe* is repeated by the higher and shriller E-flat clarinet.	Timpani and bass drum at first. After the loud tutti, the theme is accompanied by rhythmic pattern in woodwinds.

It's worth pausing to note the extent to which the melody contributes to the effect, both structural and narrative, of each movement. The *idée fixe* is the main theme of the main part of "Reveries—Passions" (movement I). When the hero sees his beloved, the *idée fixe* is heard for the first time, played by flutes and first violins in unison, with barely any accompaniment except for a sort of throbbing in the lower strings.

The theme returns in the middle of the movement, this time on the flute, clarinet, and bassoon, riding a magic carpet of sound in the accompanying strings.

Toward the end of the movement, the *idée fixe* is transformed into a grand, triumphant, brassy march.

In the rest of the symphony, the *idée fixe* reappears, but is never quite complete, and is something extra added to a movement rather than being essential or intrinsic as in the first movement. In the middle of "A Ball" (movement II), for instance, the *idée fixe,* now in waltz tempo, is heard in the wind instruments (flute and oboe, later flute and clarinet). Wisps of the waltz theme float through the air, above tremolos in the strings; then the waltz returns.

In "Scene in the Country" (movement III), the *idée fixe* reappears in the midst of an impassioned instrumental recitative, as the hero meditates on his beloved. The phrases of the theme (played by flute and oboe) are separated by vigorous tremolos in the upper strings and raging, recitative-like passages in the lower strings and bassoons.

"March to the Scaffold" (movement IV) uses only the beginning of the *idée fixe*: At the very end of the movement, the solo clarinet's melody—a last thought of the beloved—is cut short by a crash suggesting the stroke of a guillotine. Musically speaking, the *idée fixe* is a coda to the march, standing outside the main movement.

At the beginning of "Dream of a Witches' Sabbath" (movement V), the *idée fixe* appears as a deformed version of itself, representing the beloved transformed into a witch. Her melody is played on an E-flat clarinet, an instrument that Berlioz deliberately chose for its strident sound, and we never hear the theme again.

Berlioz's idea of having the theme reappear in all five movements is a masterstroke. The *idée fixe* has powerful narrative value, and it makes us remember all sorts of things from one movement to the next. At the same time, the theme is integral only to the first movement. In all the others, it is a touch of color, an added event that could be removed without doing much harm to the *musical* shape of the movement in question (see Table 10.2, Appearances of the *Idée fixe*, p. 280).

SOMETHING BORROWED, SOMETHING NEW

Nothing we've said about how the *idée fixe* is simply inserted into, or tacked onto, the formal aspects of the later movements is meant to detract from Berlioz's genius. Nor should it lessen the excitement or the novelty of the symphony to know that many of its themes and other musical elements were already in existence, composed for a different purpose, when the symphony was put together. The theme of the "Scene in the Country" originally came from Berlioz's *Solemn Mass;* even the *idée fixe* is derived from the theme of a cantata written in an earlier attempt to win the Rome Prize.

Berlioz was in a hurry. The foundation, the basic program, was in place by at least April 1830, and he constructed the symphony by assembling, and altering, already existing materials. (This was nothing out of the ordinary: Bach, Handel,

Ⓢ Berlioz: *Fantastic Symphony*, I, first theme, following introduction

Ⓢ Berlioz: *Fantastic Symphony*, I, theme returns in the middle

Ⓢ Berlioz: *Fantastic Symphony*, I, recapitulation

Ⓢ Berlioz: *Fantastic Symphony*, II, *idée fixe* theme

Ⓢ Berlioz: *Fantastic Symphony*, III, appearance of *idée fixe* with recitative-like passage

Ⓢ Berlioz: *Fantastic Symphony*, IV, Coda

Ⓢ Berlioz: *Fantastic Symphony*, V, first theme, following introduction

and Mozart, for example, were recyclers of their own and other composers' music.) What all this suggests is that transformation is possible, that music can convey meaning in a great many ways. It matters less that the march was not originally a "March to the Scaffold" (it was borrowed from Berlioz's incomplete opera *Les francs-juges*) than the fact that it fits perfectly into Berlioz's storytelling and his musical structure.

The practice (common until the mid-nineteenth century) of moving music from one location and context to another raises questions that are especially relevant to program music. If music is capable of telling a story, how can music that was designed to tell one story tell another when it is transferred to a new piece? Does it tell a story only when we know in advance what the story is? How clearly does it do so? If we were to hear the *Fantastic Symphony* with no prior knowledge, and were asked to write down the story it tells, how many of us would come close to Berlioz's story? Such questions are well worth pondering, even if there are no easy answers. But this is the symphony of symphonies as far as program music is concerned, and it is remarkable that it does its job so well given the speed with which it was assembled, and the various origins of its music.

Listening to the Music

 LG 37   **FIRST MOVEMENT: "REVERIES—PASSIONS"**

The opening movement of the *Fantastic Symphony* has a meditative introduction, in which the muted violins play a beautiful melody, referencing nostalgia for home, that Berlioz had written under the spell of Estelle Duboeuf many years before. After an outburst of frantic joy, the music subsides, and the "Estelle" theme comes back again, this time stronger. Only after that does the main part of the movement, with its quick tempo, begin, with the *idée fixe* as its main theme.

A second theme is based on an alternative version of the beginning notes of the *idée fixe*; there is a ruminating development section (it has an oboe solo that Berlioz added at some point after the premier) based on a polyphonic development of the theme; and in a coda Berlioz slows down and narrows the *idée fixe* until it's just a single sound. At the end of the movement, the anguished hero experiences "religious consolations," expressed here as a series of long, slow chords, like a repeated "Amen." (See LG 37, p. 283.)

SECOND MOVEMENT: "A BALL"   LG 38

The waltz that follows, with its four harps, paints a beautiful picture of a French ballroom. The dance theme bounces from one section of the orchestra to another, at one point merging with the *idée fixe*. (See LG 38, p. 284.)

The waltz was the latest dance craze in 1830, thought to be quite racy and dangerous for young women because of the dizziness that its whirling motion often caused. There were, in fact, parents who would not let their daughters waltz, for fear the spinning would make them lose control. What's more, in the waltz the man steps between his partner's legs, which can lead to no good (see Comments on Waltzing, left).

Comments on Waltzing

"The waltz is a dance of quite too loose a character, and unmarried ladies should refrain from it altogether, both in public and private."

—From Madame Celnart's
The Gentleman and Lady's Book, 1833

"Vertigo is one of the great inconveniences of the waltz; and the character of this dance, its rapid turnings, the clasping of the dancers, their exciting contact, and the too quick and too long continued succession of lively and agreeable emotions, produce sometimes, in women of a very irritable constitution, syncopes, spasms and other accidents which should induce them to renounce it."

—From Donald Walker's, *Exercises for Ladies . . .*, 1836

LISTENING GUIDE 37   DVD

Berlioz *Fantastic Symphony*, I, "Rêveries—Passions" (Reveries—Passions)

15:50

DATE: 1830
GENRE: Program symphony

LISTEN FOR

TEXTURE: Use of orchestral color and textures as memorable structural elements

THEMES: *Idée fixe* and "Estelle" melody

EXPRESSION: Program music (imitation of sounds and evocation of emotions)

PROGRAM*

The author imagines that a young musician, afflicted with that moral disease that a well-known writer calls the *vague des passions*, sees for the first time a woman who embodies all the charms of the ideal being he has imagined in his dreams, and he falls hopelessly in love with her. Through an odd whim, whenever the beloved image appears before the mind's eye of the artist, it is linked with a *musical thought* whose character, passionate but at the same time noble and shy, he finds similar to the one he attributes to his beloved.

This melodic image and its model pursue him incessantly like a double *idée fixe*. That is the reason for the constant appearance, in every moment of the symphony, of the melody that begins the first *allegro*. The passage from this state of melancholy reverie, interrupted by a few fits of groundless joy, to one of delirious passion, with its moments of fury, of jealousy, its return of tenderness, its religious consolations—this is the subject of the first movement.

* Translations of all the program notes are adapted from Edward T. Cone, *Fantastic Symphony: An Authoritative Score; Historical Background; Analysis; Views and Comments*, Norton Critical Scores (New York: Norton, 1971), pp. 31–35.

TIME	FORM	DESCRIPTION
0:00	Introduction	Soft woodwinds, horns, strings.
	Introduction theme ("Estelle")	"Estelle" melody:
1:52	Introduction, continued	An outburst of joy.
2:38	Introduction, concluded	The "Estelle" theme again, in a richer orchestration; an agitated and passionate transition to the main portion of the movement.
5:33	First theme (*idée fixe*)	Lower strings accompany theme with evenly spaced pairs of quick notes, evocative of an excited heartbeat rhythm:
6:10	Transition	Loud outbursts alternate with lyrical passages.
6:45	Second theme	Hint of *idée fixe* followed by loud new theme:
		Strings, then added woodwinds, with constant swells in volume.

(continued)

TIME	FORM	DESCRIPTION
7:00	Repeat	Repeat of first and second themes.
8:28	Development	*Idée fixe* in lower strings; repeated loud chord; development of second theme.
8:55	Transition	Chromatic scales rising to a climax (brass are added at the top) and then falling, leading to an abrupt pause.
9:25	First theme transposed	Horn solo; strings accompany the *idée fixe* in woodwinds.
10:38	Development of second theme	Contrapuntal strings.
10:55	Return to and development of transition	Begins with soft timpani roll and upper strings.
11:41	Development of *idée fixe* as retransition	Oboe solo floats above contrapuntal version of the opening of the *idée fixe* in the lower strings.
12:36	Recapitulation of first theme	Loud, marchlike tutti.
13:51	Coda	Opening of *idée fixe* reduced to near-static quality. The movement concludes with slow chords played "religiosamente" (in a religious manner) and "as soft as possible."

LISTENING GUIDE 38 Ⓢ | DVD

Berlioz *Fantastic Symphony*, II, "Un bal" (A Ball)   6:57

DATE: 1830
GENRE: Program symphony

LISTEN FOR
RHYTHM/METER: Dance rhythm of the waltz
SCORING: Varied accompaniments as the waltz returns

THEMES: *Idée fixe* appears in the middle of the movement, combined with waltz

PROGRAM
The artist finds himself in the most varied situations—in the midst of the *tumult of a party*, in the peaceful contemplation of the beauties of nature; but everywhere, in town, in the country, the beloved image appears before him and disturbs his peace of mind.

TIME	FORM	DESCRIPTION
0:00	Introduction	Strings and harps create a sort of floating atmosphere, out of which the waltz emerges gradually.
0:40	First theme (waltz)	The waltz begins with four phrases, with a *rallentando* (slowing down) at the end of the third; here is its beginning:
1:46	Waltz theme, second appearance	Theme in violins; the accompaniment is a fast alternation, on the three beats of the waltz measure, of strings-harps-winds, strings-harps-winds.

2:16	Second theme (*idée fixe*)	The *idée fixe,* in waltz tempo, played by flute and oboe, then flute and clarinet. Strings accompany, including fragments of the waltz melody.
3:20	Waltz theme, third appearance	Theme is in second violins, violas, cellos (tenor range); accompaniment in strings, with woodwind interjections and first-violin twiddles.
4:25	Waltz theme, fourth appearance	Melody in woodwinds, with string accompaniment.
4:56	Coda, part 1	Increasing excitement by quickening the tempo and adding to the instrumentation.
5:38	Coda, part 2: *idée fixe*	Soft clarinet, with horn and harp.
6:22	Coda, part 3	The movement ends with a loud orchestral tutti that gradually speeds up. Whirlwind finish.

THIRD MOVEMENT: "SCENE IN THE COUNTRY"

 LG 39

The center of the symphony is a very long slow movement titled "Scene in the Country" (see LG 39, below). In an introduction we are placed outdoors by the sound of two shepherds playing their pipes, one echoing the other (this imagery returns in the coda, where the first shepherd is now answered by peals of thunder). The main section is a series of variations on a lyrical theme—borrowed, as it happens, from Berlioz's *Solemn Mass* written some years earlier. ("He reflects upon his isolation; he hopes that his loneliness will soon be over.") Halfway through, the idyllic music is interrupted by an agitated recitative in the cellos, double basses, and bassoons. ("But what if she were deceiving him!") Phrases of the *idée fixe,* played by the flute and oboe, alternate with recitative, until finally the recitative, now

LISTENING GUIDE 39 DVD

Berlioz *Fantastic Symphony,* III, "Scène aux champs" (Scene in the Country)

17:08

DATE: 1830
GENRE: Program symphony

LISTEN FOR

FORM: Theme and variations, but drastically modified by long introduction and coda, and by the insertion of a recitative-like passage in the middle

THEMES: Appearance of *idée fixe* in the midst of an instrumental recitative

EXPRESSION: Imitation of nature (shepherds piping, thunder, etc.)

PROGRAM

Finding himself one evening in the country, he hears in the distance two shepherds piping a *ranz des vaches* [a mountain melody] in dialogue. This pastoral duet, the scenery, the quiet rustling of the trees gently brushed by the wind, the hopes he has recently found reason to entertain—all concur in affording his heart an unaccustomed calm, and in giving a more cheerful color to his ideas. He reflects upon his isolation; he hopes

that his loneliness will soon be over. . . . But what if she were deceiving him! . . . This mingling of hope and fear, these ideas of happiness disturbed by black presentiments, form the subject of the *adagio.* At the end, one of the shepherds takes up the *ranz des vaches*; the other no longer replies. Distant sound of thunder . . . Loneliness . . . Silence.

(continued)

TIME	FORM	DESCRIPTION
0:00	Introduction	English horn and oboe duet, later accompanied by tremolo in strings.
2:03	Main theme	Flute and violin in unison, with pizzicato punctuation:

TIME	FORM	DESCRIPTION
3:11	Variation 1	Flutes and violins in thirds, with long notes in clarinet and horns.
4:31	Transition	Beginning with insistent unisons, swinging rhythm in a downward melody; a temporary shift to minor mode, leading to . . .
6:15	Variation 2	Theme in cellos, violas, bassoon (tenor range), with interjections from woodwinds, chords from strings, and filigree countermelody in violins.
7:39	Central section: *idée fixe* with recitative	A fierce tremolo leads to what sounds like an instrumental recitative by the cellos, double basses, and bassoons; their interjections alternate with phrases from the *idée fixe* in flute and oboe. Finally the recitative overpowers the *idée fixe*.
9:48	Variation 3	Pizzicato violas and violins play an altered form of the main theme; a countermelody in clarinet and interjections from flute and first violins.
10:51	Variation 4	Rather like loud machinery: fast repeated notes, short-short-long, in lower strings, meandering first violins, a countermelody in the woodwinds, all accompanying the main theme in the second violins.
12:26	Coda with *idée fixe* combined with fragments of the theme	The beginning of the main theme in imitation in strings, with the beginning of the *idée fixe* in imitation by flute and clarinet. The music gradually subsides.
14:40	Return of introduction, but altered	English horn, as at the beginning, now not answered by oboe but accompanied by four timpani (thunder); a final cadence with horn and strings.

taken up by all the strings, drowns out the melody, as though the hero's thoughts of his beloved become overwhelmed by his doubts about her. This is followed by a sobbing series of sighs, before the variations return. ("This mingling of hope and fear, these ideas of happiness disturbed by black presentiments, form the subject of the *adagio*.")

LG 40 FOURTH MOVEMENT: "MARCH TO THE SCAFFOLD"

In the fourth movement, the disconsolate hero poisons himself with opium. As Berlioz says in the program, "He dreams that he has killed his beloved, that he is condemned and led to the scaffold, and that he is witnessing *his own execution*. The procession moves forward to the sounds of a march that is now somber and fierce, now brilliant and solemn . . . ." The march is a tour de force of orchestration, with inventive effects from drums, horns, kettledrums, bassoons, trombones, and double basses. As he thinks a last "thought of love," a clarinet plays the first four measures of the *idée fixe*, before it is chopped off by a loud chord representing the fall of the guillotine's blade. (See LG 40, p. 287.)

LISTENING GUIDE 40 | DVD

Berlioz *Fantastic Symphony*, IV, "Marche du supplice" (March to the Scaffold)   6:41

DATE: 1830
GENRE: Program symphony

LISTEN FOR

MELODY: Two main themes; separate groups of instruments play successive notes of a melody (at 4:00 and 4:40)
RHYTHM: Dotted march rhythms

TEXTURE: Groups of instruments competing
SCORING: Eerie opening with muted horns and pizzicato strings
EXPRESSION: Depiction of the guillotine

PROGRAM

Convinced that his love is unappreciated, the artist poisons himself with opium. The dose of narcotic, too weak to kill him, plunges him into a sleep accompanied by the most horrible visions. He dreams that he has killed his beloved, that he is condemned to death and led to the scaffold, and that he is witnessing *his own execution*. The procession moves forward to the sounds of a march that is now somber and fierce, now brilliant and solemn, in which the muffled noise of heavy steps gives way without transition to the noisiest clamor. At the end of the march the first four measures of the *idée fixe* reappear, like a last thought of life interrupted by the fatal blow.

TIME	FORM	DESCRIPTION
0:00	Introduction	Timpani and pizzicato lower strings with soft French horns.
		The syncopated rhythm anticipates theme **B**:
0:24	First theme (**A**)	A single melodic line, moving stepwise down and up; varied in dynamics:
0:37		The theme played in thirds, countermelody in bassoon.
0:49		The theme, played twice, begins high in violins, with pizzicato accompaniment of lower strings.
1:14		The theme played with its melodic inversion, and a countermelody in bassoon.
1:32	Second theme (**B**)	Sudden loud winds and brass with prominent low trombone notes; shift to major mode:
1:57	The whole movement up to here repeated from beginning	
3:54	Development of first theme	Brass alternates with strings and winds, using rhythm from theme **A**:
4:00		First theme divided among different instruments.

(continued)

TIME	FORM	DESCRIPTION
4:10	Variation of second theme	Tutti with counterpoint in strings.
4:34	Return of opening development material	Brass (now with timpani) alternating with strings and winds; violins employ the timpani's opening rhythm.
4:40		First theme divided among different instruments.
4:47	Closing section	Development of first theme.
5:28	Coda	Dotted figure leads to very loud chords.
5:46		Alternation of major chord in winds and brass with minor chord in strings—quicker and quicker alternation, leading to a loud chords and a tumble toward a sudden pause.
6:01	*Idée fixe* conclusion	Solo clarinet plays the beginning of the *idée fixe*; a loud tutti chord (the execution) followed by pizzicato in low strings (the head dropping into the basket?). Drum roll and fanfare chords end the movement.

LISTENING GUIDE 41 | DVD

Berlioz *Fantastic Symphony*, V, "Songe d'une nuit de sabbat" (Dream of a Witches' Sabbath)   9:34

DATE: 1830

GENRE: Program symphony

LISTEN FOR

MELODY: Opening music with eerie supernatural effects

FORM: Use of contrapuntal techniques (fugue, combination of themes)

SCORING: E-flat clarinet mocks the *idée fixe*

THEMES: Use of religious funeral chant (*Dies irae*)

PROGRAM

He sees himself at the sabbath, in the midst of a frightful troop of ghosts, sorcerers, monsters of every kind, come together for his funeral. Strange noises, groans, bursts of laughter, distant cries which other cries seem to answer. The beloved melody appears again, but it has lost its character of nobility and shyness; it is no more than a dance tune, mean, trivial and grotesque; it is *she*, coming to join the Sabbath. . . . A roar of joy at her arrival. . . . She takes part in the devilish orgy. . . . Funeral knell, burlesque parody of the *Dies irae*, sabbath round-dance. The sabbath round and the *Dies irae* combined.

TIME	FORM	DESCRIPTION
0:00	Introduction	Odd effects from strings (strange tremolos, pieces of unison scales in the bass); descending chromatic chords; sounds of laughter from woodwinds, horn.
1:24	*Idée fixe* (altered)	Clarinet solo with timpani: beginning of *idée fixe*. Loud tutti (a roar of greeting to the newcomer). The *idée fixe*, in its new form, accompanied by winds; this turns into a general dance-like passage, which tapers to almost nothing.

2:48	*Dies irae*	Three notes in bells, with hints of the dance to come, lead to the *Dies irae* chant played by bassoons, ophicleide, and serpent in unison:
		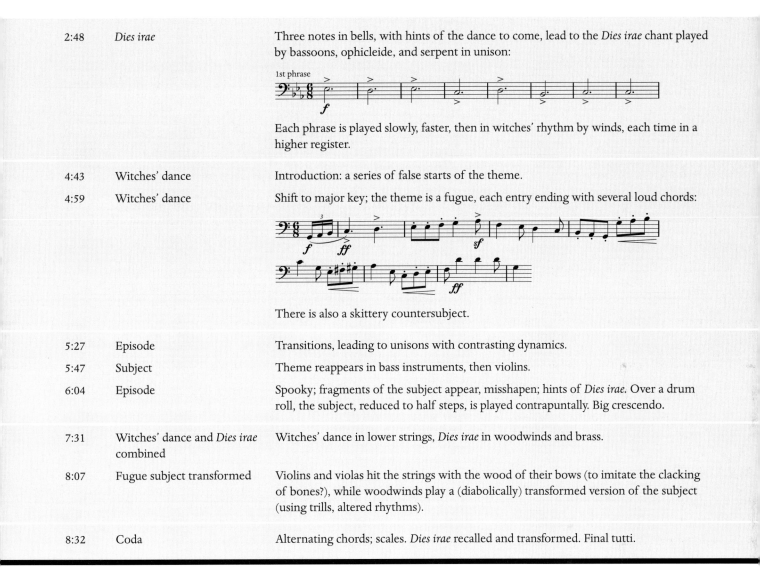
		Each phrase is played slowly, faster, then in witches' rhythm by winds, each time in a higher register.
4:43	Witches' dance	Introduction: a series of false starts of the theme.
4:59	Witches' dance	Shift to major key; the theme is a fugue, each entry ending with several loud chords:
		There is also a skittery countersubject.
5:27	Episode	Transitions, leading to unisons with contrasting dynamics.
5:47	Subject	Theme reappears in bass instruments, then violins.
6:04	Episode	Spooky; fragments of the subject appear, misshapen; hints of *Dies irae*. Over a drum roll, the subject, reduced to half steps, is played contrapuntally. Big crescendo.
7:31	Witches' dance and *Dies irae* combined	Witches' dance in lower strings, *Dies irae* in woodwinds and brass.
8:07	Fugue subject transformed	Violins and violas hit the strings with the wood of their bows (to imitate the clacking of bones?), while woodwinds play a (diabolically) transformed version of the subject (using trills, altered rhythms).
8:32	Coda	Alternating chords; scales. *Dies irae* recalled and transformed. Final tutti.

FIFTH MOVEMENT: "DREAM OF A WITCHES' SABBATH"

 LG 41

The final movement is diabolical; beginning with spooky noises, it features a sinister version of the *idée fixe*. ("The beloved melody appears again, but it has lost its character of nobility and shyness; it is no more than a dance tune, mean, trivial, and grotesque: it is *she*, coming to join the sabbath.")

As church bells ring in this final movement, a Gregorian chant for the funeral service (accompanied by the churchly serpent) is transformed into a sacrilegious dance. Then the movement gets down to its main business, the witches' dance (a lively fugue), which at the climax gets combined with the *Dies irae* chant. "We have religious music, and plenty of it," commented one listener; "but impious music: has anybody composed any before Berlioz? We think not. A subject for weeping and gnashing of teeth." Berlioz is showing the relation of the witches' sabbath to the world of true morality and emotion by transforming two themes, those of religion and of love, into a fiendish dance. (See LG 41, p. 288.)

How Did It Go?

Press coverage of the concert was modest, and opinion was divided as to whether Berlioz was a genius or a charlatan. *Le Figaro* called the *Fantastic Symphony* "the most bizarre monstrosity one can possibly imagine," while *Le National* predicted that it would "be a milestone in the memory of lovers of true music." Most writers discussed the program of the symphony, and the general idea of program music, without giving much idea of whether the performance was a good one. The reviewer for *Le Temps* may have exaggerated when he described the audience's reaction:

> How we shivered in horror before the scaffold, rendered by such beautiful images of such startling veracity that they aroused, right in the middle of the execution, a thunder of applause that nothing could stop; and how everyone laughed at the sabbath at the laughter of the monsters, and how we looked at each other struck with surprise listening to this truly infernal music—these cries, these wailings, the outbreaks of laughter and these efforts of rage! . . . Mr. Berlioz, if he matches this beginning, will one day be worthy to take his place alongside Beethoven.

The *Fantastic Symphony* was inspiring to some and shocking, even repugnant, to others. Among the latter was Fétis, who published his reaction to the *Fantastic Symphony* several years later:

> At last came the day when M. Berlioz gave a concert to let us hear his compositions. . . . The audience . . . was small, and there was scarcely anyone in the hall who was not either a friend or a guest. It was here that we heard for the first time the *Fantastic Symphony*. The audience thought it was having a nightmare during the whole performance; but they did notice the "March to the Scaffold" for its novel effects and applauded it. From this moment I began to form my opinion of M. Berlioz: I saw that he had no taste for melody and but a feeble notion of rhythm; that his harmony, composed by piling up tones into heaps that were often monstrous, was nevertheless flat and monotonous.

As for Berlioz himself, he looked back on the concert in his memoirs as "a great success." The symphony seems to have been fairly well received, and he remembered that Liszt "was conspicuous for the warmth of his applause and his generally enthusiastic behavior." The composer continued:

> The performance was by no means perfect—it could hardly be, with works of such difficulty and after only two rehearsals. But it was good enough to give a reasonable idea of the music. Three of the movements of the symphony, the "Waltz," the "March to the Scaffold," and the "Witches' Sabbath," created a sensation; the "March" especially took the audience by storm. The "Scene in the Country" made no impression at all.

The audience applauded after each movement, which was standard procedure, and there was a prolonged ovation after the "March to the Scaffold." Habeneck refused to repeat the movement, surely because most of the players had a later engagement at the Opéra. At the end of the concert there were shouts and enthusiastic stamping of feet, but whether this was for the symphony, for Berlioz, or for the concert as a whole is impossible to say.

The *Fantastic Symphony* Then and Now

Paris was only beginning to experience the excellent performances produced by the splendid Conservatory orchestra and the incomparable Habeneck; many of those in Berlioz's audience may have been hearing the orchestra for the first time. One can only imagine the excitement of being part of a new venture, the sounds of new and unusual instruments, and the sheer effect of the music.

A whole evening of music organized by a single young composer was fairly novel in Paris. Still more unusual was the notion that orchestral music could tell a story; many of Berlioz's contemporaries were used to thinking of a symphony as music, pure and simple, not as a narrative.

What may have struck listeners most in hearing the *Fantastic Symphony* for the first time, however, might have been how up-to-date it was, in both sound and conception. This "symphony" was not just a formal composition made of abstract musical materials—themes, developments, codas, rhythmic patterns, and so on—according to established conventions. It was also a work made out of fantasy, that is, out of the composer's spontaneous imagination, with the inner life of the artist as its subject. The fantasy takes him where it does without regard to traditions, rules, or anything else that restricts our freedom to create. (Of course, *all* music is in some sense the product of imagination.)

If Berlioz *did* choose to follow guiding principles from the past, he did so as a free agent. He did compose a symphony, after all, which was a highly traditional form. He wrote a fugue at the end, as composers had always done in oratorios and other great pieces of church music, both to express religious feeling and to show the experts that they could write good counterpoint. He included a traditional march and a fashionable waltz that his audience would recognize and enjoy. In short, the *Fantastic Symphony* was new and familiar at the same time, just as Beethoven's Fifth was in 1808.

It's easy to forget that Beethoven had died only three years before Berlioz wrote his groundbreaking symphony. Did the Frenchman have the sounds of Beethoven's "Pastoral" Symphony (subtitled "Scenes of Country Life") in his head when creating his own pastoral fantasy? We do know that Berlioz seized on Beethoven's discovery that symphonic music was capable of describing nature and human experience, or even expressing philosophical and political ideas. The door that Beethoven cracked open in his symphonies was flung wide by Berlioz, never to be shut again.

Blending sound and narrative

For Berlioz, the *Fantastic Symphony* was just the beginning. He went on to write a sequel called *Lélio*, for voices and orchestra, which describes the artist's "return to life" after the trauma of witnessing his own execution. (The two works were meant to be paired under the collective title *Episode from the Life of an Artist.*) In 1834 he composed *Harold in Italy*, which features a solo violist in the role of another antihero, this time drawn from Byron's poem *Childe Harold's Pilgrimage* (in reality, it is based on Berlioz's own travels in Italy). Five years later, he produced *Romeo and Juliet,* a symphony with chorus inspired by Shakespeare (and, no doubt, Harriet Smithson). Each of these works blends symphonic music and narrative in a different way.

Nor was Berlioz alone in following in Beethoven's footsteps. The idea that orchestral music could tell a story was so widely accepted by the mid-1830s that a leading German critic actually defined a symphony as "a story, developed within a psychological context, of some particular emotional state of a large body of people."

Expanding the symphonic tradition

In 1835, Robert Schumann published a famous review of the *Fantastic Symphony* (actually, it was a review of Liszt's widely circulated piano transcription of the work) in which he argued generally that the "dimensions and goals of the symphony" had been exhausted after Beethoven's Ninth. Others, however, saw the symphonic tradition as anything but a dead end. The range of subject matter deemed suitable for symphonic treatment gradually expanded to the point that Gustav Mahler, perhaps the last of the great Romantic symphonists (he died in 1911), declared that "the symphony must be like the world; it must be all-embracing." All of the composers we'll meet later in this book who wrote works using the word *symphony* in their titles are, in some sense, Berlioz's heirs.

Beethoven, as we saw in Chapter 8, demonstrated that the symphony could be a vehicle for lofty thoughts and emotions, as well as entertainment. Berlioz enlarged its scope to embrace the private struggles and passions of an individual human being—the symphony as biography (or autobiography). That focus on the individual is as central to our culture as it was to the Romantic movement. For many modern listeners, the *Fantastic Symphony* brings music into the world of our own feelings and experiences.

Chapter Review

Summary of Musical Styles

- Much of what is true of Beethoven's symphonic style is true also of Berlioz's: multimovement symphonies, each movement based on more than one theme, moving to different keys, with developmental sections that use motives from themes and combine them in new ways and with many changes of key.

- The musical shape of the symphony is like Beethoven's, with an added movement to provide an additional dance movement, and to make the symphony symmetrical:

Beethoven	*Berlioz*
I. Fast	I. Fast
	II. Waltz
II. Slow	III. Slow
III. Scherzo	IV. March
IV. Fast	V. Fast

- The recurrence of music throughout a multimovement work is of particular importance here and will become a frequent practice of later composers. Here the theme that Berlioz calls an **idée fixe** recurs in a variety of transformations in the course of several movements.

- Each of the movements of the symphony begins with some sort of introduction and ends with a coda; these are sometimes in a different tempo from the main part of the movement. For example, the introduction to the first movement is distinguished by tempo, while that of the march is a brief run-up to the main theme.

- **Orchestration** is an important part of Berlioz's technique: sometimes we recognize themes almost as much for their instrumental sound as for their melody. Elsewhere, the carefully crafted accompaniments to themes (consider the various versions of the waltz theme) show Berlioz's colorful imagination. A melody may be passed from instrument to instrument, sometimes having almost each new note played by a new instrument or group (a famous place is in the march).

ⓢ Multimedia Resources and Review Materials on StudySpace

Visit wwnorton.com/studyspace for review of Chapter 10.

What Do You Know?

Check the facts for this chapter. Take the online **Quiz**.

What Do You Hear?

Listening Quizzes and **Music Activities** will help you understand the musical works in this chapter.

🎙 Author Videos

- Berlioz's *idée fixe*

Interactive Listening Guides

LG 37 Berlioz: *Fantastic Symphony*, I, "Rêveries—Passions" (Reveries—Passions)
LG 38 Berlioz: *Fantastic Symphony*, II, "Un bal" (A Ball)
LG 39 Berlioz: *Fantastic Symphony*, III, "Scène aux champs" (Scene in the Country)
LG 40 Berlioz: *Fantastic Symphony*, IV, "Marche du supplice" (March to the Scaffold)
LG 41 Berlioz: *Fantastic Symphony*, V, "Songe d'une nuit de sabbat" (Dream of a Witches' Sabbath)

Flashcards (Terms to Know)

antecedent phrase	*idée fixe*
conjunct	orchestration
consequent phrase	program music
disjunct	

CHAPTER 11

THURSDAY, MARCH 13, 1845, LEIPZIG:

Felix Mendelssohn's Violin Concerto in E Minor

🎵 CORE REPERTOIRE	🎙 AUTHOR VIDEOS	
• **LG 42** First movement, Allegro molto appassionato	• Basic techniques in violin playing	
• **LG 43** Second movement, Andante	• A demonstration of violin virtuosity in Mendelssohn's Violin Concerto	
• **LG 44** Third movement, Allegro molto vivace		

Introduction

"It pleased extraordinarily; everyone said it was one of the most beautiful pieces in this genre; but it also fulfills all the requirements that can be demanded of a concert piece to the highest degree, and players of the violin cannot thank you enough for this gift."

—Ferdinand David to Felix Mendelssohn, January 2, 1845

The concerto

The concerto is a genre that combines two of the nineteenth century's favorite musical pleasures: grand orchestral music and virtuoso showmanship. We have seen the concerto in its Baroque form in the hands of Bach, who seemed to have the same combination of elements in mind. By the time of Mozart and Beethoven, in the late eighteenth and early nineteenth centuries, the concerto had become a vehicle for the interplay of tensions between a David and a Goliath, that is, between the dazzle of a single player and the power of the orchestra.

We might even go one step further and place the Romantic concerto in terms more typical of its time—as a depiction of the individual against society. This was a favorite theme of nineteenth-century composers, novelists, artists, playwrights, and philosophers. In music, the figure of the lone, heroic revolutionary was epitomized by Beethoven and Wagner (see Chapters 8 and 13). Felix Mendelssohn had few such antisocial tendencies. By nature and by upbringing, he fit into his upper-middle-class environment; and yet he certainly had issues of identity, especially spiritual ones, as he grew up.

Concertos have been written for virtually every instrument, from accordion to zither, as well as for two or more instruments—for example, Bach's Concerto in F Major for Harpsichord, Two Recorders, and Strings (see Chapter 6). The solo group of Beethoven's Triple Concerto consists of piano, violin, and cello, and Schumann wrote a remarkable concerto for four horns and orchestra. Mendelssohn himself wrote "double" concertos for two pianos and for piano and violin. But the preeminence of the violin and piano in Western music has ensured that solo concertos for these two instruments remain the timed-honored staples.

The challenge of writing a concerto lies not so much in making the solo part difficult—many concertos are essentially showpieces for the soloist more than they are serious musical explorations—as in constructing a piece of music that has real substance, while still providing the brilliance that gives the concerto its excitement. Mendelssohn's Violin Concerto is one such piece, and it has been a favorite of audiences and violinists since it was first performed in 1845.

The only other violin concertos that rival Mendelssohn's in popularity in the modern repertoire are those by Beethoven (1806), Brahms (1878), and Tchaikovsky (also 1878). Each is a carefully constructed piece of music, not just a showpiece for the instrument, and each is the only concerto that its composer wrote for violin. (Mendelssohn actually composed another violin concerto when he was thirteen, but he did not consider it part of his mature legacy.) Just as Mendelssohn followed in Beethoven's footsteps, so Brahms and Tchaikovsky learned from Mendelssohn how to combine sizzling virtuosity with symphonic grandeur.

Ⓢ Brahms: Violin Concerto in D Major, I

Ⓢ Tchaikovsky: Violin Concerto in D Major, III

FIG. 11.1 Leipzig about 1850, showing the Town Hall with its tower.

The Setting

LEIPZIG IN 1845

The Leipzig that Mendelssohn knew was one of Europe's leading cultural centers, as it had been in Bach's time a century earlier. The great writer Johann Wolfgang von Goethe described the German city as "a little Paris." St. Thomas's Church and the venerable university continued to dominate Leipzig's spiritual and intellectual landscape (see Figure 11.1). The recent completion of Germany's first long-distance railroad, which connected Leipzig with Dresden, together with the famous trade fairs, made the city a hub of Central European traffic and commerce.

Leipzig was also home to a burgeoning publishing industry. The composer Robert Schumann, Mendelssohn's close friend and contemporary, boasted that the city supported no fewer than 150 bookshops, fifty printing plants, and thirty periodicals, including the *Neue Zeitschrift für Musik*, Germany's most influential music magazine, which the composer Robert Schumann had edited since 1834. The presence of such luminaries as Mendelssohn and Schumann helped make Leipzig audiences even more musically sophisticated than in the days when Bach's Collegium Musicum was performing in Zimmermann's coffeehouse.

In 1781, thirty-one years after Bach's death, Leipzig opened its first concert hall, known as the Gewandhaus (see Figure 11.2). It occupied one floor of the Cloth Hall (*Gewandhaus*, in German), next door to the university and a few blocks from St. Thomas's Church. The rather austere rectangular auditorium seated about five hundred people—roughly the size of an average recital hall today. Because the rows of chairs were placed at right angles to the stage, listeners had to crane their necks to see the performers and the edifying inscription from the Latin philosopher Seneca overhead: *Res severa verum gaudium* (Seriousness alone is true amusement).

The resident orchestra of the Gewandhaus grew steadily in importance during the late eighteenth and early nineteenth centuries. Mozart performed with it in 1789, and Beethoven's symphonies were played in Leipzig soon after their premieres in Vienna. In 1842 the Gewandhaus was remodeled, with balconies added along both sides. It was in this enlarged hall that Mendelssohn's Violin Concerto had its first performance three years later. (The building has been rebuilt several times; Leipzig's current principal concert hall—built while Leipzig was part of East Germany during the Cold War, and on another site—is still called the Gewandhaus, and its famous orchestra remains active to this day.)

Mendelssohn, who was named director of the Gewandhaus concerts in 1835, not only greatly improved the quality of the orchestra but also built their series into events that no one in Leipzig could ignore. The orchestra played twenty concerts a year, on Thursday evenings, from October until Easter (see Mendelssohn's Schedule in Leipzig, left). Mendelssohn planned all of the programs and conducted most of them. (Before that time, conductors were used mostly for large choral pieces; instrumental music was often led by the concertmaster from his chair as first violinist, as in Bach's day.) By all accounts, Mendelssohn was a superb conductor, liked and respected by the

Mendelssohn's Schedule in Leipzig

In October 1839, the composer urged his friend Eduard Devrient to visit Leipzig:

Here you would hear a great deal of music, and much of it, I believe, you would like; the finished way in which we play the symphonies of Mozart and Beethoven, I know would please you. We have not very much music during the summer; it begins with the autumn, and from now to November is at its height, when all are assembled, and both executants and listeners have gathered fresh love and power in the long recess. By New Year's Day there is almost too much of it, and when spring returns one feels quite exhausted and surfeited with music, so that a stop is very welcome.

musicians. He had a photographic memory, and was one of the earliest conductors to use a baton.

Mendelssohn's choice of music had much to do with the formation of the orchestral repertory that we now consider the norm. He programmed works by Bach, Mozart, and Beethoven; much of his own music; and pieces by contemporaries such as Schumann, Louis Spohr, the Danish composer Niels Gade, and Hector Berlioz, whom he had met in Rome in the early 1830s (see Chapter 10). As was common at the time, Mendelssohn's Gewandhaus concerts included not only orchestral music but also vocal pieces, scenes or acts from operas, and chamber and solo works. The program that included the first performance of his Violin Concerto was typically varied (see p. 302).

FIG. 11.2 The interior of the Gewandhaus (Cloth Hall), the concert hall of Leipzig. Unlike the arrangement of most modern concert halls, the seats were arranged in facing rows along the long side of the hall.

FELIX MENDELSSOHN

Felix Mendelssohn was born into a distinguished German-Jewish family known for its intellectual and artistic accomplishments (see biography, p. 298). His father, Abraham, was a banker and philanthropist and the son of Moses Mendelssohn, a leading philosopher of the Enlightenment. Abraham Mendelssohn is supposed to have quipped, "Once I was the son of a famous father, now I am the father of a famous son."

Despite their eminence, the Mendelssohns suffered from the social and legal discrimination against Jews in Germany at the time (see Letter from Mendelssohn's Teacher Carl Friedrich Zelter, right). Felix's parents decided to convert to Christianity for the sake of their children, all four of whom were baptized in 1816, when Felix was seven. They even appended the "Christian" surname Bartholdy to the family name, and for the rest of his life Felix signed himself Mendelssohn Bartholdy (though he balked at his father's request that he drop the name Mendelssohn entirely). Nevertheless, anti-Semitism plagued the composer throughout his life and, as we will see, continued to haunt his name after death.

When Mendelssohn was two, the family moved from Hamburg to Berlin, where he grew up in a hotbed of musical activity. His older sister Fanny, whom his father initially thought more talented, was an excellent pianist and composer (see Fanny Hensel and Clara Schumann, p. 299). Felix studied piano with his mother and composition with the eminent Carl Friedrich Zelter. Another of his teachers was the famous composer and piano virtuoso Ignaz Moscheles, who later became a close friend and colleague. Felix was considered an affable and pleasant child, who often put others at ease.

Mendelssohn became a fluent and dazzling pianist before turning ten. In his early teens he wrote symphonies, concertos, and chamber works of high quality. Goethe heard both Mozart and Mendelssohn perform as children and compared them in unequivocal terms:

> Musical prodigies, as far as mere technical execution goes, are probably no longer so rare: but what this little man [Mendelssohn] can do in extemporizing and playing at sight, borders on the miraculous, and I could not have believed it possible at so early an age. "And yet you heard Mozart in his seventh year at Frankfurt?" said Zelter.

Letter from Mendelssohn's Teacher Carl Friedrich Zelter

Felix is a good, handsome boy, happy and obedient. He may be certainly the son of a Jew, but no Jew. The father, with significant sacrifice, has not circumcised his sons and brings them up properly as it should be done. It would really be a rare thing if an artist came out of the son of a Jew.

FELIX MENDELSSOHN (1809–1847)

Felix Mendelssohn was a prolific and gifted composer of many talents who achieved international fame. As a child prodigy in an intensely intellectual and musical family, he developed his performing skill, his abilities as a composer, and his literary and cultural expertise in highly favorable surroundings. From his teens he composed works that are still favorites with audiences.

Born in Hamburg, Germany, in 1809, Felix grew up in Berlin with his brother and two sisters. Under the tutelage of Carl Friedrich Zelter, the director of Berlin's prestigious Singakademie (Singing Academy), he rapidly matured as a composer; his earliest extant composition was written at age ten. When Felix was twelve, he met the poet Goethe in Weimar and struck up a friendship that would be deeply meaningful for them both.

By his late teens, Mendelssohn's compositional technique was fully developed; he also excelled in art (he was a skillful painter, see Figure 11.3), literature, languages, and philosophy. Mendelssohn spoke German, English, and French fluently, and read voraciously in each of those languages, as well as in Latin and Greek.

In 1829, Mendelssohn organized and conducted an important revival of Bach's *St. Matthew Passion* at the Singakademie. The revival of serious interest in the music of Bach was largely the result of Mendelssohn's pioneering efforts.

By the 1830s Mendelssohn was internationally known as a composer, pianist, and conductor. In 1837 he married Cécile Jeanrenaud (see box, p. 300, and Figure 11.4), also an amateur painter, with whom he had five children. By all accounts it was a happy and successful union.

Mendelssohn's illustrious career was capped by his appointment as director of the Leipzig Gewandhaus in 1835. Eight years later, in 1843, he founded the Leipzig Conservatory; despite his onerous administrative duties, he maintained a busy schedule of appearances as pianist and conductor all over Europe. As a result of his peripatetic lifestyle, he was absent from the premiere of his own Violin Concerto. In 1847, after the death of his beloved sister Fanny, the composer suffered a series of devastating strokes and died in November, at age thirty-eight.

Mendelssohn's music is elegant, lyrical, and beautifully crafted. He is particularly remembered for his oratorios *Saint Paul* and *Elijah*; his piano music, chamber music, and symphonies (the *Italian* and *Scotch* symphonies are among today's favorites); and his music for Shakespeare's *Midsummer Night's Dream,* which includes the famous Wedding March.

Ⓢ Mendelssohn: *Elijah* (oratorio)

MAJOR WORKS: Orchestral work, including 5 symphonies; 1 violin concerto, 2 piano concertos, 4 overtures, and incidental music to 7 plays; 2 oratorios (*Saint Paul* and *Elijah*); chamber music, including string quartets, piano trios, and cello sonatas; numerous works for piano and for organ; choral works; and songs.

FIG. 11.3 A watercolor by Felix Mendelssohn, done in 1847, in Thun, Switzerland.

FIG. 11.4 A portrait of Cécile Jeanrenaud, painted around the time of her 1837 marriage to Mendelssohn.

Fanny Hensel and Clara Schumann

Four years older than her famous brother, Fanny Mendelssohn Hensel (1805–1847; see Figure 11.5) was his lifelong confidant and artistic counselor. Although Felix recognized her exceptional talent as a composer and pianist, both he and their father discouraged her from venturing outside the traditional domestic sphere. As a married woman, Fanny contented herself with running an artistic salon at her home in Berlin. Not until the end of her life did she assert her independence by publishing a collection of songs without first seeking Felix's approval.

Fanny's experience mirrored that of another outstanding female composer, Clara Schumann (1819–1896; see Chapter 12). She, too, lived in the shadow of a famous man—her husband, Robert—but, unlike Fanny, Clara's social background did not prevent her appearing in public, and she had a socially acceptable outlet in her piano playing. (She was one of the leading concert artists of her day.) As a rule, composing was not considered a suitable occupation for women in the nineteenth century. The Leipzig Conservatory, which Felix founded in 1843, restricted women to a two-year course in music theory "especially organized for their requirements," and the Paris Conservatory barred its doors to women composers until the 1870s.

"Yes," [I] answered; "at that time I myself had only just reached my twelfth year, and was certainly, like all the rest of the world, immensely astonished at his extraordinary execution; but what your pupil [Mendelssohn] already accomplishes, bears the same relation to the Mozart of that time, that the cultivated talk of a grown-up person does to the prattle of a child."

The Mendelssohns presented grand musical matinees on alternate Sunday mornings in their dining room on Berlin's fashionable Leipziger Strasse, with a small orchestra that Felix conducted. (At first he was so small that he needed to stand on a stool.) For each of these occasions Felix produced new works; he or Fanny played the piano while another sister, Rebecka, sang and their brother Paul played the cello.

By the time Mendelssohn was eighteen, he already had several major works to his credit, including his timeless Overture to Shakespeare's *Midsummer Night's Dream* Ⓢ and his astonishingly precocious Octet for Strings. Starting in his twenties, he began composing a stream of piano pieces called *Songs without Words* Ⓢ, which have become perennial favorites with performers and listeners alike.

Few composers in history have been more admired and better liked by their contemporaries than Mendelssohn. There are many accounts of his modesty, sensitivity, cultivated manners, and gift for friendship and love. His marriage to Cécile Jeanrenaud, the daughter of a protestant pastor in Frankfurt, seems to have been an ideal match (see Letter to His Sister, p. 300). A fountain of energy, Mendelssohn was naturally athletic and throughout his short life enjoyed swimming and hiking. A pupil at the Leipzig Conservatory who knew him in the mid-1840s left this description:

Mendelssohn had a slender, delicately framed figure. His dexterous and agile bodily movements were extraordinarily lively. . . . The dark eye blazed like lightning. It could just as quickly assume a friendly, benevolent and cheerful expression as a sharply penetrating one or a serious and thoughtful one. . . . The high, beautifully domed forehead was framed by black hair, which fell in curls to the sides and behind. The face that tapered towards his chin was bordered by thick sideboards. The moderately curved nose was of the Roman type and betrayed his oriental [Jewish] ancestry. The extremely

FIG. 11.5 Felix Mendelssohn's sister Fanny Hensel, a pianist and composer, with her son Sebastien in her arms, 1832.

Ⓢ Mendelssohn: *A Midsummer Night's Dream*, Overture

Ⓢ Mendelssohn: *Songs without Words*, No. 6, "Spring Song"

Letter to His Sister

On July 24, 1836, Mendelssohn wrote a letter to his sister Rebecka, proclaiming his love for "this charming girl":

The present period is a very strange one, for I am more desperately in love than I ever was in my life before, and I do not know what to do. I leave Frankfurt the day after tomorrow, but I feel as if it would cost me my life. At any rate I intend to return here and see this charming girl [Cécile Jeanrenaud] once more before I go back to Leipzig. But I have not an idea whether she likes me, or not, and I do not know what to do to make her like me, as I have already said. But one thing is certain, that to her I owe the first real happiness I have enjoyed this year, and now I feel fresh and hopeful again for the first time.

FIG. 11.6 The violinist Ferdinand David, concertmaster of the Leipzig Gewandhaus Orchestra and the soloist who first performed Mendelssohn's Violin Concerto in 1845.

finely formed mouth made a striking impression. When he opened it in conversation or laughter, two rows of dazzlingly white teeth could be seen. Everything combined in Mendelssohn to make his appearance as a whole attractive and charming.

FERDINAND DAVID

The eminent violinist Ferdinand David (1810–1873; see Figure 11.6), for whom Mendelssohn wrote his concerto, had been a friend of the composer's for almost twenty years; he was actually born in the same apartment house in Hamburg as Mendelssohn, less than a year later. Although their parents were acquainted, the two boys did not meet until later in life, when each had achieved a certain degree of success. David was a violinist at the Königstadt Theater in Vienna (1826–29), where he became friendly with Mendelssohn. When Mendelssohn became director of the Gewandhaus concerts in 1835, he invited David to come to Leipzig as **concertmaster**, a post that the violinist would occupy for thirty-seven years.

Well known as a concert artist, David was also a famous teacher (he joined the faculty of the Leipzig Conservatory in 1843) and the author of an influential textbook on violin playing. His students included Joseph Joachim, who premiered Brahms's Violin Concerto, and August Wilhelmj, Wagner's concertmaster at Bayreuth. David's musical taste was as wide-ranging as Mendelssohn's. He became a tireless promoter of Schubert, whose chamber music he played in numerous Leipzig concerts. He also championed the late string quartets of Beethoven, the early works of Brahms, and music of Bach and other composers of earlier periods.

David himself composed more than forty works, which he often played on his tours. An English reviewer of one of his violin concertos praised both the performance and the music: "His tone is most pure, his cantabile expressive, his intonation perfect, and his bowing such as all English players should endeavor to imitate. His composition—well adapted to exhibit the powers of the violin—fully justifies us in pronouncing it the work of a scholar and a musician of genius."

NIELS GADE

Another of Mendelssohn's close musical associates was the Danish composer and conductor Niels Gade (1817–1890; see Figure 11.7). It was he who had the honor of conducting the first performance of Mendelssohn's Violin Concerto in March of 1845, while the composer himself was enjoying a hard-earned holiday with his family in Frankfurt.

Having failed to get his first symphony performed in Copenhagen, Gade had sent the score to Mendelssohn, who liked it very much. Mendelssohn began a correspondence with Gade, and performed the symphony in 1843. Gade then won a Danish government grant to travel to Leipzig, where he met Mendelssohn, conducted another performance of his symphony, and was hired by Mendelssohn as assistant conductor at the Gewandhaus. He also taught at the Leipzig Conservatory.

After Mendelssohn's death in 1847, Gade was appointed his successor at the Gewandhaus. A year later war broke out between Germany and Denmark, and Gade prudently returned to Copenhagen. There he established a first-rate orchestra and remained the leading figure of the musical life in Denmark until shortly before his death in 1890, composing eight symphonies, a number of overtures, and other works strongly indebted to Mendelssohn's musical style.

The Performance

PREPARATIONS

Even though Mendelssohn was an expert pianist, organist, and conductor who had written concertos from an early age, he always seemed to have trouble dealing with the fundamental problem associated with the genre: striking a balance between technical and purely musical demands. He was also hampered by the fact that he was not a fan of virtuosity for its own sake, as he made clear in a letter to the pianist Ignaz Moscheles:

> But why should I hear those Variations by Herz [Henri Herz, a piano virtuoso] for the thirtieth time? They give me as little pleasure as rope dancers or acrobats: for with them at least there is the barbarous attraction that one is in constant dread of seeing them break their necks. . . . I only wish it were not my lot to be constantly told that the public demand that kind of thing. I, too, am one of the public, and demand the very reverse.

Mendelssohn had been intending to write a violin concerto for some time. He wrote to David in 1838, after their third season of working together at the Gewandhaus, "I'd like to do a violin concerto for you next winter; one in E minor is running through my head, and the opening of it will not leave me in peace." Later in the same letter he noted that the concerto was swimming around in his brain in a shapeless condition, but that a day or two of work would bring it into focus.

David, barely able to contain his eagerness, pleaded with Mendelssohn to

FIG. 11.7 Niels Gade, the Danish composer and conductor who led the first performance of Mendelssohn's Violin Concerto.

> have pity and write a violin concerto—you have produced so many lovely things for pianists, orchestras, choruses, clarinetists and basset-horn players. Just once do something for us, particularly for me. You are the right man for it, it would cost you fourteen days and you would earn eternal gratitude, but do it soon, before my fingers become stiff and my *saltando* [a technique of bouncing the bow on the string] ridden with gout.

But Mendelssohn would not be rushed. "Now that is very nice of you to press me for a violin concerto!" he wrote to David while vacationing near Koblenz. "I have the greatest desire to write one for you, and if I have a few favorable days here I shall bring you something of the sort. But it is not an easy task. You want it to be brilliant, and how is such a one as I to manage that?"

Writing a serious concerto for a famous violinist, collaborator, and friend whom he wanted to please was not something that Mendelssohn took lightly. When he finally showed the score to David in September of 1844, the violinist immediately arranged to have parts made for orchestral performance. By November, David was ready to audition the solo part for Mendelssohn. "I'll play your concerto for you when you come," he wrote. "The score is ready for you; but it is more difficult than I thought at first glance."

David worked closely with Mendelssohn on the technical details of the violin part and how it should look in the published version. (Mendelssohn was an excellent violinist—Zelter thought he could have been a great one—but he did not have David's virtuoso technique.) The concerto was published, in the form of a solo part with piano accompaniment, shortly after the first performance. In keeping with Mendelssohn's international reputation, the publication bore the joint imprints of three distinguished publishing houses in Leipzig, London, and Milan.

THURSDAY, MARCH 13, 1845

Mendelssohn's concerto was the second work on the twentieth and final subscription concert of the Gewandhaus season. The program, as reported in the papers, consisted of the following:

Overture and Introduction from the opera *Euryanthe* by *C. M. von Weber*
Concerto for the violin, composed by *F. Mendelssohn Bartholdy* (new, manuscript)
    performed by Herr Concertmaster *David*
Recitative and Aria from *Figaro* by *Mozart,* sung by Fräulein *Hennigsen*
Introduction and Variations on a Scottish Folksong for the violin, composed and
    performed by Herr Concertmaster *David*
Music to *Kotzebue's* "Ruins of Athens," composed by *L. van Beethoven,* with
connecting poetic verses spoken by Fräulein *Baumeister*

Note that David's own music appeared alongside Mendelssohn's new concerto. Not every composer would openly invite comparison with Weber, Beethoven, Mozart, and Mendelssohn—and as it happens, David's music has not stood the test of time. Note, too, that the orchestra program contains no symphony. Mozart is represented by an aria from his opera *The Marriage of Figaro*, Beethoven by his powerful incidental music to a play by the German dramatist August von Kotzebue. All interest, though, was focused on the new concerto.

 Basic techniques in violin playing

The Music

"We know," wrote one reviewer about the score of Mendelssohn's concerto, "that in the case of many famous virtuosos whose concertos have become known as effective solo pieces, they just write the melodies themselves, and leave the instrumentation, and the *tutti* [orchestra] passages to somebody else."

But what about a concerto whose composer is not a distinguished performer on the solo instrument, as in the case of Mendelssohn's Violin Concerto? The same reviewer addressed this very question:

> If a composer who is not a virtuoso and is not making the composition for himself to play, undertakes to write a violin concerto, he can do what the art of music is all about: he can easily allow himself to be freer and more poetic than the composing virtuoso, who always more or less lets himself be led by what is most effective for the instrument and most grateful for his own performing talents. . . . A piece like [Mendelssohn's] is to be gratefully treasured not only for itself, but also because, by departing from the very narrow tracks of convention, it gives the genre itself an impulse and provides it with a refreshed life.

Perhaps only those who have heard one too many bad, bombastic concertos from the nineteenth century can know how grateful Mendelssohn's contemporaries must have been to hear a balanced concerto like his. In avoiding virtuosity for its own sake, Mendelssohn provided a model for later concerto composers to emulate. But this is not to say that his Violin Concerto is devoid of showmanship. On the contrary, it afforded many opportunities for David and his fellow virtuosos to demonstrate the tricks of their trade.

VIRTUOSITY

All concertos written for a solo instrument—whether by Bach, Mendelssohn, or any other composer—have one basic thing in common: they pit a single person (the soloist) against many people (the orchestra). The smaller combatant, as it were, needs to compensate in wile and agility for lack of heft. The soloist in a concerto—who, obviously, can never play as loudly as the orchestra—uses **virtuosity**, the ability to perform dazzling feats of difficulty, to make the instrument heard, to attract our attention, and to create a balance between size and nimbleness (see The Cult of the Virtuoso, right).

How does a violinist show off her or his virtuosity? Essentially, there are four techniques: playing high up on the instrument, playing loudly, playing quickly, and playing more than one note at a time. In short: high, loud, fast, and multiple.

In Mendelssohn's concerto, the violin begins almost immediately with the beautiful first theme, played in the upper register: not at a stratospheric level—that will come later—but high enough so that it feels as if the violin is soaring and that the instrument possesses a power that sets it apart from the orchestra. Later in the concerto, the violin plays notes so high that you are not sure if you are really hearing them.

One reason playing high is more difficult than playing low is because the higher you go on the violin, the closer together the notes become and the harder it is to play in tune. Watching the fingers of a virtuoso violinist crawl over the upper reaches of the fingerboard is like watching an acrobat doing a high-wire act; it requires a similar level of skill, agility, balance, and precision, as well as a certain fearlessness. In order to understand this, you will need to become familiar with the basic mechanics of violin playing first (see Violin Playing, p. 304).

Playing loudly poses a different set of challenges. To accomplish this, the violinist generally exerts more pressure on the bow and moves it more quickly across the string. The player can also do other things to give the impression of loudness, such as increasing the rate or width of the **vibrato**—the pulsation given to sound by rhythmically wiggling the left hand back and forth, thus slightly changing the pitch of the note. (As a rule, string players in Mendelssohn's time used vibrato more sparingly than they do today.) Some notes last longer than the bow stroke, and the violinist has to be clever at changing from down-bow (moving the bow arm away from the violin) to up-bow (moving the bow arm toward the violin) in an almost imperceptible way.

Playing fast comes in many forms, and much of its success depends on knowing how the instrument works. For example,

A demonstration of violin virtuosity in Mendelssohn's Violin Concerto

The Cult of the Virtuoso

The Italian word *virtuoso* (from a Latin root meaning skill) originally denoted a person who was proficient at something; it might be fencing, music, cooking, or practically any other activity. By the nineteenth century, it had come to mean a performer with almost super-human skill as a singer or instrumentalist. There had been concertos, and expert players, long before Mendelssohn, but it was not until the early nineteenth century that the virtuoso performer came to inspire the kind of hero worship we now associate with an elite group of rock musicians and other pop idols.

In the 1830s, Niccolò Paganini dazzled all of Europe with his violin acrobatics; he performed what seemed to be miracles—indeed, some thought he was in league with the Devil, or was the Devil himself. At the same time Franz Liszt achieved such mastery of the piano, and was such a skilled showman, that he was worshiped as a kind of demigod. Paganini, Liszt, and a few other superstars achieved a fame comparable to that of the most illustrious opera singers. The virtuoso was somehow set off from reality by an ability to do what was seemingly impossible.

Mendelssohn, himself a celebrated keyboard virtuoso, admired Liszt and even invited him to give three special concerts at the Gewandhaus in 1840. But the pianist's view that "virtuosity is not a secondary outgrowth, but an indispensable element of music" was fundamentally alien to Mendelssohn's artistic philosophy. When Liszt boasted that he could imitate a full orchestra at the keyboard, Mendelssohn expressed skepticism to a fellow composer: "Well if I could only hear the first eight bars of Mozart's G minor Symphony, with that delicate figure in the [violas], rendered on the piano as it sounds in the orchestra—I would believe it."

Violin Playing

Aperformer plays a note on the violin by pressing a string down onto the fingerboard while making it sound, or vibrate, with the bow (see figures below). Pressing the finger on the fingerboard shortens the length of the vibrating string; the higher the note is, the shorter the string needs to be. (Think of how the piano's strings get shorter as you move toward the right, or high, end of the keyboard.)

The spacing on the fingerboard is proportional. The violin's highest string sounds the second E above middle C (the top space on the treble staff; see p. A-3). To play the E above that, you divide the string in half with your finger. To hear the E above *that*, you divide the remaining part of the string in half, thus vibrating only a quarter of the string's full length. All the notes between the first E and the second E thus occupy half the length of the string, while all the notes between the second E and the third E occupy only a quarter of the string; the notes get closer together as you play higher and the vibrating string gets shorter. What this means for the violinist is that playing in the high register requires a measure of precision that is very difficult to achieve. If you do not place your finger in exactly the right place, the note is out of tune—and everyone hears it. The same is true in the violin's lower register, of course, but there the margin for error is much greater.

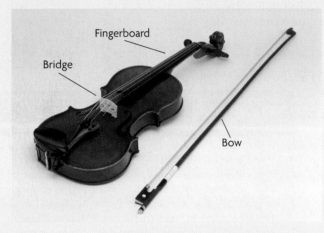

FIG. 11.8 A violin and a violin bow.

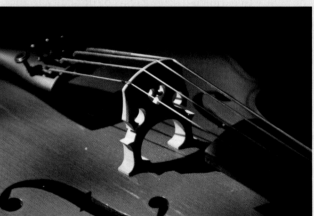

FIG. 11.9 The bridge of a violin is curved so that each string can be played separately.

Slur

many notes can be connected on a single bow stroke. If the fingers move nimbly on the string, the notes will change without altering the direction of the bow. Such passages are written in the violinist's part with a **slur** over them. In cases where each note gets its own bow stroke, you can tell when the player is going fast by the way the bow moves furiously back and forth.

The first fast playing that the soloist does in Mendelssohn's concerto is with triplets—three notes in the space of two. They are grouped in sets of six at first, and later in groups of three. Part of the challenge—and the fun—in this varied virtuoso writing and playing is seeing how many different ways of doing something fancy can be devised. Some notes, like the triplets just mentioned, are fast, but more or less melodic; others take advantage of the fact that adjacent strings produce different notes, so that sweeping the bow across all the strings produces a

Arpeggio

dazzling, **arpeggio** effect (cascading chord-tones—think of the sound of a harp), as in the first-movement **cadenza** (an elaborate solo passage that usually comes just before the end of a concerto movement). For more on this and the following virtuoso techniques, listen to the Author Videos on StudySpace.

Double-stopping

Playing two strings at the same time (called **double-stopping**) is another way of producing a louder sound. This technique involves a certain acrobatic element, because the violin was not specifically designed for playing several notes at the same time. The violin, like the viola, cello, and double bass, is essentially a *melody* instrument; its four strings, tuned to four different notes, are stretched across a curved bridge (see Figures 11.8 and 11.9) in such a way that each string can be played separately (if the bridge were flat, you could not play the two middle strings by themselves). By carefully drawing the bow across two adjacent strings, however, you can actually make two notes sound simultaneously. Mendelssohn does this at the beginning of the first movement, where the violinist plays a series of octaves (that is, two notes an octave apart, played simultaneously on adjacent strings).

Mendelssohn also uses another technique to give the listener an impression of hearing multiple notes. In the middle section of the slow movement, the violinist executes a **tremolo** between two notes (a fast alternation produced by putting a left-hand finger down and lifting it up) on one string while playing a sustained melody on another using the other fingers of the left hand. The effect is almost like hearing three-part harmony. *Tremolo*

In Mendelssohn's concerto, the violin alternates between lyrical melodies and brilliant fast patterns. The tunes are beautiful, but the orchestra can play them too. What it cannot do is match the virtuosity of the soloist.

Listening to the Music

Mendelssohn's concerto has the luminous orchestral color that we associate with music by Beethoven and Berlioz, and a lyricism that may remind us of some of the pieces we've heard by Mozart and Schubert. Mendelssohn's challenge was to combine the lyrical and the symphonic with the virtuosity that is characteristic of concertos, adding the lightning and excitement without losing the beauty and the drive in a flurry of empty showmanship.

The form of Mendelssohn's Violin Concerto is innovative in at least three respects. The first is the absence of breaks: the whole concerto is played without any sort of pause—the three movements are stitched together by linking passages, producing a more or less seamless flow of music (recall that Beethoven connected the last two movements of his Fifth Symphony). The second innovation relates to the structure of the first movement: for the opening of his concerto, Mendelssohn reversed the traditional tutti and solo; the concerto begins with the solo, and then the tutti (admittedly abridged) follows. (There are of course other concertos, which Mendelssohn may well have known, that experiment with traditional form.) The third innovation is Mendelssohn's treatment of the first-movement cadenza. We will look at all three of these features more carefully below. *Form*

FIRST MOVEMENT: ALLEGRO MOLTO APPASSIONATO   🎧 LG 42

Most concertos, from Bach's time onward, begin with the orchestra playing a ritornello that includes the principal theme or themes of the first movement. Only then does the soloist enter, having been, as it were, provoked to action—to comment on or do battle with or collaborate with the orchestra.

In Mendelssohn's concerto, famously, there is only a soft chord and a throb before the violin plays the very high and beautiful first theme. From here on, the orchestra is not so much the soloist's partner as it is an accompanist and punctuator. Mendelssohn's skill with the orchestra, gained from years of experience as a composer and conductor, is apparent in the way he alters and tightens the traditional first-movement concerto form. (For a summary of the following discussion, see Table 11.1, Concerto First-Movement Form, p. 306.)

TABLE 11.1

Concerto First-Movement Form

STANDARD FORM (Late 18th Century)

	Tutti exposition	Solo exposition	Development	Recapitulation	Coda
Themes	Theme 1, transition, Theme 2, closing theme	Theme 1, transition, Theme 2, closing theme	Various	Theme 1, transition, Theme 2, closing theme, **cadenza**	Final cadence
Performers	Orchestra	Soloist (+ orchestra)	Soloist + orchestra	Soloist + orchestra, soloist	Orchestra

MENDELSSOHN'S VIOLIN CONCERTO (19th Century)

	Combined tutti and solo exposition	Development	Recapitulation	Coda
Themes	Theme 1, transition, Theme 2, closing theme	Various themes, **cadenza**	Theme 1, transition, Theme 2, closing theme	Final cadence
Performers	Soloist, then orchestra	Soloist + orchestra, soloist	Orchestra + soloist	Orchestra + soloist

The basic structure of a standard Classical first-movement concerto form is similar to the sonata form used for symphonies and other works. The main difference is that a typical eighteenth-century concerto—a form inherited by nineteenth-century composers—has *two* expositions instead of one. The first exposition is by the orchestra, which lays out all the themes and stays in the home key. The second or "solo" exposition, occurs when the soloist enters and, with the orchestra, goes through the musical material again, this time moving to a second key, as in sonata-allegro form. A development section follows (just as in a symphony), which uses material from the exposition, moves through many keys, and arrives at the recapitulation, where the home key and the original themes are repeated, without changing key.

Mendelssohn makes several important changes to this template. To begin with, he dispenses with the orchestral exposition and combines it with the solo exposition, so that violinist and orchestra alternate in presenting the main thematic material. Then he blurs the division between the exposition and the development section by means of a sort of insider joke, where the violin climbs up into the stratosphere at the end of the closing theme and refuses to come back down to earth for the full cadence that we are waiting for.

Mendelssohn has another trick up his sleeve later on. Audiences in 1845 knew pretty much what to expect in a concerto: at the end of the recapitulation, the music stops just before the orchestra arrives at the final cadence of the closing theme. This is the soloist's cue to perform an unaccompanied *cadenza* (Italian, for cadence), an elaborate, virtuosic display of all the fireworks he or she can muster.

Cadenzas were what audiences waited for. In earlier times, they were improvised by the performer (who was often the composer) and, because nothing was written out, there was an element of surprise that mitigated the predictability of the form. Cadenzas traditionally finish with a trill on the sound of a dominant chord, whereupon the orchestra comes back in with a crash and finishes off the concerto with a rousing coda. In a sense, then, the "standard" cadenza is really a cadence—an ending.

LISTENING GUIDE 42

Mendelssohn Violin Concerto in E Minor, Op. 64, I
(Allegro molto appassionato)   13:44

DATE: 1845
GENRE: Concerto

LISTEN FOR
MELODY: Virtuoso techniques in solo part
RHYTHM/METER: Duple meter, fast pace that gains speed

FORM: Surprise placement of violin cadenza
Departures from standard first-movement concerto form

TIME	FORM	DESCRIPTION
	Exposition	
0:00	Theme 1, soloist	As the orchestra provides an opening harmony, the violin launches straight into the opening theme in E minor:
0:37	Soloist's extension	Virtuosic introductory material. The violin shows what it can do: triplets, octaves, triplets and octaves combined.
1:09	Theme 1, orchestra	
1:43	Transition	An angular transition theme begun by orchestra and taken up by violin:
1:59		Virtuoso figuration in violin.
3:00	Theme 2	Exposition moves to key of C major for Theme 2, which begins in woodwinds while the violin holds its very lowest note pianissimo. Even though it's the opposite of what the soloist normally does—high and loud and fast—the violin is very clearly heard:
3:26		Violin states Theme 2.
4:28	Closing theme	Variant of Theme 1, with extensions; violin ends in very high register. At this point, we expect a trill from violin and final cadence. We get the trill, from the orchestra, but the harmony is changed so that cadence cannot be final.

(continued)

TIME	FORM	DESCRIPTION
Development		
4:40	Blurred boundary	Instead, repetition of trill merges into beginning of the development, without ever having had a complete cadence.
5:50	Derived from transition	Material from transition theme.
6:05	Derived from Theme 1	Violin performs figuration, while orchestra deconstructs first theme.
6:36	Anticipation of recapitulation	Violin returns to opening of Theme 1. Everyone is poised for a return to tonic key . . .
7:38	Cadenza	But recapitulation is unexpectedly delayed by placing cadenza here (instead of in its usual place, at end of recapitulation). A series of arpeggios finally leads to the return of Theme 1, in its original key.
Recapitulation		
9:22	Theme 1	Violin continues its arpeggios while orchestra reprises Theme 1.
9:42	Transition	Orchestra, then violin with extension.
10:17	Theme 2	
11:41	Closing theme	Another version of Theme 1, with extensions. After a cadence (delayed, as before) . . .
Coda		
13:13		The music speeds up, growing more excited, combining Transition theme and beginning of Theme 1.

But Mendelssohn's cadenza is different. For one thing, it comes at an unexpected place—at the end of the *development*, as a lead-in to the recapitulation, instead of just before the final orchestral close. The early arrival of the cadenza is a surprise to those who "know" how a concerto ought to proceed. Not only is Mendelssohn's cadenza written out, it also begins not, like most cadenzas, after a break, a stop, in the orchestra, but directly out of the orchestra's ongoing crescendo. And it ends with a series of arpeggios that are clearly leading somewhere, anticipating an arrival. The arrival, of course, is the return to E minor and the opening theme, now played by the orchestra. The violin doesn't stop as it would at the end of a "normal" cadenza, but continues with its arpeggios while the orchestra plays the first theme that starts the recapitulation, giving a new and transfigured quality to the melody (see LG 42, p. 307).

🔊 LG 43   SECOND MOVEMENT: ANDANTE

At the end of the first movement, after all the instruments play their final fortissimo chord, the bassoon holds onto its B and then moves up a half step to C. Other instruments enter, each playing a half step, until we arrive at the key of the slow movement, C major. After these slightly unsettling shifting sounds, there is a sense of calm and stability when the strings begin the accompanimental figure for the main theme.

LISTENING GUIDE 43 | DVD

Mendelssohn Violin Concerto in E Minor, Op. 64, II (Andante)   8:30

DATE: 1845
GENRE: Concerto

LISTEN FOR

MELODY: Violin theme like "song without words"
HARMONY: Modulation to new key at beginning

FORM: Simple, three-part form (**ABA**)
Continuous transition from previous movement

TIME	FORM	DESCRIPTION
	Transition	
0:00		Bassoon continues its note from first movement; other instruments enter (flute, violas, violins, cellos), each moving a half step, and gradually modulating to C major and beginning the accompaniment.
	A section	
	First theme, in four phrases	
0:44	First phrase	
1:04	Second phrase	
1:24	Third phrase	Almost the same as first phrase:
1:44	Fourth phrase	Similar to second phrase, but considerably extended:
	First theme, varied	
2:13	First phrase	Violin begins a version of first phrase, much extended.
2:50	Fourth phrase	Version of last phrase, much extended.
	B section	
3:51	Transition	Violin extension leads to trill and cadence, orchestra begins with a fanfare of horns and trumpets.

(continued)

TIME	FORM	DESCRIPTION
4:09	Second theme, phrase a	Orchestra (tremolo in violins anticipates what the soloist will do).

TIME	FORM	DESCRIPTION
4:24	Second theme, phrase b	
	Phrases a and b with extension	Violin solo, playing its own tremolo accompaniment:

TIME	FORM	DESCRIPTION
4:47	Phrase a	Exchanges between orchestra and violin.
5:02	. . . extension	Solo violin; characteristic repeated rhythm from timpani.
5:22	Phrases a and b	Orchestra and violin now alternate.
5:30	. . . extension	Solo violin in double-stops alternates with phrase b in orchestra; violin extension leads back to home key of C major and reprise of **A section**.
	A section	
5:55	Return of first theme	The orchestra continues the tremolo accompaniment from middle section; only two phrases now, the last extended. Addition of pizzicato in the lower strings.
7:25	. . . extension	Violin extends last phrase.

The second movement is a straightforward three-part form, **ABA**, with a memorably lyrical beginning and ending, and a more passionate middle section. The main theme is monopolized by the solo violin, which never really shares it with the orchestra. This lovely melody is quintessential Mendelssohn; it might come from one of his *Songs without Words* for solo piano.

The middle section, moving to different keys and somewhat more agitated than the first theme, features alternations between violin and orchestra, and more of the multiple-string playing described earlier. There is also an impressive passage in octaves for the soloist. When the main melody finally returns, it is still played by the violin, which now performs some of the music in a very high register (see LG 43, p. 309).

THIRD MOVEMENT: ALLEGRO MOLTO VIVACE

 LG 44

A little **intermezzo** (a term meaning interlude), marked *Allegretto non troppo* (not too fast), in which the violin seems to meditate wistfully on three repeated notes reminiscent of the opening of the first movement's main theme, leads without interruption into the last movement (*Allegro molto vivace* means very fast).

A brass fanfare, like the beginning of a great triumphal march, introduces the elfin, scherzo-like main theme of the finale. This sound is one of Mendelssohn's specialties; he used it to represent the fairy world of Shakespeare's *Midsummer Night's Dream*, in the scherzo movements of much of his chamber music, and in many other works.

Ⓢ Mendelssohn: *A Midsummer Night's Dream,* Scherzo

The third movement is a sonata form in E major, contrasting with the E minor of the first movement. The skittering first theme contrasts with the almost pompous second theme (which confirms the solemnity of the opening fanfare). Despite their different characters, the second theme is interspersed with figures from the first; in addition, Mendelssohn finds brilliant ways to make the two themes intertwine in the G-major development section.

The recapitulation adds sprightly new countermelodies to the now familiar material, and an exciting coda includes a bravura section showing off the violinist's trills, while the woodwinds reprise the opening melody. The concerto comes to a close with a sweeping arpeggio from the violin (see LG 44, p. 312).

How Did It Go?

The premiere was considered sufficiently newsworthy to attract members of the press from far and wide. The local reviewer for the influential music journal *Allgemeine musikalische Zeitung* praised the work in carefully measured terms: "Mendelssohn's as yet unpublished Violin Concerto struck us immediately on first hearing as a dignified and attractive work, as we are accustomed to expect from the pen of the revered master."

A writer named Herrmann Hirschbach disagreed, dismissing the Violin Concerto as trite and lightweight (a criticism that was frequently leveled against Mendelssohn's music):

> Mendelssohn has rather too little human pain in his pieces; they are mostly music for those who are as fortunate as he. . . . This concerto is a work on a declining trajectory. . . . [It] is a well-made and not very difficult piece in E in three movements (the first movement is in the minor, the second in C, the third in E major), but which in respect of invention presents me with nothing impressive. The ideas are too superficial; straightaway, with the theme of the first movement, one feels that the composer is not serious about seriousness, the theme of the Andante is uninteresting, and that of the last movement displays only contrived cheerfulness.

On the other hand, no less a composer (and critic) than Robert Schumann reportedly congratulated David on having performed a concerto that he himself would like to have written.

Two weeks after the premiere, a contrite but ecstatic David wrote to Mendelssohn:

> I should have reported to you long ago about the result of my first public performance of your violin concerto; forgive me that I do so only now. It pleased extraordinarily;

LISTENING GUIDE 44 Ⓢ | DVD

Mendelssohn Violin Concerto in E Minor, Op. 64, III
(Allegro molto vivace) 7:15

DATE: 1845
GENRE: Concerto

LISTEN FOR

MELODY: Meditative intermezzo at beginning
TEXTURE: Mendelssohn's characteristic "scherzo" sound

SCORING: Intertwining of themes in development and recapitulation sections

TIME	FORM	DESCRIPTION
	Transition	
0:00	Transition to last movement	Violin muses wistfully on 3 repeated notes reminiscent of the opening of the first movement's main theme.
0:46	Introduction, E major!	Loud fanfares from brass, quick, quiet arpeggios from the violin.
	Exposition	
0:58	First theme, E major	Mendelssohn's signature elfin, scherzo-like sound; delicate woodwind accompaniment. A fairly typical **AABA** phrase-shape (not shown here), with extensions before the return to **A**:
1:48	Transition	Violin patterns; orchestra uses motives from first theme.
2:10	Second theme, B major	A quick alternation of fanfare and violin figure from the first theme:
2:46	Closing theme	Solo violin becomes more lyrical, while orchestra continues material from first theme.
	Development	
2:54	Section 1	Based on second theme; winds and brass play versions of second theme (later, strings take over) while violin has rapid scales, then chords and pizzicato; modulates through various keys.
3:26	Section 2	Based on opening theme (but now in G major); violin begins the theme, then plays a new lyrical countermelody whose opening rhythm is based on opening fanfare:
3:53	Section 3	Orchestra plays the countermelody; violin figurations based on opening theme. Violin leads back to . . .

	Recapitulation	
4:17	First theme, E major	Violin now accompanied by the lyrical countermelody from the development:

4:38	Transition	
4:44	Second theme, E major	
5:15	Closing theme	

	Coda	
6:13		Begins like the development; features bold trills in violin, including one that is sustained while a version of the second theme is played. Toward the end, the more lyrical closing theme is now fortissimo, with very high notes from violin; then an excited rush to the end, based on the opening of the second theme.

everyone said it was one of the most beautiful pieces in this genre; but it also fulfills all the requirements that can be demanded of a concert piece to the highest degree, and players of the violin cannot thank you enough for this gift. I above all have you to thank, since I am not a little proud to have brought such a work before the public for the first time. All that I can tell you about my playing is that I had no accidents, and that I was so well prepared that I did not have to think about mechanical things, but could give myself completely to the performance. According to all reports the solo violin could be clearly heard, even in the places with the thickest instrumentation. The additional small changes and simplifications that you found for the solo part, I had to use, in order to be able to play without any embarrassment; I beg you to forgive it if they don't have your approval, but it was too important for me that I play as impeccably as possible. May the success of this work be so great that you will someday once again think of us poor fiddlers.

Mendelssohn wrote no more solo music for "fiddlers" in the remaining two and a half years of his life, although he did compose a magnificent string quartet in which the violin naturally features prominently. David and Gade were among the pallbearers at the composer's funeral in 1847. Years later, a statue of Mendelssohn was erected in front of the Gewandhaus; an angel playing the violin stood at its base (see Figure 11.10).

The Violin Concerto Then and Now

Mendelssohn's contemporaries immediately recognized the Violin Concerto as a masterpiece. Thanks to the artistry of Ferdinand David and other violinists, it won a secure place in the hearts of music lovers from which it has never been dislodged. It is in the repertory of every concert violinist, and is one of a small number of Mendelssohn's works that everyone acknowledges as a masterpiece.

Today visitors to Leipzig can tour the house where Mendelssohn and his family

FIG. 11.10 A replica of the monument to Felix Mendelssohn in front of the Leipzig Gewandhaus; the original was destroyed in the Nazi era.

spent the last two years of his life. (They moved there in the fall of 1845, several months after the premiere of the concerto.) The bronze statue of the composer that once stood at the entrance of the Gewandhaus was melted down by the Nazis in 1936 as part of their campaign of anti-Semitic terror (in 2009 a modern replica was unveiled near the Thomaskirche; see figure at left). Performances of Mendelssohn's music, along with that of other composers of Jewish extraction, were proscribed in Germany during the Third Reich (1933–45).

Mendelssohn's posthumous persecution is ironic in light of his childhood conversion to Christianity, the sincerity of his religious faith, and his habit of heading his compositions with a prayer. Yet the composer could never forget that his Jewish background set him apart from other Germans, even in the eyes of his closest friends. His genius and popularity did not prevent him from being targeted by anti-Semites in the nineteenth and twentieth centuries, notably Richard Wagner, whose virulently racist tract *Judaism in Music* (1850) was read by Adolf Hitler and his followers.

But the Nazi period could not remove Mendelssohn from his permanent niche in the musical pantheon, and the Violin Concerto is one of his greatest works. It combines his gift for singing melody, his ability to produce brilliant, glittering music (as in the last movement), and his perfect sense of form. It has both the rollicking energy of some of his other perennial favorites—the *Midsummer Night's Dream* Overture and the *Italian* Symphony—and the lyrical beauty of his *Songs without Words*.

Mendelssohn has sometimes been called the Romantic Mozart—he is brilliant, full of playfulness, and a consummate craftsman, just like Mozart. But he is a also a composer whose contribution to the Romantic music of the nineteenth century is unforgettable and stands on its own, without need of comparison. Mendelssohn's Violin Concerto has been a cornerstone of the repertory ever since David gave the first performance. Violinists never tire of learning to play it, and audiences never fail to love listening to it.

Chapter Review

Summary of Musical Styles

- A **concerto** is a piece, usually in three movements, for one or more solo instruments with orchestra. A typical Romantic concerto used first-movement concerto form, then a three-part **ABA** form for the second movement, and the sonata form for the finale.

- **Virtuosity** is a feature of all concertos; the soloist provides spectacular feats of difficulty to counterbalance the large volume of the orchestra.

Mendelssohn's Violin Concerto has some unusual features:

- The three movements are connected so that they are played without a pause.
- The first movement, rather than beginning with an exposition for orchestra alone, begins with an exposition for violin and orchestra together.
- The **cadenza**, instead of coming at the end of the first movement, comes nearer its center, at the end of the **development** section.

Some general characteristics of Mendelssohn's musical style include

- a sense of elegance and balance;
- a gift for lyrical, songlike melody;
- an ability to create light, quick, elfin-sounding music.

⊛ Multimedia Resources and Review Materials on StudySpace

Visit wwnorton.com/studyspace for review of Chapter 11.

What Do You Know?

Check the facts for this chapter. Take the online **Quiz**.

What Do You Hear?

Listening Quizzes and **Music Activities** will help you understand the musical works in this chapter.

⦿ Author Videos

- Basic techniques in violin playing
- A demonstration of violin virtuosity in Mendelssohn's Violin Concerto

Interactive Listening Guides

LG 42   Mendelssohn: Violin Concerto in E Minor, Op. 64, I (Allegro molto appassionato)

LG 43   Mendelssohn: Violin Concerto in E Minor, Op. 64, II (Andante)

LG 44   Mendelssohn: Violin Concerto in E Minor, Op. 64, III (Allegro molto vivace)

Flashcards (Terms to Know)

arpeggio	slur
cadenza	tremolo
double-stop	vibrato
intermezzo	virtuosity

CHAPTER 12

SATURDAY, MARCH 29, 1862, PARIS:

Clara Schumann Performs Robert Schumann's *Carnaval*

◐ **CORE REPERTOIRE**	◉ **AUTHOR VIDEOS**
▪ **LG 45** *Carnaval*, "Préambule" ▪ **LG 46** *Carnaval*, "Arlequin" ▪ **LG 47** *Carnaval*, "Eusebius" ▪ **LG 48** *Carnaval*, "Florestan" ▪ **LG 49** *Carnaval*, "Chopin" ▪ **LG 50** *Carnaval*, "Pause" and "Marche des Davidsbündler contre les Philistins"	▪ The Sphinxes and the A-S-C-H motive in Schumann's *Carnaval*

Introduction

> *"A masquerade is perhaps the most perfect form in which life can enact the fancies of poetry. . . . All things which are normally separate from each other, even the different seasons and religions, those who are friends and those who are enemies, are drawn into a single, vibrant, happy circle."*
>
> —Jean Paul, *Flegeljahre*, 1804–05

In this chapter, we will meet one of greatest pianists of the nineteenth century and listen to one of the most beloved and characteristically Romantic compositions for solo piano. The pianist is not the composer, but the two people together make one of the most interesting and productive Romantic partnerships—that of the composer Robert Schumann and his wife, the virtuoso pianist Clara Wieck.

Clara's performance, an 1862 recital in the concert hall of the Paris piano manufacturing company Érard, featured works of her husband Robert, including his *Carnaval*, a charming collection of short pieces that he had written and published some years before and that might have been familiar to some in the audience.

Clara was a published composer and the first woman to break into the world of touring piano virtuosos that was such an important part of nineteenth-century musical culture. A tireless champion of Robert's music, both before and after their marriage, Clara gave the first performances of many of his most successful works. Their names are inextricably linked, not only as husband and wife, but also as composer and interpreter.

Romantic partnership

The piano was the solo instrument par excellence of the Romantic period. Under the fingers of a wizard like Franz Liszt, it was all but transformed into a symphony orchestra. According to a contemporary account, Liszt once conducted the "March to the Scaffold" from Berlioz's *Fantastic Symphony*, then "sat down and played his own arrangement for the piano alone, of the same movement, with an effect even surpassing that of the full orchestra, and creating an indescribable *furore*." Virtuoso pianists were the musical superstars of their day, celebrated far and wide for their astonishing technique and consummate showmanship.

ⓢ Berlioz, arr. Liszt: *Fantastic Symphony*, II

Robert Schumann's *Carnaval* is a series of piano pieces tied together by their overarching literary theme and by shared musical material. The pieces in *Carnaval*, like those in Schumann's other such collections (*Papillons*, *Noveletten*, *Davidsbündlertänze*, *Album für die Jugend*), are charming and short, with descriptive and often fanciful titles. Such brief, evocative compositions are often called **character pieces**. Like similar music by Mendelssohn, Schubert, Brahms, and others, these works, often in a songlike lyrical style form, were intended for private entertainment as much as for public performance and were an important element of nineteenth-century music-making.

Character pieces

Some of the pieces in *Carnaval* are named after people Schumann knew, some after characters associated with Carnival (the festive season that precedes Lent in the church calendar), and two after well-known composers whom he admired. Schumann imagines that they are all guests at a masked ball, dancing to the accompaniment of lively music; many of the movements are in dance rhythms. It is this

FIG. 12.1 Clara Wieck Schumann, in a photograph taken in 1850.

ⓢ R. Schumann: Piano Sonata in F♯ Minor, I (theme from Clara's *Dance of the Phantoms*)

ⓢ C. Schumann: Piano Trio, IV (Allegretto)

FIG. 12.2 Friedrich Wieck, pianist and teacher, father of Clara Wieck; he taught both Clara and Robert Schumann, and vigorously opposed their marriage.

vivid work that Clara Schumann chose to close her piano recital in Paris in 1862, six years after Robert's death and almost three decades after *Carnaval* was composed. The path to that recital is a complicated story, as we will see, but well worth the journey.

CLARA SCHUMANN (1819–1896)

Clara Wieck (see Figure 12.1) transformed herself from a child prodigy into an international celebrity. Under the stern eye of her father, Friedrich Wieck (see Figure 12.2)—who managed her training, and also her career, until she came of age—she soon became a seasoned concert artist. After her parents divorced in 1824, she remained in the custody of her father. He arranged her formal debut at the Leipzig Gewandhaus (see Chapter 11) at age eleven, and together they set out to conquer Paris, Vienna, and the other musical capitals of Europe. Clara was made an honorary chamber musician to the imperial Austrian court and was highly esteemed by the leading musicians of the day.

She was also making a name for herself as a composer. It was common for piano virtuosos in the nineteenth century to write music for themselves to play. Most of it, however, consisted of bravura showpieces of questionable artistic merit. Clara, who early in her career had reveled in such dazzling stuff, now regarded this frivolity—and the keyboard antics that often accompanied it—as unmusical and undignified. As her experience and repertory grew, she became ever more determined to be accepted as a serious artist. Certainly she was taken seriously as a composer, not least by Robert, who valued her advice and paid her the ultimate compliment of quoting liberally from her music in his own works. In the first movement of his Op. 11 Piano Sonata, for example, a skipping theme borrowed from Clara's *Dance of the Phantoms* flits capriciously from one voice to another.

Despite her aversion to virtuosity for its own sake, young Clara produced her share of audience-pleasers: her debut recital at the Leipzig Gewandhaus featured a brilliant set of variations on a theme of her own creation, and her early Piano Concerto reflects the dramatic streak of a preternaturally self-confident teenager. But Clara also composed introspective character pieces reminiscent of the piano miniatures that both Robert and Frédéric Chopin were writing at the time. In later years she composed some wonderful songs and an intense, moody piano trio that many people consider her masterpiece.

Beginning in 1835, the mutual attraction between Clara and Robert became a matter of growing concern to her father. Wieck did his best to keep the young lovers apart by sending Clara to Dresden (where she continued to correspond with Robert, and even met him in secret). A period during which she was performing in different locations, as arranged by her father, resulted in minimal contact between them and left both of them despondent. Then, in 1839, they initiated a prolific correspondence, full of promises of love and expressions of Clara's conflicted feelings (see Clara to Robert, p. 319). Their epistolary courtship suited Robert perfectly. Surprisingly for someone so effusively articulate in both words and music, he often found himself tongue-tied in conversation.

Although Wieck recognized Robert's exceptional musical talent, he remained implacably opposed to the match and threatened to disinherit Clara if they married. Because by law Clara was too young to marry without her father's consent, a long series of lawsuits, court appearances, and legal entanglements ensued, in the course of which Wieck made formal allegations about Robert's mental instability, chronic drunkenness, and other faults. The acrimonious legal wrangling finally came to an end in August 1840, when Wieck was defeated in court. The lovers wasted no time: their long-delayed wedding took place in the village church at Schönefeld, near Leipzig, on September 12, a day before Clara's twenty-first birthday.

The Schumanns were a famously devoted couple (see Figure 12.3). They maintained a "marriage diary" together; they studied music and read novels and poetry together; they collaborated, at Robert's urging, on the joint publication of a volume of songs. Maintaining a two-career household was not always easy, however, especially after Clara and Robert settled down and began having children. They often disagreed about which concert tours she should undertake and whether he should go along. Although her father had managed her career from the beginning, since their disagreement and her 1839 trip to Paris she had been independent of his guidance. She must have found her husband's attempts to adjust her plans trying; Robert, however, wished to assume the role of sole breadwinner, and also suffered emotionally in her absences. She in turn made serious efforts to promote his music, even though Robert's pieces were not always the best-received items on her programs.

Clara continued to perform and occasionally to compose under her married name, while also devoting much of her time to her husband's career and their eight children (one of whom died in infancy).

Starting in late January 1854, Robert was driven to distraction by "painful aural disturbances" that he heard in his head. After unsuccessfully trying to kill himself by jumping into the Rhine River, he asked to be committed to a private asylum near Bonn. There he received visits from Brahms, the violinist Joseph Joachim, and other friends, but not from Clara: the doctors warned that her presence might cause a severe relapse. At last, hearing that Robert was gravely ill, she hurried to his bedside. She fed him, and thought he recognized her. Robert died two days later, on July 29, 1856.

For the next forty years, Clara loyally dedicated herself to the memory of her husband. She continued to play Robert's music on her recitals (at which she invariably wore widow's black) and edited a complete edition of his works in collaboration with Brahms. Although she herself stopped composing, she became an exceptional teacher and an even more famous performer. Over the years she played hundreds of concerts throughout Europe, finally retiring in 1891, at the age of seventy-two. By the end of her long life, Clara was seen as a model of the sort of artist who puts the music foremost and uses technique in the service of high art rather than of shallow entertainment.

Clara to Robert, April 1839

My father must be quite unhappy sometimes; he is to be pitied, and secretly I worry about it, but I can't do anything about it. People will probably say one day that I brought on my father's death—the One above will forgive me; haven't I fulfilled all my duties to him? And shouldn't you love your husband more than anything else? Oh Robert, forgive me if, later on, I am sometimes overcome by sudden melancholy thoughts about my father—it's so painful! Let me kiss you now—and come what may, I won't forsake you, and you will remain true to me, too. If you are mad at me, do tell me; you don't have to hide anything from me, even if it might make me sad. I'll always be your faithful wife, ten years from now, twenty years from now, and in all eternity—my love will never fade, nor my devotion! You will learn that yet.

FIG. 12.3 Robert and Clara Schumann, by Eduard Kaiser, from 1847.

The Setting

ROBERT SCHUMANN

Robert Schumann first met Clara in 1828, when she was nine years old and he was eighteen. Both were pupils of her father, Friedrich Wieck. At the time, Robert's ambition was to become a concert pianist, but by 1832 he had abandoned those plans and decided to make his mark as a composer and critic instead (see biography, below).

Ernestine von Fricken   In the summer of 1834, a young girl named Ernestine von Fricken (see Figure 12.4) arrived to study with Wieck. Schumann became infatuated with her, and before long they were secretly engaged. (Then but fifteen, Clara was not yet in Schumann's romantic sights.) When Baron von Fricken caught wind of the affair, he rushed to Leipzig and brought her home to the town of Asch. Schumann discovered that Ernestine was not the daughter of the wealthy baron, as she had claimed—although the baron took responsibility for her—but the illegitimate child of another man. By the next summer the engagement was off. As we will see, however, Schumann's immortalized first love is a major component of *Carnaval*.

ROBERT SCHUMANN (1810–1856)

Schumann was a performer, writer, and composer. In his own lifetime he was influential as all three, but he is remembered now for his compositions, especially his piano works and songs; there are also symphonies, chamber works, an opera, and other large-scale pieces. His music journal *Neue Zeitschrift für Musik* influenced the course of music in the Romantic period. Schumann's complex inner life, which he expressed in his music and in his journalism, was represented in a series of personalities, or characters, which corresponded to different facets of his psyche.

At the University of Leipzig he was supposedly studying law, but Schumann continued to devote himself to literature and, increasingly, music. He took lessons with the famous teacher Friedrich Wieck, through whom he met all of musical Leipzig, including the teacher's daughter Clara, whose public career would outshine his, and who would become his muse, wife, agent, editor, and heir.

Increasing literary activity with the *Neue Zeitschrift für Musik*, and increasing activity as a composer, made up for the unfortunate injury to his right hand that caused Schumann to abandon plans for a professional career as a pianist.

The Schumanns, who married in 1840, lived in Leipzig,

Dresden, and Düsseldorf, sometimes touring for Clara's performing career. Robert was at times depressed but then would recover and become very productive. Over the years, these swings would become more and more extreme.

Poor health and disputes with his musicians and his employers led to the end of his position as music director in Düsseldorf, and after a tour in the Netherlands with Clara in late 1854 Robert's condition became so bad that he was confined to an asylum, where he died in 1856.

Schumann's career was characterized by frenzies of inspired composition, often in a particular genre: songs (1840), symphonies (1841), chamber music (1842–43), oratorio, dramatic music, and church music. His symphonies and chamber music are among the treasures of the modern standard repertory.

Ⓢ Schumann: "Im leuchtendem Sommermorgen," from *Dichterliebe*
Ⓢ Schumann: Symphony No. 1, IV
Ⓢ Schumann: Piano Quintet, I

MAJOR WORKS: Orchestral works, including 4 symphonies and 1 piano concerto; various chamber works; over 300 piano works, including *Papillons*, *Carnaval*, and *Album für die Jugend* (*Album for the Young*); about 300 songs, including 2 song cycles: *Dichterliebe* (*The Poet's Love*) and *Frauenliebe und -leben* (*Women's Love and Life*); and 1 opera.

Ernestine was not the only reason that the year 1834 was so important in Schumann's life. It was also the year in which he was instrumental in founding the *Neue Zeitschrift für Musik* (New Journal for Music), an influential musical magazine that he wrote and edited almost single-handedly for the next decade. He became one of the foremost composer-critics of his day (Berlioz was another), and helped shape the musical taste and style of the Romantic era. In an early editorial, he expressed his admiration for Bach, Beethoven, and other masters, curtly dismissed the music of the recent past as trivial and mechanical, and promised to "prepare for and hasten the advent of a new, poetic future."

Schumann divided his musical contemporaries into three groups: classicists, middle-of-the road conservatives (he also referred to them, less flatteringly, as Philistines), and romantics. Among the latter—those on whom his hopes for the future rested—he counted Frédéric Chopin (see Figure 12.5), Felix Mendelssohn (see Chapter 11), and himself. (Schumann's estimate of himself turned out to be about right.) Over the years he introduced the readers of the *Neue Zeitschrift* to forward-looking composers like Berlioz and Brahms (see Schumann Praises the Young Johannes Brahms, p. 322).

In 1835, a few months after putting the finishing touches on *Carnaval,* Schumann met both Chopin and Mendelssohn; their richly poetic **piano miniatures** had provided a model for his own. Schumann's close friendship with Mendelssohn lasted until the latter's death in 1847. Chopin—whom he famously hailed as a "genius" in 1831—was one of the influences that led Schumann to envision a musical style capable of combining two apparently irreconcilable qualities: the fluid virtuosity then fashionable in piano playing, and the poetic intimacy of the miniature so popular among Romantic composers.

FIG. 12.4 Ernestine von Fricken, with whom Robert Schumann was briefly in love and who was one of the inspirations for his *Carnaval.*

Ⓢ Chopin: Prelude, Op. 28, No. 11

THE LEAGUE OF DAVID

Combining his literary and musical talents, Schumann created an imaginary world peopled with good and evil characters. He dreamed up a band of crusaders dedicated to defeating those he termed musical Philistines. Florestan and Eusebius were the ringleaders of this imaginary *Davidsbund,* or League of David. Florestan was the extroverted, lighthearted enthusiast, while Eusebius was moody, reflective, and even a little depressive. Representing the two sides of Schumann's own character, they appeared regularly in the pages of the *Neue Zeitschrift für Musik*, signing articles and carrying on earnest conversations. Other members of the league who made occasional appearances included Master Raro (modeled on Friedrich Wieck) and Chiarina (a thinly disguised Clara).

In the preface to his collected writings, Schumann explained that he invented these "contrasting artist-characters" in order to "express different points of view on artistic matters." Various members of the League of David are brought to life not only in Schumann's writings, but also in his music. Many of his compositions play on the personalities of his fictitious alter egos. In *Carnaval,* for instance, Eusebius is depicted in a calm, meditative adagio, while a restlessly driving waltz mirrors Florestan's impetuousness: accented **cross-rhythms** (the effect of two meters at once) and syncopations are prominent, contributing to a strong sense of metric ambiguity. Schumann's musical portrait of sixteen-year-old Clara is a fiery outburst, labeled *Passionato,* an unmistakable sign of the powerful attraction she held for the young composer.

FIG. 12.5 Frédéric Chopin (1810–1849), eminent composer and pianist, subject of one of the miniatures in *Carnaval.*

Schumann Praises the Young Johannes Brahms

Sitting at the piano, he proceeded to reveal to us wondrous regions. We were drawn into circles of ever deeper enchantment. His playing, too, was full of genius, and transformed the piano into an orchestra of wailing and jubilant voices. There were sonatas, rather veiled symphonies—songs, whose poetry one would understand without knowing the words . . . single pianoforte pieces, partly demoniacal, of the most graceful form—then sonatas for violin and piano—quartets for strings—and every one so different from the rest that each seemed to flow from a separate source.

Musical milieu

PARIS IN 1862

Paris in the mid-nineteenth century was the undisputed center of European musical life, though Vienna might disagree, and cities like Leipzig and St. Petersburg were rapidly developing as musical centers; London had been one since the eighteenth century. France's king Louis-Philippe had been overthrown in 1848, a victim of the same revolutionary wave in Europe that swept Richard Wagner into exile in Switzerland (see Chapter 13). Under the rule of Napoleon III, nephew of the Emperor Napoleon Bonaparte, Paris was on the threshold of its dramatic transformation into the modern metropolis that Stravinsky would know in the early twentieth century (see Chapter 15). An expansion of the city limits in 1860 swelled the population to 1.6 million, more than twice its size at the premiere of Berlioz's *Fantastic Symphony* thirty years earlier.

At the time of Clara Schumann's visit, ground had just been broken for a magnificent new opera house, the Palais Garnier. (It finally opened in 1875 and is still used for performances; see Figure 12.6.) Charles Gounod's *Faust*, premiered three years earlier at the Théâtre Lyrique, was on its way to becoming one of the most popular operas of all time. Berlioz, at odds with the French musical establishment, had granted the rights to his new comic opera *Béatrice et Bénédict* to an impresario in Baden-Baden, Germany. Gioacchino Rossini, in the twilight of his fabled operatic career, was living in venerable retirement in suburban Passy. The French were less hospitable to Richard Wagner: members of the elite Jockey Club had disrupted the Paris premiere of *Tannhäuser* in 1861 with a barrage of whistles and catcalls (see Figure 12.7).

Despite such outbreaks of cultural chauvinism, Paris retained an irresistible allure for composers and performers from throughout the Western world.

FIG. 12.6 A nineteenth-century view of the Paris opera house, designed by the architect Charles Garnier.

FIG. 12.7 Riots in the streets of Paris outside the opera house, in response to the 1861 premiere of Richard Wagner's opera *Tannhaüser*. This is an illustration on an advertising card for meat extract.

Parisian music lovers had a special affinity for the piano, and the city was home to scores of piano manufacturers, all vying to promote their own products and artists. Since at least the 1830s, Paris had been a peak destination of traveling piano soloists. Audiences repeatedly turned out to hear their favorite virtuosos. None too discriminating in their tastes, they cheered Liszt's barnstorming exhibitionism as enthusiastically as Chopin's pearly-toned refinement. Liszt, whose spellbinding technique at first awed and later repelled the Schumanns, had set new standards for visiting pianists since he gave his first solo recitals in Paris in the 1840s (see The Solo Recital, p. 324).

Clara had played to Parisian audiences since she was twelve years old. On her first visit (1831–32) to Paris, which she made with her father, she didn't get far there; her relatively modest playing style did not attract much attention in a city with a highly competitive piano-music scene. But she was by nature resolutely high-minded and did not reciprocate the Parisians' notoriously fickle admiration. "The better one gets to know the people," she wrote to Robert in 1839, on her second trip (made without her father), "the more one detests their frivolousness, their vapid philandering, their ignoble feelings—oh, I just can't stand it! At social gatherings they sit around the fireplace after supper and talk about the most uninteresting things—I could die from anger." By 1862, however, her opinion of the French had improved considerably, perhaps because they had finally come to share her enthusiasm for Robert's music. As she reported to Brahms,

Clara's first visit

Clara's second visit

> The magnificence of the scenery [at the Opéra] beggars description, it is often like magic, but the opera takes from 4 to 5 hours, it never ends before midnight. The whole manner of life here is dreadful, one goes to a party about 9:30, and towards 11 the music begins; we are seldom home before 1 o'clock. I could not stand it for long, perhaps not at all if it were not that I am greeted on all sides with a warmth and ready kindness which cannot but make me happy, not to speak of the great appreciation for Robert's works, which are far better known here than I had thought.

On this occasion—the March 29 concert in 1862—Clara performed in the Salle Érard, a small recital hall owned by the Érard company, a leading manufacturer of pianos and harps. (Paris had—and has—a number of such intimate, purpose-built halls, including the Salle Pleyel and Salle Herz.) Long and narrow, with ornate neo-classical paintings adorning the walls, the elegant, shoebox-style auditorium was designed to showcase not only star performers but also instruments—in this case, the prized Érard grand piano, with its patented double-escapement action (see The Pianoforte, p. 325) that had revolutionized piano making in the early nineteenth century.

CHOOSING A PIANO

Clara was sometimes frustrated with the pianos she found in Paris; indeed, one of the continuing annoyances of her career as a soloist was the unreliable quality of the instruments provided on her tours. This is still a problem for pianists today, but in the nineteenth century the rapidly evolving technology of piano manufacturing meant that, in principle at least, performers had a much wider range of pianos to choose among (see The Pianoforte, p. 325). Finding the right instrument was often a matter of luck and perseverance. Even if the piano was well maintained—something that experience had taught Clara not to count on—it might not be the kind she preferred.

Of the French-style pianos, Clara's favorite was the Pleyel—a preference she shared with Chopin: he felt he could make his own sound on it, while the Érard

The Solo Recital

Before the mid-nineteenth century, solo recitals as we know them today were practically unknown. A typical concert program for, say, one of the *Academies* in Beethoven's Vienna (see Chapter 8) was a combination of solo and ensemble, vocal and instrumental pieces. Even the most famous pianists and violinists shared billing with various "assisting artists" as a matter of course. Audiences were accustomed to variety, and it was thought that they wouldn't tolerate two hours of music played by a single musician, no matter how skilled or charismatic.

Franz Liszt changed all that, starting in the late 1830s. Liszt's transcendent virtuosity on the piano was guaranteed to hold an audience's attention (see Figure 12.8); perhaps, too, music lovers were hungry for a new kind of concert experience. At any rate, he made his intentions clear by advertising one of his concerts as a "musical soliloquy." Later, in London, he announced that he would give a "recital"—and the term stuck.

The novelty value of such events was still fresh when Liszt gave his first unassisted recital in Paris, on March 27, 1841, at the Salle Érard. "Twenty-five years ago such an attempt would have been impossible," one critic observed, but in this case "the artist emerged victorious." Liszt had a healthy ego and seized the opportunity to nurture his growing personality cult. Like a modern pop star, he often stepped down from the stage between numbers to mingle with his legions of adoring fans. "The concert," he declared, "is—myself."

In an age preoccupied with virtuosity and individualism, it is not surprising that the solo recital caught on quickly. Yet the old-fashioned mixed programs did not disappear overnight. As late as 1855, Clara Schumann was advised that "in England, they must always have so many expensive singers at concerts that they will not

always give Pianistes as much as they deserve." Recitals, then as now, were the test of a performer's range and ability. As one of Clara's pupils remarked after hearing her play a pair of recitals in the 1860s, she "gave a full exhibition of her powers in every kind of music."

Ⓢ Liszt: *Transcendental Etudes*, No. 4, "Mazeppa"

FIG. 12.8 This nineteenth-century caricature of Franz Liszt shows him with multiple arms and hands, a humorous comment on his dramatic and dazzling keyboard prowess.

The Pianoforte

A **pianoforte** (usually shortened to **piano**) is a keyboard instrument in which the strings are struck with padded wooden hammers that the player activates by depressing the keys. Unlike the harpsichord that Bach played, which plucks the strings with a uniform sound no matter how hard the player strikes the key, the piano sounds softer or louder depending on the player's touch. (In fact, the instrument takes its name from the Italian words *piano* and *forte*, meaning soft and loud.)

The heart of the piano is the *action* (see Figure 12.9), the mechanism that transmits the touch of the player's finger on the key to the hammer. The key throws the hammer up toward the strings. The hammer then strikes the strings, bounces off, and returns to rest; this motion is called the "escapement." As long as the hammer is in motion, it is not available for a new keystroke, which of course makes it difficult to play rapidly repeated notes. In the "double-escapement" action that Sébastien Érard invented in 1821, however, the hammer can be reengaged by the key *before* it falls back to rest, thus enabling the pianist to play repeated notes quickly and lightly.

Although the piano is essentially a string instrument, it also has some characteristics of the percussion family: for each note the pianist plays, the hammer strikes several strings (usually three) tuned in unison. A felt damper (which prevents the strings from vibrating) is raised whenever the appropriate key is depressed, and returns to position when the key is released. In this way, the player can control the precise length of time the note sounds.

For added resonance, a **sustaining pedal** raises all the dampers at the same time before any notes are struck. Another pedal shifts the entire set of hammers sideways, so that they strike only one or two of the strings for each note, with a corresponding reduction in volume. Some grand pianos are also equipped with a third pedal, which acts like a sustaining pedal, except that it raises the dampers (and thus prolongs the sound) of only those notes that are already being produced. Beethoven, Schumann, Chopin, and other Romantic composers used the pedals to produce a wide variety of imaginative special effects.

In the late eighteenth and nineteenth centuries, various traditions of piano manufacture—principally Viennese, English, and French—vied for dominance and superiority, each emphasizing a different aspect of the instrument.

Throughout Clara Schumann's career, pianos steadily increased in size and volume. Thicker strings required heavier hammers and higher tension in order to produce an ever more robust sound. Central to Clara's concerns as performer and teacher was the development of a range and control of touch, with the strength to produce tone on these larger pianos, but the delicacy for expressive playing.

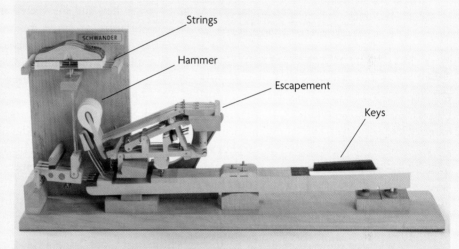

FIG. 12.9 Model of a grand piano, showing the action for three keys.

pianos made the sound for him. But choosing a piano in Paris was not simply a matter of musical taste; political sensitivities involving sponsors were in the mix as well, as Clara wrote to Robert in 1839:

> I have an Érard in my room which I can barely play; I had lost all heart, but yesterday I played on a Pleyel, and they are a lot easier. I have to practice three more weeks before I can play a single note in public. I could have three grand pianos in my room already—everyone wants me to use his. If only I knew what to do. I would like to play on the Pleyel without offending Érard who has done me every favor imaginable. I might have to play on both of them at the same time. We will probably put a Pleyel in my bedroom—but then I will no longer be able to move around.

She ultimately did play on an Érard piano on her 1839 visit.

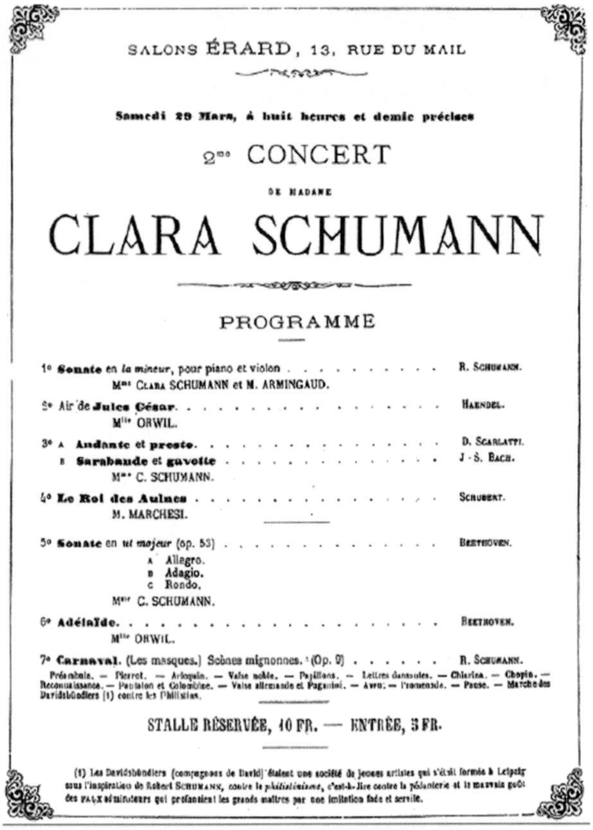
SALONS ÉRARD, 13, RUE DU MAIL

Samedi 29 Mars, à huit heures et demie précises

2me CONCERT

DE MADAME

CLARA SCHUMANN

PROGRAMME

1° **Sonate** en *la mineur*, pour piano et violon . . . . . R. SCHUMANN.
Mme CLARA SCHUMANN et M. ARMINGAUD.

2° Air de **Jules César** . . . . . HAENDEL.
Mlle ORWIL.

3° A **Andante et presto** . . . . . D. SCARLATTI.
B **Sarabande et gavotte** . . . . . J.-S. BACH.
Mme C. SCHUMANN.

4° **Le Roi des Aulnes** . . . . . SCHUBERT.
M. MARCHESI.

5° **Sonate** en *ut majeur* (op. 53) . . . . . BEETHOVEN.
A Allegro.
B Adagio.
C Rondo.
Mme C. SCHUMANN.

6° **Adélaïde** . . . . . BEETHOVEN.
Mlle ORWIL.

7° **Carnaval.** (Les masques.) Scènes mignonnes. (Op. 9) . . . . . R. SCHUMANN.
Préambule. — Pierrot. — Arlequin. — Valse noble. — Papillons. — Lettres dansantes. — Chiarina. — Chopin. — Reconnaissance. — Pantalon et Colombine. — Valse allemande et Paganini. — Aveu. — Promenade. — Pause. — Marche des Davidsbündlers (1) contre les Philistins.

STALLE RÉSERVÉE, 10 FR. — ENTRÉE, 5 FR.

(1) Les Davidsbündlers (compagnons de David) étaient une société de jeunes artistes qui s'était formée à Leipzig sous l'inspiration de Robert SCHUMANN, contre le *philistinisme*, c'est-à-dire contre la pédanterie et le mauvais goût des faux admirateurs qui profanaient les grands maîtres par une imitation fade et servile.

FIG. 12.10 The printed program of Clara Schumann's concert in Paris, March 29, 1862.

The Performance

SATURDAY, MARCH 29, 1862, AT 8:30 P.M.

For her trip to Paris in 1862, Clara had been offered a fixed fee for a series of four concerts. At first she was inclined to refuse, but Madame Érard (who had succeeded her late husband as head of the firm) urged her to reconsider, arguing persuasively that Robert's music, now in vogue in Paris, would be particularly appreciated. Ultimately Clara undertook the concerts at her own financial risk, with Madame Érard providing the hall and handling the business arrangements. In this way she hoped to clear enough profit to make the trip worthwhile.

Arriving on March 6, Clara checked into her rooms at the Hôtel des États-Unis, where she was called upon by many distinguished musicians. On her previous visit it was she who had had to do the calling, but now she was a world-famous artist. Rossini, the celebrated composer of opera, came to see her, and she visited with her old friend Pauline Viardot, famous as a singer, but also a composer and pianist.

Clara's first concert (there were finally six in all) took place in the Salle Érard on March 20. The centerpiece was a performance of Robert's Quintet in E♭ Major for Piano and Strings, in which Clara was joined by the eminent Armingaud-Jacquard String Quartet, a group known especially for its performances of Beethoven and Mendelssohn. She reported to Brahms that the concert "went excellently, enormous enthusiasm being manifested after each movement of the quintet, and so on from piece to piece." Nine days later she gave a second concert, this time assisted by a violinist and singer (see Figure 12.10, the concert program). (Not until the 1870s did Clara start giving purely solo recitals.) Once again, Robert's music had pride of place. The program was as follows:

1. Robert Schumann, Violin Sonata No. 1 in A Minor
2. George Frideric Handel, aria from *Giulio Cesare*
3. Domenico Scarlatti, Andante and Presto
4. Johann Sebastian Bach, Sarabande and Gavotte
5. Schubert, *Le Roi des Aulnes* (*Der Erlkönig*)

(Intermission)

6. Ludwig van Beethoven, Piano Sonata in C Major, Op. 53
7. Beethoven, *Adelaïde*
8. Schumann, *Carnaval*

Robert's Violin Sonata in A Minor, played by Clara and violinist Jules Armingaud, was not very well received. "When he is not inspired, when passion does not say enough to him, Schumann resorts to vague harmonies which have a harsh and bizarre effect," wrote one critic. Another writer was even more scathing: "This painful work, of an interminable length, has only an andante in which one can recognize a somewhat gracious phrase; the rest is of an obscurity which is not worth illuminating." This is the sort of thing critics often say when confronted with new or unfamiliar music. Today, it is hard to believe that anyone could have described Schumann's beautiful sonata as harsh, painful, or uninspired.

Next Clara demonstrated her commitment to the old masters by playing solo pieces by Domenico Scarlatti and J. S. Bach, whom both she and Robert admired enormously. Between them Mademoiselle Orwil, a pupil of Viardot, sang a French translation of Schubert's *Erlkönig*. Orwil also sang an aria from Handel's opera *Giulio Cesare*, accompanied by Clara. The second part of the concert opened with a big piano sonata, Beethoven's Opus 53, in C major. Here Clara showed the skills for which she was famous: poise, judgment, power in the service of expression. One writer commented that her style was "dominated by force and rhythmic clarity, rather than grace and imagination. She plays wisely, squarely and with an astonishing vigor." Another critic detected a masculine quality in her playing, noting that it had "a sort of virility that sits well with the grand and grave conceptions of the German school." Clara was no ingénue, and in the works of Beethoven and Bach, she was second to none. After Mademoiselle Orwil sang Beethoven's *Adelaïde*, Clara rounded off the program with Robert's *Carnaval*.

The Music

A MUSICAL MASQUERADE

Carnaval is a musical depiction of a masked ball. It may have been inspired by the costume-ball scene in the novel *Flegeljahre* (*The Awkward Age*) by Jean Paul, one of the great literary influences on Schumann and many others in the German Romantic movement. Schumann calls his pieces *scènes mignonnes*—little or cute scenes. Their titles are in French, even in the German edition. Some are dances or marches, scenes of physical activity, of time passing, of festivity. Others show us a particular person, real or imagined. They are not, apparently, scenes in the theatrical sense of action; they are musical pictures of characters, moments, or moods. The work does encapsulate certain autobiographical narratives, such as Robert's stance against "Philistines," and his love life.

The cast of characters in Schumann's imaginary carnival features several stock figures from the Italian **commedia dell'arte**, the improvised fairground theater that had been popular since the Renaissance. They include Pierrot, a sad clown distinguished by his long white blouse; Harlequin, in his diamond-pattern costume, the sly servant of Pantalon, the simpleminded, often-deceived character; and the beautiful Columbine (see Figure 12.11).

Everyone at the ball is in some sort of costume. For those wearing masks, there is pretense, acting, a kind of freedom; people in disguise can allow themselves to do things that they would not do otherwise. Things get even more complicated when Schumann introduces musical portraits of real-life contemporaries like Clara or Ernestine, or well-known musicians like Chopin and Niccolò Paganini.

In a sense, all the characters in *Carnaval* are impersonations: they represent Schumann himself in multiple disguises. The work is a hall of mirrors, where nothing is quite real and everything is a reflection. But words are not notes; much of *Carnaval's*

FIG. 12.11 Characters from the Italian *commedia dell'arte*: Harlequin, Pierrot, and Columbine, from a French costume book of about 1850.

inventiveness springs from a purely musical source. Schumann spent hours improvising at the piano as he tried out various melodies, textures, and patterns. How his extemporized creations crystallized into compositions we cannot be sure, but we do know that they are first and foremost pieces of music, with a thrilling variety of ideas and sounds. Schumann himself said that the suggestive "literary" titles were added later:

> The pieces were finished in short order, and this of all things during the Carnival season of 1835, incidentally in a serious atmosphere and in straitened circumstances. Later I gave titles to the pieces and called the collection *Carnaval*. If there are many things in it to please one person or another, the musical moods change too quickly to be followed by a large audience, which does not want to be startled every minute.

Even the precise number of pieces seems to have remained an open question in Schumann's mind. When he offered the collection to a German publisher in 1837, under the title *Fasching: Schwänke auf vier Noten für Pianoforte von Florestan* (*Carnival: Jokes on Four Notes for Piano by Florestan*), he indicated that he had already "pruned" several movements away. (See Titles of the Pieces in *Carnaval* as It Was Published in Germany, below.) The question of whether *Carnaval* is one big piece, or a series of miniatures, is more or less put to rest by Schumann himself—it is a

Titles of the Pieces in *Carnaval* as It Was Published in Germany (1837)

Titles in italics do not appear in the French edition.
Titles is red indicate characters from the *commedia dell'arte*
Titles in orange indicate characters from the Davidsbund
Titles in blue indicate pieces whose titles are names of musicians

Préambule (Preamble)
Pierrot
Arlequin
Valse noble (Noble Waltz)
Eusebius
Florestan
Coquette
Réplique (Reply)
Papillons (Butterflies)
A. S. C. H. – S. C. H. A. (Lettres dansantes) (Dancing Letters)
Chiarina (= Clara)
Chopin
Estrella (= Ernestine von Fricken)
Reconnaissance (Gratitude)
Pantalon et Columbine
Valse allemande (German Waltz)
Paganini
Aveu (Vow)
Promenade
Pause
Marche des Davidsbündler contre les Philistins (March of the League of David against the Philistines; also called "Finale" in the French edition)

group of intimate scenes, of individual pieces; they are arranged in an agreeable order, but not in one that is immutable. Clara herself often omitted some pieces in performance. In an intimate gathering, one might play a single piece or two.

Evidently Schumann wrote more pieces that include the musical pun on the letters A-S-C-H (see below) than got included in *Carnaval,* since a number of them are recognizable in some of his later works. These may be some of the ones he pruned.

The first German edition (1837) indicated that the work was also published in Paris—and so it was, but with nine of the pieces omitted, apparently at the publisher's request. (The omissions in the French edition are italicized in the list on p. 328.) In fact, the score came out in France slightly earlier than in Germany, and *Carnaval* was for a long time much more popular in France than in the composer's native country.

Schumann's willingness to countenance various versions, and Clara's frequent omission of some of the pieces, make clear, as we've seen, that *Carnaval* was not conceived as an unalterable whole. Even Liszt, an early and enthusiastic champion of the work, excised no fewer than twelve movements when he played it in Leipzig. Apparently Schumann approved, so one wonders what *Carnaval* really is. Is it a group of charming pieces from which pianists are free to choose? Or is it a single, integrated work, what we might call a **cycle,** and if so, in what sense? Romantic notions of fragments as having particular power, and of creating a sequence with its own meaning, may go against our own ideas of the piece as a single invariable work, but we must acknowledge that to Robert, Clara, and others, the "work" is a flexible concept.

Cycle

STRUCTURE AND THEMATIC LINKS

In *Carnaval* the individual movements are linked by a motive that appears in various versions, and the whole work is framed by opening and closing movements that are related to each other, but are different in form and style from the intervening miniatures.

Much of Schumann's music, here and elsewhere, is constructed from small motives that he combines to make a kind of musical mosaic. With the exception of the opening and closing pieces of *Carnaval,* all contain some version of a musical motive based, as we learn from a letter of Robert's, on the letters of Ernestine von Fricken's hometown, Asch. The name of Asch lends itself to portrayal in music, using German nomenclature for the notes:

The Sphinxes and the A-S-C-H motive in Schumann's *Carnaval*

$A = A$

$S = E\flat$ (Es in German)

$C = C$

$H = B\natural$

By a happy coincidence, the same four letters are part of Schumann's own name, linking him with his first love. In the score of *Carnaval,* which he subtitles *Scènes mignonnes sur quatre notes* (Little Scenes on Four Notes) he prints a series of three "Sphinxes," which he surely intends to be tantalizing riddles. (In ancient Egyptian mythology, a sphinx is a mysterious hybrid creature made from parts of various animals; but Robert's is probably the sphinx of Greek mythology, who asks riddles.)

According to German names for notes, S (that is, Es) is E♭, As is A♭, and H is B♮, so that these three "Sphinxes" are S-C-H-A (these are the only musical letters in the name SCHumAnn.), As-C-H, and A-S-C-H. All three "Sphinxes" are deeply woven into the texture of *Carnaval*; we will encounter them in several of the pieces discussed in the Listening Guides of this chapter. (See Schumann Describes the Creation of *Carnaval*, below.) Interestingly, most pianists do not play the "Sphinxes," sometimes keeping a moment of silence instead.

Schumann's asides and "Sphinxes" are surely designed for the *player*, not the listener, and are there to create and reinforce the intimate dialogue between composer and player that printed music allows. The increasing number of pianos and pianists, and the expanding distribution of music, meant that nineteenth-century piano miniatures had increasing popularity, even if the actual works themselves might never be performed on a concert stage. Many more people than could have attended Clara's concert in 1862 would certainly have purchased a copy of *Carnaval*, played it had home, and been familiar with it.

QUOTATION AND SELF-QUOTATION

Here and there in *Carnaval,* Schumann quotes from his own music and that of other composers. In "Florestan," for instance, he reuses a passage from his piano cycle *Papillons* (Butterflies) of 1831 (see LG 47). The melody of a popular folk-style song known in Germany as the "Grossvatertanz" (Grandfather's Dance) appears at the end of *Papillons* and again in the last movement of *Carnaval*, where it is identified in the score as a "seventeenth-century dance"; Schumann also used it in his *Album for the Young* in 1848. Conversely, a section of "Promenade" reappears in Schumann's *Davidsbündlertänze*, published, like *Carnaval,* in 1837.

Musical quotations

Schumann may not have intended listeners to recognize such **musical quotations;** the quotations are brief, and many players and listeners would not even have heard their sources. But this sort of quotation, including quotations of Clara's compositions, seems to be part of Schumann's inspiration; and to the extent that we do recognize the quotations, we understand something of the many connections, literary and musical, that went into Schumann's creative process.

PIANISTIC VIRTUOSITY

The piano can be a very intimate instrument, appropriate for domestic music-making, accompanying songs, and delicate playing; *Carnaval* contains many such lyrical moments. At the same time, the piano (like the violin; see Chapter 11) was one of the chief vehicles of astounding virtuosity in the hands of players like Liszt, Chopin, Thalberg, and Kalkbrenner, all nineteenth-century piano wizards.

Both Clara and Robert Schumann had been schooled in a style of piano playing that stretched the performer's capacity to the limit. Clara maintained her virtuosity at the highest level, although she was know more for her fidelity to the score than for flashy playing. Robert's ambitions as a performer ended early; later in life, he wrote a number of easier works specifically for amateur players, including his best-selling *Album for the Young. Carnaval* is not a raging concerto or a dazzling

Schumann Describes the Creation of *Carnaval*

From a letter of 1837 to the pianist and composer Ignaz Moscheles:

Carnaval came into existence almost incidentally and is constructed for the most part on the notes ASCH, which make up the name of a little place in Bohemia where a musical friend of mine lived. Strangely enough, these are also the only musical letters in my own name. The titles I added later. Indeed, is not music sufficient unto itself, eloquent in itself? "Estrella" is the kind of name one would put under a portrait so as to fix it more clearly in one's memory; "Reconnaissance" is a scene of reunion, "Aveu" a declaration of love, "Promenade" a stroll such as one might take arm-in-arm with one's partner at a German ball. All this has no artistic significance. The only interest seems to me to lie in the various different spiritual states and moods.

showpiece, but it does require virtuoso technique, even if it is not called on in every moment. The passages illustrated in the box below give some idea of the challenges the pianist faces.

There are twenty-one titled pieces in *Carnaval*. Although they are all interconnected by motives and themes, most are self-contained musical creations that can stand equally well on their own. (There are four exceptions: "Paganini" and "Valse Allemande" are a pair, as are "Coquette" and "Réplique.") Each piece deserves close attention, careful study, and repeated listening. Here we will concentrate on a few delightful examples.

Virtuosity in *Carnaval*

Schumann's music makes formidable technical demands on the performer. In "Préambule," for example, he uses octaves in both hands, including intervening notes, to provide a very full sound of crashing chords:

ⓢ Schumann: *Carnaval*, "Préambule," crashing chords

Octaves are also useful in one hand to give a melody a stronger profile:

ⓢ Schumann: *Carnaval*, "Préambule," octaves

A special trick of Schumann's (though not unknown elsewhere) is illustrated in "Reconnaissance," where the right hand plays octaves, while making quick repetitions of the lower note only with thumb and forefinger:

ⓢ Schumann: *Carnaval*, "Reconnaissance"

The **arpeggio**—from the Italian word for harp—is a chord that is broken or strummed; that is, the individual notes are played one after another, from bottom to top or vice versa. An arpeggio is not necessarily difficult to play, but it always sounds impressive. The challenge in this case lies in making the arpeggio sound smooth, even, and dynamically well shaped throughout, while continuously dividing it between the left and right hands. It is a standard accompaniment figure in piano music, as in "Chopin" from *Carnaval*:

ⓢ Schumann: *Carnaval*, "Chopin"

(continued)

Virtuosity in *Carnaval* (continued)

In "Paganini," rapid "broken" octaves in the right hand, combined with very fast alternations in the left, make a dazzling display, reminiscent of Paganini's own violin virtuosity:

Ⓢ Schumann: *Carnaval*, "Paganini"

"Pantalon et Columbine" conjures the illusion of three-handed playing (another favorite technique of the 1830s), with a central melody surrounded by an alternation of bass notes below and chords above:

Ⓢ Schumann: *Carnaval*, "Pantalon et Columbine"

In "Pause," the impression is of sheer speed, right-hand arpeggios and figuration combined with very fast left-hand oom-pah alternations; there are difficult cross-rhythms and metrical shifts:

Ⓢ Schumann: *Carnaval*, "Pause"

🎙 The Sphinxes and the A-S-C-H motive in Schumann's *Carnaval*

Listening to the Music

 LG 45   **"PRÉAMBULE"**

Schumann's "preamble" is a little suite in itself, in that it consists of a series of five overlapped sections, each with its own tempo, rhythms, and themes. A halting beginning—the same notes repeated three times, in slightly different rhythms—leads to a majestic opening section—calling the dancers to the ballroom floor—that soon turns into a quick waltz. The music gradually gets faster and faster, with lively syncopations and rippling arpeggios, culminating in an almost frantic *presto*. It is a whirling, increasingly energetic introduction to the ballroom (see LG 45, p. 333).

 LG 46   **"ARLEQUIN"**

The servant Harlequin is an incorrigible trickster. His music has a funny prancing gait, characterized by irregular syncopations, and each phrase starts with a little hiccup or hee-haw. The rhythmic jerkiness contrasts with the piece's highly regular and symmetrical **ABABA** form (see LG 46, p. 335).

Schumann *Carnaval*, "Préambule" (Preamble) 2:07

DATE: 1834–35

GENRE: Character piece (within a piano cycle)

LISTEN FOR

METER: Left-hand bass-note/chord patterns sometimes not in sync with the meter

FORM: Five overlapping sections

THEMES: Upward motive (E♭ to F at the beginning); recurs many times

EXPRESSION/DYNAMICS: Increasingly rapid tempos

TIME	FORM	DESCRIPTION
	Section 1: Introduction	Quasi maestoso ("Rather majestic")
0:00	Opening phrase	Halting beginning, crashing homophonic chords; 6-bar phrase:

TIME	FORM	DESCRIPTION
0:09	Opening phrase, repeated	
0:17	Contrasting phrases	Same halting rhythm, but melody and chords are separated at first; temporary new key; two regular 4-bar phrases:

TIME	FORM	DESCRIPTION
0:30	Opening phrase, rescored	Loud syncopated low chords added.
0:39	Final phrase	Final answering phrase:

TIME	FORM	DESCRIPTION
	Section 2: First of three interconnected waltzes	
0:45	Opening phrases: upbeat octaves at beginning	Tempo speeds up; waltz rhythm, melody and accompaniment (but left-hand pattern often doesn't follow oom-pah-pah pattern). Note 3-note motive—up-down (E♭-F-E♭) of Section 1:

(continued)

TIME	FORM	DESCRIPTION
0:48	Opening phrases repeated without upbeats	Right hand in waltz time, left hand plays duple-meter pattern: oom-pah oom-pah (bass, chord, bass, chord).
0:56	Two phrases, extended to six bars by long chord with scales in left hand, with transition to	

Section 3: Second waltz

| 1:04 | Two parallel 4-bar phrases | More lyrical version of motives of Section 2; phrases begin like those of Section 2, including 3-note motive; second halves of phrases are repeated notes moving down chromatically. Clear triple rhythm in right hand, while left hand is \|oom-pah-pah\|pah-oom-pah: |

sempre col Ped.

| 1:10 | Two more phrases, begin-ning with inversions of earlier phrases. Second phrase is much extended | Octaves in right hand, with syncopations; left hand is \|oom-pah oom-\|pah oom-pah. |
| 1:19 | Return to opening phrase of section, overlapping with . . . | Apparent return is really transition to next section, with an **accelerando** (speeding up). |

Section 4: Third waltz

| 1:23 | Two phrases of new material | Tempo is **animato** (animated). Charming effect of lightly touched octaves: |

pp   *sempre*   *più*

| 1:27 | Two phrases | Begins with 3-note motive and continues with downward cascades. |
| 1:32 | Vivo (faster still) | Right-hand arpeggios, later sweeping upward: |

vivo

Phrases are
2 + 2 bars (bass is chromatic)
4 + 4 bars (higher in right hand)
4 + extended phrase using 3-note motive and leading to **ritenuto** (holding back) . . .

Section 5: Finale

1:49   Presto (very fast): rush to end   Lots of syncopation in both hands:

Two 8-bar phrases, followed by phrase with closing chords.

LISTENING GUIDE 46 | ⑤ | DVD | 🎧

Schumann *Carnaval,* "Arlequin" (Harlequin)   1:01

DATE: 1834–35

GENRE: Character piece (within a piano cycle)

LISTEN FOR
RHYTHM: Uniform "prancing" rhythm

FORM: ABABA

TEXTURE: Hiccup start to each phrase

EXPRESSION: Strong dynamic contrasts

TIME	FORM	DESCRIPTION
	Section A	
0:00	Opening two phrases: **aabc**, where **a** begins with flip; **b** is same rhythm, tonic harmony; **c** is downward scale in octaves	A sort of prancing on tiptoe. Harlequin dances. Note jerky rhythm, with flip at the beginning of each phrase:
		Opening two phrases are on single harmony (dominant seventh chord). Dynamic contrasts between phrases.
0:06	Opening phrases repeated	Repeated phrases are an octave higher.
	Section B	Contrast of very loud and very soft.
0:10	**acac**	New harmony, new phrase pairing. Phrase **a** is loud with octave doublings of the melody; **c** has a descending scale in octaves.
0:17	Four-bar phrase made of opening flips	Starts quiet; note **ritardando** (slowing), preparing return of opening theme.
	Section A, repeated	
0:24	Return of opening two phrases	
0:30	Return of opening phrases, repeated	Repeated phrases are an octave higher.
	Section B, repeated	
0:36	**acac**, repeated	

(continued)

TIME	FORM	DESCRIPTION
0:42	Four-bar phrase made of opening flips	Note ritardando, preparing return of opening theme.
	Section A, repeated	
0:49	Return of opening two phrases	
0:54	Return of opening phrases, repeated	Repeated phrases are an octave higher.

LISTENING GUIDE 47   ⓢ | DVD | 🎙

Schumann *Carnaval,* "Eusebius"   1:54

DATE: 1834–35

GENRE: Character piece (within a piano cycle)

LISTEN FOR

RHYTHM: Unusual rhythmic groupings in melody (7, or 5, or 3 notes per duple beat)

FORM: Construction from only two phrases (**A** and **B**)

TEXTURE: Each phrase played with and without octaves

EXPRESSION: Blurring by use of sustaining pedal

TIME	FORM	DESCRIPTION
	Section 1: AABA	
0:00	First phrase (**A**)	Seven notes per measure until the four slow descending notes that end the phrase.
0:12	Second phrase (=**A**)	Repeat of first phrase.
0:24	Third phrase (**B**)	Shorter time values make this phrase sound more animated: 5 + 3 rhythm in right hand, wider range.
0:37	Final phrase (**A**)	Return to first phrase.
	Section 2: BABA	
0:51	Phrase **B**	Phrase **B**, octaves in right hand played slower, and with sustaining pedal (allows smoother motion between large rolled chords in left hand; pedal markings end when large chords disappear).
1:06	Phrase **A**	Phrase **A**, octaves in right hand, played slower, and with sustaining pedal.
1:21	Phrase **B**	Played as in Section 1, without octaves or sustaining pedal.
1:36	Phrase **A**	As at the beginning of Section 1; the piece hardly seems to end. . . .

"EUSEBIUS"

  LG 47

This dreamy miniature represents the introspective side of Schumann's character. The final chord, certainly not a tonic triad, leaves us suspended in midair, as if the piece is not quite finished, and the meandering melody similarly resists being tied down to mundane regularity: Sometimes it has five notes per beat, sometimes three, and sometimes seven. The use of the damper (sustaining) pedal heightens the pensive mood. The opening is marked "senza Pedale," that is, with no pedal at all. In a later passage, with octaves in the right hand and thick chords in the left, Schumann instructs the player to hold down the pedal throughout, producing a rich veil of sound (see LG 47, p. 336).

"FLORESTAN"

LG 48

Volatile, agitated, and changeable, "Florestan" is a musical portrait of Schumann's active, extroverted alter ego. Beginning with the notes A, E♭, C, B (the third of the "Sphinxes"), the piece is a stream of passionate impulses, each ending in a somewhat different place, musically and presumably also emotionally. Early on, Schumann quotes a theme from his *Papillons*, the work in which he first depicted Jean Paul's literary masked ball. A final frantic flurry (including a crisp, *staccato* [detached] version of the A-S-C-H motive) fails to resolve harmonically, and the music dissolves into thin air as the whirling continues (see LG 48, p. 337).

LISTENING GUIDE 48   Ⓢ | DVD | 🔊

Schumann *Carnaval*, "Florestan"   0:53

DATE: 1834–35

GENRE: Character piece (within a piano cycle)

LISTEN FOR

TEXTURE: All phrases begin with the same swirl, but lead to different musical endings. Rapid changes of tempo.

THEME: A-S-C-H motto at beginning and end

EXPRESSION: Inconclusive ending

TIME	FORM	DESCRIPTION
0:00	Opening energetic flurry	Marked "Passionate," this piece is very variable, in tempo, rhythm, and mood. Opening energetic flurry leads to slow rising scale.
0:10	Second flurry	As before, but leads to longer slow section (this is marked "Papillon?" in the score, and is a quotation).
0:24	Third flurry	Begins as before, leads to a series of regular 4 bar phrases.
0:39	Fourth flurry	Rapid notes in inner voices; rises higher and higher.
0:45	Fifth flurry	Begins as the beginning; the opening figure gets almost hysterical, dissolves, and simply stops (on dominant chord).

LG 49   **"CHOPIN"**

This charming piece evokes the music of the eminent Polish composer-pianist, whom both Robert and Clara admired. What is it about Schumann's music that sounds like Chopin's? Perhaps it is the flowing arpeggio accompaniment, the lyrical melody, the remarkable harmonic shifts. Chopin was popularly celebrated for his lyricism and surface calm. Perhaps Robert labeled this piece "Agitato" in order to reveal the underlying storminess in Chopin's music (see LG 49, below). Listen to this extract from one of Chopin's Preludes; do you think Schumann's imitation is on the mark?

Chopin: Prelude, Op. 28, No. 11

LG 50   **"PAUSE" AND "MARCHE DES DAVIDSBÜNDLER CONTRE LES PHILISTINS"**

By far the longest piece in *Carnaval*, the "March of the League of David against the Philistines" brings the cycle full circle to a rousing conclusion. Schumann reprises

---

LISTENING GUIDE 49   Ⓢ | DVD

Schumann *Carnaval*, "Chopin"   1:15

DATE: 1834–35
GENRE: Character piece (within a piano cycle)

LISTEN FOR

MELODY: Lyrical melody   **TEXTURE:** Arpeggio accompaniment
FORM: Three pairs of phrases, each pair different

TIME	FORM	DESCRIPTION
0:00	Two phrases of three bars; the second is a step higher.	Rippling arpeggios in left hand, lyrical melody (note 3-note motive, E♭-F-E♭, used in the "Préambule") in right hand:
		First phrase begins in major and ends in minor; second phrase begins in minor and ends in major, leading to an unusual cadence.
0:14	Two phrases of two bars, the second a step higher	Note Chopin-like filigree decoration at end of second phrase.
0:22	A final, chromatic lyrical phrase, with a ritardando	Last three notes are E♭, B♮, C (SHC; Sphinx no. 3).
0:32	The whole thing repeated	Repetition of sections is characteristic of Chopin, but also of Schumann and many others.

music from the opening "Préambule" and quotes a well-known German popular song, the "Grossvatertanz" (Grandfather's Dance), to represent the old guard, the old-timers, the Philistines. In a sense, the finale is a gathering up of all the characters in the ballroom, a grand march to end the masquerade and send everyone home in high spirits (see LG 50, below).

LISTENING GUIDE 50 | DVD

Schumann *Carnaval*, "Pause" and "Marche des Davidsbündler contre les Philistins" (March of the League of David against the Philistines)   3:50

DATE: 1834–35
GENRE: Character piece (within a piano cycle)

LISTEN FOR
FORM: Introduction; March; repeated 3-part interior section; Coda   **EXPRESSION:** Use of acceleration for excitement
THEMES: Quotation of popular German song. Reprise of theme from "Préambule"

TIME	FORM	DESCRIPTION
	Introduction	
0:00	"Pause": introduction to march	Much of it is quoted from the opening movement.
	March of the League of David	
0:18	Opening of march	Note triple meter (odd for a march). First three notes are A♭, C, B♮ (the A-S-C-H motive). The homophonic chords recall opening of "Préambule."
	First interior section	
1:19	Molto più vivo (much livelier), leading to . . .	Dotted figure, accelerating.
1:36	"Grossvatertanz"	Quoted in bass, then treble.
1:55	Animato—Vivo	Quoted from opening movement; pianissimo, rushing. Vivo takes its main figuration from "Pause."
	Second interior section Repeats the first in varied form	
2:17	Return of Molto più vivo	Different key; again leading to . . .
2:32	"Grossvatertanz"	Quoted in bass, then treble.
2:51	Return of Animato—Vivo	Different key. Leads to repeated jagged triple figure of Molto più vivo.
	Coda	
3:19	Coda: heightened energy, speed; syncopated	Quoted from opening movement.

How Did It Go?

Clara had played *Carnaval* in private many times, but not until 1856, near the end of Robert's life, did she perform it in public. Even then, she apparently felt obliged to abridge *Carnaval* for popular consumption. In Paris, she omitted five of the pieces: "Eusebius," "Florestan," "Coquette," "Réplique," and "Estrella."* Perhaps she considered the music too difficult for the average listener; or perhaps the allusions to Ernestine von Fricken in the last three pieces brought back unhappy memories. In any case, in later years she changed her mind and insisted that "I myself would always play the work in its entirety."

The reviewer for the *Revue et gazette musicale* was delighted with *Masques* (as *Carnaval* was sometimes called in France—the name means "carnival scenes") and with Clara's performance, describing the latter with adjectives typically gendered feminine:

> . . . what spirit, what imagination, what melodic abundance! It is not, if you insist, a composition in the accepted form of the word; it is rather a true magic lantern, where verve and *humor* harmoniously follow tenderness and all the outbursts of a lively sensibility.
>
> In this sort of satire, in our opinion, more melodic than really gay, more amiable than mordant, more agreeable than spicy—for in fact for epigram and irony notes can't do what words can, and even need an explanatory program—Madame Clara Schumann deployed all the coyness, all the seductions of her style and demonstrated all its suppleness. . . . Mme Schumann gave a taste, with this delicious carnival, of all that imagination offers of brilliance, caprice, finesse and originality.

On the other hand, the critic for the *Ménéstrel* deemed Schumann's music so avant-garde that it belonged to "the mists of the future" (even though *Carnaval* was already a quarter-century old!). Schumann, he added, "is a composer one has to take into consideration, without rushing, by bringing a great maturity and judgment. He does not lack ideas, as witness the bouquet of little pieces that Mme Schumann played us. It is difficult for a composer-pianist to arouse more interest with so few notes." This comment would have pleased Schumann, concerned as he was with the Romantic concept of fragments—tiny bits of inspiration (not necessarily complete) that, when taken together, can add up to or even exceed a long and fully developed sonata.

The praise was not unanimous, however. The critic of the *Art musical*—evidently one of Schumann's despised Philistines—dismissed *Carnaval* as the incoherent ravings of a lunatic; this was not uncommon after Schumann's death when it was known that he had died in an asylum (see A Vituperative Review of *Carnaval*, left).

Despite such criticism, Clara's concerts in Paris were enormously successful, financially as well as artistically. A week after this recital she was honored by being

A Vituperative Review of *Carnaval*

I t would be impossible for us to say what it was, that composition for the piano, by Robert Schumann, called *Carnaval*, with which Mme Schumann ended her concert. This piece, which is divided into 16 episodes with the following titles: *Préambule—Pierrot—Arlequin—Valse noble—Papillons—Chiarina*, etc., etc., is a sort of fantastic, humorous epic, in the style of Callot [engraver of carnival scenes] or of [E. T. A.] Hoffmann, the storyteller. It is impossible to have an idea of such an assemblage of raw dreams, without hearing this strange composition played by Mme Schumann, who alone understands, they say, the music of her husband! The piece lasts at least a half-hour, and your panting imagination, your worn-out ear, can barely catch a motive, a design, an image, a striking rhythm. It is the nightmare of a sick person, the dream of a hallucinator, who gets tied up in his story and makes you participate in all the transports he experiences in trying to articulate something intelligible. I saw the moment when the distinguished audience of this concert was about to get up and leave the room, out of boredom and impatience. That is however what they love in Germany, what the connoisseurs in Leipzig, in Berlin, in Dresden, admire, and what we're told is the latest and supreme transformation of the art of pleasing people by the combination of sounds. We are surely sick, in France, but it's better to applaud the trivialities of *Giralda* [an opera by Adolphe Adam] and the ariettas of *La Chatte merveilleuse* [an operetta by Albert Grisar] than to succumb to the sick daydreams of a Robert Schumann.

---

* In order to meet two of Schumann's imaginary characters, however, we have pretended that she actually played "Eusebius" and "Florestan" in Paris.

invited to perform Beethoven's Fifth Piano Concerto in an orchestral concert at the Paris Conservatoire. (Soloists normally had to apply to perform in this series.) Three further concerts followed, one of which featured Viardot both playing piano duets with Clara and singing. Clara also taught many lessons in Paris (for which she charged very high fees) and held a series of musical soirées.

Carnaval Then and Now

Carnaval is a multifaceted piece, with different levels of meaning—masks, portraits, dances, imitations, hidden and not-so-hidden references. The work also represents the double nature of nineteenth-century piano music

That double nature lies in the private and public sides of the instrument. On the one hand, the piano became the domestic instrument of choice during the nineteenth century; on the other, it was the thundering, diabolical, seductive instrument of the great virtuosos.

In the sixteenth century every gentleman and lady played the lute, and, as we saw in Chapter 3, the repertory for that instrument is enormous and beautiful. In the seventeenth and eighteenth centuries, the lute was eclipsed by the harpsichord and clavichord. The nineteenth century was the century of the piano, as the twentieth century was the century of the guitar, the emblem of folk, rock, and pop music. (So far, the twenty-first century seems to be the century of electronic instruments, but how it will end is anybody's guess.)

It was in the 1800s that classical music first became widely available to a large segment of society. Public concert halls are the creations of the nineteenth century, and it was largely through them that a taste for music and music-making became an important part of public culture. Bach's and Mozart's audiences were restricted to the upper strata of society; but a series of revolutions in America and Europe, and the growing economic, political, and cultural power of the middle classes, greatly expanded access to the arts and made music a domestic commodity. Well-brought-up people learned to play and sing, and to do so they needed to have pianos in their homes.

From the time of Beethoven onward, publishers had sought relatively easy music to sell to the growing market of amateur musicians. As a result, composers began to think in terms of writing two different kinds of music: music that only Liszt, Clara Schumann, Thalberg, and Kalkbrenner could possibly play, and music that you or I or anybody else could play if we took lessons and practiced regularly.

In the chapter on Mendelssohn's Violin Concerto, we explored the public side of performance and the cult of the virtuoso that grew up around Paganini, the dazzling violinist who was thought to be possessed by the Devil—how else to explain his diabolical dexterity? The piano was even more popular than the violin as a vehicle for solo virtuosity: it needed no accompaniment, and as technology made pianos louder and more responsive at the same time, it became possible to perform seemingly superhuman musical feats for very large public audiences.

There is a risk for composers in catering to showmanship, of course, and a great deal of showy piano music was designed to make an instantaneous effect, rather than have lasting artistic value. Robert Schumann and his League of David railed against this kind of shallow, self-serving virtuosity, while Clara Schumann sought to rise above it. It is in music like *Carnaval* that the two tendencies meet in the middle, blending artistic merit with technical dazzle.

Carnaval is no easy music—far from it. Parts of it are very difficult indeed, which is one of the reasons virtuoso pianists frequently feature it on their recitals. Another is that Schumann's music seeks to reach the listener, not by dazzling or overwhelming us, but by captivating and seducing us. He grabs our attention with a variety of moods and effects, producing a succession of evanescent moments that are often not quite what they seem.

When the French critics insisted that *Carnaval* needed to be heard more than once to be understood, and characterized it as music of the future, they were right on both counts. Schumann's music is always new because there is always more to hear, so long as the listener is in a receptive frame of mind. The fact that *Carnaval* has stood the test of time proves that it belonged—and still belongs—to the future. Like much of the rest of Schumann's music, it occupies a place of honor in the rarefied world of nineteenth-century piano miniatures, and in the world of large-scale musical accomplishments.

Chapter Review

Summary of Musical Styles

Schumann's *Carnaval* shares several characteristic of nineteenth-century piano music:

- The work is composed of short pieces (**miniatures** were a favorite Romantic notion).
- *Carnaval* displays a variety of different styles (one of the reasons for calling such works **character pieces**).
- Each piece has a characteristic or descriptive title.
- The music, including asides from Schumann and the mysterious "Sphinxes," seems designed as much for the private player as for the concert stage.
- Like the music of Mendelssohn and Schubert, the pieces are often songlike and lyrical in style.

In addition, *Carnaval* has its own distinct musical characteristics:

- The whole consists of substantial opening and closing pieces ("Préambule" and "Marche des Davidsbündler contre les Philistins") surrounding a series of brief character sketches and dance-tempo movements.
- Except for the opening and closing works, each piece makes some use of the musical motto A-S-C-H.

⑤ Multimedia Resources and Review Materials on StudySpace

Visit wwnorton.com/studyspace for review of Chapter 12.

What Do You Know?

Check the facts for this chapter. Take the online **Quiz**.

What Do You Hear?

Listening Quizzes and **Music Activities** will help you understand the musical works in this chapter.

Author Videos

- The Sphinxes and the A-S-C-H motive in Schumann's *Carnaval*

Interactive Listening Guides

LG 45 Schumann: *Carnaval*, "Préambule" (Preamble)
LG 46 Schumann: *Carnaval*, "Arlequin" (Harlequin)
LG 47 Schumann: *Carnaval*, "Eusebius"
LG 48 Schumann: *Carnaval*, "Florestan"
LG 49 Schumann: *Carnaval*, "Chopin"
LG 50 Schumann: *Carnaval*, "Pause" and "Marche des Davidsbündler contre les Philistins" (March of the League of David against the Philistines)

Flashcards (Terms to Know)

animato
arpeggio
character pieces
commedia dell'arte
cross-rhythms
cycle

musical quotations
pianoforte (piano)
piano miniatures
ritenuto
sustaining pedal

CHAPTER 13

MONDAY, AUGUST 14, 1876, BAYREUTH:

Richard Wagner's *The Valkyrie* (*Die Walküre*)

⚙ CORE REPERTOIRE

- **LG 51** Act 1, Prelude (Storm)
- **LG 52** Act 1, Scene 1, Siegmund and Sieglinde Meet and Fall in Love ("Wess' Herd dies auch sei")
- **LG 53** Act 1, Scene 2, Sieglinde and Siegmund in Love, and Siegmund's Sense of Foreboding
- **LG 54** Act 1, Scene 3, "Winterstürme wichen dem Wonnemond"
- **LG 55** Act 1, Scene 3, "Siegmund heiss' ich"

▶ VIDEOS

- Act 1, Scene 3: "Winterstürme wichen dem Wonnemond"
- Act 1, Scene 3: "Siegmund heiss' ich"
- Act 3, Prelude: Ride of the Valkyries— "Hojotoho!"
- Act 3, Scene 3: Magic Fire Music

Introduction

"From the scenic point of view it interested me greatly, and I was also much impressed by the truly marvellous staging of the work. Musically it is inconceivable nonsense, in which here and there occur beautiful, and even captivating, moments."

—Peter Ilyich Tchaikovsky, August 14, 1876

In August 1876, a very long work (it took four evenings to perform) called *The Ring of the Nibelung (Der Ring des Nibelungen)* was given its first complete performance in the town of Bayreuth, in southern Germany. Everybody in the world of classical music, and almost everybody else in the Western world, considered the premiere the most important artistic event of the age. The work's composer, Richard Wagner, was regarded by his followers as almost a god, and his disciples provided the resources needed to build him a temple—a theater on a hill, in which performances would be given to immortalize his music. Wagner's Festival Theater, or Festspielhaus, was a sort of shrine, and to this day the composer's descendants direct a summer festival there devoted to his—and *only* his—works. His music, for many listeners, strikes a perfect balance between music and drama, art and emotion, and poetry and action; it is mythic in subject matter, symphonic in musical scope, and unhampered by divisions into numbers, arias, and recitatives—divisions that have created many musical-dramatic problems in opera.

Music as drama

Nowadays we include *The Ring of the Nibelung* under the heading of opera; but Wagner—who knew something about the subject, having composed, directed, and written about operas all his life—regarded his *Ring* not as opera, but rather as drama. The difference may be a little hard to appreciate, but it involves a recalibration of the relationship between words and music, and a comprehensive attention to detail—from libretto to orchestration to stagecraft, for example—that no composer before or since Wagner has been able to command (see Figure 13.1).

Wagner's four *Ring* dramas—*The Rhinegold (Das Rheingold)*, *The Valkyrie (Die Walküre)*, *Siegfried*, and *Twilight of the Gods (Götterdämmerung)*—are the type of opera that people often make fun of. They involve women wearing horned helmets, warriors brandishing long spears, tenors who sing unbelievably loudly, and

🎙 AUTHOR VIDEOS

- The sword leitmotif in Wagner's *Valkyrie*

FIG. 13.1 A caricature of Richard Wagner, with a huge head, orchestrating the dawn of a new day.

performances that last four or five hours. They are easy to mock if you don't buy into the power of music and myth.

Wagner's idea (put more simply than he would have) is that there are basic human passions hidden inside each of us, and that music is the best, perhaps the only, way to turn these emotions into deeply gripping art. Many people feel that Wagner pulls this transformation off better than any other composer. His music is surpassingly beautiful, especially when it is allowed to do its work as part of what Wagner called a **total work of art** (in German, *Gesamtkunstwerk*), the combination of drama, poetry, music, and stagecraft in which he specialized, and for which the Bayreuth theater was built.

The four *Ring* operas are based on ancient Norse legends, tales that, like all myths, hold a timeless appeal by telling us things about ourselves, disguised as stories about ancient gods and heroes. Wagner clearly understood how to appeal to our innermost selves: even though all musical art in some sense expresses the human psyche, Wagner's great gift was the clear depiction of the interior thoughts and emotions of his characters.

The heroic and universal aspect of the *Ring* is underscored by the libretto, written by Wagner himself, which is fashioned in the so-called **Stabreim**, the alliterative verse typical of ancient Teutonic legend (and of Anglo-Saxon poems like *Beowulf*). You don't have to be able to understand German to hear the repeated consonants within each line of couplets like this:

> *Winterstürme wichen dem Wonnemond,*
> *In mildem Lichte leuchtet der Lenz;*
> *(Winter storms yield to the delightful moon,*
> *In gentle moonlight shines the Spring;)*

The central story of *The Ring of the Nibelung* is that of Siegfried, a mortal hero of the race of Walsungs fathered by Wotan, the king of the gods. *The Valkyrie* is about Siegfried's human parents, Siegmund and Sieglinde, and about Brunnhilde, daughter of Wotan, and a Valkyrie; in Norse mythology, the Valkyries were maidens who escorted the souls of slain warriors to Valhalla, the palace of the gods. We don't actually meet Siegfried himself until the third evening, *Siegfried* (during which he awakens Brunnhilde from an enchanted sleep; see Plot Summary, p. 350).

Wagner's music is closely tied to the story. This is true in all opera, of course; but Wagner's particular gift, and his extremely influential invention, is in the way he uses the music to explain what is going on in the characters' heads and hearts, and to make connections among objects, people, and events that would otherwise not be known either to the characters *or* to the audience. What appears sometimes to be a lack of "real-time" action is the exploration of the inner actions of the mind and the emotions.

Most of this interior "action" happens not in what is sung and acted on the stage, but in the music the orchestra plays. And what music it is! Wagner had a genius for creating stupendous orchestral sounds, like the famous Ride of the Valkyries which comes from the third act of this opera. ▶

▶ Video

Leitmotifs

Wagner invented a means of tying everything together with a complex web of brief themes. We recognize these themes—called **leitmotifs**—because they are memorable and because they recur often; some are melodies, some are harmonic progressions, some are rhythmic patterns, and most combine all of these elements. The leitmotifs are associated with objects, characters, emotions, and places. The strands of individual themes are woven into the "endless melody"

(Wagner's term) in the orchestra, while the characters onstage generally sing in a sort of speech rhythm that seldom uses such themes. Some people think Wagner's musical delivery of words has no lyricism at all; it certainly doesn't resemble the show-stopping arias that nineteenth-century audiences had come to expect from opera singers.

Although Wagner does not make such distinctions, we might find it useful to think of Wagner's music as consisting of three styles or modes of musical discourse. First, there is a narrative or conversational style in which characters speak to each other (or to themselves) in a speechlike melody, while the orchestra provides an accompaniment in which inner meanings and feelings can be depicted without having to be spoken aloud, or explained. Examples include the dialogues—spoken and unspoken—between Sieglinde and Siegmund.

There is also a lyrical style: Wagner's music can soar with the best of them; this style, however, is quite rare in the *Ring* operas, usually saved for moments of high intensity in which a character actually sings a beautifully flowing melody. An example is Siegmund's song "Winterstürme wichen dem Wonnemond," followed by Sieglinde's passionate "Du bist der Lenz." ▶   ▶ Video

Finally, there is a symphonic style, usually reserved for moments when the orchestra is allowed to give full voice to its music. Examples here include the opening storm, the Ride of the Valkyries, and the Magic Fire Music. ▶   ▶ Video

The combined effect of Wagner's voices and orchestra was unprecedented. Even today, many listeners who prefer operas with long lyrical songs, and lots of repetition of words and melodies, fail to understand—or at least to appreciate—what Wagner is up to. In his many writings about music and drama, he made it clear that he thought of speech and action as merely the outward aspect of **music drama**. The real, inner drama resided in the music and took place, first and foremost, in the orchestra pit. Wagner said that his dramas were "acts of music made visible."

The Setting

RICHARD WAGNER

Richard Wagner had been waiting for this moment for a long time. The sixty-three-year-old composer was enormously talented, ambitious, and ruthless. Some would say that he was relentless in his pursuit of artistic perfection, others that he let nothing stop him from getting his way.

From his early career as a composer of French-style grand operas, through his time employed at the Dresden court, where he also learned all about Italian opera, Wagner strove to develop a purely German style of music theater. After getting thrown out of Germany in 1849 (for participating in a political uprising), he fled to Switzerland and lived there for more than a decade. During his exile, he continued to turn out a stream of literary and journalistic essays that made it clear what drove him, and where he was headed (see biography, p. 348).

Wagner's iconoclastic political views were mirrored in his artistic theories and attitudes. Monumentally egotistical and self-confident, he was one of most controversial and polarizing figures in music history. His concept of music drama was part of a wider vision of "the artwork of the future," and Wagner's view of the future bore a close resemblance to *The Ring of the Nibelung*. Although as a young and ambitious composer he emulated the music of Giacomo Meyerbeer, Hector

RICHARD WAGNER (1813–1883)

Born in Leipzig into a theatrical family, Wagner studied music in Dresden and Leipzig, beginning his career in opera at an early age. He held positions as chorus master and conductor in small companies, and gained practical experience while working on his earliest operas, *The Fairies* (*Die Feen*), *The Ban on Love* (*Das Liebesverbot*), and *Rienzi*. In 1837 he became director of the opera in Riga (Latvia), shortly after marrying the actress Minna Planer. (The turbulent marriage ended with her death in 1866.) He had some unhappy years in Paris, and then worked as assistant music director in the court of Dresden, where his opera *The Flying Dutchman* (*Die fliegende Holländer*) was produced. His attachment to German and Nordic mythology, and to history and medieval legend, led to his operas *Tannhäuser* (Dresden, 1845) and *Lohengrin* (Weimar, 1850).

Exiled for political activity in 1849, Wagner lived in Switzerland, where he wrote essays and pamphlets. There, he developed the libretto for his *Ring of the Nibelung*, a version of which he published in 1854, having already started on the music and conceived of a special theater for his festival. He returned to Germany in 1860 and had the good fortune to receive the enthusiastic support of the newly crowned young Ludwig II, king of Bavaria, who idolized him. The king wanted to produce Wagner's operas in Munich, but Wagner pursued his ideal by choosing the town of Bayreuth as the place to build his Festival Theater and hold the performances of *The Ring*. His persistence, and his commitment to the project, finally succeeded, with the help of his second wife Cosima, the daughter of Franz Liszt. Cosima had a powerful sway over Wagner and would retain her influence at Bayreuth until her own death in 1930.

The Bayreuth festivals (only two of which, in 1876 and 1882, took place in Wagner's lifetime) were momentous, and continue to be so. Wagner, surrounded by his wife and children, held court at Wahnfried, their house in Bayreuth, which became the center of a cult that to some extent still exists today. He died of a heart attack in 1883 in Venice, and is buried on the grounds of Wahnfried. But the man still looms as one of the most important artistic creators of the late nineteenth century.

Ⓢ Wagner: *Tannhäuser*, Pilgrim's chorus
Ⓢ Wagner: *Tristan and Isolde*, Prelude
Ⓢ Wagner: *Die Meistersinger von Nürnberg*, Prelude

MAJOR WORKS: 13 operas (music dramas), including *The Flying Dutchman* (*Die fliegende Holländer*), *Tannhäuser*, *Lohengrin*, the four-opera cycle *The Ring of the Nibelung* (*Der Ring des Nibelungen*), *Tristan and Isolde*, *The Mastersingers of Nuremberg* (*Die Meistersinger von Nürnberg*), *Parsifal*, and others; a small amount of orchestral, vocal, choral, and piano music.

Wagner's Anti-Semitism

Wagner was far from the only person prejudiced against Jews in his time, but he was one of the most vociferous and vituperative. In 1850 he published in the *Neue Zeitschrift für Musik*, the influential musical journal founded by Robert Schumann (see p. 321), an article entitled *Judaism in Music* ("Das Judenthum in der Musik"). In it he claimed that Jews, because they cannot speak Western languages properly (they make a "creaking, squeaking, buzzing snuffle"), can therefore not express true feeling, and are incapable of creating song or music. He was particularly critical of Mendelssohn, who was recently deceased; and he criticized, without naming him, the enormously popular German-Jewish opera composer Giacomo Meyerbeer. Wagner reprinted a much longer version of his article in 1869, and it became an important landmark of German anti-Semitism.

Berlioz, and Felix Mendelssohn (see Chapters 10 and 11), he eventually cut his ties to the more established composers. His contempt for the music of Mendelssohn and Meyerbeer was later compounded by religious and racial bigotry: Wagner was a rabid anti-Semite whose opposition to Jews later made him a hero to the Nazis (see Wagner's Anti-Semitism, left).

Wagner led a less than exemplary life; wherever he went, he left a trail of unpaid debts, broken promises, broken hearts, and at least one broken marriage. He eloped with his second wife, Cosima (see Figure 13.2), while she was still married to the great conductor Hans von Bülow, one of Wagner's most ardent champions. But none of these peccadilloes dented the cast-iron faith of true believers. To them, all that mattered was the glorious body of music that Wagner created.

Wagner's musical influence on other composers was mixed; some adored his work (Camille Saint-Saëns, Anton Bruckner), others abhorred it (Giuseppe Verdi), and many were simply baffled by it. No one, however, could ignore it.

It is telling that all of Wagner's music dramas are based on

Teutonic legend rather than Greek or Roman mythology or stories drawn from the Christian tradition. Throughout his career, he was concerned with creating a native German art, free of what he saw as cultural and, later, racial impurities. Wagner's fixation with Germanness was hardly unique. In 1876, Europeans and Americans were preoccupied with the meaning of nationhood and national culture. **Nationalism** was a major theme of music and literature as well as politics. Wagner was even commissioned to write a patriotic march for the centennial of the American Declaration of Independence, which was performed in Philadelphia on May 10, 1876; less than twenty years later, Antonín Dvořák would compose his famous *New World Symphony*, a landmark of musical nationalism (see Chapter 14). Yet Wagner's efforts transcended nationalism—the ancient legends as he retells them in the *Ring* operas are really about the human condition. In this series of tales, the morals are as clear as they are universal: greed is the root of all evil; love has infinite power; it is not easy choosing between duty to self and duty to others.

FIG. 13.2   Richard Wagner with his wife, Cosima, daughter of Franz Liszt, in 1872.

THE POEM

Wagner had been working on *The Ring of the Nibelung*, and on its production, for almost three decades. In 1848 he imagined a poem and opera called *Siegfried's Death*; he envisioned a wooden theater in which it would be given a one-time festival performance, after which the theater would be dismantled. In that idea (never realized) is the kernel of what actually happened. The single, stand-alone opera multiplied into a tetralogy—or, as Wagner preferred to think of it, a prologue followed by a trilogy—and the temporary theater became a permanent temple dedicated to Wagner and his music. By 1853 Wagner had written and published a version of the text of the whole *Ring* cycle, although the music had not yet been written, and in 1863 he published the poem *Der Ring des Nibelungen*.

The plot

The plot of the *Ring* is long and involved, but a brief summary will suffice for our purposes. By the end of the four evenings, the mortal hero Siegfried has undone the wrong committed by the gods in the theft of some gold. The treasure has its rightful place at the bottom of the Rhine River, under the protection of the Rhinemaidens. It was stolen by Alberich (of a race of dwarves known as Nibelungs), stolen back by Wotan, the chief god, and then used to pay off a pair of giants for building Valhalla. The orchestral prelude to this drama, a stream of unchanging harmony that seems to rise from the depths of the mighty river, is one of the most famous moments in all opera.

Ⓢ Wagner: *The Rhinegold*, Prelude

The Rhinegold (the first of the four works, which Wagner thought of as a prelude) does more than set the scene, however; it also presents the basic philosophical problem that drives the plot of the entire *Ring* cycle: the gold, when fashioned into a ring, gives its wearer unlimited power, but only if he or she renounces love. The choice between money and love—or, if you like, ambition and truth—is one of the eternal themes of drama and literature. Sure enough, the curse of death that Alberich places on the ring begins to take effect: no sooner do they get their hands on the gold, than one of the giants (Fafner) kills his brother (Fasolt).

In the third evening, *Siegfried*, we will learn how the hoard of gold, guarded by Fafner in the form of a dragon, is rescued by the hero with the help of a sword that he has forged from broken pieces. And in the final installment, *Twilight of the Gods*,

▶ *Plot of* The Valkyrie

The opera takes place in Germany in mythological antiquity.

ACT 1

- A violent storm is raging in a forest. Siegmund, exhausted, bursts into the hut of Hunding and Sieglinde and collapses wordlessly on the floor in front of the hearth. 🔊 **LG 51**

- Sieglinde enters, takes pity on the stranger, and brings him a cup of water. Reviving, Siegmund gazes rapturously into her eyes. 🔊 **LG 52** He explains that he is fleeing a tribe of warriors, enemies who had burned his home, murdered his mother, and abducted his sister.

- Their intimate encounter is interrupted by the return of the surly Hunding. Clearly displeased to find another man with his wife, he nevertheless feels obliged to offer Siegmund food and shelter for the night. In the course of their conversation, the two men discover that they are mortal enemies. As Siegmund and Sieglinde exchange longing glances, Hunding warns his guest to prepare for combat the next day. 🔊 **LG 53**

- Hunding goes to bed, drugged by a sleeping potion that Sieglinde has given him. She seizes the opportunity to tell Siegmund about the magic sword protruding from the trunk of a tree growing in the middle of the hut. He recognizes it as the sword that his father, Wälse (Wotan), promised he would find in his hour of need.

- As moonlight floods through the open door, Siegmund and Sieglinde sing an ecstatic paean to love and spring ("Winterstürme wichem dem Wonnemond"). ▶ **Video** and 🔊 **LG 54** Realizing that Sieglinde is his long-lost sister, Siegmund triumphantly prises the sword loose from the tree, and the lovers rush out into the night ("Siegmund heiss' ich"). ▶ **Video** and 🔊 **LG 55**

ACT 2

- Wotan, king of the gods, orders his favorite daughter, Brünnhilde, to aid Siegmund in the duel with Hunding. She rallies her fellow Valkyries with the stirring battle cry "Hojotoho!"

- Fricka, goddess of marriage, rebukes Wotan for permitting Siegmund to steal Hunding's wife. She demands that he punish the lovers by condemning Siegmund—Wotan's one hope for recovering the cursed ring of the Nibelung—to death. Brünnhilde pleads for the hero's life, but Wotan angrily commands her to carry out Fricka's wishes.

- When Brünnhilde tells Siegmund that she is powerless to protect him, he defiantly vows to kill himself and Sieglinde rather than submit to his fate. Moved, the Valkyrie decides to disobey her father. However, during the fight, Wotan shatters Siegmund's sword and Hunding slays him. Brünnhilde spirits the sleeping Sieglinde away from the battlefield on horseback.

ACT 3

- In the exciting orchestral interlude known as the Ride of the Valkyries ▶ **Video** the warrior maidens gallop across the night sky on their horses, carrying the souls of fallen heroes to Valhalla. Brünnhilde arrives on the mountaintop with Sieglinde, who gathers the fragments of Siegmund's sword and escapes ahead of the vengeful Wotan.

- The other Valkyries try to hide Brünnhilde, but Wotan orders them away. In a poignant scene, he bids a tender farewell to his favorite daughter and places her in a deep trance (from which she will be awakened by the hero Siegfried in the third opera of the *Ring* cycle).

- Wotan commands the fire god to surround the sleeping Valkyrie with a protective ring of flames. In the flickering light of the Magic Fire Music ▶ **Video** the mighty god brandishes his spear to the heavens and disappears.

Brünnhilde restores the ring to the custody of the Rhinemaidens, while Wotan and his fellow immortals are swallowed up in a great cataclysm that destroys Valhalla.

But the subject of *The Valkyrie,* the second of the four *Ring* operas, is love: Sieglinde (married to the horrible Hunding), and Siegmund (lost in the raging storm that opens the opera and stumbling into Hunding's house), are thrown together by circumstance and fall in love. Ultimately, Hunding kills Siegmund, in a duel in which they are both puppets of the gods—but not before Siegmund and Sieglinde (who are, incidentally, siblings, fathered by Wotan!) have conceived the hero Siegfried (whom we will meet in the next evening).

Wagner and Tolkien

The question of whether, and to what extent, J.R.R. Tolkien's famous *Lord of the Rings* trilogy was indebted to Wagner's *Ring* will probably never be settled to the satisfaction of the works' fans. Tolkien airily dismissed any suggestions of Wagnerian influence on his fantasy, asserting that "both rings were round, and there the resemblance ceases." Yet it is a matter of record that Tolkien and C. S. Lewis (author of the *Chronicles of Narnia*) were drawn to Wagner's music dramas as students at Oxford in the 1930s; they even translated the libretto of *The Valkyrie* as the basis for an earnest scholarly analysis.

One point on which everybody agrees is that Wagner and Tolkien drank from the same well of inspiration: the great Norse and Germanic legends of the Middle Ages, including the *Nibelungenlied*, the Icelandic Eddas, and the Volsunga Saga—with perhaps a pinch of the Brothers Grimm added for good measure. According to Roger Scruton, a noted philosopher and Wagner expert, "The forests and rivers, the fires and storms, the dragons and mermaids . . . are recreated in the *Ring*, with a freshness and poetry that owe everything to music, but with a directness that recalls the rich tradition of German children's literature. . . . Looked at in that way, we can see Wagner's *Ring* cycle as a bridge between two far more humble productions: Grimm's fairy tales and the *Lord of the Rings*. . . . Indeed, the emotions that are stirred by the cinematic realisation of Tolkien's rambling story are a faint echo of what would be felt, were the *Ring* to be performed as Wagner intended. . . ."

The next time you watch the movie versions of Tolkien's novels, ask yourself: does anything in the story and the film score make you think of Wagner?

It all sounds terribly complicated and convoluted, but *The Ring of the Nibelung* is really no harder to follow than J.R.R. Tolkien's popular *Lord of the Rings* trilogy—which, by the way, draws on many of the same mythological sources that Wagner used (see Wagner and Tolkien, above). It's no accident that the epics have a common theme: the curse of a ring and the redemption of humankind. Moreover, as we will see below, Wagner has a way of simplifying things for the listener by means of a system of musical labels that clue us in to what is happening in the drama, both on stage and out of sight.

FIG. 13.3 Ludwig II (1845–86), king of Bavaria and patron of Richard Wagner.

One person who wasn't in the least daunted by the *Ring* was King Ludwig II of Bavaria, Wagner's chief patron (see Figure 13.3). Ludwig inherited his throne in 1864, at age eighteen, by which time he was a confirmed admirer of Wagner's music and ideas. Romantic medievalism combined with hero-worship led him to build fairy-tale castles, like earthly Valhallas, and to commission paintings of Wagnerian heroes. He even proposed to build an enormous opera house in his capital, Munich, to perform Wagner's works. Wagner was glad of Ludwig's support, but his plans called for a theater of his own in a small town, where the audience would come only for the beauty of the experience. When, several years before the first complete *Ring* cycle, Ludwig insisted on producing *The Rhinegold* and *The Valkyrie* in Munich, against Wagner's wishes, relations between them became a bit chilly.

After inspecting many possible sites for his theater, Wagner chose the town of Bayreuth in northern Bavaria, which had an eighteenth-century opera house that he thought might be the right place for his *Ring*. In the end, he decided the opera house wasn't suitable after all and persuaded the local authorities to donate a building lot on the edge of town. The citizens of Bayreuth helped him raise funds through a series of concerts and other activities; additional contributions came from a network of Wagner Societies that had sprung up around Europe; and Wagner also put in a lot of his own money (including his fee for writing the American *Centennial March*). A final push involved a reconciliation with King Ludwig, who provided a substantial last-minute loan that made it possible for Wagner, unlike any composer before or since, to have a theater erected according to his specifications for the performance of no other music than his own.

THE FESTIVAL THEATER

Although the cornerstone of the Festival Theater was laid in 1872, construction was delayed while Wagner devoted himself to the onerous task of fund-raising. In the end, the receipts fell short of expectations and he was forced to economize on building materials: the Festival Theater was made of timber filled in with brick. Completed in just a few months, it was said to be the largest freestanding wooden structure in the world. Wagner enlisted experts to help with the architectural plans and the mechanical aspects of the stage, but he had considerable experience in opera houses and knew what he wanted. Indeed, both the Festival Theater and the arrangements for the festival were almost exactly as Wagner had described them in the preface to his early edition of the *Ring* poem in 1863 (see Wagner's Festival Theater, below, and Figure 13.4).

Unlike traditional European opera houses, with multiple tiers of private boxes for the nobility stacked in a horseshoe-shaped curve around the orchestra floor, the Festival Theater had a (mostly) democratic seating plan. The thirty semicircular rows were gently stair-stepped, so that every seat had an unobstructed view. There were no boxes along the sides or hanging over the stage; instead, a small "Princes' Gallery" at the back of the auditorium was reserved for dignitaries (the shy King Ludwig hid there for the dress rehearsal of *The Rhinegold*), with other special guests seated in an "Artists' Gallery" above. The individual cane-bottomed chairs (said to be very uncomfortable) were finally replaced by modern theater seats in the 1960s. There was room for 1,345 spectators on the main floor. A painted canvas ceiling

FIG. 13.4 A drawing of Wagner's Festival Theater in Bayreuth; notice the very high stage house, allowing sets to be raised above the stage.

Wagner's Festival Theater

In 1863, Wagner spelled out his vision for his ideal theater in the preface to the poem Der Ring des Nibelungen:

Here a provisionary theatre would be erected, as simple as possible, perhaps only of wood, and with the interior designed only for artistic purposes. I should confer with an experienced and intelligent architect as to a plan for such a house, with amphitheatrical arrangement of the seats, and the decided advantage of an invisible orchestra. Here then, in the early spring months, the leading dramatic singers, chosen from the ensemble of the German opera houses, would be assembled, in order to study the various parts of my stage work, entirely uninterrupted by any other claims upon their artistic abilities.

On the days appointed for performance—of which I have in mind three in all—the German public would be invited to be present, as these performances, like those of our large music festivals, are to be made accessible, not only to the partial public of any one city, but to all friends of art, far and near.

A complete performance of the dramatic poem in question would take place in midsummer—of a fore-evening *Das Rheingold* and on the three following evenings the chief dramas *Die Walküre*, *Siegfried*, and *Götterdämmerung*.

To complete the impression of such a performance, I should lay great stress upon an invisible orchestra, which it would be possible to effect by the architectural illusion of an amphitheatrical arrangement of the auditorium.

gave them the impression of being inside a big tent or, as one observer described it, "a college lecture-hall on a large scale."

Equal care was lavished on the backstage facilities. The stage was equipped with all the latest technology: there were seven sets of wings, each with slots in the floor for raising and lowering scenery; fly space and equipment for drops and panoramas; and grids for raising and lowering overhead lighting equipment. In addition, there were three levels of storage space and machinery beneath the stage. The lighting consisted of 3,246 gas lamps (there was a special gas plant on the theater grounds) placed behind, beside, and above the sets, and sometimes attached to movable scenery. Different colors depended on separate gas systems; and an electric generator powered a few arc lamps for special effects, such as the projections of magic-lantern slides for the Ride of the Valkyries (see Wagner's Lighting Effects, right).

There were impressive sets for each scene in all four *Ring* operas. Some required elaborate painting and construction: the opening scene of *The Valkyrie* is set in Hunding's hut, in which the trunk of a giant ash tree seemed to be growing out of the center of the stage floor (see illustration, p. 344). All the settings were intended to present a natural image—if the term *natural* can be applied to scenes that don't exist in nature, such as the home of the gods and the underground world of the dwarves. This naturalistic style of production held sway at Bayreuth until the mid-twentieth century, when the composer's grandson Wieland Wagner turned tradition on its head by banishing meticulously detailed trees and castles in favor of abstract, modernist settings (see Figures 13.5 and 13.6).

But the chief innovation of the Festival Theater, corresponding to Wagner's idea of how the orchestra and voices should be related, was—and is—the placement of the orchestra (see Figure 13.7). Wagner wanted to create a **"mystic gulf"** between the audience and the performers; the orchestra was invisible, its sound emanating as if by magic from beneath the stage. This was

> ### Wagner's Lighting Effects
>
> *John R. G. Hassard, a correspondent for the* New York Tribune, *was at the first performance and described Wagner's magical lighting effects for his readers:*
>
> The stage is not lighted in the usual way from the wings, borders and foot-lights, but by some contrivance which I do not understand a light seems to be diffused over the whole scene. Sometimes it comes from the back. Moreover, the light is continually changing. Night and day, sunshine and storm, follow each other by nice gradations, and even when all the action takes place by day there are shifting lights and shadows as there are in nature. The cloud effects are beautiful, and Wagner employs them freely. Transparent vapors float over the heavens with incessant motion, or hover around the rocky steeps. For this purpose very thin painted gauzes are used. For heavier exhalations an illusion is produced by clouds of steam.... It is by means of steam, reddened by reflected light, and shot here and there with small flames, that the effects of fire are produced.

accomplished by submerging the players in a deep pit, mostly under and covered by the stage. The violins sat in the upper row, nearest the audience; other sections of the orchestra were placed successively lower and farther away, with the brass and percussion sunk deepest of all. As a result, the sound of Wagner's enormous orchestra was blended, and somewhat dampened, by the time it entered the auditorium through the slot in front of the stage. A hood facing the stage (installed at the last minute) directed the sound back toward the stage and helped achieve a suitable balance between orchestra and singers. (Even today, singers at Bayreuth have a hard time hearing the orchestra.)

The Performance

PREPARATIONS

Determined to have the finest performers that Germany could provide, Wagner hand-picked singers and instrumentalists from opera houses and orchestras all around the country. This was not the way things usually worked: orchestra players and singers had annual contracts with opera houses, and they could not just go off to play and sing for Wagner, no matter how great a genius he was. (Although

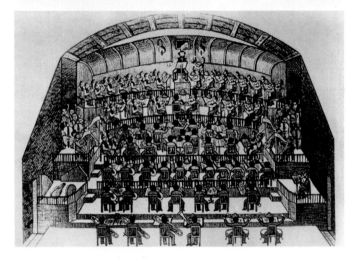

TOP, FIG. 13.5 Original set for Act 2 of *The Valkyrie*, a mountain where Hunding and Siegmund battle.

MIDDLE, FIG. 13.6 The ride of the Valkyries, bringing the bodies of fallen heroes to Valhalla, in a modern production from the English National Opera.

BOTTOM, FIG. 13.7 A drawing of the Bayreuth orchestra pit from beneath the stage; Wagner leans through an opening to talk to the conductor Hans Richter.

major opera houses today have full-time resident orchestras, leading singers are generally accustomed to appearing in many different houses in the course of a season, a freedom that few singers enjoyed in the nineteenth century.)

Wagner got around this problem by spreading the rehearsals and performances over two summers, when opera houses were closed. He made a careful plan in advance and carried it out almost exactly. In the first year (1875, as it turned out), singers would gather in July and August for a month of piano rehearsals, followed by a month of rehearsals onstage with orchestra, basic scenery, and props. It was like an intensive summer music camp, without the pressure of a performance at the end. The next summer, another long series of rehearsals, this time with the orchestra and full stage trappings, culminated in three complete performances of the *Ring* cycle in August.

Wagner made the rounds of opera houses in 1872 looking for singers, and by 1874 he had signed up the entire cast. The prestige and excitement attached to the project made singers eager to be chosen. (Although the pay he offered was minimal, the singers were led to expect a share of the profits from the festival—which, however, never materialized.) Wagner chose his singers not only for their voices, but also for their acting abilities and appearance. The demands he placed on them were heavy. It is still considered a monumental achievement to perform the role of Siegfried, Brünnhilde, or Wotan. This is partly because the singers have to make themselves heard over Wagner's large orchestra (see below), and partly because the main characters in the *Ring* are on stage for a long time and have a lot to sing. They must have power and stamina. In 1876 the same singer was expected to sing Wotan for the whole cycle, and most singers had multiple roles. Few singers today are willing to subject themselves to such an ordeal. (The 1876 cast of *The Valkyrie* is listed below; see also Figures 13.8 and 13.9.)

The Original Cast of *The Valkyrie*

Siegmund, mortal son of Wotan (tenor): Albert Niemann
Hunding, husband of Sieglinde (bass): Joseph Niering
Wotan, king of the gods (bass-baritone): Franz Betz
Sieglinde, mortal daughter of Wotan (soprano): Josephine Scheffsky
Brünnhilde, a Valkyrie and daughter of Wotan (soprano): Amalie Materna
Fricka, wife of Wotan (mezzo-soprano): Friedericke Grün
Valkyries, warrior-maidens and daughters of Wotan: eight more singers, who
    also took roles as Rhinemaidens, Norns, Erda, Freia, Waltraute, etc., in the
    other *Ring* operas

Wagner also assembled a crack team of musical assistants, conductors, copyists, and rehearsal pianists, each of whom, like the singers, felt privileged to be asked. Foremost among them was the "blond Viking" Hans Richter, who would conduct the orchestra for the performances. Piano rehearsals began in July 1875 and proceeded at the rate of one opera a week. From August 1 to 16, Wagner worked with the orchestra alone in the mornings, and with both orchestra and singers in the evenings, covering one act each day. After that came a week of staging rehearsals to work out the most difficult movements. Wagner was delighted with the effects in the theater, though it became clear that the orchestra was generally too loud, despite being covered, and would have to play more softly in performance than had been anticipated.

Wagner's stellar team of technical and design experts included Richard Fricke, ballet master at Dessau, who was engaged as a sort of stage director; Emil Doepler, professor and lecturer on costume at the universities in Weimar and Berlin, who produced the strictly authentic Teutonic costumes; Josef Hoffmann, a Viennese landscape painter, who designed the settings (which were created by the celebrated Brückner brothers from Coburg); and Karl Brandt from the theater in Darmstadt, who was in charge of technical stage furnishings. Fricke left a wonderfully informative diary in which we learn how difficult it was for some of the singers to be effective on the stage. On June 13, before the piano rehearsals began, he wrote:

FIG. 13.8   Amalie Materna in costume as the Valkyrie Brünnhilde in the original production.

> I could not get very far rehearsing with Fräulein Scheffsky. I shall try again at 11 o'clock tomorrow morning to get rid of the customary meaningless arm gestures. She is gifted, and will become a good Sieglinde. However—my good [Albert] Eilers, another story, I could never have believed how a singer and qualified musician could act on the stage for about twenty years, and still not know how to stand or walk. How I tortured myself with Eilers, how I tried to explain to him the characteristics of the part of Hunding, but—to have him imitate and repeat it all for me? He just does not comprehend it. If I were in Wagner's place, I would look for another Hunding.

In the end, Wagner did replace Eilers as Hunding; his initial judgment wasn't always faultless. (Eilers retained the role of the giant Fasolt in *The Rhinegold*.) Unlike Fricke, however, he was not at all satisfied with Scheffsky's Sieglinde. On June 22, Fricke reported that Wagner "passed by me, raging, whispering something to me. I could only make out the words 'Change it, change it. Scheffsky is terrible.'" Wagner was famous for taking charge of rehearsals, often contradicting himself from one day to the next, and showing the singers how to act. He spent a lot of time coaching Scheffsky; Lilli Lehmann, one of the Valkyries, described one such session in her memoirs:

FIG. 13.9   Hans Richter, conductor of the first performance of *The Valkyrie*.

> [Scheffsky] was big and powerful and had a big, powerful voice. She lacked poetry (and the brains to contrive to express what she lacked) and in her first scene, where Sieglinde, overcome by her wretched lot, calls back Siegmund to her, she failed totally. Her Sieglinde had no suggestion of great sorrow or inner longing. Wagner was very dissatisfied and acted the scene out for her. . . . Never since has any Sieglinde, in my experience, come near to matching him, even remotely.

In the early summer of 1876, the Festival Theater was still under construction, but rehearsals of staging, and rehearsals with orchestra, moved forward according to Wagner's carefully planned schedule. Beginning in late May there were daily rehearsals for orchestra and machinists to smooth out the thirty-six scene changes in the *Ring*. June and July saw morning rehearsals for the singers, concentrating on staging and accompanied by piano. "An army of prompters arose behind every bit of scenery and in every corner of the wings," reported Lehmann; "I myself prompted Siegmund from behind Hunding's fireplace." (Lehmann is the only member of the original cast who made recordings; she later became a great Wagnerian singer, and her account of Sieglinde's avowal of love, "Du bist der Lenz," gives some idea of the vocal sound Wagner had in mind.)

A couple of weeks of rehearsals with singers and orchestra, one act per day, gave way to rehearsals of whole operas, spaced one day apart. A final series of dress rehearsals was held from August 6 to 9, after which Wagner gave the singers three days of well-deserved rest. Then, at long last, came the first complete performance of *The Ring of the Nibelung*.

The Music

WAGNER'S ORCHESTRA

It should take nothing away from the drama on stage to say that much of the action in the *Ring* cycle takes place in the orchestra pit. Only an orchestra of gargantuan proportions could do justice to Wagner's epic conception; some 125 players or more were crammed into the sloping, subterranean pit of the Festspielhaus. (Hector Berlioz, by comparison, had 86 players at his disposal for the *Fantastic Symphony*, and Igor Stravinsky considered it a luxury to deploy 99 musicians for *The Rite of Spring*.) Besides the usual array of strings, woodwinds, brass, and percussion, there were no fewer than six harps, eight horns, an unusual bugle-like instrument called a steerhorn, and tenor and bass versions of the newfangled Wagner tuba, which the composer had designed himself. (See The Orchestra of *The Valkyrie*, below.)

Despite these impressive numbers, Wagner's writing for the orchestra is subtle, imaginative, and at times surprisingly delicate. Actually, it is not as big a problem as it sounds for the singers to make themselves heard over the orchestra, because Wagner is careful to keep the orchestra out of the way, except at key moments

The Orchestra of *The Valkyrie*

Wagner uses the same basic orchestra in all four *Ring* operas, but each of them includes a few special instruments as well. The orchestration for *The Valkyrie* calls for a steerhorn (a long, medieval bugle), as well as a set of specially made Wagner tubas.

1 piccolo	1 contrabass tuba
3 flutes (3rd doubles as 2nd piccolo)	1 steerhorn
4 oboes (4th doubles on a special alto oboe of Wagner's design)	2 pairs of timpani
	glockenspiel
3 clarinets	tenor and bass drums
1 bass clarinet	triangle, cymbals, and tam-tam
3 bassoons	6 harps
8 horns (5th and 7th double on tenor Wagner tubas, 6th and 8th double on bass Wagner tubas)	16 first violins
	16 second violins
3 trumpets	12 violas (a newly designed large viola was used)
1 bass trumpet	12 cellos
4 trombones (4th plays contrabass trombone)	8 double basses

that require all the firepower in his arsenal. Upon discovering at rehearsals that the orchestra was generally too loud, he laid down the law and ordered the musicians to play *"piano, pianissimo"* most of the time. According to one member of the team, "Wagner declared that the orchestra should support the singer as the sea does a boat, rocking but never upsetting." (Unlike most operas, *The Valkyrie* has no chorus part; in fact, the only *Ring* opera that uses a chorus is *Twilight of the Gods*.)

Edvard Grieg wrote enthusiastically—and perhaps a shade enviously—about the small army of musicians that Wagner had recruited: "There are about one hundred and twenty-five in the orchestra and what tremendous artists they all are! All of the very first rank. And with their magnificent fullness of tone each one sounds like two—so this orchestra could be taken for one of two hundred ordinary players! As they gather in the pit it comes to resemble a huge ant-hill of players and instruments."

WAGNERIAN LEITMOTIFS

If you knew nothing about Wagner, from the description of the leitmotifs you would probably think of the music of *The Valkyrie* as being somewhat like Beethoven's—constructed of brief but memorable themes, or motives, that are assembled in various patterns to make much longer stretches of music. However, thanks to Wagner's own writings and the avalanche of publicity that preceded the first performance of the *Ring*, it was the rare audience member at Bayreuth in 1876 who did not understand that Wagner used these short, characteristic themes not only as building blocks for musical architecture, but also as signposts for the audience. More important for Wagner's psychological purposes, they express the emotional state associated with the object or person at the moment, in addition to anticipating, labeling, or recalling.

We call these short themes leitmotifs (the German word *Leitmotiv* means "leading motive"), even though Wagner himself did not use the term. Each leitmotif has the job of "leading" our attention to something—an object, an emotion, a person, an event. Wagner teaches us what each leitmotif means, so that we learn without having to work very hard.

There is a moment in Act 1 of *The Valkyrie*, for example, when Siegmund mentions that his father promised him a sword in his time of direst need. A spark from the fire lights up the sword stuck in the tree; we see it, though Siegmund does not. At that moment, a trumpet in the orchestra plays a sort of fanfare in C major, and when later Siegmund pulls the sword out of the tree ▶, the sword leitmotif swells to titanic proportions. By the end of the act, whenever we hear this music, no matter how it may be understated or mixed in with other music, we know—even if the characters themselves do not—what it refers to (see The Sword Leitmotif, right).

Wagner's leitmotifs are characterized by clearly recognizable chord progressions or rhythms. Some, like the sword leitmotif, are more or less fixed—they usually occur in the same form, and often in the same key, every time they appear. Another example is the leitmotif that represents Valhalla, which is first heard in *The Rhinegold*. In the second scene of that opera, Wotan is shown with Fricka, his wife, and the towers of Valhalla rise up in the background while the noble, stately theme is played in D♭

🎙 The sword leitmotif in Wagner's *Valkyrie*

▶ Video, Wagner: *The Valkyrie*, "Siegmund heiss' ich"

The Sword Leitmotif

The leitmotif of the sword is gradually revealed as the first act progresses. (The numbers in parentheses indicate where it occurs.)

At first we do not know why Sieglinde is looking at the tree (1). We begin to associate the sound of the motive with the idea of a sword when Siegmund wonders about the sword his father promised him (2). Later, the fire brightens in the hut (3), revealing the place on the tree where the sword's hilt is protruding (though Siegmund does not yet recognize what it is). Sieglinde begins to tell the story of a weapon she is going to show him (4), and then tells how Wotan placed it there; she shows him the weapon (5). She then says that she knows who will be able to pull it out (6). Finally, at the climactic moment near the end of the act, Sigmund draws out the sword (7).

⑤ Wagner: *The Rhinegold*, the Valhalla leitmotif

⑤ Wagner: *The Valkyrie*, Sieglinde's pity leitmotif

⑤ Wagner: *The Valkyrie*, love leitmotif

⑤ Wagner: *The Valkyrie*, Hunding's leitmotif

major. Later in the *Ring*, this same music is played whenever the home of the gods is referred to, either explicitly or implicitly. In Act 1 of *The Valkyrie*, when Sieglinde says that a mysterious stranger has thrust the sword into the ash tree, the orchestral accompaniment tells us everything we need to know: the stranger was Wotan, who dwells in Valhalla.

Other leitmotifs are malleable, changing form as the situation changes. One such leitmotif, representing the ring, acts as a sort of cement that binds many elements of the music drama together. Other such leitmotifs represent pity and love; the latter plays a particularly important role in the first act of *The Valkyrie*.

All told, about twenty clearly identifiable leitmotifs recur throughout the *Ring* cycle. Another thirty or so leitmotifs are more localized, as is the case with Hunding's signature theme in *The Valkyrie*; we recognize him immediately even before we see him, by the sinister and military sound of his quartet of low brass instruments (the special Wagner tubas created for the *Ring*). When Hunding finally appears on stage, the full, loud version of this theme confirms our suspicions about his dark side.

Wagner did not invent the use of musical motives as a kind of shorthand to evoke subliminal images or associations in the listener's mind. Many opera composers in the eighteenth and early nineteenth centuries (including Wagner himself) laced their works with "reminiscence motifs" that recalled characters or situations already presented onstage (think of Berlioz's *idée fixe*), but Wagner was the first to employ leitmotifs systematically.

LARGER MUSICAL FORMS

In *The Valkyrie,* as in the other three *Ring* operas, Wagner is as concerned with larger musical forms as with the localized occurrences of leitmotifs. He is deeply aware of harmony as a propelling force, even when the harmony is static: witness the prelude to *The Rhinegold*, with its 136 bars of an unfolding E♭ major chord. The listener will likely not be aware of the means by which Wagner shapes melody, harmony, and leitmotif into large forms. Wagner's ability to delay a final cadence—for example, by substituting a different, sometimes surprising or ambiguous harmony for the final chord we expect—can keep our expectations suspended for a long time. His frequent use of **pedal points**—maintaining a single note in the bass, like a pedal note on an organ, while harmonies in the upper voices change—is another way of holding suspense in the balance.

Pedal points

Listening to the Music

🎧 LG 51

ACT 1, PRELUDE (STORM)

The Valkyrie begins with a vivid musical representation of a storm, out of which Siegmund stumbles blindly into Hunding's hut. The Storm Music, which takes the place of a conventional overture such as one finds in Mozart's *Don Giovanni*, is a terrifically effective piece of scene painting; you can almost feel the sharp lash of the rain and the surging blasts of wind. At the same time, it is a carefully constructed piece of instrumental writing; it repays careful study because it illustrates how larger stretches of music can be put together from smaller elements (see LG 51, p. 359).

By the time Wagner wrote this prelude, there was already a fair amount of storm music in the orchestral repertory—for example, in Beethoven's Sixth Symphony, Rossini's *William Tell* Overture, and Wagner's own *Flying Dutchman*—so Wagner knew that his contemporaries would instantly recognize it as such.

LISTENING GUIDE 51   ⓢ | DVD

Wagner *The Valkyrie*, Act 1, Prelude (Storm)   3:04

DATE: 1876

GENRE: Opera (music drama)

LISTEN FOR

MELODY: Many repetitions of a small motive, representing the storm:

RHYTHM/METER: Regular two- and four-bar phrases

FORM: Two climaxes; the first climax anticipates the second. The second climax has the leitmotif (from *The Rhinegold*) of Donner, the god of storms:

EXPRESSION/DYNAMICS: Large-scale crescendos and diminuendos help shape the form

TIME	DESCRIPTION
	Opening theme
0:00	A two-bar phrase, distinct for its up-and-down shape.
0:04	Two-bar phrase repeated.
0:07	First bar, four times.
0:12	Second bar, four times, the last two turn up.
0:18	Four-bar phrase, derived from previous bar, rises and falls.
0:24	Opening theme, repeated higher.
0:52	Added element: first climax, four bars, the last leading to a chord, which alternates with the rising figure.
1:03	Subsides: the scale figure, in various versions, in groups of four bars.
1:26	Second climax
	Four bars: opening figure, polyphonic, plus fanfare (Donner leitmotif, thunder and lightning, from *The Rhinegold*).
1:54	Repetitions of rumble plus version of Donner figure; decrescendo.
2:21	Opening figure, returning to home key.
2:44	Opening figure returns as at beginning.
2:55	Siegmund leitmotif, curtain up . . .

ACT 1, SCENE 1: SIEGMUND AND SIEGLINDE MEET AND FALL IN LOVE   LG 52

Siegmund has blindly sought refuge from the storm and finds himself in the home of Sieglinde and her husband. Hunding extends the customary hospitality to his guest but soon realizes that Siegmund is his enemy and that they are duty-bound to engage in mortal combat the next day. Later in the scene, Siegmund and Sieglinde fall in love and realize that they are both the children of Wotan. (Their child, the hero Siegfried, will be the protagonist of the last two operas in the *Ring* cycle.) Wagner's music for this deeply moving scene artfully combines their leitmotifs with those representing the storm and love. Sieglinde silently brings Siegmund a drinking horn filled with water. Wagner's stage directions say: "Siegmund drinks

⑤ Wagner: *The Valkyrie*, Sieglinde's pity leitmotif

⑤ Wagner: *The Valkyrie*, Siegmund's leitmotif, at end mixed with Sieglinde's

and gives the horn back. As he signs his thanks with his head, his eyes fix themselves on her with growing interest." What we hear first is a short rising figure that here is associated with Sieglinde's pity for the wayfarer. A sinking, scalar fragment of the Storm Music, associated with Siegmund's leitmotif, is repeated three times, each time higher in pitch (growing interest, perhaps); then a solo cello picks up the last note of his theme and transforms it into a beautiful melody, accompanied by cellos and double basses: Siegmund is in love (see LG 52, below). The love leitmotif will play an increasingly prominent role in Act 1, until finally it overpowers all else. But in this particular passage nobody has said a word; all the action is in the orchestra.

LISTENING GUIDE 52 ⑤ | DVD

Wagner *The Valkyrie,* Act 1, Scene 1, Siegmund and Sieglinde Meet and Fall in Love ("Wess' Herd dies auch sei")   4:57

DATE: 1876

GENRE: Opera (music drama)

LISTEN FOR

MELODY: Leitmotifs introduced (Siegmund, Sieglinde, love):

Siegmund

Love leitmotif 1

Sieglinde

Love leitmotif 2

RHYTHM/METER: Voices in speech rhythm

HARMONY: Leitmotifs used as harmonic filler, as "glue" between vocal lines

TEXTURE: Development of leitmotifs in longer orchestral passages

---

TIME	TEXT	TRANSLATION (*Wagner's stage directions in italics*)	LEITMOTIFS IN THE ORCHESTRA
	Siegmund		
0:00	Wess' Herd dies auch sei, hier muss' ich rasten.	Whoever this hearth belongs to, here must I rest.	
0:07			Siegmund's leitmotif twice; remnants of storm leitmotif.

	Sieglinde		
0:40	Ein fremder Mann? Ihn muss ich fragen.	A stranger? I must question him.	
0:49	Wer kam in's Haus, und liegt dort am Herd?	Who came in, and lies there on the hearth?	
0:58			Siegmund's leitmotif.
1:03	Müde liegt er von Weges Müh'n.	There he lies exhausted from travel.	
1:10			Siegmund's leitmotif.
1:14	Schwanden die Sinne ihm? Wäre er siech?	Is he only tired? Is he sick?	
1:20			Siegmund's leitmotif combined with Sieglinde's—each twice.
1:31	Noch schwillt ihm der Athem; das Auge nur schloss er.	He's still breathing; he has just closed his eyes.	At end, three bass notes in same rhythm as the end of Sieglinde's leitmotif.
1:41	Muthig dünkt mich der Mann	He looks brave to me	At end, three bass notes in same rhythm as the end of Sieglinde's leitmotif.
1:49	Sank er müd'auch hin.	though very tired.	
1:54			Siegmund's leitmotif: he wakens.
	Siegmund		
1:59	Ein Quell! Ein Quell!	A drink! A drink!	
	Sieglinde		
2:02	Erquickung schaff'ich.	I'll bring you water.	
2:04		(*She goes out to fill the drinking horn, and returns and offers it to him.*)	Siegmund's leitmotif combined with Sieglinde's (twice); then a development of both, ending with Sieglinde's.
2:44	Labung biet'ich dem lechzenden Gaumen:	Here's a drink for dry lips:	At end, Sieglinde's leitmotif.
2:56	Wasser, wie du gewollt!	Water, as you wished!	
3:04		(*He drinks, then gazes at her.*)	Solo cello plays Siegmund's leitmotif three times, each higher than the last; then breaks into love leitmotifs, heard for the first time as they look into each other's eyes. There are two melodies: (1) "Du bist der Lenz" first leitmotif, and (2) chromatic second leitmotif.
	Siegmund		
4:15	Kühlende Labung gab mir der Quell,	The water was refreshing,	At end, Sieglinde's leitmotif.
4:21	des Müden Last machte er leicht;	my weariness is eased;	At end, Sieglinde's leitmotif.
4:27	erfrisch ist der Muth, das Aug'erfreut des Sehens selige Lust.	my heart is renewed, my eyes are gladdened at what I see.	At end, Sieglinde's leitmotif.

LG 53   **ACT 1, SCENE 2: SIEGLINDE AND SIEGMUND IN LOVE, AND SIEGMUND'S SENSE OF FOREBODING**

Wagner seeks musical and dramatic unity at various levels through his use of recurring leitmotifs and large-scale harmonic structures. The local presence, in real time, of leitmotifs as orchestral glue allows for deep psychological moments in which we hear what the characters are thinking. Listening Guide 53 (see below) focuses on a scene from Act 1, in which for a long time nothing is spoken, but everything is understood by the audience. Wagner's stage directions, together with his music for the orchestra, bring the interior drama of the characters out into the open.

LISTENING GUIDE 53   Ⓢ | DVD

Wagner *The Valkyrie*, Act 1, Scene 2, Sieglinde and Siegmund in Love, and Siegmund's Sense of Foreboding   4:00

DATE: 1876

GENRE: Opera (music drama)

LISTEN FOR

MELODY: Leitmotifs indicate what a character is thinking. Heard before this excerpt is the leitmotif of Hunding (its rhythm will reappear in this scene):

TEXTURE: Use of leitmotifs in sequences; creation of musical material by polyphonic combinations of leitmotifs

TIME	ACTION (*Wagner's stage directions in italics*)	LEITMOTIFS IN THE ORCHESTRA
0:00	[Hunding has told Sieglinde to prepare his drink]	Bass has slow rhythm derived from Hunding leitmotif.
0:12	*Sieglinde stands a while undecided and thoughtful.*	Sieglinde (clarinet, with a minor-key turn at the end derived from the renunciation of love leitmotif, first heard in *The Rhinegold*).
0:31	*She turns slowly and goes with hesitating steps to the pantry.*	The same pattern repeated; Sieglinde's leitmotif in oboe.
0:59	*There she stops again and remains lost in thought with her face half turned away.*	Bass derived from Hunding; the leitmotif in woodwinds is that of the Walsung's woe (Siegmund sang it recently).
1:33	*With quiet resolve she opens the cupboard, fills a drinking horn, and shakes in some herbs from a box.* [She has decided to give Hunding a sleeping potion].	Sieglinde (strings), with Hunding in bass.
1:51	*Then she turns her eyes to Siegmund, to meet his eyes, which he has never taken off her.*	Love leitmotif 1 in clarinet.
2:03	*She sees Hunding watching them, and goes immediately to the bedroom.*	Hunding in bass.
2:09	*On the steps she turns again, looks passionately at Siegmund,*	Love leitmotif 1, descending, in oboe.
2:30	*and shows with her eyes, with significant earnestness, a particular place in the tree-trunk.*	Sword leitmotif (trumpet, echoed by oboe).
2:45	*Hunding gets up and chases her out of the room.*	Hunding
2:54	*With a last look at Siegmund, she goes into the bedroom and closes the door after her.*	Sword (oboe)
3:09		Hunding (tubas)
3:15	*Hunding* Mit Waffen wehrt sich der Mann. Dich, Wölfling treffe ich morgen: mein Wort hörtest du: hütte dich wohl! (A man needs weapons; I'll see you tomorrow, Wölfling. You heard me: protect yourself well!)	
3:46	*He goes into the room.*	Hunding—rhythm only, gradually fading.

ACT 1, SCENE 3: SPRING SONG—"WINTERSTÜRME WICHEN DEM WONNEMOND"

 LG 54
▶ Video

Opera for much of its history—think of Mozart's *Don Giovanni* (Chapter 7)—was full of songs, and the songs were often full of virtuosic vocal display. By the middle of the nineteenth century, however, the display was disappearing in favor of a more lyrical style. Wagner pushes this tendency even further: songs are very rare in his operas, especially the *Ring*. Instead, he gives most of his characters a kind of song-speech, avoiding long **melismas** or other purely vocal effects that hinder the understanding of the words. (In this his vocal writing resembles the speechlike **recitatives** that we remember from the music of Monteverdi, Handel, and Mozart.) Usually his characters do not sing the melodies of the leitmotifs, which are in the realm of the orchestra. Only rarely does Wagner give a singer what sounds like a traditional aria full of text repetition, smooth phrases, and soaring melody.

One such place is in Act 1, where Siegmund, enraptured by the warm breeze that enters the room when the doors of the hut are blown open, sings a song about spring and love. It has a wonderful rustling accompaniment; note too that its bass line is not unlike the storm motive—the fierce winds have changed to summer breezes.

It is at the end of this song, which closes with the word *Lenz* (spring), that Sieglinde makes it clear that the leitmotif we have heard in the orchestra is indeed the music of love—she now sings that melody, using the word that Siegmund has just uttered: "Du bist der Lenz nach dem ich verlangte" (You are the spring I have been longing for). It is one of the tenderest and most passionate moments in opera (see LG 54, below).

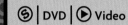 Wagner: *The Valkyrie*, "Du bist der Lenz"

LISTENING GUIDE 54   ⑤ | DVD | ▶ Video

Wagner *The Valkyrie*, Act 1, Scene 3, "Winterstürme wichen dem Wonnemond"   4:03

DATE: 1876

GENRE: Opera (music drama)

LISTEN FOR

MELODY: Sieglinde sings the love leitmotif as "Du bist der Lenz"—one of the few times a leitmotif is sung

SCORING: Rustling accompaniment of woodwinds; bass line similar to storm leitmotif in Prelude

EXPRESSION: The most lyrical, aria-like passage in the opera

TIME	TEXT	TRANSLATION	DESCRIPTION
0:00			Orchestra depicts moonlight and the rustling of leaves.
	Siegmund		
0:22	Winterstürme wichen dem Wonnemond, in mildem Lichte leuchtet der Lenz; auf linden Lüften leicht und lieblich, Wunder webend er sich wiegt; durch Wald und Auenweht sein Atem, weit geöffnetlacht sein Aug':	Spring has conquered the winter storms, springtime shines with a gentle light; On balmy breezes, light and lovely, it works miracles as it sighs; Through woods and meadows its breath blows, its wide-open eyes are smiling:	Siegmund's music is lyrical, aria-like.
0:59	aus sel'ger Vöglein Sange süss er tönt, holde Düfte haucht er aus; seinem warmen Blut entblühen wonnige Blumen, Keim und Spross entspringt seiner Kraft.	Heavenly birdsong sweetly proclaims it, its presence exhales blissful scents; its warm blood produces wonderful flowers, buds and shoots grow from its might.	Here he begins what sounds like a second strophe.
1:24	Mit zarter Waffen Zier bezwingt er die Welt; Winter und Sturm wichen der starken Wehr: wohl musste den tapfern Streichen	With weapons of charm it conquers the world; Winter and storms vanish before their strong force: And so these strong doors yield also,	The song, and the accompaniment, becomes more excited.

	die strenge Türe auch weichen, die trotzig und starr uns—trennte von ihm.	for, stubborn and hard, they kept us from the spring.	
1:50			The orchestra plays love leitmotif 1.
1:58	Zu seiner Schwester schwang er sich her; die Liebe lockte den Lenz: in unsrem Busen barg sie sich tief; nun lacht sie selig dem Licht. Die bräutliche Schwester befreite der Bruder; zertrümmert liegt, was je sie getrennt: jauchzend grüsst sich das junge Paar: vereint sind Liebe und Lenz!	To its sister here it flew; Love decoyed the spring: In our hearts it was deeply concealed; now it smiles joyfully at the light. The brother frees the sister-bride; all that kept them apart lies in ruins; Joyfully the young couple greet one another: Love and Spring are united!	Siegmund sings the leitmotif.
	Sieglinde		
3:19	Du bist der Lenz, nach dem ich verlangte in frostigen Winters Frist. Dich grüsste mein Herz mit heiligem Grau'n, als dein Blick zuerst mir erblühte . . .	You are the spring I longed for in the frosty winter cold. My heart greeted you with holy fear, when first your glance lighted upon me . . .	Sieglinde begins with love leitmotif 2, continues with music from the first part of that leitmotif.

ACT 1, SCENE 3: SIEGMUND AND THE SWORD—"SIEGMUND HEISS' ICH"

 LG 55

 Video

The sword motif in Wagner's *Valkyrie*

Act 1 culminates with the thrilling moment in which Siegmund extracts the sword from the ash tree. In a soliloquy that preceded the Spring Song, he recalled his father's promise that a sword would be his salvation in his hour of need. Thanks to the Valhalla leitmotif (which was first heard in *Rheingold*), we learned that Wotan is the "mysterious stranger" who left the sword for him to find in Hunding's hut. At the end of the first act, Siegmund christens his weapon "Notung" (Needful), and he and Sieglinde, in a frenzy of love, rush off into the forest (see LG 55, p. 366).

In this ecstatic scene, Wagner achieves his goal of the oneness of music and drama. The inner and outer aspects of the music drama are fused: the outer aspect is the spoken word and the action of the drama, which we apprehend through the characters' words and actions; the inner aspect is the world of thoughts and emotions, which is portrayed by the instrumental music. Two leitmotifs that have developed over the course of the act—the sword, first heard when Sieglinde indicated its place on the tree with her glance, and love, begun when Sieglinde looks at Siegmund over the drinking horn—reach their culmination, musically and dramatically, at the end of the act.

ACT 3, PRELUDE: RIDE OF THE VALKYRIES

 Video

Two further video excerpts (Ride of the Valkyries and Magic Fire Music) allow us to experience some of Wagner's greatest writing for orchestra. The famous Ride of the Valkyries opens Act 3, as the band of warrior-maidens gathers on a mountaintop. In the preceding act, Wotan instructed Brünnhilde to ensure that Siegmund defeated Hunding, but was overruled by Fricka, his wife. When Brünnhilde, moved by the lovers' entreaties, shielded Siegmund anyway, Wotan shattered Siegmund's sword with his spear but it is Hunding who then kills Siegmund. Now Brünnhilde has come to seek protection for Sieglinde from her sister Valkyries.

LISTENING GUIDE 55 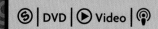 DVD | ▶ Video | 🎙️

Wagner *The Valkyrie*, Act 1, Scene 3, "Siegmund heiss' ich"   3:59

DATE: 1876

GENRE: Opera (music drama)

LISTEN FOR

THEMES: Leitmotifs introduced earlier reach a climax:
The sword is revealed, and its leitmotif
reaches a climactic fanfare, played
by trumpets, all in one harmony:

SCORING: Orchestral passages

EXPRESSION: Voices in speech rhythm

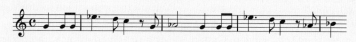

Renunciation of love leitmotif
foreshadows plot:

The love leitmotif at the end
of the scene:

TIME	TEXT	TRANSLATION (*Wagner's stage directions in italics*)	DESCRIPTION
	Sieglinde		
0:00	Siegmund: so nenn ich dich!	I name you Siegmund!	
		(*He leaps to the ash tree and grips the sword's handle*)	
	Siegmund		His excitement at the sword can be heard in the trumpet's sword leitmotif.
0:09	Siegmund heiss' ich	Siegmund I am named	
	und Siegmund bin ich!	and Siegmund I am!	
	Bezeug' es dies Schwert,	Let this sword,	
	das zaglos ich halte!	which I fearlessly hold, be a witness!	
	Wälse verhiess mir,	Wälse promised me	
	in höchster Not	that in deepest distress	
	fänd' ich es einst:	I would find it one day:	
	ich fass' es nun!	now I hold it!	
0:41	Heiligster Minne	Holiest love's	He sings the renunciation of love leitmotif; Wagner is perhaps letting us know that this love is doomed.
	höchste Not,	deepest need,	
	sehnender Liebe	yearning love's	
	sehrende Not	searing desire	
	brennt mir hell in der Brust,	burns bright in my breast,	
	drängt zu Tat und Tod:	urges me to do and die:	
1:07	Notung! Notung!	Needful! Needful!	He calls on the sword by name ("Needful").
	So nenn' ich dich, Schwert.	So I name you, sword.	
	Notung! Notung!	Needful! Needful!	
	Neidlicher Stahl!	Precious steel!	
	Zeig' deiner Schärfe	Show your sharp	
	schneidenden Zahn:	and cutting edge:	
	heraus aus der Scheide zu mir!	come from your scabbard to me!	

1:39		(*With a mighty effort he draws the sword from the tree and shows it to the astonished and enraptured Sieglinde*)	Sword leitmotif.
1:51	Siegmund, den Wälsung, siehst du, Weib! Als Brautgabe bringt er dies Schwert: so freit er sich die seligste Frau; dem Feindeshaus entführt er dich so.	It is Siegmund, the Volsung, that you see, woman! As wedding gift he brings this sword: so he weds the holiest of women; he takes you away from the enemy's house.	Note the use of brass in the orchestra.
2:23	Fern von hier folge mir nun, fort in des Lenzes lachendes Haus: dort schützt dich Notung,	Far from here now follow me, out into springtime's laughing house: there the sword Needful	The orchestra plays the music of "Winterstürme."
2:42	das Schwert, wenn Siegmund dir liebend erlag!	will protect you, even if Siegmund dies of love!	Notice the use of the love leitmotif 2 in the orchestra.
		(*He has embraced her, in order to lead her away with him.*)	
		(*She tears herself away in highest intoxication, and faces him.*)	
	Sieglinde		
2:59	Bist du Siegmund, den ich hier sehe? Sieglinde bin ich, die dich ersehnt: die eigne Schwester	Are you Siegmund, whom I see here? I am Sieglinde who longed for you: your own sister	
3:15	gewannst du zu eins mit dem Schwert!	you have won along with the sword!	Very rapid version of the love leitmotif.
	Siegmund		
3:17	Braut und Schwester bist du dem Bruder: so blühe denn, Wälsungen-Blut!	You are wife and sister to your brother; so flourish, Volsung blood!	
		(*Passionately he draws her to him; with a cry she falls on his breast. The curtain falls quickly.*)	Sword and love leitmotifs combined.

The Ride of the Valkyries, one of Wagner's most accomplished and successful orchestral interludes, was often played as an excerpt on concert programs, both before and after the premiere of the opera itself. (For this purpose Wagner needed to rewrite it a little, since orchestras were unlikely to have enough vocal soloists available to sing the parts of the Valkyries.) The Valkyries' cry of "Hojotoho!" has already been introduced to us in Act 2, and this is the moment where Wagner combines it with a magnificent orchestral movement.

The beginning of Act 3 shows the Valkyries, those daughters of Wotan who ride through the sky escorting the souls of dead heroes to Valhalla, as they cry out "Hojotoho! Heijaha!" In Wagner's production the riders were shown by projections onto a scrim. Like the storm that opens Act 1, this music is artfully constructed from a small number of ideas assembled into larger structures.

▶ Video

ACT 3, SCENE 3: MAGIC FIRE MUSIC

Wotan is deeply displeased with Brünnhilde, his favorite daughter, for siding with Siegmund in the combat with Hunding. In a long and moving scene, he explains to Brünnhilde that even the chief of the gods cannot go against what is ordained. She has disobeyed him and will be punished by being placed in a deep trance, to be awakened by whatever mortal passes by and claims her. Brünnhilde's pleas soften his heart, and he protects her with a shield and a circle of supernatural fire that only a hero can penetrate. That hero will be Siegfried, the child of Siegmund and Sieglinde.

The delicately orchestrated Magic Fire Music—preceded by an invocation of Loge, the god of fire—provides a magical and poignant ending for *The Valkyrie*. Wagner creates a sense of mystery, of time stopping, as we await the hero who will appear in the next installment of *The Ring of the Nibelung*.

How Did It Go?

MONDAY, AUGUST 14, 1876, 4:25 P.M.

"Of all the dull towns I imagine Bayreuth, in its normal state, to be the dullest," grumbled a reporter who had come all the way from London for the festival. But of course this was not the town's normal state. Everybody in the musical world knew that the performances were taking place there. A sizable contingent of royalty, from the emperor of Brazil to the emperor of Germany, was present, along with such musical notables as the composers Edvard Grieg and Peter Ilyich Tchaikovsky, and journalists from around the world. (King Ludwig attended only the last of the three cycles.) All the hotels were overcrowded, finding something to eat was said to be a mortal struggle, and there was a sense of excitement in the air.

The opening-night performance of *The Rhinegold*, on August 13, went pretty well, despite a few minor mishaps. (Wotan dropped the ring and it rolled off into the wings; a stagehand raised a curtain too soon and revealed other stagehands in shirtsleeves, destroying Wagner's illusion.) Wagner's music was marvelously well performed. At the end the audience applauded for twenty minutes, hoping that the composer would appear on stage. This did not please Wagner, who wanted the performance to be something of a ritual experience, and he promptly had a notice printed to instruct the audience not to applaud the following day. (In ordinary opera houses, it was entirely normal to applaud a favorite singer or aria, sometimes in the hope of getting the music repeated on the spot. But the Festival Theater was not an ordinary opera house.)

The Valkyrie lasted from 4:25 until 9:50 p.m. (according to Richard Fricke's watch; others reported slightly different timings). Each of the three acts was applauded at its end—despite Wagner's injunction—and the Ride of the Valkyries at the beginning of Act 3 got its own round of applause (it was already well known to concert audiences as an orchestral piece). Intermissions of about an hour separated the acts, during which the audience was welcome to stroll around the grounds or take a meal in one of the theater's two

FIG. 13.10 A drawing from 1876 depicting the battle between Hunding and Siegmund; Wotan in the background breaks Siegmund's sword as Hunding kills him; Sieglinde in the foreground looks on in horror.

restaurants (though, in fact, they had to fight for a place). A fanfare of brass instruments, playing music from the opera, called the audience back to their seats for the second and third acts.

By all accounts it was a very good performance, with fewer of the technical glitches that had detracted from *The Rhinegold*. The orchestra, under Richter's inspired direction, rose magnificently to the occasion. The big symphonic numbers—the opening storm, the Ride of the Valkyries, and the Magic Fire Music—were all calculated to produce a spectacular effect. Wagner wanted the staging to be equally impressive (see Figure 13.10). The first-act scene in Hunding's hut, with its sword-bearing ash tree, was universally admired. But as a "total work of art," the production left something to be desired. The ride of the Valkyries through the sky was depicted by projected lantern slides, but most of the audience couldn't make out the images. (At the premiere of *The Valkyrie* in Munich, King Ludwig's stable boys, mounted on real horses, had impersonated the warrior-maidens.) And the magic fire with which Wotan surrounds Brünnhilde at the end was an ineffective ring of gas jets.

FIG. 13.11   Amalie Materna as Brünnhilde poses with the horse donated by King Ludwig II of Bavaria.

By most accounts, Albert Niemann, as Siegmund, sang beautifully. Grieg called his performance "overwhelmingly good," and Lehmann praised him to the skies: "He had intellect, vocal power and incomparable expression at his command. His singing, his acting and his stage presence took possession of everyone—this Siegmund was unique and will no more come again than will another Wagner." Fricke, on the other hand, reported that Niemann's voice was not in good shape, and the American critic John R. G. Hassard didn't care for him at all ("His voice is worn and husky, and his love-making brutal"). It's remarkable how differently people heard the same singer.

Josephine Scheffsky was acceptable, if not dazzling, as Sieglinde. The strain was so telling on Franz Betz (Wotan) that it was noticed by more than one critic, and indeed the next day's performance of *Siegfried*—in which Betz was scheduled to sing the demanding role for the third day in a row—had to be postponed a day. Everybody agreed that Amalie Materna was first-rate as Brünnhilde (see Figure 13.11). A large and attractive woman, she had a warrior's build and a voice to match—what today would be called a Wagnerian voice.

Wagner left the theater before the end of the performance of *The Valkyrie*, strained and tired. Curtain calls were forbidden, as he had already announced on a placard, but the audience applauded and shouted tumultuously anyway, ignoring the oppressive summer heat inside the theater. The emperor of Germany dined at one of the theater restaurants and departed by train at 11:30 p.m. Most of the rest of the audience probably headed straight for bed, to save their strength for the two long evenings of music drama that lay ahead.

The Valkyrie Then and Now

Wagner's music has had a remarkable career since that evening in 1876, and has engendered a cult following that persists to this day. The Bayreuth Theater still stands, and it still produces Wagner's works exclusively. It is the sort of temple of music that Wagner had intended, and a monument to Wagner that surely would not displease him.

Wagner was a brilliant, gifted, inspired composer; he was also a person of selfish habits, despicable prejudices, and devious actions. His long relationship with King Ludwig of Bavaria, whose financial help ultimately made Bayreuth possible, may have been based in part on deceit. (Wagner allowed the king to think he admired him, and followed his advice, more than he actually did.)

It's not hard to see why Wagner's combination of German nationalism and blatant anti-Semitism made him a hero to the Nazis in the twentieth century. (Adolf Hitler was close with the Wagner family and regularly attended the Bayreuth Festival.) Partly for that reason, his music has long had political overtones; for example, the Israel Chamber Orchestra's decision to appear at the 2011 Bayreuth Festival set off a storm of controversy in Israel, where Wagner's works are still tainted by their association with the Holocaust.

Despite his place in history, Wagner's fame endures because of the nature of his stories and the quality of his music. The legends on which he bases his texts are, like so many myths, stories about universal human conditions, and they explain us to ourselves, whether we are German or not. The inverse relationship between power and love; the conflict that arises when duty requires one thing and passion requires another—these are human, not German, issues. We recognize Wotan's desire to get everything right, which ends up making everything go wrong. At the end, Valhalla is consumed by flames, as the Rhinegold is finally returned to its only rightful resting-place, at the bottom of the river. If it had not been disturbed, none of these troubles would have arisen—but then we would also have been deprived of four evenings of thrilling music.

Chapter Review

Summary of Musical Styles

There are three essential Wagnerian styles represented in this chapter:

- The narrative style, in which characters speak to each other (or to themselves) using a relatively speechlike melody, while the orchestra provides an accompaniment in which inner meanings and feelings are depicted without having to be spoken aloud or explained. Examples include the dialogues—spoken and unspoken—between Sieglinde and Siegmund.

- The lyrical style (quite rare in the *Ring* operas, and usually saved for moments of high intensity), in which a character sings a beautifully flowing melody. An example is Siegmund's song "Winterstürme wichen dem Wonnemond," followed by Sieglinde's passionate "Du bist der Lenz."

- The symphonic style, usually reserved for moments when the orchestra can be allowed to play at its top volume. Examples here include the opening storm, the Ride of the Valkyries, and the Magic Fire Music.

Wagner invented a means of tying everything together with a complex web of brief themes called **leitmotifs.** They can be melodies, harmonic progressions, harmonic patterns, or a combination of all three. These leitmotifs are associated with objects, characters, emotions, and places.

ⓢ Multimedia Resources and Review Materials on StudySpace

Visit wwnorton.com/studyspace for review of Chapter 13.

What Do You Know?

Check the facts for this chapter. Take the online **Quiz**.

What Do You Hear?

Listening Quizzes and **Music Activities** will help you understand the musical works in this chapter.

ⓟ Author Videos

■ The sword leitmotif in Wagner's *Valkyrie*

Interactive Listening Guides

LG 51 Wagner: *The Valkyrie*, Act 1, Prelude (Storm)
LG 52 Wagner: *The Valkyrie*, Act 1, Scene 1, Siegmund and Sieglinde Meet and Fall in Love ("Wess' Herd dies auch sei")
LG 53 Wagner: *The Valkyrie*, Act 1, Scene 2, Sieglinde and Siegmund in Love, and Siegmund's Sense of Foreboding
LG 54 Wagner: *The Valkyrie*, Act 1, Scene 3, "Winterstürme wichen dem Wonnemond"
LG 55 Wagner: *The Valkyrie,* Act 1, Scene 3, "Siegmund heiss' ich"

ⓥ Videos

Act 1, Scene 3: "Winterstürme wichen dem Wonnemond"
Act 1, Scene 3: "Siegmund heiss' ich"
Act 3, Prelude: Ride of the Valkyries
Act 3, Scene 3: Magic Fire Music

Flashcards (Terms to Know)

Gesamtkunstwerk	pedal point
leitmotif	recitative
melisma	Stabreim
nationalism	total work of art

CHAPTER 14

FRIDAY, DECEMBER 15, 1893, NEW YORK:

Antonín Dvořák's Symphony No. 9 in E Minor (*From the New World*)

🎵 CORE REPERTOIRE	🎙 AUTHOR VIDEOS	
▪ **LG 56** First movement, Adagio—Allegro molto ▪ **LG 57** Second movement, Largo ▪ **LG 58** Third movement, Scherzo: Molto vivace—Poco sostenuto ▪ **LG 59** Fourth movement, Allegro con fuoco	▪ Syncopation and the spiritual in the first movement of the *New World* Symphony	

Introduction

"Undoubtedly the germs for the best of music lie hidden among all the races that are commingled in this great country. . . . The fact that no one here as yet has arisen to make the most of it does not prove that nothing is there. . . . Nothing must be too low or too insignificant for the musician. . . . He should listen to every whistling boy, every street singer or blind organ-grinder."

— Antonín Dvořák, "Music in America," 1895

It might seem odd that one of the most famous pieces of American classical music was written by a Czech composer closely identified with the music of his homeland. Antonín Dvořák, the celebrated composer of *Slavonic Dances*, *Moravian Duets*, and other concert-hall favorites, came to New York from his native Bohemia (the modern-day Czech Republic) in 1892 to be director of the National Conservatory of Music. During his stay in the United States, which lasted until the spring of 1895, he composed a kind of symphonic valentine to the New World, inspired by American tales, landscape, and what he considered to be American elements in music.

Dvořák had been invited to New York not only because he was one of the most famous composers in the world but also because the conservatory's sponsors hoped that he would contribute to the creation of a distinctively American style of music. After all, Dvořák was well known as a **nationalist composer** who excelled at expressing the spirit of his own people in music. He believed that Native Americans and African Americans had produced the most original and characteristic American music. Accordingly, he promoted the idea that these two musical traditions (which he seems to have regarded as indistinguishable) could serve as the basis of a new American school of composition.

Nationalist composer

Today, few people would agree that Native American and African American music are closely related, or that either of these ethnic categories represents a single, unified style. Indeed, many listeners do not consider the *New World* Symphony a particularly American work—except, perhaps, for the unforgettable first theme of the slow movement. This haunting melody, played on an English horn, has a relatively simple song form reminiscent of folk music.

Ⓢ Dvořák: Symphony No. 9, II, 1st and 2nd phrases

Actually, Dvořák's theme *is* folk music in a way: you may recognize it as the melody of "Goin' Home," a popular hymn that was set to Dvořák's music after the symphony was written (many other pop and jazz standards are also based on classical compositions). This cross-cultural appeal helps explain why the *New World* Symphony has become a favorite with audiences all over the world, regardless of whether it embodies anything distinctively American.

Ⓢ "Goin' Home"

Of course, Dvořák was not simply a nationalist composer; he wrote all kinds of compositions—chamber music, concertos, church music, operas, oratorios— and much of his music is not recognizably Bohemian, even to those listeners who are familiar with folk music from that region (see biography, p. 374). During his sojourn in America, however, he took his assignment to nurture an American musical style very seriously. Although he traveled around the country a bit, and

Antonín Dvořák (1841–1904)

For many people, the Czech composer Antonín Dvořák epitomizes the spirit of Romantic nationalism in music. Like his countryman Bedřich Smetana, he wrote music in the international classical tradition, but often based on folk themes, that made him famous far beyond the borders of his native Bohemia.

Born near Prague in 1841, Dvořák was recognized as having musical talent from an early age and became an accomplished violist and violinist. Beginning in 1857 he studied organ, theory, and composition in Prague; there he joined a dance band, taught piano, and played in an orchestra conducted by Smetana. He married one of his students, Anna Čermáková; they were a devoted couple and had nine children.

In the 1870s Dvořák began to make a name for himself as a composer in his homeland. Through his friendship with the German composer Johannes Brahms, he published his first set of *Slavonic Dances* in 1878 and became an international celebrity practically overnight. The success of his choral work *Stabat Mater* in 1882 prompted an invitation to visit London, where his Seventh Symphony was performed for the first time in 1885. Later his Requiem, Eighth Symphony, and Cello Concerto would also have their premieres in England.

Dvořák's increasing renown and prosperity allowed him to buy a house in the countryside south of Prague, and to travel to London, Russia, and elsewhere. But his stay in the United States, from 1892 to 1895, was by far his longest absence.

In later years he devoted himself chiefly to writing symphonic tone poems and operas, the best known of which is the lyric fairy tale *Rusalka*. He served as director of the Prague Conservatory from 1901 until his death (from heart trouble) in 1904. Although showered with honors at home and abroad, he never lost the humility that he had expressed years earlier in a letter to a fellow musician: "Despite the fact that I have moved a bit in the great musical world, I still remain just what I was—a simple Czech Musikant."

Dvořák is best known for his nine symphonies, but he composed in most of the prevailing genres. His gift for melody and orchestral color as well as his solid understanding of forms of the Classic era make his music so popular today, and his Cello Concerto is considered one of the great canonic works for that instrument.

Ⓢ Dvořák: *Slavonic Dances*, Op. 46, No. 1
Ⓢ Dvořák: *Humoresques,* Op. 101, No. 7
Ⓢ Dvořák: *Stabat Mater*

MAJOR WORKS: Orchestral music, including 9 symphonies (No. 9, *From the New World*) and other symphonic works (*Slavonic Dances*); concertos, including 1 for cello and 1 for violin; at least 14 operas, including *Rusalka*; chamber music, including the *Dumky* Piano Trio and the *American* Quartet; choral music, including 1 Requiem, a *Stabat Mater*, songs, and dances.

even spent a few weeks in a Czech community in rural Iowa, his experience of the New World centered on New York City. And New York, then as now, was a social and musical melting pot that defied easy categorization.

The Setting

NEW YORK IN THE 1890s

After the city of New York annexed Brooklyn and the other outer boroughs in the late 1890s to form the modern city, it had a population of more than three million people. Roughly half of them were first-generation immigrants who had crossed the Atlantic in search of the freedom symbolized by the newly erected Statue of Liberty. Others were attracted to New York, as many still are, by the promise of prosperity, glamour, and a rich cultural life.

Despite America's image as a land of opportunity and equality, the gap between rich and poor was as wide as in any Old World country. In 1892 it was reported that New York counted 1,368 millionaires among its ranks; many built mansions on the Upper East Side, which was quickly replacing lower Fifth Avenue as the city's most fashionable address (see Figure 14.1).

The southern end of Manhattan was a different world. Jacob Riis, a newspaper reporter and photographer turned social reformer, had shocked the conscience of the nation in 1890 with his book *How the Other Half Lives;* it documented the squalor of the tenements on the Lower East Side, home to successive waves of Irish, German, Italian, Jewish, and other immigrant groups since the 1830s (see Figure 14.2). Dvořák and his family lived farther north, on East 17th Street, and the cross-section of humanity that he encountered on the streets of his neighborhood must have reminded him of the mishmash of nationalities that made up the Austro-Hungarian Empire.

Automobiles were still a novelty in the 1890s; most New Yorkers used the far-flung network of streetcars, cable cars, and elevated railways. (The city's first subway was approved by voters while Dvořák lived there, but didn't go into operation until 1904.)

Industrial tycoons like John D. Rockefeller, Andrew Carnegie, J. P. Morgan, and Henry Clay Frick—all of whom Teddy Roosevelt, New York's reform-minded civil service commissioner in the early nineties, would later condemn as "malefactors of great wealth"—built their empires in part by exploiting the country's inexhaustible supply of cheap immigrant labor. Workers' strikes and antitrust legislation did little to check the growing power of the monopolists and plutocrats, and the great fortunes they amassed laid the foundations for many of the city's bastions of culture, learning, and philanthropy.

Among the institutions spawned in America's late-nineteenth-century Gilded Age were the Metropolitan Museum of Art, the New York Public Library, the American Museum of Natural History, Stanford White's Moorish-style Madison Square Garden (the second entertainment facility of that name), the original Metropolitan Opera House (erected in 1883 at 39th and Broadway), and Andrew Carnegie's famous concert hall, which opened in the spring of 1891 and quickly established itself as the city's premier venue for classical music.

New York's lively musical scene in the "Gay Nineties" (an epithet for the decade of the 1890s) rivaled that of many European cities. But even though a handful of American musicians boasted international reputations, most people still looked across the Atlantic for solo performers, conductors, opera stars, and musical culture in general. The Metropolitan Opera, for example, became virtually a German opera house in the late 1880s under the direction of Anton Seidl (see biography, p. 376). One of the great Wagner conductors of the day (he had served as the composer's assistant for the first complete *Ring* cycle in 1876), Seidl introduced American audiences to many of the German master's operas, which were invariably performed in the original language and often by members of the original casts.

In 1891, when the Met responded to changing tastes by abandoning German opera in favor of French and Italian, Seidl accepted the

FIG. 14.1 A view of Fifth Avenue, photographed in 1898. This is the area of the new mansions of the very rich. Looking north from 65th Street, the John Jacob Astor mansion is in the foreground.

FIG. 14.2 An alley known as "Bandits' Roost," off Mulberry Street in New York City. Photo by Jacob A. Riis, 1887.

ANTON SEIDL (1850–1898)

Born in Budapest, the conductor Anton Seidl was a disciple of Richard Wagner, and was recognized as the world's foremost exponent of the Wagner style long before he came to the United States in 1885. (His wife, a noted soprano, sang at the Metropolitan Opera.) Seidl presided over six highly successful German-language seasons at the Met before moving to the podium of the New York Philharmonic in 1891.

Of the many European musicians who visited New York in the late nineteenth century, only a handful stayed on permanently. Seidl was by far the most eminent and enthusiastic of these cultural immigrants. He took out American citizenship, purchased a country estate in the Catskills, and devoted himself wholeheartedly to the cause of American composers and opera in English. He considered Edward MacDowell, then America's best-known classical composer, to be greater than Johannes Brahms.

Seidl was strong in his admiration for Dvořák's symphony. "I think it will serve to incite the younger American musicians to work in the lines laid down so successfully by Dr. Dvořák, and which point in the direction of the establishment of a truly national school of musical composition," he told the press. "I like the symphony. I think it is a great work. I have discovered new beauties in it at every rehearsal, but from the very first I have been deeply impressed by the adagio [Largo]. It is so sad. It seems to me so suggestive of the loneliness of the immense prairie of the Far West. And it is pathetic with the pathos of homesickness."

Seidl continued to champion Dvořák's symphony after its Carnegie Hall premiere, conducting many performances in New York and elsewhere before his death in 1898 at the relatively young age of forty-seven.

---

conductorship of the New York Philharmonic Society. The orchestra had existed since 1842—its very first concert opened with Beethoven's Fifth Symphony—and by the time Seidl took over it had grown into a large and well-rehearsed ensemble. Since 1886 the Philharmonic had played at the Metropolitan Opera House, but when a fire gutted the Met in 1892, it moved to Carnegie Hall (which would remain the orchestra's home until Lincoln Center was built in the 1960s). It was there that Seidl would lead the first performance of Dvořák's *New World* Symphony in December 1893.

THE NATIONAL CONSERVATORY

Jeannette Thurber

Another institution that played a key role in Dvořák's visit to America was the National Conservatory of Music. It was founded in 1885, mostly as a result of the single-minded efforts of Jeannette Thurber (see Figure 14.3). With the support of her wealthy husband and a number of other rich and influential New Yorkers, Mrs. Thurber organized the school along the lines of the prestigious Paris Conservatory, where she herself had studied. Her goal was to provide a top-quality musical education so that American performers would not need to travel to Europe for their training. A focused and persuasive champion of music in New York and in America, Jeannette Thurber was a compelling force in support of music, especially opera.

Initially, the conservatory focused on opera, since Mrs. Thurber wanted to provide singers to the American Opera Company, another one of her projects. Classes were offered in voice, piano, stage deportment, and solfeggio (sight-reading); the conservatory also had an orchestra and a fencing teacher (swashbuckling was apparently an important part of an opera singer's skills). But the opera company soon went bankrupt and as a consequence the curriculum expanded into instrumental instruction, music history and theory, composition, and other areas.

Occupying a pair of adjoining brownstone houses on East 17th Street, the National Conservatory was funded and run by Mrs. Thurber. She remained determined to make musical education available to anyone with talent, regardless of their ability to pay; and she was ahead of her time in seeking out physically challenged students as well as women, African Americans, and other minorities.

As a result of its generous scholarships, and Mrs. Thurber's insistence on recruiting the best teachers available (including Anton Seidl), the conservatory was constantly in financial difficulty. The first director, Jacques Bouhy, a Belgian baritone who had sung in the premiere of Bizet's *Carmen*, returned to Europe in 1889. As Mrs. Thurber looked around for a more illustrious figure to serve as nominal head of the conservatory, she set her eyes on Dvořák and hounded him until finally, after lengthy negotiations, he agreed to come to New York for a period of two years.

Dvořák's duties as the school's musical director were far from onerous: in addition to teaching a small composition class three mornings a week, he was expected to conduct four concerts with the conservatory orchestra and six concerts of his own works in other American cities. (The latter obligation was never completed.) For this he was paid the princely salary of $15,000 a year—some twenty-five times what he was making at the Prague Conservatory. Mrs. Thurber's largesse helps explain why a composer who loved his native land and his quiet domestic life agreed to uproot himself, his wife, and two young children (see Figure 14. 4) and go to live in a noisy, crowded city in a distant country.

Dvořák's most important assignment was not part of his official job description: as he wrote to a friend on the eve of his departure, "The Americans expect great things of me. I am to show them the way into the Promised Land, the realm of a new, independent art, in short a national style of music! . . . This will certainly be a great and lofty task, and I hope that with God's help I shall succeed in it. I have plenty of encouragement to do so."

FIG. 14.3 Jeannette Thurber, founder of the National Conservatory, who engaged Antonín Dvořák as its director.

ANTONÍN DVOŘÁK IN AMERICA

Dvořák was fifty-one years old when his ship made port at Hoboken in late September 1892. Already a world-famous composer, he had recently been awarded honorary doctorates by the University of Cambridge in England and the Czech University of Prague (everyone in the United States referred to him as "Dr. Dvořák"). Americans knew him primarily for music that reflected the folk culture and music of his native land, such as the *Moravian Duets* ⑤, the folk-song settings that first won him widespread acclaim, and the *Slavonic Dances,* which had been performed by orchestras all over the world.

The great man impressed his American hosts with his modesty and vitality. One journalist was pleasantly surprised to discover that Dvořák was "not an awesome personality at all. He is much taller than his pictures would imply, and possesses not a tithe of the building ferocity to be encountered in some of them. A man about 5 ft. 10 or 11 inches, of great natural dignity, a man of character, Dvořák impresses me as an original . . . . He is not beautiful in the forms of face, but the lines of his brow are so finely modeled, and there is so much emotional life in the fiery eyes and lined face, that when he lightens up in conversation, his face is not easily forgotten."

FIG. 14.4 Antonín Dvořák, with his wife, children, and friends, shortly after their arrival in America in 1892.

Dvořák's Hobbies

From the reminiscences of J. J. Kovařik, Dvořák's guide/secretary in America:

What the Master missed in America were his pigeons and locomotives.... In New York at that time, there was only one station—the others were across the river.... At the main station they did not allow anybody on to the platform except the passengers and it was in vain that we begged the porter to let us look at the "American locomotive." We travelled by overhead tram to 155th Street, a good hour from the Master's house, and there, on a bank, waited for the Chicago or Boston express to go by. Only it took up a lot of time, nearly the whole afternoon, as we always waited for a number of trains so that it would be worth the journey.

FIG. 14.5 Dvořák's house in New York, 327 East 17th Street.

When the composer and his family moved into their new home, a three-story Italianate-style row house at 327 East 17th Street (see Figure 14.5), he found a Steinway piano waiting for him, courtesy of the head of the firm. (The house was torn down in 1991, but a statue of the composer stands in nearby Stuyvesant Square Park.) Except for his light teaching and conducting responsibilities, and various public appearances required of the National Conservatory's director, most of Dvořák's time in New York was his own (including four months of paid vacation a year). His favorite pastimes were raising pigeons (see Figure 14.6) and train spotting. He loved to visit the pigeon cage in the Central Park Zoo and often rode the elevated tram to 155th Street, where he could watch trains go by (see Dvořák's Hobbies, left).

Dvořák also frequented the docks in lower Manhattan, chatting with ships' passengers and crews, pining for the day when he could return to his beloved Bohemia (see Nostalgia and the Evolution of the *New World* Symphony, p. 379). Yet on the whole his two and a half years in the United States were happy and productive, apart from the fact that his salary was often late and he had to pester Mrs. Thurber in order to get paid. "I love the American people very much," he remonstrated with her, "and it has been my desire to help Art in the United States, but the necessities of life go hand in hand with Art and though I personally care very little for worldly things, I cannot see my wife and children in trouble." Mrs. Thurber prevailed on him to renew his contract, but he stayed only a few extra months, sailing home in April 1895.

DVOŘÁK AND NATIONALISM

At the 1893 World's Columbian Exposition in Chicago, there were splendid pavilions, the first Ferris wheel, and a great many events; the organizers of the Exposition's "Czech Day" invited Dvořák to conduct a gala concert in August. Not only was he an exceptionally appealing ambassador for his people, he was also a leading exponent of a school of composition that exerted widespread influence in the late nineteenth century. Nationalism was an essential part of Dvořák's success, in both the Old and the New World. Even people who were not of Bohemian origin responded to the folk themes and other national elements in his music.

Nationalism describes a trend in which composers seek to express the identity of a place, a people, or a country. Often this involves the use of folk melodies, rhythms, or dances. Composers may also draw on national myths and folklore for their subject matter, whether or not they adopt "local" musical styles. Nationalism in music provides an important means to experience our own culture and to enjoy the characteristic music of other cultures.

The urge to express one's own culture in music is an aspect of Romanticism that was embraced by many composers, in many countries, in the second half of the nineteenth century. Edvard Grieg in Norway, Jean Sibelius in Finland, Bedřich Smetana in Bohemia, Isaac Albéniz and Enrique Granados in Spain, and Mikhail Glinka, Modest Mussorgsky, and Alexander Borodin in Russia are a few examples of composers who gave a local or regional twist to the German symphonic tradition that was the international style of their day.

As a young nation, the United States had comparatively few indigenous musical traditions to draw upon. Nonetheless, Dvořák believed that a national American music was both possible and desirable. In 1892 he read an article called "Negro

Music," published in December of that year under the pseud-
onym "Johann Tonsor," but undoubtedly the work of a certain
Mildred Hill—a composer, writer, and student of black music—
from Kentucky (and, incidentally, the author of "Happy Birthday"). The article contained theoretical descriptions of black
music (which Dvořák would later paraphrase) and six notated
examples of "Negro" music. These included "Swing Low, Sweet
Chariot," a melody similar to a prominent theme in the first
movement of the *New World* Symphony.

Dvořák took particular interest in the African American students at the National Conservatory. It was largely through one
of them, a young black singer and composer named Harry T.
Burleigh, that he came to know the **spirituals** (a kind of religious song) of African Americans. Burleigh himself was influential in bringing the spiritual to the concert stage, through his
performances and his arrangements for voice and piano.

Dvořák observed Native American singers and dancers during
his summer vacation with his family in the Bohemian community in Spillville, Iowa, in 1893. He also enjoyed performances of
Native Ameican dances at Buffalo Bill's Wild West Show, to which
Mrs. Thurber took him in hopes of inspiring an opera based on
Henry Wadsworth Longfellow's poem *The Song of Hiawatha*. The
opera never materialized, but, as we will see, some of Dvořák's
ideas for it are embedded in his Symphony No. 9.

Dvořák began work on the symphony shortly after his
arrival in the United States, in December 1892. The full score is
dated May 24, 1893, but he continued to make changes before
its premiere in December, mostly during his summer holiday in
Iowa. That spring and summer, the composer either wrote or
(since his English was imperfect) allowed to be reported from
interviews a series of magazine and newspaper articles describing his approach to national music. The following appeared in
the *Century Magazine*:

FIG. 14.6 Dvořák was a passionate breeder of pigeons.

Nostalgia and the Evolution of the *New World* Symphony

As Mrs. Thurber reported it, she took credit for the idea of the New World *Symphony:*

Anton Seidl was probably right in declaring that the intense pathos of the slow movement of the *New World Symphony* was inspired by nostalgia—by longing for home. It was at my suggestion that he composed this symphony. He used to be particularly home-sick on steamer days when he read the shipping news in the *Herald*. Thoughts of home often moved him to tears. On one of these days I suggested that he write a symphony embodying his experiences and feelings in America —a suggestion which he promptly adopted.

> All races have their distinctive national songs which they at once
> recognize as their own, even if they have never heard them before. It is a proper
> question to ask, what songs, then, belong to the American and appeal more strik-
> ingly to him than any others? What melody will stop him on the street, if he were
> in a strange land, and make the home-feeling well up within him, no matter how
> hardened he might be, or how wretchedly the tunes were played? Their number to
> be sure seems to be limited. The most potent, as well as the most beautiful among
> them, according to my estimation, are certain of the so-called plantation-melodies
> and slave-songs, all of which are distinguished by unusual and subtle harmonies, the
> thing which I have found in no other songs but those of Scotland and Ireland.

Dvořák elaborated on the subject for readers of the *New York Herald*:

> Now, I found that the music of the negroes and of the Indians was practically identi-
> cal. I therefore carefully studied a certain number of Indian melodies which a friend
> gave me and became thoroughly imbued with their characteristics—with their spirit
> in fact. It is this spirit which I have tried to reproduce in my new symphony. I have not
> actually used any of the melodies. I have simply written original themes embodying

the peculiarities of the Indian music, and, using these themes as subjects, have developed them with all the resources of modern rhythms, harmony, counterpoint and orchestral color.

During his two and a half years in the United States, Dvořák produced other music with evident American themes. In addition to the *American* String Quartet, Op. 96, and the String Quintet in E♭ Major, Op. 97, there is some vocal music: a *Te Deum* for chorus and orchestra (written in 1892 for the 400th anniversary of Columbus's discovery of America), a patriotic potboiler of a cantata called *The American Flag*, and an arrangement of Stephen Foster's song "Old Folks at Home" (better known as "Swanee River"); there is also the famous *Humoresque* No. 7 for piano (from his set of eight *Humoresques*, Op. 101), which employs the "Plantation Dance" dotted rhythm that Dvořák located in books of minstrel songs. But for most people the *New World* Symphony is synonymous with the composer's "American" period, and a landmark in the history of musical nationalism.

The Performance

CARNEGIE HALL

For $2,500, the fifty-one-year-old Peter Ilyich Tchaikovsky, internationally known Russian composer of operas, symphonies, and concertos, traveled to New York in 1891 and lent his prestige to the inaugural festivities for the new Music Hall built and endowed by industrialist Andrew Carnegie. Other cultural institutions in New York boasted fine, purpose-built homes, but orchestras for the most part had to make do with small halls run by piano manufacturers (Steinway, Chickering, and Knabe) that were inadequate for symphony and choral concerts. Even the Metropolitan Opera House, where the Philharmonic had performed since 1886, was acoustically far from ideal.

It was Walter Damrosch, conductor of the Oratorio Society, who persuaded the Scottish-born steel magnate that a major metropolis needed a first-class auditorium for orchestral music. Carnegie acquired a plot of land on Seventh Avenue, between 56th and 57th Streets—a largely undeveloped area then considered suburban—and spent some two million dollars erecting a handsome six-story building in the Italian Renaissance style, faced with buff-colored terra cotta and brick (see Figure 14.7). Carnegie, who had already endowed dozens of public libraries throughout the country, believed that the rich had a moral obligation to share their wealth with the less fortunate; at the laying of the cornerstone in 1890, he expressed hope that "all good causes may here find a platform."

Since its opening, Carnegie Hall has arguably been the most prestigious American performing venue for classical music; among those who made their American debuts there were Sergei Rachmaninoff, Vladimir Horowitz, Jascha Heifetz, Arthur Rubinstein, and Yehudi Menuhin. The opening concert, on May 5, 1891, was a social event of the first magnitude. The cream of New York society turned out to hear Tchaikovsky

FIG. 14.7 Carnegie Hall, built by the industrialist Andrew Carnegie, on the corner of 57th Street and 7th Avenue, photographed in 1891, the year of its opening.

conduct his *Festival Coronation March* (originally composed in 1883 for Tsar Alexander III's coronation) and performances of Beethoven's *Leonore* Overture No. 3 and the Berlioz *Te Deum* led by Damrosch.

FRIDAY, DECEMBER 15, 1893, AT 2 P.M.

The first performance of Dvořák's symphony was more a social than a musical occasion; one newspaper commented on "the unusually large number of tickets purchased by persons who do not attend the concerts of the [Philharmonic] society as a rule." The orchestra played the symphony twice, on Friday afternoon and Saturday evening. (The Philharmonic's Friday matinees were considered rehearsals, but they were public events to which tickets were sold.) Even though the Friday performance was the unofficial premiere, Dvořák himself was nowhere to be seen; he had reportedly given his ticket to someone who particularly wanted to hear the symphony. Instead he went on Saturday, sitting with his family in a prominent box next to one occupied by Mrs. Thurber and her husband.

FIG. 14.8 The review of the premiere of Dvořák's *New World* Symphony in the *New York Herald* (December 16th, 1893) included this sketch of Anton Seidl conducting the orchestra.

The *New World* Symphony was not the only work on the program; it was sandwiched between selections from Felix Mendelssohn's incidental music to *A Midsummer Night's Dream* and the Violin Concerto of Johannes Brahms, played by the young French violinist Henri Marteau. But it was the Dvořák that most of the eager audience had come to hear. Thanks to the extensive coverage in the press, everybody knew that they were experiencing a significant moment in New York's, and America's, musical history. The *New York Herald* described the scene at some length:

> It was essentially a "ladies'" day. The Philharmonic rehearsals always are. . . . At half-past one there were small groups of enthusiastic admirers of the Philharmonic, of music, of Dr. Dvořák, of Marteau scattered about the great hall, chatting merrily, and, to tell the truth, rather noisily, about a variety of matters—principally private, though that by no means caused them to moderate their voices.
>
> Outside there was a long line of tardy ticket purchasers. . . . And heartily tired of it all they looked long before the flutes gave the first notes of the "Midsummer Night's Dream" Overture. No one seemed quite at ease during the earlier part of the concert. There was an air of excitement pervading every one. . . .
>
> At last the moment arrives. Mr. Seidl mounts the platform. There is a moment of expectancy. Every eye is on the uplifted baton. It descends. And we are listening at last to Dr. Dvořák's symphony "From the New World." [See Figure 14.8].

Ⓢ Dvořák: Symphony No. 9, II, opening

The Music

WHAT IS AMERICAN MUSIC?

The Americanness of Dvořák's *New World* Symphony has been fiercely debated ever since its premiere. Many of the elements that nineteenth-century critics took for American had to do with literary rather than musical associations. The *New York Times* reported that it was "authoritatively informed" that the second and third movements were written as "the expression of certain moods found in American

Longfellow's *Song of Hiawatha*

The American poet Henry Wadsworth Longfellow (1807–1882) was held in high regard in the nineteenth century. Although largely unread today, his book-length epic *The Song of Hiawatha* was among the most popular poems in the English language. Generations of schoolchildren learned its intoxicatingly rhythmic lines by heart:

By the shores of Gitche Gumee,
By the shining Big-Sea-Water,
Stood the wigwam of Nokomis,
Daughter of the Moon, Nokomis.

Hiawatha tells the legend of an Indian chief who makes peace among warring tribes and counsels his people to welcome the Christian missionaries. Longfellow's romanticized portrayal of Native Americans and his richly poetic evocations of nature and mythological tales (including one in which humans are turned into birds) captivated Dvořák. In an interview in New York, the composer recalled that he first became acquainted with the poem "about thirty years ago through the medium of a Bohemian translation. It appealed very strongly to my imagination at that time, and the impression has only been strengthened by my residence here."

Dvořák was not the only musician inspired by Longfellow's fictional creation. Frederick Delius wrote a tone poem titled *Hiawatha* in 1888, and the cantata *Scenes from the Song of Hiawatha* by another British composer, Samuel Coleridge-Taylor (who was black), once rivaled Handel's *Messiah* in popularity. Interestingly, the conductor Anton Seidl also answered Mrs. Thurber's call to write a *Hiawatha* opera, and actually seems to have completed one act before he died.

literature and definitely embodied in" Longfellow's *Song of Hiawatha* (see left). Dvořák himself testified that the Largo was "a sketch for a longer work, either a cantata or an opera," to be "based upon Longfellow's 'Hiawatha,'" while the third movement "was suggested by the scene at the feast in 'Hiawatha' where the Indians dance."

Some commentators see a close parallel between the slow, second movement and Longfellow's poem; Dvořák said that the Largo depicts Hiawatha's wooing of the beautiful Minnehaha. But even though Dvořák acknowledged Longfellow as a source of inspiration, and even though his sketch for the Largo bears the suggestive title "Legend," he did not provide a narrative to go with the symphony in the manner of Berlioz's *Fantastic Symphony* and other examples of **program music**. And yet he did want his audience to know about the connection with Hiawatha, and this affected the way people listened and reacted to the symphony.

A great deal of ink has been spilled over the question of what constitutes American music. Is it defined, as Dvořák and others believed, by the explicit or implicit use of indigenous folk music? Or by the incorporation of themes drawn from American folklore and history? Or by some indefinable manifestation of the national spirit? To write American music, the composer and music critic Virgil Thomson once said, "all you have to do is to be an American and then write any kind of music you wish." By that definition, Dvořák's *New World* Symphony could never qualify as authentically American.

The issue of American musical identity took on new meaning in the twentieth century, when American musicians challenged the dominance of the European concert-hall tradition and American popular music conquered the world. Composers like Charles Ives, Aaron Copland, and Duke Ellington set out to write music that reflected the culture and character of their homeland in much the same way that Dvořák's *Slavonic Dances* did. Not all of these "American" works used indigenous materials. As we will see later in connection with Leonard Bernstein's *West Side Story* (see Chapter 18), music can be unmistakably American even when it draws on the characteristic rhythms and melodies of other cultures.

Musically speaking, the characteristics that identify Dvořák's symphony as American for the most part have to do with rhythm (especially syncopation) and melody (pentatonic scales and the lowered seventh scale note). Although these elements are found in some kinds of American music, they are actually common to many folk and traditional musics throughout the world.

Syncopation and the spiritual in the first movement of the *New World* Symphony

Dvořák: Symphony No. 9, I, 1st theme

"Swing Low" theme

Syncopation Many of the melodies in the *New World* Symphony use **syncopation**, in which a strong note comes on a weak beat (as in the two notes sung, in "Swing Low," to the last syllable of "chariot," or the notes sung to *Rudolph, the red-nosed Reindeer*"). Examples include the last two notes of the first phrase of the first main theme; and the third and fourth notes of the "Swing Low" theme. In both these cases a short note comes on the beat (where we might expect a long note), and a much longer note comes after the beat. Syncopation is a pervasive feature of later African American music (such as ragtime and jazz), and Dvořák evidently considered it characteristically American.

Pentatonic scale   A second "American" feature is the use of the **pentatonic** scale. This is a five-note scale that can be produced by playing only the black notes of the piano, or by leaving out the fourth and seventh notes of the major scale. The pentatonic scale is used in cultures around the world and figures in many Anglo-American ballad melodies. By omitting the seventh note, or leading tone, of the major scale, it weakens the feeling of returning home to the **keynote**, or **tonic**, that is so characteristic of tonal music. Listen again to the English horn solo in the symphony's slow movement: the first and last portions of the melody are pentatonic (although the middle is not); note how Dvořák sidesteps the leading tone at the final cadence.

Pentatonic scale

Dvořák: Symphony No. 9, II, 1st and 2nd phrases

Lowered seventh note   Another of Dvořák's favorite devices is the use of a **lowered seventh note**, especially in themes in minor keys. A subsidiary melody in the first movement is a good example. At least one critic, Henry Krehbiel, who was interested in folk music and often lectured on it, said of this melody that it had a "distinctively negro characteristic in the employment of the flat seventh"; he then went on to say that the melody gives a "somewhat Oriental tinge" to the movement!

Dvořák: Symphony No. 9, I, melody with lowered 7ths

Listening to the Music

THE SHAPE OF THE SYMPHONY

Like Beethoven's Fifth Symphony and many others, the *New World* Symphony has four movements, with the pattern fast-slow-scherzo-fast. The individual movements also have formal shapes that are traditional and easy to grasp. In short, Dvořák's symphony is traditional with respect to its shape; nothing about its external structure identifies it as particularly American.

In the later movements, Dvořák occasionally brings back themes from earlier in the symphony, both for their emotional resonances and to give the work a greater sense of organic unity. He may have learned the technique of thematic recurrence and transformation from Beethoven, who uses it in his Fifth and Ninth symphonies, or from Berlioz's *idée fixe*, or from Wagner, whose **leitmotifs** permeate his operas (see p. 346). By the late nineteenth century, at any rate, it had become a technique widely practiced by composers.

Thematic recurrence and transformation

THEMES

One aspect that gives Dvořák's symphony its sense of unity, and that allows the composer to bring back themes from earlier movements, is that many of his themes seem to be arrangements of the same few basic rhythmic, melodic, and harmonic ideas. These similarities make it easier for Dvořák to manipulate and repeat the themes in different contexts. This varied repetition, in turn, helps the listener to follow his train of musical thought, not just within a single movement, but over the forty minutes or so that it takes to perform the entire symphony.

Dvořák uses three main thematic building blocks in the *New World* Symphony: a *dotted rhythm* (long-short-short-long), a *simple melodic motif* (a rising minor third, like the first two notes of the theme of the Largo), and a *harmonic idea* (which sounds like a lowered seventh rather than the customary leading tone). Table 14.1 gives the beginnings of several important themes in the symphony and shows how each is related to at least one of the others.

TABLE 14.1

Unity of Themes

OPENING DOTTED RHYTHM

MELODY USING MINOR SCALE WITH LOWERED 7TH (circled)

MELODY BEGINNING WITH MINOR 3RD

Movement I, closing theme

Movement I, first theme

Movement II, first theme

Movement III, second theme

Movement I, second theme

Movement II, second theme

Movement IV, first theme

🎵 LG 56

📡 Syncopation and the spiritual in the first movement of the *New World* Symphony

FIRST MOVEMENT: ADAGIO—ALLEGRO MOLTO

Dvořák's first movement has a languorous introduction, which gives way to a contrast of themes—active, sinister, and happily sunny. Several of these themes were inspired by African American music. The second theme (G minor), in both its melody and form (insistent repetition), is close to one of "Tonsor's" themes in the article "Negro Music" (see above, p. 379); and the third theme is very close to "Swing Low, Sweet Chariot," also quoted in "Negro Music."

The movement has the typical form of a symphonic first movement, usually called sonata form (see p. 220). Remember that the general outline of such movements (including the first movement of Beethoven's Fifth Symphony) has three parts:

Exposition, where themes are presented, and the music starts in one key and ends in another (the whole Exposition is sometimes repeated).

Development, where musical material from the Exposition is presented in new ways, often featuring many changes of key and recombinations of motives.

Recapitulation, where the music returns to the home key and the opening theme, presents the other themes (but not always in the original keys), and closes in the home key.

This description is as true for Dvořák as it is for Beethoven, even though their symphonies are entirely different in their musical content. (See LG 56, p. 386.)

SECOND MOVEMENT: LARGO

 LG 57

The second movement is what most of us remember when we hear this symphony. It includes the beautiful lyrical theme that reminds us of a spiritual. A central section contains some remarkable music that sounds like birdsong (and in which Dvořák quotes robins and bluebirds from a book of American birdsong). In addition, there are a series of unforgettable harmonies (initially performed by the brass section) that have a mystical aspect. Dvořák himself said that the Largo was based on Hiawatha's wooing of Minnehaha. "It is different to the classic works in this form. It is in reality a study or a sketch for a longer work, either a cantata or an opera which I propose writing, which will be based upon Longfellow's 'Hiawatha.'"

Before we listen to the movement, let's have a look at the *first theme*, and see how Dvořák alters it in its later appearances.

The first time it occurs, the English horn plays the whole melody, consisting of six phrases, where each phrase is the same length (two measures). The first phrase and the second are the same at their beginnings, but different in their ending; the first phrase, ending on the note above the keynote (the tonic), feels incomplete, and the second phrase's ending, one note lower on the keynote itself, feels like a close.

Phrase 1 (**A**)   Phrase 2 (**A′**)

Ⓢ Dvořák: Symphony No. 9, II, 1st and 2nd phrases

The third and fourth phrases are identical, and together form a contrasting portion of the melody in a higher register and with new harmonies.

Phrase 3 (**B**)   Phrase 4 (**B**)

Ⓢ Dvořák: Symphony No. 9, II, 3rd and 4th phrases

The last two phrases are like the first two, except that the final phrase has a new ending, high rather than low.

Phrase 5 (**A**)   Phrase 6 (**A″**)

Ⓢ Dvořák: Symphony No. 9, II, 5th and 6th phrases

We might make a representation of the phrase relationships in this melody as **AA′ BB AA″** (read as "**A, A prime**," etc.), where the little strokes or "prime" signs indicate general similarity with some difference. After the theme is finished there are several repetitions of the closing notes, a means of producing a sense of finality.

When the theme returns after the second set of "mystical chords," its form is different. The strings begin with a slightly altered version of the middle phrase (**B**), played twice, with some development of that phrase. The English horn returns with the two concluding phrases. Again there are repetitions of the ending.

The theme returns in the closing section, in a form similar to its full statement at the beginning, alternating between English horn and strings as before but with some interesting alterations. The first alteration is the halting way in which the middle phrase, **B**, is played when it's repeated: there are pauses in the course of the phrase—something like sobs or sighs. A second change is in the harmony at the end—Dvořák chooses a particularly expressive chord to accompany the four notes before the final note—and as a result he has changed the next-to-last note of the melody (in the two echoes that follow, the original note is restored).

What seems like a simple melody, a song form full of repetitions, is nevertheless put to a variety of uses in the movement. Its opening three notes are a motive that permeates the whole symphony. (See LG 56, below.)

The essential shape of the second movement is quite simple: a first idea, something else, and then a return to the first idea. Each of the three larger sections consists of an alternation of two ideas (with a special one-time event in the middle), and everything in the movement (with that exception again) returns at some point.

LISTENING GUIDE 56   ⓢ | DVD | ◉

Dvořák Symphony No. 9 in E Minor (*From the New World*), I
(Adagio—Allegro molto)   11:45

DATE: 1893

LISTEN FOR

MELODY: Somber opening melody

FORM: Slow introduction leads to traditional symphonic first-movement form

RHYTHM: First and third themes begin with the same syncopated rhythm

THEMES: Three characteristic ("American") themes

TIME	FORM	DESCRIPTION
0:00	**Introduction**	A quiet, languorous melody is played first by cellos, then by flutes: The calm is shattered by a loud, jagged, syncopated passage that foreshadows the opening theme.
	Exposition	
1:51	Opening theme (Theme 1)	Horns outline an E-minor triad, rising and falling against a backdrop of shimmering chords in the strings. Woodwinds echo their crisp, dotted rhythms in response:
2:32	Transition	Tension mounts, then slowly dissipates.
2:54	Second theme (Theme 2)	Flutes and oboes introduce a lilting but ominous theme in a new key (G minor): Theme 2 is repeated . . .

| 3:11 | Transition | And extended by the strings. |
| 3:57 | Closing theme (Theme 3) | A flute solo combines elements of the first two themes in a sunny, major-key setting. Liquid triplets soften the edges of the dotted rhythm. This is the theme whose beginning suggests "Swing Low, Sweet Chariot" (the first two measures below mimic "chariot," while the third and fourth measures follow the tune of "Comin' for to carry me home"): |

Near the end, Dvořák sets up the dramatic return to the opening theme.

Exposition repeated

Development

| 7:07 | Section 1 | Strings elaborate on material from the closing theme, combining duple and triple rhythms: |

| 7:18 | Section 2 | The solo horn, piccolo, and trumpet reprise the closing theme. The rest of the section develops the crisp, dotted figure from opening theme, which the cellos condense into a reverse-dotted figure: a short note followed by a long note. |
| 7:38 | Section 3 | Violins take over from cellos, while trumpets play a variant of the closing theme: |

Then the lower instruments (bassoons, trombones, cellos, and double basses) repeat the opening theme with chromatic alterations. Throughout the section, the double basses maintain a steady, chugging rhythm that heightens the excitement.

| 7:53 | Section 4 | The music continues to modulate, changing keys restlessly as the triadic figure from the opening theme pops up again and again: |

| 8:24 | Section 5 | The figure from the opening theme is passed from one instrument to another. |

Recapitulation

8:40	Opening theme (Theme 1)	Back to the home key of E minor as the opening theme returns in the horns.
8:53	Transition	
8:16	Second theme (Theme 2)	Flutes reprise Theme 2, a half step above its original appearance:

(continued)

TIME	FORM	DESCRIPTION
	Transition	
10:18	Closing theme (Theme 3)	The closing theme comes back, now in major—first in solo flute, then in violins.
	Coda	
10:46		The harmony suddenly shifts. The closing theme (in trumpets) combines with the opening theme (in trombones) in preparation for a final, triumphal return to the home key of E minor.

LISTENING GUIDE 57   ⓢ | DVD

Dvořák Symphony No. 9 in E Minor (*From the New World*), II (Largo)   11:56

DATE: 1893

LISTEN FOR

MELODY: Famous theme, first played by English horn, thought to be "American" in feeling

HARMONY: Series of "mystical chords" at the beginning that

reappear at the end (and that will return at the end of the last movement)

TEXTURE: A central section with birdsong trills

TIME	FORM	DESCRIPTION
0:00	**Introductory material**	

The brass present a series of "mystical chords":

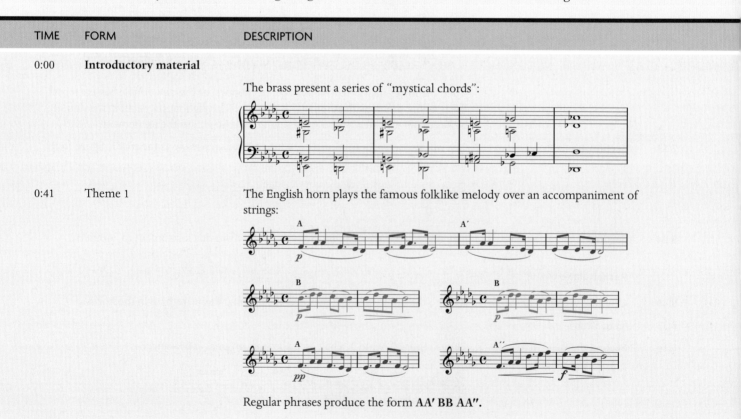

| 0:41 | Theme 1 | The English horn plays the famous folklike melody over an accompaniment of strings: |

Regular phrases produce the form **AA′ BB AA″**.

		Woodwinds reprise the chords, in a higher octave.
2:48	Theme 1 again	A variant of the folk theme returns in the strings, with an extension that leads into the two concluding phrases played by the English horn. Echoes in the strings and horns lead to the next section.

Middle section

| 4:38 | Theme 2 | The flute begins an improvisatory-sounding theme in a minor key, emphasizing a descending minor third at its beginning: |

A slow passage in woodwinds leads to . . .

| 5:38 | Theme 3 | A slow, marchlike theme by the flute, with pizzicato bass: |

6:04	Theme 2	Theme 2 returns, bigger in sound, with richer orchestration, followed by a slow passage returning to . . .
6:58	Theme 3	The marchlike theme, now slower.
8:00	New material	A one-time section in a major key, featuring many trills, like birdsong, leading to a combination of motives from the first movement with a motive from this movement's Theme 1:

Closing section

| 8:29 | Theme 1 | The movement's opening theme returns in the English horn and then strings, becoming more halting and fragmented, sometimes only in solo strings. |
| 10:34 | | The first violins play an unaccompanied pentatonic line descending to their low register . . . |

| 10:58 | | making a transition to the return of the mystical chords. The movement closes with an ascending string arpeggio and a quiet chord in the double basses. |

LG 59   **THIRD MOVEMENT: SCHERZO**

The movement is lively and in a minor key. It evokes Native American dance; Dvořák told an interviewer that the Scherzo "was suggested by the scene at the feast in *Hiawatha* where the Indians dance, and is also an essay I made in the direction of imparting the local color of Indian characters to music." The characteristic three quick repeated notes is at the basis of its energy; this is surely Dvořák's picture of Native American drumming. But a second more relaxed theme gives a sense of space, contrasting with the strong drive of the first theme. Perhaps these represent American characteristics, as Dvořák heard them.

The third movement is based on rhythmic patterns, as we might expect from knowing a Beethoven scherzo. An opening theme builds to a furious fortissimo and then relaxes into a major-key second theme (beginning with an upward minor third, like other themes in the symphony).

The movement has the shape we expect: **ABA**: Scherzo (**A**), Trio (**B**) (remember that the term "trio" is used for the second section of a scherzo, minuet, or march, regardless of instrumentation), and the repeat of the Scherzo (**A**).

The Trio (Dvořák doesn't actually call it that) is a charming interlude in the rhythm of a waltz. The music here may represent a passage in *Hiawatha* where Native Americans are turned into birds.

After the Trio, the Scherzo returns, repeated literally. Dvořák adds a short coda combining scherzo and first-movement motives. (See LG 58, below)

LG 58   **FOURTH MOVEMENT: ALLEGRO CON FUOCO**

The last movement is an inventive combination of themes culled from the entire symphony, a kind of summary and fusion of what has gone before, in a somewhat altered version of sonata form. Its first theme, like a call to arms, is played by the brass. It uses the minor third and lowered seventh that are characteristic of much of the symphony. The theme is gradually transformed into lively triplets. A series of other transformations leads to several other themes of lyrical character.

Here and elsewhere in the symphony, a lot of the thrill is due to Dvořák's imaginative orchestration. The use of strings divided into many parts, the wonderful woodwind solos, the low brass (horns and trombones) used in active thematic ways rather than as reinforcements, the addition of colorful touches of percussion, all make this a symphony that goes far beyond Beethoven, and in many ways rivals Berlioz, in its use of instrumental color.

LISTENING GUIDE 58 | DVD

Dvořák Symphony No. 9 in E Minor (*From the New World*), III

(Scherzo: Molto vivace—Poco sostenuto)   7:05

DATE: 1893

LISTEN FOR

RHYTHM: Driving rhythm of opening section, based on three quick repeated notes

MELODY: Songlike second theme

FORM: Waltzlike trio

TIME	FORM	DESCRIPTION
	Scherzo	
0:00	First theme	After an opening explosion, the first theme, based on a 3-note repeated motive,
		builds up to furious fortissimo.
0:40		The whole section is repeated; quick echoes of the 3-note motive.
1:20	Transition	Brief sense of calm.
1:28	Second theme	A shift to a major key, and a new relaxed tempo introduces an expansive second theme, which begins with a rising minor third:
2:00	Closing theme	Reprise of first theme motive, with a crescendo; hammered ending.
2:31	Transition to Trio	Borrowed music from the first movement and sweeping fragments of phrases:
	Trio	
2:54	First theme	A sprightly, waltz-tempo theme in the woodwinds; four phrases, each with the same rhythm:
		Theme is repeated.
3:18	Second theme	A new rhythm, ending with a trill:
		A transition leads back to first theme.
3:41	First theme returns	Louder, more instruments.
3:53	Second theme returns	
4:16	First theme returns	Still different orchestration; transition leads back to Scherzo.
4:34	**Scherzo**	Repeated as before.
6:25	**Coda**	Dramatic opening; the coda combines motives from the Scherzo and the first movement.

Dvořák Symphony No. 9 in E Minor (*From the New World*), IV
(Allegro con fuoco)   10:55

DATE: 1893

LISTEN FOR
MELODY: Balanced 8-phrase first theme

SCORING: Dramatic use of orchestra, especially brass

THEMES: Many combinations of themes from previous movements

TIME	FORM	DESCRIPTION
0:00	**Introduction**	From a string unison, the texture expands outward to lead to the exposition.
	Exposition	
0:14	First theme, E minor	Horns announce first theme.

Two phrases (horns and trumpets), repeated:

Two contrasting phrases (strings):

Phrases seven and eight are similar to the first two:

| 1:10 | Transition | Numerous triplets create a theme and a sense of moving forward: |

Violins

Winds

There is a contrasting section, and a return to the opening theme, before the transitional decrescendo.

1:46	Second theme, G major	A quiet, solo clarinet over shimmering strings (note the leaping punctuation in lower strings at the ends of phrases):

Strings lead to a section for full orchestra.

2:32	Closing theme, G major	Descending 3-note figure ("Three blind mice") in violins and woodwinds:

The staccato accompaniment in the low strings becomes syncopated.

Development

3:33	Section 1	Combines "Three blind mice" with first theme.
3:53	Section 2	Combines first theme with triplets of transition.
4:17	Section 3	Combines theme from Largo with first theme.
4:41	Section 4	Theme from Largo in winds, leading to brass.
4:54	Section 5	The first theme is stated at two speeds at the same time.
5:17	Section 6	Combines first theme from first movement with first theme.
5:30	Section 7	Brass play first theme from this movement, crescendo leading to . . .

Recapitulation

5:46	First theme	Abbreviated recapitulation.
5:58	Transition	The active transitional theme from the exposition is missing here; a contemplative version of the opening theme, modulating to distant keys, almost like a development, leads to the second theme.
6:34	Second theme	Cellos play the lyrical second theme now.
7:21	Closing theme	The closing theme, in flutes, is much altered; now it is relaxed, with accompaniment figures in lower strings, then bassoon.

Coda

8:08	Section 1	One horn, then several, provides various reminiscences (first theme of first movement, second theme of Scherzo, "Three blind mice" theme); trombones play the first theme of the first movement in a crescendo.
8:57	Section 2	"Mystical chords" of second movement, now loud, and with different harmonies.
9:19	Section 3	Quiet; combines Largo and Scherzo themes; fourth movement first theme in horns, with timpani accompaniment.
9:53	Section 4	Final statement of opening theme: slow unison; combined with first-movement theme and Largo theme; final fortissimo.

Coda   In the coda of the symphony Dvořák reviews the previous movements; he refers to the opening of the first movement's main theme (it has appeared in every movement!); he reprises the "mystical chords" of the Largo; the English-horn theme of the Largo is combined with the rhythmic motive of the Scherzo. In a blazing ending the basses move up and down in a sort of pentatonic arpeggio over a fortissimo E-major chord. The fiery effect, the listener's sense of familiarity and ownership of the themes, and the triumphant ending, have never failed to earn the symphony a rousing applause. (See LG 59, p. 392.)

How Did It Go?

There are conflicting accounts of the first performance. The *New York Times* observed that "the applause was exceedingly timid," adding that "to-morrow all those who did not quite know how to treat the new work yesterday will be sorry they did not express warm approval." According to the *Tribune,* on the other hand, the "usually tranquil" American audience was "enthusiastic to the point of frenzy." The response to the Saturday-night performance was even more demonstrative. The *Musical Courier* reported that the audience "threw kid glove convention to the winds" after the slow movement "and became for the moment as crazily enthusiastic as a continental one. Dvořák was yelled for and he finally did appear in one of the upper boxes and bowed to the sea of faces upturned to him and then pointed to Mr. Seidl."

No one faulted the Philharmonic's performance or doubted that Dvořák had contributed a work of lasting value to the repertory. As to the symphony's "American" quality, however, opinion was mixed. The composer-critic Reginald De Koven, writing in the *New York World,* qualified his praise of the "dreamy, languorous" second movement, which he deemed "almost too placid, too poetic, too contemplative in character to be considered characteristically national in spirit." Henry Krehbiel of the *Boston Herald* took a broader view, observing that although the symphony might be "Indian in spirit," it was "Bohemian in atmosphere. Dr. Dvořák can no more divest himself of his nationality than the leopard can change his spots."

Many critics declared that the symphony wasn't American in any way. Walter Damrosch, the conductor, was quoted along such lines: "To me it suggests nothing American. It is Dvořák." In the *Musical Courier,* James Huneker wittily turned the question on its head: "Dvořák's is an American symphony: is it? Themes from negro melodies; composed by a Bohemian; conducted by a Hungarian and played by Germans in a hall built by a Scotchman." As Huneker saw it, "the American symphony, like the American novel, has yet to be written. And when it is, it will have been composed by an American."

Years later, Dvořák's American secretary further muddied the waters by claiming that the composer had never intended to put an American stamp on his music. According to J. J. Kovařík, Dvořák, in his rush to deliver the score

FIG. 14.9 The title page of Dvořák's Ninth Symphony, bearing the inscription "from the new world" in English; a later list of Dvořák's symphonies is at left.

to Seidl, hastily scribbled "From the New World" on the title page as an after-thought (see Figure 14.9):

> There were many, and there still are, who believed and still believe that this title means "An American Symphony," and that with this title the Master somehow attached to his work an "American seal." This is an erroneous interpretation. The fact that the Master wrote, at the last moment, the title "From the New World" onto the title page was simply one of his innocent jokes—and does not mean anything more than "Impressions and greetings from the New World," as he declared more than once.

The *New World* Symphony Then and Now

In the weeks following its premiere, the *New World* Symphony was performed to enthusiastic audiences in Boston and other cities, and its popularity has never waned. In the spring of 1895 Dvořák returned to Bohemia, where he became the head of the Prague Conservatory and one of the most revered figures in Czech music. The National Conservatory in New York continued, though never with a director as famous as Dvořák. It was to fade away in the 1920s, when Mrs. Thurber's energies waned and other schools of music competed with and eventually overshadowed it.

None of these institutions, however, had as its explicit mission the creation of a distinctively national school of composition. When such a tradition finally did emerge, in the 1920s and 1930s, it was the result not of an educational curriculum but of the desire of American composers to capture the essence of their homeland, just as American writers, painters, playwrights, and dancers were doing at the same time. Virgil Thomson was right: "American" music embraced everything from John Philip Sousa's marches to Aaron Copland's *Fanfare for the Common Man*, from Scott Joplin's piano rags to George Gershwin's opera *Porgy and Bess*, from Stephen Foster's sentimental parlor songs to Bessie Smith's gut-wrenching blues. All of it went out "from the New World" to the Old and became part of the world's musical heritage.

In an article titled "Music in America," published a few months before his departure, Dvořák exhorted Americans to "listen to every whistling boy, every street singer or blind organ-grinder." Music, he seemed to be saying, is all around us, even in our crowded, cacophonous cities; all we have to do is learn to hear it. American composers took his words to heart. The culture of Native Americans inspired a whole school of "Indianist" composers in the early twentieth century. Gershwin's *American in Paris* translated the brash sounds and rhythms of New York's streets into the suave language of the French *boulevardier*. Charles Ives wove hymn tunes, band marches, and college fight songs into his multilayered musical tapestries, and Virgil Thomson wrote a slice-of-American-life ballet called *Filling Station*.

But it was the music of African Americans that was destined to develop into the dominant strain of twentieth-century popular music in the United States and much of the rest of the world. The anonymous critic of the *New York Times* almost seems to anticipate this in his review of Dvořák's symphony:

> The American people—or the majority of them—learned to love the songs of the negro slave and to find in them something that belonged to America. If those songs are not national, then there is no such thing as national music. It is a fallacy to suppose that a national song must be one which gives direct and intentional expression

to patriotic sentiment. A national song is one that is of the people, for the people, by the people. The negroes gave us their music and we accepted it, not with proclamations from the housetops, but with our voices and our hearts in the household. Dr. Dvořák has penetrated the spirit of this music, and with themes suitable for symphonic treatment, he has written a beautiful symphony, which throbs with American feeling, which voices the melancholy of our Western wastes, and predicts their final subjection to the tremendous activity of the most energetic of all peoples.

Dvořák could not know, of course, the impact that the music of black Americans would eventually have: the legacy of blues, jazz, and many other styles has made the United States a source of musical energy and renewal for the whole world. This might have pleased Dvořák in that he wished America, and the world, to embrace the music of African Americans. It is black Americans themselves—and not European composers—who created it, developed it, and turned it into one of the world's great patrimonies.

Although the *New World* Symphony did not become the great sound of American music—Americans themselves ultimately took responsibility for that—it is a milestone of Romantic nationalism. When we listen to Dvořák's music today, we hear it filtered through a century and more of authentically American music, both popular and classical. It is hard to imagine that there ever was any serious debate over what was or was not American music, or whether such a thing could even exist.

Dvořák drew inspiration from the music, all the music, that he heard around him. In the *New World* Symphony he used the forms and methods, orchestration and textures, of the European symphonic tradition to paint an American portrait. Whether this makes Dvořák more or less "American" than a Boston composer trying to write like Wagner is a question worthy of our attention. But as listeners, we can enjoy Dvořák's work simply as one of the greatest symphonies ever written, as fresh today as it was in 1893.

Chapter Review

Summary of Musical Styles

Dvořák's music is in many ways characteristic of **Romantic nationalist composers**: he uses the universal symphonic language inherited from the great German symphonists (Haydn, Mozart, Beethoven) and inflects it with folk melodies drawn from national cultures.

In Dvořák's *New World* Symphony, he uses certain procedures that are related to his effort to give this symphony an American flavor:

- the use of **pentatonic scales** in the construction of themes;
- the use of a scale with a **lowered seventh** in the construction of melodies.

Some of the other salient characteristics are those shared by many other composers, including:

- the relationships of themes to each other, many of them beginning with a rising minor third;

- transformations of themes in subsequent appearances;
- appearance of themes in more than one movement;
- polyphonic combinations of themes;
- a rich and imaginative orchestration.

ⓢ Multimedia Resources and Review Materials on StudySpace

Visit wwnorton.com/studyspace for review of Chapter 14.

What Do You Know?

Check the facts for this chapter. Take the online **Quiz**.

What Do You Hear?

Listening Quizzes and **Music Activities** will help you understand the musical works in this chapter.

🎙 Author Videos

- Syncopation and the spiritual in the first movement of the *New World* Symphony

Interactive Listening Guides

LG 56 Dvořák: Symphony No. 9 in E Minor (*From the New World*), I (Adagio—Allegro molto)

LG 57 Dvořák: Symphony No. 9 in E Minor (*From the New World*), II (Largo)

LG 58 Dvořák: Symphony No. 9 in E Minor (*From the New World*), III (Scherzo: Molto vivace—Poco sostenuto)

LG 59 Dvořák: Symphony No. 9 in E Minor (*From the New World*), IV (Allegro con fuoco)

Flashcards (Terms to Know)

keynote	program music
lowered seventh note	spirituals
nationalism	syncopation
nationalist composer	tonic
pentatonic	

THE TWENTIETH CENTURY

	HISTORICAL EVENTS	MUSICAL EVENTS
1850		1862–1918 Claude Debussy
		1874–1951 Arnold Schoenberg
1875		1875–1937 Maurice Ravel
		1881–1945 Béla Bartók
		1882–1971 Igor Stravinsky
		1883–1945 Anton Webern
		1885–1935 Alban Berg
		1891–1953 Sergei Prokofiev
1900	1900 Freud, *The Interpretation of Dreams*	1900–1990 Aaron Copland
	1905 Einstein's theory of relativity	1906–1975 Dmitri Shostakovich
		1908–1992 Olivier Messiaen
		1912–1992 John Cage
	1914–18 First World War	1913–1976 Benjamin Britten
	1920 19th Amendment passed, giving women the right to vote	1916–2011 Milton Babbitt
		1918–1990 Leonard Bernstein
1925		1923– György Ligeti
	1929 Stock market collapse	1931– Sofia Gubaidulina
	1929 Great Depression	1935– Terry Riley
	1939–45 Second World War	1939– Ellen Taaffe Zwilich
	1945 Atomic bombs explode in Japan	
		1947– John Adams
1950	1950–53 Korean conflict	1952– Kaija Saariaho
	1954 Supreme Court declares segregation unconstitutional	1953– Tod Machover
	1963 John F. Kennedy assassinated	1962– Jennifer Higdon
	1964–75 U.S. combat units in Vietnam conflict	
	1967 European Community formed	
	1968 Martin Luther King, Jr. assassinated	
	1969 Neil Armstrong walks on moon	
	1969 Woodstock Festival	
1975		
	1989 Fall of the Berlin Wall	
	1991 Collapse of the Soviet Union	
2000	2001 World Trade Center and Pentagon attacked	
	2003 United States invades Iraq	
	2008 Barack Obama elected first African American president of the United States	
	2008 The Great Recession	
2010		

Legend: ● France ● Russia ● England ● Austria ● US ● Hungary ● Finland ● Estonia

PART V

Music and Politics: Twentieth-Century Music

The twentieth century was a century of war, hot and cold; of technology ushering in drastic changes; of struggles against discrimination; of globalization in which the world became smaller. Its music was inevitably affected by these changes: warfare influenced the uses of music and its place in society; technology allowed for the dissemination of music by electronic means and for the creation of music by nonacoustic methods; social and cultural barriers between people gradually become more permeable, and the musics of the world came into fruitful contact.

Political Events

The First World War (1914–18), involving all the powers of Europe and ultimately the United States, caused devastating damage. Technology was no longer the unqualified success that would bring a bright future; instead it was employed in trench warfare, bombs, gas, and artillery, killing a large proportion of Europe's male population.

World War I

A collapse in the American stock market that started in October 1929 led to a long financial depression across the globe, which in turn contributed to the rise of extremism in Germany. There the National Socialist (Nazi) movement culminated in the dictatorial state of Adolf Hitler, whose territorial ambitions led to World War II. His attempt to eradicate Europe's Jewish population is one of the great shames of the twentieth century. Fascist totalitarian states also arose starting in the 1920s, in Italy (under Benito Mussolini), Spain (under Francisco Franco), and other countries.

World War II

Partly as a result of the unsatisfactory peace at the end of the First World War, the Second World War (1939–45) was even more global and more destructive. Pitting the Axis powers of Germany, Italy, and Japan against England, the Soviet Union, China, and other countries, the Japanese attack at Pearl Harbor in December 1941 drew Americans into the war, which was being fought on several continents and in the Pacific, destroying lives, property, and cultural heritage in London, Dresden, and many other cities. Its conclusion, the deployment of atomic bombs on Hiroshima and Nagasaki, brought to an end a horrifying chapter in human history.

Further theaters of war have involved the United States—after World War II a great superpower—in Korea, Vietnam, Iraq, and Afghanistan; these interventions in principle are in support of freedom and democracy. Elsewhere in the world—in the Balkan states, the Middle East, and in North Africa, for example—uprisings, revolutions, and wars continue.

Idealism of various kinds characterizes the best and the worst of the twentieth century. The 1917 Russian Revolution resulted in a communist government based on the ideas of Karl Marx. The Soviet Union, a powerful and repressive state, was America's ally in the Second World War but ultimately its opponent in the *The Cold War* Cold War—an ideological, economic, and political struggle for power and influence between Soviet-led communist states and Western democracies that spanned four decades (see Figure V.1, map of Europe during the Cold War, below). In the United States, fear of communism led to investigations of citizens, the inquiries of Senator Joseph McCarthy, and a continuing atmosphere of hostility, suspicion, and dread, ending with the collapse of the Soviet Union in 1991.

The twentieth century also saw the quest for justice in many places as well as

FIG. V.1 Map of Europe during the Cold War (1945–91).

continued struggles against discrimination on the basis of gender, race, or sexual orientation (see Figure V.2). The struggles continue, but much progress has been made.

Technology contributed not only to the efficiency of warfare but also to many other aspects of human life. Remarkable advances in the understanding and treatment of disease made life longer and healthier for much of the world's population. The availability of electricity, telephone, radio, automobile, and airplane have all made enormous changes in living. Instant communication, speedy travel, the Internet, and the use of machines to perform what formerly took a lot of labor, all have changed people's lives greatly.

The cinema has taken the place of many opera houses and live theaters, and recording—vinyl record, magnetic tape, CD, or electronic file—has made it possible to listen to any music, from any place in the world, at any moment. The role of music and live performance will never be the same.

Music in the Twentieth Century and Beyond

Politics and music are inextricably bound. Wars, for example, both generate music—for the military, for propaganda, and to bolster political ideals—and alter its course. The Nazis forbade music composed or performed by Jewish composers and by others considered "degenerate." The Soviet Union, along with its satellite nations, exerted severe controls over the nature of permissible music, as did the Nazis; generally, atonal, dissonant, twelve-tone, and other such music (see below) was discouraged, forbidden, or punished. And in China, the Cultural Revolution (1966–76) repressed a generation of musicians and composers.

The early twentieth century was a moment of crisis for Western art music. Classical tonality, the use of keys and the relationships among keys for the structuring of music, large and small, came to a crossroads, with tonality pushed to the extreme, far beyond Wagner's chromaticism. Composers like Gustav Mahler ⑤ and Richard Strauss chose to continue in the long and fruitful development of tonal music while some of their contemporaries, as we will see, were seeking alternative musical systems.

At the beginning of the century, **impressionist** composers Claude Debussy ⑤, Maurice Ravel, and others used a palette of unusual musical colors, exotic scales, and free association of chords to produce a musical style based more on pattern and harmonic color than on the strong attractions of tonal relationships. (See Figure V.3.)

The period between the two world wars saw the birth of musical **neoclassicism**—a trend towards a finely balanced, unromantic, objective view of music inspired by the works of Baroque and Classical composers. The avoidance of emotion and the rejection of the external references of program music, as seen in the crystalline forms of music by Igor Stravinsky, Paul Hindemith, and Sergei Prokofiev, among others, became an inspiration to listeners and to later composers like the Americans Aaron Copland and Virgil Thomson.

FIG. V.2 The twentieth century came to recognize and respect a range of sexual preferences and lifestyles. It was not until 2004 that same-sex marriage became legal in Massachusetts and, subsequently, in some other jurisdictions.

⑤ Mahler: Symphony No. 2, I (crescendo and explosion)

⑤ Debussy: *Prelude to "The Afternoon of a Faun"*

FIG. V.3 Claude Monet, *Haystacks at Sunset, Frosty Weather*, 1891. The impressionist painters, of whom Monet was a leading figure, wanted to record fleeting impressions of the effects of light; note the many colors used in the depiction of shadow.

Science and Philosophy

Although **Karl Marx** died in 1883, his writings continued to have profound and far-reaching effects; **Sigmund Freud**, already highly influential in the nineteenth century, published his most important works in the twentieth century (see p. 260); and **Albert Einstein** (1879–1955), perhaps the greatest scientist of the new century, developed a special theory of relativity which explained gravitation as an aspect of space, time, and matter. The scientific implications of his work are of tremendous significance technically as well as philosophically.

The Arts

The visual arts experienced new styles and explorations, many attached to schools, trends, and "isms." The *impressionism* of the late nineteenth century was followed by movements such as expressionism, cubism, surrealism, and abstract expressionism.

Expressionism seeks to relate an emotional experience rather than an external reality, often involving exaggeration and strong colors or shapes. The late works of Vincent van Gogh are sometimes classified as expressionist, as are the works by **Egon Schiele** (1890–1918) and **Oskar Kokoschka** (1886–1980). Arnold Schoenberg, one of the most influential composers of the twentieth century, was also an expressionist painter (see Figure 16.1, p. 435).

Georges Braque (1882–1963), **Pablo Picasso** (1881–1973), and others created **cubism** as an analytical tool to study the planes, surfaces, and volumes that go into our perception of shapes and spaces (see illustration, p. 399).

In painting as in literature, **surrealism** is the expression of the impossible, often juxtaposing familiar objects in unfamiliar ways. The purpose is to produce an unsettling or shocking effect not available in normal reality. Famous surrealist artists include **René Magritte** (1898–1967),

Salvador Dalí (1904–1989), and **Marcel Duchamp** (1887–1968).

Abstract expressionism is a postwar American style involving the absence of recognizable subject matter from nature, and the use of form, color, and composition to give a work its essence. **Jackson Pollock** (1912–1956) became one of the movement's most famous artists.

One of the greatest artists of the twentieth century was Pablo Picasso, who participated in all these styles, and many more, including *minimalism*, a movement, mostly in the visual arts and music, in which a work contains only its most simple and basic elements. Particularly associated with this movement were **Helen Frankenthaler** (1928–2012), a major figure in abstract expressionism who spearheaded a way of using color to "soak" a canvas; **Louise Nevelson** (1900–1988), known primarily as a sculptor who created "assemblages" from found objects; and the New York artists of the 1960s **Mark Rothko** (1903–1970), **Barnett Newman** (1905–1970), **Frank Stella** (b. 1936), and **Robert Motherwell** (1915–1991). These New York artists were influenced by the composer John Cage (see p. 404).

In the second half of the twentieth century, a new kind of realism appeared with the art of **Georgia O'Keeffe** (1887–1986), **Jasper Johns** (b. 1930), **Robert Rauschenberg** (1925–2008), and **Roy Lichtenstein** (1923–1997). This new realism fed directly into the movement known as **pop art**—Andy Warhol (1928–1987) is the most famous artist from this movement—which erased the distinction between "high" and "low" art by drawing its themes from everyday life: soup cans, comic books, and popular cultural icons like Marilyn Monroe.

The latter half of the century saw the increased entry into mainstream arts of women and of people of color, and the acknowledgment of non-Western art. The arts led the way toward inclusion: artists were at the forefront of raising issues of individuality—class, religion,

and sexual identity, for example—and focusing attention on the exclusion and devaluing of so many of the world's voices.

Architecture in the twentieth century is an area of significant artistic importance. Technology allowed many of the finest modern ideas to find their clearest expression. **Modernism** in architecture takes a variety of forms. The sculptural works of the American **Frank Lloyd Wright** (1867–1859) culminated in his Guggenheim Museum in New York, a giant flowerpot in which the viewer descends a long spiral ramp. The so-called **international style**, in which all superfluous ornament is avoided, and buildings show their function by their form, is represented famously by Mies van der Rohe's Seagram Building in New York. The **postmodern** trend—a reaction to the formalism of the international style—is seen in the Pompidou Center, an art museum in Paris that represents its structure by placing all the mechanical and service aspects of the building—stairways, ductwork, essential structure—on the *outside*, so as to free the interior for the display of art. The result is a building that, while entirely efficient, looks almost Baroque in its wealth of surface detail (see Figure V.4).

Literature

Like the other arts, literature from the twentieth century has had constantly shifting artistic sensibilities highlighted by fragmentation and experimentation, as well as an increasing awareness of differences and, ironically, interconnections. The century begins with works now considered classics: **Joseph Conrad** (*Heart of Darkness*, 1902), **Henry James** (*The Ambassadors,* 1903), and **Marcel Proust** (*Remembrance of Things Past*, first volume, 1913). After the First World War, writers in English on both sides of the Atlantic experimented with narrative styles and techniques, and extended the boundaries of storytelling.

These authors include **James Joyce** (*Ulysses*, 1922) and **William Faulkner** (*The Sound and the Fury*, 1929) as well as less experimental writers like **D. H. Lawrence** (*Lady Chatterley's Lover*, 1922), **Virginia Woolf** (*To the Lighthouse*, 1927), **F. Scott Fitzgerald** (*The Great Gatsby*, 1925), **Thomas Wolfe** (*Look Homeward, Angel*, 1929), **John Steinbeck** (*The Grapes of Wrath*, 1939), and **Ernest Hemingway** (*For Whom the Bell Tolls*, 1940).

Politically oriented literature, arising at the time of the Second World War, looked at the world through a lens of alienation and the conflicting impulses of human conscience: **George Orwell** (*Animal Farm*, 1945) and the French existentialists **Jean-Paul Sartre** (*Being and Nothingness*, 1943) and **Albert Camus** (*The Plague*, 1947) are only a few of the writers.

Writers in other languages include **Thomas Mann** (*The Magic Mountain*, 1924; German), **Jorge Luis Borges** (*The Aleph*, 1949; Spanish), **Gabriel García Márquez** (*One Hundred Years of Solitude*, 1967; Spanish), **Umberto Eco** (*The Name of the Rose*, 1980; Italian), and **Vladimir Nabokov** (*Lolita*, 1955), who wrote in Russian and English.

American novelists of the later half of the century include **Norman Mailer** (*The Naked and the Dead*, 1948), a proponent of creative nonfiction; the gay African American **James Baldwin** (*Go Tell It on the Mountain*, 1953); the Nobel Prize–winning **Saul Bellow** (*Herzog*, 1964); the prolific **John Updike** (*Couples*, 1968); and the identity-obsessed Jewish writer **Philip Roth** (*Portnoy's Complaint*, 1969).

Poets of the century writing in English range from the modernist **T. S. Eliot** (*The Love Song of J. Alfred Prufrock*, 1917) and **e. e. cummings** (*The Enormous Room*, 1922), to the realist **Robert Frost** (*New Hampshire*, 1923) and the "confessional" poet **Sylvia Plath** (*The Bell Jar*, 1963).

Dramatists from all schools of thought, such as naturalists, avant-gardists, realists, and modernists, include **George Bernard Shaw** (*Pygmalion*, 1912), **Samuel Beckett** (*Waiting For*

FIG. V.4 The Centre Georges Pompidou (Pompidou Center for the Arts), Paris. Architects Renzo Piano, Richard Rogers, and Su Rogers sought to express the function of the building by putting the mechanical systems, which are usually hidden, on the outside, where they become a kind of decoration.

Godot, 1953), **Eugene O'Neill** (*The Iceman Cometh*, 1940), **Tennessee Williams** (*A Streetcar Named Desire*, 1947), **Arthur Miller** (*Death of a Salesman*, 1949), and **Tony Kushner** (*Angels in America*, 1992).

Certain special writers deserve a place of their own in the century: **A. A. Milne** (*Winnie-the-Pooh*, 1926), **J.R.R. Tolkien** (*The Hobbit*, 1937), and **J. K. Rowling** (the *Harry Potter* series, 1997-2007). Genre fiction of all kinds abounds: science fiction, spy thrillers, detective mysteries, fantasy, and much more.

Cinema

One of the chief arts, new in the twentieth century, is the cinema, which ultimately combined literature, drama, music, and visual arts in a new medium. In the United States the era of the silent cinema saw works by **D. W. Griffith** (*Birth of a Nation*, 1915) and the comedies of **Charlie Chaplin** and **Buster Keaton**, among others. The addition of sound made film a complete entertainment, and a series of artists has contributed to making it high art. They include

the midcentury directors **Walt Disney** (*Fantasia*, 1940), **John Huston** (*The Maltese Falcon*, 1941), **John Ford** (*The Quiet Man*, 1952), **Elia Kazan** (*On the Waterfront*, 1954), and **Alfred Hitchcock** (*Psycho*, 1960).

Cinema has an international reach, and its luminaries have included such directors as **Akira Kurosawa** (*Seven Samurai*, 1953), **Satyajit Ray** (*Aparajito*, 1956), **Ingmar Bergman** (*The Seventh Seal*, 1957), **Federico Fellini** (*La Dolce Vita*, 1960), and the French "new wave" filmmakers of the 1950s and 1960s, including **Jean-Luc Godard** (*Breathless*, 1960) and **François Truffaut** (*Jules and Jim*, 1962).

Film continues to flourish, as entertainment and as art. Among many brilliant directors, we might single out **Steven Spielberg** (*Jaws*, 1975), **Martin Scorsese** (*Taxi Driver*, 1976), **Woody Allen** (*Annie Hall*, 1977), **Joel and Ethan Coen** (*Fargo*, 1996), and **Pedro Almodóvar** (*Talk to Her*, 2002). New forms, including 3D camera technology, are changing the face of cinema as well. Other media will almost certainly revolutionize the future of the arts.

Second Viennese School

Ⓢ Schoenberg: *Five Piano Pieces, Op. 23, V*

Twelve-tone music

Neoclassicism stands in contrast to the music of the so-called **Second Viennese School** of Arnold Schoenberg, Alban Berg, and Anton Webern (the **First Viennese School** being the group of composers including Haydn, Mozart, and Beethoven). Arnold Schoenberg, along with his students and colleagues Webern and Berg, sought to substitute for tonality a new system in which all twelve notes of the chromatic scale would have equal importance. This **atonal music**, as others called it, led to the creation of a system of **twelve-tone music**, composed by using a series of all twelve notes, and repeating the entire series, in a variety of transpositions and inversions, before any note is repeated. Provided that the composer chose the **series**, or **tone row**, carefully, this system gave a sense of unity and a systematic approach to the structure of music, while avoiding the sounds that would remind the listener of classical tonality.

Later in the century, Schoenberg's twelve-tone system became enormously influential, extending the technique of ordering a series of pitches to other aspects of music—rhythm, timbre, attack, and dynamics, for example. Composers wrote "serial" music in which most of the events of a piece were determined by a series of pre-compositional decisions.

Aleatoric music

Diametrically opposed to this, but curiously similar in effect, is the **aleatoric music** of John Cage and others (*aleatoric* means dependent on chance or indeterminate elements). Cage, an influential composer and philosopher, tried to expand horizons by producing music out of silence, out of a group of radios, out of a toy piano. Some of his music is composed by chance processes—flipping a coin, consulting the traditional Chinese I Ching, and so on. These processes are then used to determine the notes, their lengths, and other parameters.

Other twentieth-century composers invented a generally astringent, angular musical style, sometimes based on the music of their own culture; these include Béla Bartók in Hungary; Benjamin Britten in England; and the Russians Sergei Prokofiev, who left his native land only to return years later, and Dmitri Shostakovich, who navigated a complex career in the Soviet Union.

Ⓢ Shostakovich: *String Quartet No. 8 in C Minor, II*

In the latter part of the century, the availability of various means of generating sound electronically (manipulation of recorded sound, synthesizers, computer-generated tones) led composers to experiment with music that mixes live and electronic sounds, as well as music that is generated purely electronically; such electronic music eliminates acoustic instruments, and no performer is involved—the composer communicates directly to the listener through loudspeakers. Important voices in this ever varied and expanded medium include Edgard Varèse, Milton Babbitt, and Tod Machover.

Ⓢ Varèse: *Deserts*, excerpt 7

For much of the twentieth century, composers made an effort to create a new sound-world with each composition. The result is a wide-ranging variety of sounds and systems that make it difficult to characterize the nature of twentieth-century music. Variety is at the core of its character.

In the second half of the twentieth century a mixture of new trends in music sought alternatives to the atonal, serially organized music. The aleatoric music of Cage and others was one such attempt. The music of Britten, Bartók, and the Russians was another. Musical **minimalism** was still another, employing the gradually shifting patterns of multiple repetitions to create longer shapes. (See Figure V.5.) Much twentieth-century music had avoided repetition almost completely (as it had avoided tonality), but in minimalist style, repetition of patterns is essential. A classic of the genre is Terry Riley's *In C*, for any number of melody instruments, in which each performer uses the same series of fifty-three short musical phrases, each

Minimalism

Ⓢ Reich: *New York Counterpoint*

repeated as many times as the players choose. The effect is of a shifting, patterned, polyphonic swirl of music in C major. Philip Glass, Steve Reich Ⓢ, John Adams and other composers have adopted aspects of minimalism.

At the end of the century, the term **neoromantic** became popular to describe the works of composers who since much earlier in the century had imbued their works with the emotional intensity so characteristic of nineteenth-century music and used lush harmonies and orchestration reminiscent of that previous century. Such composers include Americans Samuel Barber, John Corigliano, Ellen Taaffe Zwilich, and Jennifer Higdon; England's Ralph Vaughan Williams and Benjamin Britten; Germany's Wolfgang Rihm; Hungarian-born György Ligeti; Estonian-born Arvo Pärt (whose music is also reminiscent of Gregorian chant); Polish composer Krzysztof Penderecki; and the Finnish composer Kaija Saariaho.

Art music in the twentieth century has also been much influenced by its neighboring non-Classical music. **Jazz** and **blues**, both originating in African American culture, have not only been at the root of a great deal of popular music, but also have influenced composers from Maurice Ravel to Leonard Bernstein.

In the music of this final section, we will traverse a number of these styles, from the savage and folk-oriented *Rite of Spring* by Igor Stravinsky, through the expressionistic atonality of Alban Berg, to the mystical music of Olivier Messiaen and the pop-inspired Leonard Bernstein. It is a century of experiment, of variety, and of change, full of excitement for the listener.

FIG. V.5 Frank Stella, *Marrakech*, 1964. Stella's fluorescent colors and simple repeating patterns are typical of minimalist art; a similar movement in music employs slowly shifting, repetitive musical patterns.

Style Comparisons at a Glance

ROMANTIC MUSICAL STYLE	TWENTIETH-CENTURY MUSICAL STYLE
Traditional instruments continue to be used	Technology provides new instruments and electronic techniques
Themes and melodies are often folklike	Many melodies are disjunct, awkward to sing
Regular rhythmic patterns and meters	Much use of irregular rhythms
Harmonies based on chromatic scale, changes of major-minor modes, unusual key contrasts	Widespread abandonment of traditional harmony in favor of atonality, serial music, and other techniques
Genres: many miniatures—piano solos, songs, character pieces—as well as symphonies, program pieces, concerto, and opera	In addition to traditional forms, a wide variety of experimental, indeterminate, and open-form music
Music seeks to express personal, interior emotional experiences	A new objectivism pervades much twentieth-century music
Music seeks to express local, cultural, and national traditions	Music sometimes seeks to express political realities; there is still some late-Romantic nationalism

CHAPTER 15

THURSDAY, MAY 29, 1913, PARIS:

Igor Stravinsky's *The Rite of Spring* (*Le sacre du printemps*)

🔧 CORE REPERTOIRE	🎙️ AUTHOR VIDEOS
■ **LG 60** "Introduction" ■ **LG 61** "Signs of Spring: Girls' Dance" ■ **LG 62** "Spring Rounds" ■ **LG 63** "Procession of the Oldest and Wisest One" ■ **LG 64** "Glorification of the Chosen Victim" ■ **LG 65** "Sacrificial Dance"	■ Folklike melodies from *The Rite of Spring* ■ New sounds in "Signs of Spring: Girls' Dance," from *The Rite of Spring* ■ The building blocks of "Glorification of the Chosen Victim," from *The Rite of Spring*

Introduction

The first performance of *The Rite of Spring* (*Le sacre du printemps*, to use its proper French name) is probably the most famous premiere in the history of Western music. Igor Stravinsky wrote his score to accompany a ballet, and both the music and the dancing were so revolutionary that they nearly set off a riot in the theater. As soon as the curtain went up, the audience began screaming and laughing and protesting so loudly that the dancers on stage could hardly hear the enormous orchestra playing just below them in the pit. And yet Stravinsky's score contains some of the loudest unamplified music ever written.

Sergei Diaghilev, the legendary chief of the Russian Ballet (or Ballets Russes), wanted the ballet to be provocative: after all, the more scandal the public anticipated, the more tickets he stood to sell. When he commissioned the score from Stravinsky, he thought he knew what he would get. The young Russian composer had already written two enormously successful ballets for the company, *Firebird* and *Petrushka*. Moreover, the **choreography** (that is, the composition of the dance movements) for the new work was created by Vaslav Nijinsky, the most celebrated male dancer in the world at that time. *The Rite of Spring* was a collaboration of giants, and the musical result has fascinated listeners ever since.

The Rite of Spring was a lavish stage spectacle that involved a story, lots of dancing, and colorful settings and costumes. Only later did Stravinsky detach his score from its theatrical context and give it a second life in the concert hall. Indeed, the *Rite* has become, along with *Firebird*, one of the most frequently performed works in the orchestral repertory.

Subtitled *Pictures from Pagan Russia*, the ballet depicts ancient Slavic rituals enacted by a primitive tribe in prehistoric times. The pagan rites are enacted in order to appease the earth and ensure that spring will come again. At the end of the ballet, a chosen sacrificial victim is required to dance herself to death so that the earth will be fertile. The costumes and scenario—by Russian archaeologist, cultural expert, and painter Nicholas Roerich—attempted to make a realistic and authentic portrayal of ancient customs.

This ballet is a reflection of a trend we now call **primitivism**, a movement that valued the arts of non-Western and tribal peoples. Traditional Western approaches held that such peoples had no art or, at best, inferior art. But the paintings of Paul Gaugin (1848–1903)—borrowing motifs from the Tahitian people he visited—and the discovery of the arts of sub-Saharan Africa and other areas, provided a widened scope for aesthetic appreciation.

It will help to understand the ballet, and Stravinsky's music, if we bear in mind

Ⓢ Stravinsky: *The Rite of Spring*, "Procession of the Oldest and Wisest One"

Choreography

The ballet

Primitivism

that it is *supposed* to look and sound primitive and ritualistic (although it uses entirely new and modern sounds). The choreography is deliberately just the opposite of what we expect from ballet; it is all group movement, flat-footed, knock-kneed, with little use of the arms. It takes only a moment to understand also what the composer is doing. *The Rite of Spring* is full of simple melodies that might be bits of folk songs—as, in fact, some of them are. Other elements of the score—rhythmic and melodic patterns, repetitions, juxtapositions—contribute to the ballet's ritualistic atmosphere.

Ritual   A ritual usually involves some sort of ceremony, one that follows a set of prescribed rules or conventions. Certain ceremonies—the crowning of a king, the swearing-in of a president, a wedding, or a religious Mass such as the one we witnessed at Notre Dame Cathedral—must be performed in a specific way, with all the elements in a given order. A ritual is not designed to please or to sound nice; it simply accomplishes a job.

There is something impersonal and unemotional about the performance of a ritual. Stravinsky seeks to capture those qualities in *The Rite of Spring*. At the same time, the sheer visceral impact of the music gives it a breathtaking sense of immediacy. For a piece that is a century old, it still sounds shockingly modern—or perhaps shockingly primordial.

The Setting

PARIS IN 1913

Paris at the dawn of the twentieth century was one of the most exciting and cosmopolitan cities in the world, renowned for its tree-lined boulevards, stately office and apartment buildings, parks adorned with fountains and statuary, and stylish restaurants and cafes (see Figure 15.1). Then as now, the skyline was dominated by the thrusting steel spire of the Eiffel Tower, constructed for the great exposition of 1889. Equally eye-catching were the twin landmarks of the 1900 World's Fair, the

FIG. 15.1 A photograph from about 1900 of the Arc de Triomphe at the top of the Avenue des Champs-Élysées; by 1913 there would be more motor cars.

Grand Palais and the Petit Palais. At every turn, old buildings were coming down and new ones were going up in a frantic effort to keep pace with a population of nearly three million that was growing by the day.

Long a fabulously beautiful city, the French capital had lately been transformed into an ultramodern showplace. A stream of automobiles, electric streetcars, bicycles, buses, and carriages filled the streets. A vast network of railways brought the world to the city's doorsteps through the portals of its palatial train stations. Since the turn of the century, the underground metropolitan railway (the *métro* for short) had connected Paris's twenty administrative districts, or *arrondissements*.

Technology reigned supreme, its potential seemingly limitless. (Nobody knew that millions of people would soon die in a terrible war waged by means of the most technologically advanced weaponry.) Streets were lit with electric lights; telephones and other modern conveniences were becoming increasingly affordable. By subscribing to the *théâtrophone*, a service that brought a listening device into the home, Parisians could hear live performances of concerts, plays, and operas in their own living rooms. For a small fee, they could sample the novel delights of recorded music in one of the city's many *cabinets de phonographes*. The newest form of electronic media, the cinema, was rapidly gaining ground. Already Paris boasted some two hundred movie houses, many of them former theaters and music halls.

Technology

All this, and much more—circuses, wax museums, cycling and horseracing tracks—made Paris an international capital of culture and fashion. But nothing symbolized the glamorous, forward-looking spirit of the *belle époque* ("beautiful period") more brilliantly than Diaghilev's Russian Ballet.

Belle époque

SERGEI DIAGHILEV AND THE RUSSIAN BALLET

Since 1909, the annual visit of Diaghilev's troupe of Russian dancers had been one of the highlights of Paris's artistic calendar. The company held the stage for several weeks each spring, after the regular season of theater and opera was finished. The repertoire consisted mainly of ballets, both new and old, but Diaghilev was also an

SERGEI DIAGHILEV (1872–1929)

Sergei Diaghilev was born into a prominent family in provincial Russia that nurtured his early interest in literature and music. As a student in St. Petersburg in the 1890s, he thought of becoming a composer, only to see his hopes crushed when the great Nikolai Rimsky-Korsakov ridiculed his early efforts as "absurd." Turning instead to painting, Diaghilev set himself up as an art critic, organized exhibitions of modern art, and founded an influential journal called *World of Art*. By this roundabout route he came to his real calling as an impresario—or, as one observer described him, "the greatest magician in the world of art."

In 1907 Diaghilev organized a series of seven concerts devoted to Russian music at the Paris Opéra. The following year he returned to stage a season of operas, and in 1909 he imported a group of dancers on leave from the imperial ballet in St. Petersburg. The Russian Ballet remained a popular fixture on the Parisian scene until 1914, when it temporarily relocated to the United States. After the war, Diaghilev reassembled his troupe, now Russian in name only, and cemented his place in history by commissioning such masterpieces as the Stravinsky–George Balanchine ballet *Apollo* (originally *Apollon musagète*), which breathed new life into the classical language of both music and dance.

Both adored and detested by the artists he patronized, Diaghilev died in Venice in 1929, at the peak of his fame. Forty-two years later, Stravinsky was laid to rest a few yards away.

opera producer. The 1913 season included two works by Modest Mussorgsky, *Boris Godunov* and *Khovanschina*, as well as *Ivan the Terrible* by Stravinsky's old teacher, Nikolai Rimsky-Korsakov.

Whether in opera or ballet, Diaghilev was a master of his art, which was to assemble an all-star team of composers, dancers, choreographers, designers, and musicians; coax, cajole, and browbeat them into working together; and whip the public into a frenzy of anticipation for their collaborations. In a word, he was an *Impresario* **impresario** (see biography, p. 409).

In the two decades of the Russian Ballet's existence (it disbanded after the death of its founder in 1929), Diaghilev presented an astounding number of creations of lasting importance. The roster of the company's set and costume designers includes the artists Pablo Picasso, Henri Matisse, Georges Braque, Maurice Utrillo, and the pioneering fashion designer Coco Chanel. Among the composers from whom Diaghilev commissioned scores were Claude Debussy, Maurice Ravel, Richard Strauss, Francis Poulenc, and Serge Prokofiev—plus, of course, Stravinsky, who wrote no fewer than eight ballets and three operas for the Russian Ballet between 1910 and 1928.

Diaghilev emphasized the traditional themes and folk imagery of his native Russia, which Parisian audiences found tantalizingly exotic. But above all he wanted the Russian Ballet to be associated with whatever was new, imaginative, and exciting. Both the company and Diaghilev's productions had a glitter and sizzle that would be the envy of any impresario or promoter today. In addition to his managerial skills, Diaghilev had a powerful, persuasive, and often abrasive personality.

His homosexuality was known but not mentioned; and it was partly his infatuation with Vaslav Nijinsky (who was deeply conflicted about his own sexuality) that led him to name his star dancer the company's exclusive choreographer in 1913. In doing so, he displaced the far more experienced Michel Fokine, who had been responsible for most of the Russian Ballet's early successes, including Stravinsky's *Firebird* and *Petrushka*. Many people faulted Diaghilev's judgment, but the results were as stunning as they were controversial.

FIG. 15.2 Vaslav Nijinsky as the Faun in the 1912 ballet version of *Afternoon of a Faun*. Design is by the Russian painter and set and costume designer Léon Bakst.

VASLAV NIJINSKY

Handsome and phenomenally athletic, the twenty-three-year-old Nijinsky was one of the Russian Ballet's chief attractions. (Only the great ballerina Anna Pavlova rivaled his star power, but by 1913 she had left to start her own company.) Critics described him as feline, jaguar-like, and he was famous, as many male ballet stars are, for leaps that seemed to defy gravity. In *The Specter of the Rose*, one of Nijinsky's star turns, a young lady comes home from the ball and sets a single rose beside her. The rose comes to life (Nijinsky executing a spectacular leap through the window), they dance together, and the rose disappears (another spectacular leap out the window).

Nijinsky made his debut as a choreographer in 1912 with *The Afternoon of a Faun*. Audiences expecting to see the rounded, fluid gestures of classical ballet were disappointed. Instead, he copied the flat, static look of a Grecian frieze, with the dancers' bodies seen frontally, their heads in profile, and their arms twisted to the sides. Nijinsky himself played the languorous, satyr-like faun (see Figure 15.2) who encounters (or perhaps only dreams about) a group of young women in a forest. One of the nymphs touches his arm, then coyly pulls away, and the ballet closes with the faun making a shocking masturbatory gesture.

VASLAV NIJINSKY (1890–1950)

As both dancer and choreographer, Vaslav Nijinsky looms large in the history of ballet and modern dance. Trained at the Imperial Ballet School in St. Petersburg, he was steeped in the classical tradition that had made Russia the center of the dance world in the late nineteenth century. But Nijinsky was something of a loner, and in his early years he was rebellious enough that the authorities at the Maryinsky Theater fired him. (The official reason for his dismissal was indecent exposure—appearing on stage in an immodest costume.) In 1911 he moved to Paris to join his friend Diaghilev, who had been similarly ostracized in Russia for his homosexuality.

By all accounts, Nijinsky projected an electrifying presence on stage. He was known not only for his fabulous leaps but for the catlike smoothness and agility of his dancing. Ironically, one of his most famous roles—as the pathetic clown in Stravinsky's *Petrushka*—made no demands on his virtuosity. His sister, herself a famous dancer and choreographer, recalled: "Only the swinging, mechanical, soul-less motions jerk the sawdust-filled arms or legs upwards in extravagant movements to indicate transports of joy or despair." Nijinsky refined this angular, stylized movement in the four ballets he created between 1912 and 1916 that constitute his total choreographic achievement: *The Afternoon of a Faun* (danced to Claude Debussy's *Prelude to "The Afternoon of the Faun"*), *Jeux* (also Debussy), *The Rite of Spring*, and *Till Eulenspiegel* (Richard Strauss).

In 1913 Nijinsky married a Hungarian woman he met on tour in Buenos Aires. Romola de Pulszky was a devoted wife and bore him two children. Diaghilev, feeling jilted, reacted by angrily firing his prize dancer. Although Nijinsky continued to perform, he proved incapable of managing a career on his own. After his final public performance in 1917, he gradually lost his grip on reality, and by 1919 he was declared insane. He languished in various mental institutions until his death in 1950, leaving a diary signed "God Nijinsky."

Like Diaghilev, it seems, Nijinsky was a born provocateur (see biography, above). In 1913, the year he was made choreographer of the Russian Ballet, he created a dance that appears to depict a game of tennis, but is really about love. *Jeux*, which premiered two weeks before *The Rite of Spring*, involves one male dancer (Nijinsky) and two females. The women dance on the balls of their feet, almost on tiptoe, as if in a tennis service. The ballet begins with a tennis ball bouncing onto the stage and ends with a famous three-way kiss suggestive of Nijinsky's sexual ambivalence. Years later, the dancer wrote: "*Jeux* is the life of which Diaghilev dreamed—three young men making love to each other."

The music for both *Jeux* and *The Afternoon of a Faun* is by Claude Debussy, whose delicately perfumed, **impressionistic style** is strikingly unlike Stravinsky's. Yet the two composers established a good rapport. There is a famous story about them playing through Stravinsky's four-hand piano arrangement of *The Rite of Spring* at the home of the music writer Louis Laloy in the summer of 1912. "We were struck dumb," Laloy recalled, "overwhelmed as by a hurricane springing up from the depths of the ages to take our life by the roots."

Ⓢ Debussy: *Prelude to "The Afternoon of a Faun"*

Nijinsky's choreography for the *Rite* was more daring than that of his earlier ballets. This time he turned classical ballet vocabulary almost literally inside out: the dancers stood with knees together, heels apart, toes pointed inward, and arms held close to their bodies—essentially the opposite of ballet's so-called first position. Moreover, all the dancing is group dancing—there are no solos comparable to those in traditional ballets, except for the famous sacrificial dance at the end. It is a pathbreaking piece of choreography, designed to look tribal and primordial, and it had a huge impact on the younger generation of choreographers who were inventing a new style of movement known as modern dance.

Choreography for the Rite

IGOR STRAVINSKY

Igor Stravinsky, the thirty-year-old Russian composer who was busily transforming himself into a Parisian and a man of the theater, had come to Diaghilev's attention in 1909, when the impresario attended the premiere of his orchestral tour de force *Fireworks* in St. Petersburg. A series of orchestral arrangements that Stravinsky made for the Russian Ballet convinced Diaghilev that he was ready for a more important assignment. The upshot was the two ballets that made Stravinsky's name in Paris, *Firebird* (1910) and *Petrushka* (1911), both based on Russian legends.

IGOR STRAVINSKY (1882–1971)

Stravinsky was one of the most performed and most influential composers of the twentieth century, moving through several countries (Switzerland, Russia, France, the United States) and several musical styles (from **neoclassicism** to **serialism**), but always retaining his characteristic acerbity and color. Wherever he was, he remained a Russian composer. He is, perhaps with Tchaikovsky, the only composer to achieve fame by composing ballet music.

Raised in St. Petersburg, Russia, Stravinsky was the child of a famous operatic bass and a strict mother who was a fine pianist. Although young Igor studied law, as most Russian men of the upper classes did, he was committed to music from the time of his studies with the distinguished composer Nikolai Rimsky-Korsakov. In 1906 he married his cousin Katya Nosenko, with whom he remained until her death in 1939. Later he married Vera Sudeykina, who is thought to have been his mistress since about 1921.

A fastidious dresser, Stravinsky wore his hair parted in the middle and prided himself on his trim physique. He seemed taller than he really was because, as one contemporary observed, "he carries his head in the air and his look dominates his interlocutor; he speaks from on high, and his eyes wander over objects and persons with a divergence and a mobility that surround them like a sudden rainshower." Diaghilev commissioned the ballet scores that catapulted Stravinsky to fame in Paris. After the electrifying premiere of *The Rite of Spring* in 1913, Stravinsky realized that his future lay not so much in Russia as in being a Russian composer in the West. For the next twenty-six years, he spent most of his time in Paris, even becoming a French citizen.

Despite his tolerance of the Nazis and his sympathy for Italian dictator Benito Mussolini, the 1930s proved difficult for Stravinsky in Paris. In 1939 he and Vera emigrated to the United States, living first in Los Angeles and later in New York. (He became an American citizen in 1945.) Stravinsky enlarged his fame with further major works, recordings, and performances as both conductor and pianist. He also produced a series of writings, mostly in the form of conversations with Robert Craft, his American amanuensis, assistant, and ultimately close friend and biographer.

Late in life Stravinsky overcame his resistance to the atonal technique of his fellow émigré Arnold Schoenberg and composed several moving works, including *Threni*, *Canticum sacrum*, and the *Requiem Canticles*.

A lifelong hypochondriac, Stravinsky was also obsessed with his financial affairs, musical copyrights, and posthumous reputation, even after he had become the most famous composer of classical music in the world. After his death in New York on April 6, 1971, he was buried on an island in Venice near his old benefactor Diaghilev.

Stravinsky was always a man of the theater, and his range was astonishing. Among his later ballets are the Russian-style *Wedding*, the neo-Romantic *Apollo*, the Tchaikovskian *Fairy's Kiss*, the neoclassical *Orpheus*, and the almost atonal *Agon*. He wrote a neo-Baroque opera, *The Rake's Progress*, as well as many other works of a ceremonial or religious nature, such as the **oratorio** *Oedipus Rex*, a Mass, and the *Symphony of Psalms* (all set to Latin texts).

Ⓢ Stravinsky: *Symphony of Psalms*
Ⓢ Stravinsky: *L'histoire du soldat*
Ⓢ Stravinsky: *Requiem Canticles*

MAJOR WORKS: Ballets, including *The Firebird*, *Petrushka*, *The Rite of Spring*; operas and other theater works, including *The Rake's Progress* and *L'histoire du soldat*; orchestral music, including Symphony in C and Symphony in Three Movements; choral music, including *Symphony of Psalms*.

Listeners who knew those richly colored scores were struck by how different *The Rite of Spring* sounded. Although many of the techniques and ideas that Stravinsky explored in the *Rite* had been tried out in *Firebird* and *Petrushka*, the ballets might almost have been written by three different composers. *The Firebird* speaks the late Romantic language of Tchaikovsky and, especially, of Stravinsky's teacher Rimsky-Korsakov; it has lush harmonies, soaring melodies, and rich orchestration. In *Petrushka* Stravinsky begins to find his own voice, emphasizing folk elements, unusual harmonies, and striking rhythmic effects. The *Rite* is something completely new—the "birth certificate of modernism," as the composer Pierre Boulez called it. (See Stravinsky's biography, p. 412.)

⑤ Stravinsky: *The Firebird*

⑤ Stravinsky: *Petrushka*

Stravinsky was not yet the most famous composer in the world, but his recent successes had given him a taste of celebrity, and he was delighted by the opportunity to work on *The Rite of Spring*, especially since Diaghilev had encouraged him to use an extra-large orchestra.

At the time of their collaboration, Stravinsky professed great respect for Nijinsky. "Nijinsky is an admirable artist," he told an interviewer. "He is capable of renewing the art of ballet. We never for a second failed to be in absolute communion of thought. Later you will see what he will do." Over the years, however, the composer apparently convinced himself that Nijinsky was a musical ignoramus. In his ghost-written autobiography of 1936, he belittled the dancer's contribution to *The Rite of Spring,* saying that he "was incapable of giving intelligible form to its essence, and complicated it either by clumsiness or lack of understanding."

Stravinsky's relationship with Diaghilev was similarly rocky. Temperamental and strong-willed, the two men seemed to thrive on conflict, and for long periods they stopped speaking to each other, even as Stravinsky continued to supply new works for the Russian Ballet. As Nijinsky noted in his diary, Diaghilev "cannot exist without Stravinsky, and Stravinsky cannot live without Diaghilev. Both understand each other. Stravinsky fights with Diaghilev very cleverly. I know both their tricks."

FIGS. 15.3A AND B Costumes for the Chosen Victim (top) and for one of the women (bottom), both designed by Nicholas Roerich for the premiere of *Le sacre du printemps.*

NICHOLAS ROERICH

Stravinsky's about-face on Nijinsky was not his only attempt to rewrite history. As time went by, he increasingly denigrated the role that Nicholas Roerich—Russia's leading authority on prehistoric Slavic culture— had played in their collaboration (see Roerich's biography, p. 414). Diaghilev had known him in St. Petersburg and helped introduce his work to the public in the pages of his journal *World of Art.* In 1909 the impresario commissioned Roerich to create the sets and costumes for one of the Russian Ballet's biggest hits, the Polovtsian Dances from Alexander Borodin's opera *Prince Igor.*

Stravinsky's germ of an idea for a ballet about a pagan ritual sacrifice prompted him to seek advice from Roerich. As he wrote to a friend, "Who else could help me, who else knows the secret of our ancestors' close feeling for the earth?" It was Roerich who drew up the scenario—the plot and action—for *The Rite of Spring,* which Stravinsky followed almost to the letter in composing the music. Roerich also designed the colorful scenery and costumes, based on what was understood at the time to be authentic Slavic folklore (see Figures 15.3–15.5).

In later years Stravinsky claimed full credit for the scenario, much as he discounted the revolutionary impact of Nijinsky's choreography after he began promoting the *Rite* as a concert piece. "The idea of *Le Sacre du printemps* came to me while I was still composing *The Firebird,*" the composer recalled disingenuously.

NICHOLAS ROERICH (1874–1947)

Trained in art, law, and archaeology, Nicholas Roerich had a long and varied career as a painter, stage designer, and cultural activist. His stylized landscapes and imaginary historical scenes, many on themes drawn from Slavic history and folklore, are distinguished by simplified outlines and flat areas of color. One of his most famous paintings, *The Forefathers*, dates from 1911, while he was working with Diaghilev and Stravinsky (see Figure 15.4). It depicts a rustic piper encircled by bears amid the rolling hills of northern Russia—a primordial image that might almost have served as a backdrop for *The Rite of Spring*.

Around the time of the Russian Revolution, Roerich emigrated first to Finland, then to England and the United States. In the late 1920s he settled in a small Himalayan village in India, where he pursued his scholarly and artistic interest in Eastern philosophy and religion. He was instrumental in drafting the Roerich Pact, an international treaty for protecting cultural treasures and institutions, which was signed by many nations in 1935. In that same year the Internal Revenue Service accused Roerich of tax fraud, forcing him to sell many of the paintings that he had used as collateral to finance his personal travel.

Known as a visionary and mystic, Roerich died in India in 1947. Eleven years later, a collection of his paintings went on display at the newly opened Roerich Museum in New York City.

FIG. 15.4 *The Forefathers* (1911) by Nicholas Roerich; this could almost have served as a backdrop for *Le sacre du printemps*.

FIG. 15.5 An oil sketch by Nicholas Roerich for the actual set of Part One of *Le sacre du printemps*.

"I had dreamed a scene of pagan ritual in which a chosen sacrificial virgin dances herself to death." In other words, what had been a collaboration, one of the most momentous in musical and theatrical history, eventually got repackaged as Stravinsky's solo act.

THE BALLET

Scenes for the Rite   Roerich outlined the scenario of *The Rite of Spring* in a letter to Diaghilev:

> [T]he first set should transport us to the foot of a sacred hill, in a lush plain, where Slavonic tribes are gathered together to celebrate the spring rites. In this scene there is an old witch, who predicts the future, a marriage by capture, round dances. Then comes the most solemn moment. The wisest ancient is brought from the village to imprint his sacred kiss on the new-flowering earth. During this rite the crowd is

seized with a mystic terror, and this our excellent Nijinsky has stylized for us admirably well.

After this uprush of terrestrial joy, the second scene sets a celestial mystery before us. Young virgins dance in circles on the sacred hill, amid enchanted rocks, then they choose the victim they intend to honor. In a moment she will dance her last dance, before the ancient old men, wrapped in bearskins, to show that the bear was man's ancestor. Then the graybeards dedicate the victim to the god Yarilo.

The ballet is in two parts, with a pause in the middle during which a curtain is lowered and the set is changed. Each part consists of a series of group rituals, games, and dances, followed by an action by a single individual. The first half, "The Adoration of the Earth," takes place in the daylight and involves male activities like simulated abduction of women and simulated warfare. It culminates in the arrival of the oldest and wisest member of the tribe, who comes forward to kiss the earth. (Stravinsky evokes the mystical significance of this moment with a soft, shimmering chord in **harmonics** played by the strings; see p. 10.) Then the stage erupts in a frenzied dance. *First Part*

The second half of the ballet, focused more on women, is set at night. "The Sacrifice" begins with a circle dance by the young women of the tribe. By a game of elimination, they select one of their number to be this year's victim. The elders arrive, the ancestors are invoked and appear mysteriously, the Chosen Victim performs her sacrificial dance, and the ballet ends with the elders holding her lifeless body up in the air. *Second Part*

Roerich's prose outline matches the stage action quite closely. What is not clear from his scenario is that the *Rite*, like many other ballets, is made up of a number of dances, each involving different personnel and each set to its own music. Likewise, Stravinsky's score is a sequence of separate but interconnected musical numbers. These numbers are actually named in the score, like chapters in a book, and they serve as a kind of running plot summary for both performers and listeners (see Titles of Musical Numbers, below).

Titles of Musical Numbers in *The Rite of Spring*

First Part: The Adoration of the Earth	Second Part: The Sacrifice
"Introduction"	"Introduction"
"Signs of Spring: Girls' Dance"	"Mysterious Circles of Girls"
"Game of Abduction"	"Glorification of the Chosen Victim"
"Spring Rounds"	"Evocation of the Ancestors"
"Games of Rival Cities"	"Ritual Actions of the Ancestors"
"Procession of the Oldest and Wisest One"	"Sacrificial Dance"
"The Kiss of the Earth"	
"Dance Overcoming the Earth"	

In the beginning, *The Rite of Spring* was not just a piece of music but a "total work of art" (*Gesamtkunstwerk*), a blend of music, dance, drama, and spectacle after the fashion of Wagner's *Walküre*. Anyone who has the opportunity to see Nijinsky's choreography as reconstructed by Millicent Hodson (see Reconstructing the *Rite*, p. 416) will understand how closely the music and dance work together, and how much action is represented in Stravinsky's music—or, to put it another way, how the music seems to be just right for what the dancers are doing. *Gesamtkunstwerk*

Reconstructing the *Rite*

Although several systems of dance notation have been devised, none is capable of capturing every nuance of a dancer's moving body. As a result, dancers cannot "read" the score of a ballet in the same way that musicians can. For the most part, they have to learn their movements by repetition, usually working directly under the supervision of the choreographer. By the same token, unless a dance happens to be preserved on film or video, the choreography stands a good chance of being irretrievably lost.

Unfortunately, no one thought to film *The Rite of Spring* in 1913; in fact, only three still photographs of the original production, taken backstage at the Théâtre des Champs-Élysées, are known to exist. Not until 1987 did the New York–based Joffrey Ballet revive Nijinsky's choreography on the basis of some inspired detective work by the dance historian Millicent Hodson based on surviving choreographic notes and interviews with dancers in the original ballet. Kenneth Archer, Hodson's husband, recreated Roerich's boldly colored sets and costumes for the Joffrey's landmark reconstruction.

The Performance

THE THÉÂTRE DES CHAMPS-ÉLYSÉES

In previous years Diaghilev had given performances in various places in Paris, including the magnificent opera house, the Palais Garnier. But 1913 saw the opening of a marvelous new facility, the Théâtre des Champs-Élysées. Its owner, Gabriel Astruc, was an impresario of skill and imagination. He had experience as a producer of concerts, operas, and other attractions (including circuses), and when Diaghilev began to present ballet in Paris, he did so in association with Astruc.

Astruc built his theater not on the grand Avenue des Champs-Élysées, but on the nearby Avenue Montaigne, an elegant address in an up-and-coming neighborhood. The building was the latest thing, with a marble facade incorporating reliefs by the well-known sculptor Émile Bourdelle (see Figure 15.6). The use of steel and reinforced concrete beams for the frame meant that the seating area was unencumbered by the forest of columns that is usually required in a theater. The décor was spare and modern, with rows of armchairs upholstered in red velvet, three tiers of free-floating balconies, a silver stage curtain, and a domed ceiling decorated with paintings of modern operas encircling a huge sun-shaped light (see Figure 15.7).

Astruc was determined to make a splash. His opening concert on April 2, 1913, featured the most famous French composers of the day (Camille Saint-Saëns, Claude Debussy, Vincent d'Indy, Gabriel Fauré, and Paul Dukas) conducting their own works. Subsequent evenings were devoted to operas, ballets, and vocal recitals. But the climax of the theater's first spring season was the appearance of Diaghilev's Russian Ballet, alternating with the first performances of Fauré's opera *Pénélope*. And the high point of the "Russian season" was the premiere of *The Rite of Spring*.

FIG. 15.6 The exterior of Théâtre des Champs-Élysées, newly opened in 1913.

PREPARING THE PERFORMANCE

Dance rehearsals Diaghilev had no incentive to skimp on rehearsal time, since Astruc had guaranteed a fee of 25,000 francs per performance, more than twice what he had paid the Russian Ballet in earlier seasons. (This is what enabled Diaghilev to give Stravinsky carte blanche to write for an exceptionally large orchestra.) More than one hundred dance rehearsals were held, beginning long before the orchestra players got their first glimpse of the music. Every rehearsal was needed, because the choreography was extremely complex and the rhythms were challenging.

Nijinsky asked for things that ballet dancers did not normally do with their bodies. Over and over again he demonstrated what he wanted, the dancers growing more exhausted and bewildered by the hour. (Nijinsky had decided not to create a role for himself in the *Rite*; he already had enough to do in the other ballets on the program.) There was a movement of some kind for virtually every event in the music, with the result that the dancing is both action-packed and highly repetitive.

Lydia Sokolova (her real name was Hilda Munnings, but this was the Russian Ballet!) described rehearsing the "Dance Overcoming the Earth" that ends the first half of the ballet: "We had to run about more or less *ad lib*, and stamp to various rhythms. We were really allotted no definite place on the stage, and the curtain came down on a stampede of humanity. . . . Some of the girls used to be running around with little bits of paper in their hands, in a panic, quarrelling with each other about whose count was right and whose wrong."

According to the dancer Anatole Bourman,

Nijinsky rehearsed like an inexhaustible demon until he nearly dropped in his tracks. Jumps were no longer completed on toes with slightly flexed knees, but flat-footed and straight-legged in a fashion to preclude the possibility of lightness, and to convey an impression of antediluvian festivity that nearly killed us. With every leap we landed heavily enough to jar every organ in us. Our heads throbbed with pain, leaving us continually with nerves jangled and bodies that ached. Nijinsky had to rehearse with every single group, and danced hour after hour, pounding his feet onto the stage with mighty thumps that must have cost him untold agony, for he had been used to dancing with the lightness and freedom of a feather tossed by the wind.

FIG. 15.7 The interior of Théâtre des Champs-Élysées. The steel-reinforced architecture permits a very open auditorium without columns.

Not surprisingly, dancers soon began to complain that they had difficulty following Nijinsky's chaotic directions (see Stravinsky Describes a Dance Rehearsal, right). Diaghilev responded by hiring Miriam Ramberg, a student from Émile Jaques-Dalcroze's school of eurhythmics near Dresden (it focused on translating rhythms into bodily movements), to interpret the actions for the dancers and help them cope with the complexities of the rhythms. (The Polish-born Ramberg, who later called herself Marie Rambert, went on to become a legendary teacher in England. The Russian Ballet dancers nicknamed her "Rhythmitchka.")

Orchestra rehearsals The orchestra of the Russian Ballet consisted of eighty-two professional musicians from various Parisian orchestras, all of which had finished their seasons by the time the ballet season began. For *The Rite of Spring*, Diaghilev

Stravinsky Describes a Dance Rehearsal

The dancers had been rehearsing for months and they knew what they were doing, even though what they were doing often had nothing to do with the music. "I will count to forty while you play," Nijinsky would say to me, "and we will see where we come out." He could not understand that though we might at some point come out together, this did not necessarily mean we had been together on the way. The dancers followed Nijinsky's beat, too, rather than the musical beat. Nijinsky counted in Russian, of course, and as Russian numbers above ten are polysyllabic—eighteen, for example, is *vosemnádsat*—in fast-tempo movements, neither he nor they could keep pace with the music.

hired seventeen additional musicians. Stravinsky had increased the orchestra's size at his request, and the result was an ensemble featuring quintuple winds and brass—that is, five players for each group of instruments—along with eight horns and a very large string section. All ninety-nine players are essential, because almost every musician has a unique part (see The Orchestra, below).

The Orchestra for the *Rite*

The score often calls on players to "double," that is, to switch between two instruments. For example, the bassoons are sometimes configured as four bassoons and one contrabassoon, and sometimes as three bassoons and two contrabassoons.

Woodwinds

Flutes (5 players): 2 piccolos, 3 flutes, 1 bass flute in G
Oboes (5 players): 4 oboes, 2 English horns
Clarinets (5 players): 1 E-flat clarinet, 1 piccolo clarinet in D, 3 clarinets in A and B, 2 bass clarinets
Bassoons (5 players): 4 bassoons, 2 contrabassoons

Horns

Horns (8 players): 2 players also play tenor tuba for the "Procession of the Oldest and Wisest One"

Brass

Trumpets (5 players): 1 piccolo trumpet, 4 trumpets in C, 1 bass trumpet in E♭
Low brass (5 players): 3 trombones and 2 tubas (sometimes joined by the 2 tenor tubas played by two of the horn players)

Percussion

5 players: piccolo timpani, 4 timpani, bass drum, triangle, antique cymbals, tam-tam, guiro, tambourine, cymbals

Strings

Stravinsky calls for specific numbers of *pupitres*, music stands of two players each:
8 stands of first violins (all 8 are needed on p. 20 of the 1913 score)
7 stands of second violins (all needed on p. 77)
6 stands of violas (all needed on p. 84)
at least 7 cellos (5 soloists plus "the others" on p. 75)
at least 6 double basses (a famous passage calls for 6 solo double basses, p. 7)

FIG. 15.8 Pierre Monteux who conducted the 1913 premiere of *Le sacre du printemps*. This photograph is from about 1918, while Monteux was conductor at the Metropolitan Opera House in New York.

The orchestra was conducted by thirty-eight-year-old Pierre Monteux (see Figure 15.8), who had begun his career as a violist and played in the Paris premiere of Debussy's opera *Pelléas et Mélisande* in 1902. As conductor of the Russian Ballet since 1911, Monteux had led the first performances of a number of major works, including Stravinsky's *Petrushka*. Later he conducted at the Metropolitan Opera in New York, became music director of the Boston Symphony and the San Francisco Symphony, and took out American citizenship. He died in Maine in 1964, aged eighty-nine, three years after signing a twenty-five-year contract with the London Symphony.

Monteux had a keen ear and boundless energy. He was in no doubt as to how he felt about the score of *The Rite of Spring*: he hated it (see Pierre Monteux Hears Stravinsky Play the *Rite*, p. 419). But Monteux knew how to rehearse an orchestra, and he got results. According to Louis Speyer, the first oboist, "When we saw the parts for the first time we couldn't believe they could be played," but the conductor "kept his admirable calm all the way." Henri Girard, a double-bass player, recalled:

> It is hard to describe the astonishment of the orchestra when we started the first rehearsal. Except for Monteux, who had studied the score with Stravinsky, everybody was confused by the complicated rhythms, atrocious dissonances, and strange sounds to which our ears were not accustomed. Musicians started to stop Monteux, asking if the parts were correctly printed, wanting to know, for example, if "my B-natural is correct as my neighbor is playing B-flat." This went on for a certain time until Monteux said angrily, "Do not stop me asking if you have a mistake. If you have one, I will let you know."

Pierre Monteux Hears Stravinsky Play the *Rite*

With only Diaghilev and myself as an audience, Stravinsky sat down to play a piano reduction of the entire score. . . . The very walls resounded as Stravinsky pounded away, occasionally stamping his feet and jumping up and down to accentuate the force of the music. Before he got very far I was convinced he was raving mad.

Stravinsky, too, was a whirlwind of energy as he pounded out his music at the keyboard during orchestra rehearsals, breaking strings right and left. (He was known to go through as many as four pianos in a single week.) The oversize orchestra could barely squeeze into the pit of the new theater, and the awkward seating arrangement made it difficult for the players to hear one another. But as the rehearsals progressed—seventeen for the orchestra alone, five more with the dancers—the production gradually fell into place.

The final dress rehearsal, on May 28, was the one to which Diaghilev invited the press. He wanted to give the critics extra time to write their reviews, and also to increase his income by reducing the number of free seats set aside for journalists at the premiere. Consequently, most of the reviews of the *Rite* make no mention of the exciting events of May 29. The critics who had been in the theater the night before had no way of knowing that a storm was about to erupt.

FIG. 15.9 Upper-class Parisian women from around 1910, dressed in the most up-to-date fashions of the time. This would have been the style of dress worn for the opening of *Le sacre du printemps*.

THURSDAY, MAY 29, AT 8:45 P.M.

Every seat in the theater was filled on the night of the premiere, even though the weather was hot and sticky and tickets cost nearly twice as much as for a normal ballet evening. The fashionable audience was a cross-section of upper-class Parisians, tourists, and people who were interested in all things modern and avant-garde (see Figure 15.9). Most of them were season ticket holders and had already seen Nijinsky's controversial *Jeux* two weeks earlier, as well as the Russian Ballet's splendid production of Mussorgsky's opera *Boris Godunov*.

A whiff of scandal was in the air. Diaghilev was probably responsible for planting the tantalizing announcement that appeared in several Parisian newspapers on the morning of the performance:

> *The Rite of Spring*, which the Russian ballet will perform for the first time tonight at the theatre of the Champs-Élysées, is the most surprising realization that the admirable troupe of M. Serge de Diaghilew has ever attempted. It is the evocation of the first gestures of pagan Russia evoked by the triple vision of Strawinsky, poet and musician, of Nicolas Roerich, poet and painter, and of Nijinsky, poet and choreographer.

One will find there the strongly stylized characteristic attitudes of the Slavic race with an awareness of the beauty of the prehistoric period.

The prodigious Russian dancers were the only ones capable of expressing these stammerings of a semi-savage humanity, of composing these frenetic human clusters wrenched incessantly by the most astonishing polyrhythm ever to come from the mind of a musician. There is truly a new thrill which will surely raise passionate discussions, but which will leave all true artists with an unforgettable impression.

The impresario had cleverly constructed the program to ensure that *The Rite of Spring* made the strongest possible impact. First came *Les Sylphides,* a "romantic reverie" set to orchestral versions of some of Chopin's most popular piano pieces. (Two of the transcriptions were by Stravinsky himself.) This was the kind of ballet that the traditionalists in the audience had come to see, with all the women wearing tutus and a terrific waltz duo for the company's star dancers, Tamara Karsavina and Nijinsky.

Les Sylphides was followed immediately by the *Rite.* After the intermission came *The Specter of the Rose,* another romantic chestnut (music by Carl Maria von Weber, arranged for orchestra by Hector Berlioz), featuring Nijinsky's famous leaps through the window. The final work was the Polovtsian Dances from Borodin's opera *Prince Igor,* a Russian-flavored showstopper danced by the entire company and sung by the chorus of the Imperial Opera of St. Petersburg.

May 29 was the anniversary of the first performance of *The Afternoon of a Faun,* which Diaghilev considered a good omen. In the back of his mind, perhaps, was the thought that Stravinsky's new ballet might reprise the éclat that had greeted Nijinsky's debut as a choreographer. The dreamy *Sylphides* was surely meant, not only as a warm-up for the company, but to prepare the ground for a shock when the same dancers appeared onstage in Nijinsky's "awkward" and "primitive" *Rite.*

The Music

In *The Rite of Spring* and other works, Stravinsky was deliberately trying to create music that is not beautiful or expressive in the conventional sense. If someone had asked him whether he wanted his music to be beautiful, he might have replied that it was the wrong question. He wanted his music to be well crafted and to have the formal and logical clarity that he admired in all works of art.

Absence of linear continuity

We might think that music "about" spring should unfold organically, the way plants grow from seeds—developing from a small idea, and becoming gradually and imperceptibly larger and broader. *The Rite of Spring,* however, lacks the kind of motivic and thematic development that we find in the music of, say, Bach or Beethoven. One of the things that puzzled listeners in 1913 was the absence of linear continuity, a sense that a melody is never quite complete, that one musical theme or passage does not follow "naturally" from another.

The title of Stravinsky's ballet provides a key to the puzzle: *The Rite of Spring* is about prehistoric rites performed in the springtime, not about spring itself. It is the ritualistic aspects of the music that Stravinsky is emphasizing—the archaic, nonexpressive quality of ideas that are repeated, not for the sake of beauty, but for the sake of ritual.

This does not mean that *The Rite of Spring* is not beautiful. Many people think it is. Stravinsky's music is exciting, visceral, maybe even savage, but it also contains moments of quiet, contemplative grace. Because these qualities are produced by techniques that Stravinsky uses in many other pieces, you might think that *all* his music sounds like pagan rituals, and in a sense it does. Diaghilev's commission was precisely the opportunity Stravinsky needed to break out of the Russian Romantic mold of his training and background—the mold that had shaped the scores of *The Firebird* and, to a lesser degree, *Petrushka*. It was the notion of ritual that set him on the track that changed his music and all the music of the twentieth century.

The hallmarks of Stravinsky's mature style are all present in *The Rite of Spring*. Before we consider the score in detail, here are a few general elements of Stravinsky's music to keep in mind:

General stylistic elements

- **Folk and folklike melodies.** The very first music we hear in the ballet—a melody played very high on a bassoon—has a rhapsodic, improvised, folklike quality. In fact, this melody, along with several others in *The Rite of Spring*, is arranged from a Lithuanian folk tune. Other folklike melodies in the score are Stravinsky's own, but they sound similarly timeless and exotic. They have irregular phrases, and the scales they use are unusual. They generally use only a few notes, rearranged in a variety of ways.

  Ⓢ Stravinsky: *The Rite of Spring,* "Introduction"

- **Ostinato**. This is the musical term (it means "obstinate" in Italian) for something repeated over and over. It might be a single chord, a melody, or a series of notes. The reiterated chord at the beginning of "Signs of Spring: Girls' Dance" is an ostinato; so is the slow, four-beat figure at the beginning of "Spring Rounds." Most interesting are the places where an ostinato continues while something else happens. Sometimes two or more ostinatos are operating, at different speeds and in different rhythms. A good example is in "Procession of the Oldest and Wisest One," where an ostinato melody played by all the tubas (in groups of *four* beats) runs parallel to an ostinato rhythm in the bass drum (which has a loud stroke every *three* beats). The result is a clockwork pattern in which the two ostinatos are sometimes in phase and sometimes out of phase. You can hear similar rhythmic combinations throughout *The Rite of Spring* (see LGs 62, 63, and 64). This sort of displacement, or misalignment, of one relatively simple element with respect to another, is one of the chief techniques that makes the music sound complex: it is the layering of simple elements in irregular alignment.

  Ⓢ Stravinsky: *The Rite of Spring,* "Procession of the Oldest and Wisest One" (tuba ostinato)

- **Static sounds**. Stravinsky composed at the piano, and one of his gifts lay in discovering chords that make new sounds. The many-times-repeated chord of "Girls' Dance" is a good example; it can be analyzed as two chords from two different keys, or in a number of other ways. But it happens to be easily playable on the piano and to make a memorable sound. Other characteristic sounds are found throughout the score; further examples include the shifting sound of the introduction to the second part. These sounds are often primary elements in Stravinsky's block construction (see below).

  Ⓢ Stravinsky: *The Rite of Spring,* "Signs of Spring: Girls' Dance"

- **Polytonality.** Stravinsky and many other twentieth-century composers experimented with combining two or more keys, or tonalities, at once. We call this technique "polytonality" (the Greek prefix *poly* means "many"). Polytonality is an important feature of *The Rite of Spring*. The ostinato chord in "Girls' Dance" is made of chords in two different keys that are superimposed on each other. There are also melodies that are played simultaneously in two keys; a good example is in "Games of Rival Cities." In those cases the effect is almost like **overtones** (see p. 10), the two versions of the melody blending as though we were listening to a strange and unfamiliar instrument.

  Ⓢ Stravinsky: *The Rite of Spring,* "Games of Rival Cities"

⑤ Stravinsky: *The Rite of Spring,* "Glorification of the Chosen Victim"

- **Block construction.** Long stretches of music in the *Rite* (and in other works by Stravinsky) are put together like patchwork quilts or mosaics. In other words, one, or more, small, invariable blocks of music return repeatedly, interspersed with other blocks, in irregular patterns. The result might look like **AAaAaAA**, where each letter stands for a block of music, repeated the same way each time. The pattern given here is that of the beginning of "Glorification of the Chosen Victim." (**A** and **a** are two versions of the same basic chord, one of Stravinsky's special discoveries; **A** is always the same, five quick beats; **a** is variable in length, rocking back and forth.) In such passages, it is as though there were tiles of various colors, except that here the tiles are short passages of music, each having its own characteristic harmony, orchestration, and rhythm. (See LG 65, p. 429).

All these elements go into making Stravinsky's astringent, sometimes impassive style. It has a captivating rhythmic variety, a great deal of rhythmic irregularity, and some absolutely fascinating sounds. A selection of some of the most characteristic scenes will give a flavor of this revolutionary piece.

Listening to the Music

⚡ LG 60

"INTRODUCTION"

🎙 Folklike melodies from *The Rite of Spring*

The ballet begins with the curtain closed. An eerie sound, like a melody from another time and a different culture, sets a folklike, improvisatory mood (see LG 60, below). We already know what it is, but for its listeners it might have seemed like an unknown instrument. Like many of the melodies in the ballet, it has the not-quite major, not-quite minor quality that we call "modal" (using a scale other than major or minor).

LISTENING GUIDE 60 | DVD | 🎙

Stravinsky *The Rite of Spring,* "Introduction" 1:07

DATE: 1913

GENRE: Ballet (performed also as orchestral work)

LISTEN FOR
MELODY: Modal melody creates folklike quality
RHYTHM: Irregular rhythms

SCORING: Bassoon in very high register; gradual increase of accompaniment

EXPRESSION: Eerie, improvisatory feeling

TIME	FORM	DESCRIPTION
0:00	First bassoon phrase:	

Unaccompanied until partway through. The effect is of 4 subphrases, each beginning on the note C and ending on the note A.

0:20	Second bassoon phrase:	(musical notation)

Begins as before, but uses many levels of triple notation to create a rhapsodic, improvisatory sound. New notes are introduced: B♭, G♭. On the G♭, the lowest note of the phrase, the clarinets begin an accompaniment in triplets.

0:33	Third bassoon phrase:	(musical notation)

Like the opening phrase, with the second (triplet) element omitted. Note the low oboe during the last bassoon note.

0:53	Fourth bassoon phrase:	(musical notation)

Consists of the ending portion of subphrases 1 and 3. Note that oboe in the accompaniment continues.

0:56   The prelude continues. Bassoon returns briefly at the very end (not heard here).

"SIGNS OF SPRING: GIRLS' DANCE"

The curtain opens on the first dance of the ballet, in which the young men of the tribe learn rituals from an old woman. The dance features the pounding repetition of a remarkable chord (it is a chord in two keys at once, known as a **polychord**). The repetition is varied by irregular accents, and occasionally by melodies that grow from the combination of chord and accent (see LG 61, below).

When Stravinsky first played this passage on the piano for Diaghilev, the impresario is reported to have said to the composer, "Will it go on a long time this way?"

🔊 LG 61

🎧 New sounds in "Signs of Spring: Girls' Dance," from *The Rite of Spring*

Polychord

LISTENING GUIDE 61   Ⓢ | DVD | 🎧

Stravinsky *The Rite of Spring,* "Signs of Spring: Girls' Dance"   1:20

DATE: 1913

GENRE: Ballet (performed also as orchestral work)

LISTEN FOR

MELODY: Melody gradually evolves from the repeated notes and accents

RHYTHM: Regular four-beat rhythm, with accents in irregular patterns

SCORING: A single chord (a polychord, in two keys at once), repeated many times

TIME	FORM	DESCRIPTION
	Prelude	Stravinsky sets a clock going, and a harmony, in the 4-note pattern of the pizzicato violins repeated five times.
0:00		A repeated chord, in 4-beat units, with accents at irregular intervals: 1234 1234 1**234** 1234 1**234** **1234** **1234** 1**234**.

(continued)

TIME	FORM	DESCRIPTION
0:09	Interlude (4 bars)	Oboe pattern returns.
0:13		The chord and accents return; melody is added to the last six 4-note groups: 1234 **1234** 1234 **1234** ⌐1234 1234 1234 1234 1234 1234.⌐
0:25	Interlude	Oboe pattern returns.
0:29	Trumpets enter	Harmony changes; trumpets repeat a new pattern.
0:38		Chords return, in same pattern as beginning: 1234 1234 **1234** 1234 **1234** **1234** **1234** 1**234**.
0:48	Bassoon and trombone enter	Bassoon and trombone begin to make a melody from the repeated notes (their melody indicated by brackets). As they move away from the chord, the accents stop. When the melody stops, the accents resume: 1⌐234 1234 1234 1⌐234 1234 1⌐234 1234 1⌐234 **1234** 1⌐234 1234 1234 1234⌐ **1234** 1234 **1234** 1**234** 1⌐234 1234 1234 1234 1234 1234 1234 1234 1234 1234.⌐

🔊 LG 62 "SPRING ROUNDS"

Later in the first part of the ballet, the young women dance "Spring Rounds." We've just seen how a pounding repeated chord gives rise to a melody in "Girls' Dance." Here, too, an opening ostinato (a four-beat pattern with a bass note, a chord played three times, and some **syncopated** melodic motion) ultimately proves to be the beginning of one of those folklike melodies that turns around on itself without quite ending or having clear phrases.

The dance itself is clearly organized into two parts: each part consists of repetitions of the ostinato (alternating with interludes) followed by a section of melody derived from the ostinato. The whole piece builds in a great crescendo to a climax of almost excruciating loudness and dissonance (see LG 62, p. 425).

🔊 LG 63 "PROCESSION OF THE OLDEST AND WISEST ONE"

Near the end of "Games of Rival Cities" (a tribal war-game of two competing groups of men), a procession enters from offstage. The Sage, the oldest and wisest member of the tribe, is slowly guided forward to the center of the group. At the end of the procession, he kneels down and kisses the earth.

"Procession of the Oldest and Wisest One" is a classic example of a Stravinsky ostinato: a repeated—and somewhat varied—melody in the tubas begins before the previous dance is over, and continues to the end of the procession. While this tuba melody proceeds on its plodding course, a variety of other ostinatos, in various rhythms, pile on top of it in a stupendous crescendo (see LG 63, p. 426).

The Sage's kiss is followed by "Dance Overcoming the Earth," which concludes the first part of the ballet. Stravinsky describes the dancers first "rolling like bundles of leaves in the wind," then "stomping like Indians trying to put out a prairie fire."

Stravinsky *The Rite of Spring*, "Spring Rounds"   2:42

DATE: 1913

GENRE: Ballet (performed also as orchestral work)

LISTEN FOR

MELODY: What begins as an ostinato becomes a melody

RHYTHM: Heavy string chords; regular beat with syncopation

FORM: ABA'B'

SCORING: Shifting instrumentation in a long crescendo

The piece is made in two large sections, using segments of the following melody:

TIME	FORM	DESCRIPTION
	Section A: ostinatos	
0:00		Opening ostinatos: A very heavy bass note, followed by a chord played three times, with lower strings moving on **offbeats**:
0:05		The same, repeated.
0:09		The same, repeated.
0:14	(1) Interlude	Interlude in winds (shorter version).
0:18		Return to repeated chords.
0:28	(2) Interlude	Interlude in winds (longer version).
0:35		Return to repeated chords; horns.
	Section B: ostinato becomes melody	
0:45		Ostinato becomes melody; the three notes become the beginning of a folklike tune, here played by strings:
0:54		Horns play the melody:
1:07		Strings, with flute trills:

(continued)

TIME	FORM	DESCRIPTION
	Section A′ (variant of A)	
1:26		Ostinatos: return of opening chords.
1:36	(1) Interlude	Interlude (shorter version).
1:41		Opening chords.
1:45	(2) Interlude	Interlude (longer version).
	Section B′ (variant of B)	
1:52		Melody returns. Very loud orchestration; chord at end suddenly louder, added notes:
2:06		More instruments, especially brass:
2:20		Brass added:
2:27		More instruments added:
2:32		Melody is almost swamped:

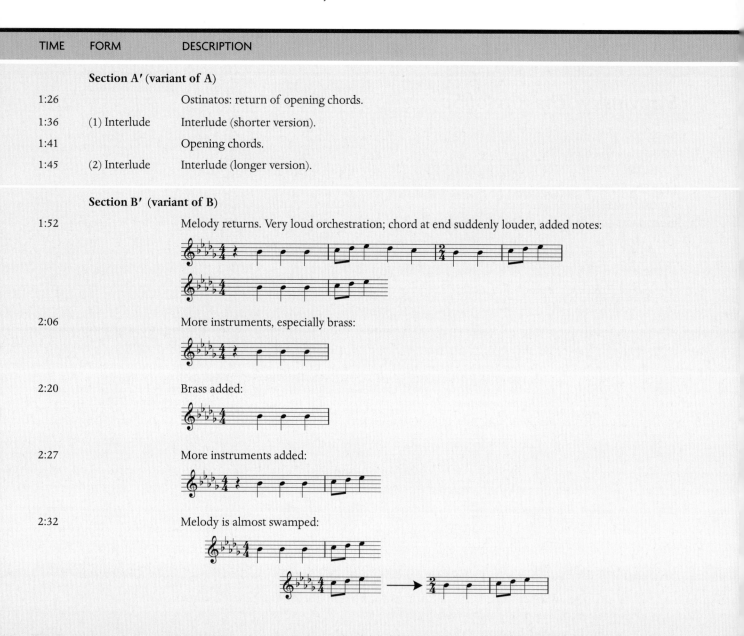

LISTENING GUIDE 63   ⓢ | DVD

Stravinsky *The Rite of Spring,* "Procession of the Oldest and Wisest One"

1:43

DATE: 1913

GENRE: Ballet (performed also as orchestral work)

LISTEN FOR

MELODY: Repeated melody (ostinato) in tubas; melody has variable beginning, invariable end

TEXTURE: Various ostinatos (bass drum, trombones, oboes, trumpets) are added in a gradual crescendo

TIME	FORM	DESCRIPTION
0:00		End of "Games of Rival Cities"
0:12	1 aabc	The tubas begin with a long G♯, hardly noticed until it moves to G♮, and then from G♯ to F♯. The ostinato always begins with one of these two combinations, and always ends with the same four notes: G♯, A♯, C♯, A♯. String melody continues.
0:20	2 abbc	Note bass drum stroke every three beats.
0:27	3 bc	Upper brass added.
0:30	4 bac	Note the trombone ostinato.
0:35	5 aabc	"Procession of the Oldest and Wisest One" (overlaps "Games of Rival Cities") begins.
0:42	6 abbc	New instruments; dotted rhythm.
0:49	7 abbc	More and more instruments and ostinatos added; sounds are very confused and noisy.
0:56	8 abbc	Trumpets added.
1:02	9 abbc	
1:16	10 abbc	The procession stops suddenly; a throbbing as the Sage kneels, and a chord in string harmonics as he kisses the earth.

"GLORIFICATION OF THE CHOSEN VICTIM"

Slow, quiet ritual dances of the young women open the second part of the ballet. One of the women fails to execute the dance correctly and is thereby chosen to sacrifice her life in order that spring will come again. She stands trembling in the middle of the circle while the other women dance around her.

"Glorification of the Chosen Victim" is a savage dance, and along with the final "Sacrificial Dance" it is one of the most characteristic and innovative pieces in the score. The music is made of a mosaic of small, almost invariable musical elements, each with its own unique harmony and rhythm. Before hearing the whole piece, listen to each of the individual elements (see Author Video; the elements are described in LG 64) and try to fix them in your mind. Stravinsky assembles these elements into patterns that, despite their highly irregular rhythms, form a large, coherent, three-part structure (see LG 64, p. 428).

 LG 64

The building blocks of "Glorification of the Chosen Victim," from *The Rite of Spring*

LISTENING GUIDE 64 | DVD |

Stravinsky *The Rite of Spring*, "Glorification of the Chosen Victim"

1:48

DATE: 1913

GENRE: Ballet (performed also as orchestral work)

LISTEN FOR

FORM: Three-part structure, **ABA'** (Note that these letters are *not* the same as the letters A-F used below for the six motifs in this piece.)

THEMES: Juxtaposition of several small elements, each used many times, and assembled into larger patterns

EXPRESSION: Changing harmonies, rhythms, and colors

TIME	FORM	DESCRIPTION
0:00		The dance is preceded by eleven repetitions of a fortissimo chord.
	Section A	
0:17	$A_5A_5a_9A_5a_2A_5A_5$	Alternation of motives A and a. "A" is dynamic, always five quick beats beginning with a bass note; "a" is the same harmony, rocking back and forth statically.
0:25	$B_4C_7B_4C_7A_5B_4C_6$	Motive B (an upward rushing) and motive C (a rocking figure on a new harmony); note the fakeout A_5 in the middle, which might make you think that the earlier music is returning.
0:40	$a_6A_5a_9A_5A_5a_2A_5A_5$	Return to the sound of A, with some new patterns.
	Section B	
0:47	$D_{4\frac{1}{2}}D_{5\frac{1}{2}}D_{7\frac{1}{2}}E_5D_9(D)_2$	Two new harmonies: D begins with a bass drum stroke; (D) is accompanied by trumpets. E is pizzicato strings and percussion.
1:03	$E_5E_6E_5E_6E_5$	E only.
1:14	$E_5(D)_3E_6(D)_2E_3(D)_3$	The two new harmonies combined.
	Transition	
1:25	F_5B_3	F, heard only here, is followed by the dynamic upward rush of B_3.
	Section A' (related to Section A)	
1:30	$A_5A_5a_9A_5a_2A_5A_5$	Same as **Section A**, part 1.
1:38	$a_6A_5a_9A_5A_5a_2A_5A_5$	Same as **Section A**, part 3.

LG 65   **"SACRIFICIAL DANCE"**

The final "Sacrificial Dance" opens with a single loud chord punctuating the Chosen Victim's single spasmodic movement before she dances herself to death. Stravinsky composed this piece, like almost everything he wrote, at the piano; he said that at first he knew how to play it, but not how to write it down. The difficulty, surely, is in the highly irregular meter, with groups of two, three, four, and five beats in unpredictable patterns.

Like "Glorification of the Chosen Victim," this dance is highly structured, despite its seeming irregularity. It is shaped something like a **rondo**, with an opening section that comes back twice, alternating with contrasting sections. The main, repeating section is changed a little each time, as the dancer grows more and more tired. The second time it appears it is a half-step lower than before (this is not something that most of us hear, but it makes the sound somewhat darker). The last repetition is very low, and some of the patterns are turned upside-down.

Rondo

In the closing measures, the ancestors of the tribe lift the victim on high, and the curtain falls (see LG 65, below).

LISTENING GUIDE 65   Ⓢ | DVD

Stravinsky *The Rite of Spring,* "Sacrificial Dance"   4:37

DATE: 1913

GENRE: Ballet (performed also as orchestral work)

LISTEN FOR
RHYTHM: Irregular meter
FORM: Rondo form, **ABA′CA″**

TEXTURE: Telltale phrase ending of three descending notes

TIME	FORM	DESCRIPTION
		Opening spasm of the dancer; a leap, throwing her legs back.
	Section A	
0:00		Loud string and brass chords, irregular metrical patterns of two, three, four, and five beats. In this diagram, large numbers indicate units that begin with a bass note, small numbers those that begin with a rest. Each of the phrases ends with the unit "4," whose last three descending notes are easily recognized. Boxed sections have extra instruments added.
0:29	**Section B**	Repeated chords in irregular patterns. The first pattern might be heard as 2 1 3 1 1 2 3 1 2 1 1 etc. A trombone melody is interjected. The volume of the repeated notes is increased. Then there is a return to softer repeated chords; trombone melody; whirling effect.
1:55	**Section A′**	**Section A** repeated a half-step lower.
2:23	**Section C**	Percussion, roaring low brass, crescendo. Note the fakeout inclusion of a moment of **Section A** in the middle.
3:32	**Section A″**	**Section A** music returns, but in a much lower register, and reorchestrated.
4:27	**Coda**	She dies: sudden silence; a flute scale as she is lifted up by the ancestors; a loud chord ends the piece.

How Did It Go?

The noise, the murmurs and shouting, started almost as soon as the house lights dimmed. The audience hardly could have objected to the haunting bassoon melody in the opening measures, or to choreography that had not yet been seen. (The curtain does not rise until the hammered repeated chords of "Signs of Spring: Girls' Dance.") They must have been primed for a scandal. Stravinsky certainly thought so, and he was furious:

Protests

Mild protests against the music could be heard from the very beginning of the performance. Then, when the curtain opened on the group of knock-kneed and long-braided Lolitas jumping up and down (*Dance of the adolescents* [the opening dance]), the storm broke . . . and a few minutes later I left the hall in a rage; I was sitting on the right near the orchestra, and I remember slamming the door. I have never again been that angry. The music was so familiar to me; I loved it, and I could not understand why people who had not yet heard it wanted to protest in advance. I arrived in a fury backstage, where I saw Diaghilev flicking the house lights in a last effort to quiet the hall. For the rest of the performance I stood in the wings behind Nijinsky holding the tails of his *frac* [frock-coat], while he stood on a chair shouting numbers to the dancers, like a coxswain.

Adolphe Boschot's Negative Review of the *Rite*

Imagine people decked out in the most garish colors, pointed bonnets and bathrobes, animal skins or purple tunics, gesturing like the possessed, who repeat the same gesture a hundred times: they stamp in place, they stamp, they stamp, they stamp, and they stamp. . . . They break in two and salute. And they stamp, they stamp, they stamp. . . . Suddenly a little old woman falls down headfirst and shows us her underskirts. . . . And they stamp, they stamp. . . .

And then there are groups that develop close-order drills. The dancers are up against each other, packed like sardines, and all their charming heads fall on the right shoulders, all congealed in this contorted pose by a unanimous crick in the neck. . . .

In the second act, here is a delicious dancer, Mademoiselle Piltz. The choreographer destroys her at will: he deforms her legs making her stand still with her toes turned in as far as possible. It's hideous. . . . And later, when she does move, she must hold her head in both hands, and glue it to her shoulder, as if to show that she suffers from a toothache combined with that same crick in the neck which is the signature of the "poet-choreographer."

Obviously, all this can be justified: what that is is prehistoric dance. The uglier and more deformed it is, the more prehistoric.

Perhaps the audience was protesting the dismissal of Michel Fokine, the Russian Ballet's former choreographer in chief. (Fokine had choreographed everything on the program except the *Rite*.) Or perhaps they were upset by Nijinsky's inability (or refusal) to give them a conventionally beautiful classical ballet. If that is what they had in mind, they were right. Fokine had been fired, and Nijinsky's choreography was nothing like Fokine's. In the *Rite*, Nijinsky was deliberately trying to make the dancers look unballetic, a point recognized even by reviewers who panned the ballet (see Adolphe Boschot's Negative Review, left).

There are dozens of reports about the premiere, some of them written by people who were probably not there but wish they had been. The conflicting testimony raises as many questions as it answers: Were the police called? Did Astruc really come on stage between the two parts of the *Rite* to offer the spectators a refund? Did Diaghilev switch the house lights on and off to try to calm the audience down? Were even half of the insults and jeers that were reported actually uttered?

One thing everyone agrees on is that there was a colossal din in the theater, which is why Nijinsky was shouting rehearsal numbers at the dancers from the wings and Stravinsky had to restrain him from rushing onto the stage during the performance. Fortunately, the musicians had the unflappable Monteux to follow. "On hearing this near riot behind me," the conductor wrote later, "I decided to keep the orchestra together at any cost, in case of a lull in the hubbub. I did, and we played it to the end absolutely as we had rehearsed it in the peace of an empty theater."

Even the great "Sacrificial Dance" at the end was disrupted, but only momentarily. More than one report mentions the doctor-dentist joke shouted at Marie Piltz (to whom Nijinsky had reassigned the solo role after his sister, Bronislava Nijinska, became pregnant):

She stood on the stage, her chin leaning on her folded hands, and just trembling for some nineteen bars of music. Someone called, "Un docteur!" another, "Un dentiste!" Then, "Deux dentistes!" It seemed that pandemonium would prevail, but the power of the dance which Nijinsky had composed for Piltz communicated itself to the spectators; they became silent and shared for a little while the torment and the ecstasy of the girl singled out for sacrifice.

The "Sacrificial Dance" is an amazing piece of choreography, the only solo dance in the ballet. "Then in this magic circle," wrote one sympathetic critic, "the victim until that moment motionless, wan under her white fillet, begins the death dance. And I recall Marie Piltz facing calmly a hooting audience whose violence completely drowned out the orchestra. She seemed to dream, her knees turned inward, the heels pointing out—inert. A sudden spasm shook her body out of its corpse-like rigor. At the fierce onward thrust of the rhythm she trembled in ecstatic, irregular jerks" (see Figure 15.10).

At the end of the performance, Stravinsky, Nijinsky, and Monteux came on stage for four or five curtain calls. Then the two Russians joined Diaghilev for a late-night supper, after which they all piled into a cab and drove to the Bois de Boulogne, Paris's Central Park, where the impresario recited Pushkin's poetry and burst into tears. That, at least, is how the playwright Jean Cocteau, who claimed to have been there, remembered the evening. According to Monteux, Stravinsky simply vanished after the performance, "to wander disconsolately along the streets of Paris." The composer himself reported only the scene in the restaurant, with a satisfied Diaghilev declaring, "Exactly what I wanted!"

FIG. 15.10 One of a series of drawings made by the artist Valentine Gross during performances of *Le sacre du printemps* in 1913; here there are several sketches of Marie Piltz in the "Sacrificial Dance," and a drawing of four men in the middle.

The Rite of Spring Then and Now

Stravinsky was haunted by *The Rite of Spring*. For decades, people talked and asked him about it incessantly. Interviewed for a television documentary in 1966, when he was eighty-three, the composer was still grumbling about the obtuseness of the Parisian audience. It was not the music that had incited the riot, he maintained, "but what the audience saw on stage. They came for *Scheherazade*, they came to see beautiful girls, and they saw *Le sacre du printemps*, and they were shocked. They were very naïve and very stupid people."

Nijinsky's *Rite* ran for a mere eight performances before it was dropped from the Russian Ballet's repertoire. (The dancer's marriage in 1913, and his subsequent estrangement from Diaghilev, probably had something to do with the ballet's disappearance.) After World War I, the impresario revived the *Rite* with new choreography by Nijinsky's successor, Léonide Massine. Meanwhile, Stravinsky continued to write ballets for Diaghilev's company: *The Song of the Nightingale, Pulcinella, The Fox, The Wedding*, culminating in his neoclassical masterpiece *Apollon musagète* (later shortened to *Apollo*) in 1928.

By then *The Rite of Spring* was firmly established as a concert piece, albeit one that other choreographers felt free to "interpret" in their own way. One wonders how Stravinsky—or Nijinsky—would have reacted to Paul Taylor's 1980 *Le Sacre du Printemps (The Rehearsal)*, in which the pagan sacrifice was transformed into a gangland-style bloodfest, to say nothing of Molissa Fenley's solo version (1988), danced topless and renamed *State of Darkness*.

Interpretation of the Rite

Ever since its creation, *The Rite of Spring* has appealed to the avant-garde, people who are (or think of themselves as being) in front of the pack. A number of the pieces that we are examining in this book, from *Orfeo* to *West Side Story*, had a similar cutting-edge impact in their time. Claudio Monteverdi and Leonard Bernstein thrived on plowing new ground. Other composers prefer to work in a style that has comfortable and understandable conventions and boundaries, as Handel did in *Messiah*, Schubert in his songs, and Mendelssohn in his Violin Concerto.

In the eyes of its Parisian audience, Diaghilev's Russian Ballet represented everything that was new and trendy in dance, music, and art. Paradoxically, the novelty of *The Rite of Spring* had as much to do with its ancient pagan subject matter as with its sophisticated, ultramodern style. Primitivism was an important element of avant-garde art in the early twentieth century, as Nicholas Roerich and other painters extolled the supposed virtues and simplicities of "primitive," non-Western cultures.

Many critics who had liked both Stravinsky's *Firebird* and *Petrushka* thought that the *Rite* represented a grotesque exaggeration of the novelties that had made those pieces so charming. Few of them would have agreed with the composer Florent Schmitt in hailing Stravinsky as "the Messiah we have waited for since Wagner." And practically no one foresaw that *The Rite of Spring* would become one of the most influential pieces of music of the twentieth century, or that Stravinsky's primordial rhythms, colors, and gestures would pass into popular culture when Walt Disney used the *Rite* as the sonic backdrop to the creation of the earth in his animated movie *Fantasia* of 1940.

In a sense, the afterlife of *The Rite of Spring* illustrates the adage that yesterday's avant-garde becomes today's establishment. And yet Stravinsky's astonishing score still epitomizes the "modern music" that many concertgoers find difficult to understand, much less to like. One measure of the ballet's greatness is that it has not lost its power to attract (or repel) listeners in a visceral way. But it does not diminish Stravinsky's timeless achievement to acknowledge that it originated in an almost mythical collaboration of great Russian artists for a Parisian audience in 1913.

Chapter Review

Summary of Musical Styles

Stravinsky's style, here and in much of his other music, shares some basic elements:

- **melodies** that are relatively simple, using modes that are not major or minor, and that have irregular phrases and repetition or smaller elements. This gives them a non-Western, folklike quality.

- **block construction**, in which an invariable few moments of music are repeated exactly, or recur unchanged. Longer sections of music may be constructed by juxtaposing a small number of elements that repeat and alternate.

- **rhythms** that seem irregular because they do not fit into a regular duple or triple meter. They may, however, be made of regular repetitions of irregular patterns.

- **harmonies** made of complex chords, which are often static and repeated, and usually have a characteristic and memorable sound.
- **ostinatos**, repeated patterns of rhythm, melody, or some other element, whose continuous repetition makes them a noticeable stylistic element whenever they are present.

ⓢ Multimedia Resources and Review Materials on StudySpace

Visit wwnorton.com/studyspace for review of Chapter 15.

What Do You Know?

Check the facts for this chapter. Take the online **Quiz**.

What Do You Hear?

Listening Quizzes and **Music Activities** will help you understand the musical works in this chapter.

⎙ Author Videos

- Folklike melodies from *The Rite of Spring*
- New sounds in "Signs of Spring: Girls' Dance," from *The Rite of Spring*
- The building blocks of "Glorification of the Chosen Victim," from *The Rite of Spring*

Interactive Listening Guides

LG 60 Stravinsky: *The Rite of Spring*, "Introduction"
LG 61 Stravinsky: *The Rite of Spring*, "Signs of Spring: Girls' Dance"
LG 62 Stravinsky: *The Rite of Spring*, "Spring Rounds"
LG 63 Stravinsky: *The Rite of Spring*, "Procession of the Oldest and Wisest One"
LG 64 Stravinsky: *The Rite of Spring*, "Glorification of the Chosen Victim"
LG 65 Stravinsky: *The Rite of Spring*, "Sacrificial Dance"

Flashcards (Terms to Know)

block construction	polychord
choreography	polytonality
harmonics	primitivism
ostinato	syncopated
overtones	

CHAPTER 16

MONDAY, DECEMBER 14, 1925, BERLIN:

Alban Berg's *Wozzeck*

🎵 CORE REPERTOIRE	▶ VIDEOS	🎙 AUTHOR VIDEOS
▪ **LG 66** Act 1, Scene 3, March and Lullaby	▪ Act 3, Scene 2: "Dort links geht's in die Stadt"	▪ The use of note and rhythm in Act 3 of Berg's *Wozzeck*
▪ **LG 67** Act 3, Scene 2	▪ Act 3, Scene 3: "Tanzt Alle; tanzt nur zu"	
▪ **LG 68** Act 3, Scene 3	▪ Act 3, Scene 4: "Das Messer? Wo ist das Messer?"	
▪ **LG 69** Act 3, Scene 4	▪ Interlude and Act 3, Scene 5: "Ringel, Ringel, Rosenkranz, Ringelreih'n!"	
▪ **LG 70** Act 3, Interlude		
▪ **LG 71** Act 3, Scene 5		

Introduction

"Apart from my desire to make good music, to fulfill musically the spiritual content of Büchner's immortal drama, to transpose his poetic language into a musical one—apart from these things I had nothing else in mind when I decided to write an opera . . . than to return to the theatre what is the theatre's."

—Alban Berg, "Das 'Opernproblem,'" 1928

Alban Berg's opera *Wozzeck*, like many of his other works, has an enthusiastic following. Its atonal musical language—avoiding establishing keys and familiar harmonies—and its subject matter of oppression, jealousy, murder, and guilt, make it characteristic of the strand of twentieth-century art called **expressionism**.

As a work of art, *Wozzeck* has an immediate appeal; the listener is moved by the plight of the characters even without understanding the technical aspects of the score. The many levels of musical and dramatic complexity in the opera reveal themselves only gradually. *Wozzeck* is a puzzle, a maze, and at the same time a gripping story. You do not have to be an expert to recognize the almost miraculous fit of Berg's musical style with the drama of social dysfunction and inequality.

Berg clearly intends us to understand the tragedy of Wozzeck and Marie as a timeless commentary on the human condition. At the same time, however, the opera is a response to a particular set of historical circumstances. Berg's audiences, traumatized by the unprecedented brutality of World War I and the economic devastation of Germany in the 1920s, came to the opera house with a very specific frame of reference. For them, *Wozzeck* was not only a harrowing drama of an individual's conflict with society but a universal parable of humankind's inherent stupidity and cruelty.

Alban Berg was part of a group of Viennese composers, led by Arnold Schoenberg (1874–1951), who sought to free music from what they considered the moribund traditions of harmony—traditions that governed most of the music we have considered up to now in this book—and to substitute a new kind of musical structure based on the equality of all twelve notes of the chromatic scale (see Appendix, p. A-6). At the same time, Berg was part of the larger artistic community referred to as **expressionists.**

Expressionism in painting, especially in the German-speaking lands of the early twentieth century, emphasized an attempt to privilege a shared subjectivity over objective reality. Harsh colors, strong linear effects, and deliberate distortions served the painter's purpose better than the lighter colors, soft brushstrokes, and decorative subject matter favored by the preceding generation. The expressionists' often cruel and brutal images made it clear that the expression of the artist, rather than the pleasure of the viewer, was the principal goal.

The term *expressionism* is sometimes applied to music as well, especially to that of Schoenberg, Berg, and Anton Webern (1883–1945). Collectively, these three men were later called the **Second Viennese School**, a name echoing the **First Viennese School** of Vienna-based composers (Mozart, Haydn, and Beethoven) who wrote in the Classical style. Berg and Webern were pupils of

Expressionism

FIG. 16.1 Alban Berg in a portrait by his teacher Arnold Schoenberg.

Schoenberg, who also happens to have been an accomplished painter (see Figure 16.1).

Ⓢ Berg: *Wozzeck*, Act 3, Scene 3, Wozzeck's descent into madness

Wozzeck may be the first music that many of us have ever heard—at least the first music in the classical tradition—that portrays brutality and abuse, anger and madness. But this same atonal music, which is sometimes thought to be inherently ugly, is also capable of reflecting tenderness, maternal devotion, and passionate love. It is Berg's poetic use of this musical language, coupled with an engrossing and fast-paced story, that keeps audiences on the edge of their seats.

The Setting

VIENNA IN 1925

Wozzeck premiered in Berlin but was born in Vienna. Alban Berg himself was born in that city, into a well-to-do family that participated in the thriving industry and commerce of the time (his father ran an export business, his mother a shop selling religious objects). A former imperial capital, Vienna was a metropolis of some two million people, but its business and cultural life still centered on the medieval quarter, where most of the coffeehouses and the principal office buildings, shops, and theaters stood (see Figure 16.2).

World War I

The First World War (1914–18) had changed everything. Hundreds of thousands of Berg's compatriots perished in battle, and the vast empire of Austria-Hungary (population fifty million) was reduced to the small republic of Austria. Vienna held about a third of Austria's population; its stately imperial buildings, including the great nineteenth-century theaters, museums, and opera house, survived as reminders of the city's bygone glory. No wonder so many Austrians in the bleak postwar period looked back nostalgically on the grandeur and spectacle they had lost.

Social and political milieu

As a result of rampant inflation, many people who, like the Berg family, had lived comfortably before the war were thrown into genteel poverty or worse. Influenza and hunger became widespread. The Marxist government of "Red Vienna" struggled to meet the needs of veterans, widows, and orphans; funds for public housing and other social services were raised by taxing the rich. Political opposition from the "Black" Christian Socialist party on the right, and from the growing communist party on the left, often led to violence. At the time of the premiere of *Wozzeck,* which coincided with the publication of Adolf Hitler's *Mein Kampf,* Austria's National Socialist (Nazi) party was already beginning to make its influence felt.

Although early-twentieth-century Vienna remained a deeply tradition-bound society, it was also a hotbed of new ideas. Sigmund Freud formulated his theories of the unconscious there, laying the foundation for modern psychoanalysis; the philosophers of the Vienna Circle developed a school of thought that emphasized the importance of logic and science; the artist Gustav Klimt embraced the protomodernist style known as Vienna Secession; and a group of architects

FIG. 16.2 A view of Vienna in the 1920s (compare Fig. 8.3, p. 211).

that included Walter Gropius sought a newer, cleaner modernism. Meanwhile, the expressionists, led by Egon Schiele in painting and Arnold Schoenberg in music, were creating works based on a new aesthetic.

ARNOLD SCHOENBERG AND ATONALITY

The Viennese enjoyed a night at the opera almost as much as they loved to waltz. The composer Gustav Mahler presided over the Vienna Court Opera from 1897 to 1907. Berg, sitting in the cheap seats, often watched him conduct (and once even spoke to the great man in a coffeehouse). Wagner was still a popular favorite, but by the 1920s his fans were among the more conservative operagoers. The newest and most avant-garde music was associated with the circle around Berg's teacher.

It was Schoenberg who first systematically explored how to abandon traditional harmony in order to create new musical structures. Composers like Wagner and Mahler had extended the language of harmony into highly chromatic territory in which all keys seemed equally related. But the presence of a key, a tonal center, even a shifting one, continued to be felt by virtue of the way the notes of a given scale related to the tonic, the final note toward which the other notes are pulled (see Appendix, p. A-6). Schoenberg and his students believed that these traditional tendencies were regressive, a burden from which music needed to be liberated; this was their motivation for experimenting with various sorts of **atonal** music (see Arnold Schoenberg on Musical Expressionism, right).

Atonal does not mean that the music has no tones, but that it shuns **tonality**, the centering of harmony on one particular note. A piece of tonal music almost always ends on the tonic or a chord built on the tonic; in fact, a piece would sound unfinished without it. (To understand what this means, try singing the first two phrases of "Twinkle, Twinkle, Little Star" and stop before you get to the last note.) Atonal music has no such predictable trajectory. It can be lyrical, sad, agitated, or anything else that tonal music can be. To appreciate those qualities, however, requires a willingness to listen for aspects of the music other than traditional harmonies and melodies. The absence of traditional harmonic constraints encourages the use of motivic development, and much of atonal music consists of a remarkable richness of melody; not necessarily soaring melody within the traditional tonal scales, but an extended horizon of possibilities and combinations. To get a sense of this, listen to some examples of atonal music by Berg's contemporaries.

BERG, *WOYZECK*, AND *WOZZECK*

The poets, journalists, playwrights, painters, architects, and musicians with whom Berg associated in Vienna's bustling coffeehouses and cabarets represented the artistic and intellectual leadership of the Viennese generation that came of age before World War I. The far-flung web of his friendships reflects his commitment to artistic progress, as well as the close-knit quality of intellectual life in the Austrian capital (see biography, p. 438).

One of Berg's friends was the great satirist Karl Kraus, who ridiculed the smug complacency of Viennese society in his periodical *Die Fackel* (*The Torch*). Kraus was a champion of the contemporary dramatist Frank Wedekind, two of whose plays would serve as the basis of Berg's second opera, *Lulu*. Kraus also helped

---

Arnold Schoenberg on Musical Expressionism

Schoenberg describes his decision, around 1908, to abandon tonal harmony and other traditional ways of achieving clarity of design in music:

It seemed at first impossible to find pertinent substitutes for these through musical means. Unwittingly, and therefore rightly, I found help where music always finds it when it has reached a crucial point in its development. *This, and this alone,* is the origin of what is called Expressionism: a piece of music does not create its formal appearance out of the logic of its *own* material, but, guided by the feeling for internal and external processes, and in *bringing these to expression*, it supports itself on their logic and builds upon that.

ⓢ Webern: Five Pieces for Orchestra, Op. 10, No. 4

ⓢ Schoenberg: Five Pieces for Orchestra, Op. 16, No. 4, *Farben*

ALBAN BERG (1885–1935)

The young Alban Berg was a tall, rangy man with serious grey eyes. Despite his fit appearance and robust good looks, his health was never good. As a junior officer in the Austrian army during the war, he suffered a physical breakdown, probably exacerbated by his chronic asthma and chain smoking. While composing, he would puff away on one cigarette after another, reportedly using the inside of the piano as an ashtray (and inviting visitors to do the same).

Music played a very personal role in Berg's life. His String Quartet, Op. 3, for example, musically expressed his relationship with Helene Nahowski (like Clara Schumann's father, Helene's father did not approve of his daughter's choice). But after a difficult and long courtship, Berg and Helene were married on May 3, 1911.

They maintained good relations with Alma Mahler, the influential widow of the famous composer Gustav Mahler, and later wife of the architect Walter Gropius. (Her third husband was the equally famous playwright Franz Werfel.) The Gropi-uses became Berg's closest friends; his last completed work, the marvelous Violin Concerto, is a memorial to their daughter, who died tragically at age eighteen. Werfel's sister, Hanna Fuchs-Robettin, was possibly Berg's lover in his later years and certainly the secret dedicatee of his *Lyric Suite*.

The success of *Wozzeck* transformed Berg from a leading light of Austrian music into a composer of international fame. Further performances, commissions, concert appearances, and service on musical committees gave him a measure of financial security in the last decade of his life. Shortly after finishing the Violin Concerto in the summer of 1935, he fell ill as a result of complications from an insect bite, and he died the day before Christmas.

Berg's lyricism provided a post-Romantic quality to his work, and his devotion to formal clarity, combined with the semi-autobiographical nature of his music, gave it a popular appeal.

Ⓢ Berg: Violin Concerto, I
Ⓢ Berg: *Lyric Suite*, Allegro misterioso

MAJOR WORKS: 2 operas: *Wozzeck* and *Lulu* (unfinished); orchestral and chamber works, including Three Orchestral Pieces, *Lyric Suite*, and the Violin Concerto.

---

rediscover and popularize the early-nineteenth-century writer Georg Büchner. Berg was in the audience when Büchner's *Woyzeck* was first performed in Vienna in May 1914. Moved by "the fate of this poor man, exploited and tormented by *all the world*," he decided to transform the play into an opera (for the plot of Berg's *Wozzeck*, see p. 444).

Setting to work on the libretto, Berg selected fifteen of Büchner's twenty-six fragmentary scenes, arranging them to suit his dramatic and musical purposes. *Woyzeck* was the product of a very different era, but its stark realism and trenchant social commentary spoke directly to Berg. Unfortunately, no sooner had he started work on the opera than he was drafted into the Austrian army. He served for the duration of the war, mostly in a tedious clerical job at the War Ministry in Vienna, which kept him out of harm's way but left no time for composing.

Berg's army experience may have brought Büchner's character closer to him. "There is a bit of me in his character," he wrote to his wife; "since I have been spending these war years just as dependent on people I hate, I have been in chains, sick, captive, resigned, in fact humiliated. Without this military service I should be as healthy as before. . . . Still, perhaps but for this that musical expression wouldn't have occurred to me."

Berg may also have responded to the play's political message about the oppression of the lower classes and the economic factors that contribute to it. Not least, he must have noticed his own similarity to Wozzeck, being himself the father of an illegitimate child as a result of an affair with a maid at his family's estate when he was seventeen.

That he selected a stage play says something about Berg's intentions. Most operas have texts specially created or adapted by poets for musical setting. Up to this time, libretti had been mostly in rhymed verse (Wagner's alliterative verse was an exception) that allowed for regular phrasing, lovely arias, and relatively simple action. But Berg did not want rhymes, regular phrases, or anything that might suggest arias. He was writing an opera of social commentary in which an oppressive environment is at the root of personal troubles. Büchner's brutally realistic language was just what he needed (see George Büchner's *Woyzeck*, right).

Berg's mentor, Schoenberg, was taken aback when he found out that Berg had his heart set on Büchner's play: "I was greatly surprised when this soft-hearted, timid young man had the courage to engage in a venture which seemed to invite misfortune: to compose *Wozzeck*, a drama of such extraordinary tragedy that it seemed forbidding to music. And even more: it contained scenes of everyday life which were contrary to the concept of opera which still lives on stylized costumes and conventionalized characters."

Although the opera was controversial at its premiere in Berlin in 1925, it soon became an international success, and royalties from performances worldwide made Berg independent and comfortable. The debut of *Wozzeck*, at the most important opera house in the most important city in German-speaking Europe, represented an accomplishment that neither Schoenberg nor Webern ever equaled.

The Performance

PREPARATIONS

Berg finished the full score of *Wozzeck* in 1922 (and a very full score it is, with quadruple winds and brass, and a lot of percussion.) A condensed piano-vocal score was finished later that same year (see Keeping Score on Scores, p. 440). Berg brought it out himself, with a dedication to Alma Mahler (who raised the money for its publication), and sent copies to various influential people to call attention to his work, in hopes of securing a performance.

The conductor Hermann Scherchen, who had heard some of Berg's music, urged him to arrange a concert suite from *Wozzeck* as a way of whetting the public's appetite for the opera. Berg did so, choosing mostly music associated with Marie, and Scherchen conducted the suite in 1924. But it was Erich Kleiber, the new music director of the Berlin State Opera, who undertook the first performance of *Wozzeck*. Kleiber loved Büchner's play, and scheduled a piano run-through of Berg's score. "It's settled!" he reportedly announced in the middle of the first act. "I am going to do the opera in Berlin, even if it costs me my job."

Kleiber was not only an excellent conductor but a man of high principle; years later, when the Nazi party banned Berg's second opera, *Lulu*, he resigned his post in protest. (The title character of *Lulu*—a femme fatale who lures men to their deaths and ends up falling victim to Jack the Ripper—was even more repellent to conventional sensibilities than Wozzeck.) When Kleiber discovered in 1939 that Jews were not allowed to perform at La Scala in Milan, he refused to conduct in

Georg Büchner's *Woyzeck*

Georg Büchner (1813–1837), the child of a German physician, studied medicine in Strasbourg before taking up a literary career. A passionate advocate of human rights, he decried the oppression of the underclass in his small body of writings, which included *Woyzeck* and two earlier plays.

Büchner was appointed to the faculty of the University of Zurich in 1836, only to die of typhus a few months later. Among his papers was the fragmentary manuscript of *Woyzeck*. Although Büchner's messy handwriting was finally transcribed in the 1870s (the spelling of the protagonist's name, Wozzeck, arose from the editor's misreading), the play did not reach the stage until 1913, a few months before Berg saw it in Vienna.

Woyzeck was inspired by the true story of Johann Christian Woyzeck, a former soldier who was executed (by hanging) in Leipzig in 1824 for murdering his mistress. During his trial, Woyzeck was examined to see if he was of sound mind. The doctor appointed by the court found him to be sane, but physically and morally "degenerate."

Most of the characters in the play are members of the working and servant classes, and their oppression by authority is Büchner's main theme. (His sympathy for the downtrodden prompted him to portray Woyzeck as a victim rather than a criminal.) Büchner left *Woyzeck* as a series of unconnected scenes, and their ordering is still uncertain. The rough, unfinished quality of the play was an advantage for Berg, since it allowed him to select and order the scenes as he thought best.

Keeping Score on Scores

The score of a complex opera or orchestral piece may go through several stages. A composer typically starts by jotting down ideas for the principal themes and other important passages, much as an artist makes preparatory sketches for a painting. The next stage, after the music is fully worked out, is a **short score**, in which the harmonies and orchestration are indicated, but only in an abbreviated way. Last comes the **full score**, which shows all the vocal and instrumental parts and every note that the composer wants to notate. Since full opera scores are large and cumbersome to use, publishers generally issue piano-vocal versions in smaller formats, with the orchestra part arranged for keyboard. Some sections of *Wozzeck* are so dense with musical material that the piano "reduction" calls for four hands.

Italy's leading opera house as well. He moved to Buenos Aires in 1937 and worked at the Teatro Colón for a dozen years before returning to Europe, where he died in 1956.

The Berlin State Opera House, built in 1844, was known as "Unter den Linden," after the elegant boulevard on which it stood (see Figure 16.3). Formerly the home of the Prussian Court Opera, it had been converted to a publicly supported opera house after the First World War, with the enterprising Max von Schillings as general manager. Schillings, and later Kleiber (see Figures 16.4 and 16.5), worked hard to wean the State Opera from its traditional diet of surefire crowd-pleasers. This was not easy in the German republic between the two world wars, during a period of runaway inflation, when the company was beset by orchestra and ballet strikes. Nevertheless, an impressive number of modern works by composers such as Ferruccio Busoni, Leoš Janáček, and Paul Hindemith were staged during those years.

The administration's policies were not universally admired, however. Kleiber and Schillings were responsible to the Ministry of Culture, which was more concerned with the bottom line than with artistic innovation. As a public theater, the opera had an obligation not only to perform regularly but, in the view of some people, to present works that would attract the largest possible number of paying customers. (This argument is familiar to every opera and orchestra director in the world.) Schillings was not happy about submitting his ambitious plans to the scrutiny of penny-pinching bureaucrats.

It was Schillings who had engaged Kleiber after the conductor's impressive guest appearance at the State Opera in 1923. The ministry thought that Kleiber would serve as a useful counterweight to Schillings, but in the matter of *Wozzeck* manager and conductor were of one mind: both agreed that the production would be an important event. As the big day drew near (see Figure 16.6), though, Schillings decided he had fought the bureaucracy long enough, and he resigned in November 1925, a month before the premiere.

The general manager's untimely departure represented one battle in a larger war waged by friends and enemies of Berg, Schillings, and Kleiber. The dispute was partly about *Wozzeck*, partly about modern music versus old favorites, and mostly

FIG. 16.3 A photograph of the German State Oper Unter den Linden from about 1920; the building, constructed in the eighteenth century, was the site of the premiere of *Wozzeck*.

about politics and power. All sorts of things were printed in the local newspapers, including exaggerated reports of huge numbers of rehearsals (actually there were thirty-four orchestral rehearsals and fourteen ensemble rehearsals—which in fact *is* a lot) and of shouting and rioting at the dress rehearsal.

Berg, who was still in Vienna, remained largely above the controversy (though he probably kept track of it); he was simply delighted that his opera was finally going to be produced. Arriving in Berlin on November 12, he wrote to his wife Helene that the cast was "splendid" (the singers were regular members of the State Opera) and that the premiere had aroused "terrific anticipation."

FIG. 16.4 Max von Schillings, conductor and composer, who was director of the State Opera until shortly before the premiere of *Wozzeck*.

FIG. 16.5 Erich Kleiber, conductor of the Berlin State Opera, who led the first performance of *Wozzeck*.

I spent my first rehearsal . . . under the megalomaniac impression that *Wozzeck* is something really great, and that accordingly the performance too will be something really great. I never dreamed I could find such understanding as a musician and dramatist as I am finding with Kleiber; and of course this gets transmitted to the singers, who are almost all first-class. The sets (at least on paper) are magnificent, the direction (and what direction!) is really Kleiber's. . . . Everybody concerned is enthusiastic in the highest degree.

When he returned to Berlin in December, Berg was nervous about how his music, which he had only heard in piano rehearsals, would sound in its full orchestral dress. "Be glad you weren't at the first rehearsal!" he told his wife. "True, I had the joy of at last hearing the thing played by the orchestra, but I also had the torment of all the points which are still wrong. If I didn't know that one can't judge after such a rehearsal, I should be very apprehensive, if not downright depressed. But from everybody's assurances, and above all the terrific eagerness of all concerned, I'm sure everything will be all right and just as I imagined it."

As we saw with Stravinsky's *Rite of Spring,* productions of new and complicated theatrical works often fall apart before they come together, and so it was with *Wozzeck.* Berg reported that "the orchestra rehearsal with the complete stage 'effects' was really chaotic, I really don't know how everything's going to work in a week's time." But Kleiber was staking his reputation on the opera's success, and insisted on hard work and perfection from everyone involved.

THE PREMIERE

The dress rehearsal took place on the morning of Saturday, December 12. Some of those at the dress rehearsal reported a certain amount of noise and protest in the theater, which the critic H. H. Stuckenschmidt tried to put in the best possible light: "In spite of a

FIG. 16.6 A newspaper announcement of the premiere of *Wozzeck*.

FIG. 16.7 The Doctor's study (Act I, Scene 4), a sketch by Panos Aravantinos for the sets for the original production of *Wozzeck*.

few die-hards, who had already rudely abused the hospitality of the theatre in the dress rehearsal, the public was overwhelmed by the work."

The sets, costumes, and staging of the original *Wozzeck* are not easy to reconstruct. Virtually all we know is that the scenery was created by the State Opera's resident designer, Panos Aravantinos (see Figure 16.7), and that it was more stylized than naturalistic. As one critic pointed out:

> Between the scenes, which flash by like cinema, there is barely two minutes' pause, and so all the sets have been reduced to suggestions. A pair of wings suddenly comes together, whose execution fully matches the slipshod quality of the music. . . . The opera-house's trademark, the uncannily large moon, which we see in every production, did not disappoint us this time. That yesterday it was a sun is unimportant. It was not of course a sun at all.

On the evening of the premiere, Monday, December 14, there was a competing concert of Wagner's music featuring the soprano Barbara Kemp. Since she was Max von Schillings's wife, the audiences may well have chosen which performance to attend at least partly for political rather than musical reasons. Berg, in Berlin, writes to his wife in Vienna on the eve of the first performance:

> The press is only printing things unfavorable to Kleiber. He is still conducting three times before the 14th, so we shall see if the audiences are against him. I don't notice any sort of friction in the company or the orchestra—far from it. They feel too strongly what a big personality he is. And it would be sheer lunacy to give up the chance of a production with Kleiber, Schützendorf and the orchestra (though that could still happen even at 6 p.m. on the 14th!).

The Music

OVERVIEW

Plot To the average listener, the most striking aspect of *Wozzeck* is the way the music expresses the devastating drama of the libretto. The protagonist, a poor soldier named Franz Wozzeck, is living a life of sullen obedience in the army, abused by the Captain (who treats him with scorn), experimented on by the Doctor (who tries out his dietary theories on him), and deceived by his common-law wife, Marie (who has eyes for the Drum Major). Ultimately, Wozzeck stabs Marie in a fit of jealous madness and drowns himself while trying to hide the bloody knife in a pond. The opera ends with children in the street taunting Marie's uncomprehending son: "Your mother is dead!" (See Plot of *Wozzeck*, p. 444.)

Structure Less obvious, but a perpetual source of fascination to music analysts, is the opera's highly formal and complex musical structure. Each of the three acts consists of five scenes, corresponding to an equal number of self-contained musical forms (there is also an extended orchestral interlude in Act 3). The five "character pieces" in Act 1, five "symphony" movements in Act 2, and six "inventions" in

Act 3 not only help ensure musical coherence and continuity, but also relate directly to the unfolding of the story. The resulting musical and dramatic scheme, as shown in Table 16.1 (see p. 445), does not seem at all artificial or contrived in the opera house. On the contrary, *Wozzeck* is a vivid and chillingly realistic depiction of the conflict between the individual and modern society.

Wozzeck provides a wonderful illustration of Berg's flexible and innovative use of the atonal language developed by his teacher, Arnold Schoenberg. It also makes extensive use of **Sprechstimme**, German for "speech-voice," a technique in which the singer observes the rhythms and melodic contour as indicated in the score, but instead of remaining on a given pitch for the indicated length, the voice slides up or down from one pitch to the next. The effect is something like a musically heightened speech.

Ⓢ Schoenberg: *Pierrot lunaire*, No. 1, *Mondestrunken* (Moon-drunk), Sprechstimme

Sprechstimme

FORMAL COHERENCE

We have seen how, in the musical language of Monteverdi, Mozart, and Wagner, the return of a "home" key or a sequence of harmonies signals musical events like endings, pauses, and surprises to the listener. Since traditional keys and harmonies are avoided in atonal music, it follows that the patterns that are so recognizable in tonal music were unavailable to the composer of *Wozzeck*.

In addition to the carefully wrought formal design outlined above, Berg uses a number of other devices to give his opera large-scale coherence of the sort previously provided by tonal harmony and make it more accessible to listeners. For example, *Wozzeck* includes a number of tonal melodies and passages. These sections provide the first-time listener with points of reference to more familiar musical forms and situations. Listen to the jaunty march played by the onstage military band in Act 1; perhaps, Berg seems to suggest, the distance between tonal and atonal music is not so great after all.

Ⓢ Berg: *Wozzeck*, Act 1, Scene 3, March

Berg laces his score with folksongs (both genuine and imitation) for much the same reason. Often he juxtaposes these relatively tuneful melodies with atonal music for dramatic effect. In the second scene of Act 1, Andres (Wozzeck's happy-go-lucky friend) sings a traditional hunting song, while the increasingly deranged protagonist prattles on in sing-songy, slightly surreal Sprechstimme.

Ⓢ Berg: *Wozzeck*, Act 1, Scene 2, Andres's hunting song

Sprechstimme is one of a number of vocal styles that Berg uses in *Wozzeck*, including the customary pitched singing voice and the spoken voice in notated rhythms. In *Wozzeck* speech and song are entirely merged in musical structure as well. Wagner, as we saw earlier, blurred the distinction between recitatives and arias; Berg did away with it altogether—which is one more reason why he felt the need to compensate by giving his opera a sturdy structural framework.

USE OF RECURRING MELODIES AND PITCHES

Another technique that Berg uses to provide musical coherence is to weave recurring melodies, rather like Wagnerian leitmotifs, into the fabric of his score. Some of these melodies are attached to specific characters; others are related to scenes and moods. They are not obvious at first hearing, but they served Berg, as they serve the listener, as a means of achieving musical coherence.

Melodies

In addition to these dramatically significant *melodies*, Berg also matches specific *pitches* to particular meanings. For example, the note B—just the note, not the key or the harmony of B—is often associated with Wozzeck. (The second scene of Act 3, in which he murders Marie, focuses obsessively on this one pitch.)

Pitches

▶ *Plot of* Wozzeck

ACT 1

- **Scene 1** The soldier Wozzeck is giving a shave to the Captain, who chides him for living an immoral life, in particular for fathering a child out of wedlock. Wozzeck protests, saying that it is very difficult to be virtuous when one is so poor.

- **Scene 2** Wozzeck and Andres, his fellow soldier, are working together in the fields when Wozzeck starts hallucinating. Andres tries unsuccessfully to calm his friend.

- **Scene 3** A military band passes outside Marie's window. Marie waves to the Drum Major, and her neighbor Margret taunts her for flirting with the soldiers. Upset with her neighbor, Marie slams the window in Margret's face and starts singing a lullaby to her son (Wozzeck's illegitimate child). Wozzeck appears and tells Marie the terrible visions he is having, fearing something dire is about to occur. 🔊 **LG 66**

- **Scene 4** Wozzeck is examined by the Doctor, who has been conducting dietetic experiments on his patient. Wozzeck has agreed to these strange restrictions—which contribute to his mental unbalance—because he is desperate for money to support Marie and his child. When the Doctor hears of Wozzeck's visions, he is delighted, since he thinks his dietary regimen has caused them; the Doctor only cares for his own fame, not Wozzeck's welfare.

- **Scene 5** At twilight the Drum Major arrives outside Marie's room. He makes advances, which she initially rebuffs, but she then gives in to him and disappears, with the Drum Major, into her room.

ACT 2

- **Scene 1** Marie is trying to get her child to fall asleep while, at the same time, admiring a set of earrings given her by the Drum Major. Wozzeck enters unannounced, and, suspicious about her earrings, asks Marie where she got them. She tells him she found them. He does not believe her but gives Marie the money from the Doctor anyway. He leaves, and Marie berates herself for lying.

- **Scene 2** The Captain and the Doctor meet each other in the street. When Wozzeck walks by, the two men drop some not-so-subtle hints that Marie is unfaithful.

- **Scene 3** Wozzeck confronts Marie, who does not deny his suspicions. He is about to hit her, when her statement "Better a knife in me than your hands on me" plants the idea of revenge in Wozzeck's deranged mind.

- **Scene 4** In a tavern, Wozzeck sees Marie dancing with the Drum Major. Two drunken men approach Wozzeck, telling him they "smell blood."

- **Scene 5** In the barracks at night, Wozzeck is unable to sleep. He begins talking to Andres. The Drum Major then enters, bragging about his seduction of Marie. The two men fight, and Wozzeck is injured.

ACT 3

- **Scene 1** Alone in her room at night, Marie reads from the Bible, crying out for mercy and forgiveness because of her sinful behavior.

- **Scene 2** Wozzeck and Marie walk by the shore near a pond. Marie is anxious to leave, but he restrains her. As a blood-red moon rises, he shouts "Not me, Marie, but not anybody else either!" He stabs her and she dies. 🔊 **LG 67** ▶ **Video**

- **Scene 3** Wozzeck returns to the tavern. People are dancing to a frenetic polka played on an out-of-tune piano. A half-mad Wozzeck starts dancing with Margret, then pulls her onto his lap. She notices blood on his hands and his arm. Others point to Wozzeck, who flees. 🔊 **LG 68** ▶ **Video**

- **Scene 4** Wozzeck returns to the scene of the crime to collect his knife and throw it into the pond. Fearing he may not have thrown it far enough from shore—and wanting to wash the blood from his clothes and hands—Wozzeck wades into the pond and drowns. The Doctor and the Captain pass by. Thinking they hear something, they hurry off, presumably in fright. 🔊 **LG 69** ▶ **Video**

- **Interlude** 🔊 **LG 70** ▶ **Video**

- **Scene 5** A children's song, reminiscent of Marie's lullaby to their son in Act I, is heard. It is the next morning. The son rides his hobbyhorse, playing with the other children, who hear the news of Marie's death. "Your mother is dead," they tell him, in a brutal but matter of fact manner. But he does not understand. The children run off to look at the corpse, while the son continues to ride and sing. Then noticing he has been left alone, he calls "Hop, hop," and rides off after the other children. 🔊 **LG 71** ▶ **Video**

TABLE 16.1

Dramatic and Musical Structure in *Wozzeck*

DRAMA		MUSIC
Exposition	**Act 1**	**Five character pieces**
Wozzeck and Captain	Scene 1	Baroque suite
Wozzeck and Andres	Scene 2	Rhapsody and hunting song
Wozzeck and Marie	Scene 3	March and lullaby
Wozzeck and Doctor	Scene 4	Passacaglia
Wozzeck and Drum Major	Scene 5	Rondo
Development	**Act 2**	**Symphony in 5 movements**
Marie and child; Wozzeck	Scene 1	Sonata movement
Captain and Doctor; Wozzeck	Scene 2	Fantasia and fugue on 3 themes
Marie and Wozzeck	Scene 3	Largo
Garden of a tavern	Scene 4	Scherzo
Guard room in the barracks	Scene 5	Rondo with introduction
Catastrophe and Epilogue	**Act 3**	**Six inventions**
Marie and child	Scene 1	Invention on a theme
Marie and Wozzeck ▶	Scene 2	Invention on a note
A tavern ▶	Scene 3	Invention on an irregular rhythm
Death of Wozzeck ▶	Scene 4	Invention on a chord
Interlude ▶		Invention on a key
Children playing ▶	Scene 5	Invention on a regular rhythm

Similarly, Marie is often identified with the note F. By extension, the interval between B and F—the **tritone,** or **augmented fourth,** perhaps the most disso- *Tritone* nant interval in tonal music—represents the relationship, always difficult and ulti- mately tragic, between the two characters. Even for listeners who lack the ability to pick out these two notes, the interval of the tritone creates a particular sound that reflects the two characters and their relationship.

INSTRUMENTATION

The orchestra in *Wozzeck* is extremely large, although Berg often breaks it down into small chamber groups, such as the fifteen-player ensemble that accompanies Wozzeck in his confrontation with Marie in Act 2, Scene 3. (The instrumentation is identical to that of Schoenberg's first Chamber Symphony and expresses Berg's homage to his teacher.) Especially impressive are the interludes for full orchestra between the opera's scenes.

 Onstage instruments add further color to the score. In Act 2, Scene 4, for instance, a tavern band plays a pair of dances, one of which quotes the minuet from Mozart's *Don Giovanni,* a famous piece of onstage music that Berg might have expected his listeners to recognize (see Chapter 7). Then Andres sings a little serenade, accompanied by one of the guitars. Meanwhile, the pit orchestra expresses Wozzeck's inner torment as his suspicions of Marie grow, until seeing her dance with the Drum Major finally convinces him of her infidelity.

Listening to the Music

Ideally, the listener should experience the entire opera—it runs about ninety minutes—in a theater. Only in this way can one feel the full effect of each scene and appreciate Berg's carefully planned development of music, character, and drama. For our purposes, however, we will concentrate on two especially powerful sections: the third scene of Act 1, in which Marie ogles the Drum Major and sings to her child; and the sequence of scenes in Act 3, where the final catastrophe plays itself out.

🎵 LG 66   ACT 1, SCENE 3: MARCH AND LULLABY

Musically and dramatically, the third scene of Act 1 is one of the most effective in the opera. At the beginning, we hear an approaching military band playing a march in the background. Marie stands at the window, her child in her arms, admiring the handsome figure of the Drum Major while exchanging insults with her neighbor. Angered by Margret's insinuations, Marie abruptly slams the window shut and sings her son to sleep. (Her beautiful lullaby is modeled on a traditional melody that Berg might have expected his listeners to know.) At the end of the scene, Wozzeck appears outside the window, mutters darkly, and rushes off.

The musical effects of this scene are many: the brass band that approaches slowly from offstage; the sudden change when the window is closed and the strings return; the beautiful melody of Marie's lullaby, with its accompaniment of solo strings; the magical chords, with harp, that accompany her refrain "Eia popeia"; and the orchestra musings that follow her song (see LG 66, p. 447).

 The use of note and rhythm in Act 3 of Berg's *Wozzeck*

ACT 3: INVENTIONS

Now that we have seen how skillfully Berg combines music and drama in a short scene, we are ready to listen to a long stretch of Act 3 as a single dramatic unit. In musical terms, Berg structures the act as a series of six "inventions," alluding to Johann Sebastian Bach's famous collection of keyboard pieces. Like Bach, Berg bases each invention on a single musical idea: in this case, a theme, a note, an irregular rhythm, a chord, a key, and a regular rhythm.

The musical structure of Act 3, for those who analyze it closely, is marvelously organized. Most listeners, though, are caught up in the opera's tragic dénouement: Wozzeck murders Marie, goes back to find the knife, and drowns himself, leaving their orphaned child singing an innocent nursery tune. We begin with Scene 2, following an opening scene in which Marie reads her Bible, talks to her child and herself; the music of that first scene is a series of variations, finishing with a fugue.

🎵 LG 67   ▶ Video

Scene 2 (Invention on a Note) The note in question is the B associated with Wozzeck, as mentioned above. He and Marie walk by the shore of a pond. The sound of the celesta and xylophone suggests the chill and the dew; the musical picture of the moonrise (string chord and pianissimo brass, "like a bloody knife") is haunting. Ultimately, Wozzeck murders Marie, shouting, "Not me, Marie, but not anybody else either!"

LISTENING GUIDE 66 | DVD

Berg *Wozzeck*, Act 1, Scene 3, March and Lullaby   4:53

DATE: December 14, 1925
TEXT: Georg Büchner

LISTEN FOR

MELODY: Strophic song of Marie's lullaby

TEXTURE: Different vocal styles (singing, half-singing, Sprech-stimme)

SCORING: Onstage band plays a military march

EXPRESSION: Chords of "Eia popeia"

TIME	TEXT	TRANSLATION	DESCRIPTION
	Marie		
0:00	Tschin, Bum, Tschin, Bum, Bum Bum Bum! Hörst, Bub? Da kommen sie!	Ching boom, ching boom boom boom boom! So you hear, child? Here they come!	A military band in the street below Marie's window plays a traditional march, which gets louder as the band approaches. **Tonal** music (representing the familiar, outside world) clashes with **atonal** music (disturbed, interior world of Marie and Wozzeck).
0:13	Was ein Mann! Wie ein Baum! Er steht auf seinen Füssen wie ein Löw'!	What a man! Like a tree! He stands up on his feet like a lion!	Marie glimpses the Drum Major, as music swells. She is using **Sprechstimme**, the speaking voice passing through specific pitches.
	Margret		
0:24	Ei was freundliche Augen, Frau Nachbarin! So was is man an ihr nit gewohnt!	Ah, what eyes you make at him, Miss Neighbor. He seems to be fond of you!	Sassy piccolo joins band.
	Marie		
0:37	Soldaten, Soldaten sind schöne Burschen!	Soldiers, soldiers are handsome lads!	Marie sings along with the band. Her music is elated: tuneful and rhythmical.

Sol - da - ten, Sol - da - ten sind schö - ne Bur - schen!

	Margret		
0:48	Ihre Augen glänzen ja!	Your eyes are shining!	The women's shouting match continues over the march.
	Marie		
	Und wenn! Was geht Sie's an? Trag' Sie ihre Augen zum Juden[,] und lass Sie sie putzen: vielleicht glänzen sie auch noch, dass man sie für zwei Knöpf' verkaufen könnt'.	As if! What's with you? Take your eyes to the Jews and get them polished; maybe they are still shiny enough that they can sell them for you cheap.	

(continued)

TIME	TEXT	TRANSLATION	DESCRIPTION
	Margret		
	Was Sie, Sie "Frau Jungfer"?! Ich bin eine honette Person, aber Sie das weiss Jeder, Sie guckt sieben Paar lederne Hosen durch!	What's with you, miss? I'm an honest person, but you, everybody knows, can go through seven pairs of leather pants!	
	Marie		
	Luder!	Busybody!	
1:19	Komm, mein Bub! Was die Leute wollen! Bist nur ein arm Hurenkind und machst Deiner Mutter doch so viel Freud' mit deinem unehrlichen Gesicht! Eia popeia . . .	Come, my child! Some people! You're just a poor bastard, and you make your mother so happy with your funny face! Lullaby . . .	Sudden quiet as Marie slams window shut. The orchestra in the pit resumes playing. Marie sings to her child, beginning the lullaby with calming nonsense phrase, "Eia popeia."

Marie

TIME	TEXT	TRANSLATION	DESCRIPTION
2:06	Mädel, was fangst Du jetzt an? Hast ein klein Kind und kein Mann! Ei, was frag' ich darnach, Sing' ich die ganze Nacht:	Maiden, what are you doing? With a little child and no husband? That's what I ask myself, and sing the whole night long:	Then comes first verse of lullaby itself, which is based on an existing melody that Berg's listeners might have known; it has rhythm and regular phrases of folksong. Note that it includes F and B-natural.

TIME	TEXT	TRANSLATION	DESCRIPTION
2:30	Eia popeia, mein süsser Bu', Gibt mir kein Mensch nix dazu!	Lullaby, my sweet child, nobody gives me anything for this!	Lush chords for this lovely refrain.
2:52	Hansel, spann Deine sechs Schimmel an, Gib sie zu fressen auf's neu, Kein Haber fresse sie, Kein Wasser saufe sie, Lauter kühle Wein muss es sein! Lauter kühle Wein muss es sein!	Little Hans, harness up your six white horses, There'll be no feed for them, No oats will they eat, No water will they drink; It must be pure fresh wine! It must be pure fresh wine!	Second verse of lullaby. Note Marie's repetition of last phrase, moving from very high to very low. Her child falls asleep at the end. Marie is lost in reverie, suggested by orchestra's magical chords (with harp).
4:50	Wer da? . . .	Who's there? . . .	The mood is interrupted when Wozzeck knocks at the window, mutters confusedly, and stalks away.

Throughout Scene 2, the note B appears variously as a low, sustained sound; in rising and falling octaves; as a stationary note in the upper registers; and as a steady beat in the timpani, an ominous death knell for Marie that grows louder and louder along with the rest of the orchestra. The scene culminates in a pair of famous crescendos. In the first, the instruments pile up one by one on a unison B that builds to an ear-splitting chordal explosion. Then the solo bass drum hammers out the jagged rhythm that will be associated with Wozzeck's madness in the following scene. After a pause, the full orchestra makes a unified crescendo, this time on Bs that are spread far apart (see LG 67, below).

Act 3, Scene 2

LISTENING GUIDE 67   Ⓢ | DVD | ▶ Video

Berg *Wozzeck*, Act 3, Scene 2, Invention on a Note   5:15

DATE: December 14, 1925
TEXT: Georg Büchner

LISTEN FOR

SCORING: Long-held note (B) appearing in different instruments, culminating with a crescendo of all the instruments on a single note

EXPRESSION: Growing intensity of the dramatic action

TIME	TEXT	TRANSLATION	DESCRIPTION
	Twilight, a forest path by a pond; Marie and Wozzeck		
	Marie		
0:00	Dort links geht's in die Stadt. 's ist noch weit. Komm schneller!	There to the left is the way to town; it's still far. Come faster!	Very low, ominous B in four trombones. A nervous bassoon melody introduces the scene. Pitch comes from very low Bs played by double basses at end of preceding change of scene.
	Wozzeck		
0:13	Du sollst dableiben, Marie. Komm, setz' Dich.	You should stay here, Marie; come, sit down.	Very low B in double basses. Strings accompany.
	Marie		
	Aber ich muss fort.	But I must go.	
	Wozzeck		
	Komm.	Come.	
0:26	Bist weit gegangen, Marie. Sollst Dir die Füsse nicht mehr wund laufen.	You have gone far, Marie. You shouldn't hurt your feet any more.	B ceases and the tempo slows down.
0:42	's ist still hier! Und so dunkel.—	It is still here! And so dark.—	Very low B in bassoon and contrabassoons as first tempo resumes. Very low B in double basses.
0:58	Weisst noch, Marie, wie lang es jetzt ist, dass wir uns kennen?	Do you know, Marie, how long it's been since we met?	Low B stops: effect is of tense expectation; winds play rhythm of Marie's lullaby. Very high B from muted first violin heard as separated notes.

(continued)

TIME	TEXT	TRANSLATION	DESCRIPTION
1:10	*Marie* Zu Pfingsten drei Jahre.	Three years at Whitsun.	
	Wozzeck Und was meinst, wie lang es noch dauern wird?	And how long do you think it will last?	B as falling octaves in harp.
1:22	*Marie* Ich muss fort.	I must go.	Tension again. Contrabass tuba, and then double bass, wander around the note B.
	Wozzeck Fürchst Dich, Marie? Und bist doch fromm! Und gut! Und treu!	Are you afraid, Marie? But you are devout! And good! And faithful!	Very low B in double basses, which slide up to higher pitches while continually returning to the low B. **Glissando** (sweeping through all the notes) in strings, harp, and celesta.
1:49	Was Du für süsse Lippen hast, Marie! Den Himmel gäb' ich drum und die Seligkeit, wenn ich Dich noch oft so küssen dürft!	What sweet lips you have, Marie! I'd give up the bliss of heaven if only I could kiss you!	Triangle announces the end of the glissando and the arrival on very high B in violins.
	Aber ich darf nicht!	But I can't!	Drastic change of mood. B, in falling octaves, in first violins. High B, in fluttering flutes.
2:33	Was zitterst?	Why are you shivering?	
	Marie Der Nachttau fällt.	The dew is falling.	
	Wozzeck Wer kalt ist, den friert nicht mehr!	One who is cold doesn't freeze.	Low B, in trombones.
	Dich wird beim Morgentau nicht frieren.	You won't feel cold in the morning.	B in rising octaves in clarinets.
	Marie Was sagst Du da?	What are you saying?	
3:03	*Wozzeck* Nix.	Nothing.	All instruments stop; Wozzeck sings low B by itself.
3:10	*Marie* Wie der Mond rot aufgeht!	How red the moon rises!	B played very softly in many octaves by strings and as a long-held note. Pianissimo brass make moonrise seem spooky.
3:39	*Wozzeck* Wie ein blutig Eisen!	Like a bloody knife!	Lower strings gradually drop out, and sound diminishes to just first violins.

	Marie		
3:49	Was zitterst?	Why are you shivering?	B heard in timpani as steady beat that grows
	Was willst?	What do you want?	louder with rest of orchestra while Wozzeck
	Wozzeck		stabs Marie.
	Ich nicht, Marie!	Not me, Marie,	
	Und kein Andrer auch nicht!	But not anybody else either!	
	Marie		
4:03	Hilfe!	Help!	As Marie utters her final cry for help, she sings
			high B that quickly drops to low B.
4:11			As she dies, timpani gradually becomes softer, and
			beating becomes like a dirge on this pitch.
	Wozzeck		
4:24	Tot!	Dead!	Timpani stops; B heard very softly in lowest
			notes of harp.
			Two enormous and almost heart-stopping crescendos: first on single B, then next, using all available Bs: between them, bass drum announces rhythm of next scene.
4:52			*Change of Scene*

Scene 3 (Invention on an Irregular Rhythm) An out-of-tune tavern piano plays a frenetic **polka** (a quick dance in duple time), incorporating an irregular, pulsing rhythm that sounds like Morse code. The rhythm appears at different speeds and in various instrumental combinations. People are dancing, encouraged by a half-crazed Wozzeck. He sings a drinking song; the polka begins again, as Wozzeck chats to Margret; she sings her own folksong, then notices blood on Wozzeck's hand and arm. Other people point at Wozzeck (see LG 68, p. 452).

 LG 68
▶ Video

Scene 4 (Invention on a Chord) This haunting scene shows Wozzeck hunting for the knife and taking his own life. Berg's musical depiction of the drowning, as seen from Wozzeck's point of view, is especially graphic: rising chords, becoming slower and slower, seem to represent the water engulfing his gradually sinking body. Frogs croak at the edge of the pond, bringing us back to the surface and the world of impassive nature. The Doctor and the Captain, passing by, think they hear something and hurry off (see LG 69, p. 454).

 LG 69
▶ Video

Interlude (Invention on a Key) In this passionate orchestral interlude, which provides a transition between Wozzeck's death and the final scene, Berg presents us with what is surely his own meditation on the tragedy. Using themes associated with the main character, he provides a music of mourning, not so much for Wozzeck as for the world that brings such circumstances into existence. This highly dramatic music is in D minor, stretching the idea of tonality almost to the limit. In Berg's own words, the interlude should be appreciated both "as the composer's confession, breaking through the framework of the dramatic plot" and "as an appeal to the audience, which is here meant to represent Humanity itself." The music we hear is Berg weeping, singing to us (see LG 70, p. 457).

 LG 70
▶ Video

Berg *Wozzeck*, Act 3, Scene 3, Invention on an Irregular Rhythm   3:01

DATE: December 14, 1925
TEXT: Georg Büchner

LISTEN FOR
MELODY: References to folksongs, popular dances (polka, waltz)
RHYTHM: Irregular rhythmic pattern that permeates the entire scene

SCORING: Music played by instruments on stage.
Music performed/heard by characters in the play

TIME	TEXT	TRANSLATION	DESCRIPTION
	Night; a tavern, dimly lit; Wozzeck, a piano player, Margret, apprentices, girls		
0:00			Out-of-tune barroom piano plays a fast **polka**, setting the scene. Over steady 8th notes in bass, we hear the rhythm in the right hand:
	Wozzeck		
0:03	Tanzt Alle; tanzt nur zu, springt, schwitzt und stinkt, es holt Euch doch	Dance, everybody! Dance, jump, sweat and stink, the Devil	Wozzeck yells at dancers.
0:12	noch einmal der Teufel!	has got you once more!	Wozzeck sings in this rhythm: Immediately, timpani play more detached version of the same pattern, but begin off the beat.
0:17	"Es ritten drei Reiter wohl an den Rhein,	"Three horsemen rode to the Rhine	Wozzeck begins to sing a drinking song that uses a contrasting rhythm:
	Bei einer Frau Wirtin da kehrten sie ein.	And stopped at the woman's inn.	Melody begins with same notes as lullaby that Marie sang to her son in Act 1, Scene 3 (see LG 66). The piano player is shouted down by Wozzeck, but the rhythmic pattern is still heard in fast version beaten three times by small drum and in a slow version played twice by strings:
0:24	Mein Wein ist gut, mein Bier ist klar, Mein Töchterlein liegt auf der . . ."	My wine is good, my beer is clear, my little daughter is lying in the . . ."	Piano player performs slow version of the pattern, trying to find proper accompaniment for Wozzeck's song. It is out of sync with the voice, however:

0:32	Verdammt! Komm, Margret!	Damn! Come, Margret!	As Wozzeck breaks off his song, the pattern is heard in upper brass and then at half-speed in lower brass. Fast polka begins again in out-of-tune piano, but suddenly breaks off.
0:39	Komm, setz Dich her, Margret!	Come, sit here, Margret!	
0:48	Margret, Du bist so heiss. Wart nur, wirst auch kalt werden! Kannst nicht singen?	Margaret, you are so warm. Wait a little, and you'll be hot! Can't you sing?	As Wozzeck chats up Margret, triplet version of the pattern is heard in strings, ornamented by trills.
1:10	*Margret* "In's Schwabenland, da mag ich nit, Und lange Kleider trag ich nit,	"In Swabia I do nothing, and I don't wear long dresses,	Margret sings a stage-song accompanied by the onstage piano, which plays steady rhythm of quarter notes. Against this, Margret sings original pattern, followed by quick version (not shown): *(musical notation: In's Schwa-ben-land, da mag ich nit,)*
1:25	Denn lange Kleider, der spitze Schuh, Die kommen keiner Dienstmagd zu."	The long dresses, the pointed shoes, they don't suit a serving girl."	She sings the same music, down a half-step.
1:40	*Wozzeck* Nein! keine Schuh, man kann auch blossfüssig in die Höll' geh'n! Ich möcht heut raufen, raufen . . .	No! No shoes, one can also go to Hell barefoot! Today I'm in a rage . . .	Rhythmic pattern is heard overlapping in brass, violins, and woodwinds.
1:56	*Margret* Aber was hast Du an der Hand? *Wozzeck* Ich? Ich? *Margret* Rot! Blut! *Wozzeck* Blut? Blut? *Margret* Freilich . . . Blut!	But what do you have on your hand? I? I? Red! Blood! Blood? Blood? Of course . . . blood!	As Margret notices blood on Wozzeck's hand, ominous fast notes rise and fall, followed by near silence, with only low strings playing the rhythmic pattern.
2:18	*Wozzeck* Ich glaub', ich hab' mich geschnitten, da an der rechten Hand . . . *Margret* Wie kommt's denn zum Ellenbogen? *Wozzeck* Ich habs daran abgewischt. *A Lad* Mit der rechten Hand am rechten Arm?	I believe I've cut myself, there on the right hand . . . Then how did it get on your elbow? I smeared it there. From the right hand to the right arm?	As Margret's suspicion escalates, the rhythmic pattern is heard many times. Listen to this passage closely: notice who plays or sings the pattern; their different speeds; if the repetitions are out of sync between instruments or voices, and what sort of melody is used for the pattern.

(continued)

TIME	TEXT	TRANSLATION	DESCRIPTION
	Wozzeck		
	Was wollt Ihr?	What's it to you?	
	Was geht's Euch an?	What's the matter with you?	
	Margret		
	Puh! Puh! Da stinkt's nach Menschenblut!	Phew! It smells like human blood.	
	Wozzeck		
	Bin ich ein Mörder?	Am I a murderer?	
	Lads		
	Blut, Blut, Blut, Blut!	Blood, blood, blood, blood!	
	Girls		
	Freilich, da stinkt's nach Menschenblut!	Of course it smells like human blood.	
	Wozzeck		
	Platz! oder es geht wer zum Teufel!	Out of my way, or somebody's going to the Devil.	

LISTENING GUIDE 69   Ⓢ | DVD | ▶ Video

Berg *Wozzeck*, Act 3, Scene 4, Invention on a Chord   4:36

DATE: December 14, 1925
TEXT: Georg Büchner

LISTEN FOR
EXPRESSION: Musical depiction of nature: frogs, moonlight, and water

TEXTURE: Chords rising and falling through chromatic motion

THEMES: Repetition of short motives

TIME	TEXT	TRANSLATION	DESCRIPTION
	Night; forest path by the pond; Wozzeck, Captain, Doctor		
	Section 1		Scene begins with 6-note chord played as repeated notes by woodwinds and horns.
0:00	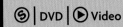		
	Wozzeck		
	Das Messer? Wo ist das Messer?	The knife! Where is the knife?	
	Ich habs dagelassen. . . .	I left it over there. . . .	

	Näher, noch näher.	Closer, closer still.	Wozzeck's Sprechstimme is accompanied by descending chromatic scales in violins.
0:16	Mir graut's da. Regt sich was.	I'm terrified! Something's moving.	Wozzeck's sense of horror is accentuated by persistent patterns in flutes, resembling croaking of frogs.
0:24	Still!	Silent!	After Wozzeck whispers this word loudly, we hear 6-note chord very softly in violins and violas.
	Alles still und tot . . .	Everything silent and dead. . . .	Wozzeck sings word "tot" (dead) on his signature pitch, B, which is not part of the 6-note chord.
0:36	Mörder! Mörder! Ha! Da ruft's. Nein, ich selbst. Marie! Marie! Was hast Du für eine rote Schnur um den Hals? Hast Dir das rote Halsband verdient, wie die Ohrringlein, mit Deiner Sünde? Was hängen Dir die schwarzen Haare so wild?	Murder! Murder! Ha! Something there. No, it's just me. Marie! Marie! What sort of red string is that around your throat? Did you earn it, like the earrings, with your sins? Why is your black hair so wild?	Glissandos in harp.
1:17	Mörder! Mörder! Sie werden nach mir suchen . . .	Murder! Murder! They will be looking for me. . . .	At shout of "Mörder! Mörder!" loud trills in woodwinds and percussion, plus loud and brassy playing of chord by trumpets and trombones. This chord is not part of the 6-note chord that has been heard throughout the scene.
	Das Messer verrät mich! Da, da ist's.	The knife betrays me! There: there it is.	Violas and cellos now play the 6-note chord as harmonics in their highest register.
			Falling orchestral lines accompany Wozzeck's discovery of the knife, coming to rest on repeated chords resembling those at beginning of scene (but played in lower octave by lower strings).
1:36	So! Da hinunter. Es taucht ins dunkle Wasser wie ein Stein.	Aha! Down there. It dives into the dark water like a stone.	These same repeated chords, but much slower, are thrown back and forth between brass and woodwinds.

Section 2

Ascending line in harp signifies rising of blood-red moon through clouds.

1:51

Aber der Mond verrät mich . . . der Mond ist blutig.	But the moon betrays me . . . the moon is bloody.

(continued)

TIME	TEXT	TRANSLATION	DESCRIPTION
	Will denn die ganze Welt es ausplaudern?!— Das Messer, es liegt zu weit vorn, sie findens beim Baden oder wenn sie nach Muscheln tauchen.	So will the whole world be talking about it?!— The knife, it's too far away, they'll find it when they go swimming or diving for mussels.	Then first violins descend chromatically. Six solo violins divide from group, falling at different speeds.
2:28	Ich find's nicht . . . Aber ich muss mich waschen. Ich bin blutig. Da ein Fleck . . . und noch einer. Weh! Weh! ich wasche mich mit Blut! Das Wasser ist Blut . . . Blut.	I can't find it. But I must wash myself. I am bloody. There's a spot . . . and another. Woe! Woe! I am washing myself with blood! The water is blood . . . blood.	Undulating water heard in orchestra, first as surface ripples, then as slower and deeper movement in horns and harp. As Wozzeck drowns, the orchestra ascends chromatically like water rising over his body.

Section 3

TIME	TEXT	TRANSLATION	DESCRIPTION
	Captain		
3:07	Halt!	Stop!	
	Doctor		
	Hören Sie? Dort!	Do you hear? There!	
	Captain		
	Jesus! Das war ein Ton.	Jesus! That was a sound.	As Captain and Doctor speak (rather than sing), the accompaniment's upward motion repeated many times, becoming slightly slower each time.
	Doctor		
	Ja, dort!	Yes, there!	
	Captain		
	Es ist das Wasser im Teich. Das Wasser ruft. Es ist schon lange Niemand ertrunken. Kommen Sie, Doktor! Es ist nicht gut zu hören.	It is the water in the pond. The water is calling. It has not drunk anyone in a long time. Come, Doctor! It is not good to hear.	
	Doctor		
3:45	Das stöhnt als stürbe ein Mensch. Da ertrinkt jemand!	It groans as if someone were dying. Someone is drowning.	An atmosphere of stillness and eeriness. The waves stop; croaking toads in clarinets are heard over a sustained 6-note chord in a few of the strings. At the mention of someone drowning, a descending line is added to the texture by celesta and harp. At the same time, the low strings play the rising line of the moon's appearance. Finally, there is a low oscillation between two notes as the sustained 6-note chord begins to fade.
	Captain		
	Unheimlich! Der Mond rot und die Nebel grau. Hören Sie? Jetzt wieder das Ächzen.	Eerie! The moon red and the mist grey. Do you hear? Again the groaning.	
	Doctor		
	Stiller . . . jetzt ganz still.	Silent . . . now completely silent.	
	Captain		
	Kommen Sie! Kommen Sie schnell.	Come! Come quickly.	

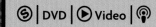

LISTENING GUIDE 70   Ⓢ | DVD | ▶ Video | 🎧

Berg *Wozzeck*, Act 3, Interlude, Invention on a Key   3:48

DATE: December 14, 1925
TEXT: Georg Büchner

LISTEN FOR

SCORING: "Romantic" orchestral writing: lyrical melodies, dynamic contrasts and broad sweeps; chords and dissonance against them

HARMONY: Wide emotional swings over a stable harmonic base

THEMES: The return of leitmotifs associated with Wozzeck

TIME	FORM/DESCRIPTION

Section A

0:00   The 6-note chord that ended the previous invention alters some notes and slips into the key of D minor, providing harmonic resolution to Wozzeck's death. This is the only place in the opera where Berg uses a key signature. A rising theme, the main theme of the interlude, emerges in lower strings:

0:24   answered by a falling theme in violins:

0:33   and transformed into different versions by flutes:

0:48   and violins:

A triplet version of the rising theme appears in horns:

The rising and falling themes overlap.

At end of this section, the music suddenly grows in speed and volume.

(continued)

TIME	FORM/DESCRIPTION

Section B

1:12   The middle section moves away from D minor, and the key signature disappears. There is further development of the opening theme, and principal leitmotifs associated throughout the opera with various characters reappear. (Only those who hear the whole opera with concentrated attention would likely recognize these.) These leitmotifs include:

2:01   DOCTOR (played by trumpets):

2:09   CAPTAIN (violins):

2:23   SEDUCTION (oboes, violins, and violas):

2:32   FIGHT (horns and bassoons, followed by trumpets and strings):

2:47   WOZZECK (At the very end, Wozzeck's own leitmotif is played very loudly by trombones, harp, and upper woodwinds):

Section A′

3:06   Return to D minor. Main theme is heard in lower winds, brass, and strings:

while their higher counterparts play the KNIFE motif:

3:41   Descending chords gradually fade, and Interlude ends quietly on the D-minor sonority on which it began.

🎧 LG 71   **Scene 5 (Invention on a Regular Rhythm)** The devastating final scene, which
▶ Video   Berg describes as a "perpetuum mobile" (perpetual motion) in $\frac{12}{8}$ time, features a children's song reminiscent of Marie's lullaby in Act 1. Wozzeck's son rides a hobbyhorse (a child's toy horse, often made of a long wooden stick with a horse's head on top), oblivious to the taunts of the other children, who finally run off to gawk at his dead mother's body.

Berg *Wozzeck*, Act 3, Scene 5, Invention on a Regular Rhythm   1:27

DATE: December 14, 1925
TEXT: Georg Büchner

LISTEN FOR

MELODY: Children's song   **THEMES:** Inconclusive ending
RHYTHM: "Perpetual motion" rhythm

TIME	TEXT	TRANSLATION	DESCRIPTION
	Day, in front of Marie's dwelling; bright morning sunshine; Marie's child; other children		
	Children		
0:00	"Ringel, Ringel, Rosenkranz, Ringelreih'n! Ringel, Ringel, Rosenkranz, Rin . . ."	"Ring around the rosy . . ."	Upward glissando in clarinets, celesta, and harp makes a sudden transition to the steady triplet rhythm of the concluding scene:

Against this constant rhythm, children sing a song. Prominent use of flutes and celesta provides a feeling of a children's song:

TIME	TEXT	TRANSLATION	DESCRIPTION
	One of Them		
0:12	Du, Käthe! . . . Die Marie . . .	You, Cathy! . . . Marie . . .	Song abruptly stops; spoken dialogue from children.
	Second Child		
	Was is?	What?	
	First Child		
	Weisst' es nit? Sie sind schon All 'naus.	Don't you know? They've all gone out there.	
	Third Child		
	Du! Dein Mutter ist tot!	You! Your mother is dead!	Child's statement to Marie's son that his mother is dead is accompanied by the DEATH leitmotif, a series of open fifths, in the strings:

(continued)

TIME	TEXT	TRANSLATION	DESCRIPTION

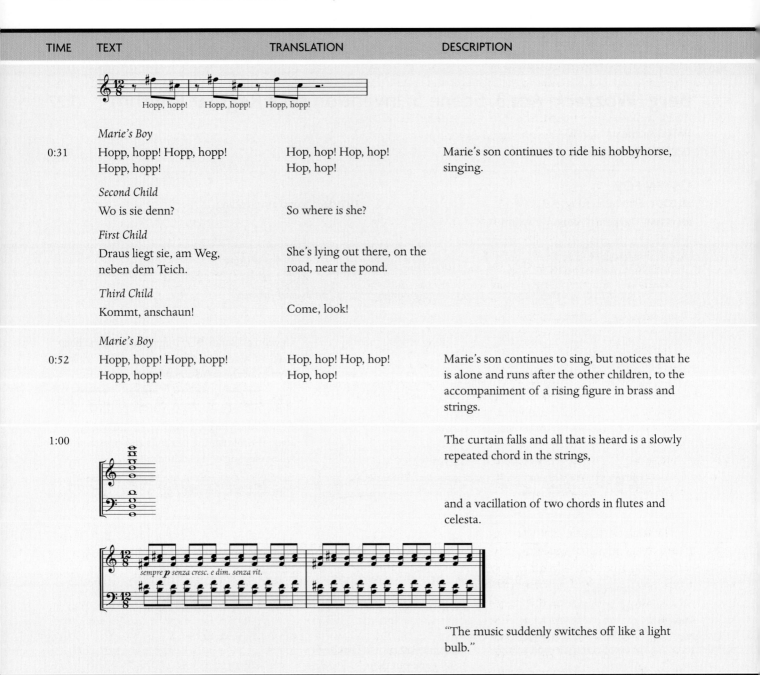

	Marie's Boy		
0:31	Hopp, hopp! Hopp, hopp! Hopp, hopp!	Hop, hop! Hop, hop! Hop, hop!	Marie's son continues to ride his hobbyhorse, singing.
	Second Child		
	Wo is sie denn?	So where is she?	
	First Child		
	Draus liegt sie, am Weg, neben dem Teich.	She's lying out there, on the road, near the pond.	
	Third Child		
	Kommt, anschaun!	Come, look!	
	Marie's Boy		
0:52	Hopp, hopp! Hopp, hopp! Hopp, hopp!	Hop, hop! Hop, hop! Hop, hop!	Marie's son continues to sing, but notices that he is alone and runs after the other children, to the accompaniment of a rising figure in brass and strings.
1:00			The curtain falls and all that is heard is a slowly repeated chord in the strings,
			and a vacillation of two chords in flutes and celesta.
			"The music suddenly switches off like a light bulb."

Act 3, Scene 5   The shimmering chord that closes the opera—the same chord we heard at the end of the first two acts—sounds as if it could continue forever, but instead suddenly switches off like a light bulb. In a lecture about the opera, Berg said that "although the music steers again into the cadential haven of the final chord it almost looks as if it was to go on. And it really does go on! As a matter of fact, the initial bars of the opera could easily link up with these final bars and thereby close the circle."

The open-ended quality of the music extends to the drama as well: Berg seems to suggest that the tragedy of *Wozzeck*—of "Wir arme Leut" (we poor folk)—is destined to repeat itself endlessly (see LG 71, p. 459).

How Did It Go?

The first performance of *Wozzeck* seems to have been one of the classic scandals that often greet the arrival of particularly unconventional and challenging works. Hans Heinsheimer, director of the opera department of the influential Austrian music publisher Universal Edition (Berg's future publishing house), recalled the occasion in his memoirs:

> At the première there were fisticuffs and verbal duels between the stalls and the boxes, derisive laughter, hissing and shrill whistling; for a time it seemed as though the enemies of the work might overwhelm the few—finally victorious—adherents of the composer. Did we—we who applauded and shouted so valiantly until the lights were turned out and the safety curtain was lowered—did we really understand what was new, great and revolutionary about the work? Perhaps a few did, but most of us did not. So what was it that moved us so? There is an inner ear—an invisible receiving apparatus—which may not necessarily perceive all the technical refinements of a composition, but is nevertheless stirred in some magical way by beauty, power and strength, and can distinguish between the resounding steps of the giant and the hasty gallop of the busy dwarf. The violent differences of opinion continued in the newspapers for days and weeks. On the one side high praise and humble recognition of the work's greatness and its creator's importance, and on the other, hate-filled and almost hysterical condemnation.

The first-night reviewers were generally baffled, although many critics acknowledged that they had witnessed a musical event of uncommon significance (see Figures 16.8 and 16.9, from opening night). No one doubted that Kleiber had led an excellent performance, that Berg's use of instruments was brilliant (as distinct from what was seen as his problematic writing for voices), that the cast had done its job superbly, or that the orchestra's playing left nothing to be desired. One influential critic, Oskar Bie, hailed Wozzeck as "no experiment, but a masterwork of art, seriously considered, and convincingly worked out." Stuckenschmidt agreed:

> It is difficult to do justice to the strange perfection and uniqueness of this work within the limits of a review. There can never before have been chosen for an opera a libretto whose literary value so completely corresponds to the

„Wozzeck", Oper von Alban Berg, Staatsoper, Berlin
Sigrid Johanson (Marie) und Leo Schützendorf (Wozzeck)

TOP, FIG. 16.8 A 1926 photograph from the Berlin premiere of *Wozzeck*, with Leo Schützendorf as Wozzeck and Sigrid Johanson as Marie.

BOTTOM, FIG. 16.9 A haunting image of Leo Schützendorf in the title role of *Wozzeck*.

possibilities of musical interpretation as does that of this magnificent fragment by Georg Büchner.

. . . Berg has succeeded in writing a music for this libretto that not only does not diminish the value of the literary work but actually enhances it to an unheard-of degree. It is a music that brings latent matters to the surface and uncovers the most secret psychological factors without waiving the most important things, namely the dramatic conception and the musical unity. The fact that Berg has done this is evidence of genius, and places him right next to the most important music-dramatists of our time. . . . Not only was the evening the greatest sensation of the season, it was a significant event in the history of music-drama in general.

For the most part, the negative reviews took issue with the music, not the performance. Berg's was not the sort of music one is accustomed to, the naysayers wrote; it lacked beauty, it was offensive to one's sense of good taste, and so on. One example, titled "Stuttering at the State Opera," will convey the flavor of this critical assault:

Leaving the State Opera House *Unter den Linden* last evening, I had the feeling that I was not leaving a public institute of art but a public mad-house. On the stage, in the orchestra, in the stalls: a lot of madmen. . . . *Wozzeck* by Alban Berg was the battle-cry—the work of a chinaman from Vienna. For these massed attacks and convulsions of instruments had nothing to do with European music and its development . . . . In the whole vocal score of *Wozzeck* I cannot find a single instance that would indicate honest and genuine inspiration. . . . In Berg's music there is not the slightest trace of melody. There are only scraps and shreds, sobs and belches. Harmonically, the work cannot be discussed, for every single thing sounds wrong. . . . The instrumentation is varied. He runs through all the possibilities between the last gasp of violin harmonics and the bass tuba's meanest grunt. A whole zoological garden is opened up. . . . I consider Alban Berg a musical impostor, and a treacherously dangerous composer. Yes, one seriously has to consider the question, whether and to what extent activity in music can be criminal. This is a matter of a capital crime in the field of music.

Wozzeck Then and Now

Berg's audience was—and still is—divided. Today, most people who are willing to give *Wozzeck* a chance do so in the spirit of experiencing, or maybe standing in awe of, an acknowledged masterpiece. But despite its vividly dramatic qualities, Berg's music is not easy to grasp on a single hearing. The lack of conventional melodies—recognizable tunes that anybody can sing—frustrates some listeners and infuriates others. Of course, the claim that certain operas lack "melody" has been a commonplace of music criticism for centuries. (It was even said of Bizet's *Carmen*, perhaps the most popular and tuneful opera ever written.) What such comments usually mean is that the composer's style is too new and unfamiliar to be described by the standard critical vocabulary.

After its premiere (and eight subsequent performances in Berlin later that season), *Wozzeck* seemed to pop up almost everywhere, from Vienna, Prague, and Leningrad to New York and Philadelphia. Berg traveled far and wide to introduce his work to audiences; it made both his reputation and his fortune. Had the Nazis not come to power, who knows what further successes might have come Berg's way. But the Nazi regime forbade performances of his music, along with that of other allegedly "degenerate" composers (including Mendelssohn; see Chapter 11). Berg, although he was not Jewish, might well have followed his teacher into exile in the United States if he had not died, prematurely, in 1935, in the midst of orchestrating the last act of his opera *Lulu*.

In an essay written three years after the premiere, Berg explained what he hoped audiences would take away from a performance of *Wozzeck*:

> However much one may know about the musical forms to be found in this opera—how strictly and logically it is all "worked out," how ingeniously planned in all its details . . . from the moment when the curtain rises until it descends for the last time, there must not be anyone in the audience who notices anything of these various fugues and inventions, suite movements and sonata movements, variations and passacaglias. Nobody must be filled with anything else except the idea of the opera—which goes far beyond the individual fate of Wozzeck. And that—so I believe—I have achieved.

The impact the war had on Berg's generation may be difficult to imagine, unless we are aware of the pain and suffering on far-off battlefields. Today, when a berserk soldier goes on a murderous rampage, we treat it as an isolated tragedy. But in the aftermath of World War I, hundreds of thousands of Wozzecks roamed the streets of Berlin, Vienna, and other European cities, unable to put behind them the horror they had experienced.

That horror is central to the "idea" of *Wozzeck*, but so too is the bittersweet beauty of Marie's lullaby and the childish innocence of the final scene. Unlike composers such as Stravinsky, who avoided the emotional and expressive associations of late-Romantic tonal music, Berg exploited those associations to trigger certain emotional reactions. The march, lullaby, barroom piano tunes, passionate symphonic music, music in recognizable styles, and often in traditional forms,

FIG. 16.10 The San Diego Opera production of *Wozzeck* in 2007, showing a moment in Act 3, Scene 4.

but with Berg's new musical content and atonal harmonies—all of these familiar devices serve to lead the listener into unfamiliar musical territory.

Over the years, the story of Wozzeck has continued to resonate with those concerned with oppression, subjugation, and abuse. A film of Büchner's play made by Georg Klaren in postwar East Germany had special meaning for people living under Soviet domination; there is also a gripping film of the play by Werner Herzog (1979). Dimitri Mitropoulos's pioneering 1951 recording of Berg's opera brought the human drama of Wozzeck, as well as the horror, to a wide audience. A 1970 film made by the Hamburg State Opera, and television films directed by Joachim Hess in 1971 and by Brian Large in 1987, are a few of many performances and recordings that continue to re-envision, and help us to re-experience, Berg's ever-modern masterpiece (see Figure 16.10).

Wozzeck is expressionism at its best, proof that the artist's vision and the viewer's pleasure need not be mutually exclusive. The subject can be both shocking and tender, and so can the music. In a good performance, the interior theater of the mind shocks and transforms us as powerfully as it did audiences in the 1920s. For Berg was a master of the theater who never forgot that the purpose of opera is to entertain. When he lectured about Wozzeck in various cities where it was being presented, he always closed with a plea to the audience: "Ladies and gentlemen—I beg you to forget all theory and musical aesthetics before you attend the performance!"

Chapter Review

Summary of Musical Styles

Wozzeck is characterized by several features that are not unique to this opera but when combined with the dramatic play create an unforgettable effect.

- Vocal delivery comes in several forms, including traditional singing, speaking, and the new technique of **Sprechstimme**, thus providing a wide variety of dramatic effects.

- Motivic construction allows Berg to create lyrical lines, complex polyphonic textures, and an ongoing, varying web of textures, all spun from a limited number of motives; this is a further development of Wagnerian style.

- **Atonal** composition allows for a variety of sounds ("harmonies" we might call them if they were meant to sound "harmonious") that broaden the expressive palette of the composer.

- Reference to recognizable musical styles and forms (march, lullaby, dance-hall polka, barroom piano) makes the listener feel somewhat at home in this new sound-world.

⑤ Multimedia Resources and Review Materials on StudySpace

Visit wwnorton.com/studyspace for review of Chapter 16.

What Do You Know?

Check the facts for this chapter. Take the online **Quiz**.

What Do You Hear?

Listening Quizzes and **Music Activities** will help you understand the musical works in this chapter.

Author Videos

- The use of note and rhythm in Act 3 of Berg's *Wozzeck*

Interactive Listening Guides

LG 66 Berg: *Wozzeck*, Act 1, Scene 3, March and Lullaby
LG 67 Berg: *Wozzeck*, Act 3, Scene 2, Invention on a Note
LG 68 Berg: *Wozzeck*, Act 3, Scene 3, Invention on an Irregular Rhythm
LG 69 Berg: *Wozzeck*, Act 3, Scene 4, Invention on a Chord
LG 70 Berg: *Wozzeck*, Act 3, Interlude, Invention on a Key
LG 71 Berg: *Wozzeck*, Act 3, Scene 5, Invention on a Regular Rhythm

Videos

Act 3, Scene 2: "Dort links geht's in die Stadt"
Act 3, Scene 3: "Tanzt Alle; tanzt nur zu"
Act 3, Scene 4: "Das Messer? Wo ist das Messer?"
Interlude and Act 3, Scene 5: "Ringel, Ringel, Rosenkranz, Ringelreih'n!"

Flashcards (Terms to Know)

atonal	First Viennese School
augmented fourth	short score
expressionism	Sprechstimme
full score	tritone
Second Viennese School	polka

CHAPTER 17

WEDNESDAY, JANUARY 15, 1941, STALAG VIIIA, ZGORZELEK, POLAND:

Olivier Messiaen's
Quartet for the End of Time

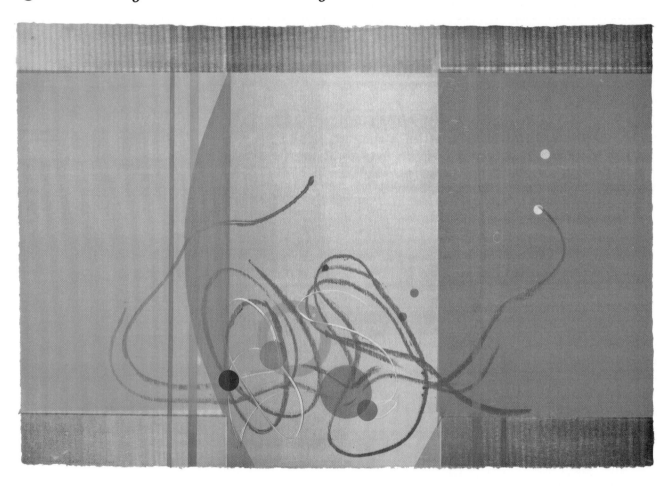

⚙ CORE REPERTOIRE

- **LG 72** I. "Liturgie de cristal" (Liturgy of Crystal)
- **LG 73** II. "Vocalise, pour l'Ange qui annonce la fin du Temps" (Vocalise, for the Angel Who Announces the End of Time)
- **LG 74** III. "Abîme des oiseaux" (Abyss of the Birds)

- **LG 75** IV. "Intermède" (Interlude)
- **LG 76** V. "Louange à l'Éternité de Jésus" (Praise to the Eternity of Jesus)
- **LG 77** VI. "Danse de la fureur, pour les sept trompettes" (Dance of Fury, for the Seven Trumpets)

- **LG 78** VII. "Fouillis d'arcs-en-ciel, pour l'Ange qui annonce la fin du Temps" (Tumult of Rainbows, for the Angel Who Announces the End of Time)
- **LG 79** VIII. "Louange à l'Immortalité de Jésus" (Praise to the Immortality of Jesus)

Introduction

"The camp of Görlitz . . . Barrack 27B, our theater. . . . Outside, night, snow, misery. . . . Here, a miracle. . . . The quartet 'for the end of time' transports us to a wonderful Paradise, lifts us from this abominable earth. Thank you immensely, dear Olivier Messiaen, poet of Eternal Purity."

—Étienne Pasquier, 1941

The *Quartet for the End of Time (Quatuor pour la fin du Temps)* was given its first performance by four French prisoners in a German prison camp in the early years of World War II. One of the performers was the composer himself, Olivier Messiaen (pronounced messy-**ahn**, with the "ahn" nasalized), who was already a well-known musician in Paris.

How the four Frenchmen came to be prisoners of war in the same camp; how the authorities came to permit entertainment, including music; how the prisoners managed to obtain instruments; how Messiaen assembled this piece for the musicians at hand; and how the performance, given in an underheated barracks for several hundred prisoners and German officials, form the background to one of the most impressive, and influential, musical compositions of the twentieth century.

The title of the work might seem like a play on words: prisoners longing for the end of their time in captivity; or perhaps a composer seeking to escape the domination of regular meter and rhythm, as Messiaen admitted he was.

But Messiaen did not just intend a musical play on words. The *Quartet*, as we will see, was Messiaen's mystical vision of the Apocalypse—of the Christian prophecy, in the last book of the New Testament, announced by an angel clad in a rainbow, that all time shall end. In addition to being a composer interested in musical systems—in procedures of scales and of exotic rhythms—Messiaen was a deeply religious Catholic, and a great deal of his music is also a meditation on religious mysteries. His *Quartet* is no exception. His ability to combine the systematic and the sublime is one of Messiaen's greatest gifts.

Title of work

Ⓢ Messiaen: *Quartet for the End of Time*, "Dance of Fury"

Ⓢ Messiaen: *Quartet for the End of Time*, "Praise to the Eternity of Jesus"

⦿ AUTHOR VIDEOS

- The nightingale and the blackbird in "Liturgie de cristal," from Messiaen's *Quartet for the End of Time*

The Setting

World War II

The escalating imperialistic threats of Germany, under the authority of its ruling National Socialist (Nazi) party and the absolute dictator Adolf Hitler, were realized when Germany invaded Poland in 1939. France and England declared war within days, and within a short time World War II had become widespread, engaging the efforts of the Soviet Union, the United States, and others, against the forces of Germany and Italy in Europe, and against Japan in the Pacific.

By the time war was declared, Messiaen had been organist of the church of La Trinité in Paris for eight years; he had taught at two music schools in Paris, the Schola Cantorum and the École Normale de Musique; and he had won first prizes in several categories at the Paris Conservatory: counterpoint, piano accompaniment, organ, and composition. This relatively young man was poised for a great career in music as an innovative composer (see biography, below). But everything changed not only for him but also for his compatriots when World War II entered French territory.

Messiaen was drafted in August 1939 and assigned to the medical corps in a simple and relatively safe job. But the sudden German invasion of Belgium and the Netherlands in May of 1940 led to the fall of both countries, and a German

---

OLIVIER MESSIAEN (1908–1992)

Olivier Messiaen, organist, pianist, composer, is among the most admired and influential composers of the twentieth century. He is especially revered by the French, and his music is strongly influenced by their culture.

Messiaen was born in Avignon, to an intellectual family: his mother was a poet, and his father, an English teacher, translated Shakespeare's plays into French. At the age of eleven, Messiaen entered the Paris Conservatory, where he studied with some of the great French composers of the time. While still a student, he published his first work, eight *Preludes* for piano, using musical techniques like modes of limited transposition (see p. 476) and nonretrogradable rhythms (see p. 477) that he would employ throughout his compositional life.

Messiaen's music is characterized by a deeply felt religious expression. It is also noted for an emphasis on the use of birdsongs as melodic material; for the elaborately constructed rhythmic systems that allow the music to sound at times so free; and for the colorful harmonic palette derived at least in part from the exploration of scales outside the traditional musical system.

He published a substantial amount of organ music (although as an organist he himself usually improvised), and his works are at the core of the modern organist's repertory. Their titles

reflect his ongoing spirituality. But his exploration of religious subjects was not limited to organ music. In the 1940s he wrote a number of works featuring solo piano, designed for himself and his second wife, Yvonne Loriod, to play. His solo piano cycle *Vingt regards sur l'enfant-Jésus* (*Twenty Gazes on the Child Jesus*) lasts about two hours.

Large orchestral pieces by Messiaen include the enormous *Turangalîla-symphonie* and the twelve-movement *Des canyons aux étoiles . . .* (*From the Canyons to the Stars . . .*), inspired by a trip to Bryce Canyon in Utah. His one opera, *Saint François d'Assise* (*Saint Francis of Assisi*), was commissioned by the Paris Opera, and its writing took up much of his time in the 1970s. It is a huge and somewhat static, contemplative work.

Messiaen did not develop themes in his work, but rather juxtaposed ideas. He retained his modest demeanor, his spiritual focus, and his devotion to his art throughout his life, and reflected the same in his music.

Ⓢ Messiaen: *L'Ascension,* "Transports de joie d'une âme devant la gloire du Christ qui est la sienne"
Ⓢ Messiaen: *Turangalîla-symphonie*

MAJOR WORKS: Orchestral work, including *Turangalîla-symphonie* and *Oiseaux exotiques* (*Exotic Birds*); chamber music, including *Quatuor pour la fin du Temps*; choral music, including *La transfiguration de Notre Seigneur Jésus Christ*; vocal music; 1 opera; keyboard and organ music; and theoretical writings.

advance into France from the east captured many French soldiers, including Messiaen, while he and others were walking in a forest from Verdun to Nancy. They were held in a camp for a time awaiting transportation, and finally sent to a German prison camp called Stalag VIIIA in Zgorzelek, Poland, some one hundred miles southeast of Berlin. Prior to the outbreak of the war, it had been a camp for Hitler youths.

France signed an armistice with Germany in June 1940; according to its terms a large northern part of France would be occupied by Germany, and a smaller southern portion, with a capital at Vichy, would be under nominal French control. A puppet government would see to administrative affairs, but Germany would set policy.

In Stalag VIIIA, prisoners contended with hunger, cold, and forced labor. They were mostly interned in barracks, though some were assigned to forced-labor details. It was in Stalag VIIIA, in January 1941, that the prisoner Olivier Messiaen, along with three fellow French prisoners—the cellist Étienne Pasquier, the clarinetist Henri Akoka, and the violinist Jean Le Boulaire—first performed his *Quartet for the End of Time*.

STALAG VIIIA

The prison camp to which Messiaen and others were assigned was not one of the extermination camps that were part of the horrific Nazi campaign to eliminate all Jews and other "undesirables" from Europe, and that made the middle years of the twentieth century such a nightmare for humankind. It was, rather, a prison for forced laborers.

The prison camp

Stalag is short for *Stammlager*, "Mannschafts*stamm-* und Stra*flager*"—personnel holding and prison camp. Stalag VIIIA (see Figures 17.1 and 17.2) was only one of a number of such camps, designed to house prisoners of enemy armies, and to put them to work in nearby factories and fields. During the time Messiaen was there, approximately 30,000 prisoners were in Stalag VIIIA, though most were housed outside the camp.

The camp had only recently been opened, and although barracks were being built at a fierce rate, there were still many prisoners housed in tents. The first occupants of the camp, in late September 1939, were 10,000 Poles. There were many prisoners from other Eastern European countries as well; these easterners were segregated from the Western European prisoners, mostly a large influx of French

FIG. 17.1 A view of Stalag VIIIA in the winter of 1942.

FIG. 17.2 A plan of Stalag VIIIA. The theater barracks, where the *Quartet for the End of Time* was first performed, is indicated near the center top.

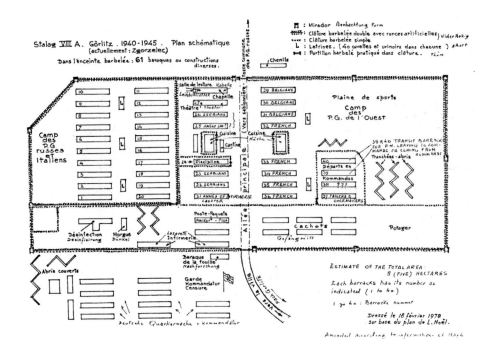

Conditions

prisoners near the end of 1939. Prisoners were segregated by country as well, and sometimes by profession. There was also a barracks for priests.

Food was scarce, and all who were at the prison camp say that there was never enough to eat. Pasquier reported a standard day as beginning with *Ersatzkaffee*, a coffee substitute; later in the day they were given one piece of black bread with some fat on it; that was all. As the months wore on and the camp became better organized, stews of cabbage, potatoes, or turnips appeared, but conditions remained harsh. The cold was fierce in the winter, and although the finished wooden barracks, where men slept in triple-bunk beds, had stoves, these never truly warmed the buildings or the men (see Figure 17.3).

FIG. 17.3 The interior of one of the barracks at Stalag VIIIA.

By early 1941, at the time of the *Quartet's* premiere, the camp seemed to be keeping some of the prisoner-workers in relatively good condition. There were infirmaries, kitchens, latrines, and a barracks set aside as a theater and another as a chapel and library. After Messiaen's release (in May 1941), the camp expanded even more, to include an orchestra of Polish musicians, a jazz band, a newspaper, and a series of art exhibitions.

There are reports that the German officers and guards who ran the prison camp seem to have had respect for the professional men whom they held captive. Musicians especially were supported and encouraged. Messiaen in particular was somewhat protected, both by his captors and by his fellow prisoners. According to his second wife, Messiaen related having been locked into the camp latrine so that he could compose in quiet (presumably during times when the prisoners were working). The inmates did what they could to lighten his duties, and the authorities even placed a guard nearby so that he would not be disturbed while he composed.

FIG. 17.4 Étienne Pasquier (left) as a member of the Pasquier Trio.

The Performance

THE PERFORMERS

The *Quartet* ensemble was assembled at the prison camp, but Messiaen had met two of his fellow prisoners, the cellist Pasquier (see Figure 17.4) and the clarinetist Akoka (see Figure 17.5), in Verdun before their capture. And indeed some aspects of the *Quartet* began to take shape before its personnel was complete.

Étienne Pasquier, born in 1905, was already a famous cellist. With his two brothers he was a member of the Trio Pasquier, a string trio that toured and recorded, and whose international fame was already considerable. In September 1939 Pasquier was drafted, and after a time was transferred to Verdun, where he commanded a group of four musicians, one of whom was Olivier Messiaen. Pasquier was able to accommodate the birdsong-obsessed Messiaen by assigning him the dawn watch so that he could be awake to hear the birds as the sun rose.

Clarinetist Henri Akoka was twenty-seven when he met Messiaen. Born into a French-Jewish family in Algeria, he moved to France in 1926. He, like Pasquier and Messiaen, took first prize at the Conservatory. Akoka played in the Radio Symphonic Orchestra of Strasbourg before being drafted and sent to Verdun to play in the military orchestra.

FIG. 17.5 Henri Akoka, the clarinetist for the *Quartet*.

Akoka—again, like Pasquier—met Messiaen before they were prisoners together. The clarinetist urged Messiaen to write a composition for him, and Messiaen did so, inspired by his dawn sessions of listening to birdsongs. The "Abyss of the Birds," the third movement of the *Quartet*, had its origin as a solo clarinet piece for Akoka.

When Germany attacked, the musicians, along with many others, fled Verdun on foot, trying to reach Nancy—a trek of about fifty miles; during this time Akoka helped maintain morale, as well as providing physical help to Messiaen and the others. It was only after they were captured that Akoka tried the clarinet piece for the first time, as Pasquier recalled:

FIG. 17.6 Jean Le Boulaire, the violinist for the *Quartet*.

FIG. 17.7 The title page of the 1941 manuscript of the *Quartet for the End of Time*, which reads, beneath the title, "in homage to the Angel of the Apocalypse, who raised his hand to heaven, saying, 'There will be no more time.'"

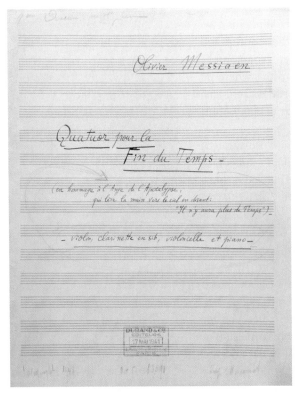

It's in this open field that Akoka sight-read the piece for the first time. I was the "music stand," that is to say, I held the music for him. He would grumble from time to time, as he found that the composer gave him difficult things to do. "I'll never be able to play it," he would say. "Yes, yes, you will, you'll see," Messiaen would answer.

After the transfer of the prisoners to Stalag VIIIA, the idea of the *Quartet* began to form. Akoka, Pasquier, and Messiaen found themselves together, and with time enough to compose and to play. A violinist, Jean Le Boulaire (see Figure 17.6), was also at the prison. He might not have been Messiaen's violinist of choice—he had not won a first prize and had never quite achieved the musical career of the other players—but he was a competent violinist, and as a French soldier he had also been captured by the Germans and sent to Stalag VIIIA.

Most prisoners labored in work details outside the camp; those who remained in the camp had jobs such as cook or tailor, and had to perform other chores as well. But musicians seem to have escaped the worst treatment. Pasquier was originally sent to an outside granite quarry, where he loaded tombstones onto wagons; but when it was discovered that he was a musician he was returned to the camp and set to work as a cook.

The violinist Le Boulaire found himself in the same barracks as Akoka, and from Akoka he learned that Messiaen was a fellow prisoner. Akoka had managed to hang on to his clarinet, but there was no violin, no cello, no piano, for the other musicians.

It seems to have been a French-speaking German guard, the lawyer Karl-Albert Brüll, who provided writing materials to Messiaen (see Figure 17.7) and found instruments for the players, including a violin for Le Boulaire. (Pasquier says it was the camp commandant who arranged for instruments—and in any event his permission would surely have been needed.) Pasquier was allowed to pick out a cello in the town of Zgorzelek, and he entertained his fellow prisoners with favorite solos.

The Germans sought to keep the prisoners in reasonably good spirits. One of the barracks was designated for use as a theater. The lavatory section in the middle was used as a stage, and seating was on benches ranging back to one end of the long barracks building.

In addition to plays, variety shows and concerts were held on Saturdays; classical music began at 6 p.m., and at 7 p.m. the variety show started, with songs, dances, skits, or comedians (see Figure 17.8). Everything ended in time for the 9 p.m. curfew.

There were also films—a lot of propaganda films—and lectures by camp inmates. One such lecture was given by Messiaen himself, on the subject of color in the Book of Revelation. "I was very surprised to be listened to so attentively," Messiaen later said. "It was this [lecture], this angel [he means the angel crowned with a rainbow, from the Apocalypse; see below] finally that rekindled my desire to compose." The lecture is closely related to the *Quartet*, with its vision of the Angel, and the color associations that Messiaen makes with certain of the passages and movements.

While in the camp, Messiaen had composed a trio for his three musician friends, a short piece that became the "Intermède" of the *Quartet*. There was no piano as yet, but there were opportunities to play, and as Messiaen put it,

I wrote for them at once a short trio without anything larger in mind, which they played for me in the lavatories, because the clarinetist had brought his instrument with him and the cellist had been given a gift of a cello with three strings. Emboldened by these first sounds, I retained this little piece as an interlude and added to it in succession the seven movements that surround it, thus carrying the total number of movements of my *Quartet for the End of Time* to eight.

(Messiaen continued to tell this story for many years, maintaining that Pasquier managed the cello part with only three strings, while Pasquier insisted that he could not possibly have done so, and that his cello, like any cello, always had all four strings.)

It is true that this trio, the "Intermède" (Interlude) of the *Quartet*, has a lighthearted, whimsical, relatively simple quality not shared by the other movements. But the "Intermède" is not the earliest part of the *Quartet* he composed, since we have seen that at least some version of the clarinet solo "Abyss of the Birds" had been written for Akoka earlier. And indeed the sources go farther back, since two movements are arrangements of music Messiaen had composed in Paris.

In November 1940 a piano arrived at the theater barracks. This upright (Messiaen says it had keys that stuck) was used for the variety shows and other concerts. It allowed Messiaen to perform a Beethoven trio with Akoka and Pasquier in one of the classical-music concerts; others remember a performance of a transcription of Beethoven's Seventh Symphony. No doubt Messiaen performed in other concerts as well. It was an odd place to be playing chamber music; these were not exactly Schubertiades, but music seemed to be important to performers and audience alike.

FIG. 17.8 A photomontage poster of the different theatrical and musical performances in Stalag VIIIA.

REHEARSALS AND PERFORMANCE

Messiaen must have anticipated the arrival of a piano, because he had evidently been working on the *Quartet* before the instrument appeared; when the piano was finally delivered, rehearsals began right away. The quartet rehearsed after Pasquier finished his job in the kitchen at 6 p.m., so there were three hours available every day for rehearsals. An additional hour every day was allotted to the musicians, which they could use for solo practice. There were also two hours on Saturday afternoons when prisoners had free time, and the quartet used this time as well. Generally the rehearsals were in the theater barracks, except when the space was needed for other rehearsals or for Saturday evening shows.

It was no easy matter to read Messiaen's difficult music, to coordinate the four instrumental parts, or to get the rhythms, the pitches, and the details of attack, articulation, and dynamics right. Le Boulaire remembered:

> The first great difficulty was to read the piece. It wasn't easy. The second was to play it together. That wasn't easy either. From the ensemble standpoint, we had a lot of trouble. Messiaen would give us cues, but that did not make it any less difficult. There are some extraordinary young people today, who certainly manage much better than we did. But we, Pasquier included, ran across something that we had never seen before, and we all stumbled a little.

For Henri Akoka it was extremely difficult to find the breath control for the long notes, for the very quiet sound Messiaen required in very high notes, and for the extreme fortissimos. "He would say to the clarinetist," says Pasquier, "'Hold that note until you can't blow anymore at all. Enlarge the sound.' Or, he would tap on the piano. He wanted terrifying *fortissimos*."

The two extremely slow movements—the two Praise movements for piano and cello and for piano and violin—both caused trouble for their players; Messiaen insisted on tempos that each player felt were unattainable. "He wanted it *very* slow," said Pasquier. "Even a slowness that verges on the impossible. So, I would debate with him, because you cannot manage to sustain the bow at that tempo. 'But yes, you're doing it,' he would insist."

THE PREMIERE

The premiere of the *Quartet*, with the permission of the commandant of Stalag VIIIA, was scheduled for January 15. This was a Wednesday, not the usual Saturday evening 6 p.m. concert preceding a variety show or a film. It was a special occasion, the *Quartet* being the only event of the evening.

Henri Breton, one of the prisoners, designed printed invitations and a program to be distributed by the performers and others, giving the name of the camp, the date, the title, and the names of the performers (see Figure 17.9). Special permission was given for the attendance of the separately housed French prisoners who were about to be released as a result of the Armistice signed between France and Germany in 1940.

There are many reports as to how many people were at the performance. Messiaen himself reports thousands of listeners. But the barracks surely could not have held more than about four hundred. Officers sat in the front row; also at the front were wounded prisoners on stretchers.

It was a very cold night—not unusual for January in this part of Poland—with snow on the ground, wind howling at frosted windowpanes, and an indoor temperature not ideal for musicians who need nimble fingers.

FIG. 17.9 A printed program from the Stalag VIIIA performance of the Messiaen *Quartet*.

The performers were dressed like the other prisoners. "I had a jacket from Czechoslovakia," recalled Pasquier, "with pockets everywhere. We wore wooden clogs that made our feet hurt, but that was all there was. But the wood kept us warm. Messiaen had a jacket that was all patched up. He was very badly dressed, thanks to me. I'm the one who helped him find clothes"

The audience, like the auditorium, was an unusual one for a piece like the *Quartet for the End of Time*. There were people of all sorts, diverse in background and experience. On the whole, however, the French were more interested in hearing the music of their famous compatriots than the large contingent of Poles were. But many, including the French, had no experience at all with modern music. Some had attended the camp's concerts of classical music (along with the more popular offerings), but there had been very little contemporary music.

It was not easy to get the crowded room quiet, but Messiaen stood and addressed the audience:

I told them first of all that this quartet was written for the end of time, without any play on words on the length of captivity, but for the end of the notion of past and future, that is to say, for the beginning of eternity, and that the work is based on the magnificent text of the Apocalypse in which Saint John says: "And I saw another mighty angel coming down from heaven, wrapped in a cloud, with a rainbow on his head. . . ."

Messiaen evidently went on to describe something of his musical style, his unusual scales and harmonies, and particularly his rhythms, whose irregularity and independence from regular meter helped to create a sense of escape or freedom from the regular march of time. There is no way to know how effective this was in preparing the audience for what followed.

The Music

Messiaen's music has an allure all its own. Even though he composed all types of music, from solo keyboard works—for organ or piano—to chamber music of various kinds to orchestral works to opera, common threads run through his work. His sound ranges from a tranquil, timeless melodiousness to an energetic, rhythmic irregularity; throughout Messiaen's compositions, the use of birdsong captures the ear and the imagination.

Messiaen was said to experience **synesthesia**, or a fusion of the senses; he experienced specific colors in relation to musical sound. In his introductions to the movements of the *Quartet*, Messiaen refers to "sweet cascades of blue-orange," "enormous blocks of purple fury," "flows of blue-orange lava." These images are clearly visual, auditory, and spiritual at the same time. In the introduction to one of the movements (VII. "Tumult of Rainbows"), Messiaen describes how this imagery works for him: "In my dreams, I hear and see arranged chords and melodies, understood colors and forms; then, after this transitory stage, I pass into the unreal and suffer with ecstasy a dizziness, a spinning superhuman mixture of sounds and colors."

Synesthesia

ASPECTS OF MESSIAEN'S MUSICAL STYLE

It is too simple to characterize Messiaen's style as consisting of birdcalls, unusual musical scales, and rhythmic patterns, but each of these was important to Messiaen, so we should pay attention to them.

Religious inspiration Foremost, for Messiaen, was the religious aspect of his music—each composition represents an attempt to elucidate a theological truth. It is perhaps natural that a church organist should write religious music, and Messiaen's output for organ includes a great many compositions with religious, sometimes mystical, titles. But much of his other music—music intended for secular concert audiences—also explores religious themes. Works like *Visions de l'Amen* for two pianos, and *Trois petites liturgies de la présence divine* (*Three Little Liturgies of the Divine Presence*), for women's chorus, orchestra, and piano, are his attempts to express religious truths. "I was born a believer," he said, "and the Scriptures impressed me even as a child. This illumination of the theological truths of the Catholic faith is the first aspect of my work, the noblest, and no doubt the most useful and most valuable—perhaps the only one I won't regret at the hour of my death."

The *Quartet* is directly inspired by a passage from the Book of Revelation, as we will see in detail below. How to make connections between sounds and images, ideas, or emotions is always a mystery in music, but Messiaen, in his talk to the audience at the premiere, in his remarks before each movement at the subsequent

Paris premiere, and in the preface to the published edition, tried to make this transparent. In the preface to the *Quartet* he wrote that the piece

> was directly inspired by this quotation from the Apocalypse [he has just cited a passage from the Book of Revelation]. Its musical language is essentially immaterial, spiritual, Catholic. Certain modes, melodically and harmonically realizing a sort of tonal ubiquity, bring the listener closer to eternity in space or infinity. Special rhythms, beyond any regular meter, contribute powerfully to removing the temporal. (All of this being only attempts and stammerings, if one thinks of the overpowering grandeur of the subject.)

Messiaen was certain that his musical-technical procedures, his modes, his rhythms, and his melodies, contributed to the religious expression he so profoundly sought.

Modes and Harmony   The word "mode" is generally used in music to refer to scales other than the major and minor ones. To Messiaen, however, "mode" meant something rather special. He was particularly interested in what he called **modes of limited transposition.**

Modes of limited transposition

An example of what he meant may help. A **whole-tone scale**—a scale consisting of whole steps—has six tones per octave (see Appendix, pp. A-4–A-6). For example, this is a whole-tone scale:

C–D–E–F♯–G♯–A♯

If you begin a whole-tone scale on any of these notes, it will produce the same six notes, for example:

E–F♯–G♯–A♯–C–D

If you play the scale starting one semitone higher (for example, on C♯ instead of C), then you get the other six notes of the chromatic scale: C♯–D♯–F–G–A–B; and likewise this produces the same six notes whenever you begin the pattern with one of these notes. If you move it up another semitone, you have the first scale again: hence, "limited transposition." This scale is symmetrical: that is, no matter where you start in the scale, you will always see the same series of intervals. The whole tone and other "limited transposition" modes lack the sense of a strong tonic or final note, and thus give a nondirectional, floating effect; time and directionality are suspended or ended. For Messiaen, this concept reflects God as the alpha and the omega, as timeless and infinite. (If you take all 12 notes—the chromatic scale—and arrange them around a circle you produce a clocklike image that is handy for visualizing what Messiaen was describing. See Figure 17.10, at left). Other modes used by Messiaen have similar qualities. The eight-note **octatonic scale** alternates half steps and whole steps and has four transpositions, as does the nine-note *enneatonic* scale, featuring a pattern of two semitones followed by a whole tone. There are seven such modes altogether, and Messiaen used them, especially the octatonic scale, to generate melodies and harmonies. Several movements of the *Quartet* have the characteristic sound of one or another of these modes.

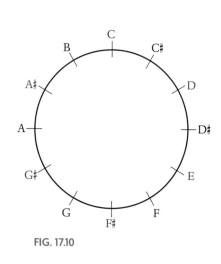

FIG. 17.10

Rhythm   Messiaen was fascinated by rhythm, and in those places where his rhythm seems most rhapsodic or improvisatory, it is often highly structured.

Messiaen's rhythmic procedures include added-value and nonretrogradable rhythms. **Added-value rhythms** are created by starting with a regular pattern and making it irregular by adding a single short note or rest. Thus a pattern of four quarter notes produces a very regular duple rhythm (♩ ♩ ♩ ♩), but adding

Added-value rhythms

an eighth note makes a curious pattern (♩ ♩ ♪♩ ♩) Such rhythms may sound to us irregular—and of course we have already heard many irregular rhythms—but some of what we hear in Messiaen is actually generated by very systematic thinking, whether we hear the system or not.

Nonretrogradable rhythms are rhythmic patterns that are palindromic—the same backward as forward ("Madam, I'm Adam"; "Able was I ere I saw Elba"). Rhythmic examples might be the following:

Nonretrogradable rhythms

♩ ♩ ♪ ♪ ♪ ♩ ♩
or
♩. ♪ ♩ ♪ ♩.

In the *Quartet*, such rhythms are used in the middle section of "Danse de la fureur" (Dance of Fury), among other places. In the example below, from that movement, each measure consists of one of these rhythms; note that each group consists of an odd number of notes, with one central value that is not duplicated. (Tied notes—two notes on the same pitch connected with a curved line, such as the second and third notes of the first example, quarter-note A tied to sixteenth-note A—are a single tone equal to the sum of the lengths.)

The pitches are not palindromic, only the rhythms:

For Messiaen, nonretrogradable rhythms also represented a kind of cosmic philosophy: just as it is impossible to go back in time or to change events from the past, so too with these rhythms. They do not change when played backward but rather repeat themselves—an echo of the irreversibility of time.

Birdsong Messiaen's attraction to birds as God's greatest musicians was serious and lifelong. He studied, recorded, and notated birdsongs all his life, and his reproduction of the sounds of birds in his music became more and more specific and literal. He did feel, however, that birdsongs are often too fast, too high, and too compressed in pitch to be completely intelligible in music. He often slowed down the rhythm; if the song was in a very high register difficult for the human ear to grasp or at the extreme of an instrument's capability, he transposed it to a lower register more usual for music; and if its pitches were minutely close together, smaller than a half step, he spread the pitches apart so that they were playable on a piano or another instrument. He also harmonized the birdsong so as to approximate its timbre.

The wonder of birds for Messiaen was one of freedom. "If you want symbols," he said, "let us go on to say that the bird is the symbol of freedom. We walk, he flies. We make war, he sings. . . . I doubt that one can find in any human music, however inspired, melodies and rhythms that have the sovereign freedom of birdsong." The quartet's violinist, Jean Le Boulaire, recalled that Messiaen "would

Messiaen and birds

spend hours, entire mornings listening to birds. And when he described birdcalls he would whistle. He whistled very, very well. He would also give indications at the piano saying: 'This is a nightingale.' And I don't know if it was because we were trying to penetrate his mind or what, but somehow we would manage to hear a nightingale at the piano."

There are pieces by Messiaen that consist of almost nothing but transcriptions of birdsongs, and pieces that are focused on birds as their main subject. These include *Le réveil des oiseaux* (*Dawn Chorus,* piano and orchestra, 1953); *Oiseaux exotiques* (*Exotic Birds,* solo piano and orchestra, 1955–56), and *Catalogue d'oiseaux* (*Catalogue of Birds,* piano, 1956–58). Many other pieces contain elements of birdsong as part of their texture.

In the first movement of the *Quartet* ("Liturgy of Crystal"), the clarinet and violin both play birdsong fragments (we learn from Messiaen that the clarinet is a blackbird and the violin is a nightingale). The clarinet bird music returns in the third movement, a solo entitled "Abyss of the Birds" (at one point the score indicates "sunlit, like a bird"), and again in the fourth movement ("Interlude"), woven into the scherzo-like texture.

Listening to the Music

Messiaen's *Quartet for the End of Time* spans a variety of instrumental groupings and musical styles. Four of the eight movements use all four players, but the third is for solo clarinet, the fourth omits the piano, the fifth is for cello and piano, and the eighth for violin and piano (see Table 17.1, Movements of the *Quartet,* p. 479). We hear dances, meditations, texture reminiscent of fourteenth-century music in the first movement and an almost Wagnerian melody in the last. Some of the movements are easier to perform than others; some seem focused on their harmonies, others are driven by their rhythms.

Le Boulaire said there were two ways of appreciating Olivier Messiaen:

> There's the mystic and there's the man, and the *Quartet* is split between these two things. There's the pure man, that is, the bird-lover, the nature-lover, but there are also some extremely harsh things, which makes one understand very well why there was so much criticism of Messiaen: at moments, it's unlistenable. It's severe, jolting. There's no harmony, no song, no melody, just this harshness. . . . So, we were a little dumbfounded by his music, because, amid all this severity, suddenly, a song would arise.

Le Boulaire might have been right about the mystic and the man, but he was wrong about the split. Messiaen's music is deeply felt, yet highly structured; it combines the heart and the head, the celestial and the earthly, in a way that, for Messiaen and for many of his listeners, is not a division but a magical fusion. As we discuss the music, it's possible to point out structural elements, but the spiritual and the emotional content is what Messiaen wants us to hear.

Book of Revelation   Messiaen's inspiration for the *Quartet for the End of Time* is from the tenth chapter of the Book of Revelation; at the beginning of his preface to the score, he cites which sections he used for inspiration (the numbers are the biblical verses):

> 1   *And I saw another mighty angel come down from heaven, clothed with a cloud; and a rainbow was upon his head, and his face was as it were the sun, and his feet as pillars of fire:*
> 2   *. . . and he set his right foot upon the sea, and his left foot on the earth, . . .*

TABLE 17.1

Movements of the *Quartet for the End of Time*

I. "Liturgie de cristal" (Liturgy of Crystal)	Full quartet. Birdsong in clarinet and in violin; repeating patterns of glissandos (cello) and chords (piano).
II. "Vocalise, pour l'Ange qui annonce la fin du Temps" (Vocalise, for the Angel Who Announces the End of Time)	Full quartet. Clarinet has birdsong elements found in the movements I, III, and IV.
III. "Abîme des oiseaux" (Abyss of the Birds)	Clarinet solo. Composed as a solo for Akoka.
IV. "Intermède" (Interlude)	Clarinet, violin, cello. Composed at Stalag VIIIA before the piano arrived. Includes birdsong material related to movements I–III.
V. "Louange à l'Éternité de Jésus" (Praise to the Eternity of Jesus)	Cello and piano. Originally for four *ondes Martenot* (an electronic instrument).
VI. "Danse de la fureur, pour les sept trompettes" (Dance of Fury, for the Seven Trumpets)	Full quartet. All in unison.
VII. "Fouillis d'arcs-en-ciel, pour l'Ange qui annonce la fin du Temps" (Tumult of Rainbows, for the Angel Who Announces the End of Time)	Full quartet. Recalls music from movement II.
VIII. "Louange à l'Immortalité de Jésus" (Praise to the Immortality of Jesus)	Violin and piano. Originally for organ.

5 *And the angel which I saw stand upon the sea and upon the earth lifted up his hand
   to heaven,*
6 *And sware by him that liveth for ever and ever, . . . that there should be time no longer:*
7 *But in the days of the seventh angel, when he shall begin to sound, the mystery of
   God should be finished. . . .*

Some of the movements bear specific relationships to passages in this text; others are meditative; one has a strictly musical title ("Interlude"). Table 17.1 (see above) lists the movements, and indicates the relations among them.

I. "LITURGIE DE CRISTAL" (Liturgy of Crystal)

The opening piece is made up of independent patterns, each instrument having a different role to play. Clarinet and violin exchange birdsongs, blackbird and nightingale, respectively. The piano plays soft chords (created from two repeating cycles, of 17 note lengths and 29 chords). The cello plays a 15-note melody repeated over and over, in a nonretrogradable rhythm, which does not coincide with either of the piano patterns; the melody is written as **harmonics** (making a string vibrate at one of its higher overtones, by touching it at a particular point), with **glissandos** (sliding the finger while bowing the string). The abrupt ending—long before the four parts could ever resynchronize—adds to the meditative timelessness of the movement. (See LG 72, p. 480.)
Messiaen's note in the score reads as follows:

*Between 3 and 4 o'clock in the morning, the birds awaken: a solo blackbird or a nightingale
improvises, surrounded by sound-dust, by a halo of trills lost high in the trees. Transpose that
to the religious plane: you have the harmonious silence of heaven.*

 LG 72

The nightingale and the blackbird in "Liturgie de cristal," from Messiaen's *Quartet for the End of Time*

LISTENING GUIDE 72 ⑤ | DVD | 🎙

Messiaen *Quartet for the End of Time,* I. "Liturgie de cristal" (Liturgy of Crystal)

2:39

DATE: January 15, 1941

LISTEN FOR

MELODY: Clarinet and violin have independent parts imitating birdsong; cello repeats 15-note pattern in harmonics, including several glissandos

TEXTURE: Rich, sustained piano chords played quietly throughout, in irregular rhythm

SCORING: Independent sounds and rhythms of the four instruments: two birds, cello pattern, piano pattern

TIME	DESCRIPTION	COMMENT
0:00	Clarinet begins with what Messiaen calls his song of a blackbird.	Note the end, with three fast notes and two repeated high notes. This will return.
0:03	Piano has joined.	The piano's chords are actually highly patterned: a repeating, irregular 17-duration rhythm; the harmonies themselves repeat in a 29-chord cycle.
0:08	Cello enters.	Cello plays in slow, irregular rhythm. Pattern is a 15-note melody that repeats continuously. The cello melody sometimes makes the violin and clarinet birdsong melodies difficult to hear.
0:11	Violin begins nightingale song.	Three short notes, then eight fast, high notes; usually followed by 3-note figure:
0:20		Nightingale figure repeats.
0:24	Clarinet begins version 2 of its opening figure.	
0:28		The birds answer back and forth, as piano and cello continue.
1:05	Clarinet begins version 3 of its opening melody.	

2:23	Each instrument plays its characteristic ending.	
2:25	Piano and cello continue.	
2:30		Farewell to blackbird.
2:33		Farewell to nightingale.

II. "VOCALISE, POUR L'ANGE QUI ANNONCE LA FIN DU TEMPS" (Vocalise for the Angel Who Announces the End of Time)

 LG 73

Vocalise

The term **vocalise** is used for a melody that is sung or "vocalized" without words. Sergei Rachmaninoff wrote a famous one for voice, later transcribed for orchestra; in this latter usage the term can indicate the vocal quality of an instrumental piece; in the *Quartet* the song seems to be the one sung by the violin and cello, playing very quietly, with mutes, in a manner that Messiaen specifies as "impalpable, distant." While they play a melody that Messiaen calls quasi-plainchant (see p. 41), the piano plays slow cascades of chords, which he calls "drops of water in a rainbow." The effect is one of timelessness, and the end of their song—the repeated ending, in a decrescendo—really does seem to stop time altogether.

The song is bookended by jagged, powerful, almost terrifying sections, each composed of a series of surprising and contrasting events—certainly the might of the angel. The clarinet includes birdcall elements from the previous movement. (See LG 73, below)

Messiaen's preface says:

> *The first and third parts (very short) evoke the power of this strong angel, with rainbow on his head and clothed in cloud, who places one foot on the sea and one foot on the earth. The "middle," those are the impalpable harmonies of heaven. In the piano, sweet cascades of blue-orange, surrounding the quasi-plainchant of the violin and cello with their distant carillon.*

LISTENING GUIDE 73 | DVD

Messiaen *Quartet for the End of Time,* II. "Vocalise, pour l'Ange qui annonce la fin du Temps" (Vocalise, for the Angel Who Announces the End of Time) 5:02

DATE: January 15, 1941

LISTEN FOR
MELODY: Clarinet recalls birdsong from first movement
HARMONY: Series of quiet "rainbow" chords in piano
FORM: Three-part form, **ABA'**

TEXTURE: Introduction and Postlude sections are short, jagged, and powerful
SCORING: All four instruments; central section, a lyrical melody, played by muted violin and cello

(continued)

TIME	FORM	DESCRIPTION
	Introduction	
0:00	Section 1	Piano crash.
0:04		Clarinet flourish.
0:08		Violin and cello play same line two octaves apart, adding clarinet birdcalls.
0:13	Section 2	Same sequence of events, altered and abbreviated.
0:32	Section 3	Cello and violin rise in a crescendo, leading to trills in violin, cello, clarinet.
0:46		Crash from piano.
		Piano chords—final note, clarinet and piano.
0:55	**Main Section**	Very quiet section that is nearly continuous and very mesmerizing. Regular piano chords, mostly in descending groups, occasionally changing to repeated chords. Muted cello and violin play slow lyrical melody, two octaves apart. Rhythms are irregular but not jarring. Only twice do they pause for a rest.

TIME	FORM	DESCRIPTION
4:17	Ending	Last few notes repeated; even fewer notes, repeated again, even more quietly; silence.
4:36	**Postlude**	Events from Introduction's final section: cello and violin crescendo (now downward), to trills in cello, violin, clarinet.
4:46		Crash from piano.
4:50		Piano chords—final note, clarinet and piano.

LG 74   III. "ABÎME DES OISEAUX" (Abyss of the Birds)

This movement, for solo clarinet, was written while Messiaen and Henri Akoka were prisoners but before they were transferred to the prison camp. Pasquier remembers holding the music for Akoka while he tried to play Messiaen's difficult piece (see above, p. 472). It was conceived in a series of sections that return in varying order; these returns, whether in literal or altered form, are easily recognizable. The movement is marked "Slow, expressive and sad."

Whether or not the version we have in Messiaen's published score is the same as what was played in the open air will probably never be known. As published, "Abyss of the Birds" contains many elements found in the other movements: specific bird-songs (related to the opening movement, and to others), suggestions of harmony (even though the piece is for a solo instrument), and irregular rhythms. The flourish that precedes the second big crescendo (and is heard inverted just before the end) appears also in the "Vocalise" (the clarinet's first sounds) and repeatedly in the "Interlude." This movement may well have served as the germ for the whole piece; or perhaps elements of it were changed when it became part of the *Quartet*, to integrate it into the larger work.

This is the only movement for a single instrument. The two string players, violin and cello, have beautiful solos in the two Praise movements, but there they are accompanied by piano. And there is a movement in unison ("Dance of Fury, for the Seven Trumpets") that is like this movement in being monophonic—but there all the instruments play, always in unison. (See LG 74, below.)

Again, we look to Messiaen's preface:

Clarinet alone. The abyss is Time, with its sadnesses, its weariness. The birds are the opposite of Time; they are our desire for light, for stars, for rainbows and for jubilant song!

LISTENING GUIDE 74 | DVD

Messiaen *Quartet for the End of Time*, III. "Abîme des oiseaux" (Abyss of the Birds)   8:22

DATE: January 15, 1941

LISTEN FOR
MELODY: Reminiscences of birdsong

SCORING : Solo clarinet

TEXTURE: Use of extreme range of the clarinet, with quiet high notes—very difficult to perform

EXPRESSION/DYNAMICS: Intense, very long crescendos, always on the note E

TIME	FORM	DESCRIPTION
0:00	**A.** Lent (slow)	Lyrical melody, whose opening long note (E) is heard three times in the opening phrase.
0:56	(**A**, phrase 2)	Beginning on a high E, a wider range, with diminuendo.
1:22	(**A**, phrase 3)	Beginning very soft and low, a long phrase concluding with music from the opening phrase.
2:42	**B.** Crescendo	Single note (high E) goes very slowly from softest possible sound to loudest. Marked "Without rushing, progressive and powerful."
2:56	**C.** Presque vif, gai, capricieux (Almost fast, gay, capricious)—Pressez (Speed up)	Fast notes, trills, flips; swoop of accelerating notes; recalls clarinet birdsong of "Liturgy of Crystal" (see LG 72).
3:24	**B.** Crescendo	Same crescendo and note as before.

(continued)

TIME	FORM	DESCRIPTION
3:36	**C.** Presque vif; pressez	Similar rhythms and birdcalls; pressez section is longer.
4:00	**D.** Modéré (moderate)	Arpeggio of seven even notes, echoed; then a loud to soft decrescendo; three separate, long notes; and a trill that slows to nothing.
4:54	**A.** Lent (slow)	Opening music returns, beginning an octave lower, and later slightly altered.
7:40	**B.** Crescendo	Same crescendo on high E.
7:56	**D.** Modéré	Arpeggio of seven even notes, echoed; a kind of inversion of earlier Modéré section.
8:07	**C.** Presque vif	Final, brief birdsong.
8:10	**A.** Lent	Four loud notes—same pitches as notes 2 through 5 of piece.

🎧 LG 75   ### IV. "INTERMÈDE" (Interlude)

The fourth movement, for violin, clarinet, and cello, is in some ways the simplest. It has regular phrases, regular meter, and witty alternations of texture. It is a sort of scherzo—a lighthearted relief from the other movements of the work.

This, according to Messiaen, is the movement he composed and rehearsed before the piano arrived at the prison camp, later adding the other movements to this one. But it seems that the clarinet solo ("Abyss of the Birds") already existed, and two of the movements existed in earlier forms and would be arranged for the quartet. So perhaps this piece, now an "Interlude" in the larger piece, was first conceived as a separate work; it lacks most of the complexities of the others, and gives very little sense either of the infinite, or of the end of time. Perhaps, if anything, it represents the regular passage of earthly, mortal time. And it makes a wonderful contrast in the context of the larger work. (See LG 75, p. 485.)

Messiaen's preface reads:

> *A Scherzo, of a more extroverted character than the other movements, but linked to them nonetheless by several melodic reminiscences.*

🎧 LG 76   ### V. "LOUANGE À L'ÉTERNITÉ DE JÉSUS" (Praise to the Eternity of Jesus)

This is a lyrical, meditative movement, of great beauty and length. Like the other Praise song (the last movement), this one is for piano and one other instrument (here it is the cello: the last movement is for violin and piano). Messiaen marks the score "Infinitely slow, ecstatic."

This piece is actually a transcription of a movement from *Fête des belles eaux* (*Festival of the Beautiful Waters*) commissioned from Messiaen by the city of Paris in 1937 to accompany a timed display of fountains in connection with the great International Exposition.

Messiaen *Quartet for the End of Time,*
IV. "Intermède" (Interlude)

1:41

DATE: January 15, 1941

LISTEN FOR
MELODY: Clarinet flourish and birdcall heard in previous movements; regular phrases
RHYTHM/METER: Regular duple rhythm

TEXTURE: Contrast of unison, harmony, and counterpoint
SCORING: Piano is absent

TIME	FORM	DESCRIPTION
	Opening Theme	
0:00	Phrase 1	All instruments in octaves; unusual scale:

Décidé, modéré, un peu vif (♩ = 96 env.)

Violin

Clarinet in B♭

Cello

TIME	FORM	DESCRIPTION
0:05	Phrase 2	Unison continues.
0:10	Repeat opening theme	
0:13	Phrase 1	Louder; switches to harmony.
0:16	Echo of phrase 1	Lower register.
0:18	Clarinet flourish, trills, birdcall	Cello and violin punctuate clarinet flourish.
0:24	Opening theme Phrase 1, varied	Violin and clarinet only.
	Lyrical Section	The violin plays pizzicato below the cello; clarinet has arpeggios.
0:30	Phrase 1: cello	
0:35	Phrase 2: violin	
0:40	Phrase 3: clarinet	
0:47	Clarinet flourish, trills, birdcall	
0:53	Clarinet repeated figure	Cello and violin in octaves, syncopated melody (related to movement VI).
0:59	Answering phrase, extended	Clarinet has lyrical syncopated melody.
1:05	Clarinet repeated figure, taken up by others	
1:08	Clarinet flourish	Three times.

(continued)

TIME	FORM	DESCRIPTION
	Opening Theme	
1:12	Phrase 1	Harmonized.
1:17	Phrase 2	Returns to octaves.
1:28	**Coda**	Three pizzicato notes; trills; glissando with birdcalls; cello pizzicato.

LISTENING GUIDE 76 | DVD

Messiaen *Quartet for the End of Time,*
V. "Louange à l'Éternité de Jésus" (Praise to the Eternity of Jesus)   8:18

DATE: January 15, 1941

LISTEN FOR
MELODY: Slow, high cello melody

HARMONY: Piano plays repeated chords; E major tonality

RHYTHM/METER: Chord changes vary in speed

SCORING: Cello and piano only

EXPRESSION/DYNAMICS: Slow decrescendo at the end

TIME	FORM	DESCRIPTION
	Theme	
0:00	Phrase 1	Cello begins alone (score says "majestic, composed, very expressive"), in tenor register; piano joins with repeated notes (piano has slight accent at each chord change).
1:14	Phrase 2	Begins like phrase 1, but somewhat extended upward and in dynamic shape, crescendo to middle section.
	Middle Section	
2:26	Phrase 1	Begins loud. Cello has same rhythm as previous phrases, but with piano accompaniment. Cello begins phrases with characteristic long-short-short-long rhythm four times, last time extended.
3:47	Phrase 2	New rhythms. Moves downward.
4:33	Phrase 3	Cello has long upward melody, with big crescendo in cello and piano.
	Conclusion	
5:44	Phrase 1	Suddenly very soft. Opening phrase played without vibrato, and with some harmonics, for first six notes; vibrato added thereafter.
7:14	Phrase 2	A kind of echo of what preceded; slow upward notes, fading away to nothing.

This movement is in the key of E major. It has an opening theme of two very long phrases, a central portion of three phrases (whose chords seem to be in the dominant, and whose melodies are in a sense developments of the theme), and a final section, suddenly soft, that returns to the music of the beginning, and disappears into the heights, and into silence. (See LG 76, p. 486.)

The high register of the cello, and the very long phrases, make this piece difficult to play, and perhaps the work's almost-timeless ethereal intent, combined with the audible difficulties of the cello part, have something to do with Messiaen's association with Jesus as the Word ("In the beginning was the Word . . ."). Messiaen's preface tries to explicate this connection:

> *Jesus is considered here in terms of the Word. A grand phrase, infinitely slow, from the cello, magnifies with love and reverence the eternity of this powerful and sweet Word, "whose years will not fail." Majestically the melody unfolds in a sort of tender and sovereign distance. "In the beginning was the Word, and the Word was with God, and the word was God."*

VI. "DANSE DE LA FUREUR, POUR LES SEPT TROMPETTES" (Dance of Fury, for the Seven Trumpets)

♪ LG 77

This energetic piece, all in unison, was called "Fanfare" at the first performance. A fanfare, of course, is a blast of trumpet music to announce something; the later title is a more poetic description of a fanfare, but the fury, and the fanfare effect, were part of the work from the beginning.

As Messiaen himself wrote, the instruments are supposed to sound like gongs and trumpets (see below); they perform in unison throughout. Rhythmically, this piece is predominantly set in phrases with notes of irregular length, each fairly short phrase ending with a longer note. There are just enough notes of extra-short or slightly longer duration to throw off any sense of regularity or of meter. Even when things get going a bit faster, the irregularity persists.

A central section, played quietly ("Distant," says the score), is one of Messiaen's most systematically structured passages. It is based on a series of his non-retrogradable rhythms—patterns of duration that are palindromic, an ordered series of sixteen pitches, which he presents slightly more than seven times. The pitch and rhythm series are of different lengths, and thus never combine in the same way. As a result, everything sounds new, rhapsodic, almost improvised, even though it is actually the working-out of pre-planned shapes. Although it might be possible to notice the palindromic rhythmic patterns, the changing relationship of rhythm to pitch makes it almost impossible to hear that the pitch series is actually repeating over and over. Messiaen does not intend for us to hear these patterns. (See LG 77, p. 488.)

His preface reads:

> *Rhythmically the most characteristic of the series. The four instruments in unison take on aspects of gongs and trumpets (the first six trumpets of the Apocalypse followed by various catastrophes, the trumpet of the seventh angel announcing the completion of the mystery of God). Use of added values, augmented and diminished rhythms, nonretrogradable rhythms. Music of stone, formidable sounding granite; irresistible movement of steel, enormous blocks of purple fury, of frozen intoxication. Listen above all to the terrible fortissimo of the theme in augmentation and changes of register of its different notes, towards the end of the piece.*

Messiaen *Quartet for the End of Time,* VI. "Danse de la fureur, pour les sept trompettes" (Dance of Fury, for the Seven Trumpets) 6:17

DATE: January 15, 1941

LISTEN FOR

MELODY: Recurrent melody based on whole-tone scale; three-note motive based on the "other" whole-tone scale: all chromatic pitches are thus used, perhaps conveying the universal and eternal

FORM: Clearly sectional structure

TEXTURE: Perpetual unison (octaves) throughout

SCORING: All instruments play throughout

TIME	FORM	DESCRIPTION
0:00	**Section 1**	Begins in unison; note irregular patterns: Six phrases, each ending with longer note. Score says "Decided, vigorous, granitic, fairly lively."
0:22	**Section 2**	Begins like section 1 and includes three of its phrases. Has total of five phrases, each ending on long note; notes grow longer and have faster values; toward end, decrescendo.
1:00	**Section 3** (Repeat of 1)	Repeat of section 1, first three phrases soft.
1:23	**Section 4**	Begins like section 1; gradual uses of shorter values, acceleration and crescendo.
	Section 5—Lyrical Section	Less frantic; pianissimo; begins with slightly longer notes:
1:52	Part 1	
2:15	Part 2	Same rhythm as part 1, different notes.
2:41	Transition	Upward rush; four downward cascades in even notes; second and third phrases of section 1, followed by long, low F♯.
	Section 6	Fast notes alternate three times with versions of a loud 3-note "gong" motive ("bronzed, brassy") in piano and clarinet. Rhythms of gong motive different each time, but always consists of shorter note between two others of equal length. Openings of three parts are varied.
2:56	Part 1	1) Begins with opening notes of the piece, but in regular rhythms; gong motive twice.
3:08	Part 2	2) Begins with a downward cascade like those in earlier transition; gong motive six times.
3:25	Part 3	3) Begins, like part 1, with the opening notes of the piece, but in regular rhythms; gong motive eight times—note octave displacements at end.

	Section 7		
3:47	Part 1	Hammered rapid notes.	
3:56	Part 2	Opening notes, in even rhythm, developed.	
4:06	Part 3	Cascades leading to trills.	
4:16	Part 4	Fast notes accelerating and crescendo.	
4:32	Part 5	Upward scale.	
4:36	Part 6	Trills, slowing and crescendo.	

	Section 8		
4:59	Part 1	Very loud, terrifying, stretched version of opening four phrases, with octave displacements. "Terrible and powerful," says the score.	
5:48	Part 2	Lyrical section reprised.	
5:53	Part 3	Four cascades.	
5:59	Part 4	Six even notes, fortissimo, and final F♯.	

VII. "FOUILLIS D'ARCS-EN-CIEL, POUR L'ANGE QUI ANNONCE LA FIN DU TEMPS" (Tumult of Rainbows, for the Angel Who Announces the End of Time)

🎧 LG 78

This movement can be considered the climax of the piece. It depicts the appearance of the angel who announces of the end of time. The work brings back music from the second movement and features an alternation between a slow lyrical theme (the first theme)—which is heard four times, in a sort of series of variations—and a much livelier, percussive theme (the second theme).

The first theme, played by cello and piano at the opening of this movement, is reminiscent of a theme in the second movement—same tempo, same regular chords in the piano, similar rhythms in the melody. It is interesting to note that in both cases the subject is rainbows (in the second movement, "drops of water in a rainbow").

The second theme, featuring a quicker tempo and regular sixteenth-note rhythm, is a regularization of the opening piano music of the second movement; and the continuation of the piece alternates these two themes; much of their harmonic materials is made by quotations and rearrangements of the chords in the second movement, as Messiaen himself points out in his *Technique of My Musical Language*. The listener is probably not supposed to notice the specific borrowings but to have a sense of a similar harmonic sound, and perhaps a subtle sense of familiarity that helps to make the disparate movements of the piece fit together.

The two themes are treated somewhat differently. The first, quasi-lyrical theme recurs as a series of variations, with the theme almost always fully intact, the variations having to do with the accompaniment. The second theme, when it reappears, is treated to a more Beethovenian development, with extensions, repetitions at different pitch levels, and other similar techniques. (See LG 78, p. 490.)

The overall result is that the high level of structure sounds intellectual, while in fact the piece arrives at an emotional climax, a sort of dizziness of colors and superhuman sounds that Messiaen describes in his preface:

Ⓢ Messiaen: *Quartet for the End of Time,* "Vocalise"

Ⓢ Messiaen: *Quartet for the End of Time,* "Tumult of Rainbows"

Here certain passages from the second movement return. The powerful angel returns, and above all the rainbow which covers him (the rainbow, symbol of peace, of wisdom, and of all vibration of sound and light).—In my dreams, I hear and see chords and melodies arranged, understood colors and forms; then, after this transitory stage, I pass into the unreal and suffer with ecstasy a dizziness, a spinning superhuman mixture of sounds and colors. These swords of fire, these flows of blue-orange lava, these brusque stars: there is the tumult, there are the rainbows!

LISTENING GUIDE 78   ⓢ | DVD

Messiaen *Quartet for the End of Time,*
VII. "Fouillis d'arcs-en-ciel, pour l'Ange qui annonce la fin du Temps" (Tumult of Rainbows, for the Angel Who Announces the End of Time)   7:19

DATE: January 15, 1941

LISTEN FOR

FORM: Alternation of two main themes

THEMES: First theme, a lyrical melody, recurs in varied forms. Second theme, more active, is developed differently each time

SCORING: All four instruments. Accumulation of musical elements builds up to almost unbearable complexity and volume

TIME	FORM	DESCRIPTION
0:00	Main theme 1	Three phrases in cello, each beginning with similar rhythm and having similar contour. Piano provides accompaniment in repeated chords in different registers:

1:32	Secondary theme 1	(a) Percussive repeated notes; piano begins with opening riff of second movement; (b) continued regular rhythm; (c) piano flourishes followed by trills (during which cello provides glissandos); (d) regular piano chords, slowing down.
2:13	Main theme 2	Lyrical section reprised; theme now in violin; piano chords as before; clarinet provides counter-melody.
3:44	Secondary theme 2	All instruments participate; this version is more extended, ends with quick rhythmic alternation between piano and others.

4:26	Main theme 3, phrase 1	Piano and violin flourishes precede clarinet playing first phrase of theme, with cello *col legno* (striking the strings with wood of the bow).
4:34	Main theme 3, phrase 2	Piano and violin flourishes precede clarinet playing second phrase of the theme, with cello *col legno* and continued violin flourishes.
4:58	Secondary theme 3	Climactic section includes more references than we can hear: a commentary on secondary theme in piano (from earlier in the piece), plus a rhythm from first theme in violin. Piano swoops with violin rhythm expanded to clarinet and cello. Trills and glissandos alternating with chords moving up (instruments) and down (piano). Piano continues with music adapted from this movement, with much other material superimposed, including clarinet flourishes, backward and forward, building to huge fortissimo.
5:22	Main theme 4	First theme played by violin, clarinet, and cello using trilled notes, very loud; piano flourishes accompany.
5:41	Coda	Beginning of secondary theme; five squawks, and a crash.

VIII. "LOUANGE À L'IMMORTALITÉ DE JÉSUS" (Praise to the Immortality of Jesus)

 LG 79

Like the fifth movement, this is a very slow—and very long—solo accompanied by regular piano chords. Here the violin, in four exceedingly long phrases, twice rises to a high point. At the end of the fourth phrase, the piano and the violin, both quite high in their ranges, fade away into an eternal, timeless silence.

Again, like the fifth movement, this piece is transcribed from an earlier work: in this case, the *Diptyque* for organ (1930). The "Louange" is in a different key than the *Diptyque*, and instead of sustained organ chords, Messiaen wrote mesmerizing double chords for the piano.

The score is marked "Extremely slow and tender, ecstatic"; "ecstatic" was also applied to the fifth movement. These two Praises, each concerned with an aspect of Jesus, are also concerned with the aspect of time. At the beginning of this movement, the violin part is marked "expressive, paradisiacal." We can extrapolate from his writings that this so-called paradise stands outside of this world and outside of time as well—representing for Messiaen the twin rubrics of the eternal and the timeless. The second and fourth violin phrases are marked "with love." One wonders how the violinist can make this clear.

Messiaen often spoke about his desire to get away from the regular rhythmic beats of traditional music—birdsong, Indian rhythms, and other techniques helped him to do so. Here is a piece, however, with an absolutely regular repeated pattern (in the piano). But the pattern becomes so much a part of the background, of the universe of the sound in this movement, that it somehow allows us to consider a time without time—perhaps an End of Time. (See LG 79, p. 492.)

Messiaen's preface closes with this description:

A broad solo for violin, matching the cello solo of the 5th movement. Why this second Praise? It concerns in particular the second aspect of Jesus, to Jesus-Man, to the Word made flesh, resurrected immortal to communicate his life to us. It is all love. Its slow ascent to very high range is the ascent of man towards his God, of the child of God towards his Father, of the creature made divine towards Paradise.

LISTENING GUIDE 79 | DVD

Messiaen *Quartet for the End of Time,* VIII. "Louange à l'Immortalité de Jésus" (Praise to the Immortality of Jesus)   6:27

DATE: January 15, 1941

LISTEN FOR

MELODY: Four phrases; violin solo in very long phrases

HARMONY: Mesmerizing piano harmonies, slowly changing; almost ecstatic

SCORING: Violin and piano only

EXPRESSION: Gradual ascent to very high range

TIME	FORM	DESCRIPTION
0:00	Phrase 1, part 1	Lyrical phrase over a single piano harmony.
0:37	Phrase 1, part 2	Same rhythmic profile as first half-phrase; piano harmony changes.
1:12	Phrase 2	Long phrase gradually soaring to very high notes, gradually descending.
2:56	Phrase 3	Begins softly. Music same as first phrase, in two similar halves.
4:08	Phrase 4	Begins *mezzo forte*, with same music as second phrase, soaring higher and higher—but this time does not descend. Movement ends as quietly as possible.

How Did It Go?

Obviously, there weren't any "reviews" of the concert, but we do have comments from two prisoners who were in the audience at the time. The first comment, written in 1942, one year after the first performance, describes the attitude of the performers:

> The musicians, next to the young master, are bent over their instruments. Étienne Pasquier, in a tender gesture, caresses his cello. Jean Le Boulaire prepares his violin, and Henri Akoka, his clarinet resting on his knees, looks around the room and smiles at his comrades. He already knows that when he returns to his barrack his friends will mock him for a long time, because Olivier Messiaen has just stated that the clarinet constitutes *l'élément pittoresque*"("the picturesque element"). . . . Perhaps a new nickname will stay with him after this premiere, *"Monsieur Pitto."*

The second comment comes from one Charles Jourdanet, who recalled the premiere sixty years later:

> A cello solo, then a grand violin solo with a long ascent toward the high register: these are the final notes that resonate throughout the "concert hall" as well as through the hearts of the listeners. There is silence . . . no immediate applause. Members of the audience . . . approach the composer on stage. Outside, it is minus twenty degrees [Celsius]. Inside, despite several primitive heaters, winter military apparel (hoods, helmets, and mufflers) is everywhere. The temperature cannot be more than five degrees. . . .

On this memorable day for the several hundred spectators so honored to witness not just a musical premiere but a world premiere, it was daily life as usual. At six o'clock: distribution of ersatz [coffee substitute]. From eight o'clock to noon: the prisoners attend to their assigned duties. At noon: cabbage soup for all. From one to four o'clock: various chores. At five o'clock: more ersatz is distributed, along with a fifth of a loaf of black bread with a little *fromage blanc* and quite a bit of grease. . . . Finally, at six o'clock: the concert—in barrack 27—which, for several months, has served as "the theater." . . . On this cold night in January 1941, seated on benches in barrack 27, we listened, some moved by the unexpected fervor, others agitated by rhythms and sonorities to which they were unaccustomed—to the creation of what Messiaen called a "great act of faith."

Everybody understood that they were hearing something significant, something with deep meaning, at least for its composer, and that it included a variety of sounds, some lyrical and tender, others savage and dissonant; it was a music that few if any of them had ever heard the likes of before.

There was apparently a moment of silence at the end of the performance. (Could they be sure it was over? The final piece, even if they had carefully kept track of the movements, ends so quietly that one can't be sure.) And then there was applause, first hesitant, and then loud. Prisoners and others crowded around, mostly wanting to see, or congratulate, or speak with Messiaen.

AFTERWARD

Less than a month after the *Quartet*'s premiere, Messiaen was liberated from the camp and returned to Paris, where he was reunited with his wife, the violinist Claire Delbos, and their son. After recuperating for a time from his captivity, he set about the activities that would occupy him for the rest of his life: teaching, playing at La Trinité, and composing. He was appointed to teach harmony at the Paris Conservatory, where he continued to serve for many years; it might seem odd that his appointment was in harmony, not in composition—but that post had become free, owing to the effects of anti-Jewish regulations. Messiaen's wife grew increasingly unstable (she had lost her memory after an operation) and had to be institutionalized, leaving Messiaen to care for young Pascal.

Messiaen

As to the other members of the quartet, Pasquier left Stalag VIIIA at the same time as Messiaen, both being returned to France because of their professional status. He returned to his string trio, with which he performed for many years, and to his wife, the singer Suzanne Gouts, and once again played in the orchestra of the Paris Opera.

Pasquier

Akoka was about to leave the camp in the group with Pasquier and Messiaen but was detained because he was Jewish. He had earlier tried to escape and had asked Messiaen to come along with him, but the composer replied that he had been put in prison by God. On a second attempt, Akoka succeeded in escaping; along with some other prisoners, he had made his way some 350 kilometers, almost to the Czech border, when they were caught and returned to the camp. Akoka was put into solitary confinement, where he characteristically looked on the bright side by saying that at least it was well heated, and people left him alone.

Akoka

Akoka's subsequent adventures involved passing himself off as an Arab, a further escape by leaping from a train, a clandestine visit to Paris, and getting to the Free Zone, where he played in the Marseille Radio Orchestra until 1943. He survived the difficulties of the war (although his father, Abraham Akoka, was

tragically deported and put to death at Auschwitz). He lived until 1975. His clarinet never left his side.

Le Boulaire   Le Boulaire, who was not among those released as musicians (he escaped in 1941), eventually had a successful career in film and television as the actor Jean Lanier.

In Paris, Messiaen prepared his *Quartet* for publication, and in 1942 the publisher Durand brought out the score. It is hard to know what changes, if any, Messiaen adopted between the premiere at Stalag VIIIA and the publication. A piece written for a specific occasion with unusual circumstances may not be the piece one would compose if everything were possible. However, there is little evidence that much had changed. The titles of two of the movements were altered: what was originally called "Fanfare" became "Dance of Fury for the Seven Trumpets"; and the "Second Praise to the Eternity of Jesus" became "Praise to the Immortality of Jesus."

Messiaen added a preface in three parts: an introduction in which he gives the background of the piece, and descriptions and explications of the various movements (these indications are translated in the discussion of the music above; see pp. 479–91); a "Little Theory of My Rhythmic Language," in which he introduces his rhythmic ideas (also discussed above; see pp. 476–77); and finally, some brief advice to performers. Mostly he advises performers to read his commentaries, to play the music carefully, but not to fear exaggerating the nuances of tempo and dynamics.

Paris premiere   The Paris premiere of the work was given on June 24, 1941, after the score was already at the printer's. It was part of a concert of Messiaen's music celebrating his return to Paris. Given at the Théâtre des Mathurins (see Figure 17.11), near the church of the Madeleine (see Figure III.5), the concert featured the *Quartet* along with some of his other chamber music for piano with violin or voice and for solo piano. Messiaen was the pianist, and Étienne Pasquier and his brother the violinist Jean Pasquier joined clarinetist André Vacellier for the *Quartet*. As he had done in Stalag VIIIA, Messiaen gave brief spoken introductions to each of the movements. These commentaries did not please all the listeners, some feeling that they interrupted the continuity and that they were too religious in tone.

The *Quartet* Then and Now

What does it mean for music to express religious truths? What does it mean, in fact, for music to "express" anything at all? Most such expression is surely by association. When we hear slow organ music we sometimes think of a church, because that is where many of us have heard an organ. But there is nothing inherently religious in the sound of the organ itself; it is by association that we connect the two.

There are of course some things that we "get" right away when listening to music: a piece can sound fast and smooth, fast and irregular; slow; dissonant; harmonious; regular in rhythm or jagged. Each of these characteristics may well convey some emotional content too—but not always the same feeling to each person. Slow for me may be sad; for you it may be romantic. Loud and fast may be threatening, or it may be triumphant.

It is far from clear that music's message can be precise. This is perhaps why Messiaen chose to speak about each of the movements at the first performance (and at the Paris premiere), why he gives them such expressive titles, and why he writes poetic commentaries in the preface to the score. When we think of these titles, when we muse on the mysteries that fascinated Messiaen, it may well be that the music succeeds in making its religious message felt, in part because Messiaen made the effort to be precise. Much as Berlioz's *Fantastic Symphony* takes on particular meanings when we know the related story, this music might also have a different effect if we were not aware of Messiaen's message. But Messiaen was supremely confident that music *could* express the divine, a belief he had in common with Leoninus and Perotinus, whose swirling sounds filled the Cathedral of Notre Dame eight centuries earlier.

It may seem paradoxical that such a mystical composer should also be so systematic, experimental, and full of patterns and repeating elements; and yet mysticism is as full of pattern as anything else—pattern and repetition are characteristic of liturgy and might be perfectly normal in a "mystical" composer. Inspired improvisation is always based on acquired technique; it is not a matter of letting the music write itself in a kind of divine frenzy—Messiaen was always very controlled, and his treatise called *Technique of My Music Language* (1944) includes many examples from the *Quartet* in which he demonstrates not theological truths but rather musical techniques: modes, scales, rhythms, melodic formulas, "chord on the dominant with appoggiatura," and other technical matters. That the two should go together so well is one of the mysteries (and glories) of classical music.

The title of the treatise includes the telling word "my": it is about his own musical language. His music is his alone; this is of course also true of other composers and their music, and it says something about the expanding landscape of musical style in the twentieth century to consider how different Berg, Stravinsky, and Messiaen are, compared to, say, Beethoven, Mozart and Schubert.

There is nevertheless something French about Messiaen's music. He was a great admirer of the French composers called **Impressionists** (Claude Debussy, Maurice Ravel, and others); the characteristic sound he invents, the intense association of sound with color, and his evocation of nature reflects his French musical heritage.

Music suffered in wartime: the Nazis banned "degenerate" music, including jazz; they limited performances of French music even in France; and they outlawed Jewish composers. At the same time, they cherished Germany's status as the home to many great composers. They loved classical music; perhaps that explains in part why Messiaen was encouraged to compose in the camp.

Ⓢ Debussy: "Jeux de vagues," from *La mer* (*The Sea*)

The *Quartet*, written by one of the quietest of composers, has had a successful career. It is a milestone of twentieth-century music, and for many listeners it represents serenity in the midst of the horrors of the Second World War, an expression of hope for fellow prisoners, a reminder of optimism in a context that saw the devastation of Europe and the extermination of millions of its citizens. It is spiritual music in an age of secularism. For Messiaen, this work was not about war but about peace; he moved calmly forward in the midst of war and captivity, seeking to create a world where time and sound were stretched to their limits, to depict a rainbow, to make us experience the End of Time. In the sense that his *Quartet* has an enduring presence among us, he succeeded.

Chapter Review

Summary of Musical Styles

Olivier Messiaen's style is a combination of the rhapsodic and the systematic. Often what sounds improvised is the result of highly organized structures. Chief characteristics of his music, here and elsewhere, include

- **Birdsong.** Messiaen loved and studied birds his entire life, and he transcribed and included their song in his music. In the *Quartet*, the blackbird and the nightingale, played by clarinet and violin, are chief characters in the first movement, and the clarinet blackbird returns in the third and fourth movements.

- **Modes.** Messiaen is especially interested in **modes of limited transposition**, patterns of intervals that are symmetrical and can be replicated only a few times. Examples are the **whole-tone scale** (which exists in just two transpositions) and the **octatonic scale** (alternating whole steps and half steps—four possible transpositions). The use of these scales to make melodies and harmonies gives Messiaen's music much of its special character.

Rhythmic patterns. Two ideas important to Messiaen contribute to the perpetual interest of his rhythm, owing to its frequent irregularity:

- **Added-value rhythms** is the process of inserting a single short note or rest into an otherwise regular rhythmic pattern, such as ♩ ♩ ♪♩ ♩

- **Nonretrogradable rhythms** are patterns of rhythm that are symmetrical, with a central note-value surrounded on each side by values of equal length, making the rhythm read the same forward as backward. An example is ♩. ♪ ♩. ♪ ♩. Such rhythmic patterns are found in the "Danse de la fureur" and in other movements.

The overall mood of Messiaen's is rhapsodic and improvisatory-sounding. Much of the systematic compositional procedure is designed more to help the composer achieve his effects than to be heard by the listener.

ⓢ Multimedia Resources and Review Materials on StudySpace

Visit wwnorton.com/studyspace for review of Chapter 17.

What Do You Know?

Check the facts for this chapter. Take the online **Quiz**.

What Do You Hear?

Listening Quizzes and **Music Activities** will help you understand the musical works in this chapter.

🎙 Author Videos

- The nightingale and the blackbird in "Liturgie de cristal," from Messiaen's *Quartet for the End of Time*

Interactive Listening Guides

LG 72 Messiaen: *Quartet for the End of Time*, I. "Liturgie de cristal" (Liturgy of Crystal)

LG 73 Messiaen: *Quartet for the End of Time*, II. "Vocalise, pour l'Ange qui annonce la fin du Temps" (Vocalise, for the Angel Who Announces the End of Time)

LG 74 Messiaen: *Quartet for the End of Time*, III. "Abîme des oiseaux" (Abyss of the Birds)

LG 75 Messiaen: *Quartet for the End of Time*, IV. "Intermède" (Interlude)

LG 76 Messiaen: *Quartet for the End of Time*, V. "Louange à l'Éternité de Jésus" (Praise to the Eternity of Jesus)

LG 77 Messiaen: *Quartet for the End of Time*, VI. "Danse de la fureur, pour les sept trompettes" (Dance of Fury, for the Seven Trumpets)

LG 78 Messiaen: *Quartet for the End of Time*, VII. "Fouillis d'arcs-en-ciel, pour l'Ange qui annonce la fin du Temps" (Tumult of Rainbows, for the Angel Who Announces the End of Time)

LG 79 Messiaen: *Quartet for the End of Time*, VIII. "Louange à l'Immortalité de Jésus" (Praise to the Immortality of Jesus)

Flashcards (Terms to Know)

added-value rhythms	nonretrogradable rhythms
glissando	octatonic scale
harmonics	vocalise
Impressionists	whole-tone scale
modes of limited transposition	

CHAPTER 18

THURSDAY, SEPTEMBER 26, 1957, NEW YORK:

Leonard Bernstein's *West Side Story*

 CORE REPERTOIRE	 **AUTHOR VIDEOS**	
▪ **LG 80** Prologue ▪ **LG 81** "Jet Song" ▪ **LG 82** "Dance at the Gym" ▪ **LG 83** "Tonight" ▪ **LG 84** "America"	▪ Meter and rhythms in "America," from Bernstein's *West Side Story*	

Introduction

> *"As ugly as the city jungles and also pathetic, tender and forgiving. . . . Everything contributes to the total impression of wildness, ecstasy and anguish."*
>
> — Brooks Atkinson, *The New York Times*, September 27, 1957

Because *West Side Story* now holds an important place in popular culture, and its songs have become standards, we easily forget that its premiere was a watershed in the history of the Broadway musical: it joined music, dance, and story seamlessly; it showed tragedy as well as comedy on stage; and it prepared the way for musicals to address serious, contemporary themes. Its composer, Leonard Bernstein, wanted to bridge the gap between popular culture and the classical music that he loved. In fact, it was the Hollywood film version of *West Side Story*, starring the then-unknown Natalie Wood, that made the musical into a runaway international hit.

West Side Story explores the twin themes of ethnic conflict and urban violence, both pervasive issues of the 1950s. It centers on two fictional New York gangs, the Jets and the Sharks. The Jets pride themselves on being all-American guys (although they might strike us as defiant punks, and they are surely the children or grandchildren of immigrants), whereas the Sharks, as Puerto Ricans, are considered outsiders (even though Puerto Rico is a self-governing territory of the United States) and second-class citizens. At the time, the Puerto Rican population in the continental United States was large and growing, especially in New York City, where cheap airfares and a supportive community made immigration possible and attractive.

Themes

The music that Bernstein wrote for the rival gangs reflects these ethnic differences and tensions. The Sharks have a laid-back, Latin-influenced way of singing that contrasts with the Jets' edgier, in-your-face style. In the famous Latin-rhythm "I want to be in America," the Puerto Rican girls poke fun at the immigrant's desire to assimilate. On the other hand, the lovers Tony and Maria blend their "American" and Puerto Rican musical identities in the beautiful **ballad** "Tonight." (Ballads have a narrative content and are often strophic.) The all-white nature of the conflict is curiously at odds with the fact that a lot of the music is specifically African American in origin (blues, rock).

Ⓢ Bernstein: *West Side Story*, "America"

Ⓢ Bernstein: *West Side Story*, "Tonight"

The musical is an imaginative adaptation, or even a transformation, of Shakespeare's play *Romeo and Juliet*: two warring families bring tragedy on themselves after a member of one clan falls in love with a member of the other. In the case of *West Side Story*, Tony and Maria as individuals make personal what groups can't, and their story is as touching today as it was in 1957, and as Romeo and Juliet's was centuries ago.

Questions of assimilation, colonial domination, racial tension, and gang violence might seem unappealing for a Broadway musical, and the subject matter of *West Side Story* certainly shocked some of the original audience. Any sort of cultural stereotype is risky, and the Puerto Rican (as well as the "juvenile delinquent") characterizations, like many contemporaneous Latin stereotypes, are not accurate representations of Puerto Rican life, either in Puerto Rico or in New York.

The music of *West Side Story*, like its plot, is unmistakably American: Bernstein included not only popular styles, jazz, and a hint of rock 'n' roll, but also, in a nod to the "other" America, a marvelous array of Latin beats, including Hispanic musical styles and dance rhythms. The composer's distinctive classical style suffuses tunes such as "Tonight" and "Maria," which soar with operatic ecstasy. The marriage of art music and popular idioms that Bernstein set out to create more than half a century ago has stood the test of time and become, like all the other pieces we have considered in this book, a classic for the ages.

The Setting

POSTWAR AMERICA

The 1950s   The 1950s is often seen as an era of consensus and prosperity, fueled by a booming economy and the rapid expansion of America's middle class. But it was also a decade of change, anxiety, and conflict that set the stage for the social unrest of the 1960s. Two events that coincided with the premiere of *West Side Story* illustrate the challenges that confronted American society at home and abroad: one day before the show opened in New York, President Dwight D. Eisenhower called out the National Guard to protect African American students who were seeking to integrate Little Rock High School in Arkansas (see Figure 18.1); and eight days after the premiere the Soviet Union launched Sputnik, the first satellite to orbit the Earth, setting off a "space race" with the United States and a wave of paranoia about Russian technological and military dominance (see Figure 18.2).

Cold War   The escalating Cold War between the two major world powers, and the everpresent threat of nuclear confrontation, colored much of American life. Government officials and civil defense organizations urged citizens to prepare for the worst by building bomb shelters in their backyards. The House Un-American Activities Committee had launched an inquisition into the presence of communist spies and sympathizers on American soil. Although later discredited, the practice of making accusations of disloyalty, subversion, or treason without proper regard for evidence—dubbed "McCarthyism" after the communist-hunting Senator

FIG. 18.1 Nine African American students, the first to enroll at Little Rock's Central High School, escorted by National Guard in 1957.

Joseph McCarthy—tainted the lives of countless people, including Leonard Bernstein's colleague Jerome Robbins.

Americans' feelings of fear and insecurity were exacerbated by the poisonous legacy of racism. African Americans, heartened by the desegregation of the armed forces and baseball after World War II, pursued the struggle for civil rights in courtrooms and in the streets. The Supreme Court's landmark decision in *Brown v. Board of Education* (1954), which struck down state laws institutionalizing racial segregation in schools, sparked white backlash in Little Rock and many other cities. The budding civil rights movement had not yet come to embrace Puerto Ricans and other Hispanics, who constituted a sizable segment of the American population. But by the late 1950s the United States was well on its way to becoming a truly multicultural nation and casting off its recent isolationism.

As often happens in times of change and stress, many people turned to the conventional, feel-good entertainment promulgated by the mass media. *Leave It to Beaver*, a popular sitcom about an average, middle-class suburban family, premiered on CBS Television, and the quintessentially escapist film *Around the World in 80 Days* won an Oscar for best picture. The mesmerizing appeal of **rock 'n' roll**—a blend of black and white traditions of popular music—became clear in 1956, when Elvis Presley (see Figure 18.3) topped the charts with "Heartbreak Hotel." But most popular music was of a more traditional kind, with verses, an orchestral accompaniment, and voices that might be suitable for the Broadway stage or opera (see *Billboard*'s Top Songs, 1955 and 1956, p. 502).

Still, the seismic shift in time-honored cultural values left many Americans feeling nervous and defensive. Prejudices long associated with African Americans and other ethnic minorities gave rise to irrational fears that the explosive growth of popular music would promote juvenile delinquency—meaning young men (and women) skipping school and being antisocial—or threaten the American way of life. (The same fears had been stirred up in the past by ragtime and **jazz**.) Concerned citizens responded by stepping up the campaign to win more fans for classical music. No one was more visibly associated with this effort than Leonard Bernstein, who in 1958 began televising his brilliant "Young People's Concerts." Combining performances and lectures, these classical music programs sought to build a bridge between "high-brow" and "low-brow" culture in much the same way that *West Side Story* did.

NEW YORK IN 1957

The Czech composer Antonín Dvořák, himself a notable popularizer, might well have recognized much of New York more than sixty years after he wrote his *New World* Symphony. The city was bigger, of course, but still filled with people from all over the world—especially European immigrants. (Puerto

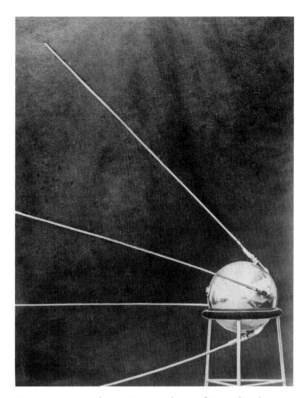

FIG. 18.2   An October 1957 press photo of Sputnik I, the Soviet satellite, displaying its four antennae, before its launch into space as the first satellite to orbit the Earth.

FIG. 18.3   Elvis Presley, 1957.

Billboard's Top Songs, 1955 and 1956

1955

1. "Cherry Pink and Apple Blossom White," Perez Prado
2. "Sincerely," McGuire Sisters
3. "Rock Around the Clock," Bill Haley & His Comets
4. "Sixteen Tons," "Tennessee" Ernie Ford
5. "Love Is a Many-Splendored Thing," Four Aces
6. "The Yellow Rose of Texas," Mitch Miller
7. "The Ballad of Davy Crockett," Bill Hayes
8. "Autumn Leaves," Roger Williams
9. "Let Me Go, Lover," Joan Weber
10. "Dance with Me Henry," Georgia Gibbs

1956

1. "Don't Be Cruel," Elvis Presley
2. "Hound Dog," Elvis Presley
3. "Singing the Blues," Guy Mitchell
4. "The Wayward Wind," Gogi Grant
5. "Heartbreak Hotel," Elvis Presley
6. "Rock and Roll Waltz," Kay Starr
7. "The Poor People of Paris," Les Baxter
8. "Memories Are Made of This," Dean Martin
9. "Love Me Tender," Elvis Presley
10. "My Prayer," The Platters

Ricans didn't start arriving in significant numbers until after the Spanish-American War in 1898.) It had maintained its standing as a capital of finance and of the arts. The Metropolitan Opera was still going strong; the New York Philharmonic was still giving splendid concerts in Carnegie Hall (Lincoln Center for the Performing Arts would not be built until the 1960s; the filming of *West Side Story* in the precise future location of Lincoln Center delayed its construction); and the Statue of Liberty, symbol of freedom and democracy, continued to look protectively over the city's "huddled masses."

FIG. 18.4 A photo, possibly staged, of a New York street gang bragging to a potential new member. Photo by Carl Purcell, about 1955.

Another thing that hadn't changed very much since the 1890s was the problem of street gangs. Urban culture—with its crowding, poverty, and difficult assimilation of immigrants—often led to street crime. Gangs engaged in turf warfare and fights called "rumbles," using weapons like switchblade knives and "zip guns" (homemade firearms). Drugs, especially heroin, would soon change the nature of gang warfare; but for now, violence was mostly about territory and ethnicity; gangs were primarily composed of young men of the same ethnic background (see Figure 18.4).

Ethnic rivalries played themselves out in a healthier way on the city's athletic fields. Sports were one of the great levelers in postwar America: African Americans, Hispanics—almost anybody with talent and drive—could participate. In 1957 there were three professional baseball teams in New York City: Whitey Ford, Yogi Berra, and Mickey Mantle were playing for the Yankees (they lost the 1957 World Series to the Milwaukee Braves); Dusty Rhodes and Willie Mays for the Giants; and Johnny Podres, Roy Campanella, and Gil Hodges for the Brooklyn Dodgers. At the end of the season, however, the Dodgers moved to Los Angeles and the Giants to San Francisco, leaving New York a one-team town for several years.

BROADWAY MUSICALS

Despite the growing popularity of movies, the professional theaters on or near Broadway continued to thrive by offering a variety of theatrical and musical entertainment, which often spun off into films, touring shows, original-cast record albums, and hit singles. In the same way that opera is indigenous to Italy, the Broadway musical is a fundamentally American creation that evolved from a long tradition of music in the theater.

FIG. 18.5 Cast members in a scene from the stage production of Rodgers and Hammerstein's musical *Oklahoma!*

A **Broadway musical**, in its classic form after 1940, is a play with music and dance in which the music is integrated into the action and the meaning of the play, and the songs, like opera arias, are utterances of the characters, sometimes of their inner feelings. *Oklahoma!* (1943; see Figure 18.5) is an historic example of the integrated musical. In that show, songs were used to advance the action by depicting someone's character ("I Cain't Say No"), by causing something to happen (Dream Sequence), or by having something happen during the song. This was the conceptual structure for *West Side Story* as well.

The songs in musicals are in a popular vein, designed—so the producers hope—to become instant favorites. The prevailing styles of the time—for example, Latin rhythms, rock, folk music, or Motown—have often been at the center of musicals. Although all musicals feature singing—and occasionally a musical is sung all the way through, without spoken dialogue (*Jesus Christ Superstar, Evita, Rent*)—musical theater often avoids adopting the styles or voices of opera.

Dance is often an important element in Broadway musicals. Sometimes the plot explicitly calls for the characters to break into dance, as in the dance-lesson number "Shall We Dance?" from the 1951 musical *The King and I*. More often, dance represents something that the composer and librettist choose not to put into words, like the Dream Sequence choreographed by Agnes de Mille in *Oklahoma!* or the scene-setting Prologue in *West Side Story*, which we'll look at more closely later on.

Dance

Broadway musicals typically begin with an overture and include a number of songs (one or two of which return later in the show as theme songs), some purely instrumental music for dance, and incidental music that leads up to a song while the characters converse. (See Numbers in *West Side Story*, p. 504.) The organization of a musical is similar to that of a Handel or Mozart opera, where speech (or, in earlier opera, recitative) advances the plot, and song reflects the emotions.

Broadway musicals are collaborations involving a lot of people. Typically there are three separate creative roles: the author (who writes the **book**—the play and its spoken lines), the **lyricist** (who writes the **lyrics**—the words to the songs), and the composer (who writes the music); sometimes a single person fulfills more than one of these functions. *West Side Story* is unusual in that the **choreographer** (creator and arranger of the dance and movement) was one of the principal creators.

Book and lyrics

Choreographer

The **producer** raises money to pay for the book, lyrics, and music. The producer (one person or a group of investors) also pays for sets and costumes, rehearsals,

Producer

Numbers in *West Side Story*

Act 1

Prologue (instrumental)
"Jet Song"
"Something's Coming"
"Dance at the Gym"
"Maria"
"Tonight"
"America"
"Cool"
"One Hand, One Heart"
"Tonight" (quintet and chorus)
"The Rumble" (instrumental)

Act II

"I Feel Pretty"
"Somewhere" (song and dance)
"Gee, Officer Krupke"
"A Boy Like That / I Have a Love"
Taunting Scene (instrumental)
Finale

changes to the show, out-of-town tryouts, publicity, theater rental, and many other items before a show can open and, with luck and talent, repay its investors. Because producers hold the purse strings and can stop a show in its tracks, they have a good deal of input as to which story is chosen, who writes and composes the music, and who is cast. They often make a significant contribution to the look and feel of a show.

Although Broadway had produced serious musicals before—*Show Boat* (1927), *Oklahoma!* (1943), and *Carousel* (1945) are a few examples—and *South Pacific* (1949) had centered on a condemnation of racial prejudice, *West Side Story* was different. What made the musical risky, in part, was that it brought it home—to an American location—while also portraying a very violent street environment. No one was quite sure how it would fare.

WRITING AND PRODUCING THE SHOW

Genesis of the show

West Side Story began with a telephone call between the choreographer Jerome Robbins and the composer Leonard Bernstein in January 1949. Robbins wanted to create an updated version of Shakespeare's *Romeo and Juliet,* set in New York City and featuring rival factions in an urban neighborhood. His original idea was to juxtapose Eastern European Jews and Irish Catholics living on New York's Lower East Side. It was after eight years, and many changes, that *West Side Story*, with its revised location—featuring gangs of "American" and Puerto Rican teenagers on the Upper West Side—opened on Broadway.

Bernstein had worked with Robbins before, and they agreed on Arthur Laurents as the author for the book. Laurents had written Broadway plays, including one called *Home of the Brave,* about anti-Semitism in the army. He knew about prejudice, and he knew about Broadway (see biography, p. 505). So did Stephen

ArtHur Laurents (1918–2011)

Laurents, the son of a lawyer and a former teacher, was born in Brooklyn, New York. After graduating from Cornell University, he began writing radio dramas. During World War II, he scripted military training films in Queens, and wrote for a military radio program. In 1945 his *Home of the Brave,* a play about anti-Semitism in the army, opened on Broadway and ran for a paltry sixty-nine performances. Another flop, *The Bird Cage* (1950), had only twenty-one performances. But he scored a success with his 1952 *The Time of the Cuckoo,* which was later adapted as a musical in *Do I Hear a Waltz?* with Stephen Sondheim's lyrics and Richard Rodgers's music.

Laurents wrote the books for *West Side Story* and *Gypsy* (a star vehicle for Ethel Merman, again with Robbins and Sondheim, music by Jule Styne). Later shows included *Hallelujah Baby!* and *La Cage aux Folles.*

Laurents also wrote Hollywood films. During the 1950s, a brush with the House Un-American Activities Committee briefly affected his ability to work in films: he refused to name people who might be members of the communist party, and was later appalled at Jerome Robbins for doing so.

Laurents's novel *The Turning Point* became a successful film. In 2000, at age eighty-two, he wrote a frank and engaging memoir, *Original Story By,* and in 2009 he returned to Broadway to direct an acclaimed revival of *West Side Story.*

Sondheim, the young, unknown lyricist whom Bernstein brought on board after work on the show had already begun. Indeed, all four collaborators were children or grandchildren of Jewish immigrants. All four happened to be either gay or bisexual as well, and knew from another angle about prejudice and being outsiders.

In writing *West Side Story,* Laurents created an artificial street slang for the gangs. He did not use current slang, fearing that it would rapidly become dated (and of course, then as now, a lot of street language would not be appropriate for general audiences). "They never used *cool* then—that word came into the language much later," he explained. "I twisted syllables and did all sorts of things because the show needed a language. It was lyric theater and if you used actual language it would have been flat." Sondheim and Bernstein appropriated some lines directly from Laurents's book and used them as the basis of songs: examples are "A Boy Like That" and "Something's Coming."

Bernstein hired two collaborators to arrange the music for the theater's resident orchestra—a common practice on Broadway. (Union rules required producers who rented a theater to pay the players in the orchestra as well.) But Bernstein felt that several of the musicians would spoil the show if they played—presumably because they were not good enough—and he therefore rearranged some of the parts, especially violin and cello, so that hired extras would play the solo parts. He also eliminated the violas entirely (that is, the viola players got paid *not* to play).

The orchestra for *West Side Story* was unusual in including a variety of instruments identified with jazz and Latin American music (see Orchestration for *West Side Story,* p. 506). Most Broadway orchestras were smaller versions of concert or opera orchestras (*Carousel* had forty players, for example) and had the usual complement of strings, woodwinds, brass, and percussion. Some recent shows had included more jazz instruments—saxophones, extra brass (trumpets and trombones), a rhythm section (piano, guitar, drums)—but this was not typical. Bernstein's score used five woodwind players to play a wide range of instruments, including five different saxophones (soprano, alto, tenor, baritone, and bass). The ensemble had an unusual number of brass players for a Broadway orchestra

Language

Ⓢ Bernstein: *West Side Story,* "Something's Coming"

Orchestration

Ⓢ Rogers and Hammerstein: *Carousel,* Overture

Orchestration for *West Side Story*

Woodwinds

Woodwind I (plays all of these): piccolo, flute, alto saxophone, clarinet in B-flat, bass clarinet

Woodwind II (plays all of these): clarinet in E-flat, clarinet in B-flat, bass clarinet

Woodwind III (plays all of these): piccolo, flute, oboe, English horn, tenor saxophone, baritone saxophone, clarinet in B-flat, bass clarinet

Woodwind IV (plays all of these): piccolo, flute, soprano saxophone, bass saxophone, clarinet in B-flat, bass clarinet

Woodwind V: bassoon

Brass

2 horns in F

3 trumpets in B-flat (2nd doubling trumpet in D)

2 trombones

Percussion

timpani

percussion (four players)*

piano/celesta

Strings

electric guitar/Spanish guitar/mandolin

7 violins

4 cellos

double bass

*traps, vibraphone, 4 pitched drums, xylophone, 3 bongos, 3 cowbells, conga, timbales, snare drum, police whistle, guiro (gourd), 2 suspended cymbals, castanets, maracas, finger cymbals, tambourines, small maracas, glockenspiel, woodblock, claves, triangle, temple blocks, chimes, tam-tam, ratchet, slide whistle

(trumpets, horns, trombones, and tuba), and plenty of percussion, including Latin instruments: a guiro (a gourd rubbed with a stick), bongos, conga, timbales (drums of various sizes), castanets, maracas (rattles), and claves (wooden clappers).

Just when the show was essentially finished, the original producers backed out. Unable to raise enough money, they felt forced to abandon the project. Perhaps the potential backers thought that *West Side Story*, with its focus on ethnic bias, was too serious, or that putting on a show that left two of the major characters dead halfway through was too risky.

It was the lyricist Stephen Sondheim who saved the day by contacting the producer Harold Prince. (Then thirty years old, Prince was on the threshold of a career that would make him a Broadway legend.) He listened to the score, liked it, and agreed to produce it with a partner. First, however, he needed two months to raise the money, hire the actors, book a Broadway theater, and prepare for out-of-town tryouts in Washington, D.C., and Boston (later changed to Philadelphia).

LEONARD BERNSTEIN

In the 1950s Leonard Bernstein, popularly known as Lenny, was America's most famous classical musician (see biography, p. 507). His picture appeared on the cover

Leonard Bernstein (1918–1990)

Born in Brookline, Massachusetts, Leonard Bernstein showed exceptional musical talent from childhood. Numerous influences—from his Jewish roots, his training at Harvard, the Curtis Institute, and the Berkshire Music Center at Tanglewood—all led to his three-pronged career as pianist, conductor, and composer. He was insatiably curious, and his ability to admire and incorporate a wide range of musical styles, from Latin dances to twelve-tone music, was a hallmark of his inclusive personality.

Bernstein's breakthrough came on November 14, 1943, when, as the assistant conductor of the New York Philharmonic, he stepped in at the last moment for the ailing Bruno Walter and became instantly famous. (The concert was broadcast nationally.) He continued conducting, in Boston and New York, while composing a wide variety of music for concert, stage, and film. Starting in 1954, he gained further renown as the host of television programs about classical music, which showcased his remarkable gifts as an educator and media celebrity. And he continued all his life to be a fine pianist, appearing as soloist, chamber musician, and entertainer at late-night parties.

In 1957—the year of *West Side Story*'s premiere—Bernstein was named co-conductor (with Dimitri Mitropoulos) of the New York Philharmonic, and from 1958 until 1969 he was its sole conductor. He traveled the world as a conductor, and in December 1989 conducted the historic "Berlin Celebration Concerts" on both sides of the Berlin Wall—while it was being dismantled. In addition, he made over four hundred recordings during his lifetime.

Bernstein the composer was as serious as he was showy: three symphonies, two operas (*Trouble in Tahiti* and *A Quiet Place*), a Mass, the *Chichester Psalms*, and a variety of chamber music and occasional pieces attest to his sense of purpose and his continuing desire to synthesize tonal traditions with modern sensibilities.

Bernstein the man spread himself over as many fields as he could master. He once wrote: "I want to conduct. I want to play the piano. I want to write for Hollywood. I want to write symphonic music. I want to keep on trying to be, in the full sense of that wonderful word, a musician. I also want to teach. I want to write books and poetry." And he did them all.

Ⓢ Bernstein: *Chichester Psalms*
Ⓢ Bernstein: *Candide* Overture
Ⓢ Bernstein: *Mass*, Alleluia

MAJOR WORKS: Orchestral work, including three symphonies; choral works, including *Chichester Psalms*; a staged *Mass*; 2 operas, *Trouble in Tahiti* and *A Quiet Place*; musicals and dramatic stage works, including *On the Town*, *Candide*, *West Side Story*, and *Fancy Free*; film score, *On the Water Front*; chamber music; piano music; and solo vocal music.

of *Time* magazine in 1957, illustrating a story about his forthcoming appointment as the first American-born conductor of the New York Philharmonic. (He served as the orchestra's co-conductor, with Dimitri Mitropoulos, for several months before assuming the title in his own right.) A magnetic, outgoing personality, combined with brilliant musical creativity, made him one of the outstanding American musical figures of the twentieth century.

One of Bernstein's ambitions was to write the Great American Opera. Perhaps *West Side Story* is that work. In keeping with Bernstein's passionate desire to communicate, it bridged the gap that separated his serious classical compositions (such as his three symphonies and the *Chichester Psalms* for chorus and orchestra) from such broadly popular works as the musicals *On the Town* and *Wonderful Town*. Like his operetta *Candide* and the highly theatrical *Mass*, *West Side Story* stakes out a middle ground between high art and popular idiom.

High art vs. popular art

JEROME ROBBINS

Jerome Robbins was a versatile dancer and choreographer who had done brilliant work on Broadway and for the ballet (see biography, p. 508). He was also a difficult

JEROME ROBBINS (1918–1998)

Jerome Robbins, the director and choreographer for *West Side Story* (and the man responsible for the original story concept), was famous as a dancer, choreographer, and director. In a theatrical career that spanned more than fifty years, he played a major creative role in several popular, and often historic, shows, including *On the Town, High Button Shoes, The King and I, The Pajama Game, Bells Are Ringing, West Side Story, Gypsy,* and *Fiddler on the Roof.*

Born in New York City, the son of a corset manufacturer, Robbins changed his name from Rabinowitz and by 1939 had given up a college major in chemistry to dance in Broadway shows. He joined the New York dance company Ballet Theatre (later known as American Ballet Theatre), where he became a soloist in his mid-twenties (1941–44). In 1944, he choreographed and danced in *Fancy Free*, to a score by Bernstein, which was transformed that same year into the musical *On the Town* and launched both men's Broadway careers.

Robbins eventually became renowned as a "show doctor,"

someone who could turn a potential flop into a hit. Among the musicals he rescued were Stephen Sondheim's *A Funny Thing Happened on the Way to the Forum* and Jule Styne's *Funny Girl* (which featured Barbra Streisand's breakthrough performance in the title role).

For many years, Robbins—like Bernstein—continued to mix high and low art: as a dancer and choreographer of serious ballet, for Broadway, and for film sequences. (Between 1949 and 1990, he was closely identified with the New York City Ballet and served for much of that period as the company's ballet master.) In the early 1950s, under the pressure of veiled threats—including the exposure of his bisexuality—Robbins named suspected communists to the House Un-American Activities Committee, an act that he regretted for the rest of his life and for which he was shunned by some of his friends.

A man of endless contradictions, Robbins was called everything from a genius to a tyrant. His dances, however, were marked by sensitivity and tenderness, even sweetness, and his contributions to American dance and theater are of enormous importance. The lights of Broadway were dimmed in tribute on the night of his death.

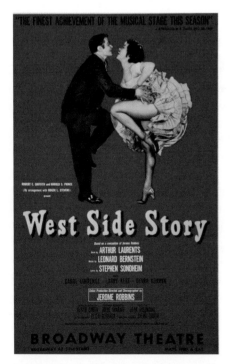

FIG. 18.6 A poster for the original Broadway production of *West Side Story*. Notice the credit lines for Jerome Robbins.

person to work with, as we will see. Lore has it that Arthur Laurents said Bernstein was afraid of only two things: God and Jerry Robbins.

Robbins insisted on special mention for himself in all posters and other materials for *West Side Story*. The words "Based on a conception of Jerome Robbins," and "Entire Production Directed and Choreographed by Jerome Robbins" had to appear, no matter what. He wanted his credit, and he deserved it (see Figure 18.6).

THE SHAPE OF *WEST SIDE STORY*

The Story From the beginning *West Side Story* was based on *Romeo and Juliet*, and despite many changes Shakespeare's plot remained the backbone of the story. Both works feature two warring families (in *West Side Story*, two rival gangs, Jets and Sharks) and a pair of lovers (the newly arrived Puerto Rican Maria and the white Tony). The fight in *Romeo and Juliet* in which Tybalt kills Mercutio, after which Romeo kills Tybalt, is echoed in *West Side Story* by the rumble in which Bernardo kills Riff in a knife fight, followed by Bernardo's death at Tony's hands. The poignant *Romeo and Juliet* balcony scene is moved to an inner-city fire escape, with Maria and Tony singing the incomparable ballad "Tonight." (See p. 509 for Plot of *West Side Story*.)

There are many other parallels to the late-sixteenth-century play, but Shakespeare's plot is not followed slavishly. Most important, Maria survives in the end (unlike Juliet, who kills herself when she finds out that Romeo is

Plot of West Side Story

Bernstein's West Side Story *is a twentieth-century adaptation of Shakespeare's* Romeo and Juliet, *in which two warring families bring tragedy on themselves when a member of one clan falls in love with a member of the other.*

ACT I

- Prologue. 🔊 **LG 80**
- Two gangs, the Jets and the Sharks, are in the midst of a turf war.
- Riff, leader of the Jets, decides to confront Bernardo, the Sharks' leader, that night at a neighborhood dance.
- The Jets ("Jet Song") decide to challenge the Sharks at the dance. 🔊 **LG 81**
- Riff convinces Tony, the Jets' former leader, to come to the dance; Tony is dreaming of an unknown but magical future ("Something's Coming").
- Maria, newly arrived in America and engaged to marry Chino, works at a bridal shop with Anita, Bernardo's girlfriend. At the dance, Tony sees Maria and time stops ("Dance at the Gym"). Riff and Bernardo agree to negotiate terms of a fight at Doc's candy store, where Tony works. 🔊 **LG 82**
- Tony finds Maria's apartment building and serenades her ("Maria"), after which they sing a duet ("Tonight"). 🔊 **LG 83**
- The Puerto Rican girls discuss the merits of living in America ("America"). 🔊 **LG 84**
- At Doc's, the nervous Jets are calmed by Riff ("Cool"). The Sharks arrive and a deal is struck for a "fair fight."

- Tony visits the bridal shop the next day, and he and Maria imagine their wedding ("One Hand, One Heart"). She asks Tony to stop the fight.
- A multithemed anticipation of events to come ("Tonight" quintet) leads to the rumble. Bernardo stabs Riff; Tony kills Bernardo. At the end, the bodies of Riff and Bernardo are left on the stage.

ACT II

- Maria sings of her happiness ("I Feel Pretty"). Chino arrives with the news that Tony has killed Bernardo.
- Tony arrives and is rebuffed by Maria. Finally Maria relents, and they sing a sort of dream song ("Somewhere").
- The Jets make fun of the police ("Gee, Officer Krupke"). They learn that Chino is planning to shoot Tony.
- Anita joins Maria and reproaches her for loving the killer of Anita's boyfriend ("A Boy Like That"). Maria convinces her of her love ("I Have a Love").
- Maria is questioned by the police, and Anita goes to Doc's to ask Tony to wait for Maria. The Jets taunt—almost rape—Anita before Doc stops them. Anita, furious, says that Chino has killed Maria.
- When Doc tells Tony that Maria is dead, Tony rushes out to find Chino and beg him to kill him too. Just as he sees that Maria is alive, Chino shoots him.
- Picking up Chino's gun, Maria holds the dying Tony ("Somewhere" reprise). The Jets and Sharks, all violence ended, form lines and carry his body offstage.

---

dead), even though she will have to live without Tony, who managed to get himself killed when he believed, falsely, that Maria was dead.

Laurents inserted placeholder lyrics at the end of the book, expecting there would be a song for Maria to close the show. But Sondheim and Bernstein never could find the right song. Laurents explained it this way:

Final scene

I meant for the girl to sing again at the very end when she picks up the gun. The dialogue I wrote was meant as a rough outline for a dummy lyric for what she should sing. And that's what she says to this day—they just never wrote the song, they decided that there shouldn't be one. One thing that Jerry [Robbins] wanted was for the girl to take sleeping pills like Juliet did, but to me it just *didn't work in contemporary terms—it just didn't make sense.*

Here is Bernstein's take on the ending:

Maria has a speech holding the gun. I don't know how many times I tried to musicalize that. It cries out for music. This is the climax, and suddenly there's no music there. I remember writing a hard-boiled piece and something that sounded like a sick Puccini aria. Everything just sounded wrong. I still feel it should be musicalized, but I wouldn't know how to do it.

The Lyrics Bernstein was extremely busy with other things (the New York Philharmonic, his show *Candide*—a flop—and much else, including, at Robbins's persuasive insistence, the creation of more dance music than he had bargained for). He agreed that he could not finish all the lyrics, as he had planned, so the talented young composer-lyricist Stephen Sondheim was hired to collaborate on them.

Sondheim in his teen years had worked under the mentorship of Oscar Hammerstein II, the lyricist for *Oklahoma!* and many other shows, and even though he did not want to be only a lyricist, Hammerstein convinced him that he should take the job. (Sondheim went on to become one of America's great composers for the Broadway stage; see biography, below.)

Sondheim's acid, realistic taste in lyrics did not always match Bernstein's more heart-on-sleeve style. A case in point is what Sondheim wrote about the song "Tonight": "I had two street kids singing, 'Today the world was just an address, a place for me to live in.' Now, you know, excuse me, that's okay for Romeo and Juliet, that's a perfectly good line, but . . . . That was Lenny's idea of poetry, very purple."

Sondheim felt that Bernstein's music was so romantic that the lyrics needed to provide a contrast in order to avoid being too emotional. So he rewrote some of

---

STEPHEN SONDHEIM (B. 1930)

If Stephen Sondheim had not moved from New York City to Pennsylvania after his parents' divorce, he might never have met the famous Broadway lyricist Oscar Hammerstein II, whose summer home was nearby. And perhaps he would never have become the greatest Broadway composer and lyricist of his—and our—time.

Hammerstein taught and encouraged the young Sondheim in a sort of apprenticeship, in which he wrote musicals as a training exercise (a musical based on a play he liked, for example). After college Sondheim, who had won a prestigious senior prize at Williams College, studied composition with the ultra-modernist Milton Babbitt. He worked a bit in television and was involved with Broadway projects as well, but *West Side Story* was his first Broadway break.

It was at the opening of Hammerstein's hit show *South Pacific* (1949) that Sondheim met the producer-director Harold Prince, with whom he was to work on many later shows. At the age of twenty-five, he was invited to provide lyrics for *West Side Story*. In 1959, he wrote the lyrics for another hit musical, *Gypsy*. Sondheim wanted to write the music as well, but Ethel

Merman, the star, insisted on a composer with a track record, and the well-known Jule Styne was hired instead.

Sondheim finally scored a hit in a show with his lyrics *and* music for *A Funny Thing Happened on the Way to the Forum* (1962), although the music was not especially well received. As lyricist he worked with composer Richard Rodgers on the 1965 show *Do I Hear a Waltz?* (for which Arthur Laurents wrote the book, based on his own play). In the 1970s, Sondheim collaborated with Harold Prince on a string of musicals: *Company, Follies, A Little Night Music, Pacific Overtures,* and *Sweeney Todd.* He won Tony awards for best music score three years in a row. His 1984 *Sunday in the Park with George* was considered stylistically avant-garde and was greeted with mixed reviews, although it won a Pulitzer Prize. But all of these works have become classics of the modern musical.

Sondheim has worked in movies and in Off-Broadway shows. His musicals have been revived, translated into many languages, and performed by symphony orchestras. And he has become the same kind of commanding figure that his mentor Hammerstein was—in fact, Sondheim is *both* Rodgers and Hammerstein, one of those creators who is equally skilled in lyrics and music alike.

FIG. 18.7 "The Rumble," the climax of Act I, showing the street fight between the Jets and the Sharks, in a photo from the original Broadway production of *West Side Story*.

Bernstein's existing lyrics, including those for Maria's "I Feel Pretty," in which he has Maria's friends, who act as a sort of chorus, mock her in the middle section of the song, suggesting that she is out of her mind. (Bernstein's lyrics had them supporting and agreeing with Maria instead of making fun of her.)

The Dance Jerome Robbins's dance vocabulary was exceptionally rich. He knew classical ballet, he knew the tap dance and kicklines of Broadway, he knew the modern dance that Agnes de Mille had used in *Oklahoma!* and other shows, and he was interested in all sorts of other styles. For *The King and I* he had studied the dance of Asia. In *West Side Story*, though, he wanted teenage slouch and arrogance to be the basis of the movement—anger disguised with languor.

Story and dance

Much of the story is told in dance. The opening Prologue, which originally was planned as a song, seemed so complicated that it gradually got simplified, and the whole turf war between the Jets and the Sharks—their pride, anger, and slouching—is explained wordlessly in the opening sequence. Likewise the scene of the dance at the gym—an obvious place for a good deal of dancing anyway—has a frozen moment in the middle: Tony and Maria see each other for the first time from across the room, approach each other, and fall in love. It is all told in music and dance, with just a few words between the lovers. And "The Rumble," the climax of Act 1, including two murders, is also mostly without words (see Figure 18.7).

The narration through dance meant that Laurents's book for *West Side Story* is perhaps the shortest of any full-length Broadway show.

The Performance

REHEARSALS

Casting the musical was problematic, since all the characters in *West Side Story* are teenagers, except for a handful of adults like Doc and the policemen (who neither sing nor dance). Bernstein wanted actors who did not have trained "operatic" voices. Robbins, on the other hand, urgently needed experienced dancers, because

FIG. 18.8 Jerome Robbins (in white) rehearsing dancers for the film version of *West Side Story*.

so much of the action was told in dance. And Laurents wanted actors who could deliver his lines convincingly.

In the end, the cast consisted mainly of young, unknown performers. Perhaps because neither Bernstein nor Laurents nor anyone else would stand up to Robbins, most of the auditions were for dancers (see Figure 18.8). If they could also sing and act reasonably well, they got the call. Most reviewers saw the point, but more than one said that the show was not well sung.

At the time, a Broadway musical normally got four weeks of rehearsal, followed by a round of out-of-town tryouts, before opening in New York. This period—perhaps six weeks in all—was an intense time, and time is big money. Robbins insisted on four extra weeks of rehearsals—an expensive proposition, but one he considered indispensable for a show that had so much complicated movement.

Robbins could be devastatingly critical in rehearsal. He felt free to do whatever he thought necessary to bring the show up to his exacting standards, including changing lines and rewriting music. He insisted on keeping the two gangs apart at all times: the Jets and Sharks were not allowed to talk to each other, eat together, or mix in any way, except in rehearsal. The idea was to create two separate communities whose antagonism would be clearly readable onstage.

"I know I'm difficult," Robbins said to the performers. "I know I'm going to hurt your feelings. But that's the way I am." And he was right: by the time the show opened, the cast despised him.

Leonard Bernstein, in His Own Words

The morning after opening night in Washington, Bernstein wrote in his journal:

The opening last night was just as we dreamed it. All the peering and agony and postponements and re-re-re-writing turn out to have been worth it. There's a work there; and whether it finally succeeds or not in Broadway terms, I am now convinced that what we dreamed all these years *is* possible; because there stands that tragic story, with a theme as profound as love versus hate, with all the theatrical risks of death and racial issues and young performers and "serious" music and complicated balletics—and it all added up for audience and critics. I laughed and cried as though I'd never seen or heard it before. And I guess that what made it come out right is that we all really *collaborated*; we were all writing the *same* show. Even the producers were after the same goals we had in mind. Not even a whisper about a happy ending has been heard. A rare thing on Broadway. I am proud and honored to be a part of it.

FIG. 18.9 An ecstatic Leonard Bernstein under the theater marquee on the opening night of the Washington, D.C., tryout of *West Side Story*.

FIRST PERFORMANCE

Out-of-town tryouts began in Washington, D.C., on August 19, 1957. The entire cast and crew had worked themselves raw; they were hopeful but apprehensive. The early signs were encouraging. The enthusiasm of the first-night audience augured well (see Carol Lawrence and Arthur Laurents, in Their Own Words, p. 512), and Bernstein was ecstatic (see Leonard Bernstein, in His Own Words, above, and Figure 18.9).

Inevitably, a number of things got changed, tightened up, added, and deleted, before the New York opening. (Extensive revisions, up to and even past opening night, are routine in Broadway musicals, as they were for operas in Handel's day.) Bernstein felt confident about the show's Broadway debut and wrote to a fellow composer, "If it goes as well in New York as it has on the road, we will have proved something very big indeed and maybe changed the face of American Musical Theater."

Listening to the Music

There are all kinds of musical styles in *West Side Story*, each designed to let us hear the world in which the characters act: Latin rhythms (mambo, tango, cha-cha, paso doble), waltz rhythms, jazz, one silly vaudeville song, classic ballads, and a lot of music that is more dissonant, and more demanding, than is usual for a Broadway show, at least one written in 1957.

ⓢ Bernstein: *West Side Story,*
"Cool," fugue

The song-and-dance "Cool" gives Bernstein a chance to show his familiarity with the jazz styles associated with postwar artists like Miles Davis (as distinct from the bebop style, or the "hot" jazz that came out of New Orleans at the turn of the century). In the dance section he treats us to a **fugue** in the atonal style of Alban Berg (see Chapter 16) but using swinging jazz rhythms.

There is even a hint of rock 'n' roll, although that style was barely on the scene at the time. (If Bernstein were writing the show today, he would surely use both rock and hip-hop; the idea was to refer to music that teenagers actually listened to.)

Tritone

The **tritone**—two notes that are three whole-tones apart, such as C and F♯—(see Appendix, p. A-4) permeates Bernstein's score. Like the minor second (notes a half step apart), the tritone is considered dissonant in tonal harmony. A composer would normally try to avoid using it in a melody, and in a chord it usually appears only where it can be "resolved" by moving immediately to a more stable and consonant harmony.

ⓢ Bernstein: *West Side Story,*
"Maria"

The tritone is easy to remember: it consists of the first two notes in the chorus of "Maria." Listen to it; does it seem dissonant to you? Probably not. Nor does it sound dissonant in other places throughout the score—for example, the first two notes of "Gee, Officer Krupke" or of "Cool" ("Boy, Boy, Crazy Boy") and in the melody that characterizes the Jets. In many cases Bernstein, like composers before him, resolves the tritone by moving to a more stable note—like the third note of "Maria." But he has also taught us simply to listen to it and like it.

A good deal of the music in *West Side Story* is designed to be danced, and each dance contains both gritty, dissonant music and expressive moments of great beauty. The dance sequences are part of reality, of real time, of action and plot. The most hauntingly lyrical moments in the score, though, are imaginary or somehow outside of time—the frozen moment when Tony and Maria first see each other at the gym, the make-believe wedding they act out, the song "Somewhere," the dream ballet sequence. That beauty is a beauty hoped for, imagined, but not achieved.

Now let's take a closer look at how Bernstein's score is actually put together. We'll listen to five numbers in the score—three songs and two that are primarily dance numbers.

🎵 LG 80

PROLOGUE

The show begins with a danced instrumental number called the Prologue, which introduces the Jets and the Sharks: the two gangs taunt each other, a Shark trips a Jet, and Bernardo, leader of the Sharks, draws blood by cutting the ear of one of the Jets. The Prologue also presents many of the musical motives and styles that will be important throughout *West Side Story*. In short, it sets the tone for the entire show (see LG 80, p. 515).

We soon learn that each gang has its characteristic whistle—casual and mostly downward for the Jets, tense and upward for the Sharks. These two signature tunes, and two or three other musical motives, will reappear throughout the show in a variety of settings and combinations. (Bernstein's use of recurrent motives associated with characters or themes may remind you of Wagner's musical techniques—see Chapter 13.)

Incidentally, if you know the movie version of *West Side Story*, you may notice that the music differs from the Broadway score—which is what we use here—in certain respects. For example, the Prologue is significantly longer on screen, although it contains the same basic elements as the original score. The visual nature of the film medium encouraged Robbins and Bernstein to set the scene in a more leisurely fashion before the police arrive and the real drama begins.

LISTENING GUIDE 80 | DVD

Bernstein *West Side Story*, Prologue   3:50

DATE: 1957
GENRE: Broadway musical

LISTEN FOR

MELODY: Small number of clear themes

METER: Switch of tempo and meter in the middle

TEXTURE: Combinations and development of themes

SCORING: No dialogue; all is done with music and dance

FIVE MAIN THEMES:

RHYTHM THEME: Syncopated rhythm, a sort of ka-thunk, ka-thunk, opening Prologue:

JETS THEME: Lazy whistle (the interval of **tritone** between fourth and fifth notes):

JETS SWAGGER: Jazzy melody associated with the Jets:

SHARKS THEME: Nervous, rising signature tune (the first two intervals are tritones):

SHARKS DOUBLE-TIME: Double-time theme (twice as fast as the previous theme) derived from Sharks Theme:

TIME	ACTION	THEMES
0:00		After an opening fanfare of Jets Theme, Rhythm Theme is introduced.
0:17	Jets	Jets Theme joins Rhythm Theme.
		Jets Swagger joins other two themes.
0:44	Bernardo enters	Sharks Theme.
0:57	Return to Jets Theme	Sharks Theme recedes and other three themes—Rhythm, Jets, and Jets Swagger—come back.
1:22	Sharks Theme	Drums develop Rhythm Theme, combined with Sharks and Jets themes.
2:15	Sharks and Jets	Change of tempo: regular double-time meter sets in, starting with Sharks Theme and developing into Sharks Double-Time. Note the quick, pulsing bass line.

(continued)

TIME	ACTION	THEMES
2:46		New jazzy trombone theme.
2:58		New theme with repeated notes, derived from Sharks Double-Time.
3:15	Bernardo cuts ear of Jet and police arrive to break up the fight	Loud chord.

 LG 81   "JET SONG"

This song and another one we will consider, "America," both use a combination of meters, simultaneous or alternating, for rhythmic interest.

The "Jet Song" begins with a verse sung by Riff ("When you're a Jet . . ."), followed by two more verses involving an overlap and a change of rhythm.

The first part of each verse is sung in ¾ time (simple triple), three even beats in a measure, while the accompaniment is in ⁶⁄₈ (compound duple), with two beats per measure, using the same ka-thump, ka-thump that we know from the beginning of the Prologue and the introduction to this song. This explains why the vocal part, which is so simple, sounds as if it is floating over a different accompaniment.

In the middle section of each verse the voice switches to ⁶⁄₈ time (and the tune is that of the Jets Theme, which we also know from the Prologue). The switch of meter is clever, and it keeps a sort of frenetic momentum going (see LG 81, below).

LISTENING GUIDE 81 · Ⓢ | DVD

Bernstein *West Side Story,* "Jet Song"   2:11

DATE: 1957

GENRE: Broadway musical

LISTEN FOR

MELODY: Introduction using three themes from the Prologue   **FORM:** Strophic form with three verses, slightly compacted

METER: Combination of meters

TIME	FORM	TEXT	DESCRIPTION
0:00	**Introduction**		Three themes from Prologue associated with the Jets (Rhythm Theme, Jets Theme, Jets Swagger), with spoken dialogue.
0:03	**Verse 1** Part A	When you're a Jet, / You're a Jet all the way, / From your first cigarette / To your last dyin' day.	The accompaniment, derived from the Rhythm Theme, is in ⁶⁄₈ time, the song melody in ¾ .
0:09	Part A, slightly varied	When you're a Jet, / If the spit hits the fan, / You got brothers around, / You're a family man!	

0:16	Part B	You're never alone, / You're never disconnected! / You're home with your own; / When company's expected, / You're well protected!	Voice switches to $\frac{6}{8}$ time.
0:25	Part A, repeated	Then you are set / With a capital J, / Which you'll never forget / Till they cart you away.	Return to original meter.
0:31	Coda	When you're a Jet, / You stay a Jet!	
0:40	**Interlude**		Same materials as Introduction; spoken dialogue.
1:04	**Verse 2** Part A	When you're a Jet / You're the top cat in town, / You're the gold medal kid / With the heavyweight crown!	Same as in Verse 1.
1:10	Part A, repeated	When you're a Jet, / You're the swingin'est thing, / Little boy, you're a man, / Little man, you're a king!	Same as in Verse 1.
1:17	Part B	The Jets are in gear, / Our cylinders are clickin', / The Sharks'll steer clear, / 'Cause ev'ry Puerto Rican / 'S a lousy chicken!	Meter switches to $\frac{6}{8}$.
1:26	**Verse 3** (elided with Verse 2) Part A	Here come the Jets / Like a bat out of hell. / Someone gets in our way, / Someone don't feel so well.	Meter changes here to $\frac{2}{4}$, but with highly syncopated melody. This marks the conclusion of Verse 2's **AABA** form and the beginning of new **ABBA** verse.
1:32	Part A, repeated	Here come the Jets: / Little world, step aside! / Better go underground, / Better run, better hide.	
1:38	Part B	We're drawin' the line, / So keep your noses hidden! / We're hangin' a sign, / Says "Visitors forbidden," / And we ain't kiddin'!	Meter switches to $\frac{6}{8}$.
1:48	Part A	Here come the Jets, Yeah! / And we're gonna beat / Ev'ry last buggin' gang / On the whole buggin' street!	Meter returns to $\frac{2}{4}$.
1:53	**Coda**	On the whole ever-mother-lovin' street!	Coda.

"DANCE AT THE GYM"

LG 82

In this dance sequence, Bernstein gives his audience—and us—the pleasure of recognizing a series of musical styles that were popular in 1957. The number begins with a **blues**—an African American form based on a simple, repetitive structure— heavy on the brass and with pounding triple rhythm, and with the direction "rocky" (meaning that it should sound like rock 'n' roll). The rhythm 'n' blues of the 1950s had this same sound when rock music was in its infancy. "Rock Around the Clock" appeared in 1955, Elvis Presley came on the scene in 1956, and pop music was in a confused transition, including crooners like Perry Como, Dean Martin, and Pat Boone, as well as black and white harmony groups such as the Platters and the Four Aces. The future was heralded by "Hound Dog" and "Heartbreak Hotel," both of them Elvis recordings (see *Billboard*'s Top Songs, 1955 and 1956, p. 502).

Blues

After a failed attempt to get the Jets and the Sharks to dance together (Bernstein provides a pompous **paso doble**, a strutting duple-meter dance), a **mambo** (a syncopated dance in $\frac{4}{4}$) follows (this is where LG 82 begins). This Cuban dance might seem

Paso doble and mambo

LISTENING GUIDE 82   ⓢ | DVD

Bernstein *West Side Story,* "Dance at the Gym"   3:06

DATE: 1957
GENRE: Broadway musical

LISTEN FOR
FORM/RHYTHM: Series of dances in characteristic rhythms, with spoken dialogue and occasional shouts of "Mambo!" Dances in order:
   Mambo / Cha-cha

TEXTURE: Woodwinds in dialogue with brass
SCORING: Use of bongos and cowbells to impart Latin flavor
THEMES: Version of "Maria" as a cha-cha

TIME	ACTION	DESCRIPTION
0:00	Mambo: this is the driving, up-tempo dance the gang members have wanted to dance all along. At end of the mambo, lights dim as Tony and Maria catch sight of each other across the room.	Lively bongos and cowbells set the frenetic melodies of the mambo in motion, with shouts of "Mambo!" serving as a sort of punctuation.
1:40	The lovers come together and talk, as if frozen in time. They dance to the rhythm of a light cha-cha.	The woodwinds and strings play an instrumental version of Tony's love song "Maria" (which has not yet been heard), in the characteristic rhythm of a cha-cha. Note the delicate use of the triangle.

more appropriate for the Sharks, but in fact it was the universal dance craze of the moment in the mid-1950s. Bernstein's mambo (punctuated with cries of "Mambo!" from both the Jets and the Sharks) is accompanied by lots of Latin percussion.

Cha-cha   An offshoot of the mambo was the **cha-cha**, which swept through Havana and New York in 1954 and found its way into *West Side Story* as a frozen moment when Tony and Maria meet for the first time. Those familiar with the show will recognize the cha-cha as a stylized version of the song "Maria," which of course has not been sung yet—Tony does not even know her name. Bernstein's formal, almost balletlike dance is lightly scored for woodwinds and strings, and the rest of the world disappears.

As the lights come up after Tony and Maria are separated, the paso doble returns. Bernstein follows it with a "jump," a loud, big-band blues that was another precursor of rock 'n' roll. (See LG 82, above.)

🔊 LG 83   "TONIGHT"

The lyrical "Tonight" has the easily recognized form of so many popular songs: an introduction followed by a chorus—the part that gets repeated (in this song, three times, with different words, but always beginning with "Tonight"). This duet is a key moment in *West Side Story,* just as the balcony scene is a central episode in Shakespeare's *Romeo and Juliet.*

Tony has just finished singing his rapturous "Maria"—whose music serves as a transition to this very moment—when Maria appears on the fire escape and they declare their love. An introductory section has Maria, and then Tony, sing an ecstatic pair of lines about the other, concluding with "you and me." The pulsing accompaniment leads to the main chorus, sung first by Maria, and then—after a first kiss—by the two of them (see LG 83, below).

"Tonight" recurs later in the show. It is performed instrumentally during a conversation between Tony and Doc, where it seems to represent Tony's hopes. It is also one of the threads in the wonderfully dramatic quintet in which the Jets, the Sharks, Anita, Tony, and Maria all express their excitement about what (they think) is about to happen that night, when the Jets and the Sharks plan to meet under the bridge.

LISTENING GUIDE 83 | DVD

Bernstein *West Side Story*, "Tonight" 3:56

DATE: 1957

GENRE: Broadway musical

LISTEN FOR

MELODY: Highly disjunct melody

FORM: Introduction (verse) and three times through the chorus. Choruses are a much-modified **AABA** form

EXPRESSION: Tension between developing love scene and static musical pattern

---

TIME	FORM		TEXT	DESCRIPTION
0:00	**Introduction:**		*Maria*	Maria makes a declaration of love, which is echoed by Tony.
0:05	Part 1		Only you, you're the only thing I'll see forever. In my eyes, in my words and in ev'rything I do, Nothing else but you. Ever!	
			Tony And there's nothing for me but Maria, Ev'ry sight that I see is Maria.	
			Maria Tony. Tony. . . .	
	Introduction:		*Tony*	Tony begins with the same music as Maria's. The mood becomes increasingly excited, then relaxes a bit as the pulsing rhythm transitions to that of the main song.
0:34	Part 2		Always you, ev'ry thought I'll ever know, Ev'rywhere I go, you'll be, you and me!	
			Maria All the world is only you and me! *(They kiss.)*	
	Chorus 1:		*Maria*	Light accompaniment, with lush use of strings. Melodic range increases. Crescendos at end of Chorus 1.
0:54	Key of B♭	A	Tonight, tonight, It all began tonight, I saw you and the world went away.	
		A	Tonight, tonight, There's only you tonight, What you are, what you do, what you say.	

(continued)

TIME	FORM		TEXT	DESCRIPTION
		B	Today, all day I had the feeling A miracle would happen. I know now I was right.	
		A	For here you are, And what was just a world is a star Tonight!	
	Chorus 2:		*Both*	
1:59	Key of A	A	Tonight, tonight, The world is full of light, With suns and moons all over the place.	The accompaniment slows as Maria and Tony kiss again. The second chorus (which they sing in unison) begins very slowly and accelerates, mirroring the lovers' breathless ecstasy.
		A	Tonight, tonight, The world is wild and bright, Going mad, shooting sparks into space.	
		B	Today the world was just an address, A place for me to live in, No better than all right,	
		A	But here you are, And what was just a world is a star Tonight!	
3:13	**Coda:** **Chorus 3**		*Both* Good night, good night, Sleep well and when you dream, Dream of me . . . Tonight!	Interruption. Maria is called indoors (the music continues instrumentally under the spoken dialogue). Before Tony leaves, the lovers reprise the final lines of the song.

 LG 84

Meter and rhythms in "America,"
from Berstein's *West Side Story*

"AMERICA"

In the comic "America," Bernstein creates a big song-and-dance number for Rosalia (who misses Puerto Rico) and Anita (who doesn't). He uses Latin dance rhythms, featuring mixed meters and cross-rhythms. The claves and guiro, important Latin percussion instruments, contribute to the Hispanic quality of this song. (See LG 84, p. 521.)

The music features the same ambiguity of $\frac{6}{8}$ and $\frac{3}{4}$ meter as in the "Jet Song," but with a different twist: here the meter switches constantly but regularly. This alternation or juxtaposition of twos and threes in music is called **hemiola**, a Greek term meaning half as much again. Two Latin rhythms are used for the two parts of the song. The smoky introduction is a **seis**—a slow line dance in duple meter, traditionally danced by six couples—in which the accompaniment is in two meters at once. The lively main part of the song is a **huapango,** a Mexican dance rhythm played by mariachi bands. It is a dance in two alternating meters: one measure of $\frac{6}{8}$—six fast syllables ("I like to be in A-")—is followed by one measure of $\frac{3}{4}$—three slow syllables ("-me-ri-ca"). It is the same pair of meters used in the "Jet Song," but here they are alternating rather than superimposed. The pattern that emerges is

Seis and huapango

6⁄8			3⁄4	
1 2 3	**4** 5 6		**1** 2 **3** 4 **5** 6	
I like to	be in A-		-me- ri- ca	
O. K. by	me in A-		-me- ri- ca	
Ev'rything	free in A-		-me- ri- ca	
For a small	fee in A-		-me- ri- ca	

6⁄8			3⁄4	
1 2 3	**4** 5 6		**1** 2 **3** 4 **5** 6	
I like the	ci—ty of		San Jua-an	
I know a	boat you can		get on	
Hundreds of	flowers in		full blo-om	
Hundreds of	people in		each ro-om	

The mixture of musical styles in *West Side Story*, of urgent street life and yearning lyricism, provides a panorama of midcentury American musical styles, maintaining a sense of unity through the use of a small number of recognizable melodic and rhythmic patterns. It is a world, meant to be modern, that has now become timeless.

LISTENING GUIDE 84   Ⓢ | DVD | 🎙

Bernstein *West Side Story,* "America"   4:35

DATE: 1957

GENRE: Broadway musical

LISTEN FOR

RHYTHM: Latin American dance rhythms: **seis** (slow), **huapango** (fast)

METER: Conflicting meters, both simultaneous and alternating

SCORING: Many Latin percussion instruments

EXPRESSION: Anita and Rosalia use same music to express opposite feelings

Tempo di huapango

(continued)

TIME	FORM	TEXT (ABBREVIATED)		DESCRIPTION
0:00	Introduction: Tempo di seis			
0:17	Verse 1	*Rosalia*		Latin-flavored percussion begins, with apparently irregular rhythm. (Actually, the accompaniment is in two meters—$\frac{6}{8}$ and $\frac{3}{4}$—at once.) The vocal melody is quite disjunct, not particularly tuneful.
		Puerto Rico,		
		You lovely island. . . .		
0:37	Verse 2	*Anita*		Anita sings the same melody but with different words that convey the opposite meaning.
		Puerto Rico,		
		You ugly island. . . .		
		I like the island Manhattan. . . .		
1:15	Tempo di huapango: Chorus 1	I like to be in America. . . .		Alternating meters ($\frac{6}{8}$ and $\frac{3}{4}$). Clapping and shouts are part of the rhythm. Note the rattle accompaniment.
1:32	Verse 1	I like the city of San Juan. . . .		Rosalia and Anita alternate lines, using the same alternating metric pattern as in the chorus, except that Bernstein adds a measure after each pair of lines, making a five-bar phrase.
1:43	Chorus 2	Automobile in America. . . .		Return to regular alternating meters.
1:57	Verse 2	I'll drive a Buick through San Juan. . . .		
2:08	Chorus 3	Immigrant goes to America. . . .		
2:20	Instrumental dance section			Orchestra maintains the metric alternation. Note percussion and brass. Section ends with instrumental version of the chorus.
2:56	Verse 3	I'll bring a TV to San Juan. . . .		
3:07	Chorus 4	I like the shores of America. . . .		
3:20	Instrumental dance section			Same as before.
3:57	Verse 4	When I will go back to San Juan. . . .		
4:09	Chorus (instrumental)			Flutes, high cries; then louder version of the chorus, with a short coda.

How Did It Go?

When *West Side Story* finally opened at New York's Winter Garden Theater on September 26, it was not the smash hit of the decade, but it did well. The reviews were mixed, as they almost always were for musicals; but the show ran for 752 performances anyway, making its backers happy. After it was turned into a movie that won ten Oscars in 1961 (it was also revived on Broadway in 1960, 1964, 1980, and 2009), *West Side Story* became an icon of American culture. But in 1957 the critics weren't sure what to make of it.

Harold Clurman, of the *Nation*, was outraged by the very idea of mixing high art and popular entertainment: "I did not enjoy it. In fact, I resented it: I thought it a phony. I am not above enjoying the phony on occasion, but I could not do so here. I do not like intellectual slumming by sophisticates for purposes of popular showmanship. It is vulgar, immature, unfeeling."

Not everybody liked the music. "Mr. Bernstein is an able and intelligent craftsman," wrote Henry Hewes in the *Saturday Review*, "but when his music is sad it seems tired, and when it is gay it seems nervous." Wolcott Gibbs advised readers of the *New Yorker* not to expect to hear tunes that could "be reproduced more or less accurately in the taxi on the way home." Today, most people would agree that there are many beautiful, hummable melodies in *West Side Story*, even though Bernstein's score has frequent dissonances and complex rhythms.

Brooks Atkinson of the *New York Times* sounded a more positive note: "Everything contributes to the total impression of wildness, ecstasy and anguish. The astringent score has moments of tranquility and rapture, and occasionally a touch of sardonic humor. And the ballets convey the things that Mr. Laurents is inhibited from saying because the characters are so inarticulate." Walter Kerr's review in the *New York Herald Tribune* was more equivocal but also singled out Robbins's choreography for praise: "The show is, in general, not well sung. It is rushingly acted. . . . But the dancing is it. Don't look for laughter or—for that matter—tears."

The magazine *Theatre Arts* agreed with Bernstein—and with the judgment of posterity—that the show was an important step forward for Broadway:

> Perhaps the musical's most striking quality is its sheer animal vitality. . . . Another striking impression conveyed by the work is its capacity for riveting one's attention. . . . The ingredients are all of a piece. Nearly everything is economical, streamlined and vital. And this not only results in a sense of immediacy but actually pushes the American musical theater several steps closer to that ultimate goal of integration of component parts, about which we hear so much nowadays from certain high priests who have all but taken the fun out of going to these shows.

West Side Story Then and Now

In the same month that *West Side Story* opened in New York, Leonard Bernstein accepted the music directorship of the New York Philharmonic. Although Carnegie Hall, then the Philharmonic's home, at Fifty-seventh Street and Seventh Avenue, was only a few blocks from the Broadway theaters, it might as well have been a different world. It was Bernstein's hope that his innovative synthesis of popular and classical styles in *West Side Story* would lead to a new form of American opera or a different relationship between theater and music. Whether this has happened or not is a matter for history. Fifty years is a long time for the jury to be out; perhaps readers of this book can answer the question for themselves.

The Tony Award for best musical of 1957 did not go to *West Side Story* but to a much more conventional show called *The Music Man*. *West Side Story* had a respectable run at the Winter Garden Theatre, and the show was reasonably successful by Broadway standards. But the release of the movie four years later changed the picture: United Artists launched a barrage of publicity and saturated the radio waves with Bernstein's songs. As a result, most people who know *West Side Story* today know it from the movie. The film differs from the show in several ways. For one thing, Natalie Wood, who plays Maria, could neither sing nor dance (although there is a lot of camera motion to give the impression that her simple footwork is more

FIG. 18.10 The poignant final scene of *West Side Story*, from the original production: Maria laments over the body of Tony.

than that). The film was shot partly on the streets of New York, which gave it an entirely different feeling from the stage musical, and some of the numbers in the score were rearranged, sometimes for new choreography, sometimes for the timings required by the difference between a film cityscape and a stage setting. For example, the film has an expanded Prologue, and "Gee, Officer Krupke" comes much later than it does in the show. Robbins, who was codirector with Robert Wise, was eventually fired for taking up too much time with detail (he got his Oscar anyway).

West Side Story has become part of the collective unconscious of Americans. It is revived everywhere—the band Metallica, the TV show *The Simpsons,* even Pixar's recent animation *Toy Story 3,* all have references to *West Side Story*— and everybody knows the film. A 2009 Broadway revival presented some of the lyrics in Spanish, allowing the Sharks to be heard for the first time in their own language. In the same year the *New York Times* ran a front-page article headlined "Under Broadway, the Subway Hums Bernstein." What riders hear as their train pulls out of the station are the opening three notes of "Somewhere" (on the words "There's a place"): a rising minor seventh and a falling half step. It is a fluke of engineering and has to do with electric currents and frequencies, but subway riders recognize the snippet of melody instantly. "Once heard," the author of the article wrote, "it is unmistakable: an echo of 'Somewhere.'" And to hear a love song from the undercarriage of a train—in New York—is fitting tribute to a show that is not only in the air, but indeed in the ground under our feet.

Chapter Review

Summary of Musical Styles

Leonard Bernstein's style in *West Side Story* is an amalgam of his own mid-twentieth-century modernism with allusions to various musical styles, especially popular music.

- The work is tinged with modernism (dissonances, polychords) and quotations of other styles (**jazz,** Latin dance music, **rock 'n' roll**).
- Orchestration with lots of woodwind, brass, and percussion (as opposed to the traditional strings-centered orchestration), along with snappy rhythmic patterns, gives the music a brightness and clarity. Expressive lyrical sections rank with some of the best-loved songs.
- Stephen Sondheim's lyrics create a clever, and sometimes astringent, quality, and contribute considerably to the rhythms of the music. The vocal lines are generally "singable," that is, relatively similar to what singers of popular

and concert music are often called upon to do (unlike the demands, say, of *Wozzeck*).

- Its larger musical forms are those of more or less standard **verse-chorus** songs, along with dance forms where appropriate (consisting usually of a series of repeated strains); certain other larger shapes, like the **fugue** in "Cool," are imports from Bernstein's classical background.

- *West Side Story* has rich polyphonic moments: songs that are heard separately first, and then sung simultaneously (Anita and Maria's "A Boy Like That/I Have a Love"), or the "Tonight" ensemble in which various individuals and groups describe, in turn and then all at once, what they expect later in the evening.

⊚ Multimedia Resources and Review Materials on StudySpace

Visit wwnorton.com/studyspace for review of Chapter 18.

What Do You Know?

Check the facts for this chapter. Take the online **Quiz**.

What Do You Hear?

Listening Quizzes and **Music Activities** will help you understand the musical works in this chapter.

⦿ Author Videos

- Meter and rhythms in "America," from Bernstein's *West Side Story*

Interactive Listening Guides

LG 80 Bernstein: *West Side Story*, Prologue
LG 81 Bernstein: *West Side Story*, "Jet Song"
LG 82 Bernstein: *West Side Story*, "Dance at the Gym"
LG 83 Bernstein: *West Side Story*, "Tonight"
LG 84 Bernstein: *West Side Story*, "America"

Flashcards (Terms to Know)

ballad	choreographer	paso doble
blues	huapango	rock 'n' roll
book	jazz	seis
Broadway musical	lyricist	tritone
cha-cha	mambo	verse-chorus form

CHAPTER 19

Coda: Into the Twenty-First Century

▶ **VIDEOS**

- John Adams: *Doctor Atomic,* Act 1, Scene 3, "Batter my heart"

Introduction

The aim of music is not to express feelings but to express music. It is not a vessel into which the composer distills his soul drop by drop, but a labyrinth with no beginning and no end, full of new paths to discover, where mystery remains eternal.

—Pierre Boulez

All the works discussed in this book were considered modern music in their day, and all have gone on to become favorites, even monuments, in the world of classical music. But when they were new, they were unknown works being heard for the first time by people eager to experience something fresh, cutting-edge, and exciting. This book, then, has not only been about our musical past but also about the present—the *now,* and the act of making music *as it happens.*

Most of the pieces in this book have been around for a long time; they've had a considerable history of appreciation, analysis, and explanation; and their styles are very familiar to us, even though we live in a period well past their own time. In fact, many of us are far more familiar with classical music from earlier eras than with classical music from our own. By contrast, nineteenth-century audiences listened to very little besides music from their own time—their "modern music"— written by their contemporaries.

This is not to say that all of the earlier music we hear sounds entirely comfortable and unchallenging to us; indeed, Monteverdi's *Orfeo,* Stravinsky's *Rite of Spring,* and Berg's *Wozzeck* were all decidedly challenging works in their day, and they remain challenging to many modern listeners.

What *is* the music of our time? The answer is different for each of us. In terms of sheer quantity—simply by measuring purchases, downloads, and other listening habits— popular music, usually rap or rock, occupies the majority of our time. Other sorts of music—jazz, folk, and classical—occupy increasingly smaller portions of the world's attention.

Today's classical music composers are the heirs of Schubert and Stravinsky, of Berlioz and Berg; like composers of earlier times—indeed like all artists—they are interested not only in capturing our attention but also in helping to make sense of the times we live in. We owe it to ourselves to hear what they have to say. Who knows? We may be living in a new golden age of music.

Do we know what to expect when we hear a piece of new music? Perhaps, but it depends on whether we choose something by a composer whose music we already know and like, or music in a style that we recognize. If we do pick something familiar, we are on relatively solid ground. But as often as not, a new piece of music is designed to take us by surprise.

Some composers want their music to sound as different as possible from any other, and many avoid traits that are characteristic of music from the past or even from the present: repetition, melody, harmony, regular rhythm, anything that might be considered traditional or predictable. Composers do this on purpose—such things don't happen by failing to pay attention—and they do it for a reason. We can't always say what that reason is, but often it is to get us to shed our preconceptions, to expect the unexpected, to enter a sound world the likes of which nobody has heard before. The music may be difficult to understand, even challenge our idea of what music is, but it almost always seeks to gain and keep our interest.

MUSIC IN REAL TIME

The computer and the Internet have connected the entire world in ways unimaginable when Stravinsky's *Rite of Spring* premiered a century ago. Wireless, GPS, and cell phones have made us all connected all the time. Social networking combines the universal with the personal, and we can now create a world according to our own wishes. And we can listen to any music, any time.

But still, there are times when we want to be together. Even when we are surrounded by music—mp3 players, video-game music, music videos; even when music is widely available at any moment; even when we have an amazing variety of music to listen to, we have to make choices, and often we choose live music. What was normal for people in the eighteenth and nineteenth centuries—to make music together, and to gather for public concerts or attend opera—is now a conscious choice. We have film, television, and recorded music at our command, and yet we still like to gather for real-time entertainment. Whether we attend sporting events, Broadway musicals, or intimate concerts, we savor the anticipation, relish the skill of the performers, enjoying the pleasure of the *now*, of being there, of not knowing the outcome in advance because it hasn't happened yet. There is something about live performance, about people performing for other people, that continues to be important and irreplaceable.

As you read this book, there is a good chance that you are a student in a college or university. Your school probably has a department of music, or a school of music, with a rich selection of new music available for listening. While many of the composers of past eras were able to compose because of the patronage of nobility or employment by churches, today's composers are often supported by colleges and universities where they are faculty and students. This means that you yourself can be present at performances of freshly composed musical compositions on a fairly

FIG. 19.1 A scene from Tod Machover's futuristic opera *Death and the Powers* from its U.S. premiere at the American Repertory Theater in Boston, 2011. From Operabots to special sound-producing Hyperinstruments to a new technique called Disembodied Performance, more than 40 computers and over 140 speakers run the production and create the sonic environment.

regular basis. It may be that down the corridor from you, or in the same building, a world premiere is being performed right now. So take some time to experience the magic of something new (see Figure 19.1).

Listening to Modern Music

There are many variables in a piece of new music. Among the things to think about when listening to new and unfamiliar music are the following:

Where does the sound come from?

Is the piece performed by traditional acoustic instruments?

Does it use any nontraditional instruments or instruments from other cultures?

Does it use electronic media? These may include prerecorded portions played during the performance; electronic manipulation or amplification of acoustical instruments; electronic instruments; and computer-generated sound.

Is the music predetermined?

Do the performers play from written parts, or a score, in which their actions are specified?

Are there elements of improvisation, in which the performers create sounds within specified parameters but whose sonic outcome is not specified?

Is the music made of notes?

Traditional score-based music uses a notational system familiar to all the composers in this book. That system draws on the notes of the chromatic scale (the notes on the piano keyboard). Many composers, particularly those writing for traditional instruments, use this sound-world and its notational system. But others do not. They do not use specific pitches but rather choose sounds, noises, or sonic events from the full range of experience and possibility, arranging them in patterns that provide a different type of experience.

Are traditional or familiar elements present?

Much modern music seeks to effect some sort of rapprochement between different kinds of music; there are composers who cite their own national folk music; composers of jazz-influenced music; rock musicians who compose oratorios; and many other crossovers and mixes that make modern music complex and interesting.

Can you recognize traditional technical features?

Are there melodies?

Are there repetitions of phrases, melodies, or sections?

Is there a meter?

Is the rhythm regular or irregular?

What is the effect?

Does the music have any sort of general emotional or descriptive effect?

Does is sound placid, active, aggressive?

Do you like it? Do you not like it? Why?

(These last questions are subjective, and the answers are different for each of us.)

John Adams's *Doctor Atomic*

⏵ Video, Adams: *Doctor Atomic,* Act 1, Scene 3, "Batter my heart"

Let us now listen to a work from the twenty-first century, and then ask ourselves some of the questions posed above. No single example can be representative of all music from our time, but we've selected a piece that brings together a number of threads in this book as well as aspects from our own culture.

The work is an opera called *Doctor Atomic,* by the American composer John Adams, which premiered in San Francisco on October 1, 2005. Adams is one of this century's best-known American composers of opera, having previously written *Nixon in China* (1987) and *The Death of Klinghoffer* (1991), among others, as well as his 2003 memorial piece for the victims of the attacks of September 11, 2001—*On the Transmigration of Souls.*

Doctor Atomic is about the Manhattan Project, the secret American effort to produce an atomic bomb during World War II, and the project's chief scientist, J. Robert Oppenheimer. In strict secrecy, at Los Alamos, New Mexico, a team of scientists rushed to produce and test the ultimate instrument of war. The opera ends with the successful detonation known by the code name "Trinity"—but not, as listeners might expect, with the simulation of a nuclear explosion.

Adams's opera, like all good drama, is really about the human condition. Oppenheimer is a learned, cultivated lover of poetry, art, and music, and is deeply conflicted about his role in creating weapons of destruction. The opera is told from many points of view (that of Oppenheimer's wife, for example, and their Native American servant) and includes various musical styles; the libretto is assembled by Peter Sellars from numerous sources, including secret documents, poems from many periods of history, and Native American song.

A compelling aria, combining aspects of old and new, interior and exterior, concludes the first act. Oppenheimer sings a sonnet by the English poet John Donne (1572–1631), expressing both the speaker's deep love for God and his own inability to resist the things that make him turn from God (Oppenheimer was an avid reader of John Donne and apparently had a copy of Donne's poems with him at the test site):

> *Batter my heart, three-person'd God; for you*
> *As yet but knock, breathe, shine, and seek to mend;*
> *That I may rise and stand, o'erthrow me, and bend*
> *Your force, to break, blow, burn, and make me new.*
> *I, like an usurp'd town to another due,*
> *Labour to admit you, but O, to no end.*
> *Reason, your viceroy in me, me should defend,*
> *But is captiv'd, and proves weak or untrue.*
> *Yet dearly I love you, and would be lov'd fain,*
> *But am betroth'd unto your enemy;*
> *Divorce me, untie, or break that knot again,*
> *Take me to you, imprison me, for I,*
> *Except you enthrall me, never shall be free,*
> *Nor ever chaste, except you ravish me.*

The poem is a cry of pain, a wish that God would "batter" the poet so that he might regain a sense of oneness with the God he has rejected. By giving Donne's words to Oppenheimer, Sellars and Adams show us the agony of the physicist's turning away from his moral duty in order to fulfill his scientific and patriotic one.

He knows only too well that he is about to unleash terrible destruction on human-kind. (In an interview years later, Oppenheimer would quote from the *Bhaga-vad Gita,* an ancient Hindu text, which Adams also uses in his opera: "Now I am become Death, the destroyer of worlds.")

As you watch the Metropolitan Opera video, notice that Oppenheimer is alone on stage, with only his invention suspended behind him, just a short time before its detonation; here is one of the few still moments in his trouble-filled and sorrowful interior and exterior life (see Figure 19.2).

If we apply some of the questions posed above, we can observe that the music is fairly traditional, in that it is performed by a singer and an orchestra; it is prede-termined (written down in advance); and it is composed of notes from traditional scales.

The music in the aria, in a reflection of the text itself, makes use of familiar materials from the past. A D-minor sonority, a sound that would not have been out of place in the eighteenth century, permeates the piece, and there are many repetitions of words and musical sections, as in a Baroque aria.

There is also a framing ritornello for the aria, used in a way that Monteverdi would have recognized. In this case, it is a single pitch (D), beginning in low strings, adding a higher D in the strings, and then chords, rhythms (timpani, repeated wind chords), and additional notes, first on the D-minor harmony and then dissonant notes. More and more elements are added to produce an active, loud sound; this sound—the business of the outer world—returns twice more.

Ritornello
    "Batter. . . . "
Ritornello
    "Batter" (repeated, varied)
    "I, like a usurp'd town"
Ritornello

FIG. 19.2 A scene from New York's Metropolitan Opera 2009 produc-tion of *Doctor Atomic* showing Oppenheimer alone on stage, with the atomic bomb looming behind him.

The opening lines of text are repeated in two sections; the first section has many repetitions of the words "knock, breathe" from the second line; then, after an intervening ritornello of the loud (worldly) noise, the singer begins from the beginning ("Batter my heart"), this time repeating the "break, blow" of the fourth line. Each of the repeated words is sung to a two-note descending figure, a motive of lament of a kind often used in Baroque music. Only after this opening ritornello-verse pair does the aria continue with the rest of the text ("I, like a usurp'd town"). The accompaniment becomes more active and pulsing; a high, rhapsodic climax is reached on "dearly I love you" before the singer closes with his plea. A version of the ritornello returns, and its sudden stop (with a drum stroke) closes the act.

The aria—and the opera—mixing as it does music and politics, technology and tenderness, is characteristic of the music of our time, and at the same time returns us to some musical roots. The idea of vocal sections with framing ritornellos is nothing new, and yet with John Adams's imaginative content, the new music and old words combine in ways that break down temporal barriers and let us hear compositional practices from the past in a fresh way.

There is no way of telling what music historians of the future might say about our century, about our period. People in what we call the Renaissance did not describe their music as Renaissance music, nor did those in Bach's Leipzig think they were listening to Baroque music—they thought of it as music, as contemporary music. One day in the future, someone may give the music of this current period a name as well—Post-Notational music? Music of the Electronic Age? Globalized music? What we do know is that what is new now will become old. What we don't know is whether that piece of music you're listening to now could become part of the classical music canon of the future. You might well be listening to the next *Orfeo, West Side Story*, Beethoven's Fifth, or Messiaen *Quartet*.

Chapter Review

⑨ Multimedia Resources and Review Materials on StudySpace

Visit wwnorton.com/studyspace for review of Chapter 19.

What Do You Know?

Check the facts for this chapter. Take the online **Quiz**.

What Do You Hear?

Listening Quizzes will help you understand the musical work in this chapter.

⏵ Videos

- John Adams, *Doctor Atomic*, Act 1, Scene 3, "Batter my heart"

Musical Notation

Like music itself, musical notation has two fundamental parameters: time and pitch. They are represented graphically by the placement of symbols on a five-line **staff** (plural, staves; see p. A-3, below). In this book, the use of musical notation has been deliberately held to a minimum, but you will get more out of both the text and the Listening Guides if you realize that reading music is simply a matter of understanding how a few basic symbols translate into sound.

TIME

We read music from left to right, just as we read English prose or poetry. The passage of time is indicated by the horizontal placement of the notes, with the duration of each note indicated by its shape. The longest note value is a whole note ○, and all the other note values—half notes ♩, quarter notes ♪, eighth notes ♪, and so on—are expressed as subdivisions of the whole note (see Figure A1, below). The circular part of the note is called the **note head**; it is usually attached to a vertical line, or **stem**, which may point up or down**.** A hook-shaped **flag** added to the stem indicates that the note value is halved. More than one flag may be used. Flags on successive notes may for convenience and clarity be replaced by a horizontal bar, or **beam**. (See Figure A2, below.)

Note head, stem, flag, and beam

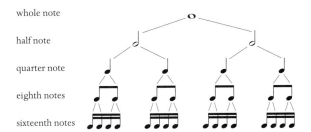

whole note

half note

quarter note

eighth notes

sixteenth notes

FIG. A1 Subdivision of the whole note

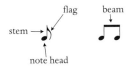

stem →

flag

beam

note head

FIG. A2 Parts of a note

   This system makes it easy to notate the rhythm of things that are divided in half, as we see below:

Here is a familiar example that uses notes to indicate the rhythm:

More complex rhythms can be written with the addition of two very useful

Tie   elements: ties and dots. A curved line called a **tie** indicates that two or more notes on the same pitch are to be joined together into a single note; for example, a quarter note tied to an eighth note ♩♪ is equal to a note as long as the two lengths together. A **dot** added after a note adds half again to its length; for example, a dot-

Dot   ted quarter note is equal in length to a quarter note plus an eighth note ♩. = ♩+♪, and a dotted eighth note is equal to an eighth note plus a sixteenth note ♪. = ♪+♬.

Thus it becomes possible to write more irregular values, like this, from the tune "Old Folks at Home":

(See more on "Dotted Rhythms," p. A-3.)

Meter and time signatures   Such rhythms are normally written in the context of a **meter**, with a time signature. In Chapter 1 we discussed meter as a regular grouping of beats. **Time signatures,** which are given at the beginning of a piece, tell the performer what the meter is and how it is notated. Basic time signatures include these:

These all tell how many notes (top number) of what sort of note (bottom number)

Measure   will fill a **measure** (a measure is a basic unit of meter, the yardstick of a piece): two quarter notes, six eighth notes, and so on.

Say, for example, there are four beats in a measure. This is most commonly notated using the time signature ⁴₄, meaning that each beat is represented by a quarter note, and there are four beats in each measure. We normally give a time signature at the beginning, and separate the groups of beats with vertical lines (called **bar lines),** so that we can identify the strong beat at the beginning of each **measure,** as shown here:

bar line   measure or bar

Here is what the example above, "Old Folks at Home," looks like with the addition of a time signature and bar lines (as well as a staff to show pitch, discussed in the next section):

Dotted Rythms In Chapter 1 we mentioned a long-short rhythm that is characteristic of many melodies and accompaniments. It is the "happy" rhythm of the word "Happy" every time it occurs in the song "Happy Birthday," but it is used in many different ways: for example, in the smooth melody that opens the slow movement of Beethoven's Symphony No. 5 (Listening Guide 30), and in the raucous "March of the Scaffold" from Berlioz's *Fantastic Symphony* (Listening Guide 40).

Ⓢ Beethoven: Symphony No. 5, II, opening

Ⓢ Berlioz: Fantastic Symphony, IV, "March to the Scaffold," march theme

As you saw in the notation of "Old Folks at Home" ("down upon the"), this rhythm is indicated using a dotted note followed by a very short note. Because of this notation, we conventionally refer to the rhythm as a **dotted rhythm**. Here is how we would notate the rhythm of the beginning of "Happy Birthday":

Hap-py birth-day to you,   hap-py birth-day to you,

PITCH

In musical notation we indicate pitch—the sequence of notes A, B, C, D, E, F, and G—by means of a **staff**: a sort of grid that was invented in the eleventh century by an Italian monk named Guido of Arezzo (see Early Musical Notation, Chapter 2, p. 33). Our modern musical staff consists of five horizontal lines:

Each line and each space is associated with one note. So the five lines, with the spaces above and below, give room for eleven notes (which was plenty for music of the Middle Ages). We indicate the association of notes with lines or spaces by putting a **clef** at the left-hand side of the staff. In the example below, the clef is a fancy letter G that shows the location of the note G. (Notice how the curlicue wraps around the second line from the bottom.) The G clef (also called a treble clef) provides the location of all the other lines and spaces in the staff:

Clef

C D E F G A B C D E F G A B C D

If the music calls for more notes than the staff can accommodate, we can insert short **ledger lines** above or below the staff, as in the example above. Another way of expanding the range of the notation is by using a different clef. The bass clef is a fancy letter F, with two dots indicating that F is on the fourth line from the bottom:

Ledger lines

C D E F G A B C D E F G A B C D

The treble and bass clefs are used together for keyboard music. The *grand staff* (which is really two staves combined) encompasses almost any note the human voice can sing:

The notation shown above, however, accounts only for the *white keys* of the piano (see Figure A3, below). What if we want to indicate black keys that lie

between the white keys? Simple: we put a sharp sign (♯) or a flat sign (♭) in front of the note in question. For example, a C♯ would be notated this way in bass clef:

The note shapes that indicate rhythm are placed at the correct height (line or space) and in the correct *horizontal* position on the staff, and the result is a notation that represents both time and pitch. With that basic concept in mind, try reading along with the notation as you listen to a familiar piece of music:

 "Old Folks at Home"

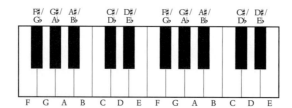

Way   down up-on the Swa - nee Ri-ver,   far,   far a - way,

Intervals

The musical distance from one note to another, the difference between their pitches, is called an **interval**.

An interval is not just a measurement of distance; it is also a sound—the sound of two pitches occurring at a given distance. An interval can be either *melodic* (if the pitches occur one after the other) or *harmonic* (if they sound together).

In learning to identify intervals by ear, it may help to visualize them on a keyboard. As shown in the illustration below (Figure A3), a piano has white keys and black keys. (This is only a small section of the keyboard, of course; a full piano keyboard has 88 keys.) The white keys correspond to the notes A, B, C, D, F, and G, while the black keys are the in-between notes designated by sharps and flats. As we saw earlier (see pp. 4–5), intervals are described as ascending or descending a certain musical distance: a second, a third, a fourth, and so on.

FIG. A3 Piano Keyboard

Octave

Notice that the sequence of notes repeats at the eighth note, the interval known as the **octave.** Notes an octave apart—say, the two A's on the keyboard above—sound both different (one high, one low) and at the same time, the same (in fact, when men, women, and children sing a melody together, even though they sing an octave apart, we say they are singing the same notes). Intervals larger than the octave are possible, of course; we usually describe them as an octave plus a smaller interval—an octave and a minor third, for example.

Minor second

Note, too, that there is no black key between E and F or between B and C. This is because all the piano keys, both white and black, are arranged so that adjacent keys are a **minor second** apart (we also call this interval a **half step** or a **semitone**). Thus, the distance from C to C♯ is the same as the distance from C♯ to D or from E to F. The minor second is the smallest interval used in traditional Western classical music, although smaller intervals are found in other musical cultures, such as that of India.

A **major second** (or a **whole step**) consists of two adjacent half steps. (The adjectives *major* and *minor* come from the Latin words meaning "greater" and "lesser.") It's a good idea to remember that there are half steps between E and F and between B and C, and that all the other pairs of adjacent white keys are a whole step apart. Any note can be raised a half step by making it a **sharp** (D♯ is played using the black key to the right of D), or lowered a half step by making it a **flat** (D♭ is played using the black key to the left of D). You can see that the black keys are used for both sharps and flats; the black key between C and D can be used for C♯ and also for Db.

Major second

A **major third,** the characteristic sound of the major scale and the major triad (we will get to triads in a moment) is made of two whole steps; the distance from C to E, or F to A, or any two other whole steps. A **minor third** consists of a whole step and a half step (as D to F, C to E♭, or any other such combination); it is the characteristic sound of the minor scale and the minor triad.

Major third

Minor third

Perhaps the most important interval for Western music is the **fifth**, the distance between two notes five letter names apart, like C to G or D♭ to A♭. The most usual size of the fifth, called a **perfect fifth**, is three and a half steps in size.

Perfect fifth

Major and Minor Scales and Keys

Scales

A scale is a collection of notes arranged stepwise in ascending or descending order, with the first and last an octave apart. The two most commonly used scales in Western music are the **major** and **minor** scales. These scales, which consist of eight notes (seven different notes and then the octave) are really summaries of the notes that we use to make melodies and harmonies.

Do	re	mi	fa	sol	la	ti	do
1	2	3	4	5	6	7	8

A **C major scale** looks like this:

The notes are spaced in such a way that there are whole steps between adjacent notes, except between notes 3 and 4 and notes 7 and 8 (marked here with angle brackets), which are separated by half steps. The placement of the half steps is what gives the major scale its characteristic sound. You can begin a major scale on any note whatever, so long as the order of the whole and half steps remains the same. A major scale beginning on D, for example, looks like this:

Major scale

In a **minor scale**, the half steps occur in a different position—between notes 2 and 3 and notes 5 and 6. Here, for example, is the scale of C minor:

Minor scale

In minor scales, the seventh scale note is often altered by raising it a half step, so that there is a semitone between the last two notes. This "leading-tone" effect pushes the melody toward the final note, the **tonic note** of the key (in this case, A).

A   B   C   D   E   F   G♯   A

Key

Examples using major scales
Ⓢ Bach: Suite in D Major, Bourrée
Ⓢ Mozart: *Don Giovanni*, Act 1, Scene 9, "Là ci darem la mano"
Ⓢ Schubert: *Die Forelle*, first verse

Examples using minor scales
Ⓢ Schubert: *Der Erlkönig*
Ⓢ Mendelssohn: Violin Concerto in E Minor, I, first theme
Ⓢ Handel: *Messiah*, "He trusted in God," opening

Example using chromatic scale
Ⓢ Berlioz: *Fantastic Symphony*, I, opening

Titles of classical works often mention a **key**: Mendelssohn's Violin Concerto in E Minor; Bach's Prelude and Fugue in C Major. This means that the music is composed using the notes of that scale, and the harmonies (see below) that can be made from them. We hear the note of the key (called the tonic) as a resting place or a goal; regardless of how the music starts, it will end on that note.

The sound of music in a major key (using a major scale) is readily distinguishable from that in a minor key. Listen now to some examples from this book that use major scales.

And here are some examples of music using minor scales.

A **chromatic scale** is a scale consisting entirely of semitone intervals—that is, a scale that uses all twelve white and black keys on the piano, instead of just the seven different notes of the major and minor scales. It is a way of describing the complete palette of notes that are available for making melodies or harmonies in Western classical music. (There is no music in "chromatic" keys; but in the twentieth century composers began to experiment with music using all the notes rather than privileging those of a major or minor scale: see Part Opener III and Chapter 16.) Listen to the opening of Berlioz's *Fantastic Symphony*, which uses a chromatic scale.

If we want to notate music in a particular key—say, D major—we normally use a **key signature** instead of continuing to insert sharps or flats every time the key requires them. Key signatures are placed at the beginning of every staff. The key signature for D major, shown below, tells us that every F should be an F♯, and every C should be a C♯, until further notice.

 Harmony

Harmony

Harmony refers to the use of simultaneous notes to produce pleasing sounds. Harmony may be the result of two notes that together produce a **consonant** interval (that is, an interval that produces a pleasing sound), or several melodies sounding together, or a melody with an accompaniment. Three or more notes sounding at the same are called a **chord**. The selection of chords, and their order and timing, is a central element in the construction and perception of music.

Chord

Triad

By far the most common chord is a **triad**. It consists of three alternating notes of a scale (the first and third and fifth notes, for example). The triad built on the first scale note (called the **tonic triad**) is a major triad—containing the intervals of a major third and a fifth—in a major key, and a minor triad—containing a minor third and a fifth—in a minor key. It is made of the first, third, and fifth notes of the scale. Triads can be based on any note of the scale, but the most common ones are those built on the first scale note (the **tonic chord**), the fifth note (the **dominant** note, whose triad is called the **dominant chord**), and the fourth note of the scale (the **subdominant** note, whose triad is called the **subdominant chord**).

Tonic, dominant, and subdominant

These three chords define a key, and go a very long way toward organizing our sense of musical progression. Many pieces consist of harmonies made of these three chords. We'll describe all three here, and you will probably find them familiar and relatively easy to recognize in music that you know, and also in music that is unfamiliar.

Tonic harmony is the sound of a final chord: almost all of the pieces that we will encounter in this book conclude with a tonic chord. Here are two examples, one each of a major and minor tonic chord.

Dominant harmony is the sound of the next-to-last chord in almost any piece (but the chord is used in many other places as well). A dominant chord is suspenseful and tends to make the listener want, and expect, a tonic chord to follow. Listen to the example from Berlioz's *Fantastic Symphony.*

A **subdominant** chord also tends to push toward the tonic, but in a less forceful way; it is the sound of the first harmony in the "Amen" that ends so many Christian hymns, or of the chord on the syllable "lu" in the opening of Handel's "Hallelujah" chorus. (The harmony on the other syllables is the tonic chord.)

The sounds of these three harmonies are well known to those of us who have grown up on Western classical, folk, or popular music. They are the sounds of the harmony that accompanies the following words when they are sung, and perhaps you can imagine them in your mind's ear just by thinking of the harmony you expect at the places indicated here:

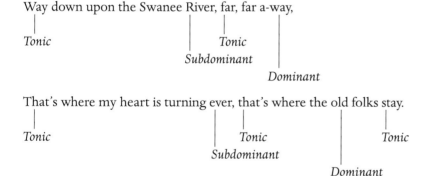

The way the harmony shifts in conjunction with a melody is one of the things that make listening to music fascinating. Sometimes the harmony shifts very regularly, as in songs like Schubert's *Die Forelle.*

Sometimes it changes quite rapidly, as in many hymns, or in the magical chords that begin the slow movement of Dvořák's *New World* Symphony. Here, although the tempo of the piece is very slow, the harmony changes with each note. Indeed, the harmony is essentially all there is to listen to.

Sometimes a composer likes to shift the harmony in a variety of rhythms. An interesting case is this passage from Berlioz's *Fantastic Symphony,* near the end of the "March of the Scaffold." The alternation between two harmonies gets faster and faster.

A piece of music does not have to stay in a single key. One way to construct longer pieces is to have the music move to another key and then return to the beginning key. The process of moving from one key to another is called **modulation**. A modulation can be sudden, as when Handel repeats the opening music of the "Hallelujah" chorus, with five "Hallelujahs" in the tonic key followed by five in the dominant.

Music can also modulate more gradually, so that we are not sure whether we

ⓢ Byrd: Agnus Dei, from Mass for Four Voices, final major chord

ⓢ Handel: *Messiah,* "He trusted in God," final minor chord

ⓢ Berlioz: *Fantastic Symphony,* IV, "March to the Scaffold," dominant chord

ⓢ Handel: *Messiah,* "Hallelujah" chorus

ⓢ Schubert: *Die Forelle,* instrumental version

ⓢ Dvořák: Symphony No. 9, II, opening

ⓢ Berlioz: *Fantastic Symphony,* IV, harmonic alternation

ⓢ Handel: *Messiah,* "Hallelujah" chorus

Beethoven: Symphony No. 5, II, modulation

Berg: *Wozzeck,* Act 1, opening

are still in the original key until the new key is firmly established. Beethoven makes a wonderful modulation in the slow movement of the Fifth Symphony, where a theme begins in one key, seems to wander a bit, and then arrives triumphantly in a new key (the keys are A♭ major and C major).

Some music is not in any key: notes can be used in many ways, and the use of keys is a convention, a preference, but not a requirement. In the early twentieth century, some composers began to experiment with dissonances and novel arrangements of notes, sometimes with the specific goal of avoiding the impressions of keys and traditional harmony, as Alban Berg did in his tragic opera *Wozzeck.*

This section on music notation, time, pitch, intervals, scales, and harmony is just a starting point. Many of the elements discussed here, and in Chapter 1, can be heard on the various Author Videos on StudySpace. The more you know about music and how it works, the greater your appreciation will be.

accompanied song *Texture* in which a single *voice* has the main melodic interest, accompanied by other voices or instrument(s).

added-value rhythm *Rhythm* created when a regular rhythmic pattern is altered by an addition within a rhythmic unit. Used in twentieth-century music.

affect In the Baroque period, a human passion, expressed through stylized gestures in dance, and through specific *tempo*, *tonality*, melodic gestures, and other aspects of music.

Agnus Dei Portion of the *Ordinary* of the *Mass*.

aleatoric music Music created using chance or other indeterminate elements.

Alleluia Portion of the *Proper* of the *Mass*.

alto Lower range for female or child's voice.

andante Moderately slow, "walking" *tempo*.

animato Animated (*tempo*).

antecedent phrase In music, a "question" phrase that is "answered" by a *consequent phrase*.

antiphonal Sung by alternating sides of the *choir; also* antiphonally.

aria Elaborate piece for *voice* and orchestra in an *opera*, *cantata*, or *oratorio*.

arpeggio (Italian *arpa*, "harp") *Chord* that is strummed or played one note after another, from bottom to top or vice versa.

arrangement Version of a piece of music for some other medium.

art song Vocal work for solo *voice* and accompaniment.

atonal See *atonal music*.

atonal music Music written with an avoidance of a sense of *tonality*; atonal.

atonality Musical language that avoids establishing *keys* and familiar harmonies.

augmented fourth See *tritone*.

ballad Song with a long narrative text, usually *strophic*; term is used for an old English folk song, a type of *lied*, and a slow, romantic popular song of the twentieth century.

bar See *measure*.

bar line Vertical line on a *staff* that separates *measures*.

bass Lowest range for male *voice*; also applied to the lowest instrument of an ensemble.

bass line Lowest sounding musical line in a piece, for example played by the lowest instrument or by the left hand of the *piano*.

basso continuo Continuous *bass line* and *chords*, used in the Baroque period to accompany one or more melodic lines, and most often played by a bass melody instrument and a keyboard instrument, for example cello and *harpsichord*.

beat Regular unit of musical time, also called pulse; usually in a range from about 40 to 200 per minute.

bel canto (Italian, "beautiful song") Italian style of singing, associated with early nineteenth-century *opera*, characterized by a lyrical and highly ornamented style.

bitonality Use of two *keys* (*tonalities*) at the same time.

block construction Technique of composing music in which short segments are treated as unvarying blocks that recur like a pattern in a patchwork quilt.

blues African American musical style generally based on a simple, repetitive harmonic structure, often of twelve *measures*.

book Text of a play, especially of a *musical*.

bourrée Popular Baroque dance in a quick four-beat *meter*, with a single *upbeat*.

brass *Wind* instruments such as trumpet and trombone, usually made of brass, in which sound is produced by buzzing one's lips into a cupped mouthpiece.

brass instruments See *brass*.

Broadway musical Genre developed in twentieth-century American theater, in which music and dance, generally in a popular vein, are integrated into a spoken play.

cadence Close of a musical *phrase* or statement.

cadenza Elaborate solo passage that usually comes just before the end of a *concerto movement*, generally as an expansion of the final *cadence*.

canon Musical procedure in which *voices* or instruments follow each other in continuous and literal *imitation*, as in a round.

cantata General name for a musical composition made up of several *movements* and featuring chorus and/or solo *voice*, usually with orchestral accompaniment, for church or concert performance.

cantor Highest ranking musical officer of a cathedral.

cantus firmus (Latin, "fixed melody") Preexisting chant or other *melody* presented in one voice of a *polyphonic* work, often in slow time values, while other voices weave melodies around it.

cantus firmus technique See *cantus firmus*.

capellmeister German term for the music director of a European court or church.

castrato Male singer who was castrated before his voice changed, often featured in Italian *opera* of the Baroque.

celesta Keyboard instrument in which pressing a *key* causes a hammer to strike a tuned metal bar.

cha-cha Dance from Cuba prevalent in the 1950s, an offshoot of the *mambo*.

chamber music Music performed by a small number of people; originally intended for a small audience.

character piece Brief, evocative composition, often for *piano* solo and intended for private entertainment; the mood or theme is often indicated by a fanciful title. Common in the nineteenth century.

choir Group of singers performing as a group, often as part of a church service; also, the name of the part of the cathedral in front of the main altar, where the singers were positioned and the services were performed.

chord Collection of three or more pitches sounded together to produce a pleasing sound.

choreographer Person who creates a dance for a ballet, *musical*, or other stage work.

choreography Design of dance for stage performance.

chromatic Colored with melodic notes or harmonies that are not in the normal *tonality*.

chromatic scale *Scale* made up of all twelve pitches of the Western system, all a *half step* apart.

chromaticism Style of inflecting music with harmonies created using *chromatic* notes.

clavichord Expressive but very quiet keyboard instrument of the Baroque period, in which pressing down a *key* causes a metal blade to strike a string.

coda (Italian, "tail") Ending section of a *first-movement sonata* or other *movement*.

collegium musicum Musical society, often associated with a university, in which members perform music for their own pleasure.

commedia dell'arte Improvised theater of Italian fairgrounds, prevalent from the Renaissance onward; staple characters such as Pierrot and Columbine appear in literature and theater.

concertmaster Leader of the first violin section of a symphony orchestra, who plays the solo passages and often serves as assistant to the conductor.

concerto Piece for one or more *virtuoso* solo instruments with orchestra, usually in three *movements*.

conjunct In *melody*, moving by step to adjacent pitches (compare *disjunct*).

consequent phrase Musical phrase that answers another phrase, called an *antecedent phrase*, to form a larger unit.

consonance Quality of *intervals* that sound well together.

consort music Name used in England in the Renaissance and Baroque for music written for instrumental ensemble (consort), often made up of a family of one type of instrument, such as *viola da gamba*.

contradanse *Duple-meter* dance, derived from the English country dance, common in Mozart's time.

cornett Popular *wind* instrument in the Baroque period and earlier, made of wood and often curved, with finger holes like a *woodwind* instrument but played with a cupped mouthpiece like a *brass* instrument.

counterpoint (Latin, *punctus contra punctum*, "putting one note against another") The art of creating simultaneous independent melodies.

countersubject In a *fugue*, a musical line that is presented every time the fugue *subject* appears.

countertenor Very high male *voice*, often using falsetto.

Credo Portion of the *Ordinary* of the *Mass*.

cross-rhythms Effect of two *meters* at once.

cycle In the nineteenth century, a single, integrated work, often for *voice* and *piano* (song cycle) or solo piano, made up of a collection of smaller pieces.

da capo aria *Aria* in a three-part **ABA** form, prevalent in the Baroque period.

development Process of exploring and reworking different musical materials; in *first-movement sonata forms*, the main middle section, in which melodies and *motives* from the first section (*exposition*) are fragmented, recombined, and used in combination with *modulation*.

discant See *discant style*.

discant style Style of *organum* in which all *voices* move together and in regular *rhythms*; used for portions of chant that are *melismatic*.

disjunct In *melody*, moving by skip between pitches (compare *conjunct*); disconnected.

dissonance Quality of *intervals* that sound harsh.

Divine Office The eight daily services performed by medieval Roman Catholic clergy at specified hours of the day.

dominant Fifth note of a *scale*, or the *chord* built on that note; besides the *tonic*, the most important note in any *key*.

dominant seventh chord Four-note *chord* built on the *dominant*, consisting of a *major triad* and a *minor* seventh.

dominant-tonic (**V–I**) Common harmonic progression, from the *dominant chord* to the *tonic chord*.

dot In the notation of *rhythm*, a dot following a note increases the note's duration by half.

dotted figure See *dotted rhythm*.

dotted rhythm Long-short *rhythm*, notated with a dotted note followed by a much shorter note.

double bass Lowest bowed *stringed instrument*, regularly used both in *jazz* and in orchestras.

double-stop On a *violin* or other bowed *stringed instrument*, playing two strings at the same time.

downbeat First *beat* in each grouping of beats of a *meter*; in notated music, the first beat of a measure.

Doxology In church *liturgy*, verse of praise to the Father, the Son, and the Holy Spirit that is often added to the end of psalms.

dramma giocoso (Italian, "playful drama") Play or *libretto* that mixes serious and comic elements.

duple meter *Meter* that is made up of two-beat (or four-beat) groupings.

dynamics Level of loudness, and changes of loudness, in music.

E-flat clarinet Small, high-pitched clarinet.

English horn Tenor-range oboe.

episode Portion of a *fugue* in which the complete *subject* is not present but which acts as a bridge between full *subject* statements.

exposition In a *fugue*, the opening section, in which each *voice* states the *subject*; in *first-movement sonata form*, the opening section, in which the main *themes* are presented, starting in the home *key* but then establishing the *dominant* or another new key area. Also *statement*.

expressionism (expressionists) Trend or style in twentieth-century art emphasizing the depiction of a shared subjectivity and emotions over objective reality; the term was generalized from the visual arts to the music of Arnold Schoenberg and Alban Berg.

figured bass Shorthand notation representing the chordal accompaniment of the *basso continuo*.

finale Last *movement* of a *symphony* or other composition; in *opera*, a large *movement* that ends an act, in which many characters, and plot elements, come together onstage.

first-movement sonata form Form most often used in first movements of *symphonies*, *sonatas*, and other instrumental works of the late eighteenth and early nineteenth centuries, consisting primarily of *exposition*, *development*, *recapitulation*, and *coda*.

First Viennese School Name applied to composers centered in Vienna in late eighteenth and early nineteenth century, including Haydn, Mozart, and Beethoven. Compare *Second Viennese School*.

flat Pitch lowered by a *half step*, or the sign ♭ to indicate it.

forte Loud.

fortepiano Early name for the modern *piano*.

fortissimo Very loud.

fugue *Polyphonic* composition based on a single *theme* or *subject*, which is introduced in *imitation* in all *voices* at the beginning of the piece and recurs thereafter in various voices. In the *exposition*, each voice enters in turn with a *statement* of the subject; between later entries of the subject, there may be *episodes* in which the subject is absent or is given only in fragmented form.

fundamental pitch Lowest *partial* of the *harmonic series*; the pitch that is perceived as the sounding pitch.

galliard Lively dance popular in the Renaissance, characterized by leaping movements, in *triple meter* and often employing *hemiola*.

gavotte Popular Baroque dance with four-beat *phrases*, always beginning with two *upbeats* followed by a strong *downbeat*.

Gesamtkunstwerk See *total work of art*.

gigue Popular Baroque dance in quick *triple meter*.

glissando Quick slide between two melodic pitches, used for expression or special effect.

Gloria Portion of the *Ordinary* of the *Mass*.

Gradual Portion of the *Proper* of the *Mass*.

Great Book of Organum (Magnus liber organi) Manuscript of two-voice *organum* from the late twelfth century, reputedly compiled by Leoninus for Notre Dame Cathedral in Paris.

Gregorian chant *Monophonic* religious *melody* (chant) sung in Latin, without instrumental accompaniment; its *rhythm* is not notated.

half cadence *Cadence* ending on the *dominant harmony* and lacking a feeling of finality.

half step Distance between the notes E and F, and B and C (or between any adjacent keys on the piano) in Western music; also called a *semitone*.

harmonic rhythm *Rhythm* of *chord* changes; the speed at which the *harmony* changes in a piece of music.

harmonic series Series of pitches contained within a sounding tone, consisting of a *fundamental tone* along with the series of *overtones* created by the secondary vibrations of a string or column of air. The harmonic series is dictated by simple mathematic proportions.

harmonics On *stringed instruments*, the *overtone* pitches produced by lightly touching the string with one hand while plucking or bowing with the other.

harmony Choice of *chords* and their relationship to each other.

harpsichord Keyboard instrument in which strings are plucked when a *key* is depressed; common in the Renaissance and Baroque periods.

hemiola Effect, particularly prevalent in Baroque music, in which a slow group of three *beats* substitutes for two fast groups of three beats.

homophony Musical *texture* in which all *voices* move in the same *rhythm*; homophonic.

huapango Mexican dance *rhythm* played by mariachi bands.

idée fixe (French, "fixed idea") Recurrent *melody*, used obsessively in different forms throughout the piece, in Berlioz's *Fantastic Symphony*.

imitation Process of having one *voice* sing or play the music that another voice has just finished. See also *imitative polyphony*.

imitative polyphony Type of *polyphony* in which each of the *voices'* (or instruments') melodies is of more or less of equal importance, and in which voices imitate each other in succession, often at different pitch levels.

impressionism Term adopted from European visual arts of the late nineteenth century and applied to the musical style of composers Claude Debussy and Maurice Ravel, in which orchestral and harmonic color are emphasized, and music is often used to evoke moods and images of the natural world.

intermedio (plural: *intermedi*) Instrumental interlude performed between acts of Renaissance and early Baroque plays.

intermezzo Musical interlude, generally a separate *movement* within a larger work.

interval Distance between two musical pitches, also thought of as the relationship between pitches; basic building block of *melody* and *harmony*.

Introit First part of the *Proper* of the *Mass*, chanted to accompany the procession of the celebrant from the sacristy to his place in front of the altar.

jazz Type of music or musical style that developed in the United States in the early twentieth century from elements of African and European American music, and often characterized by rhythmic intricacy and improvisation.

kettledrum Large drum with a parchment (often now plastic) head and metal kettle-shaped body, able to be tuned to a specific pitch; used in much orchestral music.

key *Tonality*; also, on a keyboard instruments such as *piano* and on *wind* instruments, a moving part that is used to play or change a pitch.

keynote See *tonic*.

Kyrie First part of the *Ordinary* of the *Mass*; unlike other *movements*, its short text is in Greek.

leitmotif (German: *Leitmotiv*, "leading motive") Recurring musical *motive* used to represent a person, thing, or idea, particularly in the *operas* of Richard Wagner.

libretto (Italian, "little book") Text of an *opera*.

lied (German, "song"; plural: *lieder*) Short musical composition, generally for solo *voice* and *piano*, often based on a poem.

liturgy Ceremonies and rituals, words and music, that make up a sacred service.

lowered seventh note The seventh note of a *major scale* lowered in pitch by a *half step*.

lute Pear-shaped, flat-topped instrument held like a guitar and played by plucking the six (or more) sets of strings.

lyricist (lyrics) Person who writes the words for songs, as for *musicals*; many musicals are written by a composer-lyricist pair, such as Rodgers (composer) and Hammerstein (lyricist) or Lerner (lyricist) and Loewe (composer).

madrigal *Polyphonic* setting of a secular poem.

major key *Tonality* based on the notes of a *major scale*.

major scale Seven-note scale (the eighth note is the *octave*) whose character comes primarily from the raised third scale degree, two *whole steps* above the *tonic*.

mallet instruments *Percussion* instruments with metal or wood bars or other shapes, tuned to individual pitches, and struck with mallets (short-handled hammer with a head); mallet instruments such as marimba and xylophone are capable of playing both *melody* and *harmony*.

mambo *Syncopated* dance in $\frac{4}{4}$ time, from Cuba, and very common in the 1950s.

Mass Central service of Christian worship, commemorating the Last Supper and the death and resurrection of Jesus.

measure Basic unit of *meter*; also called *bar*. In written music, measures are separated by *bar lines*.

melisma Florid *melody* sung on a single syllable; melismatic.

melody Series of musical notes designed to be sung or played in succession, generally characterized by *rhythm*, general contour, and *conjunct* or *disjunct* motion.

meter Regular grouping of *beats*; in classical music and in folk music of the western European tradition, most commonly *duple* (groups of two beats) or *triple* (groups of three beats).

metronome Mechanical or electronic device to indicate *tempo*, in terms of number of *beats* per minute.

miniature Small, intimate solo or *chamber work*, suitable for performance in a salon, common in the nineteenth century.

minimalism Mid-twentieth-century cultural movement: in visual arts, art is created from only its simplest and most basic elements; minimalist music employs gradually shifting patterns of multiple repetitions to create longer shapes.

Minnesinger In late-medieval Germany, poet-composer of secular *monophonic* song.

minor key *Tonality* based on the notes of a *minor scale*.

minor scale Seven-note scale (the eighth note is the *octave*) whose character comes primarily from the *half steps* between the second and third notes and the seventh and eighth notes.

minuet and trio Commonly, in the eighteenth century, a *movement* of a *symphony*, *string quartet*, or other work; the "trio" is a contrasting minuet, after which the first minuet returns.

minuet Popular dance of the seventeenth and eighteenth centuries, in moderate *tempo* and *triple meter*.

mode of limited transposition Term used by Olivier Messiaen for any symmetrical musical *scale* that, because of its symmetry, exists in only one or a few distinct transpositions: for example, the *whole-tone scale* and the *octatonic scale*, as distinct from *major* and *minor scales*.

modified strophic form Strophic song form that that incorporates some alteration in the strophic repetition.

modulation Process of moving from one *key* to another.

monophony Musical *texture* in which one or more voices or instruments perform a single *melody* in *unison*; monophonic.

motet *Polyphonic* vocal piece on a sacred Latin text; originally, a vocal piece created by adding texts to the melismas accompanying the chant setting.

motive Characteristic musical *phrase* or fragment that is used as a building block of a musical composition.

movement Self-contained section of a larger musical work, generally characterized by its own *tempo* (in French, *mouvement*).

music drama Wagner's term for his own works in the genre of *opera*, meant to indicate a deep exploration of character and emotion, and a full integration of music, literature, and other theatrical elements.

musical See *Broadway musical*.

musical quotation The deliberate incorporation of recognizable material from one musical composition in another.

nationalism Promotion of common identity based on political state, language, or commonly held culture; in music, a trend (particularly in the nineteenth century) in which composers seek to express the identity of a place, a people, or a country.

nationalistic composer One who excels at expressing the spirit of his or her own people in music.

neoclassicism Return to an earlier ideal of classical order and simplicity; in eighteenth-century visual arts, movement away from the decorative aspects of the Baroque toward the order, symmetry, and simplicity of the arts of classical Greece and Rome; in twentieth-century music, movement away from the emotional expressiveness of Romantic music toward the moderation and balance associated with eighteenth-century (Classical) music.

neumatic Style of chant or other vocal setting having two or three notes per syllable.

nonretrogradable rhythm Term used by Olivier Messiaen to describe rhythmic pattern that is the same backward and forward.

Notre Dame repertory Compilation of liturgical music from Paris, late twelfth and early thirteenth centuries; one of the first great collections of music whose composers are known to us.

octatonic scale Eight-pitch scale built of strictly alternating *half* and *whole steps*, prevalent in European music of the late nineteenth century.

octave Relationship (*interval*) between two pitches with the same letter name, one vibrating exactly twice as fast as the other.

Office See *Divine Office*.

opera Drama for the stage in which all characters sing their parts.

opera buffa Type of Italian *opera* of the eighteenth century with a comic plot, generally in two acts.

opera seria Type of Italian *opera* of the eighteenth century with a serious (often historical or mythological) subject matter, generally in three acts.

ophicleide *Bass brass* instrument of the nineteenth century, lacking *valves* but having holes and *keys* like a *woodwind*.

oratorio Large-scale musical setting of a religious drama, generally in operatic style but unstaged.

orchestration Art of assigning melodies, *counterpoint*, accompaniment, and so on, to the various instruments of the orchestra.

Ordinary Sung portions of the *Mass* text that do not vary according to the church calendar: *Kyrie, Gloria, Credo, Sanctus, Agnus Dei*.

organ Keyboard instrument that sounds by means of air passing through pipes.

organum Style of medieval *polyphonic* liturgical music; see *discant style* and *sustained-note organum*.

ostinato Short *motive* or melodic fragment that is repeated continuously throughout a *movement* or section of a movement.

overtone Pitch created by the secondary vibrations of a string, air column, and the like; an aspect of the *tone color* of a *voice* or instrument.

overtone series See *harmonic series*.

paired imitation *Imitative* procedure in which pairs of *voices* imitate each other.

partial A pitch of the *harmonic series*.

paso doble Lively, *duple-meter* dance.

Passion Musical setting of the account of the crucifixion of Jesus from one of the four Gospels of the New Testament.

pastoral drama Play set in idealized rural setting, often in an-

tiquity, written in verse with incidental music and songs; popular in the Renaissance through the eighteenth century.

patter song Comic song from musical theater characterized by rapid delivery of tongue-twisting text.

pavan Slow, stately, *duple-meter* dance of the Renaissance.

pedal point Single note maintained in the *bass*, as with a pedal of a church organ, while harmonies in the upper *voices* change.

pentatonic scale Five-note *scale* with no *half steps*, and that can be produced with all *piano* black keys, or by leaving out the fourth and seventh notes of a *major scale*; common in many cultures worldwide.

percussion General term for instruments that are played by striking; they produce sound using vibrating membranes (drums), or metal or wooden bars struck by a *mallet* (chimes, xylophone), or that vibrate as a whole, such as gongs and triangles.

percussion instruments See *percussion*.

phrase Segment of a *melody* or other musical passage that is distinct; phrases are often in pairs in the form of question (*antecedent*) and answer (*consequent*).

piano *Dynamic*, meaning soft.

piano miniature See *miniature*.

pianoforte, piano (Italian, "soft-loud") Keyboard instrument in which strings are struck with padded wooden hammers that are activated when a player depresses the *keys*.

piston In trumpets and some other *brass* instruments, a cylindrical type of *valve*, invented in the nineteenth century; the valve alters the length of the sounding tube.

pizzicato Effect of plucking on *stringed instruments* (such as violin) normally played with a bow.

plainchant, plainsong See *Gregorian chant*.

point of imitation Procedure by which each voice of a *polyphonic texture* enters using the same *motive*, in *imitation*.

polka Quick dance in *duple time*, originating in central Europe.

polychord Sounding of two or more different, generally clashing, *chords* at once, suggesting *polytonality*.

polyphony Musical *texture* made up of a web of independent melodic lines; polyphonic.

polytonality Effect of layering of music from different *keys* at once, so that no one key dominates.

prelude Introductory *movement* of an *opera* or other musical work; also, an independent work of unspecified form, most often for solo keyboard instrument.

prelude and fugue In the music of J. S. Bach and others, a keyboard prelude followed immediately by a *fugue* in the same *key*; Bach's *Well-Tempered Clavier* consists of preludes and fugues in each *major* and *minor key*.

prima donna (Italian, "first lady") Leading woman of an *opera* company.

primitivism Movement of the late nineteenth and early twentieth centuries that valued and imitated the arts of non-Western and tribal peoples

program music Instrumental music that is intended to describe a scene or tell a story.

Proper Texts for certain chants of the *Mass* which vary from day to day, according to the church calendar: *Introit, Gradual, Alleluia, Sequence,* Offertory, Communion.

pure organum See *sustained-note organum.*

recapitulation Third main section of *first-movement sonata form,* paralleling the *exposition,* but ending in the home *key.*

recitative Passage in *opera* and *oratorio* in which solo singers deliver text at a speed and in a *rhythm* that is intended to follow normal speech, accompanied by *chords,* most often short punctuating chords played by *harpsichord, organ,* or *piano.*

recitative style See *recitative.*

recitativo accompagnato (Italian, "accompanied recitative") Recitative in which the orchestra provides an accompaniment, and generally reserved for moments of high intensity or importance.

recitativo secco (Italian, "dry recitative") Recitative in the most usual sense, in which words are sung in a spoken *rhythm,* with simple *chordal* accompaniment played by keyboard instrument, sometimes with cello.

recorder End-blown flute, prevalent during the Renaissance and Baroque periods.

rest Indication of silence (for one *voice* or instrument or for all) within a piece of music.

retransition In *sonata form,* passage at the end of the *development* that leads to the *recapitulation.*

rhythm Sequence of events in musical time, or pattern of note durations, generally with respect to *beat* and *meter.*

ritenuto *Tempo* indication meaning held back, slower.

ritornello Passage of music that recurs within a *movement.* In a Baroque *concerto,* movements typically begin and end with the ritornello, which also recurs, in various *keys,* between solo passages.

rock 'n' roll Popular music originating in the United States in the 1940s and 1950s, blending traditions of black and white music, including rhythm and blues and country music.

rondo form Musical form characterized by returns of a fully stated *theme.*

sackbut Renaissance trombone.

salon Gathering of artists and intellectuals in a private home, for the sharing of art and ideas.

saltarello (Italian *saltare,* "to jump") Fast dance, originating in medieval Italy.

Sanctus Portion of the *Ordinary* of the *Mass.*

scale Arrangement of notes, usually adjacent and in ascending or descending order, that serves as the material for *melodies* and harmonies; the *major* and *minor scales* are those most frequently used.

scherzo (Italian, "joke") Term applied variously to different types of musical compositions, but most often to a lively dancelike *movement* of a *symphony* or other instrumental work.

Schubertiade Intimate social gathering, named for Franz Schubert, and featuring the composer and his friends providing music and poetry.

score Fully written-out version of a musical composition, with all vocal and instrumental parts and every note are indicated.

Scotch snap Rhythmic figure in which an accented short note is followed by a long note.

Second Viennese School Vienna-based composers of the early twentieth century, including Schoenberg, Berg, and Webern. Compare *First Viennese School.*

seis (Spanish, "six") Latin American line dance in *duple meter,* traditionally danced by six couples, in which the slow accompaniment is in two *meters* at once.

semitone See *half step.*

sequence Short passage of music that is repeated several times, at progressively higher or lower pitches; also, in Christian *liturgy,* a long poem appended to the *Alleluia* of the *Mass,* with a *syllabic* musical setting.

serenade Composition for chamber group or orchestra, usually meant for light entertainment, and often with more than four movements.

serialism Method of composition using a repeating series of all twelve notes of the *chromatic scale* (*twelve-tone method*); sometimes including series of other parameters (durations, dynamics, etc).

series, or **tone row** Sequence of tones used in *twelve-tone* music.

serpent S-shaped *bass* instrument with a *brass* mouthpiece but finger holes like a *woodwind,* used in church services and military bands of the eighteenth and nineteenth centuries.

sharp Pitch raised by a *half step,* or the sign ♯ to indicate it.

shawm Double-reed instrument, precursor of oboe.

short score Sketch of an orchestral composition in which full harmonies are given but the *orchestration* is indicated in abbreviated form.

siciliana Moderate-tempo Italian dance, generally in *meter* of $\frac{6}{4}$ or $\frac{6}{8}$, and associated with pastoral scenes.

slur Smooth connection of notes in a melodic line, indicated in music notation by a curved line; in violin playing, accomplished by playing all the notes on a single bow stroke.

sonata Piece generally for solo instrument (often, *piano*) or a small group of instruments, most often in three *movements.*

sonata form See *first-movement sonata form.*

song cycle See *cycle.*

soprano Highest range for female or child's voice.

spiritual Folk hymn; most often, a religious song originating among African American slaves and passed down by oral tradition.

Sprechstimme (German, "speech-voice") Technique in which singer observes the *rhythms* and pitches indicated in the score, but slides through rather than sings the pitches.

Stabreim Alliterative verse typical of ancient Teutonic legend, and used by Richard Wagner in *The Ring of the Niebelung.*

staff (plural: staves) Set of five horizontal lines on which musical notes are placed to indicate pitch.

statement See *exposition*.

stile recitativo See *recitative*.

stretta Concluding part of an *opera aria* or ensemble in which *tempo* increases; commonly used in an opera finale, with all the characters singing at once.

stretto In a *fugue*, a passage in which the *subject* is used as a *counterpoint* to itself.

string bass See *double bass*.

string quartet Ensemble of two violins, viola, and cello, or a musical composition written for this ensemble.

string instruments Musical instruments that produce sound by plucking or hitting a string, or stroking it with a bow.

strophic See *strophic form*.

strophic form Form of song that uses the same music for each verse (strophe) of poetry.

strophic variation Repetition of same basic melodic shape and series of harmonies, with variations.

subdominant Fourth note of a *scale*, or the *chord* built on that note.

subject Main *theme* of a *fugue*.

suspension Note held over from a preceding *consonance* that becomes *dissonant* with the new *harmony*.

sustained-note organum Style of organum in which a higher *voice* or voices sing many notes against each note of the chant; compare *discant style*.

sustaining pedal Pedal of a *piano* that raises all the dampers; when subsequent notes are played, the strings ring until the pedal is released.

syllabic Text setting in which each syllable has one note.

symphony Piece for orchestra, usually in four *movements*, especially important in the Classic period.

syncopation Rhythmic effect of shifted emphasis, when a strong note occurs on a normally weak *beat* of a *measure*.

temperament System of tuning keyboard instruments to make their sound more pleasing in particular *keys*. Most modern tuning is in "equal temperament," in which the *octave* is divided into twelve equally spaced *semitones*.

tempo Speed of musical *beat* or pulse, often given as a *metronome* marking, indicating the number of beats per minute.

tenor High male voice.

text painting See *word painting*.

texture Overall sonic effect in a musical passage of the number and types of instruments and *voices*, and the ways their *rhythms*, pitch ranges, *melodies*, and *chords* sound together; for various kinds of texture see *accompanied song*, *homophony*, *imitative polyphony*, *monophony*, *polyphony*.

thematic transformation Nineteenth-century compositional technique of variation and transformation of musical material as part of a larger structure.

theme *Melody* or other music material that forms the basis of a musical work such as a *movement* of a *symphony*.

thoroughbass Name used in English for *basso continuo*.

through-composed form Formal procedure in which there is no repetition of earlier music.

timbre See *tone color*.

time signature Notation (such as $\frac{3}{4}$) used to indicate *meter*.

timpani See *kettledrum*.

toccata Instrumental showpiece, most often for keyboard instrument, often improvisatory in sound, and common in the Baroque period.

tonality The centering of *harmony* on one particular pitch (*tonic*).

tone color The recognizable quality of a musical sound; for an instrument, this results from its construction and the manner in which sound is produced on it.

tonic Home note of a *key*, heard as the goal or place of *rest*.

total work of art (German: *Gesamtkunstwerk*) Richard Wagner's name for the ideal of a combination of music, drama, and stagecraft.

transcription Arrangement of music written for one instrument or group of instruments for another.

tremolo Fast repetition of a note or alternation between two notes, often used to create dramatic effect.

triad *Chord* composed of three different pitches, generally three nonsuccessive notes of a scale such as 1, 3, 5.

trio Any ensemble of three singers or instrumentalists, or portion of music using a trio ensemble; also the contrasting minuet in a *minuet-and-trio* movement.

triple meter *Meter* made up of three-beat groupings.

triplet Group of three equal notes, often subdividing a *beat*, occurring in place of two equal notes.

tritone *Interval* formed by two notes that are three *whole steps* apart; one of the most *dissonant intervals* in tonal music; the tritone occurs naturally in *major scales*, between 4 and 7 (*augmented fourth*)

trope Medieval interpolated musical meditations or glosses on liturgical texts.

troubadour Poet-musician in southern France of the twelfth and thirteenth centuries, composing secular *monophonic* songs in the language of Old Provençal.

trouvère Poet-musician in northern France of the twelfth and thirteenth centuries, composing secular *monophonic* songs in the language of Old French.

tutti (Italian, "all, everyone") Indication that everyone is to play together; generally used in orchestral music to indicated passages of massed sound.

twelve-tone method (twelve-tone music) Method of composing, developed by Arnold Schoenberg, using a predetermined series of all twelve *chromatic* notes in a variety of permutations, avoiding the repetition of tones.

unison All *voices* and / or instruments singing or playing the same notes.

upbeat Last *beat* of a *measure*, leading into the next measure; compare *downbeat*.

valve In *brass* instruments, mechanism to open and close additional lengths of tubing to change the pitch, operated by a *key* or *piston*.

variation form Musical form in which a *melody*, harmonic structure, or other musical thematic material is presented, followed by a series of variants (*variations*).

variation Alteration of a preexisting musical idea. See *variation form*.

verse-chorus form Standard *strophic* form of a song in which there is a regularly recurring refrain (chorus).

vibrato Expressive pulsation of tone produced by changing a pitch slightly and rapidly, using variation in breath (*wind* instruments, *voice*) or finger placement (*stringed instruments*).

viol See *viola da gamba*.

viola da gamba Bowed *stringed instrument* popular in the sixteenth through eighteenth centuries, with six strings and frets, held vertically like a cello, and made in several sizes, from treble (high) to contrabass (low).

virginal Small, portable keyboard instrument in which strings are plucked, much like a *harpsichord*; common in Renaissance England.

virtuoso (**virtuosity**) Instrumentalist or singer whose performance is distinguished by a display of technical proficiency.

vocalise *Melody* that is sung without words.

voice Term used for individual melodic line, whether played by an instrument or sung.

waltz Popular dance of the nineteenth century, in lively *triple meter*.

whole step *Interval* of two *half steps*.

whole-tone scale Scale built only of *whole steps*.

wind General name for any musical instrument in which sounds are produced by a vibrating column of air; includes *brass* and *woodwind* instruments.

woodwind instruments See *woodwinds*.

woodwinds *Wind* instruments (not necessarily made of wood) in which tone is produced by blowing across an edge (flute) or vibrating one or two reeds (clarinet, oboe, bassoon).

word painting Use of music to imitate images and sounds described in the text.

CHAPTER 1

3. "Music expresses that which cannot be said": Victor Hugo, *William Shakespeare*, trans. A. Baillot (London: Hurst & Blackett, 1864), p. 73.

PART I

20. From *The Rule of St Benedict* (box): Leo Treitler, ed., *Strunk's Source Readings in Music History*, rev. ed., trans. James McKinnon (New York: W. W. Norton, 1998), p. 159.

CHAPTER 2

31. "For nothing so uplifts the mind": Leo Treitler, ed., *Strunk's Source Readings in Music History*, rev. ed., trans. Oliver Strunk, rev. James McKinnon (New York: W. W. Norton, 1998), p. 123.

43. "For he that singeth praise": Sanctus Augustinus, *Enarratio in Psalmum 72*, 1: CCL 39, 986 (PL 36, 914); LXXIII (Latin LXXII), Philip Schaff, ed. (Grand Rapids, MI: Wm. B. Eerdmans Publishing Company) Christian Ethereal Library: Nicene and Post-Nicene Fathers, series I, vol. 8, p. 668.

48. "was in use until the time": Jeremy Yudkin, trans. and ed., *The Music Treatise of Anonymous IV: A New Translation* (Nenhausen-Stuttgart: Hänsler-Verlag, 1985), p. 39.

CHAPTER 3

57. "I am not satisfied with our Courtier": Baldassare Castiglione, *The Book of the Courtier* (1528), trans. Charles S. Singleton (Garden City, NY: Doubleday, 1959), p. 74.

58. Music in an Elizabethan Country House (box): The mysterious R. B. [Richard Brathwaite], *Some Rules and Orders for the Government of the House of Earle* (London, 1821), p. 44; quoted in Mark Girouard, *Life in the English Country House: A Social and Architectural History* (New Haven: Yale University Press, 1978), p. 89.

58. On reaching this gentleman's house: Richard Wilson, *Secret Shakespeare: Studies in Theatre, Religion and Resistance* (Manchester: Manchester University Press, 2004), p. 12.

59. Mr Byrd, the very famous musician and organist: ibid.

59. "she might die as gaily as she had lived": Jacques Bonnet, *Histoire de la musique et de son effets* (1715), citing the memoirs of the Abbé Victorio Siri (1677–79); cited and trans. David Scott, "Elizabeth I, Queen of England,"

Grove Music Online (www.oxfordmusiconline.com), consulted June 30, 2011.

60. My lords, you must know that I am not content with the Courtier: Castiglione, *The Book of the Courtier*, p. 74.

75. The pavane is easy to dance: Thoinot Arbeau, *Orchésographie* (1588); cited in Alan Brown, "Pavan," *Grove Music Online* (www.oxfordmusiconline.com), consulted June 30, 2011.

CHAPTER 4

91. "Tomorrow evening the Most Serene Lord the Prince": Iain Fenlon, "Correspondence Relating to the Early Mantuan Performances," in John Whenham, ed., *Claudio Monteverdi, Orfeo,* Cambridge Opera Handbooks (Cambridge: Cambridge University Press, 1986), trans. Stephen Botterill, p. 170.

93. because of his responsibility for both church and chamber music: preface to Claudio Monteverdi's *Scherzi musicali* of 1607, trans. Thomas Kelly.

94. "the fortune I have known in Mantua": Denis Stevens, ed., *The Letters of Claudio Monteverdi* (Cambridge: Cambridge University Press, 1980), p. 58, translation adapted by Thomas Kelly.

94. "His Highness the Prince": Stevens, *Letters of Monteverdi,* p. 81.

95. "all actors are to sing their parts": Fenlon, "Correspondence," in Whenham, ed., *Claudio Monteverdi, Orfeo,* p. 170.

99. The three letters are from Fenlon: ibid., pp. 167–71.

99. "little priest" ("pretino"): Angelo Solerti, *Musica, ballo, et drammatica alla corte medicea dal 1600 al 1637,* trans. Thomas Kelly (Florence: Bemporad, 1905, repr. Bologna: Forni, 1969), p. 55.

99. "that signor Francesco Rasio": Eugenio Cagnani, *Raccolta d'alcune rime di scrittori mantovani* (Mantua, 1612), p. 9; quoted in Warren Kirkendale, "Zur Biographie des ersten Orfeo, Francesco Rasi," in Ludwig Finscher, ed. *Claudio Monteverdi. Festschrift Reinhold Hammerstein zum 70. Geburtstag,* trans. Thomas Kelly (Laaber: Laaber, 1986), pp. 304–06.

99. "with a range consisting of many notes": Carol MacClintock, ed. and trans., *Hercole Bottrigari: Il desiderio . . . Vincenzo Giustiniani: Discorso sopra la musica* (Rome: American Institute of Musicology, 1962), p. 69.

115. Having recounted as well as I know: Mantova, Archivio di Stato, Archivio Gonzaga 2706, trans. Thomas Kelly, transcribed in Susan Parisi, "Ducal Patronage of Music in Mantua 1587–1627: An Archival Study" (Ph.D. diss., University of Illinois at Urbana-Champaign, 1989), vol. 1, p. 189.

116. Monteverdi is here in Milan, staying with me; and every day we talk: Fenlon, "Correspondence," in Whenham, ed., *Claudio Monteverdi, Orfeo*, p. 172.

CHAPTER 5

119. "Handel wore an enormous white wig": Charles Burney, *An Account of the Musical Performances in Westminster-Abbey* (London, 1785); repr. with intro. by Peter Kivy (New York: Da Capo Press, 1979), p. 36.

122. A London Critic Goes to the Oratorio (box): Otto Erich Deutsch, *Handel: A Documentary Biography* (New York: W. W. Norton, 1955), p. 301.

125. The Nobility did me the Honour: ibid., p. 530.

125. The *Dublin Journal* and *Dublin News-Letter* Announce the First Performance of *Messiah* (box): ibid., pp. 542–43.

125. "Mr. Handell's new Grand Sacred Oratorio": ibid., p. 545.

125. "the Flower of Ladyes": ibid., p. 530.

126. Susannah Cibber in the Eyes of Contemporaries (box): "a mere thread": Burney, *An Account*, pp. 26–27; "Woman, for this": Richard Luckett, *Handel's Messiah: A Celebration* (New York: Harcourt Brace, 1992), p. 128.

127. "I have form'd an other": Deutsch, *Handel*, p. 530.

127. Charles Burney Describes Handel Playing the Keyboard (box): Burney, *An Account*, p. 35.

142. On Tuesday last: Deutsch, *Handel*, p. 546.

143. Rising to the "Hallelujah" Chorus (box): Donald Burrows, *Handel: Messiah* (Cambridge: Cambridge University Press, 1991), p. 28.

143. An *Oratorio* either is: Deutsch, *Handel*, pp. 563–64.

CHAPTER 6

147. "Musicum Collegium is a gathering": Christoph Wolff, *The New Bach Reader: A Life of Johann Sebastian Bach in Letters and Documents* (New York: W. W. Norton, 1998), p. 203.

148. "There I had a gracious Prince": ibid., p. 151.

149. C. P. E. Bach Describes His Father's Reputation (box): ibid., p. 366.

150. wherein the lovers of the clavier: ibid., pp. 97–98.

151. Bach's Keyboard Playing (box): Johann Nicolaus Forkel, in Wolff, *The New Bach Reader*, p. 203.

151. "The water systems": Johann Christian Crell, *Das In gantz Europa berühmte, galante und sehenswürdige Königliche Leipzig in Sachsen*, trans. Thomas Kelly (Leipzig: August Martini, 1725), p. 54.

153. Public Concert Series (box): "this present Monday":

Hugh Arthur Scott, "London's Earliest Public Concerts," *Musical Quarterly* 22/14 (1936), p. 454.

153. The participants in these musical concerts: Wolff, *The New Bach Reader*, p. 186.

153. "a serving of chocolate": Friedrich Zarncke, ed., *Leipzig und seine Universität im 18. Jahrhundert. Aufzeichnungen des Leipziger Studenten Johann Heinrich Jugler aus dem Jahre 1779. . .* , 2nd ed. (Leipzig: Breitkopf & Härtel, 1909), pp. 106–07.

154. "In conducting he was very accurate": Wolff, *The New Bach Reader*, p. 306.

154. The placing of an orchestra: ibid., pp. 396–97.

156. "acquired such a high degree": ibid., p. 434.

159. C. P. E. Bach Describes How His Father Listened to Fugues (box): ibid., p. 397.

CHAPTER 7

177. "As the company is so small": Emily Anderson, ed., *The Letters of Mozart and His Family*, 4th ed. (New York: W. W. Norton, 1989), pp. 911–12.

179. "Nowhere does one find": Friedrich Ernest Arnold, *Beobachtungen in und über Prag von einem reisenden Ausländer*, 2 vols. (Prague: W. Gerle, 1787); quoted in Thomas Forrest Kelly, *First Nights at the Opera* (New Haven: Yale University Press, 2004), p. 119.

180. A Description of Pasquale Bondoni (box): Arnold, *Beobachtungen*, pp. 136–38; quoted in Kelly, *First Nights at the Opera*, p. 74.

182. "At once the news of his presence spread": Franz Xaver Niemetschek, *Mozart: The First Biography*, trans. Helen Mautner (Oxford and New York: Berghahn Books, 2007), p. 26.

182. "I looked on": Anderson, ed., *The Letters of Mozart*, p. 903.

183. "poetry is the door to music": Lorenzo Da Ponte, *An Extract from the Life of Lorenzo Da Ponte with the History of Several Dramas Written by Him* (New York: J. Gray and Company, 1819), p. 27.

183. "as perfectly as a well-made suit": Anderson, *The Letters of Mozart*, p. 497.

185. "He anticipated the day": August Meissner, *Rococo-Bilder*, 1870; quoted in Rodney Bolt, *The Librettist of Venice: The Remarkable Life of Lorenzo Da Ponte* (New York: Bloomsbury, 2006), p. 177.

185. "The stage personnel here": Anderson, *The Letters of Mozart*, pp. 911.

185. "The worth of this artist": *Allgemeine musikalische Zeitung*, April 2, 1800, col. 789; quoted in Bitter, *Wandlungen in den Inszenierungsformen des Don Giovanni von 1787 bis 1928* (Regensburg: Gustav Bosse, 1961), p. 14; translated in Kelly, *First Nights at the Opera*, p. 105.

186. Mozart on Zerlina's Scream (box): Wilhelm Kuhe, *My Musical Recollections* (London: Richard Bentley and Son, 1896), pp. 9–10.

186. "a complete beginner": Zdenka Pilková, "Prager Mozartsänger in Dresdener Quellen," *Festschrift Christoph-Helmut Mahling zum 65. Geburtstag*, ed. Axel Beer et al. (Tutzing: Hans Schneider, 1997), vol. 2, p. 1096; quoted in Kelly, *First Nights at the Opera*, p. 95.

186. "acting and singing": Bitter, *Wandlungen in den Inszenierungsformen*, p. 13; translated in Kelly, *First Nights at the Opera*, p. 98.

187. Mozart grows Impatient (box): Anderson, *The Letters of Mozart*, pp. 911–12.

190. "Everybody sings": Lorenzo Da Ponte, *Memoirs of Lorenzo Da Ponte,* ed. Arthur Livingston, trans. Elisabeth Abbott (Philadelphia: J. B. Lippincott, 1929; repr. New York: Da Capo Press, 1988), p. 133.

204. [On] Monday the 29th: *Prager Oberpostamtszeitung*, November 3, p. 178; Otto Erich Deutsch, *Mozart: A Documentary Biography*, trans. Eric Blom, et al., 2nd ed. (Stanford: Stanford University Press, 1966), pp. 303–04.

205. "Long live Da Ponte": Da Ponte, *Memoirs*, p. 179.

205. "I cannot settle the argument": *Allgemeine musikalische Zeitung,* October 24, 1798, cols. 51–52; quoted in Bolt, *The Librettist of Venice*, p. 187.

205. "The opera is divine": Da Ponte, *Memoirs*, p. 180.

CHAPTER 8

209. "Notwithstanding the fact that several mistakes were made": Elliott Forbes, *Thayer's Life of Beethoven* (Princeton: Princeton University Press, 1967), p. 454.

210. The English Physician Richard Bright Describes Vienna in 1814 (box): *Travels in Vienna . . . in the year 1814*; cited in John Lehmann and Richard Bassett, *Vienna: A Travellers' Companion* (New York: Atheneum, 1988), pp. 55–56.

211. Rents were paid twice a year: Alice M. Hanson, *Musical Life in Biedermeier Vienna* (Cambridge: Cambridge University Press, 1985), p. 15.

211. Apartments were crowded: ibid., p. 14.

212. Beethoven, who lived to the age of fifty-six: ibid., p. 10.

213. Letter (1808) from Beethoven to Joseph Sonnleitner, Complaining about His Apartment in the Theater an der Wien (box): Forbes, *Thayer's Life of Beethoven*, p. 347.

213. Dinner followed: Oscar Sonneck, ed. *Beethoven: Impressions of Contemporaries* (New York: G. Schirmer, 1926), p. 44.

213. He was usually in bed: Anton Felix Schindler, *Beethoven As I Knew Him,* ed. Donald W. MacArdle (Chapel Hill: UNC Press, 1966), pp. 385–86.

213. "Short and thickset": Lewis Lockwood, *Beethoven: The Music and the Life* (New York: W. W. Norton, 2003), p. 190.

216. An Advertisement for Beethoven's Concert: *Thayer's Life of Beethoven*, rev. and ed. Elliot Forbes, 2 vols. (Princeton: Princeton University Press, 1970), vol. 1, p. 446.

217. An Account, Perhaps Exaggerated, of an Incident at the Concert (box): Louis Spohr, *Louis Spohr's Autobiography: Translated from the German* (London: Longman, Green, Longman, Roberts, & Green, 1865), pp. 186–87.

217. Notwithstanding the fact that several mistakes were made: Forbes, *Thayer's Life of Beethoven,* p. 454.

218. An Eyewitness to the First Performance of the Fifth Symphony: Johann Friedrich Reichardt, Composer and Writer (box): ibid., p. 448.

226. "Thus Fate pounds on the gate": Anton Schindler, *Biographie von Ludwig van Beethoven*, trans. Thomas Kelly (Münster: Aschendorff, 1860), p. 158.

231. The Critic and Composer E. T. A. Hofmann on Beethoven's Fifth Symphony, 1810 (box): *Allegemeine musikalische Zeitung* (Leipzig: 1810), trans. Martyn Clarke, in David Charlton, ed. *E.T.A. Hoffmann's Musical Writings: Kreisleriana, The Poet and the Composer, Music Criticism* (Cambridge: Cambridge University Press, 1989), pp. 97–98.

CHAPTER 9

235. "I went to Spaun's": Otto Erich Deutsch, *Schubert: A Documentary Biography*, trans. Eric Blom (London: J. M. Dent, 1946), pp. 571–72.

236. J. F. Reichardt on the Viennese Theater (box): Leo Treitler, ed. *Strunk's Source Readings in Music History*, rev. ed. (New York: W. W. Norton, 1998), pp. 1039–41.

236. Music-Making in the Home (box): Hans Normann, *Wien wie es ist*, 1833, in Mary Sue Morrow, *Concert Life in Haydn's Vienna: Aspects of a Developing Musical and Social Institution* (Stuyvesant, NY: Pendragon Press, 1989), p. 118.

237. strongly developed, firm bones and firm muscles: Otto Erich Deutsch, *Schubert: Memoirs by His Friends*, trans. Rosamond Ley and John Nowell (New York: A. & C. Black, 1958), p. 51.

237. Because of his short sight he always wore spectacles: Anselm Hüttenbrenner, "Fragments from the Life of the Song Composer Franz Schubert (1854)," in Deutsch, *Schubert: Memoirs by His Friends*, pp. 182–83; quoted in Craig Wright and Bryan Simms, *Music in Western Civilization* (Belmont, CA: Thomson/Schirmer, 2006), p. 477.

237. Anyone who has seen him of a morning: Deutsch, *Schubert: Memoirs by His Friends*, p. 138.

239. I was sitting thus in my den: Deutsch, *Schubert: Memoirs by His Friends*, p. 227.

239. "a double nature": Christopher Howard Gibbs, *The Life of Schubert* (Cambridge: Cambridge University Press, 2000), p. 95.

239. "Falsity and envy were utter strangers": Deutsch, *Schubert: Memoirs by His Friends*, p. 14.

239. "halfway between a gentle tenor": Deutsch, *Schubert: Memoirs by His* Friends, p. 227.

239. "without being a virtuoso": Deutsch, *Schubert: Memoirs by His Friends*, p. 226.

240. Vogl sang so splendidly: Deutsch, *Schubert: Memoirs by His Friends,* p. 186.

240. "excellently sung by Vogl": Gibbs, *The Life of Schubert*, pp. 78–79.

240. "bold performance broke down": the comment is by Albert Stadler, 1853: Deutsch, *Schubert: Memoirs by His Friends*, p. 215.

240. has set to music several songs by the best poets: Gibbs, *The Life of Schubert*, p. 79.

241. An Article about "Gretchen" (box): Deutsch, *Schubert: A Documentary Biography,* p. 177.

241. "My peace is gone, my heart is sore": Deutsch, *Schubert: A Documentary Biography,* p. 339.

241. I have wept for him as for a brother: Deutsch, *Schubert: A Documentary Biography,* p. 829.

242. Franz [von Schober] invited Schubert in the evening: Deutsch, *Schubert: A Documentary Biography,* p. 162.

244. "That's not bad": Deutsch, *Schubert: Memoirs by His Friends,* p. 217.

253. "To see and hear him play": Deutsch, *Schubert: Memoirs by His Friends,* p. 216.

CHAPTER 10

264. Berlioz's manuscript score and the printed program give the title "Marche du supplice" (March of the scaffold). The published score of 1845 changes the name to "Marche au supplice" (March to the scaffold). Here we adopt the latter translation, to avoid confusion; the movement clearly describes a process toward the place of execution.

265. "How we shivered in horror": *Le Temps*, December 26, 1830, trans. Thomas Kelly.

270. "The impression made on my heart": Hector Berlioz, *The Memoirs of Hector Berlioz*, trans. and ed. David Cairns (New York: Alfred A. Knopf, 1969; repr. 2002), p. 70.

270. "by the third act": ibid., p. 73.

271. Movement titles: *Revue musicale*, vol. 10, November 27, 1830, p. 89, trans. Thomas Kelly.

272. "When the day came for the rehearsal": Berlioz, *The Memoirs of Hector Berlioz*, pp. 104–05.

273. "Ten million curses on all musicians": ibid., pp. 117.

275. The precision of the orchestra's playing: Henry Fothergill Chorley, quoted in Harold C. Schonberg, *Great Conductors*, (New York: Simon & Schuster, 1967), p. 99.

275. "At every wrong note": Charles de Boigne; quoted in Thomas Forrest Kelly, *First Nights: Five Musical Premieres* (New Haven: Yale University Press, 2000), p. 198.

276. This is the first time that anyone has tried: *Le Figaro*, December 4, 1830, p. 3, trans. Thomas Kelly; quoted in Kelly, *First Nights*, p. 240.

276. "It is perhaps a misunderstanding": *Revue musicale,* vol. 10, November 27, 1830, p. 89, trans. Thomas Kelly; quoted in Kelly, *First Nights*, p. 241.

276. It is not at all a matter of copying: quoted in Kelly, *First Nights*, pp. 250–51.

276. "At precisely two o'clock": *Le Temps*, December 26, 1830; quoted in Kelly, *First Nights*, p. 244.

277. Here is a young man, lanky, rough-complexioned: ibid.

278. "Beethoven, he declared": Hugh Macdonald, "Berlioz, (Louis-) Hector, 2. 1821–30, (New York: Oxford University Press, 2012).

278. Through an odd whim: *Revue musicale*, vol. 10, November 27, 1830, p. 89, trans. Thomas Kelly; quoted in Kelly, *First Nights*, p. 249.

282. Comments on Waltzing (box): Madame Celnart, *The Gentleman and Lady's Book of Politeness and Propriety of Deportment . . .* (Boston: Allen and Ticknor, 1833), p. 187; and Donald Walker, *Exercises for Ladies, Calculated to Preserve and Improve Beauty, and to Prevent and Correct Personal Defects, Inseparable from Constrained or Careless Habits* (London: Thomas Hurst, 1836), p. 142.

289. "The beloved melody appears again": quoted in Kelly, *First Nights*, p. 250.

289. "We have religious music": *Le Figaro*, December 4, 1830, p. 3; translated in Kelly, *First Nights*, p. 240.

290. "the most bizarre monstrosity": *Le Figaro*, December 7, 1830, pp. 3–4; translated in ibid., p. 243.

290. "be a milestone": *Le National,* December 6, 1830, p. 3, translated in ibid., p. 248.

290. How we shivered in horror before the scaffold: *Le Temps*, December 26, 1830; translated in ibid., p. 245.

290. At last came the day: Francois Joseph-Fétis, *Revue musicale*, February 1, 1835, trans. in Edward T. Cone, *Berlioz: Fantastic Symphony* (New York: W. W. Norton, 1971), p. 27.

290. a great success": Berlioz, *Memoirs*, p. 119; translated in Kelly, *First Nights*, p. 243.

290. The performance was by no means perfect: ibid.

291. "a story, developed within a psychological context": Gottfried Fink, quoted in Mark Evan Bonds, "The Symphony as Pindaric Ode," in Elaine Sisman, ed. *Haydn and His World* (Princeton: Princeton University Press, 1997), p. 149.

292. "the symphony must be like the world": Erik Tawaststjerna, *Sibelius*, vol. 2, 1904–14, trans. Robert Layton (Berkeley: University of California Press, 1986), p. 77.

CHAPTER 11

295. "It pleased extraordinarily": Julius Eckardt, *Ferdinand David und die Familie Mendelssohn-Bartholdy,* trans. Thomas Kelly (Leipzig: Duncker & Humblot, 1888), pp. 232–33.

296. Mendelssohn's Schedule in Leipzig (box): Eduard Devrient, *My Recollections of Felix Mendelssohn-Bartholdy and His Letters to Me* (London: Richard Bentley, 1869), pp. 206–07.

297. Letter from Mendelssohn's Teacher Carl Friedrich Zelter (box): quoted in Leon Botstein, "The Aesthetics of Assimilation and Affirmation: Reconstructing the Career of Felix Mendelssohn," in R. Larry Todd, *Mendelssohn and His World* (Princeton: Princeton University Press, 1991), p. 40, n. 37.

297. Musical prodigies, as far as mere technical execution goes: R. Larry Todd, *Mendelssohn: A Life in Music* (New York: Oxford University Press, 2003), p. 89.

299. Mendelssohn had a slender, delicately framed figure: Clive Brown, *A Portrait of Mendelssohn* (New Haven: Yale University Press, 2003), p. 8.

300. Letter to His Sister (box): Sebastian Hensel, *The Mendelssohn Family (1729–1847) from Letters and Journals*, trans. Carl Klingemann (New York: Harper & Brothers, 1882), vol. 2, p. 23.

300. "His tone is most pure" "Ferdinand David (1810–1873)," *The Musical Times* 47/761 (July 1, 1906), p. 458.

301. But why should I hear those Variations by Herz: Wulf Konold, *Felix Mendelssohn Bartholdy und seine Zeit* (Laaber, 1984), p. 13; quoted in Steve Lindeman, "The Works for Solo Instrument(s) and Orchestra," in Peter Mercer-Taylor, ed., *The Cambridge Companion to Mendelssohn* (Cambridge: Cambridge University Press, 2004), p. 113.

301. "I'd like to do a violin concerto": ibid., p. 127.

301. have pity and write a violin concerto: Letter of July 16, 1839, in Eckardt, *Ferdinand David*, p. 114.

301. "Now that is very nice of you": "Ferdinand David (1810–1873)," *The Musical Times* 47/761 (July 1, 1906), p. 459.

301. "I'll play your concerto for you": Eckardt, *Ferdinand David*, p. 230.

302. The program, as reported in the papers: *Allgemeine musikalische Zeitung*, March 1845, col. 204.

302. "We know": *Allgemeine musikalische Zeitung*, trans. Thomas Kelly, December 1846, col. 873.

302. If a composer who is not a virtuoso: ibid.

303. "virtuosity is not a secondary outgrowth": Franz Liszt, "Clara Schumann," *Gesammelte Schriften aus den Annalen des Forschritts: Konzert- und Kammermusikalische Essays*, ed. L. Raman (Leipzig: Breitkopf & Härtel, 1882), p. 192.

303. "Well if I could only hear": R. Larry Todd, *Mendelssohn: A Life in Music*, p. 392.

311. "Mendelssohn's as yet unpublished Violin Concerto": *Allgemeine musikalische Zeitung,* March 1845, p. 204; quoted in Clive Brown, *A Portrait of Mendelssohn* (New Haven: Yale University Press, 2003) p. 406.

311. Mendelssohn has rather too little human pain: H. H. [Herrmann Hirschbach], *Repertorium 2* (1845), p. 217; quoted in Brown, *A Portrait of Mendelssohn*, pp. 407–08.

311. I should have reported to you long ago: Eckardt, *Ferdinand David*, pp. 232–33.

CHAPTER 12

317. "A masquerade is perhaps the most perfect form": Jean Paul, *Flegeljahre*, trans. Ronald Taylor, *Robert Schumann: His Life and Work* (New York: Universe Books, 1982), p. 117.

317. "sat down and played": Harold C. Schonberg, *The Great Pianists: From Mozart to the Present*, rev. ed. (New York: Simon & Schuster, 1987), p. 170.

319. Clara to Robert, April 1839 (box): Eva Weissweiler, *The Complete Correspondence of Clara and Robert Schumann*, trans. Hildegard Fritsch, Ronald L. Crawford, and Harold P. Fry, 3 vols. (New York: P. Lang, 1994–2002), vol. 2, pp. 170–71.

321. "prepare for and hasten": John Daverio and Eric Sams, "Schumann, Robert" *Grove Music Online* (www.oxfordmusiconline.com), consulted June 24, 2011.

321. "contrasting artist-characters": John Daverio, *Robert Schumann: Herald of a "New Poetic Age"* (New York: Oxford University Press, 1997), p. 127.

322. Schumann Praises the Young Johannes Brahms (box): Jan Swafford, *Johannes Brahms: A Biography* (New York: Vintage, 1999) p. 84.

323. "The better one gets to know the people": Clara to Robert, February 25, 1839, in Weissweiler, *Complete Correspondence,* vol. 2, p. 76.

323. The magnificence of the scenery: Berthold Litzmann, *Clara Schumann: An Artist's Life, Based on Material Found in Diaries and Letters*; trans. and abridged from the 4th ed. Grace E. Hadow (London: Macmillan, 1913; repr. New York: Da Capo Press, 1979), vol. 1, p. 205.

324. "musical soliloquy": William Atwood, *The Parisian*

Worlds of Frederic Chopin (New Haven: Yale University Press, 1999), p. 179.

324. "Twenty-five years ago": ibid.

324. "The concert, he declared": William Weber, "Recital," *Grove Music Online* (www.oxfordmusiconline.com), consulted June 24, 2011.

324. "in England, they must always": James Parakilas, *Piano Roles: Three Hundred Years of Life with the Piano* (New Haven: Yale University Press, 1999), p. 195.

324. "gave a full exhibition of her powers": William Weber, "Recital," *Grove Music Online* (www.oxfordmusiconline.com), consulted June 24, 2011.

325. I have an Érard in my room which I can barely play: Weissweiler, *Complete Correspondance,* vol. 2, p. 53.

326. "went excellently": Litzmann, *Clara Schumann: An Artist's Life,* vol. 2, p. 204.

326. "When he is not inspired": *Revue et gazette musicale,* April 6, 1862, p. 116, trans. Thomas Kelly.

326. "This painful work": P. Scudo, *L'Art musical,* April 3, 1862, p. 139, trans. Thomas Kelly.

327. "dominated by force and rhythmic clarity": ibid.

327. "a sort of virility that sits well": *Revue et gazette musicale,* April 6, 1862, p. 116, trans. Thomas Kelly.

328. The pieces were finished in short order: Wolfgang Boetticher, *Robert Schumanns Klavierwerke,* vol. 2, p. 78, in *Robert Schumann, Carnaval, Opus 9,* ed. Ernst Hertrich (Munich: G. Henle, 2004) p. v.

330. Schumann Describes the Creation of *Carnaval* (box): Taylor, *Schumann,* p. 114.

340. "I myself would always play": Boetticher, *Robert Schumanns Klavierwerke,* vol. 2, p. 78, in *Robert Schumann, Carnaval, Opus 9,* p. v.

340. what spirit, what imagination, what melodic abundance: *Revue et gazette musicale,* April 6, 1862, p. 116.

340. A Vituperative Review of *Carnaval* (box): P. Scudo, *L'Art musical,* April 3, 1862, pp. 139–40.

340. "the mists of the future": *Le Ménéstrel,* April 6, 1862, pp. 116, 117, trans. Thomas Kelly.

CHAPTER 13

345. "From the scenic point of view it interested me greatly": Robert Hartford, ed., *Bayreuth: The Early Years: An Account of Early Decades of the Wagner Festival as Seen by Celebrated Visitors and Participants* (Cambridge: Cambridge University Press, 1980), p. 52.

348. "creaking, squeaking, buzzing snuffle": Richard Wagner, *Richard Wagner's Prose Works,* trans. William Ashton Ellis (London: Kegan Paul, Trench, Trübner & Co., 1907), vol. 3, p. 85.

351. "The forests and rivers, the fires and storms": Roger Scruton, "Desecrating Wagner," *Prospect* (April 20, 2003), vol. 85, p. 40.

352. Wagner's Festival Theater (box): Hartford, *Bayreuth: The Early Years,* pp. 20–21.

353. "a college lecture-hall on a large scale": Joseph Bennett, *Letters from Bayreuth: Descriptive and Critical of Wagner's "Der Ring des Nibelungen"* (London: Novello, 1877), p. 29.

353. Wagner's Lighting Effects (box): John R. G. Hassard, *Richard Wagner at Bayreuth; The Ring of the Nibelungs—A Description of the First Performance in August 1876 (reprinted from the New York Tribune)* (New York: Francis Hart, 1877), pp. 12–13.

355. I could not get very far rehearsing with Fräulein Scheffsky: Richard Fricke, *Wagner in Rehearsal: The Diaries of Richard Fricke, 1875–1876,* trans. George R. Fricke, ed. James Deaville with Evan Baker (Stuyvesant, NY: Pendragon Press, 1998), p. 72.

355. "passed by me, raging": ibid., p. 77.

355. [Scheffsky] was big and powerful: Lilli Lehmann, *Mein Weg* (Leipzig: S. Hirzel, 1913), trans. in Hartford, *Bayreuth,* p. 51.

356. "An army of prompters arose behind every bit of scenery": ibid., p. 49.

357. "piano, pianissimo": Carl Friedrich Glasenapp, *Das Leben Richard Wagners* (Leipzig: Breitkopf & Härtel, 1894–1911), trans. William Ashton Ellis as *Life of Richard Wagner* (London: Kegan Paul, Trench, Trübner, 1900–08) vol. 5, p. 287.

357. "Wagner declared that the orchestra should support the singer": Heinrich Porges, *Wagner Rehearsing the* Ring: *An Eyewitness Account of the Stage Rehearsals of the First Bayreuth Festival,* trans. Robert L. Jacobs (Cambridge: Cambridge University Press, 1983), p. 13.

357. "There are about one hundred and twenty-five in the orchestra": from Grieg's 1876 reports in the *Bergenpost,* trans. Hartford, *Bayreuth: The Early Years,* p. 63.

368. "Of all the dull towns I imagine": Joseph Bennett, *Letters from Bayreuth* (London: Novello 1877), p. 23.

369. The ride of the Valkyries through the sky: Hassard, *Richard Wagner at Bayreuth,* p. 34.

369. (At the premiere of *The Valkyrie* in Munich. . . .): Steven Cerf, "Wagner's Ring and German Culture: Performances and Interpretations On and Off Stage," in *Inside the Ring: Essays on Wagner's Opera Cycle,* ed. John Louis DiGaetani (Jefferson, NC: McFarland, 2006), p. 159.

369. Grieg called his performance "overwhelmingly good"; quoted in Hartford, *Bayreuth: The Early Years,* p. 68.

369. "He had intellect, vocal power": Lehmann, *Mein Weg,* p. 48.

369. ("His voice is worn and husky. . . ."): Hassard, *Richard Wagner at Bayreuth,* p. 35.

CHAPTER 14

373. "Undoubtedly the germs for the best of music": Antonín Dvořák, "Music in America," *Harper's New Monthly Magazine,* February 1895; cited in Leo Treitler, ed., *Strunk's Source Readings in Music History,* rev. ed. (New York: W. W. Norton, 1998), p. 1256.

374. "Despite the fact that I have moved a bit": John Clapham, *Antonin Dvořák: Musician and Craftsman* (New York: St. Martin's Press), p. 14.

374. In 1892 it was reported: *New York Tribune Monthly,* June 1892, cited in Frederic Cople Jaher, *Nineteenth-Century Elites in Boston and New York, Journal of Social History,* 6 (1972), pp. 32–37, at p. 38.

376. "I think it will serve to incite the younger American musicians": *Musical Record* 385 (February 1894), p. 2.

377. "The Americans expect great things of me": Otakar Šourek, *Antonín Dvořák, Letters and Reminiscences,* trans. Roberta Finlayson Samsour (Prague: Artia, 1954; repr. New York: Da Capo, 1985), p. 152.

377. "not an awesome personality at all": from *The Musical Standard;* quoted in Clapham, *Antonín Dvořák: Musician and Craftsman,* p. 18.

378. Dvořák's Hobbies (box): Hans-Hubert Schönzeler, *Dvořák* (London: Marion Boyars, 1984), pp. 143–44.

378. "I love the American people very much": quoted in John Clapham, "Dvořák's Ordeal During the American Depression," *The Musical Times* 130/1761 (1989), p. 672.

379. The article contained theoretical descriptions of black music: Michael Brim Beckerman, *New Worlds of Dvořák: Searching in America for the Composer's Inner Life* (New York: W. W. Norton, 2003), pp. 95–98.

379. Nostalgia and the Evolution of the *New World* Symphony (box): Jeannette Thurber, "Dvořák As I Know Him," *The Etude* 37, No. 11 (November 1919); cited in John Clapham, "The Evolution of Dvořák's Symphony 'From the New World,'" *Musical Quarterly* 44/2 (1958), p. 170.

379. All races have their distinctive national songs: H. C. Colles, "Antonín Dvořák. III—In the New World," *The Musical Times* 82 (1941), p. 209.

379. Now, I found that the music of the Negroes and of the Indians: "Dvořák on His New Work," *New York Herald,* December 15, 1893, p. 11.

380. "all good causes may here find a platform": Andrew Carnegie, *A Carnegie Anthology,* ed. Margaret Barclay (published privately: New York, 1915), p. 69.

381. "the unusually large number of tickets": "Dr. Dvorak's American Compositions," *New York Tribune,* December 24, 1893, p. 22.

381. It was essentially a "ladies'" day: "Dr. Dvorak's Great Symphony," *New York Herald,* December 16, 1893, p. 8.

381. "authoritatively informed": *The New York Times* (December 17, 1893); quoted in Michael Beckerman, "Dvořák's 'New World' Largo and 'The Song of Hiawatha,'" *19th-Century Music* 16/1 (1992), p. 37, n. 7.

382. "a sketch for a longer work": *New York Herald,* December 15, 1893; quoted in ibid., p. 36.

382. "about thirty years ago": Jack Sullivan, *New World Symphonies: How American Culture Changed European Music* (New Haven: Yale University Press, 1999), p. 51.

382. Interestingly, the conductor Anton Seidl: Joseph Horowitz, "Dvořák and the New World: A Concentrated Moment," in *Dvořák and His World,* ed. Michael Beckerman (Princeton: Princeton University Press, 1993), pp. 93, 97.

382. "all you have to do is to be an American": Virgil Thompson "On Being American," in *Music in the Western World: A History in Documents,* ed. Piero Weiss and Richard Taruskin, 2nd ed. (New York: Schirmer Books, 2007), p. 438.

383. "distinctively negro characteristic": Michael Beckerman, "Henry Krehbiel, Antonín Dvořák, and the Symphony 'From the New World,'" *Notes* 49/2 (1992), p. 464.

385. A central section contains some remarkable music: Beckerman, *New Worlds,* p. 227.

385. "It is different to the classic works in this form": ibid., p. 26.

390. "was suggested by the scene": quoted in John Clapham, "The Evolution of Dvořák's Symphony," p. 168.

394. "the applause was exceedingly timid": "The Philharmonic Society: First Performance from Manuscript of Dvořák's American Symphony," *New York Times,* December 16, 1893, p. 8.

394. "usually tranquil": *New York Tribune,* December 24, 1893.

394. "threw kid glove convention to the winds": quoted in Beckerman, "Henry Krehbiel, Antonín Dvořák," p. 450, n. 4.

394. "dreamy, languorous": *New York World,* December 16, 1893.

394. "Indian in spirit": *Boston Herald,* May 28, 1893; quoted in John Clapham, "Dvořák and the American Indian," *The Musical Times* 107/1484 (1966), p. 865.

394. "To me it suggests nothing American": *Musical Record,* 385 (February 1894), p. 2.

394. "Dvořák's is an American symphony": quoted in Beckerman, *New Worlds,* p. 88.

395. There were many, and there still are: Michael Beckerman, "The Master's Little Joke: Antoníin Dvořák and the Mask of Nation," in Beckerman, *Dvořák and His World,* pp. 134–35.

395. "listen to every whistling boy": Leo Treitler, *Strunk's Source Readings in Music History,* rev. ed. (New York: W. W. Norton, 1998), p. 1256.

395. The American people—or the majority of them: "Dr. Dvorak's Latest Work," *New York Times,* December 17, 1893, p. 19.

CHAPTER 15

407. "Stravinsky's music is disconcerting": Adolphe Boschot, "Le 'Sacre du printemps': Ballet de MM. Roerich, Stravinsky et Nijinsky," *L'Écho de Paris,* May 30, 1913, translated in Thomas Forrest Kelly, *First Nights: Five Musical Premieres* (New Haven: Yale University Press, 2000), p. 258.

407. "Whatever else there is": Jean Cocteau, *Le coq et l'arlequin* (Paris: Éditions de la sirène, 1918; repr. Paris: Stock, 1979), p. 88; translated in Kelly, *First Nights,* p. 258.

411. "Only the swinging": Bronislava Nijinska, *Early Memoirs* (New York: Holt, Rinehard and Winston, 1981), p. 373–74.

411. "*Jeux* is the life": Vaslav Nijinsky, *The Diary of Vaslav Nijinsky,* ed. Romola de Pulszky Nijinsky (Berkeley: University of California Press, 1971), pp. 140.

411. "We were struck dumb": *Louis Laloy (1874–1944) on Debussy, Ravel, and Stravinsky,* ed. and trans. Deborah Priest (Aldershot, England: Ashgate, 1999), p. 272.

412. "he carries his head in the air": Henri Postel du Mas, "Un entretien avec M. Stravinsky," *Gil Blas 25* (June 4, 1913), translated in Kelly, *First Nights,* p. 329.

413. "Nijinsky is an admirable artist": Igor Stravinsky, "Gloires et misères du théâtre actuel," *Montjoie,* May 29, 1913, translated in Kelly, *First Nights,* p. 297.

413. "was incapable of giving intelligible form": Igor Stravinsky, *Igor Stravinsky: An Autobiography,* (New York: Simon and Schuster, 1936; repr. New York: W. W. Norton, 1962), p. 74.

413. "cannot exist without Stravinsky": Romola Nijinska, *The Diary of Vaslav Nijinsky,* p. 39.

413. "Who else could help me:" Peter Hill, *Stravinsky: The Rite of Spring* (Cambridge: Cambridge University Press, 2000), p. 4.

413. "The idea of *Le Sacre du printemps* came to me": Igor Stravinsky and Robert Craft, *Expositions and Developments* (London: Faber & Faber, 1962), p. 140.

414. [T]he first set should transport us to the foot of a sacred hill: Serge Lifar, *Diaghilev: His Life, His Work, His Legend* (London: Putnam, 1940), p. 278.

417. "We had to run about more or less": Lydia Sokolova, *Dancing for Diaghilev,* ed. Richard Buckle (London: J. Murray, 1960), p. 42.

417. Nijinsky rehearsed like an inexhaustible demon until he nearly dropped: Anatole Bourman with D. Lyman, *The Tragedy of Nijinsky* (New York: McGraw-Hill, 1936), p. 216.

417. Stravinsky Describes a Dance Rehearsal (box): Stravinsky and Craft, *Expositions,* pp. 142–43.

419. "When we saw the parts for the first time": Truman Bullard, "The First Performance of Igor Stravinsky's 'Sacre du Printemps,'" 3 vols., (Ph.D. diss., Eastman School of Music, University of Rochester, 1971; Ann Arbor: University Microfilms), vol. 1, p. 98.

419. Pierre Monteux Hears Stravinsky Play the *Rite* (box): Doris Monteux, *It's All in the Music: The Life and Work of Pierre Monteux* (London: William Kimber, 1965), p. 91.

419. It is hard to describe the astonishment of the orchestra when we started: Bullard, "The First Performance," vol. 1, p. 97.

419. *The Rite of Spring,* which the Russian ballet will perform for the first time: "Le sacre du printemps," *Le Figaro,* May 29, 1913, translated in Kelly, *First Nights,* p. 263.

424. "rolling like bundles of leaves in the wind": Robert Craft's notes ("Genesis of a Masterpiece," preface to Igor Stravinsky, *The Rite of Spring: Sketches, 1911–1913.* Facsimile reproductions from the autographs [London: Boosey & Hawkes, 1969]), p. xxi.

430. Mild protests against the music could be heard: Stravinsky and Craft, *Expositions,* p. 143.

430. Adolphe Boschot's Negative Review of the *Rite* (box): quoted in Kelly, *First Nights,* pp. 305–06.

430. "On hearing this near riot behind me": D. Monteux, *It's All in the Music,* p. 90.

431. She stood on the stage: Mary Clarke, *Dancers of Mercury: The Story of the Ballet Rambert* (London: A. and C. Black, 1962), p. 27.

431. "Then in this magic circle": André Levinson, "Stravinsky and the Dance," *Theater Arts Monthly* 8 (1924), pp. 741–54; repr. in Bullard, "The First Performance," vol. 1, p. 152.

431. "to wander disconsolately along the streets of Paris": John N. Burk, "Le Sacre du Printemps," *Boston Symphony Orchestras Programmes (1950–51),* p. 664, citing Pierre Monteux in *Dance Index* 6, nos. 10–12 (1947), p. 242.

431. The composer himself reported only the scene in the restaurant, with a satisfied Diaghilev declaring, "Exactly what I wanted!": Igor Stravinsky and Robert Craft, *Conversations with Igor Stravinsky* (Garden City, NY: Doubleday, 1959), p. 48.

431. "but what the audience saw on stage": Charles M. Joseph, *Stravinsky & Balanchine: A Journey of Invention* (New Haven: Yale University Press, 2002), p. 26.

432. "the Messiah we have waited for": Florent Schmitt, "*Les Sacre du Printemps,* de M. Igor Strawinsky, au Théâtre des Champs-Élysées," *La France,* June 4, 1913, translated in Kelly, *First Nights,* p. 314.

CHAPTER 16

435. "Apart from my desire to make good music": Alban Berg, in Willi Reich, *Alban Berg: mit Bergs eigenen Schriften und Beiträgen von Theodor Wiesengrund-Adorno und Ernst Krenek* (Vienna, 1937), p. 175; quoted in Douglas Jarman, "Berg, Alban," *New Grove Music Online.*

437. Arnold Schoenberg on Musical Expressionism (box): Joseph Henry Auner, *A Schoenberg Reader: Documents of a Life* (New Haven: Yale University Press, 2003), p. 137.

438. "the fate of this poor man": Alban Berg, in Willi Reich, "Aus unbekannten Briefen von Alban Berg an Anton Webern," *Schweizerische Musikzeitung* XCIII/2 (February), p. 50; quoted in George Perle, *The Operas of Alban Berg, vol. 1: Wozzeck* (Berkeley: University of California Press, 1980), p. 20.

438. "There is a bit of me in his character": Alban Berg, *Letters to His Wife,* trans. and ed. Bernard Grun (London: Faber & Faber, 1971), p. 229.

439. "I was greatly surprised": *Style and Idea: Selected Writings of Arnold Schoenberg,* (New York: St. Martin's Press, 1975), p. 474.

439. "It's settled": Willi Reich, *The Life and Work of Alban Berg* (London: Thames & Hudson, 1965), p. 58.

441. I spent my first rehearsal: Berg, *Letters,* p. 344.

441. "Be glad you weren't at the first rehearsal": ibid., p. 353.

441. "the orchestral rehearsal with the complete stage": ibid., p. 353.

441. "In spite of a few die-hards": Douglas Jarman, *Alban Berg, Wozzeck* (Cambridge: Cambridge University Press, 1989), p. 70.

442. Between the scenes, which flash by like cinema: Paul Zschorlich, "'Wozzeck' von Alban Berg," *Deutsche Zeitung,* Berlin, Dec. 25, 1925, reproduced in Konrad Vogelsang, *Dokumentation zur Oper Wozzeck von Alban Berg: die Jahre des Durchbruchs 1925–32* (Laaber Verlag, 1977), p. 24.

442. The press is only printing things unfavorable to Kleiber: Berg, *Letters,* p. 350.

451. "as the composer's confession": Perle, *The Operas of Alban Berg,* pp. 88–89.

460. "although the music steers again": Douglas Jarman, *The Music of Alban Berg* (Berkeley: University of California Press, 1979), p. 238.

461. At the première there were fisticuffs: Reich, *Life and Work,* pp. 60–61.

461. "no experiment, but a masterwork of art": Jarman, *Alban Berg, Wozzeck,* p. 70.

461. It is difficult to do justice to the strange perfection: Reich, *Life and Work,* p. 62.

462. Leaving the State Opera House: ibid., pp. 61–62.

463. However much one may know about the musical forms: ibid., p. 66.

CHAPTER 17

467. "The camp of Görlitz": Rebecca Rischin, *For the End of Time: The Story of the Messiaen Quartet* (Ithaca, NY: Cornell University Press, 2003), p. 70.

472. It's in that open field: ibid., p. 12.

472. "I was very surprised": ibid., pp. 35–36.

473. I wrote for them at once: ibid., p. 16.

473. But the "Intermède" is not the earliest part of the Quartet: ibid., pp. 16–17.

473. The first great difficulty: ibid., p. 39.

474. "He would say to the clarinetist": ibid., p. 41.

474. "He wanted it *very* slow": ibid.

474. "I had a jacket": ibid., p. 63.

474. I told them first of all: ibid., p. 64.

475. "In my dreams": all translations of textual material in the score are by Thomas Kelly.

475. "I was born a believer": Rischin, *For the End of Time,* p. 49.

477. "If you want symbols": ibid., p. 60.

477. "would spend hours, entire mornings": ibid., p. 41.

478. There's the mystic and there's the man: ibid., p. 40.

492. The musicians, sitting next to the young master: ibid., pp. 64–65.

492. A cello solo: ibid., pp. 67–68.

493. He had earlier tried to escape: ibid., p. 45.

CHAPTER 18

499. "As ugly as the city jungles": Brooks Atkinson, "The Jungles of the City," *The New York Times,* September 27, 1957, p. 14.

505. "They never used *cool* then": Craig Zadan, "Sondheim & Co.," repr. *Readings on West Side Story,* ed. Mary E. Williams (San Diego: Greenhaven Press, 2001), p. 51.

507. "I want to conduct": Donal Henahan, "Leonard Bernstein, 72, Music's Monarch, Dies," *The New York Times,* October 15, 1990, p. A1.

509. I meant for the girl to sing again: Zadan, "Sondheim & Co.," repr. Williams, *Readings,* pp. 50–51.

509. Maria has a speech holding the gun: Mel Gussow, "'West Side Story': The Beginnings of Something Great," *The New York Times,* October 21, 1990, p. H5.

510. "I had two street kids singing": Meryle Secrest, *Stephen Sondheim: A Life* (New York: Knopf, 1998), p. 115.

512. Carol Lawrence and Arthur Laurents, in Their Own Words (box): Sara Fishko, "The Real-Life Drama Behind *West Side Story,*" radio broadcast, January 7, 2009 (www.npr.org/2011/02/24/97274711/the-real-life-drama-behind-west-side-story)

512. "I know I'm difficult": Humphrey Burton, *Leonard Bernstein* (London: Faber & Faber, 1995), p. 275.

513. Leonard Bernstein, in His Own Words (box): August 20, 1957, from Bernstein Estate (www.westsidestory.com/site/level2/archives/journal/excerpts.html)

513. "If it goes as well in New York": to David Diamond; cited in Humphrey Burton, *Leonard Bernstein* (London: Faber & Faber, 1995), p. 276.

523. "I did not enjoy it": October 12, 1957, repr. *The Collected Works of Harold Clurman*, ed. Marjorie Loggia and Glenn Young; intro. Robert Whitehead (New York: Applause Books, 1994), p. 336.

523. "Mr. Bernstein is an able and intelligent craftsman": Henry Hewes, *Saturday Review*, October 5, 1957, repr. Williams, *Readings*, p. 119.

523. "be reproduced more or less accurately": Wolcott Gibbs, *New Yorker*, October 5, 1957, repr. Williams, *Readings*, p. 115.

523. "Everything contributes to the total impression of wildness": Brooks Atkinson, "Theatre: The Jungles of the City," *The New York Times*, September 27, 1957, p. 14.

523. "The show is, in general, not well sung": Walter Kerr, *New York Herald Tribune*, September 27, 1957, p. 10.

523. Perhaps the musical's most striking quality: Zadan, *"Theater Arts*, December 1957," repr. Williams, *Readings*, p. A1.

524. "Once heard": Jim Dwyer, "Under Broadway, the Subway Hums Bernstein," *The New York Times*, February 21, 2009, p. A1.

Every effort has been made to contact the rights holders for each image. Please contact W. W. Norton with any updated information.

CHAPTER 1

Page 2: © Peggy Badenhausen, *Blue Bucket 1*, 2009, oil and graphite on canvas, 36" x 48"; **p. 4**: Shutterstock; **p. 14**: Mark Lyons. Courtesy of Cincinnati Symphony.

PART OPENER I

Page 18 (top left, down): HIP / Art Resource, NY; Réunion des Musées Nationaux / Art Resource, NY; AAAC / Topham / The Image Works; Huntington Library / SuperStock; (top right, down): Bridgeman Art Library; Snark / Art Resource, NY; **p. 19**: The New York Public Library / Art Resource, NY; **p. 22**: Age Fotostock / SuperStock; **p. 23**: Richard List / Corbis; **p. 24** (left side, down): Scala / Ministero per i Beni e le Attività culturali / Art Resource, NY; Scala / Art Resource, NY; Lebrecht / ColouriserAL / The Image Works; (right side, down): Granger Collection; Scala / Art Resource, NY; **p. 28**: Scala / Ministero per i Beni e le Attività culturali / Art Resource, NY; **p. 29**: National Gallery, London / Bridgeman Art Library.

CHAPTER 2

Page 30: Museu Nacional d'Art de Catalunya, Barcelona, Spain / Photo © AISA / Bridgeman Art Library; **p. 31** (top): Erich Lessing / Art Resource, NY; (bottom): The Print Collector / Alamy; **p. 34**: Alamy; **p. 35** (top): Map of Paris. David Monniaux. http://en.wikipedia.org/wiki/Public_domain; (bottom): imagebroker.net / SuperStock; **p. 36** (top): Bridgeman Art Library; (bottom): Guiziou Franck / Photolibrary; **p. 37** (top): Age Fotostock / SuperStock; (bottom): Yoshio Tomii / SuperStock; **p. 38**: Science, Industry & Business Library, The New York Public Library, Astor, Lenox and Tilden Foundations; **p. 49**: Firenze, Biblioteca Medicea Laurenziana; **p. 51**: Firenze, Biblioteca Medicea Laurenziana. Ms. Plut. 29.1, c. 2r. Su Concessione del Ministero per i Beni e le Attivita Culturali.

CHAPTER 3

Page 56: V&A Images, London / Art Resource, NY; **p. 58**: Cornerstone Photos / Alamy; **p. 60** (top): Berkeley Castle, Gloucestershire, UK / Bridgeman Art Library; (bottom): Erich Lessing / Art Resource, NY; **p. 62**: Granger Collection; **p. 71**: Musikhistorisk Museum, Copenhagen, Denmark. Carl Clausius Collection; **p. 73**: By Permission of the Folger Shakespeare Library, STC 7091, fol. C verso–C2 recto: V. "Can She Excuse My Wrongs?": **p. 74** (top): Johnny Van Haeften Ltd, London / Bridgeman Art Library; (bottom): akg-images; **p. 75**:

By kind permission of Viscount De L'Isle from his private collection at Penshurst Place, Kent, England.

PART OPENER II

Page 82 (left side, down): Granger Collection; Bridgeman Art Library; Granger Collection; (right side, down): Galleria dell' Accademia / Cameraphoto Arte Venezia / Bridgeman Art Library; Roger-Viollet / The Image Works; Hulton Archive / Getty Images; Granger Collection; **p. 83**: Scala / Art Resource, NY; **p. 85** (left): Alinari / Art Resource, NY; (right): Giraudon / Bridgeman Art Library; **p. 86** (top): Scala / Ministero per i Beni e le Attività culturali / Art Resource, NY; (bottom): Andrea Jemolo / Scala / Art Resource, NY; **p. 88**: Photolibrary; **p. 89**: Alinari / Bridgeman Art Library.

CHAPTER 4

Page 90: Scala / Art Resource, NY; **p. 91**: Galleria dell' Accademia, Italy / Cameraphoto Arte Venezia / Bridgeman Art Library; **p. 93** (top): Palazzo Ducale, Italy / Bridgeman Art Library; (bottom): CuboImages srl / Alamy; **p. 94**: (top): Adam Woolfitt / Corbis; (bottom): Photo © Hans Thorwid / Nationalmuseum, Stockholm; **p. 95**: Lebrecht Music and Arts Library; **p. 96** (top): Gilles Mermet / Art Resource, NY; (bottom): Lebrecht Music and Arts Photo Library / Alamy; **p. 97**: Gift of Annalee Newman, 1992 Accession Number: 1992.179.1 Rights and Reproduction: © 2011 Artists Rights Society (ARS), New York. Image copyright © The Metropolitan Museum of Art / Art Resource, NY; **p. 101**: Lebrecht Music & Arts; **p.102**: Musée de la Musique, Paris, Photo: Dominique Santrot.

CHAPTER 5

Page 118: British Museum / Art Resource; **p. 119**: British Library, R.M.20.f.1; **p. 120**: Granger Collection; **p. 121**: Derek Bayes / Lebrecht Music & Arts; **p. 123** (top): Lebrecht Music & Arts / The Image Works; (bottom): Private Collection / Christie's Images / Bridgeman Art Library; **p. 124** (top): Lebrecht Music & Arts / The Image Works; (bottom): Beinecke Rare Book & Manuscript Library, Yale University; **p. 125**: Gerald Coke Handel Collection, Foundling Museum, London / Bridgeman Art Library; **p. 126** (top): Historical Picture Archive / Corbis; (bottom): Lebrecht Music & Arts / The Image Works.

CHAPTER 6

Page 146: Photoservice Electa Mondadori / Art Resource, NY; **p. 147**: Lebrecht Music & Arts / The Image Works; **p. 148** (top): Foto Marburg / Art Resource, NY; (bottom): akg-images; **p. 149**: Getty Images; **p. 150**: akg-images; **p. 151** (top): Granger Collection; (bottom): akg-images; **p. 152** (top): ullstein bild /

Granger Collection; (bottom): Lebrecht Music & Arts; **p. 154** (left): Bildarchiv Preussischer Kulturbesitz/Art Resource, NY; (right): Lebrecht Music & Arts/The Image Works; **p. 156** (left): akg-images/The Image Works; (top right): Bridgman Art Library; (bottom right): Munchner Stadtmuseum.

PART OPENER III

Page 168 (left side, down): Stock Montage/Getty Images; Granger Collection; Goethe National Museum/Bridgeman Art Library; Stock Montage/Getty Images; (right side, down): (3) Granger Collection; Imagno/Getty Images; **p. 169**: *The Foursome*, c. 1713 (oil on canvas), Watteau, Jean Antoine/Fine Arts Museums of San Francisco/Bridgeman Art Library; **p. 171**: Musée de la Ville de Paris/Bridgeman Art Library; **p. 172**: Roger-Viollet/The Image Works; **p. 173** (left): The Bloomsbury Workshop/Bridgeman Art Library; (right): Apic/Getty Images; **p. 174**: Erich Lessing/Art Resource, NY.

CHAPTER 7

Page 176: Alfredo Dagli Orti/The Art Archive at Art Resource, NY; **p. 178**: Alfredo Dagli Orti/The Art Archive at Art Resource, NY; **p. 179**: Lebrecht Music & Arts; **p. 180** (top): Musée Conde, Chantilly, France; (bottom): Imagno/Getty Images; **p. 182**: Imagno/Getty Images; **p. 183**: Lebrecht/ColouriserAL/The Image Works; **p. 185**: Lebrecht Music & Arts; **p. 186**: Granger Collection; **p. 187**: Copyright © 2007 President and Fellows of Harvard University; **p. 188** (top): Erich Lessing/Art Resource, NY; (bottom): Getty Images; **p. 205**: Laurie Lewis/Lebrecht Music & Arts.

CHAPTER 8

Page 208: Erich Lessing/Art Resource, NY; **p. 209**: Imagno/Getty Images; **p. 211**: (top): Granger Collection; (center): Alamy; (bottom): Universal Images Group/Art Resource, NY; **p. 213**: Music Division, The New York Public Library for the Performing Arts, Astor, Lenox and Tilden Foundations; **p. 214**: Universal History Archive/Getty Images; **p. 215**: Imagno/Getty Images; **p. 217**: Granger Collection.

CHAPTER 9

Page 234: Erich Lessing/Art Resource, NY; **p. 237**: Erich Lessing/Art Resource, NY; **p. 238**: Erich Lessing/Art Resource, NY; **p. 239**: Erich Lessing/Art Resource, NY; **p. 240**: Erich Lessing/Art Resource, NY; **p. 242** (top): Joseph Freiherr von Spaun; http://en.wikipedia.org/wiki/Public domain; (bottom): Erich Lessing/Art Resource, NY; **p. 243** (top): Erich Lessing/Art Resource, NY; (bottom): akg-images.

PART OPENER IV

Page 256: (left side, down): bpk, Berlin/Staatsbibliothek zu Berlin, Stiftung Preussischer Kulturbesit/Art Resource, NY; Bridgeman Art Library; Time Life Pictures/Getty Images; SSPL/Getty Images; (right side, down): Universal History Archive/Getty Images; Lebrecht Music and Arts Photo Library/Alamy; Hulton Archive/Getty Images; Fotosearch/

Getty Images; Popperfoto/Getty Images; **p. 257**: bpk, Berlin/Hamburger Kunsthalle/Elke Walford/Art Resource, NY; **p. 258**: The National Trust/Photolibrary/Alamy; **p. 260**: National Gallery, London/Art Resource, NY; **p. 261**: Image copyright © The Metropolitan Museum of Art/Art Resource, NY; **p. 262**: Interfoto/Alamy.

CHAPTER 10

Page 264: Erich Lessing/Art Resource, NY; **p. 266** (top): Scala/White Images/Art Resource, NY; (bottom): ND/Roger-Viollet/Getty Images; **p. 267**: Hulton/Getty Images; **p. 268**: Giraudon/Bridgeman Art Library; **p. 269**: Reproduced with permission from the Hector Berlioz Website (www.hberlioz.com); **p. 270** (top): DeA Picture Library/Art Resource, NY; (bottom): Yale Center for British Art, Paul Mellon Collection/Bridgeman Art Library; **p. 271**: Lebrecht Music & Arts/The Image Works; **p. 274** (top): Lebrecht Music and Arts Photo Library/Alamy; (bottom): National Trust Photographic Library/Andreas von Einsiedel/Bridgeman Art Library; **p. 275** (top): Aldo Tutino/Art Resource, NY; (bottom): Mary Evans Picture Library/The Image Works; **p. 276**: Bibliothèque nationale de France.

CHAPTER 11

Page 294: © Fine Arts Museums of San Francisco; **p. 296**: bpk, Berlin/Art Resource, NY; **p. 297**: Mary Evans Picture Library/The Image Works; **p. 298** (top): bpk,/Staatsbibliothek zu Berlin, Stiftung Preussischer Kulturbesitz, Art Resource, NY; (bottom left): bpk, Berlin/Mendelssohn-Archiv, Staatsbibliothek zu Berlin, Stiftung Preussischer Kulturbesitz/Art Resource, NY; **p. 298** (bottom right): akg-images; **p. 299**: bpk, Berlin/Mendelssohn-Archiv, Staatsbibliothek zu Berlin, Stiftung Preussischer Kulturbesitz/Art Resource, NY; **p. 300**: Lebrecht Music & Arts/The Image Works; **p. 301**: Peter Joslin/ArenaPAL Topham/The Image Works; **p. 304** (left): JTB Photo Communications, Inc./Alamy; (right): Radius Images/Corbis; **p. 314**: Julie g. Woodhouse/Alamy.

CHAPTER 12

Page 316: bpk, Berlin/Kunstbibliothek, Staatliche Museen/Knud Peterson/Art Resource, NY; **p. 318** (top): Granger Collection; (bottom): akg-images; **p. 319**: Lebrecht/ColouriserAL/The Image Works; **p. 320**: Bridgeman Art Library; **p. 321**: (top): Lebrecht Music & Arts/The Image Works; (bottom): Bridgeman Art Library; **p. 322**: Stapleton Collection/Corbis; **p. 323**: Lebrecht Music & Arts/The Image Works; **p. 324**: Mary Evans Picture Library/The Image Works; **p. 325**: Lebrecht Music and Arts Photo Library/Alamy; **p. 326**: Bibliothèque Nationale, Paris, France; **p. 327**: akg-images.

CHAPTER 13

Page 344: Colette Masson/Roger-Viollet/The Image Works; **p. 346**: Réunion des Musées Nationaux/Art Resource, NY; **p. 348**: Adoc-photos/Art Resource, NY; **p. 349**: Lebrecht Music & Arts/The Image Works; **p. 351**: Private Collection/Bridgeman Art Library; **p. 352**: Bettmann/Corbis; **p. 354** (top): Lebrecht

Music & Arts/The Image Works; (center): Photo Stage; (bottom): Lebrecht Music & Arts; **p. 355** (top): Granger Collection; (right): Bridgeman Art Library; **p. 368**: akg-images; **p. 369**: Lebrecht/The Image Works.

CHAPTER 14

Page 372: Terra Foundation for American Art, Chicago/Art Resource, NY; **p. 374**: Time Life Pictures/Getty Images; **p. 375** (top): Granger Collection; (bottom): Jacob A. Riis/Museum of the City of New York/Getty Images; **p. 376**: Library of Congress; **p. 377** (top): Granger Collection; (bottom): Lebrecht/The Image Works; **p. 378**: akg-images; **p. 379**: Lebrecht/The Image Works; **p. 380**: Gabriel Hackett/Archive Photos/Getty Images; **p. 381**: Lebrecht/The Image Works; **p. 394**: Title page of *New World* Symphony, in Dvorak's hand, showing "From the New World" http://commons.wikimedia.org/wiki/Public_domain.

PART OPENER V

Page 398 (left side, down): Réunion des Musées Nationaux/Art Resource, NY; APAGetty Images; Dennis Hallinan/Alamy; AP Photo; (right side, down): Imagno/Getty Images; Mary Evans Picture Library/Alamy; Erich Auerbach/Getty Images; **p. 399**: Private Collection/Photo © BEBA/AISA/Bridgeman Art Library; **p. 401** (top): Peter Dazeley/Getty Images; (bottom): Gianni Dagli Orti/The Art Archive at Art Resource, NY; **p. 403**: Idealink Photography/Alamy; **p. 405**: © 2012 Frank Stella/Artists Rights Society (ARS), New York. Image copyright © The Metropolitan Museum of Art. Image source: Art Resource, NY.

CHAPTER 15

Page 406: © 2012 Artists Rights Society (ARS), New York/ADAGP, Paris. V&A Images, London; **p. 408**: Granger Collection; **p. 409**: Bettmann/Corbis; **p. 410**: Musée d'Orsay, Paris, France. Réunion des Musées Nationaux/Art Resource, NY; **p. 411**: Bettmann/Corbis; **p. 412**: Réunion des Musées Nationaux/Art Resource, NY; **p. 413** (top): Lebrecht/The Image Works; (bottom): Erich Lessing/Art Resource, NY; **p. 414**: (top left): E. O. Hoppe/Hulton Archive/Getty Images; (top right): *The Forefathers*, 1912 (oil on canvas); Rerikh, Nikolai; © Ashmolean Museum, University of Oxford, Bridgeman Art Library; (bottom right): The Art Gallery Collection/Alamy; **p. 416**: Albert Harlingue/Roger-Viollet/Getty Images; **p. 417**: Graham Salter/Lebrecht Music & Arts; **p. 418**: Granger Collection; **p. 419**: Library of Congress; **p. 431**: © 2012 Artists Rights Society (ARS), New York/ADAGP, Paris. V&A Images, London/Art Resource, NY.

CHAPTER 16

Page 434: Photo by Ken Howard. © 2007 The Metropolitan Opera; **p. 435**: © 2012 Belmont Music Publisher, Los Angeles/ARS, New York/VBK, Vienna. Erich Lessing/Art Resource, NY; **p. 436**: Lebrecht Photo Library; **p. 438**: Imagno/Getty Images; **p. 439**: akg-images; **p. 440**: akg-images; **p. 441** (left):

Mary Evans Picture Library/The Image Works; (right): ArenaPal/Topham/The Image Works; (bottom): Metropolitan Opera Guild/*Opera News*; **p. 442**: Courtesy of Universal Edition, Vienna; **p. 461** (top): Lebrecht/The Image Works; (bottom): Private Collection/Lebrecht Music & Arts; **p. 463**: Turtle Julian.

CHAPTER 17

Page 466: © Peggy Badenhausen, *Winter Curve 2, 2009*, monotype, 24" x 37"; **p. 468**: Mary Evans Picture Library/Alamy; **p. 469**: Courtesy of Hannalore Lauerwald from Rebecca Rischin, *For the End of Time: The Story of the Messiaen Quartet,* Cornell University Press, 2003; **p. 470** (top): Courtesy of Hannalore Lauerwald from Rebecca Rischin, *For the End of Time: The Story of the Messiaen Quartet,* Cornell University Press, 2003; (bottom): Alexander Turnbull Library; **p. 471** (top): Courtesy of Etienne Paquier from Rebecca Rischin, *For the End of Time: The Story of the Messiaen Quartet,*Cornell University Press, 2003; (bottom): Courtesy of Yvonne Dran from Rebecca Rischin, *For the End of Time: The Story of the Messiaen Quartet,* Cornell University Press, 2003; **p. 472** (top): Courtesy Jean Lanier from Rebecca Rischin, *For the End of Time: The Story of the Messiaen Quartet,* Cornell University Press, 2003; (bottom): Bridgeman Art Library; **p. 473**: United States Holocaust Memorial Museum, courtesy of Sonia Beker; **p. 474**: Courtesy of Etienne Pasquier from Rebecca Rischin, *For the End of Time: The Story of the Messiaen Quartet,* Cornell University Press, 2003; **p. 494**: Glenn Harper/Alamy.

CHAPTER 18

Page 498: Roger Wood/Corbis; **p. 500**: Bettmann/Corbis; **p. 501** (top): Bettmann/Corbis; (bottom): Charles Trainor/Time & Life Pictures/Getty Images; **p. 502**: Carl Purcell/Three Lions/Getty Images; **p. 503**: George Karger/Pix Inc./Time Life Pictures/Getty Images; **p. 505**: Photofest; **p. 507**: Erich Auerbach/Getty Images; **p. 508** (top): The Kobal Collection/Art Resource; (bottom): Artcraft Poster Collection, Prints and Photographs Division, Library of Congress; **p. 510**: AP Photo; **p. 511**: NYPL Digital; **p. 512**: United Artists/Courtesy of Getty Images; **p. 513**: Photo by Robert H. Phillips, Leonard Bernstein Collection, Music Division. Courtesy of the estate of the photographer; **p. 524**: Paul Fusco/Magnum Photos.

CHAPTER 19

Page 526: Chad Matthew Carlson/Alamy; **p. 528**: Photo by: Jonathan William; **p. 531**: Photo Stage.

MUSIC AND TEXTS

Alban Berg: Berg, *Wozzeck.* © 1926 Universal Edition A.G., Wien. © Renewed. All rights reserved. Used by permission of European American Music Distributors Company, U.S. and Canadian agent for Universal Edition A.G., Wien.

Leonard Bernstein: "America" © Copyright 1956, 1957, 1958, 1959 by Amberson Holdings LLC and Stephen Sondheim. Copyright renewed. Leonard Bernstein Music Publishing

Note: Page numbers in *italics* indicate a photograph or an illustration.

Abduction from the Seraglio, The (Mozart), 181

absolute monarchy, 84, 172

absolute music, 272

abstract expressionism, 402

Academies (public concerts), 215–16, 324

Accademia degl'Invaghiti (club), 92, 102–3

accelerando, 8, 334

accompanied song, 72–73, 76–77, 80

action (piano), 325

Adams, John, 405

    Doctor Atomic, 530–32

added-value rhythms, 476–77, 496

Adelaïde (Beethoven), 326, 327

affects, 86, 220, 232

Afghanistan, 400

African American music, 373, 380, 382, 384, 395–96, 405, 517

Afternoon of a Faun, The (Nijinsky ballet), 410, *410*, 411, 420

Age of Reason, 171

Agnus Dei, 28, 40

    from Byrd's Mass for Four Voices, 9, 62–68

Agon (Stravinsky), 412

"Ah! Perfido" (Beethoven), 216

Aida (Verdi), 262

"Air on the G String" (Bach), 162

Akoka, Abraham, 493–94

Akoka, Henri, 469, *471*, 471–74, 482, 492, 493–94

Albéniz, Isaac, 378

Alberti, Leon Battista, 29

Alcott, Bronson, 261

Alcott, Louisa May, 261

aleatoric music, 404

Alembert, Jean le Rond d', *Encyclopédie,* *172*

Aleph, The (Borges), 403

Alexander III, Pope, 37

Alleluia, 39–40, 46, 47, 49, 50

Allen, Woody, *Annie Hall,* 403

Allgemeine musikalische Zeitung, 311

Almodóvar, Pedro, *Talk to Her,* 403

alto flute, 11

alto (voice), 63, 144

amateur musicians

    in Classic era, 236–37, 244

    in Renaissance, 57

Ambassadors, The (James), 402

"America," *West Side Story* (Bernstein), 520–22

American Centennial March (Wagner), 349, 351

American Flag, The (Dvořák), 380

American in Paris, An (Gershwin), 395

American music, definitions of, 381–83, 395

American Opera Company, 376

American Revolution, 171, 172, 174, 214

American String Quartet (Dvořák), 380

Ancient era, 19

andante, 195

"And the glory of the Lord," from *Messiah* (Handel), 89, 136–38

Angels in America (Kushner), 403

Animal Farm (Orwell), 403

animato, 334

Annie Hall (Allen film), 403

antecedent phrase, 279

Antheil, George, 4

antiphonal performance, 39, 44–45

anti-Semitism, 297, 314, 348, 370, 399, 439–40, 495

Aparajito (Ray film), 403

Apollo (Stravinsky), 409, 412, 431

Apprenticeship of Wilhelm Meister, The (Goethe), 173

Aquinas, Thomas, 53

    Summa Theologica, 22

Aravantinos, Panos, 442, *442*

Archer, Kenneth, 416

architecture

    in Baroque era, 85, 89

    in Classic era, 173

    in Middle Ages, 22–23, 36

    of Notre Dame Cathedral, 37–38, 53, 269

    in Renaissance, 29

    in twentieth century, 402

Arena Chapel (Padua), 23

aria(s)

    of Adams, 530–32

    da capo, 136

    in Mozart's *Don Giovanni,* 190–91, 192, 193, 196, 197–98, 206

    in operas, 190–91, 206, 530–32

    in oratorios, 122, 130–36, 144, 220

    ritornello form for, 167

    term, 130

Armingaud, Jules, 326–27

Armingaud-Jacquard String Quartet, 326

Around the World in 80 Days (film), 501

"arpa doppia," 100

arpeggio(s), 304, 331

arrangements, 74–75, 77–79

art

    in Baroque era, 85–86, 89

    in Classic era, 172–73

    in Middle Ages, 22–23

    in Renaissance, 29

    in Romantic era, 260–61

    in twentieth century, 402

Art musical, 340

Art of Fugue, The (Bach), 149, 157

art songs, 243. *See also* lieder

Asch, Germany, 329–30

Assisi, basilica of, 23

astronomy, 28

Astruc, Gabriel, 416, 430

a tempo, 8

Atkinson, Brooks, 499, 523

atonal music, 404, 437, 443, 445, 447, 464, 514

Auber, Daniel François Esprit, 263

    La muette de Portici, 267, *267*, 277

augmented fourth, 445

Augustine, St., 43

Austen, Jane, 173

Austria, 209–10, 436. *See also* Vienna

    in Baroque era, 84

    in Classic era, 174

    in Romantic era, 258

Austro-Hungarian Empire, 178, 436

avant-garde, 432

Avignon, France, 21
Avolio, Christina Maria, 124, 126

Babbitt, Milton, 404, 510
Bacchini, Girolamo, 99
Bach, Anna Magdalena, 149
Bach, Carl Philipp Emanuel, 149, *151*, 154, 159
Bach, Johann Sebastian, 83, *149*
   The Art of Fugue, 149, 157
   basso continuo use, 101
   biography, 149
   Brandenburg Concertos, 148, 149, 151, 155, 163
   career path of, 147–51
   church music of, 151
   "Coffee Cantata," 153, 155
   Concerto in F for Harpischord, Two Recorders, and Strings, 133, 155, 163–65, 295
   Goldberg Variations, 150
   Inventions, 446
   keyboard music, 150
   keyboard virtuosity of, 150, 151, 163, 262
   The Little Organ Book, 150
   Mass in B Minor, 65, 151, 166
   Mendelssohn and, 166
   Passions, 149, 151, 166, 298
   pre-existing music used by, 281–82
   Prelude and Fugue in C Minor, from *The Well-Tempered Clavier,* 9, 155, 156–60
   reception of, 165–66
   Sarabande and Gavotte, 326, 327
   Suite for Orchestra in D Major, 125, 128, 155, 160–63
   as teacher, 150–51
   timpani used by, 12
   The Well-Tempered Clavier, 148, 149, 150, 155, 156
   at Zimmermann's Coffeehouse, 146
Bach, Wilhelm Friedemann, *151*
Bach family, 148, 149
Baglioni, Antonio, 186
Bailey, James, 127
Bakst, Léon, *410*
Balanchine, George, 409
Baldwin, James, *Go Tell It on the Mountain,* 403
Balkan states, 400

ballad, 499
ballet, 406–33
Ballets Russes, 407, 409–10, 412, 416–20, 430–31
Balzac, Honoré de, 261
Banister, John, 153
Ban on Love, The (Wagner), 348
Barbaja, Domenico, 241
Barber, Francis, 172, *173*
Barber, Samuel, 405
Bardi, Giovanni de', 94
Baroque era, 82–167
   affects in, 86, 220, 232
   art and architecture in, 85–86, 89
   historical overview, 83–85
   instruments in, 11
   literature in, 85
   map of Europe in, *84*
   musical style in, 86–89
   philosophy in, 88
   politics in, 84
   Renaissance compared with, 83, 86
   science in, 84–85, 88
   style compared with Classic era, 175
   style compared with Renaissance, 87
   term, 83–84
   timeline, 82
Bartók, Béla, 404
bass clarinet, 11
bass drum, 12
bass flute, 11
Bassi, Luigi, 185, *185*
bass line, 87
basso continuo, 87, 100, 101, 111, 115, 128, 174
bassoon(s), 11, *74*, 124–25, 274
bass trumpet, 12
bass (voice), 63, 144
Baudelaire, Charles, 261
Bauernfeld, Eduard von, *237, 239,* 242
Bayreuth Festivals, 345, 348, 351, 352–53, 368–69
beat, 5
Beatrice and Benedict (Berlioz), 270, 322
Beatriz de Dia, 32
Beaumarchais, Pierre, 189
bebop, 514
Beckett, Samuel, *Waiting for Godot,* 403
Beethoven, Karl von, 213
Beethoven, Ludwig van, 169, 170, *213, 214*

Adelaïde, 326, 327
"Ah! Perfido", 216
biography, 214
career path of, 171, 212–13
chamber music of, 214, 252
Choral Fantasy, 216, 218
concertos, 295
as conductor, 217
Eroica Symphony, 170, 214
Fidelio, 214
First Viennese School and, 404
influence of, 262, 265, 278, 291
Leonore Overture No. 3, 381
living conditions, 211–12
Maelzel and, 8
Masses of, 65, 214, 216
"Pastoral" Symphony, 291
as pianist, 214, 216, 217, 231, 262
Piano Concerto No. 4, 216, 217, 231
Piano Concerto No. 5, 341
Piano Sonata in C Major, Op. 53, 326, 327
Romantic elements in style of, 259
Ruins of Athens, 302
Schubert and, 238–39
Septet for Strings and Winds, 223
songs of, 243
string quartets, 300
symphonies of, 209, 214, 296
Symphony No. 5, 7, 13, 208–33, 268, 272, 376, 384
Symphony No. 9, 15, 170, 173, 214, 240, 292, 383
as teacher, 212
timpani used by, 12
Triple Concerto, 295
in Vienna, 212–15
Violin Concerto, 295
Being and Nothingness (Sartre), 403
bel canto, 180
Belgium, 27. *See also* Low Countries
Bellini, Vincenzo, 262
Bell Jar, The (Plath), 403
Bellotto, Bernardo, 174
   The Mehlmarkt, 211
Bellow, Saul, *Herzog,* 403
Belvedere Palace (Vienna), 210, *211*
Benedict of Nursia, 20
Benvenuto Cellini (Berlioz), 270
Berg, Alban, 404, 405, *435, 438,* 514
   biography, 438

Lulu, 437, 438, 439, 463
Lyric Suite, 438
Schoenberg and, 272
String, Quartet, Op. 3, 438
Violin Concerto, 438
Wozzeck, 191, 434–65, 527
Bergman, Ingmar, *The Seventh Seal,* 403
Berlin State Opera, 439–42, *440,* 461–62
Berlioz, Hector, *270*
arrangement of Weber's music, 420
Beatrice and Benedict, 270, 322
Beethoven's influence on, 278
Benvenuto Cellini, 270
biography, 270
career path of, 267–68, 269
description of, 277–78
Fantastic Symphony, 5, 9, 12, 13, 263, 264–93, 317, 356, 495
Les francs-juges, 270, 282
Gewandhaus Orchestra performances of works by, 297
Harold in Italy, 270, 291
as journalist, 321
Lélio, 291
La mort de Sardanapale, 273, 277
Prix de Rome won by, 273, 276
Romeo and Juliet, 291
Solemn Mass, 270, 281, 285
symphonies of, 262
Te Deum, 381
timpani used by, 12
Les Troyens, 263, 270
Wagner influenced by, 347–48
women and, 269–71, 282
Berlioz, Louis-Joseph, 269
Bernart de Ventadorn, 32
Bernini, Gian Lorenzo, 89
David, 85, 86
Bernstein, Leonard, 405, 432, *507, 513*
biography, 507
career path of, 506–7
as conductor, 501, 507, 523
Mass, 65
on opening of *West Side Story,* 513
West Side Story, 12, 382, 498–525
Betz, Franz, 354, 369
Bianchi, Giulio Cesare, 101
Bie, Oskar, 461
Biedermeier, Gottfried, 236
Biedermeier period, 236
Bird Cage, The (Laurents), 505

birdsongs, 388, 477–78, 479, 491, 496
Birth of a Nation (Griffith film), 403
bisexual(ity), 505, 508
Bismarck, Otto von, 258
Bizet, Georges, *Carmen,* 462
Black Death, 21
Bleak House (Dickens), 261
block construction, 421, 422, 432
blocks, 12
blues, 5, 395, 405, 517, 518
Boccaccio, Giovanni, *Decameron,* 23
Bohème, La (Puccini), 262
Bohemia, 178, 263
Bold, Richard, 58–59, 61, 65, 71
Boleyn, Anne, 59
Bondini, Caterina, 185–86
Bondini, Pasquale, 180–81, 182
Bondini Opera Company, 180–81, 183, 204
book (for musicals), 503
Book of the Courtier, The (Castiglione), 25–26
Borges, Jorge Luis, *The Aleph,* 403
Boris Godunov (Mussorgsky), 410, 419
Borodin, Alexander, 378
Polovtsian Dances from *Prince Igor,* 413, 420
Borromini, Francesco, *88,* 89
Boschot, Adolphe, 407, 430
Boston Herald, 394
Boswell, James, 173
Bouhy, Jacques, 377
Boulez, Pierre, 413, 527
Bourdelle, Émile, 416
Bourman, Anatole, 417
bourrée, 162
bowed string instruments, 10–11
"Boy Like That, A," *West Side Story* (Bernstein), 505, 525
Brahms, Johannes, 326, 374
character pieces, 317
Schumann's views on, 321, 322
Violin Concerto, 295, 300, 381
Bramante, Donato, 29
Brandenburg Concertos (Bach), 148, 149, 151, 155, 163
Brandt, Karl, 355
Braque, Georges, 402, 410
brass instruments, 10, 11–12
Breathless (Godard film), 403
Breton, Henri, 474

Bright, Richard, 210
Britten, Benjamin, 404, 405
Broadway musicals, 498–525. *See also West Side Story*
Brothers Karamazov, The (Dostoevsky), 261
Browning, Robert, 261
Brown v. Board of Education, 501
Brubeck, Dave, *Take Five,* 6
Bruckner, Anton, 348
symphonies of, 262
Brüll, Karl-Albert, 472
Brunelleschi, Filippo, 29, 85
Büchner, Georg, *Woyzeck,* 438, 439, 462, 464
Bülow, Hans von, 348
Burgundy, 20, 25
Burleigh, Harry T., 379
Burney, Charles, 119, 126, 127
Busoni, Ferruccio, 440
Byrd, William, 27, *62,* 83, 86
biography, 62
career of, 60–61
at Harleyford Manor, 57–59
Mass for Four Voices, 9, 56, 61, 62–68
My Ladye Nevells Booke, 62
polyphonic music of, 157
Psalmes, Sonets, and Songs of Sadnes and Pietie, 60
reception of, 79–80
"This sweet and merry month of May," 61, 68–70
Byron, George Gordon, Lord, 205, 261
Childe Harold's Pilgrimage, 270, 291

cadence(s), 63, 89, 132, 165
cadenza(s), 144
in concertos, 304, 305, 306, 308, 314
vocal, 135
Cage, John, 402, 404
Cage aux Folles, La (Herman), 505
Calderón de la Barca, Pedro, 89
Calvin, John, 28
Campion, Thomas, 57
Camus, Albert, *The Plague,* 403
Candide (Bernstein), 507, 510
Candide (Voltaire), 172
canon (imitative form), 66
canons (clerics), 39
Canova, Antonio, 172, 260
"Can she excuse my wrongs" (Dowland), 61, 64, 72–73, *73,* 76–77

"Can she excuse my wrongs" (Dowland; instrumental arrangements), 74–75, 77–79
cantatas (of Bach), 149, 151, 153, 166
Canterbury Tales (Chaucer), 23, 31
Canticum sacrum (Stravinsky), 412
cantor, 38–39, 40
cantus firmus, 23, 27
cantus firmus technique, 64
Caprichos (Goya), 173
Carmen (Bizet), 462
Carnaval (Schumann), 316, 326, 327–42
 "Arlequin," 332, 334–35
 A-S-C-H motto, 329–30, 337, 342
 associations in, 317–18, 321, 327–29
 "Chopin," 331, 338
 "Coquette," 331
 "Eusebius, 336–37
 "Florestan," 330, 337
 "Marche des Davidsbündler Contre les Philistins," 338–39, 342
 "Paganini," 331, 332
 "Pantalon et Columbine," 332
 "Pause," 332, 338–39
 "Préambule," 331, 332, 333–34, 339, 342
 publication, 329
 quotation and self-quotation, 330, 337, 339
 reception, 340–42
 "Reconnaissance," 331
 "Réplique," 331
 "Sphinxes," 329–30, 342
 structure and thematic links, 329–30
 titles of pieces, 328
 "Valse Allemande," 331
 virtuosity in, 330–32
Carnegie, Andrew, 375, 380
Carnegie Hall (New York), 375, 376, 380, 380–81, 502
Carousel (Rodgers and Hammerstein), 504, 505
Casanova, Giacomo, 184–85
Castiglione, Baldassare, *The Book of the Courtier*, 25–26, 57, 59–60
castrato, 99
Catalogue Aria, from *Don Giovanni* (Mozart), 190, 192, 196, 197–98
Catalogue d'oiseaux (Messiaen), 478
cathedrals, 20, 22, 23, 31, 53. *See also* Notre Dame Cathedral
Catherine of Aragon, 59

Catholic Church
 in Baroque era, 84
 in contemporary life, 53
 Messiaen as practicing Catholic, 467
 in Middle Ages, 21, 22, 31, 32, 34–38
 in Renaissance, 26, 27, 28, 57–59, 61, 62, 65, 70–71
Cattaneo, Claudia, 91
Caullery, Louis, *60*
celesta, 10, 459
cello, 11
Čermáková, Anna, 374
Cervantes, Miguel de, 85
 Don Quixote, 89
Cézanne, Paul, 261
cha-cha, 513, 518
chamber music
 of Beethoven, 213, 214
 in Classic era, 169, 235, 252–53
 forms in, 223
 of Mozart, 181
 of Schubert, 239
 of Schumann, 320
Chamber Symphony No. 1 (Schoenberg), 445
chancellor, 38–39
Chanel, Coco, 410
Chapel Royal, 59, 61, 62
Chaplin, Charlie, 403
character pieces, 317, 318, 342
Charitable Music Society, 123
Charlemagne, 20–21
"Charming Brute, The" (Goupy), *121*
Chartres Cathedral, 31, *31*
Chaucer, Geoffrey, *Canterbury Tales*, 23, 31
Cherubini, Luigi, 267–68, 277
Chichester Psalms (Bernstein), 507
Childe Harold's Pilgrimage (Byron), 270, 291
chimes, 12
China, 400, 401
chitarroni, 100
choir (part of cathedral), 37–38
Chopin, Frédéric, *321*
 music used in *Les Sylphides,* 420
 paraphrases of Mozart's *Don Giovanni,* 205–6
 piano music, 318
 piano virtuosity of, 330
 Schumann's depiction of in *Carnaval,* 327

 Schumann's views on, 321
Choral Fantasy (Beethoven), 216, 218
chords, 7
choreographer (for musicals), 503, 507–8, 511
choreography, 407–8, 411, 413, 417
choruses
 in operas, 357
 in oratorios, 136–42, 144
Christianity. *See also* Catholic Church
 in Middle Ages, 20–23
 rise of, 19–20
Christmas Mass at Notre Dame Cathedral (1198), 30–55, 65
 Alleluia, 46, 47, 49, 50
 Gradual, 46, 49, 51–53
 Introit, 40–41, 42–43
 Kyrie, 44–45
 Mass structure and shape, 39–40
 service, 38–53
 singers for, 38–39
chromaticism, 165, 262, 401
chromatic scale, 435
Church of England, 59
Cibber, Susannah, 124, *126*, 126
Cincinnati Symphony Orchestra, *14*
cinema, 403
cities, growth of, 21, 26
Civil War, American, 258
clarinet, E-flat, 275
clarinet(s), 11
Classic era, 169–255
 art and architecture in, 172–73
 larger forms in, 218, 219, 220–22, 223
 literature in, 173
 map of Europe in, *170*
 musical style compared with Baroque, 175
 musical style compared with Romantic, 259, 263
 musical style in, 174–75, 219–20, 254
 politics in, 171, 174
 timeline, 168
clavichord, 155, *156*
clemenza di Tito, La (Mozart), 179
cleric(s), 20, 39
clerks of Matins, 39
Cluny, abbey of, 23
Clurman, Harold, 523
Cocteau, Jean, 407, 431
coda, 221, 223, 225, 231, 311

Coen, Joel and Ethan, *Fargo,* 403
coffeehouses, 153–54, 155–56, 172
Cold War, 400, 500
Cole, Thomas, 261
Coleridge, Samuel Taylor, 261
Coleridge-Taylor, Samuel, *Scenes from the Song of Hiawatha,* 382
Collegium Musicum (Leipzig), 147, 150, 151–55, 160, 296
colonialism, 258–59
Columbus, Christopher, 28
Comédie Française (Paris), 266
"Comfort ye, my people," from *Messiah* (Handel), 130, 131, 132
commedia dell'arte, 327
communism, 400
Communist Manifesto, The (Marx and Engels), 260
concerto delle donne, 98
Concerto for Four Horns and Orchestra (Schumann), 295
Concerto in F for Harpsichord, Two Recorders, and Strings, BWV 1057 (Bach), 133, 155, 163–65, 295
concerto(s)
    in Baroque era, 121, 155, 163–65, 166, 295
    of Beethoven, 217
    in Classical era, 223, 295
    first-movement form, 306
    in Romantic era, 294–314
concerts, private, 235, 236, 239, 299
concerts, public
    in Baroque era, 153
    in Classic era, 171, 172, 212, 215–16, 231
    contemporary, 528–29, 532
    solo recitals, 324, 341
Confessions of an English Opium Eater (De Quincey), 269
Congress of Vienna (1815), 174, 236
conjunct motion, 5, 279
Conrad, Joseph, 402
consequent phrase, 279
Conservatory of Music (Paris), 267–68, 273–78, *274,* 341, 468
consonance, 7
consort music, 57, 71, 75, 79
contrabass(es), 100. *See also* double bass
contrabassoon, 11, 218 19, 228
contradance, 201
"Cool," *West Side Story* (Bernstein), 514, 525

Cooper, James Fenimore, 238
Copernicus, Nikolaus, 28, 88
Copland, Aaron, 382, 401
    Fanfare for the Common Man, 395
Corigliano, John, 405
Corneille, Pierre, 85, 89
cornett(s), 72, *74,* 100, 275
Corot, Jean-Baptiste, Camille, 261
Così fan tutte (Mozart), 177, 181, 183, 189
counterpoint, 48, 64, 149, 157
Counter-Reformation, 26
countersubject, 159–60, 167
countertenor, 126
Count Nostitz's Theater (Prague), *179,* 179–80, 181, 186–88, *187*
Couples (Updike), 403
Courbet, Gustave, 261
courses, 72
courtiers, 25–26, 27
Credo, 28, 40, 65
cross-rhythms, 321
Crusades, 20–21
cubism, 402
Cultural Revolution, 401
cummings, e. e., *The Enormous Room,* 403
cycle, 329
cymbals, 4

da capo aria, 136
Dalí, Salvador, 402
damper pedal. *See* sustaining pedal
Damrosch, Walter, 380–81, 394
"Dance at the Gym," *West Side Story* (Bernstein), 517–18
dance in Broadway musicals, 503, 511
dance notation, 416
Dance of the Phantoms (Clara Schumann), 318
Dante, *Divine Comedy,* 23
Da Ponte, Lorenzo, *183*
    biography, 183
    librettos of, 170, 177–78, 181, 182–83, 184–85, 189
Darwin, Charles, 260
David, Ferdinand, *300*
    as composer, 300, 302
    as violinist, 295, 300, 301–2, 311, 313
David, Jacques-Louis, 173, 260
David (Bernini), 85, *86*
David (Michelangelo), 29, 85, *86*
Davidsbund. See League of David

Davis, Miles, 514
"Death and the Maiden" String Quartet (Schubert), 241, 252
Death and the Powers (Machover), *528*
Death of a Salesman (Miller), 403
Death of Klinghoffer, The (Adams), 530
Death of Sardanapalus, The (Delacroix), 268
Debussy, Claude, 401, 410, 416, 495
    Prelude to "The Afternoon of a Faun," 411
    Jeux, 411, 419
    Pelléas et Mélisande, 418
Decameron (Boccaccio), 23
Declaration of Independence, 171, 172
De Koven, Reginald, 394
Delacroix, Eugène, 260
    The Death of Sardanapalus, 268
Delbos, Claire, 493
Delcaration of the Rights of the Man, 172
Delius, Frederick, *Hiawatha,* 382
de Mille, Agnes, 503, 511
Denmark, 263
De Quincey, Thomas, *Confessions of an English Opium Eater,* 269
Des canyons aux étoiles . . . (Messiaen), 468
Descartes, René, 88
    The Passions of the Soul, 88
Descent of Man, The (Darwin), 260
des Pres, Josquin, 27
deus ex machina, 103
Deutscher, 202
development
    in concerto form, 306, 314
    in sonata form, 220, 222, 223, 224–25, 230, 232, 384
Devereaux, Robert, 72
devin du village, Le (Rousseau), 172
Devrient, Eduard, 296
Diaghilev, Sergei, 407, *409*
    biography, 409
    as impresario, 409–10, 413, 416–18, 430–31
Dickens, Charles, 261
Dickinson, Emily, 261
Diderot, Denis, *Encyclopédie,* 172
Dies irae, 272, 275, 289
Dies sanctificatus (Leoninus), 46, *49, 50*
d'Indy, Vincent, 416
dioceses, 20
Diptyque (Messiaen), 491
discant style, 48, 49, 53, 54

disjunct motion, 5, 279

Disney, Walt, 432

   Fantasia, 403

dissonance, 7

Divine Comedy (Dante), 23

Divine Office, 44

divisions, 75

Doctor Atomic (Adams), 530–32

Doepler, Emil, 355

Do I Hear a Waltz? (Rodgers and
   Sondheim), 505, 510

Dolce Vita, La (Fellini film), 403

dominant-tonic progression, 87

Dominican order, 21

Don Giovanni (Mozart), 170, 176–207, 263,
   265

   Act 1, Scene 1, ensemble, 192, 194–95

   Act 1 finale, 191, 196, 199–204

   "Ah! Chi mi dice mai," 190

   arias in, 190–91

   Catalogue Aria, 190, 192, 196, 197–98

   "Dalla sua pace," 190

   "Deh, vieni alla finestra," 190

   Don Juan story as basis, 177–78

   ensembles in, 191, 206

   "Fin ch'han del vino," 190

   "Il mio tesoro," 190

   instrumentation, 191–92, 206

   "Là ci darem la mano," 174, 191, 196,
      198–99, 220

   libretto for, 182–83

   melodic phrases in, 6

   mood changes in, 178

   "Non ti fidar, o misera," 191

   "Notte e giorno faticar," 190, 192, 193

   "Or sai chi l'onore," 190

   Overture, 358

   performance preparations, 181–86

   plot, 184

   premiere, 186–88

   reception, 204–6

   sets for, 188

   stage band in, 191, 199, 445

Don Giovanni Tenorio (Goldoni), 183

Donizetti, Gaetano, 262

Don Juan (Strauss), 205

Donne, John, 85, 530

Don Quixote (Cervantes), 89

Dostoevsky, Fyodor, 261

dotted rhythm, 6, 161, 198, 382, 383, 387

double bass, 11

double-escapement action, 325

double-reed instruments, 11

double-stopping, 304–5

Dowland, John, 57, 60, 70–75, 83

   biography, 71

   "Can she excuse my wrongs," 61, 64,
      72–73, *73,* 76–77

   "Can she excuse my wrongs"
      (instrumental arrangements), 74–75,
      77–79

   "Flow, my tears," 71

   Lachrimae, 75

   reception of, 80

   "Semper Dowland, semper dolens," 71

downbeat, 6

Doxology, 40

dramma giocoso, 182

drums, 4, 12

Dryden, John, 89

Dublin, Handel in, 120–21, 122–27,
   142–43

Duboeuf, Estelle, *269,* 269–70, 271, 275,
   282

Dubourg, Matthew, 124, 127

Duchamp, Marcel, 402

duet chorus, 141–42, 145

Dufay, Guillaume, 27

Dukas, Paul, 416

Durand firm, 494

Dvořák, Antonín, *374, 377*

   The American Flag, 380

   American String Quartet, 380

   biography, 374

   "Goin' Home" melody, 373

   hobbies, 378, *379*

   Humoresques, 380

   Longfellow's *Hiawatha* and, 381–82

   Mass of, 65

   Moravian Duets, 373, 377

   "Music in America," 395

   nationalism and, 263

   New World Symphony, 11, 263, 349,
      372–97

   in New York, 375, 377–78, 501

   program music and, 272

   Slavonic Dances, 373, 374, 377, 382

   symphonies of, 262

   Te Deum, 380

dynamics, 8

Eco, Umberto, *The Name of the Rose,* 403

education

   in Middle Ages, 20, 31, 33, 34–35

   in Romantic era, 267–68, 273–78, 298,
      300, 341, 376–77, 395, 468

Edward VI, King of England, 59

E-flat clarinet, 11, 275

Eilers, Albert, 355

Einstein, Albert, 402

Eisenhower, Dwight D., 500

electronic music, 404

Elijah (Mendelssohn), 298

Eliot, George, 261

Eliot, T. S., *The Love Song of J. Alfred
   Prufrock,* 403

Elizabeth I, Queen of England, 57, 59–60,
   60, 61, 62, 68, 71, 72, *75*

Ellington, Duke, 382

embellishment

   in Baroque era, 111

   in Middle Ages, 46, 53

   in Renaissance, 28, 75

Emerson, Ralph Waldo, 261

Emile, or On Education (Rousseau), 172

Emma (Austen), 173

Encyclopaedia Britannica, 172

Encyclopédie, 172, *172,* 213

Engels, Friedrich, 260

Engerth, Eduard, Orpheus mural, *96*

England. *See also* London

   in Baroque era, 84, 85, 89, 119–20

   in Classic era, 172–73, 174

   in Middle Ages, 20, 21

   in Renaissance, 25, 27, 56–80

   in Romantic era, 260, 261

   in twentieth century, 400

English horn, 11, 274, 385

English National Opera, *354*

English Shakpespeare Company, 277

Enlightenment, 171–73, 189, 213–14

Enormous Room, The (cummings), 403

Entführung aus dem Serail, Die (Mozart),
   181

episodes (in fugue), 140, 157, 167

Epistle, 39

Érard, Sébastien, 325

Érard firm, 317, 323–26, 325

Erdödy, Countess Marie, 210, 213

Erlkönig, Der (Schubert), 240, 242, 243,
   249, 250–51, 326, 327

Eroica Symphony (Beethoven), 170, 214

escapement, 325

Essex, Earl of, 61, 75, *75*
Este family, 26
Eugene of Savoy, Prince, 210
Europe, maps of
    1815–1848, *170*
    ca. 1610, *84*
    ca. 1871, *259*
    Cold War era, *400*
    medieval, 20, *21*
    Renaissance, *25*
Euryanthe Overture and Introduction
    (Weber), 302
Evita (Lloyd Webber), 503
"Ev'ry valley," from *Messiah* (Handel),
    133–36
exploration of world beyond Europe, 28
exposition
    in concerto first-movement form, 306
    in fugue, 140, 160, 167
    in sonata form, 220, 222, 224, 230, 232,
      384
expressionism, 402, 435, 436, 464
Expulsion of the Bonacolsi, The (Morone),
    93

Fackel, Die (periodical), 437
Fairies, The (Wagner), 348
Fairy's Kiss (Stravinsky), 412
"Fall of the House of Usher, The" (Poe),
    261
Fancy Free (Bernstein), 508
Fanfare for the Common Man (Copland), 395
Fantasia (Disney film), 403, 432
Fantastic Symphony (Berlioz), 263, 264–93
    "A Ball" (movement II), 9, 281, 282,
      284–85, 290
    Beethoven's influence on, 278
    conductor for premiere, 275
    Dies irae in, 272, 275, 289
    "Dream of a Witches' Sabbath"
      (movement V), 281, 288–89, 290
    hall for premiere, 273, *274*
    idée fixe in, 278–81, 282–89, 292, 358,
      383
    instrumentation, 12, 13, 274–75, 356
    Liszt's piano transcription of, 317
    "March to the Scaffold" (movement
      IV), 281, 282, 286–88, 290, 317
    melody in, 5
    orchestra's arrangement for, 273–74
    pre-existing music used in, 281–82

premiere, 272–78
press and audience for premiere, 276
as program music, 265–66, 382, 495
program of, 271–72
reception, 265, 290–91
"Reveries—Passions" (movement I),
    281, 282, 283–84
"Scene in the Country" (movement
    III), 281, 285–86
Schumann's review, 292
structure, 278, 292
women as muses for, 269–71, 275, 282
Fargo (Coen brothers film), 403
Fascism, 399
Faulkner, William, *The Sound and the*
    Fury, 403
Fauré, Gabriel, 416
Faust (Goethe), 173, 245–46, 269, 272, 277
Faust (Gounod), 263, 322
favola in musica, 95
Fellini, Federico, *La Dolce Vita,* 403
Fenley, Molissa, 431
fermata, 6
Ferrara, 26
Ferrari, Cherubino, 116
Festival Coronation March
    (Tchaikovsky), 381
Festival Theater (Bayreuth), 345, *352,*
    352–53, 355–56, 368–69
Fête des belles eaux (Messiaen), 484
Fétis, François-Joseph, 276, 290
feudal system, 20, 21
Fidelio (Beethoven), 214
Figaro, Le (Paris newspaper), 276, 290
figured bass, 101
film. *See* cinema
finale (in symphonies), 221–22, 230–31,
    232
Finland, 263
Firebird (Stravinsky), 407, 412, 413, 421,
    432
Fireworks Music (Handel), 120
First Booke of Consort Lessons (Morley), 71
first-movement concerto form, 306, 314
first-movement sonata form, 219, 220–21,
    222–23, 224–25, 232, 306
First Viennese School, 404, 435
Fitzgerald, F. Scott, *The Great Gatsby,* 403
flats, 5
Flaubert, Gustave, 261
Flegeljahre (Jean Paul), 317, 327

Florence, 26, 29
"Flow, my tears" (Dowland), 71
flute(s), 11, *71,* 72
Flying Dutchman, The (Wagner), 348, 358
Fokine, Michel, 410, 430
folk music, 527
Ford, John, *The Quiet Man,* 403
Forefathers, The (Roerich), 414, *414*
Forelle, Die (Schubert), 243, 245, 246–47,
    252
Forkel, Johann Nikolaus, 156
forte, 8
fortepiano, 8, 155, *156*
For Whom the Bell Tolls (Hemingway), 403
Foster, Stephen, 395
    "Old Folks at Home," 15, 380
Fox, The (Stravinsky), 431
Fra Diavolo (Auber), 263
France. *See also* Low Countries; Paris
    in Baroque era, 84, 85, 89
    in Classic era, 171, 172–73, 174
    in Middle Ages, 20, 21
    in Renaissance, 25, 27
    in Romantic era, 258, 260, 261, 263
    in twentieth century, 468, 493–96
Franciscan order, 21
Franco, Francisco, 399
Franco-Prussian War, 258
francs-juges, Les (Berlioz), 270, 282
Frankenthaler, Helen, 402
Franklin, Benjamin, 172–73, 213
Franks, 20
French horn, 12
French overture, 128, 160–61, 162
French Revolution, 171, 172, 189, 214,
    236, 266
Freud, Sigmund, 260, 402, 436
Frick, Henry Clay, 375
Fricke, Richard, 355, 368, 369
Fricken, Ernestine von, 320, *321,* 329,
    340
Frost, Robert, *New Hampshire,* 403
Fuchs-Robettin, Hanna, 438
fugue choruses, 140–41, 144
fugue(s)
    in Baroque era, 128, 140, 162–63, 167
    paired with preludes, 156–60, 166
    in twentieth-century music, 514, 525
full score, 440
fundamental pitch, 10
Funny Girl (Styne), 508

Funny Thing Happened on the Way to the Forum, A (Sondheim), 508, 510

Gade, Niels, 297, 300, *301*
Gahy, Josef von, 242
Galilei, Galileo, 28, 84, 88
galliard, 75
García Márquez, Gabriel, *One Hundred Years of Solitude,* 403
Garnet, Henry, 58, 61
gavotte, 162
gay. *See* homosexuality
Gazzaniga, Giuseppe, 183
"Gee, Officer Krupke," *West Side Story* (Bernstein), 514, 524
George I, King of England, 84, 120
George II, King of England, 120
Géricault, Théodore, 260
German Bach Society, 166
Germany. *See also* Berlin; Leipzig
    in Classic era, 174
    in Romantic era, 258, 261, 262–63, 344–71
    in twentieth century, 399–400
Gershwin, George
    An American in Paris, 395
    Porgy and Bess, 395
Gesamtkunstwerk, 346, 415
Gesang des Geistes uber den Wassern (Schubert), 240
Gewandhaus (Leipzig), 296–97, *297*, 298, 300, 318
Gibbs, Wolcott, 523
gigue, 162
Gilded Age, 374–75
Giotto, 23, 31
    The Raising of Lazarus, 31
Girard, Henri, 419
Giulio Cesare (Handel), 326, 327
Glass, Philip, 405
Glinka, Mikhail, 378
glissando(s), 450, 479
Gloria, 28, 39, 40, 45, 65
Godard, Jean-Luc, *Breathless,* 403
Goethe, Johann Wolfgang von
    Der Erlkönig, 249
    Faust, 245–46, 269, 272, 277
    Leipzig described by, 296
    Mendelssohn and, 298
    Mendelssohn and Mozart compared by, 297, 299

writings of, 173, 213
"Goin' Home," 373
Goldberg Variations (Bach), 150
Goldoni, Carlo, *Don Giovanni Tenorio,* 183
gongs, 12
Gonzaga, Ferdinando, 97, 99
Gonzaga, Francesco, 94, *94,* 97, 99
Gonzaga, Vincenzo, 91, 92, 98
Gonzaga family, 92–93
Görner, Johann Gottlieb, 152–53
Go Tell It on the Mountain (Baldwin), 403
Götterdämmerung (Wagner), 345, 349–50
Gounod, Charles, 263
    Faust, 322
Goupy, Joseph, "The Charming Brute," *121*
Gouts, Suzanne, 493
Goya, Francisco de, 260
    Caprichos, 173
Gradual, 39–40, 46, 49, 51–53
Granados, Enrique, 378
Grapes of Wrath, The (Steinbeck), 403
Graupner, Johann Christopher, 149
Great Book of Organum (Leoninus), 48, 49
Great Depression, 399
Great Gatsby, The (Fitzgerald), 403
Greece, ancient, 19, 28, 94
Gregorian chant, 6, 9, 22–23, 32, 41, 43, 54
Gregory the Great, Pope, 41
Gretchen am Spinnrade (Schubert), 240, 241, 243, 245–46, 247–48, 265
Grieg, Edvard, 357, 368, 369, 378
Griffith, D. W., *Birth of a Nation,* 403
Grillparzer, Franz, 242, 254
Gropius, Walter, 437, 438
Gross, Valentine, *431*
Grün, Friedricke, 354
Guardasoni, Domenico, 204, 205
Guggenheim Museum (Wright), 402
Guidonian hand, 33, *33*
Guido of Arezzo, 33
Guillaume Tell (Rossini), 267
Guillou, P., *102*
guitar, 10
Gypsy (Styne and Sondheim), 505

Habeneck, François-Antoine, 268, 275, *275,* 276–77, 290–91
Halévy, Jacques Fromenthal, *La Juive,* 269
Hallelujah Baby! (Styne), 505

"Hallelujah" chorus, from *Messiah* (Handel), 9, 86, 119, 138–40, 143
Hamburg State Opera, 464
Hamlet (Shakespeare), 270
Hammerstein, Oscar, II, 510
Hammond organ, 10
Handel, George Frideric, 83, *120, 123*
    "And the glory of the Lord," from *Messiah,* 89, 136–38
    aria from *Giulio Cesare,* 326, 327
    basso continuo use, 101
    biography, 120
    caricature of, *121*
    "Comfort ye, my people," from *Messiah,* 130, 131, 132
    "Ev'ry valley," from *Messiah,* 133–36
    fame of, 147
    Fireworks Music, 120
    "Hallelujah" chorus, from *Messiah,* 86, 119, 138–40, 143
    "He trusted in God," from *Messiah,* 140–41, 159
    keyboard virtuosity of, 127
    Messiah, 9, 13, 86, 87, 118–45, 151, 178, 189, 432
    oratorios of, 120, 122
    Overture, from *Messiah,* 127–28, 160, 162
    polyphonic music of, 159
    pre-existing music used by, 281–82
    recitatives, 128–30, 363
    "Rejoice," from *Messiah,* 86
    "There were shepherds," from *Messiah,* 129–30
    timpani used by, 12
"Happy Birthday," 6
Harleyford Manor, 57–59
harmonic rhythm, 87–88
harmonics, 415, 479
harmonic series, 10
harmony, 7
    in Baroque music, 87
    in Classic era, 245, 249
    in Romantic music, 262, 349, 358
    in twentieth-century music, 421, 423, 433, 437, 464, 476, 489, 496
Harold in Italy (Berlioz), 270, 291
harp(s), 10, *71,* 100
harpsichord(s), 10, 28, 72, *74,* 87, 100, *156*
harpischord music
    of Bach, 150, 155, 163, 166

in Renaissance, 78–79
Harry Potter series (Rowling), 403
Hartmann, Franz von, 235, 241
Harvey, William, 84
Harvington Hall, *58*
Hassard, John R. G., 353, *369*
Haydn, Franz Joseph, 169, 205, 214
    chamber music of, 252
    First Viennese School and, 404
    symphonies of, 209
Haystacks at Sunset, Frosty Weather
    (Monet), *401*
"Heartbreak Hotel" (Presley), 501, 517
Heart of Darkness (Conrad), 402
Heifetz, Jascha, 380
Heiligenstadt Testament (Beethoven),
    214
Heine, Heinrich, 261
Heinsheimer, Hans, 461
Hemingway, Ernest, *For Whom the Bell*
    Tolls, 403
hemiola, 520
Hennigsen, Fräulein, 302
Henry VIII, King of England, 59
Hensel, Fanny Mendelssohn, 297, 298,
    299
    Clara Schumann and, 299
Hernani (Hugo), 268
hertz, 4
Herz, Henri, 301
Herzog, Werner, 464
Herzog (Bellow), 403
Hess, Joachim, 464
"He trusted in God," from *Messiah*
    (Handel), 140–41, 159
Hewes, Henry, 523
Hiawatha (Delius), 382
Higdon, Jennifer, 405
Hildegard of Bingen, 35, *36*
    biography, *36*
    Ordo virtutum, 36
Hill, John, 127
Hill, Mildred, 378–79, 384
Hilliard, Nicholas, *60*
Hindemith, Paul, 401, 440
Hirschbach, Herrmann, 311
Hitchcock, Alfred, *Psycho,* 403
Hitler, Adolf, 314, 370, 399, 468
    Mein Kampf, 436
Hobbes, Thomas, 213
    Leviathan, 88

Hobbit, The (Tolkien), 403
Hodson, Millicent, 415, 416
Hofburg Palace (Vienna), 211, 215
Hoffmann, E.T.A., 205, 231, 232, 340
Hoffmann, Josef, *355*
Holland, 27. *See also* Low Countries
Holy Roman Empire, 258
    dissolution of, 209–10, 236
    in Middle Ages, 20, 21
    in Renaissance, 25
home music-making, 236, 244. *See*
    also amateur musicians; salons;
    Schubertiades
Home of the Brave (Laurents), 504, 505
homophony, 9, 64, 69, 138
homosexuality, 411, 505. *See also*
    bisexual(ity)
horn, 12
Horowitz, Vladimir, 380
Houdon, Jean-Antoine, 172
Houel, Jean, *Storming of the Bastille, 171*
"Hound Dog" (Presley), 517
House Un-American Activities
    Committee, 500, 505, 508
How the Other Half Lives (Riis), 375
huapango, 520–22
Hugo, Victor, 3, 261
    Hernani, 268
Huguenots, Les (Meyerbeer), 263, 269
Human Comedy, The (Balzac), 261
humanism, 26, 28
Hume, David, 88, 213
Hummel, Johann Nepomuk, 252
Humoresque No. 7 (Dvořák), 380
Hundred Years' War, 21
Huneker, James, 394
Huston, John, *The Maltese Falcon,* 403
Hüttenbrenner, Anselm, 240, *240*

Iceman Cometh, The (O'Neill), 403
I Ching, 404
idée fixe, 278–81, 282–89, 292, 358, 383
"I Feel Pretty," *West Side Story*
    (Bernstein), 511
"I Have a Love," *West Side Story*
    (Bernstein), 525
illuminations, 22
imitation, technique of, 9, 27, 62–63,
    65–68, 69, 80, 138, 159
imperialism, 258–59
impresarios, 180–81, 410

impressionism, 261, 401, 411, 495
incoronazione di Poppea, L' (Monteverdi),
    91
In C (Riley), 404–5
Industrial Revolution, 258
Ingres, J.A.D., 260
intermezzo, 311, 312–13
international style, 402
interval, 5
intonation, 42
Introit, 39, 40–41, 42–43
Iowa, Dvořák's sojourn in, 374, 379
Iraq, 400
Ireland, Handel's sojourn in, 120–21,
    122–27
Israel Chamber Orchestra, 370
Italian Symphony (Mendelssohn), 298,
    314
Italy
    in Baroque era, 84, 85, 89, 90–117
    in Classic era, 172–73, 174
    map of early seventeenth-century, *92*
    in Middle Ages, 21
    in Renaissance, 25 (*See also* Low
        Countries)
    in Romantic era, 258, 260, 262
    in twentieth century, 399–400
Ite missa, 40
Ivan the Terrible (Rimsky-Korsakov), 410
Ives, Charles, 382, 395
"I Want to Be in America," *West Side*
    Story (Bernstein), 499

James, Henry, 402
Janáček, Leoš, 440
Japan, 400
Jaques-Dalcroze, Émile, 417
Järvi, Paavo, 14
Jaws (Spielberg film), 403
jazz, 382, 405, 500, 501, 505, 514, 524, 527
Jean Paul, 337
    Flegeljahre, 317, 327
Jeanrenaud, Cécile, 298, *298,* 299
Jefferson, Thomas, 173, 213
Jenger, Johann Baptist, *240*
Jennens, Charles, *125,* 128
Jesus Christ Superstar (Lloyd Webber), 503
"Jet Song," *West Side Story* (Bernstein),
    516–17, 520
Jeux (Debussy), 411, 419
Joachim, Joseph, 300, 319

Joffrey Ballet, 416
Johanson, Sigrid, *461*
Johns, Jasper, 402
Johnson, Samuel, 173
Joplin, Scott, 395
Joseph II, Emperor of Austria, 178, 182, 205
Joshua (Handel), 120
Jourdanet, Charles, 492–93
journalism, music, 171, 172, 180, 296, 311, 320, 340
Joyce, James, *Ulysses,* 403
Judaism in Music (Wagner), 314, 348
Judas Maccabaeus (Handel), 120
Juive, La (Halévy), 269
Jules and Jim (Truffaut film), 403
July Revolution, 266, 273
Jungle Book, The (Kipling), 261

Kaiser, Eduard, *319*
Kalkbrenner, Friedrich, 330, 341
Kapital, Das (Marx), 260
Kärntnertortheater (Vienna), 240–41
Karsavina, Tamara, 420
Kauffman, Angelica, 173
Kazan, Elia, *On the Waterfront,* 403
Keaton, Buster, 403
Keats, John, 261
Kemp, Barbara, 442
Kepler, Johannes, 84, 88
Kerr, Walter, 523
kettledrums, 12, 124, 160, 218
keyboard instruments, 10
keynote, 383
Khovanschina (Mussorgsky), 410
King and I, The (Rodgers and Hammerstein), 503, 511
King's Theater (London), 120
Kipling, Rudyard, 261
Klaren, Georg, 464
Kleiber, Erich, 439–40, *441,* 442, 461
Klimt, Gustav, 436–37
Kokoschka, Oskar, 402
Korea, 400
Kotzebue, August von, 302
Kovařík, J. J., 394–95
Kraus, Karl, 437–38
Krehbiel, Henry, 383, 394
Kuhnau, Johann, 149
Kupelwieser, Leopold, 241, 242, *242, 243*

Kurosawa, Akira, *Seven Samurai,* 403
Kushner, Tony, *Angels in America,* 403
Kyrie, 28, *39,* 40, 44–45, 65

Lachner, Franz, *237*
Lachrimae (Dowland), 75
"Là ci darem la mano," from *Don Giovanni* (Mozart), 174, 191, 196, 198–99, 220
Lady Chatterley's Lover (Lawrence), 403
Lafayette, Marquis de, 266
Laloy, Louis, 411
Lamb, William, 127
Large, Brian, 464
Lassus, Orlande de, 27
    Masses by, 65
Last Supper, The (Leonardo da Vinci), 29
Latin dance music, 500, 505, 513, 517–18, 520–22, 524
Latin language, 20, 23, 28, 34
laudesi, 32
Laurents, Arthur, 504–5, *505,* 508, 509, 510, 512, 513
    biography, 505
Lavoisier, Antoine, 172
Lawrence, Carol, 512, 513
Lawrence, D. H., *Lady Chatterley's Lover,* 403
League of David, 321, 341
Leave It to Beaver (TV show), 501
Le Boulaire, Jean, 469, *472,* 472–74, 477–78, 492, 494
lectern, 39
Lehmann, Lilli, *355,* 356, 369
Leibniz, Gottfried, 88
Leipzig
    in Baroque era, 146–66, *147, 148,* 148–56, *152,* 165–66
    ca. 1845, *296,* 296–97
    Gewandhaus in, 296–97, *297,* 298, 300, 318
    Mendelssohn Monument, *314*
    Mendelssohn's house in, 313–14
    Schumann in, 320–21
Leipzig Conservatory, 298, 300
leitmotifs, 346–47, 357–58, 360–67, 370, 383, 443
Lélio (Berlioz), 291
Leonardo da Vinci, 29
    The Last Supper, 29
    The Virgin of the Rocks, 29, *29*

Leoninus, 39–40, 49, 53, 54, 64, 495
    biography, 48
Leonore Overture No. 3 (Beethoven), 381
Leopold II, King of Bohemia, 179
Le Sueur, Jean-François, 277
Leviathan (Hobbes), 88
Lewis, C. S., 351
liberal arts, 22, 33
libretto, 182–83, 346
Lichtenstein, Roy, 402
lieder (of Schubert), 239, 243–51, 254, 432
Ligeti, György, 405
Linnaeus, Carl, 172
Liszt, Franz, *324*
    Berlioz's *Fantastic Symphony* premiere attended by, 277, 290
    paraphrases of Mozart's *Don Giovanni,* 206
    in Paris, 323
    performances of Schumann's *Carnaval,* 329
    piano transcription of Berlioz's *Fantastic Symphony,* 292, 317
    piano virtuosity of, 262, 303, 317, 323, *324,* 330, 341
    Wagner and, 348
literature
    in Baroque era, 85, 88–89
    children's, 261
    in Classic era, 173
    in Middle Ages, 23
    in Renaissance, 28–29
    in Romantic era, 261
    Romantic poetry, 261
    in twentieth century, 402–3
Little Organ Book, The (Bach), 150
Little Women (Alcott), 261
liturgy, 43–44
Lobkowitz, Franz Joseph Maximilian von, 210, 218
Locke, John, 88
Lohengrin (Wagner), 348
Lolita (Nabokov), 403
Lolli, Giuseppe, 186
London
    in Classic era, 169
    Handel in, 119–20, 143
    public concerts in, 153
Longfellow, Henry Wadsworth, 261
    The Song of Hiawatha, 379, 382

Look Homeward, Angel (Wolfe), 403

Lord of the Rings (Tolkien), 351

Loriod, Yvonne, 468

Louis-Philippe, King of the French, 266, *266*, 276, 322

Louis XIV, King of France, 84, 89

Love Song of J. Alfred Prufrock, The (Eliot), 403

Low Countries, 20, 27

lowered seventh note, 383, 396

Lucia di Lammermoor (Donizetti), 262

Ludwig II, King of Bavaria, 348, *351*, 351–52, 369, 370

Lulu (Berg), 437, 438, 439, 463

lute(s), 10, 28, *60*, *71*, *72*

lute songs, 71–73, 74, 76–77

Luther, Martin, 26, 28, 59

lyricist (for musicals), 503, 504–5, 506, 508, 509, 510–11, 524–25

lyrics (for musicals), 503, 510–11, 524–25

Lyric Suite (Berg), 438

Lyser, Johann Peter, drawing of Beethoven, *213*

MacDowell, Edward, 376

Machiavelli, Nicolò, *The Prince*, 25

Machover, Tod, 404
    Death and the Powers, *528*

Maclaine, Mr., 127

Maclaine, Mrs., 126–27

Madame Bovary (Flaubert), 261

madrigal(s), 59, 61, 68–70, 115

Maelzel, Johann Nepomuk, 8

Magellan, Ferdinand, 28

Magic Flute, The (Mozart), 181, 216

Magic Mountain, The (Mann), 403

Magli, Giovanni Gualberto, 99

Magno, Carlo, 91

Magnus liber organi (Leoninus), 48, 49

Magritte, René, 402

Mahler, Alma, 438, 439

Mahler, Gustav, 401, 437, 438
    symphonies of, 262, 292

Mailer, Norman, *The Naked and the Dead*, 403

mallet instruments, 12

Maltese Falcon, The (Huston film), 403

Malton, James, *A Picturesque and Descriptive View of the City of Dublin*, *123*

mambo, 513, 517–18

mandolin, 10

Manet, Edouard, 261

Manhattan Project, 530

Mann, Thomas, *The Magic Mountain*, 403

Mansfield Park (Austen), 173

Mantua, 25, 91–94, 97–103, 115–16, 188

"Maria," *West Side Story* (Bernstein), 500, 514, 518

Maria Theresa, Archduchess of Austria, 185

marimbas, 12

Marlowe, Christopher, 57

Marrakech (Stella), *405*

Marriage of Figaro, The (Mozart), 177, 181
    Don Giovanni reception compared with, 204–5
    excerpts, 302
    libretto, 189
    Prague production, 180, 182, 183, 185, 187
    quoted in *Don Giovanni*, 199

Marteau, Henri, 381

Marx, Karl, 260, 400, 402

Mary I, Queen of England, 59, 62

Mason, John, 127

Mass(es). *See also* Christmas Mass at Notre Dame Cathedral (1198)
    Alleluia, 39–40, 46, 47, 49, 50
    of Bach, 65, 151, 166
    of Beethoven, 214, 216
    of Berlioz, 270, 281, 285
    of Bernstein, 507
    Credo, 65
    of Dvořák, 65
    Gloria, 45, 65
    Gradual, 46, 49, 51–53
    Introit, 40–41
    Kyrie, 44–45, 65
    liturgy and, 43–44
    in Middle Ages, 30, 32, 33–34
    of Mozart, 65
    in Renaissance, 27, 28, 56, 61
    Sanctus, 65
    of Stravinsky, 412
    structure of, 39–40, 41

Mass for Four Voices (Byrd), 9, 56–80

Massine, Léonide, 431

Materna, Amalie, 354, *355*, 369, *369*

Matins, 39

Matisse, Henri, 410

Mayrhofer, Johann Baptist, 242

Mayseder, Joseph, 277

McCarthy, Joseph, 400, 500–501

Medici family, 26

medieval period. *See* Middle Ages

Mehlmarkt, The (Bellotto), *211*

Mein Kampf (Hitler), 436

melismas, 142, 144, 363

melismatic style, 43, 44–45, 49, 51, 54

melodic rhythm, 88–89

melody, 4–5
    in Baroque music, 86, 87, 157
    in Berg's *Wozzeck*, 443, 445, 462
    in Classical music, 174, 222, 254
    combining pitch and rhythm, 6–7
    in Gregorian chant, 44–45
    in Renaissance music, 73
    in Romantic music, 262, 385–86
    in Stravinsky's *Rite of Spring*, 421, 432
    in twentieth-century music, 479, 481, 496
    of Wagner, 346–47, 370

Melville, Herman, 261

Memoirs (Da Ponte), 183

Mendelssohn, Abraham, 297

Mendelssohn, Fanny. *See* Hensel, Fanny Mendelssohn

Mendelssohn, Felix, *298*
    appearance, 299
    Bach and, 166
    biography, 298
    career path of, 297–300
    character pieces, 317
    Classic elements in style of, 259
    double concertos, 295
    house of, 313–14
    incidental music for *Midsummer Night's Dream*, 298, 299, 311, 314, 381
    life in Leipzig, 296–97
    monument to, *314*
    Nazi ban on music by, 314, 463
    Octet for Strings, 299
    oratorios of, 298
    piano virtuosity of, 303
    Schumann's views on, 321
    sociality of, 295, 299–300
    Songs without Words, 310, 314
    string quartets, 313
    symphonies of, 298, 314
    Violin Concerto, 9, 294–315, 432
    Wagner influenced by, 348
    watercolor by, *298*

Mendelssohn, Moses, 297
Ménestrel, 340
meno mosso, 8
Menuhin, Yehudi, 380
Merman, Ethel, 505
Messiaen, Olivier, 405, *468*
  biography, 468
  Catalogue d'oiseaux, 478
  Des canyons aux étoiles . . ., 468
  Diptyque, 491
  Fête des belles eaux, 484
  "Little Theory of My Rhythmic
    Language," 494
  musical techniques used by, 475–78,
    494
  Oiseaux exotiques, 478
  organ music, 468
  Preludes for piano, 468
  as prisoner of war, 468–75, 492–93
  Quartet for the End of Time, 9, 466–97
  religiosity of, 467, 475–76, 495
  Le réveil des oiseaux, 478
  Saint François d'Assise, 468
  Technique of My Musical Language, 489,
    495
  Trois petites liturgies de la présence divine,
    475
  Turangalîla-symphonie, 468
  Vingt regards sur l'enfant-Jésus, 468
  Visions de l'Amen, 475
Messiah (Handel), 118–45, 151, 432
  "And the glory of the Lord," 89, 136–38
  arias in, 130–36, 220
  autograph, *119*
  choruses in, 136–42
  "Comfort ye, my people," 130, 131, 132
  "Ev'ry valley," 133–36
  "Hallelujah" chorus, 9, 86, 119, 138–40,
    143
  "He trusted in God," 140–41, 159
  instrumentation, 13, 124–25
  moods in, 178, 220
  Overture, 127–28, 160, 162
  performance preparations, 123–25
  premiere of, 125–26
  reception of, 142–44
  recitatives in, 128–30, 189
  "Rejoice," 86
  singers for, 123–24
  text of, 128
  "There were shepherds," 129–30

three-part form of, 128
meter, 5–6. *See also* rhythm and meter
metronome, 8
Metropolitan Opera (New York), 375–76,
  380, 418, 502, *531*
Meyerbeer, Giacomo, 263, 277, 347–48
  Les Huguenots, 269
  Robert le diable, 263, 269
Micelli, Caterina, 186
Michelangelo, 29
  David, 29, 85, *86*
Middle Ages, 18–23, 30–55
  anonymous creators in, 22
  art and architecture in, 22–23, 53
  historical overview, 19–21
  instrumental music in, 32
  literature in, 23
  map of Europe in, 20, *21*
  Mass in, 30–55
  musical style, 22–23
  notation in, 22, 32, 33
  Paris in, 35–37
  religion in, 21, 22, 31, 34–38
  science in, 33
  secular music in, 31–32
  style compared with Renaissance, 29
  term, 19, 31
  timeline, 18
Middle East, 400
Middlemarch (Eliot), 261
Midsummer Night's Dream incidental
  music (Mendelssohn), 298, 299, 311,
  314, 381
Mies van der Rohe, Ludwig, 402
"Mighty Fortress Is Our God, A" (hymn),
  88
Milan, 26
Miller, Arthur, *Death of a Salesman*, 403
Milne, A. A., *Winnie-the-Pooh*, 403
Milton, John, 85, 89
miniatures, 254, 262
  piano, 321, 327–42, 342
minimalism, 402, 404–5
Minnesänger, 22, 32
minor key, 195
minuet and trio, 219, 221, 222, 232
Missa solemnis (Beethoven), 214
Mitropoulos, Dimitri, 464, 507
Moby-Dick (Melville), 261
modal quality, 422
modernism, 402

modes of limited transposition, 468, 476,
  496
modified strophic setting, 244, 249
Moke, Camille, 270, *271*, 277
Molière, 85, 89
Molina, Tirso de, 89
monasteries, 20, 22, 34, 36
Monet, Claude, 261
  Haystacks at Sunset, Frosty Weather, *401*
monophony, 9
  in Baroque music, 138
  in Gregorian chant, 22, 32, 49, 54
  in medieval secular songs, 32
Monroe, Marilyn, 402
Monteux, Pierre, *418*, 418–19, 430, 431
Monteverdi, Claudio, *91*, 432
  biography, 91
  L'incoronazione di Poppea, 91
  L'Orfeo, 9, 83, 86, 90–117, 121, 163, 178,
    189, 192, 275, 527
  "Possente spirto," from *Orfeo*, 110–15
  recitatives, 107, 109–10, 363
  ritornellos used by, 163, 531–32
  Il ritorno d'Ulisse in patria, 91
  Scherzi musicali, 91, 115
  "Tu se' morta," from *Orfeo*, 107, 109–10
  Vespers of the Blessed Virgin, 91
  "Vi ricorda, o boschi ombrosi," from
    Orfeo, 102, 106–7, 108–9
Monteverdi, Giulio Cesare, 93
Moravia, 263
Moravian Duets (Dvořák), 373, 377
Morgan, J. P., 375
Morley, Thomas, 27, 57, 60
  First Booke of Consort Lessons, 71
Morning after the Wreck, The (Turner), *260*
Morone, Domenico, *The Expulsion of the
  Bonacolsi*, *93*
mort de Sardanapale, La (Berlioz), 273,
  277
Moscheles, Ignaz, 297, 301, 330
motet(s)
  in Middle Ages, 23
  in Renaissance, 27, 28, 59
Motherwell, Robert, 402
motives, 7, 63, 65–66, 80, 132
  of Beethoven, 7, 220, 222, 226, 232, 357
  of Schumann, 329
movements (of symphonies), 175, 219
Mozart, Leopold, *181*, 182
Mozart, Maria Anna ("Nannerl"), *181*

Mozart, Wolfgang Amadeus, 169, 170, *181*

  Act 1, Scene 1, ensemble, from *Don Giovanni,* 192, 194–95

  Act 1 finale from *Don Giovanni,* 191, 196, 199–204

  biography, 181

  career path of, 171

  Catalogue Aria, from *Don Giovanni,* 190, 192, 196, 197–98

  chamber music of, 252

  concertos, 295

  Così fan tutte, 177, 181, 183, 189

  Don Giovanni, 6, 170, 176–207, 263, 265, 358, 445

  First Viennese School and, 404

  keyboard virtuosity of, 262

  "Là ci darem la mano," from *Don Giovanni,* 174, 191, 196, 198–99, 220

  The Magic Flute, 181, 216

  The Marriage of Figaro, 177, 180, 181, 182, 183, 185, 187, 189, 204–5, 302

  Masses by, 65

  Mendelssohn compared to by Goethe, 297, 299

  "Notte e giorno faticar," from *Don Giovanni,* 190, 192, 193

  operas of, 178, 179, 181, 183, 216

  performances with Gewandhaus Orchestra, 296

  "Prague" Symphony, 182

  pre-existing music used by, 282

  recitatives of, 86, 189–90, 363

  Requiem, 12

  Romantic elements in style of, 259

  songs of, 243

  symphonies of, 209

Mr. Neale's Music Hall (Dublin), 123, *124,* 125–27

Muette de Portici, La (Auber), 267, *267,* 277

Müller, Wilhelm, 241

Munich, 27

Musical Courier, 394

musical forms, 13, 15–16. *See also specific types*

musical instruments, 4, 10–12. *See also specific instruments and types*

musical quotations, 330, 339

musical staff, 33

Music Man, The (Willson), 523

music of the spheres, 33

Mussolini, Benito, 412

Mussorgsky, Modest, 378

  Boris Godunov, 410, 419

  Khovanschina, 410

"My Country, 'Tis of Thee," 5

My Ladye Nevells Booke (Byrd), 62

mystic gulf, 353

Nabokov, Vladimir, *Lolita,* 403

Nahowski, Helene, 438, 441

Naked and the Dead, The (Mailer), 403

Name of the Rose, The (Eco), 403

Napoleon I, Emperor of the French, 170, 174, *174,* 210, 214, 236, 266

Napoleonic Wars, 236

Napoleon III, Emperor of the French, 322

Nation, 523

National, Le (Paris newspaper), 290

National Conservatory (New York), 376–77, 395

nationalism, 258, 263, 396

  Dvořák and, 373–74, 378–80, 396

  Wagner and, 349, 370

Native American music, 373, 379–80, 390, 395

nave, 37

Nazism, 314, 348, 370, 399, 401, 412, 439, 462–63, 468, 495

"Negro Music" (Hill), 378–79, 384

neoclassicism, 173, 260, 401, 412

neoromantic music, 405

Neue Zeitschrift für Musik, 296, 320, 321, 348

neumatic style, 43, 54

Nevell family, 62

Nevelson, Louise, 402

New Hampshire (Frost), 403

Newman, Barnett, 402

  The Song of Orpheus, 97

Newton, Isaac, 84, 88

New World Symphony (Dvořák), 15, 263, 349, 372–97, 501

  Americanness of, 381–83

  First Movement, 384, 386–88

  Fourth Movement, 390, 392–94

  "mystical chords" in, 385, 388, 394

  premiere, 381, *381*

  reception, 394–96

  Second Movement, 11, 385–86, 388–89

  shape of, 383

  syncopation in, 382

  themes, 383–84, 396–97

  Third Movement, 390–91

  title page, *394*

New York, New York

  1890s, 374–78

  ca. 1957, 501–3

New York City Ballet, 508

New York Herald, 379–80, 381

New York Herald Tribune, 523

New York Philharmonic, 376, 502, 523

New York Times, The, 381–82, 394, 395–96

New York Tribune, 394

New York World, 394

Nibelungenlied, 351

Niemann, Albert, 354, 369

Niering, Joseph, 354

Nijinska, Bronislava, 430

Nijinsky, Vaslav, 407, *410,* 410–11, *411,* 413, 417, 419–20, 431

  biography, 411

Nixon in China (Adams), 530

noise, 4

nonretrogradable rhythms, 468, 477, 479, 487, 496

Norma (Bellini), 262

North Africa, 400

Nosenko, Katya, 412

notation

  development of, 23, 32, 48–49

  in Middle Ages, 22, 32, 33, 48–49

  in Renaissance, 72, *73*

note, 4–5

Notre Dame Cathedral (Paris), 23, 32, 33, 37–38, 495

  central portal, *37*

  Christmas Day at, 38–40

  Christmas Mass at, 30–55, 65

  diagram of, *38*

  enduring presence of, 53

  facade, *35*

  interior with rose window, *34*

  Leoninus and Perotinus at, 48

  restoration of, 269

  rose window, *37*

Notre Dame de Paris (Hugo), 261

Notre Dame repertory, 34

"Notte e giorno faticar," from *Don Giovanni* (Mozart), 190, 192, 193

nozze di Figaro, Le (Mozart). *See Marriage of Figaro, The*

oboe(s), 11, 124–25, 160

Ockeghem, Johannes, 27

octatonic scale, 476, 496

octave, 5

Octet for Strings (Mendelssohn), 299

Ode to Joy (Schiller), 15, 170, 173

Oedipus Rex (Stravinsky), 412

offbeats, 425

Office, 44

Oiseaux exotiques (Messiaen), 478

O'Keeffe, Georgia, 402

Oklahoma! (Rodgers and Hammerstein), 503, *503,* 504, 511

"Old Folks at Home" (Foster), 6, 15, 380

Old Provençal, 32

Oliver Twist (Dickens), 261

One Hundred Years of Solitude (García Márquez), 403

O'Neill, Eugene, *The Iceman Cometh,* 403

On the Origin of Species (Darwin), 260

On the Town (Bernstein), 507, 508

On the Transmigration of Souls (Adams), 530

On the Waterfront (Kazan film), 403

opera buffa, 189, 206

Opéra-Comique (Paris), 267

Opéra (Paris), 266–67, *267,* 322, *322*

opera(s)

    of Adams, 530–32

    in Baroque era, 85, 86, 89, 91–92, 94–116, 121, 531–32

    beginnings of, 86, 94–95, 115, 180

    of Berg, 434–65

    Broadway musical structure compared with, 503

    in Classic era, 170, 176–207

    of Dvořák, 374

    in England, 119

    impresario's role in, 180–81

    of Messiaen, 468

    of Mozart, 170, 176–78

    "number" *vs.* "through-composed," 192

    oratorio compared with, 122, 143–44

    in Romantic era, 262–63, 267, 344–71

    stage bands in, 191–92, 199, 445–46, 451, 452–54

    stage machinery and set design, 188

    term, 91–92

    in twenty-first century, 530–32

    Wagner's music dramas, 192, 344–71

opera seria, 121, 189, 206

ophicleide, *274,* 274–75

Oppenheimer, J. Robert, 530–32

Oppersdorf, Count Franz von, 210

oral transmission, 32, 33

oratorio(s), 119, 120, 122, 143–44. *See also Messiah*

    of Mendelssohn, 298

    of Stravinsky, 412

orchestra

    in Classic era, 169, 191–92, 206, 218–19

    in Romantic era, 262, 268, 273–74

    standard ensemble, 12–13

    typical seating plan, *14*

orchestra pit, 216

orchestration

    of Berlioz, 293

    of Bernstein, 505–6, 524

    of Dvořák, 390

    of Handel, 162–63

    of Stravinsky, 418

    of Wagner, 356–57

Ordinary of the Mass, 40, 44

Ordo virtutum (Hildegard of Bingen), 36

Orfeo (Monteverdi), 83, 86, 90–117, 121, 527

    basso continuo in, 101

    first performance of, 102–3

    instrumentation, 100–101, 275

    moods in, 178

    performers in premiere, 97–99

    plot, 98

    "Possente spirto," 110–15

    Prologue, 104–6

    reception, 115–16

    recitatives in, 107, 109–10, 189

    ritornellos in, 163

    Toccata, 9, 103–4

    trombones in, 100, 192

    "Tu se' morta," 107, 109–10

    "Vi ricorda, o boschi ombrosi," 102, 106–7, 108–9

organ(s), 10, 100, 101, 127

organ music

    in Baroque era, 127, 149, 150, 151

    of Messiaen, 468

    in Renaissance, 28

organum, 48, 49, 54

ornamentation. *See* embellishment

Orpheus myth, 95–97

Orpheus (Stravinsky), 412

Orwell, George, *Animal Farm,* 403

Orwil, Mademoiselle, 327

ostinato, 421, 424–26, 433

overtones, 4, 10, 12, 421

overtone series, 160

overture(s)

    in Baroque era, 127–28, 160–61, 162

    in Broadway musicals, 503

    in *Don Giovanni,* 358

Paganini, Niccolò, 262, *262,* 303, 341

    Schumann's depiction of in *Carnaval,* 327

paired imitation, 64

Palais Garnier (Paris), 322, *322,* 416

Palazzo del Capitano (Mantua), *94*

Palestrina, Giovanni Pierluigi da, 27

    Masses by, 65

papacy, 20, 21, 25, 84

papal schism, 21

Papillons (Schumann), 330, 337

Paris

    ca. 1830, 265, *266,* 266–68

    ca. 1862, 322–27

    ca. 1913, *408,* 408–9

    in Classic era, 169

    in Middle Ages, 35–37, *35*

    Notre Dame in, 23, 32, 33, *34, 35*

Pärt, Arvo, 405

partial, 10

paso doble, 513, 517–18

Pasquier, Étienne, 467, 469, 470, *471,* 471–74, 482, 492, 493, 494

Pasquier, Jean, 494

Passions (of Bach), 149, 151, 166, 298

passions, in Baroque era, 85–86, *87,* 88–89

Passions of the Soul, The (Descartes), 88

"Pastoral" Symphony (Beethoven), 291, 358

patronage

    in Baroque era, 92–94, 120, 148

    in Classic era, 181, 212, 214

    in Renaissance, 25, 26, 27, 57–59, 60–61

    in Romantic era, 348, 351–52, 376–77

patter song, 186

Paumgartner, Sylvester, 252

pavans, 71, 75

Pavlova, Anna, 410

Pazzi Chapel (Florence), 85, *85*

pedal points, 358

Pelléas et Mélisande (Debussy), 418

Penderecki, Krzysztof, 405

Pénélope (Fauré), 416

pentatonic scale, 383, 396

percussion instruments, 10, 12

Perotinus, 39–40, 49, 53, 54, 64, 495

    biography, 48

    Sederunt, 48

    Viderunt omnes, 40, 48, *51*, 51–53

perpetuum mobile, 458

Petrarca, Francesco, 28

Petre, Sir John, 61

Petrushka (Stravinsky), 407, 411, 412, 413,

    418, 421, 432

Philippe Auguste, King of France, 36

philosophy

    in Baroque era, 88

    Enlightenment, 172

    in Romantic era, 260, 261

    in twentieth century, 402

phrases, 5, 6, 385

Piano, Renzo, Pompidou Center (Paris),

    403

Piano Concerto No. 4 (Beethoven), 216,

    217, 231

Piano Concerto No. 5 (Beethoven), 341

piano (dynamic), 8

pianoforte, piano(s), 8, 187, *188*, 212, *325*

    Érard firm, 317, 323–26

    mechanism, 10, *325*

piano music. *See also* miniatures

    in Romantic era, 262, 316–43, 321–42

    of Schubert, 239, 254

    of Schumann, 316–43

Piano Sonata, Op. 11 (Schumann), 318

Piano Sonata in C Major, Op. 53

    (Beethoven), 326, 327

piano trios (of Beethoven), 213

Picasso, Pablo, 402, 410

piccolo, 11, 218–19, 228

piccolo trumpet, 12

*Picturesque and Descriptive View of the City

    of Dublin, A* (Malton), *123*

Piero della Francesca, 29

Piltz, Marie, 430–31, *431*

pitch

    definition of, 4

    melody and, 405

più mosso, 8

Plague, The (Camus), 403

plainchant, plainsong. *See* Gregorian

    chant

Planer, Minna, 348

Plath, Sylvia, *The Bell Jar*, 403

Plato, 28

Pleyel firm, 324–25

Polovtsian Dances, from *Prince Igor*

    (Borodin), 413, 420

plucked string instruments, 10–11

Poe, Edgar Allen, 261

point of imitation, 63, 80

politics

    in Baroque era, 84

    in Classic era, 171, 174

    in Renaissance, 26

    in Romantic era, 258, 348

    in twentieth century, 370, 399–401, 436

polka, 451, 452, 464

Pollock, Jackson, 402

polychord, 423

polyphony, 9

    in Baroque music, 115, 138, 157

    imitative, 9, 62–63, 65–68, 69, 138, 159

    in medieval music, 22–23, 39–40,

        46–53, 54

    in Renaissance vocal music, 27, 62–65,

        80, 86

    in twentieth-century music, 525

polytonality, 421

Pompidou Center (Paris), 402, *403*

Ponziani, Felice, 186, 199

pop art, 402

popes. *See* papacy

popular music, 1950s, 501, 502

Porgy and Bess (Gershwin), 395

Portnoy's Complaint (Roth), 403

Portugal, 21

"Possente spirto," from *Orfeo*

    (Monteverdi), 110–15

postmodernism, 402

Poulenc, Francis, 410

Poussin, Nicolas, 86, 89

Praetorius, Michael, treatise on musical

    instruments, *74*

Prague, *178–79*, 178–82, 186–88, 204–5

Prelude and Fugue in C Minor, from

    Well-Tempered Clavier, The, BWV 847

    (Bach), 9, 155, 156–60

Prelude to "The Afternoon of a Faun"

    (Debussy), 411

preludes and fugues, 156–60, 166

Presley, Elvis, 501, *501*, 517

Pride and Prejudice (Austen), 173

prima donna, 185

primitivism, 407–8, 432

Prince, Harold, 506, 510

Prince, The (Machiavelli), 25

Prince Igor, Polovtsian Dances from

    (Borodin), 413, 420

principe, Il (Machiavelli), 25

printing press, invention of, 26

producer (for musicals), 503–4

program music, 265–66, 271–72, 278–89,

    382, 495

Prokofiev, Sergei, 401, 404, 410

Proper of the Mass, 40

Protestantism, 26

Proust, Marcel, 402

*Psalmes, Sonets, and Songs of Sadnes and

    Pietie* (Byrd), 60

psalms, 39, 41

psychoanalysis, 260

Psycho (Hitchcock film), 403

Puccini, Giacomo, 262

"Puer natus est," 9, 32, 34, 40–41, 42–43

Pulcinella (Stravinsky), 431

Pulszky, Romola de, 411

Purcell, Carl, *502*

pure organum. *See* sustained-note

    organum

Pushkin, Alexander, 206

Pygmalion (Shaw), 403

Quadrivium, 33

Quartet for the End of Time (Messiaen),

    466–97

    "Abîme des Oiseaux," 9, 482–84

    Book of Revelation as inspiration for,

        478–79

    "Danse de la Fureur, pour les Sept

        Trompettes," 487–89, 494

    "Fouillis d'arcs-en-ciel...", 489–91

    "Intermède," 9, 484, 485–86

    "Liturgie de Cristal," 479–81

    "Louange à l'Éternité de Jésus," 484,

        486–87

    "Louange à l'Immortalité de Jésus,"

        491, 492, 494

    movements, 479

    Paris premiere, 494

    performers for premiere, 469, 471–73

    premiere, 474–75

    reception, 492–94

    rehearsals, 473–74

Quartet for the End of Time (continued)
   style elements, 475–78, 494
   title page, *472*
   "Vocalise, pour l'Ange qui annonce la
      fin du Temps," 481–82
quartet(s), 223
Quiet Man, The (Ford film), 403
Quiet Place, A (Bernstein), 507
Quintet in E-flat Major for Piano and
      Strings (Schumann), 326
quintet(s), 223, 243, 252–53

Rachmaninoff, Sergei, 380, 481
Racine, Jean, 85, 89
racism in America, 501
ragtime, 382, 395, 501
Raising of Lazarus, The (Giotto), 31
Rake's Progress, The (Stravinsky), 412
rallentando, 8
Ramberg, Miriam, 417
rap, 527
Rasi, Francesco, 99, 111
rationalism, 88
Rauschenberg, Robert, 402
Ravel, Maurice, 401, 405, 410, 495
Ray, Satyajit, *Aparajito,* 403
realism, 29, 261
recapitulation
   in concerto form, 306, 308
   in sonata form, 220–21, 222, 225, 230–
      31, 232, 384
Recio, Marie, 270
recitation, 42
recitative, 194
   in operas, 189–91
   in oratorios, 122, 128–30, 144
   of Wagner, 363, 370
recitative style, 86, 91, 115, 116, 119
recitativo accompagnato, 129–30, 144,
      190
recitativo secco, 128–29, 144
recorder(s), 11, 72, 100, 163
recusants, 58–59, 61, 62, 65
Reformation, 26, 28, 58, 59
regal (organ), 101
Reich, Steve, 405
Reichardt, Johann Friedrich, 218, 236
Reiche, Gottfried, 160
"Rejoice," from *Messiah* (Handel), 86
religion. *See also* Catholic Church;
      Christianity

   in Baroque era, 143–44
   in Middle Ages, 21, 22, 31, 34–38
   in Renaissance, 26, 28
   in twentieth century, 467, 475–76, 495
Rembrandt van Rijn, 86, 89
Remembrance of Things Past (Proust), 402
Renaissance, 19, 25–29, 56–80
   art and architecture in, 29
   Baroque compared with, 83, 86
   courtly behavior in, 25–26, 27, 57–60
   dances in, 75
   historical overview, 25–26
   instrumental music in, 11, 61, 62,
      71–75, 77–79
   literature in, 28–29
   map of Europe in, *25*
   Mass in, 56–80
   musical style, 26–28
   politics in, 26
   religion in, 22, 27, 28
   science in, 28
   secular music in, 28, 57, 61
   style compared with Baroque, 87
   style compared with Middle Ages, 29
   term, 25
   timeline, *24*
Rent (Larson), 503
Requiem Canticles (Stravinsky), 412
Requiem (Mozart), 12
rest, 64
retransition, 220
réveil des oiseaux, Le (Messiaen), 478
Revue et gazette musicale, 340
Reynolds, Joshua, *Study of a Black Man,*
      172, *173*
rhetoric, Handel's use of, 132
Rhinegold, The (Wagner), 345, 349, 351,
      352, 357, 368, 369
rhythm and meter, 5–6
   in Baroque music, 88–89, 101–2
   cross-rhythms, 321
   development of, 23
   dotted rhythm, 6, 161, 198, 382, 383,
      387
   galliard, 75
   in Gregorian chant, 22, 32
   irregular, 421, 423, 427, 428–29, 432
   nonretrogradable rhythms, 468, 477,
      479, 487, 496
   notation and, 48–49
   in Renaissance music, 73

   syncopation, 382, 424
   in twentieth-century music, 476–77,
      479, 487, 491, 494, 496
Richter, Enoch, 153
Richter, Hans, *354, 355, 355, 369*
Rienzi (Wagner), 348
Rigoletto (Verdi), 262
Rihm, Wolfgang, 405
Riis, Jacob, 375
Riley, Terry, *In C,* 404–5
Rimbaud, Arthur, 261
Rimsky-Korsakov, Nikolai
   Ivan the Terrible, 410
   Stravinsky influenced by, 409, 412, 413
Ring of the Nibelung, The (Wagner), 345–
      47, 348. *See also Valkyrie, The*
   central story, 346–47
   leitmotifs in, 357–58
   libretto source, 346, 349, 351
   plot, 349–51
   theater built for, 352–53
Rinuccini, Ottavio, 96
Risorgimento, 258
ritardando, 8, 335
ritenuto, 334
Rite of Spring, The (Stravinsky), 405,
      406–33, 527
   absence of linear continuity, 420
   block construction in, 421, 422, 432
   choreography for, 407–8, 411, 413, 417
   costumes for, *413*
   "Dance Overcoming the Earth," 424
   dance rehearsals, 416–17
   folk and folklike melodies in, 421, 432
   "Games of Rival Cities," 421, 424
   "Glorification of the Chosen Victim,"
      422, 427–28
   instrumentation, 11, 12, 13, 356, 418
   "Introduction," 7, 421, 422–23
   irregular meter in, 6, 421, 423, 427,
      428–29, 432
   musical elements, 420–22
   musical numbers, 415
   orchestra rehearsals, 417–19
   ostinato use, 421, 424, 426, 433
   polyphony in, 9
   polytonality in, 421
   premiere, 419–20, 441
   primitivism in, 407–8
   "Procession of the Oldest and Wisest
      One," 421, 424, 426–27

reception, 407, 430–31
reconstruction of, 415, 416
ritual in, 408
"Sacrificial Dance," 427, 428–29
scenario for, 413–15
"Signs of Spring: Girls' Dance," 421, 423–24
"Spring Rounds," 421, 424, 425–26
static sounds in, 421, 433
subject, 407–8
ritornello
Adams's use of, 531–32
Bach's use of, 133, 163–65, 166–67
Handel's use of, 133, 135, 136, 144
Monteverdi's use of, 104–5, 111, 116, 163, 531–32
ritorno d'Ulisse in patria, Il (Monteverdi), 91
ritual, 408
Robbins, Jerome, 501, 504, 505, 507–8, *508,* 509, 511, 512, *512,* 524
biography, 508
Robert le Diable (Meyerbeer), 263, 269
rock, 527
"Rock Around the Clock," 517
Rockefeller, John D., *375*
rock 'n' roll, 500, 501, 514, 524
Rodin, August, 260
Roerich, Nicholas, 407, *414,* 419, 432
biography, 414
Prince Igor sets and costumes, 413
Rite of Spring costumes, *413*
Rite of Spring scenario, 413–15
Rogers, Richard and Su, Pompidou Center (Paris), *403*
Roman empire, 19
Romanesque architecture, 22–23
Romantic era, 256–397
arts in, 260–61
literature in, 261
map of Europe in, *259*
philosophy in, 260, 261
politics, economics, and technology, 258–59, 260, 348
science in, 260
timeline, 256
Romanticism, 257
individual's struggle against society, 295
musical style, 259, 262–63
in Paris, 268–69

program music and, 265–66, 271–72
style compared with Classical, 259, 263
style compared with twentieth-century music, 405
Rome, 26, 27
papacy and, 84
Sistine Chapel in, 29
Romeo and Juliet (Berlioz), 291
Romeo and Juliet (Shakespeare), 269, 270, 499, 504, 508–9
rondo form, 7, 219, 221–22, 246, 429
Roosevelt, Teddy, 375
Rosenkavalier, Der (Strauss), 263
Rossini, Gioacchino, 241, 322, 326
William Tell, 267
William Tell Overture, 358
Roth, Philip, *Portnoy's Complaint,* 403
Rothko, Mark, 402
Rousseau, Jean Jacques, 172
Le devin du village, 172
Emile, or On Education, 172
Social Contract, 172
"Row, row, row your boat," 46, 88
Rowling, J. K., *Harry Potter* series, 403
Royal Academy of Music, 120
Rubens, Peter Paul, 86, 89
Rubini brothers, 101
Rubinstein, Arthur, 380
Ruhe, Ulrich, 160
Ruins of Athens (Beethoven), 302
Rule of St. Benedict, The, 20
rulers of the choir, 39
"Rumble, The," from *West Side Story* (Bernstein), 511, *511*
Rusalka (Dvořák), 374
Russia. *See also* Soviet Union
Napoleon's invasion of, 174
nationalism in, 263
in Romantic era, 261
Russian Ballet. *See* Ballets Russes
Russian Revolution, 400

Saariaho, Kaija, 405
sackbut(s), 72
sacre du printemps, Le. See Rite of Spring, The
Sacre du Printemps (The Rehearsal), Le (Taylor ballet), 431
sacristy, 39
Saint François d'Assise (Messiaen), 468
St. Germain des Prés (Paris), 36
St. John Chrysostom, 31

St. Mark's Basilica (Venice), 91
St. Mary Magdalene Church (Paris), *173*
St. Nicholas Church (Prague), 179
Saint Paul (Mendelssohn), 298
St. Peter's Basilica (Rome), 26, 29, 85, *85,* 89
Saint-Saëns, Camille, 348, 416
St. Stephen's Cathedral (Vienna), 210, 211
Saint Teresa in Ecstasy (Bernini), 89, *89*
St. Thomas School (Leipzig), 149, *150,* 152
St. Thomas's Church (Leipzig), 149, 150, *150,* 296
Salieri, Antonio, 237
Salle Érard (Paris), 324, 326–27
Salle Herz (Paris), 324
Salle Pleyel (Paris), 324
salons, 235, 236, 239
saltarello, 32
San Carlo alle Quattro Fontane (Rome), 88, 89
Sanctus, 28, 40, 65
San Diego Opera, *463*
Santa Maria del Fiore (Florence), 23, 29
Sant'Angelo in Formis, *22*
Santorii, Santorio, 85
Saporiti, Teresa, 186, *186*
Sarabande and Gavotte (Bach), 326, 327
Sartre, Jean-Paul, *Being and Nothingness,* 403
Satie, Erik, 4
Saturday Review, 523
saxophone, 11
scales, 5
Scarlatti, Domenico, 326, 327
Scenes from the Song of Hiawatha (Coleridge-Taylor), 382
Scheffsky, Josephine, 354, 355, 369
Scherchen, Hermann, 439
Scherzi musicali (Monteverdi), 91, 115
scherzo, 15, 221, 226, 228, 229, 390–91
Schiele, Egon, 402, 437
Schikaneder, Emanuel, 216
Schiller, Johann Friedrich, 173
Ode to Joy, 15, 170, 173
Schillings, Max von, 440, *441,* 442
Schindler, Anton, 226
Schmid, Julius, 174
Schober, Franz von, 242, *242*
Schoenberg, Arnold, 404, 435–36
Chamber Symphony No. 1, 445
as painter, 402, *435*

Schoenberg, Arnold (*continued*)
program music rejected by, 272
Stravinsky and, 412
Scholasticism, 22, 26, 53
Schönbrunn Palace (Vienna), 210
schöne Müllerin, Die (Schubert), 241
Schubart, Christian Friedrich Daniel, 245
Schubert, Ferdinand, 236
Schubert, Franz, 169, *237, 238, 240, 243*
Beethoven and, 238–39
biography, 238
career path of, 171
chamber music of, 252–53
character pieces, 317
Classic elements in style of, 254
contemplative music of, 170–71
David and, 300
"Death and the Maiden" String
Quartet, 241, 252
Das Dörfchen, 240
Der Erlkönig, 240, 242, 243, 249, 250–51,
326, 327
Die Forelle, 243, 245, 246–47, 252
Gesang des Geistes uber den Wassern, 240
Gretchen am Spinnrade, 240, 241, 243,
245–46, 247–48, 265
lieder of, 240, 432
life in Vienna, 237–43, 263
Romantic elements in style of, 254
Die schöne Müllerin, 241
"Trout" Quintet for piano and strings,
243, 252–53
"Unfinished" Symphony, 241
"Wanderer" Fantasy, 252
Winterreise, 241
Die Zauberharfe, 240
Die Zwillingsbrüder, 240, 243
Schubert circle, 174, 237, 241–43
Schubertiades, 234–55, 238, 239, 241–44,
253
Schumann, Clara Wieck, 297, *318, 319,*
438
as composer, 317, 318
concerts in Paris, 323–27, 340–41
Hensel and, 299
life and career path, 318–19
marriage, 319
as pianist, 316–17, 340–41
pianos played by, 324–25
Schumann, Robert, 319, *319,* 320
Album for the Young, 330

Berlioz's *Fantastic Symphony* reviewed
by, 292
biography, 320
Carnaval, 316–43
character pieces, 317
Concerto for Four Horns and
Orchestra, 295
Gewandhaus Orchestra performances
of works by, 297
illness of, 319
as journalist, 296, 320, 321, 348
lieder of, 244
Mendelssohn's Violin Concerto viewed
by, 311
Papillons, 330, 337
Piano Sonata, Op. 11, 318
program music and, 272
Quintet in E-flat Major for Piano and
Strings, 326
Violin Sonata No. 1 in A Minor, 326–27
von Fricken and, 320–21
Schützendorf, Leo, *461*
Schwind, Moritz von, 239, 241, 242,
243
science
in Baroque era, 84–85, 88
in Enlightenment, 172
in Middle Ages, 33
in Renaissance, 28
in Romantic era, 260
in twentieth century, 402
Scorsese, Martin, *Taxi Driver,* 403
Scotch Symphony (Mendelssohn), 298
Scruton, Roger, 351
Seagram Building (Mies van der Rohe),
402
Secession style, 436–37
Second Viennese School, 404, 435–36
secular music
in Middle Ages, 31–32
in Renaissance, 28, 57, 61, 68–79
Sederunt (Perotinus), 48
Seidl, Anton, *375–76, 376, 377, 379, 381,
381, 394*
biography, 376
as composer, 382
seis, 520–22
Sellars, Peter, 530
"Semper Dowland, semper dolens"
(Dowland), 71
Sense and Sensibility (Austen), 173

Septet for Strings and Winds
(Beethoven), 223
sequences, 46, 89, 132, 165, 219
serenade(s), 223
serialism, 412
series, 404
serpent, 275, *275,* 289
Seven Samurai (Kurosawa film), 403
Seventh Seal, The (Bergman film), 403
Sforza family, 26
Shakespeare, William, 28–29, 57, 60, 89
Hamlet, 270
Romeo and Juliet, 269, 270, 499, 504,
508–9
"Shall We Dance?" from *The King and I*
(Rodgers and Hammerstein), 503
sharps, 5
Shaw, George Bernard, 206
Pygmalion, 403
shawm(s), 72, *74*
Shelley, Percy Bysshe, 261
short score, 440
Shostakovich, Dmitri, 404
Show Boat (Kern and Hammerstein),
504
Sibelius, Jean, 378
siciliana, 132–33
Siegfried (Wagner), 345, 346, 349
sinfonia, 209
Singakademie (Leipzig), 298
single-reed instruments, 11
Sistine Chapel (Rome), 29
slavery, abolition of, 258–59
Slavonic Dances (Dvořák), 373, 374, 377,
382
slow movement (of symphonies), 221,
227–28, 232
slur(s), 304
Smetana, Bedřich, 374, 378
Smith, Bessie, 395
Smithson, Harriet, *270,* 270–71, 277, 291
snare drum, 12
Social Contract (Rousseau), 172
Société des Concerts du Conservatoire,
268
Society of Friends of Music (Vienna), 236
Society of Musical Artists (Vienna), 236
Sokolova, Lydia, 417
Solomon (Handel), 120
"Something's Coming," from *West Side
Story* (Bernstein), 505

"Somewhere," from *West Side Story* (Bernstein), 524

sonata-allegro from. *See* first-movement sonata form

sonata form. *See* first-movement sonata form

sonata(s)
of Beethoven, 213
in Classical music, 223

Sondheim, Stephen, *510*
biography, 510
as lyricist, 504–5, 506, 508, 509, 510–11, 524–25

song cycle(s), 238

Song of Hiawatha, The (Longfellow), 379, 382

Song of Orpheus, The (Newman), *97*

Song of the Nightingale, The (Stravinsky), 431

songs, German. *See* lieder

Songs without Words (Mendelssohn), 310, 314

Sonnleithner, Leopold von, 237, 240

Sonnleitner, Joseph, 213

soprano (voice), 63, 144

Sorrows of Young Werther, The (Goethe), 173

sound, basic terms and concepts about, 3–9

Sound and the Fury, The (Faulkner), 403

South Pacific (Rodgers and Hammerstein), 504, 510

Southwell, Robert, 58, 61

Soviet Union, 400, 401

Spain
in Baroque era, 85, 89
in Classic era, 173, 174
in Middle Ages, 20, 21
in Renaissance, 25
in Romantic era, 260
in twentieth century, 399

Spaun, Joseph von, 234, *242*, 242–43

Specter of the Rose, The (Nijinsky ballet), 410, 420

Spenser, Edmund, 57

Speyer, Louis, 419

Spielberg, Steven, *Jaws*, 403

spirituals, 379, 384, 385, 387

Spohr, Louis, 297

Spontini, Gaspare, 277

Sprechstimme, 443, 447, 455, 464

Sputnik I, *501*

Stabreim, 346

Stalag VIIIA prison camp, *469,* 469–71, *470,* 492–93

"Star-Spangled Banner," 5

statement (in fugue), 140

State of Darkness (Fenley ballet), 431

steerhorn, 356

Steinbeck, John, *The Grapes of Wrath,* 403

Stella, Frank, 402
Marrakech, 405

stile recitativo, 86, 91, 115, 116, 119

Stockhausen, Karlheinz, 4

Storming of the Bastille (Houel), *171*

Strauss, Richard, 263, 401, 410
Don Juan, 205
Till Eulenspiegel, 411

Stravinsky, Igor, *412*
aesthetics of, 463
Apollo, 409, 412, 431
ballets of, 431
biography, 412
career path of, 412–13
Firebird, 407, 412, 413, 421, 432
neoclassical style, 401
Petrushka, 407, 411, 412, 413, 418, 421, 432
program music rejected by, 272
The Rite of Spring, 6, 7, 9, 11, 12, 13, 356, 405, 406–33, 441, 527

Streetcar Named Desire, A (Williams), 403

street gangs, problem of, 502–3

Streisand, Barbra, 508

stretta, 191

stretto, 165

Striggio, Alessandro, 96–97, 111

Striggio, Giovanni, 115

string bass, 11

string instruments, 10–11

String Quartet, Op. 3 (Berg), 438

string quartet(s)
of Beethoven, 300
in Classical music, 223
of Mendelssohn, 313

strophic setting, 22, 32, 72–73, 116, 244, 245, 249, 499

strophic variation, 105–6

Stuckenschmidt, H. H., 441–42, 461

Study of a Black Man (Reynolds), 172, *173*

Styne, Jule, 505, 508

subcantor, 38–39

subject (in fugue), 7, 140, 157, 167

Sudeykina, Vera, 412

Suite for Orchestra in D Major, BWV 1068 (Bach), 125, 128, 155, 160–63
Overture, 160–61, 162

Summa Theologica (Aquinas), 22

Sunday in the Park with George (Sondheim), 510

surrealism, 402

suspensions, 66

sustained-note organum, 49, 53, 54

sustaining pedal (piano), 325, 337

Svoboda, Joseph, 186

"Swanee River," 220

Swift, Jonathan, 123

"Swing Low, Sweet Chariot," 384, 387

syllabic style, 43, 54

Sylphides, Les (ballet with Chopin's music), 420

Symphonie fantastique (Berlioz). *See Fantastic Symphony* (Berlioz)

symphonies
of Beethoven, 15, 170, 208–33, 292, 358, 383
in Classic era, 170, 175, 209, 218–32, 223, 232
of Dvořák, 15, 374
form of, 15, 218, 219, 220–22
Mahler's view of, 292
of Mendelssohn, 298
of Mozart, 181
in Romantic era, 262, 264–93
of Schumann, 320

Symphony No. 5 (Beethoven), 208–33, 272
First Movement, 223–25, 226, 384
form, 15, 219, 305
Fourth Movement, 226, 228, 230–31
instrumentation, 13, 218–19
New York Philharmonic performance, 376
opening motive, 7, 226
Paris premiere, 268
premiere, 214–15, 216–18
reception, 231–32
Second Movement, 226–28
Third Movement, 226, 228, 229
unity of themes, 226, 232, 383

Symphony No. 9 (Beethoven), 15, 170, 173, 214, 240, 292, 383

Symphony of Psalms (Stravinsky), 412

syncopation, 382, 424

synesthesia, 475

synthesizer(s), 10

Take Five (Brubeck), 6

"Take Me Out to the Ball Game," 6

Talk to Her (Almodóvar film), 403

Tallis, Thomas, 59, 62

tambourine, 12

tango, 513

Tannhäuser (Wagner), 322, *323*, 348

Taxi Driver (Scorsese film), 403

Taylor, Paul, 431

Tchaikovsky, Petr Ilyich

    at Carnegie Hall, 380

    Festival Coronation March, 381

    at premiere of Wagner's *Ring* cycle,

        345, 368

    quintuple meter used by, 6

    Stravinsky influenced by, 413

    symphonies of, 262

    Violin Concerto, 295

Teatro Colón (Buenos Aires), 440

Technique of My Musical Language

    (Messiaen), 489, 495

Te Deum (Berlioz), 381

Te Deum (Dvořák), 380

Telemann, Georg Philipp, 147, 149, 153

Teltscher, Joseph, *240*

tempo, 5, 7–8

Temps, Le (Paris newspaper), 277–78, 290

Tennyson, Alfred, Lord, 261

tenor (voice), 63, 144

termination, 42

texture, 9

Thalberg, Sigismond, 330, 341

Theater an der Wien (Vienna), 213, *215*,

    215–17, *217*

Theatre Arts, 523

Théâtre des Champs-Élysées (Paris), *416*,

    416–17, *417*, 419–20

Théâtre des Mathurins (Paris), 494, *494*

Théâtre des Nouveautés (Paris), 272, 276

Théâtre Lyrique (Paris), 322

thematic recurrence and transformation,

    383

theme and variations, 7, 221, 252–53

themes, 7

    in Beethoven's Symphony No. 5, 226,

        232, 383

    in Classical symphonies, 219–20, 232

in Dvořák's *New World* Symphony,

    383–84, 396–97

"There were shepherds," from *Messiah*

    (Handel), 129–30

"This sweet and merry month of May"

    (Byrd), 61, 68–70

Thomson, Virgil, 382, 395, 401

Thoreau, Henry David, 261

thoroughbass, 87

Threni (Stravinsky), 412

through-composed setting, 244, 249

Thurber, Jeannette, 376–77, *377*, 378, 379,

    381, 382, 395

Till Eulenspiegel (Strauss), 411

timbre, 10

Time of the Cuckoo, The (Laurents), 505

timpani, 12

toccata, 103–4

Tolkien, J.R.R.

    The Hobbit, 403

    Lord of the Rings, 351

Tolstoy, Leo, 261

tonality, 437, 447, 451, 463–64, 531–32

tone color, 10, 262

tone row, 404

tonic, 383

"Tonight," from *West Side Story*

    (Bernstein), 499, 500, 508, 510,

    518–20, 525

Tosca (Puccini), 262

total work of art, 346

To the Lighthouse (Woolf), 403

transcendentalism, 261

transcriptions, 163

transepts, 37

Traviata, La (Verdi), 262

tremolo(s), 305

triangle, 4, 12

trio(s), 229. *see also* minuet and trio

    in Classical music, 223, 390

    in opera, 194

Triple Concerto (Beethoven), 295

tritone, 445, 514

Trivium, 33

Trois petites liturgies de la présence divine

    (Messiaen), 475

Trollope, Anthony, 261

trombone(s), 12, *74*, 100, 192, 199, 218–19,

    228

tropes, 46

troubadours, 22, 32

troubairitz, 32

Trouble in Tahiti (Bernstein), 507

"Trout" Quintet for piano and strings

    (Schubert), 243, 252–53

trouvères, 22, 32

Troyens, Les (Berlioz), 263, 270

Truffaut, François, *Jules and Jim*, 403

trumpet(s), 12

    Baroque, 100, 124, 160

    piston, 274

tuba, 12

tuning fork, 4

Turangalîla-symphonie (Messiaen), 468

Turner, J. M. W., 260

    The Morning after the Wreck, 260

Turning Point, The (Laurents), 505

"Tu se' morta," from *Orfeo* (Monteverdi),

    107, 109–10

twelve-tone music, 404

twentieth century, 398–525

    art and architecture in, 402

    human rights struggle, 400–401

    literature in, 402–3

    map of Europe in, *400*

    music in, 401, 404–5

    philosophy in, 402

    political events, 370, 399–401, 436

    science in, 402

    style compared with Romantic, 405

    timeline, 398

twenty-first century, 527–32

Twilight of the Gods (Wagner), 345, 349–50

"Twinkle, Twinkle, Little Star," 6, 174,

    437

Ulysses (Joyce), 403

"Unfinished" Symphony (Schubert), 241

unison, 22, 34, 43, 138, 487

United States. *See also* New York, New

    York

    in 1950s, 500–501

    in Romantic era, 260–61

Updike, John, *Couples*, 403

Urbana, Lucrezia, 101

Urbino, 25–26

Urhan, Chrétien, 277

Ut queant laxis (hymn), *33*

Utrillo, Maurice, 410

Vacellier, André, 494

Valkyrie, The (Wagner), 249, 344–71, 415

Act 1, Prelude (Storm), 358–59

Act 1, Scene 1, 359–61

Act 1, Scene 2, 362–63

Act 1, Scene 3, "Du bist der Lenz," 347, 364, 370

Act 1, Scene 3, "Siegmund Heiss' Ich," 365, 366–67

Act 1, Scene 3, "Winterstürme wichen dem Wonnemond," 347, 363–65, 370

instrumentation, 12, 356–57

lack of chorus part, 357

larger musical forms in, 358

leitmotifs in, 360–67

Magic Fire Music, 347, 368, 370

original cast, 354

performance preparations, 353–56

plot, 350

premiere, 368–69

Ride of the Valkyries, 347, 365, 367, 370

scenery and lighting effects, 353, *354*

van Gogh, Vincent, 261

Wheat Field with Cypresses, 261

Varèse, Edgard, 404

variation form, 219, 221

variations. *See* theme and variations

Vaughan Williams, Ralph, 405

Vega, Lope de, 89

Velasquez, Diego, 89

Venice, 26, 91

Verdi, Giuseppe, 262, 348

Verdun, Treaty of, 20

Verlaine, Paul, 261

Vermeer, Johannes, 89

Versailles, palace of, 85

verse-chorus form, 525

Vespers of the Blessed Virgin (Monteverdi), 91

Vézelay, abbey of, *23, 23*

Viani, Antonio Maria, 102–3

Viardot, Pauline, 326, 341

vibraphones, 12

vibrato, 303

vicars, 39

Victoria, Queen of England, 258

Viderunt omnes (Perotinus), 40, *51,* 51–53

Vienna

ca. 1826, 234–55

ca. 1925, *436,* 436–37

in Classic era, 169, 174, 182–83, 205, 209–15, *210, 211,* 231–32

Congress of (1815), 174, 236

public concerts in, 215–16

Vienna Court Opera, 437

Vietnam, 400

Vingt regards sur l'enfant-Jésus (Messiaen), 468

viola, 11

viola da gamba, 11, 72, 100

violin(s), 11, 100, *304*

playing technique, 303–5

Violin Concerto (Berg), 438

Violin Concerto (Brahms), 295, 300, 381

Violin Concerto (Mendelssohn), *9,* 294–315, 432

conductor for premiere, 300

First Movement, 305–8

form, 305

preparations for premiere, 301–2

publication of, 302

reception, 311, 313–14

Second Movement, 308–10

Third Movement, 311, 312–13

violinist for premiere, 300

virtuosity in, 302–5

Violin Concerto (Tchaikovsky), 295

violin mutes, 275

violin(s), 11, 100, *304*

playing technique, 303–5

Violin Sonata No. 1 in A Minor (Schumann), 326–27

viol(s), 11, *71,* 72, 74

virginal, 62, 72

Virgin of the Rocks, The (Leonardo da Vinci), 29, *29*

"Vi ricorda, o boschi ombrosi," from *Orfeo* (Monteverdi), 102, 106–7, 108–9

virtuosos, virtuosity

in Baroque era, 127, 147, 151, 163, 262

in Classic era, 262

cult of, 303, 341–42

in Romantic era, 262, 295, 302–5, 306, 314, 317, 323–27, 341–42

Visions de l'Amen (Messiaen), 475

Vivaldi, Antonio, 163

vocalise, 481

Vogl, Johann Michael, 240, 241, 242–43, *243,* 244, 249, 252

voices, 63

Voltaire, 172

von Gogh, Vincent, 402

Wagner, Cosima, 348, *349*

Wagner, Richard, *346, 348, 349, 354,* 437

alliterative verse of, 346, 439

American Centennial March, 349, 351

anti-Semitism of, 314, 348, 370

biography, 348

career path of, 347–49

chromaticism of, 401

cult of, 369

Flying Dutchman, The, 348, 358

influence of, 262

Judaism in Music, 314, 348

leitmotif technique, 346–47, 357–58, 370, 383, 443

music dramas of, 192, 262–63, 345–47, 348–49

program music and, 272

The Ring of the Nibelung, 345–47, 348, 375

Seidl and, 375, 376

in Switzerland, 322

Tannhäuser, 322, *323,* 348

The Valkyrie, 12, 249, 344–71, 415

Wilhelmj and, 300

Wagner tuba, 356

Waiting for Godot (Beckett), 403

Walküre, Die (Wagner). *See* Valkyrie, The

Walter, Bruno, 507

waltz(es), *9,* 282, 284–85

"Wanderer" Fantasy (Schubert), 252

War and Peace (Tolstoy), 261

Ward, Joseph, 127

Warhol, Andy, 402

Washington, George, 173

Waterloo, Battle of (1815), 174, 266

Watson, Thomas, 68

Weber, Carl Maria von

music used for *Specter of the Rose,* 420

Overture and Introduction from *Euryanthe,* 302

Weber, Constanze, 181, *182,* 184

Webern, Anton, 404, 435–36

Wedding, The (Stravinsky), 412, 431

Wedekind, Frank, 437

Weelkes, Thomas, 60

Well-Tempered Clavier, The (Bach), 148, 149, 150, 155, 156

Prelude and Fugue in C Minor, *9,* 155, 156–60

Werfel, Franz, 438

West Side Story (Bernstein), 382, 498–525, 504–25
  "America," 520–22
  "A Boy Like That," 505, 525
  "Cool," 514, 525
  "Dance at the Gym," 517–18
  dance in, 511
  film version, 499, 522, 523–24
  first performance, 513, 522
  "Gee, Officer Krupke," 514, 524
  "I Feel Pretty," 511
  "I Have a Love," 525
  "I Want to Be in America," 499
  "Jet Song," 516–17, 520
  language in, 505
  Latin rhythms in, 513, 517–18, 520–22, 524
  lyrics for, 510–11
  "Maria," 500, 514, 518
  numbers in, 504
  orchestration, 505–6, 524
  plot of, 509
  poster for, *508*
  Prologue, 12, 503, 514–16, 524
  reception, 522–23
  rehearsals for, 511–12
  Romeo and Juliet as basis for, 508–9
  "The Rumble," 511, *511*
  "Something's Coming," 505
  "Somewhere," 524
  story for, 508–10
  themes in, 499
  "Tonight," 499, 500, 508, 510, 518–20, 525
  writing and producing, 504–6
Wheat Field with Cypresses (van Gogh), *261*
Whistler, James McNeill, 260
Whitman, Walt, 261

whole-tone scale, 476, 496
Wieck, Friedrich, 318, *318*, 320, 321, 438
Wilhelmj, August, 300
Williams, Tennessee, *A Streetcar Named Desire*, 403
William Tell (Rossini), 267
William Tell Overture (Rossini), 358
wind instruments, 10, 11
Winnie-the-Pooh (Milne), 403
Winter Garden Theater (New York), 522, 523
Winterreise (Schubert), 241
Wise, Robert, 524
Wolf, Hugo, lieder of, 244
Wolfe, Thomas, *Look Homeward, Angel*, 403
women composers
  in Middle Ages, 32, 35, 36
  in Romantic era, 297, 299
Wonderful Town (Bernstein), 507
Wood, Natalie, 499, 523–24
woodwind instruments, 10, 11
Woolf, Virginia, *To the Lighthouse*, 403
Worcester, Earl of, 61
word painting
  in Baroque era, 130, 132–33
  in Classic era, 245, 246
  in Renaissance, 68
Wordsworth, William, 261
World War I, 399, 435, 436, 463
World War II, 400, 467–75, 492–94, 530
Woyzeck, Johann Christian, 439
Woyzeck (Büchner), 438, 439, 462, 464
Wozzeck (Berg), 434–65, 527
  concert suite from, 439
  dramatic and musical structure, 442–43, 445

  formal coherence, 443
  instrumentation, 445–46
  Invention on a Chord, 451, 454–56
  Invention on a Key, 451, 457–58
  Invention on an Irregular Rhythm, 451, 452–54
  Invention on a Note, 446, 449–51
  Invention on a Regular Rhythm, 458–60
  Inventions, 446, 448–60
  later productions, 463–64
  libretto source, 437–39
  March and Lullaby (Act 1, Scene 3), 446, 447–48, 458
  performance preparations, 439–41
  plot, 442, 444
  premiere, 441–42, 461
  reception, 461–64
  scenic design, 442, *442*
  stage band in, 191, 445–46, 451, 452–54
  use of recurring melodies and pitches, 445
Wright, Frank Lloyd, 402

xylophones, 12

"Young People's Concerts," 501

Zauberflöte, Die (Mozart), 181, 216
Zauberharfe, Die (Schubert), 240
Zedler, Johann Heinrich, 147
Zelter, Carl Friedrich, 297, 298, 301–2
Zimmermann, Gottfried, coffee house of, 147, *148*, 153, 155–56, 163, 296
Zwilich, Ellen Taaffe, 405
Zwillingsbrüder, Die (Schubert), 240, 243